Free Trade and
Liberal England
1846–1946

Free Trade and Liberal England 1846–1946

ANTHONY HOWE

CLARENDON PRESS · OXFORD

1997

Oxford University Press, Great Clarendon Street, Oxford OX2 6DP

Oxford New York
Athens Auckland Bangkok Bombay
Calcutta Cape Town Dar es Salaam Delhi
Florence Hong Kong Istanbul Karachi
Kuala Lumpur Madras Madrid Melbourne
Mexico City Nairobi Paris Singapore
Taipei Tokyo Toronto Warsaw
and associated companies in
Berlin Ibadan

Oxford is a trade mark of Oxford University Press

Published in the United States
by Oxford University Press Inc., New York

British Library Cataloguing in Publication Data
Data available

Library of Congress Cataloging in Publication Data
Howe, Anthony.
Free trade and liberal England, 1846–1946 / Anthony Howe.
p. cm.
Includes bibliographical references (p.   ).
1. Free trade—Great Britain—History.   2. Liberal Party
(Great Britain)—History.   I. Title.
HF2045.H68   1997
382'.71'0941—dc21   97-16509

ISBN 0–19–820146–X

1 3 5 7 9 10 8 6 4 2

Typeset by Best-set Typesetter Ltd., Hong Kong
Printed in Great Britain
on acid-free paper by
Bookcraft Ltd., Midsomer-Norton
Nr. Bath, Somerset

*In memory of my mother
and for my father*

Preface

One hundred and fifty years after the repeal of the Corn Laws, a new study of free trade in nineteenth- and early twentieth-century Britain seems overdue. For, while there have been frequent studies of the rise of free trade and of Repeal itself, free trade after 1846 has been neglected in favour of studies of its opponents, especially of Joseph Chamberlain and the tariff reformers. As a result, there has been no attempt to write a political history of free trade since F. W. Hirst's *From Adam Smith to Philip Snowden: A History of Free Trade in Great Britain* (1925), a work necessarily marked by its author's strong polemical engagement with its subject. This historical reticence has several roots, among them the unfashionability of free trade in an era of managed economies, the difficulty of studying what has been seen as an 'unspoken assumption' of the Victorians, but, above all perhaps, the daunting complexity of the task, given the potential ubiquity of the ideas and practices of free trade in the nation's economic, religious, cultural, diplomatic, political, and intellectual life. An *histoire totale* of free trade is probably beyond the scope of a single scholar, and the aims of this book are necessarily more modest. It explores for the most part two interrelated themes: the implications of the repeal of the Corn Laws for British politics, especially for the history of the Liberal Party from Gladstone to Asquith, and the vital ramifications that adherence to free trade held for Britain's position within the liberal international order. Other important facets of free trade are at best indirectly addressed, for example, the fiscal system under free trade, the relationship between free trade and economic growth, and the intellectual history of *laissez-faire*.

The study of free trade also necessarily encounters semantic problems. These, I hope, I have treated in a common-sense rather than dogmatic fashion. The term 'free trade' is used to indicate trade between nations 'free' from all but revenue tariffs. Free trade in this sense was a policy supported by Whigs, Radicals, Liberals, and many Conservatives, but dissented from by protectionists, fair traders, and tariff reformers. Yet, politically, free trade became intertwined with a second-term 'Cobdenism', for it was Cobden, the hero of the Anti-Corn Law League, rather than Peel, the executive author of Repeal, whose name became synonymous with Britain's attachment to free trade. 'Cobdenism', however, was often a term used far more by its enemies than by its friends, and it is employed here sparingly to indicate those attached closely to Cobden's leading precepts, put simply in the motto of the Cobden Club: 'free trade, peace, and goodwill.'

In undertaking this study I have benefited not only from the published works of many scholars, but also from the advice and encouragement of Colin Matthew, Peter Mandler, Frank Trentmann, Alon Kadish, and Cheryl Schonhardt-Bailey, to all of whom I am most indebted. I have also benefited from the interest of a loyal band of Cobdenites, those LSE students who over the years have grappled with 'Cobden, Free Trade, and Europe, 1846–1882'. Seminars at Oxford, the Institute of Historical Research, Sussex, the Australian National University, and Princeton University have proved helpful and fruitful, while chapters three and five first took shape in the form of a paper for the Anglo-Russian Conference of Historians in 1991. This work gained essential impetus from the tenure of visiting fellowships at the Shelby Cullom Davis Center for Historical Studies, Princeton University and the Department of History, Research School of Social Sciences, Australian National University. They provided congenial atmospheres for thought and research, as well as the informed interest of Lawrence Stone, Ken Inglis, and Allan Martin.

I am extremely grateful to the trustees, owners, and custodians of the papers cited in the bibliography and footnotes for permission to consult and quote from these unpublished materials. I am also most grateful to the staffs of many libraries and archives, whose unstinting help has made this book possible, above all, the staff of the British Library of Political and Economic Science, which has itself provided a cornucopia of materials for this book. I also thank Mr Peter Clarke, Mr Philip Mallet, and Mr Charles Smedley for making family papers available to me. The editors of *History* and Cambridge University Press have kindly allowed me to include here material which has first appeared in other forms elsewhere. I am also grateful to Tony Morris at Oxford University Press for his long and keenly sustained interest in this project.

Finally, I deeply thank my wife Catherine, for whom this book can only be a small compensation for all that she has foregone in enabling me to combine its writing with the immense enjoyment of the early years of our children, Victoria, Nicholas, and Amelia.

Contents

List of Abbreviations

ADB	*Australian Dictionary of Biography*
BDFA	*British Documents on Foreign Affairs*
BL	British Library
BLPES	British Library of Political and Economic Science
CCJ	*Chambers of Commerce Journal*
CCM	Cobden Club Minutes
CP	Cobden Papers
DBB	*Dictionary of Business Biography*
DNB	*Dictionary of National Biography*
EcHR	*Economic History Review*
EHR	*English Historical Review*
EP	Elliot Papers
FFL	Free Food League
FTA	Free Trade Association
FTL	Fair Trade League
FTU	Free Trade Union
GD	M. D. R. Foot and H. C. G. Matthew (eds.), *Gladstone Diaries*
GG Corr.	A. Ramm (ed.), *Gladstone–Granville Correspondence*
GP	Gladstone Papers
GSDA	Gold Standard Defence Association
HGP	Herbert Gladstone Papers
HJ	*Historical Journal*
HLRO	House of Lords Record Office
IFL	Imperial Federation League
ILP	Independent Labour Party
JDE	*Journal des Économistes*
LRC	Labour Representation Committee
NRU	National Reform Union
PRO	Public Record Office
RCDTI	Royal Commission, Depression in Trade and Industry
RP	Russell Papers
TRHS	*Transactions of the Royal Historical Society*
TRL	Tariff Reform League
UETL	United Empire Trade League

UFTL   Unionist Free Trade League
WFTU   Women's Free Trade Union
WG   *Westminster Gazette*
WSRO   West Sussex Record Office

I

Free Trade and the Early Victorians: The Corn Laws Repealed, 1846

A great and hazardous experiment is about to be made, novel in its character, and without the support of experience to guide or direct it, embracing and extending over unbounded interests, and pregnant with results that may prove fatal in their consequences.

Sir John Gladstone, *Plain Facts intimately connected with the intended Repeal of the Corn Laws* (1846), 30.

The question itself grew upon me from year to year; the *principle* involved in our struggle expanded into such world-wide importance that I became more and more enamoured of it.

Cobden to Grey, 1 June 1846.[1]

T HE repeal of the Corn Laws in 1846 was, in many ways, far more long-lasting in its political and economic implications than other supposedly pivotal events in nineteenth-century Britain, for example, the Reform Acts of 1832 and 1867. For, in abandoning the tariffs which had for centuries protected her agriculture, Britain launched herself upon an unprecedented course, seeking to lead the world towards a peaceful order based on free commercial exchange between individuals and nations. Subsequently, and uniquely among the leading powers of Europe, Britain declined to return to protection during the Great Depression of 1873–96, and despite the strong protectionist leanings of her self-governing colonies, the ideal of a free trade empire persisted well into the twentieth century. From 1846 British foreign policy was also based firmly and consistently on the desirability of free trade within the international system. Electorally, free trade won persistent endorsement against successive protectionist, fair trade, and tariff reform challenges. Only in 1931, in conditions of national crisis, did the Chamberlainite alternative of tariff reform and imperial preference overturn this deeply rooted political consensus. But, for the best part of a century free trade has outstanding claims to be considered the single most distinctive characteristic of the British state, joining Protestantism and empire as an indispensable hallmark of England's world 'mission'.

The Corn Laws, so decisively rejected in 1846, were themselves part of a wider protectionist structure which had sought since the seventeenth century to embrace

---

[1]   Papers of the 3rd Earl Grey, Department of Paleography and Diplomatic, University of Durham (hereafter Grey Papers).

shipping, commerce, and the colonies, as well as food supply.[2] Thus, into the 1840s the Navigation Acts still extended considerable benefits to British shipbuilders and shipowners, for not only were foreign-built ships debarred from the British regis- ter, but two-fifths of British tonnage was in trades from which foreign ships were excluded.[3] More widely, the flow of goods into and out of Britain was impeded by a huge range of prohibitions and tariffs, with a large measure of preference for important colonial products, such as sugar, timber, and coffee. While few free traders doubted that customs duties were a legitimate form of state revenue, their number, extent, and illogicality increasingly alienated merchants, Radicals, and bureaucrats: in 1840 the influential Select Committee on Import Duties reported that seventeen articles produced 95 per cent of customs revenue; over a thousand duties were deemed vexatious and readily expendable.[4]

The intellectual basis of this 'mercantilist' system had been thrown into perma- nent doubt by Adam Smith's *Wealth of Nations* in 1776, a work whose ideas exerted an early impact upon British politicians in the 1780s.[5] The Anglo-French Commer- cial Treaty of 1786 had also provided a diplomatic model for future free traders, forming part of Pitt's extensive commercial negotiations, which had seemed largely geared to the needs of an expanding industrial economy.[6] The wars against revolu- tionary and Napoleonic France (1793–1815) had not ruled out further cautious liberalization, above all with regard to trade in the East, but peace reversed this tide with the notorious Corn Law of 1815, and other protectionist impediments to trade.[7]

This protectionist revival in part stimulated the famous, if exaggerated, public

[2]   D. G. Barnes, *A History of the English Corn Laws, 1660–1846* (1930); R. L. Schuyler, *The Fall of the Old Colonial System* (Oxford, 1945); P. J. Cain and A. G. Hopkins, 'Gentlemanly Capitalism and British Expansion Overseas, I: The Old Colonial System, 1688–1850', *Economic History Review*, 2nd ser., 39 (1986), 501–26.

[3]   S. Palmer, *Politics, Shipping and the Repeal of the Navigation Laws* (Manchester, 1990), 40.

[4]   *Parl. Papers*, 1840, 5 (601), iii–vii; for a full discussion, L. Brown, *The Board of Trade and the Free-Trade Movement, 1830–42* (Oxford, 1958), esp. 141–213; D. M. Williams, 'Customs Evasion, Colonial Preference and the British Tariff, 1829–1842', in P. L. Cottrell and D. H. Aldcroft (eds.), *Shipping, Trade and Commerce, Essays in Memory of Ralph Davis* (Leicester, 1981), 99–116.

[5]   R. F. Teichgraeber III, ' "Less Abused than I had Reason to Expect": The Reception of *The Wealth of Nations* in Britain, 1776–90', *Historical Journal*, 30 (1987), 337–66; D. Winch, *Riches and Poverty: An Intellectual History of Political Economy in Britain, 1750–1834* (Cambridge, 1996), 157–62; D. Irwin, *Against the Tide: An Intellectual History of Free Trade* (Princeton, 1996), chs. 5 and 6.

[6]   W. O. Henderson, 'The Anglo-French Commercial Treaty of 1786', *EcHR*, 2nd ser., 10 (1957–8), 104–12; M. M. Donaghey, 'Textiles and the Anglo-French Treaty of 1786', *Textile History*, 13 (1982), 205–24; J. P. W. Ehrmann, *The British Government and Commercial Negotiations with Europe, 1783–93* (Cambridge, 1962); J. E. Crowley, 'Neo-mercantilism and *The Wealth of Nations*: British Commercial Policy after the American Revolution', *Historical Journal*, 33 (1990), 339–60.

[7]   A. Webster, 'The Political Economy of Trade Liberalization: the East India Company Act of 1813', *EcHR*, 2nd ser., 43 (1990), 404–19; A. J. B. Hilton, *Corn, Cash, and Commerce: The Economic Policies of the Tory Governments, 1815–1830* (Oxford Historical Monographs: Oxford, 1977). For the course of trade in the nineteenth century, see K. Harley, 'Foreign Trade: Comparative Advantage and Performance', in R. Floud and D. McCloskey (eds.), *The Economic History of Britain since 1700. Vol. 1 1700–1860* (2nd edn., 1994), 300–31.

advocacy of free trade in the London Merchants' Petition of 1820, but the Liberal Tory governments of the 1820s were to prove themselves well in advance of mercantile opinion in pursuing freer trade.[8] With Huskisson at the Board of Trade, many tariffs were lowered and abolished, a continuation of the Pittite process of administrative rationalization and financial reform designed to maximize revenue and minimize the cost of its collection.[9] Huskisson's Reciprocity of Duties Act of 1823 also reduced significantly the scope of the Navigation Acts, by allowing any nation to transport goods into Britain in return for the same privilege, from which twenty-seven reciprocity treaties had resulted by 1844.[10] Eventually, too, the Tory government defied its own agricultural supporters in modifying protection, with the Corn Law of 1828 tacitly acknowledging Britain's future dependence upon foreign supplies of corn, and the need to encourage new markets for her own manufactured goods. Freer trade, driven by the administrative pragmatism of the Liberal Tories, might itself have led to the abandonment of the Corn Laws but for the break-up of the Tory government and the return of the Whigs to office in 1830.[11]

The Whig governments of the 1830s revealed themselves as cautious and inconsistent in economic policy. They were understandably anxious not to alienate their own landed supporters. Therefore, rather than advancing the cause of free trade (save by piecemeal measures), they sought political success in measures of constitutional, religious, and social reform that were designed to consolidate their traditional stance as custodians of civil and religious liberty, as well as their growing aspirations towards the 'trusteeship of the people' in early industrial England.[12] The Whigs' own financial experts, who shared much in common with the Liberal Tories, were largely impotent, with, for example, Althorp retiring from office in 1834, and Poulett Thomson accepting premature colonial exile in 1839. Most of the momentum for free trade therefore moved from the Cabinet to the Radicals within the Board of Trade—whose ideas strongly marked the Select Committee on Import Duties in 1840—and to the parliamentary Radicals and their provincial allies—notably, from 1838 the Manchester Anti-Corn Law Association (from 1839 the formidable Anti-Corn Law League).[13] Despite some belated Whig moves to harness the electoral benefits of this movement, their defeat in the election of 1841 left

[8] T. Tooke and W. Newmarch, *A History of Prices and of the State of the Circulation from 1793 to the Present Time* (6 vols, 1838–57), vol. 5, 343; Hilton, *Corn*, 173–5; W. D. Grammp, 'How Britain turned to Free Trade', *Business History Review*, 61 (1987), 86–112; A. C. Howe, 'Free Trade and the City of London, *c.*1820–1870', *History*, 77 (1992), 393.

[9] Hilton, *Corn*, *passim*; P. Harling, *The Waning of 'Old Corruption': The Politics of Economical Reform in Britain, 1779–1846* (Oxford, 1996).

[10] Palmer, *Shipping*, 50–2.

[11] Hilton, *Corn*, 269–301, 306–7.

[12] Brown, *Board of Trade*; R. Brent, *Liberal Anglican Politics, 1830–1841* (Oxford, 1987); P. Mandler, *Aristocratic Government in the Age of Reform. Whigs and Liberals, 1830–1852* (Oxford, 1990); J. P. Parry, *The Rise and Fall of Liberal Government in Victorian Britain* (1993), 113–54.

[13] Brown, *Board of Trade*, 70–5; N. McCord, *The Anti-Corn Law League, 1838–1846* (1958).

open the way for the Liberal Tory Peel to complete the reforms of the 1820s, with the introduction of peacetime income tax in 1842, the revision of the sliding scale for corn, and a series of budgets which largely demolished the fiscal *ancien régime*, reducing 750 duties in 1842 and abolishing 450 in 1845.[14] Peel, as Hilton has argued, arrived at free trade by a different route from that taken by the Whigs, Radicals, and the Select Committee on Import Duties, but the policy prescriptions which assured his goal of a 'just economy' were now identical in the minds of many with those that sought 'an expanding one'.[15]

However, quite unlike that of the 1820s, this executive process of fiscal reform was set against the spectre of bitter class and party conflict.[16] The extra-parliamentary pressure of the Chartist movement made insistent the importance of bread prices and wages as components of the 'Condition of England' question, while the Anti-Corn Law League voiced effectively the demands of entrepreneurial politics, symbolized by its leader Richard Cobden with his 'middle class set of agitators'.[17] This struggle not only opposed the 'lords of the loom' against the 'lords of the soil', but portended a whole series of reforms in Church, State, and the colonies, designed, some feared, to root entrepreneurial values within the heart of the erstwhile 'territorial constitution'.[18] The Whigs, despite the fears of some of their landowners, were now prepared to endorse Repeal, although they were not ready in December 1845 to form a government in order to do so.[19] In January 1846, as growing fears of famine in Ireland made urgent the need for governmental action on the Corn Laws, Peel proposed to Parliament their total repeal rather than resort merely to their suspension.[20] As the debate over Repeal engulfed Parliament and the country between January and June, Peel found himself opposed by the bulk of his party and its rural supporters, a rupture that had long threatened.[21] In June 1846

[14]　Brown, *Board of Trade*, 224–30; B. Hilton, 'Peel: A Reappraisal', *Historical Journal*, 21 (1979), 585–614; N. Gash, *Sir Robert Peel: The Life of Sir Robert Peel after 1830* (1972), 295–329, 450–67; Harling, '*Old Corruption*', 240–8.

[15]　B. Hilton, *The Age of Atonement: The Influence of Evangelicalism on Social and Economic Thought, 1785–1865* (Oxford, 1988), 248; below, 11.

[16]　G. Kitson-Clark, 'Hunger and Politics in 1842', *Journal of Modern History*, 25 (1953), 355–74; A. Briggs (ed.), *Chartist Studies* (1959); J. Epstein and D. Thompson, *The Chartist Experience: Working-class Radicalism and Culture* (1982); R. Stewart, *Party and Politics, 1830–1852* (1989); Gash, *Peel*, for a very selective list.

[17]　McCord, *Anti-Corn Law League*; A. Howe, *The Cotton Masters, 1830–1860* (Oxford Historical Monographs: Oxford, 1984); J. Prest, *Politics in the Age of Cobden* (1977); G. R. Searle, *Entrepreneurial Politics in Mid-Victorian Britain* (Oxford, 1993), 17–50.

[18]　F. M. L. Thompson, *English Landed Society in the Nineteenth Century* (1963), 283; Howe, *Cotton Masters*, 208.

[19]　F. A. Dreyer, 'The Whigs and the Political Crisis of 1845', *English Historical Review*, 80 (1965), 514–37; Mandler, *Aristocratic Government*, 231–3.

[20]　For a recent study, see C. Kenealy, *This Great Calamity. The Irish Famine, 1845–52* (Dublin, 1994).

[21]　R. Stewart, *The Politics of Protection. Lord Derby and the Protectionist Party, 1841–52* (Cambridge, 1971); I. D. C. Newbould, 'Sir Robert Peel and the Conservative Party, 1832–1841', *EHR*, 98 (1983), 529–57.

more than two hundred Tory MPs voted against Repeal and were prepared shortly after to accept the return of a Whig government as more bearable than the continued leadership of their party by its 'betrayer'.

In this way the repeal of the Corn Laws was not simply the logical culmination of Liberal Tory economic reform, but became indissolubly linked with the class politics of the 1840s and the permanent scarring and division of the Tory Party. In turn, Repeal signified not simply the emergence of a new fiscal system, but became immediately and lastingly enveloped in a series of myths central to British political memory in the nineteenth and early twentieth centuries. Their starting-point was the contemporary interpretation of Repeal, hailing the victory of the League over both Peel and the aristocracy. From this grew an inveterate Victorian identification of free trade with British power and prosperity, while, for the Edwardians, the narrative of Repeal contained a central parable of the people's deliverance from the aristocratic oppression symbolized by the 'hungry forties'. Repeal therefore cast a long political shadow, still weakly discernible on its centenary in 1946, but finally dispelled in the 1950s.[22] The myth of Repeal is, however, essential to an understanding of free trade in nineteenth-century Britain, and its genesis deserves brief recapitulation before we consider the historical orthodoxies which have more recently replaced it.

The overarching free trade myth—that of the victory of the 'millocrats' of the Anti-Corn Law League over Britain's proud aristocracy—sprang from a mixed parenthood. On the one hand, it was a Tory myth, lent credibility by Peel's encomium to Cobden for his part in Repeal in 1846, but propagated above all by Disraeli's protectionist interpretation of Repeal as the betrayal of the old Tory party, as well as by his invention of the term 'the Manchester School'.[23] In Disraeli's view, Peel, acting as the League's disciple, had unnecessarily sacrificed the interests of the tenant farmers, the landed gentry, and the aristocracy to the pressures of urban England and the 'Manchester confederacy'.[24] For, in Repeal the anti-Peelite Tories saw not simply the abandonment of protection for agriculture, but a fundamental erosion of British power, based as it was on land, shipping, and the empire; above all, Repeal embodied a constitutional revolution, with Peel sacrificing the power of Parliament at the altar of the Anti-Corn Law League and its upstart millowners.

On the other hand, Radical and League-inspired accounts of Repeal were equally anxious to proclaim the 'victory' of 'Manchester man' and the defeat of 'unrighteous monopoly', themes announced in Prentice's triumphalist two-volume

---

[22] McCord, *Anti-Corn Law League*, 208–16; G. Kitson-Clark, 'The Electorate and the Repeal of the Corn Laws', *TRHS*, 5th ser., 1 (1951), 109–26; id., 'The Repeal of the Corn Laws and the Politics of the 'Forties', *EcHR*, 2nd ser., 4 (1951–2), 1–13.

[23] B. Disraeli, *Lord George Bentinck; A Political Biography* (1852; new edn., 1861); T. S. Ashton, 'The origin of the Manchester School', *The Manchester School*, 1 (1930–1), 58–90; D. Read, *Peel and the Victorians* (1987), 237 ff.

[24] Disraeli, *Bentinck*, esp. 72, 84, 142, 151, 154–5, 221.

account of the League, published in 1853.[25] Prentice's work was important in two ways. First, it provided a thorough and coherent account of the League, based on an intimate knowledge of its inner workings, which permanently established the image of the millocrats' League driving the nation forward to Repeal. However much the history of the League had been, as Cobden privately admitted, 'a blundering unsystematic series of campaigns', Prentice fulfilled Cobden's exhortation to 'Shew how vastly the power, the moral power of Manchester has been increased by having been the home of the League'.[26] Second, Prentice's book immediately replaced other, more jaundiced and chaotic accounts of the League's operations, for example that of the erstwhile League lecturer Alexander Somerville.[27] Prentice's *History* was also well complemented by that of Henry Dunckley, a youthful publicist whose book *The Charter of the Nations: or Free Trade and its Results* (1854) won the (briefly revived) League's prize competition in 1852, when a renewed drive against protectionism seemed prudent with a minority Tory government in power. For Dunckley, the merits of free trade were already incontrovertible, embodying a peaceful constitutional and social revolution, a model which, in the aftermath of the Revolutions of 1848, differentiated Britain from her continental rivals.[28]

Yet Protectionist and Radical interpretations of Repeal were rapidly joined by the myth of Peel popularized in the wake of his untimely death in 1850. Not only did Peelites such as Gladstone, Cardwell, and Stanhope re-create their own pasts, with Peel succeeding Pitt as the model of impartial executive government, but, as Read has shown, the cult of Peel became deeply and immediately rooted in middle- and working-class opinion, with artisans and factory operatives ready to acclaim him as author of their deliverance from the miseries of the 1840s.[29] Even the Leaguer and cotton master Henry Ashworth saw in the pennies subscribed for Peel memorials 'the future guarantee of a Free Trade policy'.[30] This cardinal Peelite association with Repeal, although, as we will see, increasingly submerged in the

[25]   A. Prentice, *History of the Anti-Corn Law League* (2 vols, 1853; 2nd. edn. introd. by W. H. Chaloner, 1968).
[26]   Cobden to Prentice, 8 Aug. 1853 and 13 Sept. 1851, CP-21, Cobden Papers, West Sussex Record Office (WSRO).
[27]   Somerville's *Free Trade and the League* (2 vols, Manchester, 1853) provided 'a biographic history of the pioneers of freedom of opinion, commercial enterprise, and civilization in Britain', which began with Offa and Alfred and ended with the League; *The Whistler at the Plough and Free Trade* (1852), dedicated to Lord John Russell, included many of Somerville's League writings on rural England. Somerville, however, fell out badly with the Manchester School at this time, and in 1854 published a bitter indictment of *Cobdenic Policy: The Internal Enemy of England*. A second League employee, and son-in-law of T. P. Thompson, Andrew Bisset was also at work in the early 1850s on a history of England since the Stuarts, with especial attention to the land laws. He later published *Notes on the Anti-Corn Law Struggle* (1884).
[28]   Dunckley, a Baptist preacher, later became the editor of the *Manchester Examiner*; for his career, see *Manchester Guardian*, 30 June 1896.
[29]   H. C. G. Matthew, *Gladstone, 1809–1874* (Oxford, 1986), 101; *Memoirs of the Right Hon. Sir Robert Peel*, ed. Lord Stanhope and E. Cardwell (2 vols, 1856–7); Read, *Peel and the Victorians*, passim.
[30]   Ashworth to Cobden, 19 Oct. 1850, CP 3, WSRO.

later cult of Cobden, proved long-lived. It remained powerful in the early twentieth century, and was particularly attractive to Liberal Unionists such as Arthur Elliot and Lord Northbrook, who distinguished carefully between Peelite and Cobdenite variants of free trade.[31]

In recent historiography this Peelite view has remained influential and, in many ways, prevalent.[32] Painstakingly, the encrustations of the myth of the Anti-Corn Law League have been carefully removed by the modern restorers of political art, revealing in Repeal the supreme act of enlightened Conservative statesmanship. For Kitson-Clark in 1929, as for Gash in 1972, Peel acted in a way that secured the future of traditional institutions and pointed out the path of Conservative progress, balancing the needs of working-class welfare, economic growth, and aristocratic survival.[33] Far from signifying the victory of the League's external pressure, Repeal represented only part of the seamless process of aristocratic adjustment in Victorian Britain.[34] Since some Tories were already 'liberal' in economic policy, and the Whigs were converts to a moderate fixed duty, if not repeal, in 1841, the League itself was almost an unnecessary intrusion upon parliamentary government. 'Noisy' but 'meagre' in influence and power, it may even have delayed the goal to which it was devoted.[35] Peel's own decision to propose repeal of the Corn Laws in 1846 was in this view at once far-sighted and pragmatic, the product of long-term aspirations and 'a sensible response' to both the 'Condition of England' question and the famine in Ireland.[36] Even for historians who see in Peel a more dogmatic, or abstract, approach to policy-making, Repeal represents the natural outcome of the policies of freer trade adopted in the 1820s, policies whose aim had been moderate growth and financial stability, rather than the export-led, optimistic, even millenarianist expectations of the League's supporters.[37]

This consensus upon Peel's resolute and skilful statesmanship is therefore well established, and there is no need to dissent from its recognition of the importance of Peel's vision and disinterestedness in order to emphasize the wider context in which historians and social scientists have recently sought to understand Repeal. To the agency of Peel himself and to the widespread debunking of the League myth, there have been added sophisticated explanations of the ideological, structural, parliamentary, and international determinants of the repeal of the Corn

[31] Northbrook to Elliot, 25 Sept. 1903, EP 19493, Arthur Elliot Papers, National Library of Scotland; Elliot found Thursfield's *Peel* (1893) 'good reading at the present juncture', and Parker's *Peel* (3 vols, 1891–9) 'very instructive reading just now', Diary, 24 May and 6 June 1903, EP 19526.
[32] For a suggestive context, see M. Bentley, 'Liberal Toryism in the Twentieth Century', *TRHS*, 6th ser., 4 (1995), 177–201.
[33] G. S. R. Kitson-Clark, *Peel and the Conservative Party* (1929); Gash, *Peel*.
[34] Typically, B. Kemp, 'Reflections on the Repeal of the Corn Laws', *Victorian Studies*, 5 (1961–2), 189–204; for a rare dissenting view, see J. C. D. Clark, *English Society, 1688–1832* (1985), 455.
[35] N. McCord, *British History, 1815–1906* (1991), 152–3, 169–70; Parry, *Liberal Government*, 143–7.
[36] McCord, *British History*, 165.
[37] Hilton, 'Peel: A Reappraisal', and id., *Atonement*, 248–50.

Laws. A review of such interpretations revises in important ways our understanding of free trade as a defining characteristic of Liberal England.

The Corn Laws and free trade ideology

Most simply, Repeal in 1846 has been seen as the culmination of the impact of enlightened economic ideas upon policy-making. To the early and well-documented impact of Smith has been added that of Ricardo and a host of lesser political economists, within Parliament and without, through the periodical press and the institutions of the provincial economic literati.[38] By the 1840s the Corn Laws remained as the outstanding example of artificial interference in the natural order of the economy, after the gradual rationalization of the tariff, the reform of the Poor Law, and of monetary policy. This critique had been lent added point and popularity in the 1830s by the strident writings of Tooke, Torrens, and T. P. Thompson, 'an Anti-Corn Law League of intellectuals' which Fay believed had effectively eroded the defences of the Corn Laws before Manchester came into action.[39] The Ricardian critique was also lent force by the Political Economy Club, many of whose leading members supported repeal by 1842, and by the founding of *The Economist* in 1843.[40] Within the machinery of the state itself, at the Board of Trade, a group of dogmatic free traders, led by J. D. Hume and J. MacGregor, had acted throughout the 1830s as an influential conduit for liberal ideas and policies.[41] In all these ways one may see the emergence of the secular model of free trade, a vision of unlimited growth and progress, 'expansionist, industrialist, competitive, and cosmopolitan' in its tendencies, a vision later exemplified in the writings of Mill, Fawcett, and Jevons, and an inherent part 'of the mental furniture of every educated Victorian'.[42]

However plausible this ideological explanation of Repeal, few models of policy-making have been so effectively undermined as this one in recent years. Above all, the work of Hilton has shown that within the world-view of the political élite, the ethical content of free trade derived far more from the beliefs of evangelical religion than those of political economy.[43] In the 1820s, as in the 1840s, Hilton has argued,

---

[38]   Amidst a vast literature, see M. Blaug, *Ricardian Economics. A Historical Study* (New Haven, 1958); W. D. Grampp, *The Manchester School of Economics* (1960); M. Berg, 'Progress and Providence in English Nineteenth-Century Political Economy', *Social History*, 15 (1989), 365–75; F. W. Fetter, *The Economist in Parliament, 1780–1868* (Durham, NC, 1980); Winch, *Riches and Poverty*; Irwin, *Against the Tide.*

[39]   C. R. Fay, *The Corn Laws and Social England* (Cambridge, 1932), 151; L. G. Johnson, *General T. Perronet Thompson* (1957).

[40]   *Political Economy Club. Minutes of Proceedings, 1899–1920, Roll of Members, and Questions Discussed, 1821–1920* (1921), vol. 4, 3 Mar. 1842; R. Dudley Edwards, *The Pursuit of Reason: The Economist, 1843–1993* (1993).

[41]   Brown, *Board of Trade*, 20–33.

[42]   Hilton, *Atonement*, 69; P. Adelman, *Victorian Radicalism* (1984), 25.

[43]   Hilton, *Corn*, 307–14; id., *Atonement, passim.*

'the more widespread and probably more influential' model of free trade was derived from evangelical political economy, a vision 'more cyclical, retributive and nationalist in its tendencies' than the Ricardian model. Paying particular attention to the Liberal Tories, Hilton has convincingly demonstrated that they owed little to the secular Ricardians, but much to Christian political economists such as Copleston, Senior (in his earlier career), and Chalmers. As advocates of freer trade, the Liberal Tories sought stability and morality through the removal of artificial props in the economic world, allowing the operation of the providential order, with God-given rather than man-made pains and penalties. This emphasis encouraged banking and Poor Law reform, as well as the gradual removal of protective duties. Although the depth of the evangelical commitment of some Liberal Tory politicians may be questioned, Hilton makes out a plausible case that this religious morality predominated among 'those in the City, the service economy, and the professions', all of whom subscribed to 'progressive gentry, *rentier*, and metropolitan values'.[44]

Hilton's account, however, needs to be supplemented at several points. First, it draws too sharp a dichotomy between a 'secular North' of England, and an 'evangelical South'; undoubtedly, the industrialists of the North were fully exposed to evangelical influences, both Anglican and Nonconformist, even if the balance between them differed from that in the metropolis.[45] Second, it deals less well with the strong High Church sentiment in the metropolis and universities. Rightly, Hilton suggests that this merges with evangelicalism in some cases, but that in others it sustained a different vision, of continued managerial intervention by the state, embracing policies such as the Bank Charter Act as well as continued support for protectionism.[46] Finally, Hilton limits his conclusions to the Liberal Tories, leaving in limbo those Whigs who equally belonged to the world of the progressive gentry and metropolitan élite. Here, however, his account may usefully be supplemented, for, as Mandler has shown, by the late 1820s many Whigs had gravitated towards 'liberal values', partly under the influence of evangelical religion, but also that of the Scottish Enlightenment.[47] Brent has also made out an interesting case for a distinctive Whig brand of 'liberal political economy'.[48] Exemplified above all by the Drummond Professors at Oxford after 1832, this creed foreshadowed the Whigs' rapid move towards free trade after 1840, although this movement had been

[44] Hilton, *Atonement*, esp. ix, 64–70, 135, 188–201, 260–5, 375–6, cf. review by N. Gash, *EHR*, 104 (1989), 136–40.

[45] J. Garnett and A. C. Howe, 'Churchmen and Cotton Masters', in D. J. Jeremy (ed.), *Business and Religion in Modern Britain* (1988), 72–94; M. Smith, *Religion in Industrial Society: Oldham and Saddleworth, 1740–1865* (Oxford Historical Monographs: Oxford, 1994).

[46] Howe, 'City of London', 394–5.

[47] Mandler, *Aristocratic Government*, esp. 23–33.

[48] R. Brent, 'God's Providence: Liberal Political Economy as Natural Theology at Oxford, 1825–60', in M. Bentley (ed.), *Public and Private Doctrine* (Cambridge, 1993), 85–107.

well prepared by their long exposure to the free trade ideas of Horner, Brougham, and the pages of the *Edinburgh Review*.[49]

With free trade in the ascendant in the 1840s, both in its secular and evangelical models, earlier Tory and Whig beliefs in protection and in reciprocity rapidly wilted, but by no means disappeared. Protectionism continued to be defended by some metropolitan Anglicans, university Tractarians, segments of the aristocracy, and by some evangelicals. It remained a lively force well into the 1850s, with expert financiers like Henry Burgess, as well as young aristocratic Oxonians such as Ingestre, ready to defend a 'Country' tradition in economics. Similarly, the protectionist view of national power based on shipping and the Navigation Laws continued to strike a chord in the seaports, especially in London and Liverpool.[50] Yet protectionism was unable to escape the appearance of the articulation of vested interests under threat, and the English protectionists lacked the intellectual spur provided by Hamilton and Carey in America, or by Fichte and List in Germany. Only in Ireland did protectionism produce an intellectually respectable defence: that of Isaac Butt, later to be leader of the Home Government Association, but at this point Whately Professor of Political Economy at Trinity College, Dublin. Those in favour of repealing the union with Ireland were divided, however, for some upheld the Corn Laws as a buttress of Ireland's agrarian prosperity, while others, including 'The Liberator' Daniel O'Connell, actively canvassed the cause of free trade, at least on the mainland.[51]

The leading English alternative to free trade remained, therefore, the case for reciprocity, the cornerstone of Huskissonite freer trade in the 1820s, but a policy still strongly urged by the political economist Torrens in 1844, and taken up by Disraeli in the later 1840s, as we will see in Chapter 3.[52] The case for reciprocity, and admiration for Huskisson, remained considerable in the 1840s, but the repeal of the Corn Laws in 1846 represented a broader doctrine of free trade. For Peel consciously adopted this policy not as an emergency measure dictated by the Irish famine, but as a choice between restriction and openness in world trade.[53] Openness

[49]   B. Fontana, *Rethinking the Politics of Commercial Society* (Cambridge, 1985); W. D. Sockwell, 'The Contribution of Henry Brougham to Classical Political Economy', *History of Political Economy*, 23 (1991), 645–73; K. Bourne and W. B. Taylor (eds.), *The Horner Papers. Selections from the Letters and Miscellaneous Writings of Francis Horner MP 1795–1817* (Edinburgh, 1994).

[50]   A. D. Macintyre, 'Lord George Bentinck and the Protectionists: A Lost Cause?', *TRHS*, 5th ser., 39 (1989), 141–65; Howe, 'City of London', 401–4.

[51]   R. D. Collison Black, *Economic Thought and the Irish Question* (Cambridge, 1960), 140–4; K. Nowlan, *The Politics of Repeal* (1964), 99–105; D. O'Connell, *Observations on Corn Laws, on Political Pravity and Ingratitude, and on Clerical and Personal Slander, in the shape of a Meek and Modest Reply to the Second Letter of the Earl of Shrewsbury to Ambrose Lisle Phillipps, Esq.* (Dublin, 1842); J. O'Connell, *Reflections of a Parliamentary Career* (2 vols, 1849), vol. 1, 330, 333–4, 336–46; vol. 2, 128–36, combining support for Irish manufactures with hostility to the Corn Laws.

[52]   R. Torrens, *The Budget. On Commercial and Colonial Policy* (1844; reprint, 1970); L. Robbins, *Robert Torrens and the Evolution of Classical Economics* (1958); L. Gomes, *Foreign Trade and the National Economy: Mercantilist and Classical Perspectives* (1987), 198; below, 87.

[53]   *Hansard*, 3rd ser., 83, c. 1042, 16 Feb. 1846.

now required more than a policy of reciprocal commercial treaty negotiation of the sort advocated by Huskisson in the 1820s, but whose diminishing returns had become evident to Peel and Gladstone by 1845.[54] Rather, in Peel's view Britain had now deliberately to adopt a policy of free imports as necessary to her own prosperity, and also as an 'example of liberality to other countries'. In the 1890s Peel's grandson George was to emphasize that the policy of 'free imports' was for Peel 'the discovery of a new world', necessitating the abandonment of the policy of reciprocity dear to the Liberal Tories of the 1820s.[55] Dramatically, in 1846 Peel proclaimed to the inhabitants of Elbing in Germany his conviction that 'by encouraging freedom of intercourse between the nations of the world, we are promoting the separate welfare of each and are fulfilling the beneficent designs of an all-wise Creator', with 'Commerce the happy instrument of promoting civilisation, of abating national jealousies and prejudices and of encouraging the maintenance of general peace by every consideration as well as every obligation of Christian duty'.[56]

It is arguable that in espousing unilateral free trade, Peel had at this point moved from his earlier adherence to the ethical beliefs of retributive evangelical theology within a national framework towards an endorsement of Cobden's cosmopolitanism, to a perception of the moral and material benefits of free international exchange, if not a vision of unlimited growth and progress; to some extent the two models of free trade which Hilton has so daringly analysed now overlapped in the mind of Peel himself.[57] It was this version of 'Liberal Free Trade', so close to that of the League, which so dismayed and alarmed Huskissonites such as Sir John Gladstone, for whom the 'true meaning' of free trade remained 'a reciprocal exchange of the commodities of two independent countries, each admitting the production of the other free of duty'.[58] Clearly, Peel's universal free trade now threatened to leave behind some of the evangelical caution of the earlier Liberal Tory generation, and, as Hilton allows, the Cobdenite, secular, cosmopolitan model of free trade, vociferously and widely disseminated by the League in the 1840s, now rapidly eroded the providentialist arguments of the Liberal Tories.[59] In the case of the 'last Liberal Tory' William Gladstone, it also required the Irish famine to underline the stark moral choice between Repeal and the permanent maintenance of protection, although Gladstone's support for the former had already become

[54]   F. Hyde, *Mr Gladstone at the Board of Trade* (1934), 125–8; W. E. Gladstone, *Remarks upon Recent Commercial Legislation* (1845).

[55]   C. S. Parker, *Sir Robert Peel from his Private Papers* (3 vols, 1891–9), vol. 3, 587.

[56]   Draft, Peel's reply (5 Aug. 1846) to the Elbing address (14 July), Peel Papers, Add. MS 40612, fos. 227–8; for J. Prince Smith's part in the latter, see W. O. Henderson, *Britain and Industrial Europe, 1750–1870* (Leicester, 1972), 168–70.

[57]   Hilton, *Atonement*, 248–50; or, as the Protectionist Croker put it: 'He [Peel] is much nearer to the Radicals than to any other party in the State', to Wellington, 29 June 1846 in *The Croker Papers*, ed. L. J. Jennings (3 vols, 1885), vol. 3, 114.

[58]   Sir John Gladstone, 'Free Trade', MS, 23 July 1846, Glynne–Gladstone Papers, 1187, St Deniols Library, Hawarden (Clwyd Record Office).

[59]   Hilton, *Atonement*, 68–70, 188–202, 246–8.

clear by 1845.[60] Thereafter, free trade, as Matthew has illuminatingly argued, replaced for Gladstone the Anglican Church as the key instrument through which God harmoniously adjusted the class relations of industrial society, while it also became part of Britain's providential mission to the world.[61] In these ways the decision to repeal the Corn Laws in 1846 contained important new ideological slants which would exercise a strong subsequent influence. Yet for many Victorians support for Repeal was not perhaps the elevated and painstaking ethical choice that it was for Gladstone. More frequently, historians have moved from the realms of evangelical morality and political economy to ask how far Peel's advocacy of Repeal in 1846 was open to the pressures of economic interest, the collective influence of either industry or the City, the brazen power of the League's 'Gothic invaders', or the more subtle manœuvres of the nation's 'gentlemanly capitalists'.

The Corn Laws and 'Gentlemanly Capitalism'

'Gentlemanly capitalism', that social order based on the confluence of power between the monied interest and the landed élite, which, it has been powerfully argued, dominated Britain after the Revolution of 1688, faced a stern dual challenge in the 1830s and 1840s.[62] On the one hand, free trade threatened the central prop of the old order, the protection that land had enjoyed in return for the benefits it bestowed upon its City of London allies. On the other hand, those benefits had already come under stringent scrutiny in the widespread attack upon 'Old Corruption', and free trade itself threatened the protectionist and preferential system under which many City institutions had prospered. The emergence of the Anti-Corn Law League as the spearhead of industrial opinion in favour of free trade therefore challenged both the land and the City of London for primacy in the formation of economic policy. Superficially, the repeal of the Corn Laws looks like a concession to industry, but ultimately, it has been argued, the beneficiaries of free trade would be the City and its allies. Repeal therefore neatly counterposes the forces of land, the City, and industry in a way that provides an ideal opportunity to test the applicability of the sociological model which opposes the City and industry as determinants of economic policy-making.[63] How far did the City of London, the most obvious location of Britain's gentlemanly capitalists, itself adopt a distinctive view of the Corn Laws? And how much more successful was it than the exporters

---

[60]   Hilton, *Atonement*, 350–1.

[61]   *The Gladstone Diaries*, ed. M. R. D. Foot and H. C. G. Matthew (14 vols, Oxford, 1968–94) (hereafter *GD*), vol. 3, xxxvi–xlii.

[62]   P. J. Cain and A. G. Hopkins, *British Imperialism* (2 vols, 1993); id., 'Gentlemanly Capitalism and British Overseas Expansion I: The Old Colonial System, 1688–1850', *EcHR*, 2nd ser., 39 (1986), 501–26; id., 'II: The New Imperialism, 1850–1945', ibid. 11 (1987), 1–26; cf. M. Daunton, ' "Gentlemanly Capitalism" and British Industry', *Past and Present*, 122 (1989), 119–58.

[63]   In addition to Cain and Hopkins, see G. Ingham, *Capitalism Divided: The City and Industry in British Social Development* (1984).

of the North in exerting pressure on the government? Did the City encourage the state to adopt free trade, or was it the passive beneficiary of a policy that allowed the state itself to rise above interest groups, to redefine free trade not simply as a strategy of ruling-class domination, but as an ideology which freed the state from its dependence upon 'Old Corruption' and landed power?

It is to some extent unfashionable to subject ambitious historical speculation to mere empirical investigation, but there is perhaps a case for asking how far Britain's City-based financiers did themselves seek to encourage the adoption of free trade as part of such an aggressive and purposive strategy of ruling-class domination.[64] Here, the evidence of City attitudes suggests neither a united front, firm purpose, nor covert power. As on most issues, the City spoke in several tongues, none of them particularly influential in the counsels of Whig or Tory parties. Certainly, the League's campaign for Repeal scarcely endeared it to the City's gentlemanly capitalists, with its orator A. W. Paulton reporting colourfully in 1840: 'The City does not behave well in the matter; they are a heap of rascally monopolists themselves and they are somewhat fearful of loosening the wedge that holds all the rotten rubbish of corruption together.'[65] When a Metropolitan Anti-Corn Law Association was set up in 1840, it was largely the work of Francis Place and the Philosophic Radicals, not of City types, as is indicated by Place's failure to raise more than £10 for the cause.[66] Possibly, City distaste was not so much for the goal of free trade as for the League's methods and democratic rhetoric. It is interesting in this context that the evangelical free trader W. W. Whitmore (originally from the City, but subsequently a Shropshire country gentleman) proposed to Samuel Jones Loyd (the future Lord Overstone) in 1841 a 'London-based agitation on the lines of the anti-slavery campaign, with the hope of countering the political radicalism, economic ignorance, and ethical optimism of the Anti-Corn Law League'.[67] The upshot of this, if any, is unknown, but moderate free trade did acquire growing City support in the early 1840s, just as Whig policy was moving in this direction. For example, in April 1841 George Grote, the Philosophic Radical banker, presented to the House of Commons a petition from the City in favour of the revision of import duties. The signatures, headed by that of J. H. Palmer, East India merchant and former Governor of the Bank of England, comprised the 'great leading firms in this metropolis'. This petition enabled the Whigs to claim the support both of the merchants of London and the manufacturers of the North for their wavering moves in the direction of free trade.[68] Leading City voices, both Conservative and Liberal,

[64] Cain and Hopkins, *British Imperialism*, 32–3.
[65] Quoted in McCord, *Anti-Corn Law League*, 76.
[66] Ibid. 77; *London Radicalism, 1830–43: A Selection from the Papers of Francis Place*, ed. D. J. Rowe (London Record Society, 1975), 210 ff. The League's London activities were, in part, organized from the offices of Joseph Travers and Sons, tea and sugar merchants, St Swithin's Lane. See *Joseph Travers and Sons. A Few Records of an Old Firm* (privately printed, 1924), 32.
[67] Hilton, *Atonement*, 206.   [68] *Hansard*, 3rd ser., 57, c. 1353, 30 Apr. (Labouchère).

also seem to have moved at this point behind the revamped Whig policy of a moderate fixed duty on corn.[69]

Only slowly, therefore, did gentlemanly capitalists turn towards total repeal rather than a fixed duty, and then largely as a result of League pressure and in response to changing governmental policy. Significantly, City voices in a discussion of the Corn Laws at the Political Economy Club in March 1842 saw both Radical (G. W. Norman) and evangelical (Samuel Jones Loyd, contrary to Whitmore's earlier suggestion) support for Repeal against the moderate fixed duty defended by the Russian merchant Hubbard. More dramatically, in 1843 Loyd became the first major City figure (although with Lancashire roots) to subscribe to the Anti-Corn Law League. Here was the first sign that, in the words of the Revd W. J. Fox, London might not after all be 'a cistern for the foul toads of monopoly to knot and gender in'.[70] Loyd's conversion was prompted by a by-election in the City of London which served to polarize opinion between the League brand of free trade, upheld by the otherwise moderate Whig merchant James Pattison, and the protec-tionists led by Thomas Baring, probably the City's leading figure at this time.[71] As part of its campaign in this election, the League also promoted the foundation of *The Economist* in an attempt to mobilize the monied interest behind free trade and to complement the industrial readership of its own journal, *The Anti-Bread Tax Circular*, which in September 1843 became *The League*.[72] The election itself was a triumph for the League, and in some ways a decisive turning-point in the Repeal campaign.[73] Even so, the margin of victory was small (6,532 votes to 6,367), which was evidence against any rapid crumbling of protectionism in the City. It was, for example, believed that many protectionists had abstained.[74] Moreover, the League's success was almost certainly the result of the mobilization of the popular vote in the City, through the activities of Place and P. A. Taylor, agitating in

---

[69]   J. G. Hubbard, *Vindication of a Fixed Duty on Corn* (1842); D. Salomons, *Reflections on the operation of the Present Scale of Duty for regulating the Importation of Foreign Corn* (1840); id., *The Corn Laws: Their Effects on the Trade of the Country Considered* (1841). Overstone also prominently supported Lord John Russell's candidature for the City of London in the 1841 election; D. P. O'Brien, *The Correspondence of Lord Overstone* (3 vols, Cambridge, 1971), vol. 1, 324–5.

[70]   *Political Economy Club, Proceedings,* 3 Mar. 1842; Prentice, *Anti-Corn Law League,* vol. 2, 126.

[71]   Loyd's intervention was, even so, the result of Whig, not League, pressure. Lansdowne to Loyd, 9 Oct. 1843, Overstone Papers, 804/960, University of London Library.

[72]   *The Economist,* 1843, passim; *The Economist, 1843–1943* (1943), 8–11, 31; E. I. Barrington, *The Servant of All: Pages from the Family, Social, and Political Life of My Father James Wilson* (2 vols, 1927), vol. 1, ch. 4; McCord, *Anti-Corn Law League,* 182–4.

[73]   And seen as such by the government; see Read, *Peel and the Victorians,* 128. For Cobden's views, see letter to S. Morley, 25 Mar. 1861, Cobden Papers, British Library (hereafter CP), Add. MS 43670.

[74]   O'Brien, *Lord Overstone,* vol. 1, 337–41; Joshua Bates Diary, 22 Dec. 1843, Barings' Archives, Bishopsgate, London. (I am grateful to Barings Bros. for permission to consult their archives and for the help of Dr John Orbell in doing so.) Aberdeen's appointment of the perceived Radical Henry Bulwer as minister to Spain also cost the Tories votes, according to *Elizabeth, Lady Holland to Her Son, 1821–1845,* ed. Earl of Ilchester (1946), 211. The Radical George Grote travelled from Cornwall in order to vote at this election: Mrs Grote, *The Personal Life of George Grote* (2nd edn. 1873), 153.

Common Council and Common Hall.[75] In addition, as Morier Evans reported, from among the clerks of the City, the coffee-house *habitué* 'scarcely believes the utility of not submitting to an alteration of the Corn Laws'.[76]

The shift of City opinion towards Repeal was confirmed by the line taken by the *Bankers' Magazine* on its foundation in 1844.[77] Reflecting in particular the views of the 'modern' joint-stock banks, rather than those of the 'old' private bankers, the *Bankers' Magazine* claimed to put forward the first analysis of the impact of the Corn Laws on the 'Banking Interest', proclaiming the issue not only a manufacturers' question, but also a 'Bankers' Question'. It urged Repeal, for 'we do not think that bankers can wish for the continuance of our present system of Corn Laws', although it realized that bankers who were also landowners and millionaires might well still favour them.[78] Interestingly, the necessity of Repeal was urged as an immediate consequence of the Bank Charter Act of 1844, an Act not widely supported in the City, but promoted by Peel in the interests of monetary stability. Since, under the Bank Charter Act, the state of the foreign exchanges would automatically regulate domestic money supply and credit, it became of overriding importance to avoid the rapid fluctuations in the exchanges that were widely attributed to the operation of the Corn Laws. The clear conclusion of 'practical bankers' was that 'Our present Banking Laws and our present Corn Laws could not exist together'.[79] While, therefore, accepting the Bank Charter Act as the regulatory basis of finance, the *Banker's Magazine* urged Repeal as its necessary complement. In this way government banking policy itself encouraged a shift of City opinion in the direction of free trade, and encouraged a view of a natural self-regulating order in which the Corn Laws represented an anomalous governmental interference with the regular or natural course of trade.

Yet the line taken by the *Bankers' Magazine* was probably a minority one in the City in the mid-1840s. Many bankers and merchants were still to oppose both the Bank Charter Act and free trade, as, for example, did Tom Baring and many witnesses before the 1847–8 Secret Committee on Commercial Distress. This opposition was also propagated by the *Circular to Bankers*, published by the active protectionist Henry Burgess.[80] Moreover, in the industrial North there was still little hope of spirited support from City millionaires. Thus, in December 1845

[75] *London Radicalism*, ed. Rowe, 210 ff., 232–4; see too below, 35.

[76] D. M. Evans, *The City: or the Physiology of London Business: with Sketches on the Change, and at the Coffee House* (1845), 167.

[77] Its prime movers were Sydney Waterlow, son of a prominent City stationer, and J. S. Dalton, of the Provincial Bank of Ireland. Waterlow, later a leading City figure, was a Unitarian whose views had been strongly influenced by the Revd W. J. Fox. See *Banker's Magazine*, centenary number, Apr. 1944; G. Smalley, *The Life of Sir Sydney H. Waterlow, Bart.* (1909), 13–14, 29–30.

[78] *Banker's Magazine*, June 1844, 130; Jan. 1846, 186.

[79] Ibid., Jan. 1846, 187; Feb. 1846, 262.

[80] *Parl. Papers*, 1847–48, VIII (395 and 584) SC Commercial Distress; Letters of Henry Burgess, 1841–52, Burgess Papers, New York Public Library. Burgess acted as commercial adviser to the Protectionist leader, Lord George Bentinck.

Cobden compared the City unfavourably with the Whigs: 'Contrast Lord Morpeth's conduct with that of nineteen out of twenty of the bankers and merchants of Lombard St and Broad St etc. and how much more reason have we to put faith in the aristocracy of blood than the patricians of the purse.' Cobden drew a further moral from this timidity: 'You should remind these natural leaders of the City people that if they abdicate their power now, they will risk the loss of influence for ever.'[81] The City's approach to the Corn Law debates in 1846 confirmed Cobden's fears of its powerlessness. The Repeal Bill divided members of City firms, their families, and interests both inside and outside Parliament. The Baring family, for example, was split on this issue, as was the West India interest.[82] Similarly divided was the Russia Company, whose members had been intimately involved in discussion of free trade since its advocacy by one of their number, Thomas Tooke, in 1820. Yet the Governor of the Russia Company William Thornton Astell, Protectionist MP for Bedfordshire since 1841, voted against repeal of the Corn Laws, which was ironic, since he was the only MP still in the House to have voted against their introduction in 1815. The Company itself, while welcoming the very halting steps by Tsar Nicholas towards freer trade in the 1840s, met the prospect of Repeal with justifiable apprehension in view of the likely disturbance to trade that it anticipated from large inflows of Russian grain in 1847.[83]

This polarization of City opinion clearly resulted from ideology, religion, business practice, perceived costs and benefits, and possibly from social affiliation, in that those City men, like Baring and Astell, with strong landed ties may have been the most ardent protectionists. Nevertheless, the consequence of this ambiguity and division was to render impotent the forces of gentlemanly capitalism in respect of the repeal of the Corn Laws, and to reduce the City to the position of passive recipient of a decision left squarely in the hands of the state. Typically, a leading gentlemanly capitalist William Cotton, Governor of the Bank of England in 1843–5, wrote: 'although I regret the course they have determined on with respect to the corn laws, etc. I give them full credit for honesty of purpose and a disregard of all selfish considerations.'[84] Peel's decision was in part affected by a desire for stability in the corn market, an end shared by the City, but his primary concerns, as we will see, were those of balanced economic growth, social harmony, political and constitutional order, and a peaceful international system based on the moral benefits of free exchange.

[81] Cobden to J. Dillon, 1 Dec. 1845, in Cobden Letters, Manuscript Department, William Perkins Library, Duke University, Durham, North Carolina.

[82] P. Ziegler, *The Sixth Great Power: Barings, 1762–1929* (1988), 116–18; Diary of Sir F. T. Baring, 24 Apr. 1854, Northbrook Papers, Barings' Archives; *Hansard*, 3rd ser., 85, c. 265–70, 27 Mar. 1846; 86, c. 721–6, 15 May 1846, Division Lists on Repeal.

[83] Russia Company, Court Minute Books, esp. 6, 12 June, 10 July 1846, 12 May 1847, Guildhall Library, London.

[84] Cotton to W. Cotton jun., 30 Mar. 1846, Letterbook 10, Cotton Papers, Bank of England Archives. Cotton believed that economically Repeal would not be disastrous, but 'without producing much good it will lead to a state of political disorganisation for some years to come'. See, too, Cotton to J. W. Bramston MP, 22 Mar. 1845, ibid.

Most of these goals were shared by the City, but Repeal was not considered the best means to achieve them. On the contrary, many in the City shared the view of Joshua Bates, the leading partner in Barings, that 'all the doings of Sir Robert Peel in the Tariff etc. by which he inclines towards the free trade system have been wrong, not only wrong in the abstract but wrong in reference to the condition of the country, its debt, poor laws etc.'.[85] As a result, Repeal was, at best, supported by half the City's leading men, who would, contemporaries suggested, have opposed this policy at the hands of the Whigs.[86] Undoubtedly the City respected Peel not because they had greater access to him, but largely on grounds of his acknowledged expertise in matters of trade and finance, an ability that the Whigs had conspicuously lacked when last in office.[87] It should therefore be clear that any model of decision-making which ascribes to the City a preponderant, even if only indirect, influence on economic policy must be wide of the mark in the case of the repeal of the Corn Laws. Repeal was accepted in the City as a *pis aller*, the settlement of a contentious issue, but it by no means commanded universal authority as the ideologically, politically, or economically preferred solution. That gentlemanly capitalists had good reason to be suspicious of free trade was, as we shall see, to be amply confirmed in the commercial crisis of 1847.[88]

Although gentlemanly capitalists did not exercise a preponderant influence on Repeal, the abolition of protective tariffs vitally conditioned the nature of the empire within which they had flourished. The full implications of free trade for the empire awaited the return of the Whigs to power in 1846, but the repeal of the Corn Laws, as the resistance to it revealed, already threatened the mercantilist/protectionist ideal of empire, linking land, shipping, colonies, and national power.[89] Within the City of London the keenest resistance to Repeal was voiced in terms of this concept of national power, by financiers such as Baring and shipowners such as Joseph Somes and G. F. Young. Above all they had valorized the Huskissonite ideal of imperial statesmanship, combining freer trade with reciprocity and preference, against the emerging cosmopolitan understanding of free trade.[90]

It was against this earlier imperial vision that Repeal struck vital blows, both against Canada as a colonial supplier of grain, and against the principle of preference itself. For, the logic of Repeal—the opening of the British market equally to the corn of all nations—dictated the abandonment of imperial preference. Peel had

---

[85]   Bates to Tom Baring, 24 Nov. 1843. MS 18321, HC 1.20.8., Barings' Archives, Guildhall Library, London.

[86]   For City petitions for and against, see *Hansard*, 3rd ser., 86, c. 1290, 28 May 1846; 87, c. 440, 15 June 1846. On the later occasion, Stanley claimed that the signatures of those opposing 'represented more than threefold the amount of business' transacted by those in favour.

[87]   Parker, *Peel*, vol. 3, 352.

[88]   Below, 51.

[89]   Gomes, *Foreign Trade*; B. Semmel, *The Rise of Free Trade Imperialism* (Cambridge, 1970), esp. 176–202.

[90]   For an early discussion of this, see *Hansard*, 3rd. ser., 24, c. 231, 5 June 1834, with Sandon, MP for Liverpool, seeing 'little value in setting what was called a good example [unilateral tariff reduction] . . . It was vain to hope that the progress of liberal principles would lead to liberality in trade.'

already forced upon a reluctant party the reduction of preference in favour of free-grown sugar, a policy the Whigs had also promoted.[91] The timber duties had also been reduced, while retaining preference for Canada. Yet, oddly, it was as recently as 1843 that Peel's government had extended preference to Canadian corn by the Corn Act of that year. This policy had in some ways been an inadvertent concession to Canadian opinion; in other cases, including Australia and the Ionian Islands, the Colonial Office had set its face against preference.[92] In 1846 the gesture towards Canada was summarily reversed, to the discomfiture of Stanley, the somewhat reluctant author of the 1843 Act, who in 1845 had been the only leading minister to leave the Cabinet over the issue of Repeal.[93] As we have seen, Peel now decisively embraced a policy of unilateral free trade, gravitating towards a new cosmopolitan vision that was far more in keeping with Cobden than Huskisson.[94] This reversal of policy met growing dismay in Canada, first paving the way for support for annexation with the United States, but more lastingly for a commercial *modus vivendi* embodied in the Reciprocity Treaty of 1854.[95] More widely, the end of preference signalled the removal of the cushioning by the state of the old colonial interests which, as the commercial crisis of 1847 would show, were now to be fully exposed to the harsh winds of international competition. Such interests had been vital to the City as it had existed into the 1840s, but free trade itself prefigured a restructuring of the City, encouraging the shift from colonial shipping and imperial trade to international trade and finance, centred on London's merchant bankers, an identity which shapes all modern perceptions of the City. In this sense, the repeal of the Corn Laws was not the child but the midwife of the form of gentlemanly capitalism that prospered in later nineteenth-century Britain.

The Corn Laws and the British State

The insufficiency of both ideological or structural explanations of Repeal tends to highlight Peel's own autonomy of action, a view that is entirely in line with both contemporary and subsequent emphases upon his statesmanship. Yet this itself opens up a new perspective, an explanation of Repeal in terms of the benefits it

[91] R. Stewart, 'The Ten Hours' and Sugar Crises of 1844', *Historical Journal*, 12 (1969), 35–57.

[92] D. L. Burn, 'Canada and the Repeal of the Corn Laws', *The Cambridge Historical Journal*, 2 (1928), 254. This concession was also seen to have weakened the Ricardian case for protection in return for special burdens. T. F. Lewis to G. C. Lewis, 26 Dec. 1845, Harpton Court Papers, C/1749, National Library of Wales. I owe this, and subsequent references to the Harpton Court Papers, to the kindness of Peter Mandler. For Australia, whose protests against the Canadian Bill were led by the Whig-Wakefieldians, see J. A. La Nauze, 'Australian Tariffs and Imperial Control. Part II', *Economic Record*, 24 (1948), 218–34; W. P. Morrell, *British Colonial Policy in the Age of Peel and Russell* (Oxford, new imp. 1966); for currants and Corfu, E. Calligas, 'Lord Seaton's Reforms in the Ionian Islands, 1843–48', *European History Quarterly*, 24 (1994), 12.

[93] D. Walker-Smith, *The Protectionist Case in the 1840s* (1933), esp. 69; Burn, 'Canada and Repeal'; Fay, *Corn Laws*, 124–34; Stewart, *Politics of Protection*, 41–2.

[94] In 1843 Peel dismissed preference as 'a retrograde policy', *Memoirs*, vol. 2, 218.

[95] D. C. Masters, *The Reciprocity Treaty of 1854* (1937; revised edn., 1963); R. E. Ankli, 'The Reciprocity Treaty of 1854', *Canadian Journal of Economics*, 4 (1971), 1–20.

offered to the British State.[96] Above all, Peel's statesmanship resided not merely in placing country above party and personal ambition, but in a progressive freeing of the British State from the power of vested interest groups. Here, the logic of the Liberal Tory economic policy—the emancipation of the natural order—entailed the removal of artificial props from interests such as timber, shipping, and sugar, as well as land. Land, as Peel frequently noted, was the greatest interest, which entitled it not to state privilege, but merely to the more cautious and gradual application of the principles of self-regulation.[97] For Peel, the most powerful state was the minimal state, freed from class interests, and subservient neither to the claims of patronage, the City, industry, nor the land. Within such a state the landed interest would not necessarily find itself weaker, either politically, socially, or economically. Peel, an improving farmer himself, believed agriculture could compete successfully in a new economic order, just as he believed that Repeal strengthened the Crown, aristocracy, and other established institutions.[98] Without Repeal, the ceaseless exposure of the Corn Laws as an artificial, man-made monopoly threatened, in the context of the early 1840s, the stability of society itself. In this way, the Radical attack upon monopoly, coinciding with the liberal desire to free the state from vested interests ensured that the land could no longer escape the fate of the East India Company, the timber, and the sugar trades, if the providential order were to be properly restored.[99]

Free trade here merged with the long-running campaign for economy in governmental expenditure, whereby the state would also be freed from corruption and inefficiency, enabling the emergence of a meritocratic order, of which Gladstone would become the exemplar and guardian.[100] Free trade, above all through the abolition of tariffs, would encourage economy, itself the guarantee of morality in politics. 'Public economy', as Gladstone, following Cobden, asserted, 'is part of public virtue'.[101] This link between free trade and the fiscally minimal state became well established in the Treasury in the 1840s, upheld by Peelites and evangelicals such as Arbuthnot, Clerk, and Trevelyan.[102] The Peelite model of taxation aimed at maximum revenue derived from relatively few, but highly productive sources of indirect taxation, causing the least artificial distortion of the economy and offering minimal encouragement to the formation of interest groups dependent on fiscal

---

[96]   For the broader context, see P. Harling and P. Mandler, 'From "Fiscal-Military" to *Laissez-Faire* State, 1760–1850', *Journal of British Studies*, 32 (1993), 44–70.

[97]   Peel, *Memoirs*, vol. 2, pt. 3, 214–15 [Cab. Memo. 2 Dec. 1845]; Parker, *Peel*, vol. 2, 530 [Peel to Croker, 3 Aug. 1842], 556; *Hansard*, 2nd ser., vol. 77, cc. 495–6, 14 Feb. 1845.

[98]   Parker, *Peel*, vol. 3, 194, 326; D. C. Moore, 'The Corn Laws and High Farming', *Economic History Review*, 2nd ser., 18 (1965), 544–61.

[99]   Harling, '*Old Corruption*', 251, has recently argued that Repeal was strongly influenced by 'Peel's desire to rid the government of the stigma of economic favouritism'.

[100]   P. Harling, 'Rethinking "Old Corruption" ', *Past and Present*, 147 (1995), 127–58.

[101]   To Welby, 26 Oct. 1887, Murray Papers, 1678, Blair Castle.

[102]   H. Roseveare, *The Treasury: The Evolution of a British Institution* (1969), 165–70; *DNB* for Clerk and Arbuthnot.

favour. In this model, too, the burden was shifted clearly towards direct taxation, a move towards social egalitarianism that Peel and the Radicals had long fa-voured.[103] In addition, by abolishing sources of indirect taxation, Peel consciously strove to reduce the financial resources available to government, sharing with the Radicals the belief that this acted as a deterrent to warmongering, ensuring that any decision for war would be open to the political retribution that resort to higher income tax might bring. Finally, the simplification of the tariff was also seen as a means whereby some of the last bastions of 'Old Corruption' might be stormed, for example, by reducing the peculation that some believed was rife in the London docks in the 1840s.[104] In these ways free trade became the indispensable part of the Peelite–Gladstonian ethic of good government, a model of the efficient and 'knaveproof' state, which remained well into the twentieth century the beau ideal of the Civil Service.

The arguments, therefore, that led Peel towards Repeal in 1846 were in part those shaped in the 1820s, confirmed by the success of economic reform, and consolidated by the reintroduction of income tax in 1842 as an engine of fiscal change. The continued rationalization of the tariff, and the removal of the last vestiges of protection for manufacturing, encouraged the removal of agricultural protection, both on grounds of equality with industry, and efficiency in agricul-ture.[105] Peel had ceased to believe that this protection was necessary to guarantee remunerative prices, nor had protection been a sufficient guarantee of home food supply in bad years. Aristocratic self-interest lay in agricultural improvement, not in permanent state favour; buoyant incomes were readily available to the estate management-conscious landowners, even if the race-going aristocrats might suffer appropriate retribution for neglect.[106] Peel was also open to the League's idea that foreign production of food would generate additional demand for British goods abroad, an argument that acquired renewed pertinence during the depression of 1837–42, when manufacturing unemployment had seemed to threaten mass pov-erty and insurrection.[107] Peel also shared the City's view that sudden influxes of grain (and effluxes of gold to pay for it) unnecessarily disturbed the exchanges, and distorted the money market. Repeal therefore grew in importance to Peel as a necessary step towards balanced, gradual economic growth, and towards monetary stability, goals to which his evangelical beliefs had long predisposed him.

[103]   Hilton, *Corn*, 251 ff. In his Elbing letter (Nov. 1846) Peel defended income tax as not simply a means to remedy budgetary deficit, but as a 'juster principle of taxation'. Peel Papers, Add. MS 40612, fos. 227–8.
[104]   The charge was led by the new Peelite head of the Customs, Sir Thomas Fremantle, but encountered strong City resistance. See below, 69.
[105]   e.g. T. F. to G. C. Lewis, 30 May 1841, Harpton Court MSS, C/1709; Gladstone, memorandum for Peel, 2 Jan. 1845, Peel Papers, Add. MS 44528, fos. 1–3.
[106]   Peel, *Memoirs*, vol. 2, 215; Parker, *Peel*, vol. 3, 326; Gash, *Peel*, vol. 2, 150. See, too, D. Irwin, 'Political Economy and Peel's Repeal of the Corn Laws', *Economics and Politics*, 1 (1989), 41–59.
[107]   W. R. Greg, *Not Overproduction but Deficient Consumption, the Source of Our Sufferings* (1842).

Peel also undoubtedly saw in such balanced growth the most attractive solution to the 'Condition of England' question, rejecting the more interventionist gestures of the Whigs in terms of factory and social reform. He believed that the spectre of Chartism was to be laid by prosperity, to which Repeal was a necessary means, not through lower prices and hence lower wages, but through the incentives to manufacturing employment and the investment of capital.[108] By 1845 Peel had abandoned the protectionist view that Repeal was a panacea for wage-cutting cotton lords, with lower corn prices merely prefiguring lower wages. Finally, of course, by 1845 the political benefits of Repeal were irresistible—it would be the most effective way of undercutting the growth of class tension and the rising volume of anti-aristocratic sentiment, both of which the Irish famine threatened to intensify. This could be portrayed to the Tory executive mind as a policy wholly in keeping with the best interests of the monarchy, aristocracy, and Church. More strongly, the abandonment of the shadow of protection might more deeply entrench aristocratic power, as Cobden himself used tendentiously to suggest.[109] Yet the state itself would no longer favour the landed interest, and free trade above all signified for Peel a natural order in which all interests would be removed from the back of the state, enabling it to function as, at once, a meritocratic and a providential order. This liberal view was not too far removed from the belief of the members of the Anti-Corn Law League that Repeal presaged a 'fundamentally new conception, on the part of the ruling power of these realms, of the legitimate functions of legislation and government', namely, the turning away from 'special class interests' to the 'national questions' of social reform, those of education, crime, and public health.[110]

While such important domestic considerations carried Peel towards Repeal, he could not ignore its implications for the British State in its international dimensions. For, as we have seen, the policy necessitated the abandonment of imperial preference and, as 'The Charter of the Nations', it led towards the Cobdenite goal of a peaceful world order based on the division of labour and on the Enlightenment association between peace and commerce.[111] Here, Repeal contained vast consequences for the international system, whose ramifications would arguably determine the shape and outcome of the First World War itself.[112] On the one hand, the abandonment of reliance upon domestic sources of food supply, although only rendered definitive by the fall in prices and inflow of American grain in the 1870s, left Britain largely dependent upon foreign grain, which in itself became a vital

---

[108]   Gash, *Peel*, 562–615, esp. 607.
[109]   e.g. House of Commons, 13 Mar. 1845 in J. Bright and J. E. T. Rogers, *Speeches on Questions of Public Policy by Richard Cobden* (1878), 133–46.
[110]   *The League*, 4 July 1846.
[111]   F. H. Hinsley, *Power and the Pursuit of Peace* (Cambridge, 1963), 92–113; E. Silberner, *The Problem of War in Nineteenth-Century Economic Thought* (Princeton, 1946); S. C. Neff, *Friends But No Allies: Economic Liberalism and the Law of Nations* (New York, 1990).
[112]   A. Offer, *The First World War: An Agrarian Interpretation* (Oxford, 1989).

determinant of foreign policy and military strategy.[113] The British Navy, rather than the British farmer, became the guarantor of the nation's food supply. Repeal itself, therefore, in a way encouraged the growth of the Navy in the long term, despite the fears of the protectionists that it betokened the decline of national power.

On the other hand, free trade itself offered an additional means to bolster British power within the world system, as a strategy to reshape that system in ways that favoured Britain's economic power, through both coercive means and the ideological dissemination of free trade. Theorists of 'hegemonic stability' have therefore seen free trade as a necessary part of British power in the nineteenth-century world order. In the same way, it is suggested, in the post-1945 world the United States, as the hegemonic power, adopted free trade as being in its own interest, as well as a public good for the world as a whole.[114] It would be unduly reductionist to argue that free trade was a consciously deployed tool of British domination, but its international aspects were clearly recognized by contemporaries. For example, on occasion Peel and Gladstone advocated unilateral free trade as a necessary bastion of Britain's manufacturing supremacy, which required abundance and cheap provisions.[115] But they were anxious that other nations should follow Britain's example if the maximum benefits of free trade were to be realized for all nations, although they now abandoned what had proved a rather fruitless search for reciprocity treaties in the early 1840s.[116] They were also aware that Repeal would impose costs on British colonies, and that the immediate beneficiary of this change in policy would be the United States.[117] With the settlement of the vexatious Oregon Question in 1846 in particular, the possibility of the inflow of American grain attracted considerable interest, in Britain and America.[118] Above all, this possibility seems in part to have encouraged the modification of the highly protectionist American tariff, with the Walker Act of 1846 seen by contemporaries as an early response to

[113]   Ibid. and A. Offer, 'The Working Classes, British Naval Plans, and the Coming of the Great War', *Past and Present*, 107 (1985), 204–26.

[114]   For an overview of this debate, see P. K. O'Brien and G. A. Pigman, 'Free Trade, British Hegemony, and the International Economic Order', *Review of International Studies*, 18 (1992), 89–113.

[115]   *Hansard*, 3rd ser., 83, cc. 276–8, 27 Jan. 1846; see, too, Semmel, *Free Trade Imperialism*, 149–50.

[116]   Above, 11; N. M. Gordon, 'Britain and the *Zollverein* Iron Duties, 1842–5', *EcHR*, 2nd ser., 22 (1969), 75–87. However, not all negotiations had proved fruitless, with Britain agreeing a commercial treaty with Naples in April 1845; E. Pontieri, *Il Riformismo Borbonico nella Sicilia del Sette e dell'Ottocento* (Rome, 1945), 271–347.

[117]   For arguments in favour of this interdependence, incidentally undermining slavery by its encouragement of free-grown American corn, see J. Curtis, *America and the Corn Laws* (Manchester, 1841).

[118]   The Foreign Secretary Aberdeen was Peel's keenest supporter on Repeal, with a clear belief in free trade's pacific potential; as Greville noted in November 1845, apropos of the Oregon Affair, '. . . he [Aberdeen] knows that nothing will have so great an effect in America, nothing tend so materially to the prevalence of pacific counsels, as an announcement that our Corn Laws are going to be repealed'. *The Greville Memoirs, 1814–1860*, ed. L. Strachey and R. Fulford (8 vols, 1938), vol. 5, 243–7 [5 and 6 Dec. 1845].

Britain's new openness of trade.[119] More recently, it has been argued that this modification provides a good example of the way in which a hegemonic economic power was able to encourage, rather than coerce, other countries to participate in a liberal international order, the 'second face of hegemony'.[120] Even so, in the case of the United States, this was only short-lived membership, for, although the tariff was again lowered in 1857, the Civil War dictated a more complete return to protectionism. In the immediate term, the hopes of Cobdenite and Peelite free traders for a new liberal order were necessarily centred far more on Europe than on America.

If this prospect of universal free trade proved Utopian, as the critics of 'Cobdenism' would relentlessly point out, it was an expectation that even Peel encouraged. For example, in his admiration of Cobden, in his parliamentary speeches, and in the Elbing letter, he struck a distinctly cosmopolitan note.[121] As the career of Gladstone too would show, Cobden's internationalist ideas now replaced the imperial statesmanship of Huskisson as the cynosure of the Peelites, with Gladstone himself already the leading supporter of the doctrine of free imports denounced by his father as the abrogation of 'every principle hitherto of Free Trade among nations'.[122] In the diplomatic sphere, this betokened a decisive shift towards the search for freer international trade, which would preoccupy British statesmen until the National Government of 1931 resumed the imperial quest.[123] Yet, however important this international dimension was for Peel, Cobden, and Britain, as it was also for those protectionists who lamented the threatened loss of British power, it bore only marginally on Parliament itself, 'the decisive theatre' in which class and party have often seemed more reliable guides than state and nation to political behaviour.[124]

The Corn Laws and Parliament

In March 1837 Clay's motion for a ten shilling fixed duty on corn received the support of only 89 MPs; in June 1846, 327 MPs voted for the total, if not immediate, abolition of the Corn Laws. The reasons for this parliamentary *bouleversement* have been long debated, prompting impressive, if somewhat indecisive,

[119]   Pakenham to Aberdeen, 13 Sept. 1845, no. 93, PRO FO5/428, fos. 7–12; ibid. 26 Feb. 1846, no. 18, FO5/446, fos. 131–2.

[120]   S. C. James and D. A. Lake, 'The Second Face of Hegemony: Britain's Repeal of the Corn Laws and the American Walker Tariff of 1846', *International Organisation*, 43 (1989), 1–30.

[121]   Peel's paean to Cobden in his resignation speech, normally seen as a lapse in political taste, reflected a genuine appreciation of the diplomatic value of free trade as propagated by Cobden, in noted counterpoint to Palmerstonian bluster. *Hansard*, 3rd ser., 87, c. 1053, 26 June 1846. See, too, above, 11.

[122]   Sir John Gladstone, 'Free Trade' (23 July 1846), Glynne–Gladstone Papers, 1187; *GD*, vol. 3, xxxviii–xxxix.

[123]   Interestingly, this change in British policy in 1931 forms the backcloth to Fay's account of free trade in *Corn Laws*, e.g. 134.

[124]   McCord, *Anti-Corn Law League*. ch. 8, 'The Decisive Theatre'.

quantitative analyses of legislative behaviour in the 1840s. Even so, hostility to the Corn Laws was no new phenomenon, although after 1829 it had been largely overlain by the issue of parliamentary reform. In the reformed Parliament, W. W. Whitmore, at that time MP for Wolverhampton, took up his earlier campaigns against the Corn Laws, aided by his constituency colleague, the ironmaster Fryer. In 1835 Wolverhampton elected as its MP the Benthamite brother of Lord Clarendon, C. P. Villiers, who was to become the most single-minded opponent of the Corn Laws in Parliament.[125] Villiers's fellow Wolverhampton MP Thomas Thornely, a Liverpool merchant, was keen to push for freer trade, as were Manchester's and Liverpool's MPs.[126] Thus, in 1833 Mark Philips had asserted the primacy of Repeal over Whig retrenchment and fiscal reform, while in 1834 William Ewart had linked the issue to growing support for free trade in Europe, and to the cause of peace.[127] But it was Villiers who emerged at the centre of a knot of free trade MPs, who spearheaded the movement for Repeal, which was now taken up by the London Philosophic Radicals and their associates. This group constituted the first Anti-Corn Law Association, and lay behind Clay's motion in 1837. The following year Villiers, Clay's adjutant in 1837, launched the first of his famous annual anti-Corn Law motions, on this occasion for inquiry, not repeal, gaining the support of ninety-five MPs, eleven of whom were from Lancashire. Growing provincial disquiet over the Corn Laws was seen in petitions, propaganda, and public meetings, prompting the formation of the Manchester Anti-Corn Law Association in October 1838, the fulcrum for the League of 1839.[128]

With this renewed parliamentary and provincial interest in the Corn Laws, and especially since the onset of severe depression in 1837, Whig ministers were 'prompt' to support Villiers's second motion, for considering the 1828 Corn Law in March 1839.[129] Yet the Whigs lacked any determined policy—however sympathetic to the economic and political arguments for free trade, the hostility of Melbourne as well as Lansdowne, Bedford, and others, and the equivocation of liberals such as the Chancellor Baring and, at this stage, Howick, precluded a change of policy.[130] Significantly, Poulett Thomson, unable to satisfy his Man-

---

[125]   W. O. Henderson, 'Charles Pelham Villiers', *History*, 37 (1952), 25–39; *Free Trade Speeches of Charles Pelham Villiers*, ed. 'By a member of the Cobden Club' [Agnes, daughter of Sir John, Lambert.] (2 vols, 1883).

[126]   Thornely to Villiers, 1835–7, Thornely Letters, BLPES.

[127]   *Hansard*, 3rd ser., 18, cc. 973–4, 18 June 1833 [Philips]; 22, c. 436, 19 Mar. 1834 [Ewart]: 'He was convinced the peace of the world would depend more upon the intercourse between the Seine and the Thames and the Mersey and the Hudson than on the intrigues of the diplomatists.'

[128]   For a careful study of divisions of opinion in Manchester on free trade and the Corn Laws, see M. J. Turner, 'Before the Manchester School: Economic Theory in Early Nineteenth-Century Manchester', *History*, 79 (1994), 216–41.

[129]   Parry, *Liberal Government*, 145; even so, sixty-four Liberal MPs were against, with three Tories in favour, so Thornely to Villiers, 24 Mar. 1839, Thornely Letters.

[130]   Howick only came out decisively in favour of tariff revision in May 1841. T. F. to G. C. Lewis, 4 May 1841, Harpton Court MSS, C/1704.

chester constituents, preferred retreat from the Board of Trade to Canada in 1839, lamenting that 'there is no chance of carrying the House with one of any great commercial reforms, timber, corn, sugar etc; party and private interests will prevent it. If Peel were in, he might do this.'[131] Whig immobility ended only belatedly in April 1841, when political necessity and budgetary extremity dictated a change of policy.[132] But this conversion was too late to convince important sections of the urban electorate, including that of Lancashire, that the Whigs' reforming credentials were still trustworthy, while it helped encourage a strong Tory reaction in the countryside and smaller borough seats.[133] Peel returned to office to face the challenge of reconciling a party of entrenched squirearchical reaction, the logic of his own ripening free trade sentiments, and the need to solidify the Tory support in the urban electorate that had been created in 1832.[134] This proved an impossible task. He hoped that in the longer term he might persuade the Tories to support Repeal, but the Irish famine, which precipitated his decision, also deprived him of potential support from his own party. As a result, repeal of the Corn Laws was passed not by votes from the Tories, but from the Whigs, in the ratio of two to one.

The explanation of why MPs voted in the way they did has preoccupied two generations of quantitative historians, seeking to measure the relative contributions of personal interest, constituency pressure, and political loyalty. This debate has, above all, concerned Tory MPs, with the Whig support for Repeal readily, if too simply, explained as an opportunistic switch from the fixed duty of 1841 towards total repeal in response to Russell's 'Edinburgh letter' in November 1845.[135] Nevertheless, the evolution of Whig opinion was not quite so simple, with divided counsels precluding their ability to form a government in 1845, and with strong landed hostility to Repeal in the party only gradually yielding to the imperative of electoral success in urban Britain.[136] On the Tory side, the picture has proved far more complex. Why did some Tories support Repeal, but a majority oppose their

---

[131]   Journal, 21 Sept. 1839 in *Memoir of the Life of Lord Sydenham*, ed. G. Poulett Scrope (1844), 102.

[132]   Brown, *Board of Trade*, 222–5; Brent, *Liberal Anglican Politics*, 292–8; Parry, *Liberal Government*, 147.

[133]   'What they [the Whigs] propose is anything but that [free trade], unless indeed it [a fixed duty] is meant to be merely a step to no protection at all which all the arguments, upon which they defend their course, would lead one to believe.' Lord Wharncliffe to Henry Burgess, 18 July 1841, Burgess Papers, New York Public Library. For the election, see B. Kemp, 'The General Election of 1841', *History*, 37 (1952), 146–57; E. Jaggard, 'The 1841 British General Election: A Reconsideration', *Australian Journal of Politics and History*, 30 (1984), 99–114; Howe, *Cotton Masters*, 211.

[134]   T. F. Lewis, a 'Peelite-in-waiting', thus wrote to his brother, the Whig G. C. Lewis: 'Peel is in a very embarrassing position—if he comes in now he must do so on the Corn Law part of the budget and that will increase the schism between the two sections into which the country is divided and place the battle on the very worst ground on which it could properly be fought.' 4 May 1841, Harpton Court MSS, C/1704.

[135]   Dreyer, 'Political Crisis of 1845', 514–37. C. P. Villiers's annual motion for total repeal usually gained about a hundred votes. Several leading Whigs preceded Russell's advocacy of Repeal by some years, e.g. Fox Maule, Spencer, and Howick. *The Panmure Papers*, ed. G. S. B. S. Douglas and G. D. Ramsay (2 vols, 1908), vol. 1, 21 ff; Mandler, *Aristocratic Government*, 218–19.

[136]   See Ch. 2 for further consideration of the Whigs and free trade.

leader? W. O. Aydelotte's pioneering cliometric study in the 1960s served brilliantly to demolish any simplistic explanation in terms of economic interests, social
background, or constituency pressure.[137] If anything divided Peel's supporters
from his opponents, it was their experience of office, a view conformable with
recent studies of the evolution of Liberal Toryism as an executive ethic, which was,
by definition, distanced from the sympathies of backbenchers. Here at least was
confirmation of a growing chasm between leaders and MPs, which Peel did pitifully
little to close. On the one hand, this governmental élite readily accepted the fiscal,
social, and political basis of Repeal. On the other, Disraeli and Bentinck sought to
rally the Tory nation around the romantic motifs of land, empire, and paternalism
which lay behind the protectionist case.[138] This ideological conflict, long implicit in
Tory politics, provides in some ways the most satisfactory explanation of the Tory
divisions over Repeal in 1846.

Such an ideological interpretation of Repeal has proved inadequate, however, for
more recent cliometricians who have attempted to rework Aydelotte's figures.
Their recalculations have not served fully to reinstate any clear interpretation of
Repeal in terms of economically based conflict within the Tory Party, but they have
powerfully suggested that MPs did respond, to a greater extent than Aydelotte
allowed, to their own pecuniary interests (particularly the extent of their non-
agricultural business interests) and to the interests of their constituents, measured
by factors such as their dependence upon corn, cattle, cotton, or iron, and their
exposure to public disorder in the early 1840s.[139] Much more ambitiously,
Schonhardt-Bailey has attempted to explain Repeal by reference to structural
change in Britain's economy, and rational choice in its political behaviour. First,
she has related the success of the Anti-Corn Law League as a lobbying-group both
to the growing geographical concentration of textiles, providing a solid core for the
League, and to the growing geographical spread of export-dependent industrial
interests.[140] Second, her study of portfolio diversification, based on a national
sample of death duty and income tax statistics, reveals a decisive shift of economic
interests from land towards a more varied pattern of non-agricultural investment in
the years 1835–45, among both MPs and the wealthy as a whole.[141] This evidence
suggests, rather against Aydelotte's claim, that changing economic structure in
itself provides a rational case for Repeal. But to what extent were shifts in par-

[137] W. O. Aydelotte, 'The Country Gentlemen and the Repeal of the Corn Laws', *English Historical Review*, 82 (1967), 47–60.
[138] P. Smith, 'Disraeli's Politics', *Transactions of the Royal Historical Society*, 5th ser., 37 (1989), 65–85; Macintyre, 'Lord George Bentinck'.
[139] T. McKeown, 'The Politics of Corn Law Repeal and Theories of Commercial Policy', *British Journal of Political Science*, 19 (1989), 353–80.
[140] C. Schonhardt-Bailey, 'Lessons in Lobbying for Free Trade in 19th-Century Britain: To Concentrate or Not', *American Political Science Review*, 85 (1991), 38–58.
[141] Ibid., 'Specific Factors, Capital Markets, Portfolio Diversification, and Free Trade: Domestic Determinants of the Repeal of the Corn Laws', *World Politics*, 43 (1991), 545–69.

liamentary voting influenced by such changes in economic rationality? Here, Schonhardt-Bailey unambiguously asserts the primacy of these economic shifts, providing evidence that both the personal fortunes of MPs and of their constituents had shifted decisively from land in the years before 1846. The movement towards free trade (or, more guardedly, the growing costs of protection) revealed by parliamentary divisions in the 1840s, therefore reflected this diversification. Above all, she concludes that in the divisions over Repeal MPs responded to the changing economic needs of constituencies, a 'surfacing of constituency interests at the expense of party unity'.[142] Peelites, i.e. those Tories who voted for Repeal, did so, therefore, not for reasons of personal loyalty or executive sympathy, as Aydelotte and others suggested, but in response to 'electoral and constituency changes' between 1832 and 1846, changes that even more obviously determined Whig actions.

In so closely linking economic interest and voting behaviour, this account decisively repudiates notions of both party loyalty and of the independence of MPs, for their behaviour approximates far more to that of spontaneous 'delegates', able to perceive, and ready to act in accordance with the changing balance of constituency economic fortunes. This is a rigorous world of public choice, which puts to one side influence, patronage, corruption, and leadership, suggesting that the Whigs of 1832 were far more successful than they, and certainly the Chartists believed, in creating a rational, efficient, and representative political order. Yet, in a way, this impressive and rigorous quantification proves too much, and too little. First, despite Schonhardt-Bailey's disclaimer, her argument does in part depend upon structural change only influencing parliamentary voting after 1842. In turn, it pays too little attention to explaining the 'rationality' of Conservative resurgence in the 1830s, just as the Whigs were, albeit belatedly, turning towards free trade. This posed a problem for contemporaries, for, as T. F. Lewis put it:

at this moment [May 1841] it would really seem as if a Government [i.e. the Whigs] had only to propose what is just and right, in order to secure its becoming utterly contemptible and unpopular——what is to be the result of it no human creature can guess——but it would seem as if a conservative government was to be created in order to uphold and maintain all that rational people have for years shown to be at variance with the true interests of the publick.[143]

Had constituency interests really changed sufficiently between 1842 and 1846 to make protectionism rational in 1841 and free trade so five years later?

Second, however, this revisionist account continues to focus attention on the Peelites, whereas Repeal was to be largely carried by Whig and Irish votes. In the case of the former, it is perhaps arguable that party unity came before constituency interests, especially in the case of the remaining Whig county MPs, while the

---

[142] Ibid., 'Linking Constituency Interests to Legislative Behaviour: The Role of District Economic and Electoral Composition in the Repeal of the Corn Laws', *Parliamentary History*, 13 (1994), 86–118, quote on p. 116.

[143] To G. C. Lewis, 13 May 1841, Harpton Court MSS, C/1706.

behaviour of the latter was tactical, for Ireland was to return a strong cohort of Protectionist MPs in 1847. It should also be noted that a small but significant portion of English MPs (twenty-four) who voted for Repeal were in fact disowned by their constituents in the general election of 1847, as were a number of protectionists.[144] Finally, the notion of a clear-cut constituency direction is perhaps itself misleading, for in the election of 1847, thirty-one county, thirty-five borough, and two university seats were to be divided between Liberals and Protectionists.[145] To sustain the rational choice model, therefore, a further step is required, namely to show that these divisions in constituencies reflected the rational interests of differentiated sets of voters. Until this is done, we may properly continue to assume that irrational forces—those of party, habit, deference, patronage, tradition, religion, prejudice, drink, family, and ideology—continued to influence both constituency behaviour and the voting pattern of MPs.[146]

It has long been recognized that opinion did matter in the reformed House of Commons, even if historians have been unwilling to accord it the priority implied in the rational choice model.[147] Yet in elevating the importance of political choice in the constituencies, this challenging account usefully redirects attention back to the Anti-Corn Law League, whose *raison d'être* had been to replace party perceptions by notions of a general interest above party. The League had inserted itself between party and the constituencies in the 1840s both as an educative force, the 'instructor' throughout the land, and as an electoral machine. This suggests that the importance of the League was greater than its debunkers have allowed, both as the agency of rational choice in the 1840s, and as a longer-term influence in generating popular loyalties to free trade.

The Corn Laws, the League, and popular politics

With McCord's impressive revisionist history of the Anti-Corn Law League still fresh in the historiographical tradition, it has sometimes been difficult for historians to recapture the importance of the Corn Laws as a popular political issue.[148] For McCord, the parliamentary theatre was decisive, the League a self-important irrelevance, a view that has been almost universally held ever since. This view has been challenged by Prest's account of *Politics in the Age of Cobden* (1977), but the League has remained marginal to discussions of Repeal, portrayed, at best, as an

[144] Additionally, in 1847 only 67.2% of sitting MPs chose to seek re-election, the lowest number between 1835 and 1906. G. W. Cox, *The Efficient Secret: The Cabinet and the Development of Political Parties in Victorian England* (Cambridge, 1987), 72, 73.

[145] The 1847 election also yielded the highest percentages of split voting and non-partisan plumping between 1832 and 1910: Cox, *Efficient Secret*, 103, 108, 109.

[146] See, too, I. McLean, 'Rational Choice and the Victorian Voter', *Political Studies*, 40 (1992), 496–515.

[147] Kitson-Clark, 'The Electorate'; T. J. Nossiter, *Influence, Opinion, and Idiom in Reformed England* (Hassocks, 1975).

[148] Parry, *Liberal Government*, 371. Equally, of course, Chartism has dominated perceptions of popular politics.

interesting pressure group, more a model for the future than an influence in the 1840s, or as an example of collective organization by the industrial bourgeoisie, a prototype for middle-class self-identity.[149] But in debunking the myths of the League, it is also too easy to miss its reality, not as a factor determining élite political behaviour, but as a major element in creating a popular audience for political information, in creating a serious challenge (unlike that of the Chartists) to Parliament's monopoly of political wisdom, and in creating a genuine court of appeal to the people, which later politicians would exercise. Gladstone's Midlothian campaign was, in this sense, the logical culmination of League politics.[150]

Above all, the League itself transformed free trade into a national political issue, removing it from the confines of the intelligentsia. In some sense, it never had been so narrowly confined. There had been a lively tradition of popular resistance to the Corn Laws since 1815, and support for free trade, upheld, for example, by Place and Hodgskin in the press in the 1820s.[151] In Lancashire, even after the Corn Law of 1828, the campaign for free trade continued until swallowed up in the agitation for reform.[152] In Sheffield vigorous opposition to the Corn Laws was expressed through the single-minded passion of Ebenezer Elliott, whose *Corn Law Rhymes* reached a third edition in 1831.[153] Yet for the most part, between 1828 and 1832, free trade and the attack on monopoly had become goals to be achieved through parliamentary reform, the success of which had itself encouraged apathy on other issues.[154] Even so, this was short-lived, and popular disillusionment with the reformed Parliament because of its failure to act on the Corn Laws proved the spur to the revival of the anti-Corn Law movement.[155] This was soon active, as we have seen, in provincial towns including Wolverhampton, Manchester, Liverpool, Nottingham, Sheffield, Perth, and Glasgow.[156] The campaign was not so much evidence of manufacturers' power within the reformed system as the result of their lack of power. The Reform Act of 1832 had not been followed by the expected attack on monopoly in all its forms, but by Whig policies whose benefits for the middle classes were far from obvious. For example, the monopoly of the Bank of England had been renewed, not abolished, in 1833, while reform of the Poor Law,

[149]   D. Hamer, *The Politics of Electoral Pressure* (Hassocks, 1977), ch. 5; Howe, *Cotton Masters*, esp. 208–15.

[150]   For an individual example of this symmetry, see A. Mitchell, *Political and Social Movements in Dalkeith. From 1831 to 1882* (privately printed, Edinburgh, 1882), recording his progress from Leaguer to Chairman of the Midlothian Liberals in 1880. In general, see H. Jephson, *The Platform* (2 vols, 1892).

[151]   N. W. Thompson, *The People's Science* (1984), 13–14.

[152]   Barnes, *English Corn Laws*, 216.

[153]   A. Briggs, 'Ebenezer Elliott, the Corn Law Rhymer', *Cambridge Journal*, 3 (1949–50), 686–95.

[154]   E. Elliott to J. B. Smith, 18 and 29 Oct. 1833, 7 Apr. 1835. J. B. Smith Papers, Corn Laws, vol. 3, Manchester Central Library; cf. H. Booth, *Free trade as it affects the people. Addressed to a Reformed Parliament* (Liverpool, Jan. 1833).

[155]   N. Gash, *Politics in the Age of Peel* (1953), 6; Barnes, *English Corn Laws*, 231.

[156]   See above, 24; K. J. Cameron, 'The Anti-Corn Law Movement in Scotland', unpublished Ph.D. thesis, Edinburgh (1971), ch. 4; N. Longmate, *The Breadstealers* (1984), 11 (Sheffield Anti-Bread Tax Society).

which had some very dogmatic entrepreneurial supporters, was in part promoted as a form of relief of the special burdens on agriculture, after which repeal of the Corn Laws should follow.[157] Whig policies on education, factory legislation, and Ireland, as well as the growing failure of economical and fiscal reform, alienated many middle-class Whig supporters, who now saw in Repeal a means both to challenge their own aristocratic leaders, and to bid to retain working-class support against the growing appeal of Chartism and Feargus O'Connor.[158]

This Radical alliance proved impossible in the late 1830s with the emergence of Chartist independence, but the slogan of 'the people versus the aristocracy' remained the most obvious rallying cry for the League, despite the growing adherence of aristocratic politicians to its cause. Such gentlemanly leaders, as in the Chartist movement, were acceptable in part because of their identification with the cause of the people, as in the case of Villiers. Others, however—for example, Milner Gibson—were at first suspected of being opportunistic turncoats. More generally, free trade, having re-emerged as part of a broad popular movement, was left as a single issue in the hands of the League, while working-class energies were largely, if not entirely, siphoned off to the Chartist movement. This left free trade open to Tory-Radical and later Chartist attack as a wage-cutting device of the manufacturers, a charge that was only gradually rebutted by the League.[159] But Cobden's success in promoting the broader benefits of free trade for the people paved the way for a substantial rallying of working-classs support to the League after 1843. At the same time, popular political economy, including advocacy of free trade, had largely replaced both the moral economy of the eighteenth century, and the primitive Ricardian socialism of the 1820s.[160] This facilitated both the reintegration of the Radical alliance fragmented by the impact of Chartism, and the eventual ideological triumph of the League.

The importance of the League was therefore not simply that of an all-powerful interest group able to exert irresistible pressure within Parliament, but that of a magnet able to pull to its pole large fragments of free trade—anti-monopoly sentiment. In doing so, it aimed to create a new national political community, with a better claim to represent the people than that assembled at Westminster, which had repeatedly turned a deaf ear to the people's grievances. In this there was a greater similarity between the League and the tactics of earlier Radical movements than is sometimes allowed. The League's first convention was in the style of earlier anti-Parliament movements, although under Cobden's influence this tactic was abandoned in favour of working within Parliament, especially after the Plug Plot of

---

[157]   Villiers, *Free Trade Speeches*, 15; see, too, W. J. Fox to H. Martineau, 21 Jan. 1843 in *Harriet Martineau. Selected Letters.* ed. V. Sanders (Oxford, 1990), 69.

[158]   Thornely to Villiers, 20 Nov. 1839, Thornely Letters.

[159]   Barnes, *English Corn Laws*, 246–8, 258; L. Brown, 'The Chartists and the Anti-Corn Law League', in Briggs (ed.), *Chartist Studies*, 342–71.

[160]   Thompson, *The People's Science*, 221–2; A. Kadish (ed.), *The Corn Laws. The Formation of Popular Economics in Britain* (6 vols. 1996), vol. 1, xxx–xxxi.

1842. Undoubtedly, therefore, Cobden pushed the League in the direction of respectability. But this reinforced, rather than diminished, its political stature, which, through its successful propaganda machine, was able to reshape the contours of popular political argument, and to create a new definition of the public sphere.

This redefinition of the public sphere worked at several levels. Parliament itself was central, with men such as Cobden and Bright hailed as exemplars of a new type of political leader.[161] Cobden's first Commons speech was heralded by Martineau, as 'a new era in the history of England . . . now that the People's tale had at last been told in the People's House of Parliament'.[162] Cobden, Bright, Villiers, and a host of secondary leaders, also acted as links between Parliament and the people, with their successive tours of England and Scotland, rivalling those of Cartwright and Wesley as peripatetic evangelists. Preceding Gladstone's campaigns by a generation, in the Britain of the 1840s a huge number of voters and non-voters had the opportunity to hear the case for Repeal made by popular parliamentary leaders, the first political orators of the railway age. Significantly, a large number of working-class autobiographies of the 1840s, including those of several Chartists, recall attendance at League meetings.[163] This neglected exercise in rhetoric was an essential part of the League's redefinition of the political community.[164] In this political sphere, the League's leadership was supplemented by the less well known, but equally vital work of its lecturers, usually a far more radical body than the movement's Manchester purses, but central to its popular impact.[165] Despite the often hostile reception the lecturers met in the early years, their appeal and audience undoubtedly increased. The creation of the Anti-League in 1844 was itself testimony to the growing effectiveness of the League's incursions into rural localities.[166] Finally, its hugely successful Covent Garden meetings, combining rhetorical power and metropolitan presence served most effectively to reinforce its image as the agent of a community greater than the sum of the cotton masters' purses.

The League's successful exercise in political rhetoric, stimulating a huge new audience for free trade, was replicated on an even vaster scale through print.[167] First, as is well known, the League took full advantage of the penny post to

---

[161] D. Read, *Cobden and Bright: A Victorian Political Partnership* (1967); P. Joyce, *Democratic Subjects: The Self and the Social in Nineteenth-century England* (Cambridge, 1994) for a post-modernist reading.

[162] H. Martineau, *The History of England during the Thirty Years' Peace, 1816–46. Vol. 2 1830–46* (1850), 608.

[163] C. Godfrey, *Chartist Lives* (New York, 1987), 329–31; McCord, *Anti-Corn Law League*, 210–11.

[164] Cf. H. C. G. Matthew, 'Rhetoric and Politics in Great Britain', in P. J. Waller (ed.), *Politics and Social Change in Modern Britain* (1987), 34–58.

[165] e.g. James Acland, R. R. Moore, and F. Boase, *Modern English Biography*; P. Hollis (ed.), *Pressure from Without in Early Victorian England* (1974), 13–14.

[166] M. Lawson-Tancred, 'The Anti-League and the Corn Law Crisis of 1846', *Historical Journal*, 3 (1960), 162–83.

[167] In 1843 the League effort included 9,026,000 tracts, 650 lectures, 156 deputations, 426,000 tracts placed as advertisements. Prentice, *Anti-Corn Law League*, vol. 2, 120.

inundate the electorate with its propaganda.[168] Second, this was backed up by the League's own regular publications, the *Anti-Corn Law Circular*, the *Anti-Bread Tax Circular*, and eventually *The League*, which helped orchestrate the movement's local campaigns, while providing a wider instrument of communication with the growing audience for free trade ideas. Third, partly through its meetings and *The League*, the campaign against the Corn Laws achieved a prominence in the press, besides which that of Chartism was negligible.[169] The League's impact through speech-making and in print was unprecedented for its range and ability to create an audience for economic, social, and political issues. Bagehot, a self-confessed 'worshipper of Richard Cobden', strongly influenced by attending the League's Covent Garden meetings, attested to the unique popular interest in Victorian Britain in issues of political economy: 'There has never, perhaps, been another time in the history of the world when excited masses of men and women hung on the words of one talking political economy. The excitement of these meetings was keener than any political excitement in the last twenty years, keener infinitely than any which there is now.'[170] Such interest in political economy of course had its origins before the League, and would be sustained later by a range of educational vehicles, including numerous popular lectures, school textbooks, and the university extension movement.[171] But Harriet Martineau, while not a disinterested party, was a perceptive observer in suggesting that the League's seven years' work:

approached more nearly to a genuine National Education than any scheme elsewhere at work. By the Anti-Corn Law League the people at large were better trained to thought and its communication, to the recognition of principles, the obtaining of facts, and the application of the same faculties and the same interest to their public as to their private affairs, than by any methods of intellectual development yet tried under the name of Education.[172]

In such ways, the League had successfully generated a new level of popular interest in politico-economic debate.

Even so, the League's appeal was never simply so rational and utilitarian in character. Rather, it seems that its success lay in its ability to mix the fervent language of evangelical religion with the secular thinking of the Radicals, Liberals, and Ricardians. We still await a full study of the League's language, but this intertwining is well established, through its use of biblical symbolism, the presence of many Dissenters among the League's lecturers, and the success of its famous

---

[168] McCord, *Anti-Corn Law League*, e.g. 148–50; Longmate, *The Breadstealers*, 109, 192–3.

[169] Read, *Peel and the Victorians*, 37, for the increase in newspaper stamps in the 1840s.

[170] 'Mr Cobden', *Bagehot's Historical Essays* (1965), ed. N. St John Stevas, 223–4; 'Memoir of Mr Bagehot by R. H. Hutton', *The Collected Works of Walter Bagehot*, ed. N. St John Stevas (15 vols, 1965–86), vol. 15, 88; Bagehot to E. Fry, 1 May 1843, in ibid., vol. 12, 215.

[171] For one lecturer, William Ellis, see *DNB* and R. Gilmour, 'The Gradgrind School: Political Economy in the Classroom', *Victorian Studies*, 11 (1967–8), 207–24; J. M. Goldstrom, 'Richard Whately and Political Economy in School Books, 1833–80', *Irish Historical Studies*, 15 (1966–7), 131–46. See, too, below, 115.

[172] Martineau, *History of England*, 416.

meetings of ministers at Manchester and Edinburgh in 1841–2.[173] The sentimental and exuberant rhetoric of Bright and Fox was as vital as the colder logic of Villiers and Cobden.[174] On the one hand, the League unfolded a Cobdenite vision of the future: free trade leading to economic prosperity, social harmony, and universal peace.[175] On the other hand, League oratory deployed the rhetoric of morality, justice, Providence, and retribution. As early as 1840, Sidney Smith in London noted: 'I see symptoms of the Prayer book appeals I make having effect. I believe ultimately that this will be the pivot of the question. Our enemies can dispute our political economy but their mouths are shut by our theology.'[176] Through its secular and religious language, the League thus successfully combined the 'moral cravings of the middle class' with a universalist rather than sectarian or class-based rhetoric, which underpinned its claim to speak for the people, or even the nation. By so doing it won over to the cause of Repeal large sections of national opinion, including *The Times*, and literary figures including Dickens and Carlyle, although a distaste for the League itself survived.[177] In a way, it was the very success of the League in identifying itself with Repeal as a national good that stimulated and accelerated the need for Peel to separate the one from the other, and to reappropriate free trade for Tory politics. Similarly, by 1845 Russell had recognized the necessity of Whig advocacy of Repeal as the indispensable condition of the renewal of the party's electoral popularity.

This attempt by party politicians to reappropriate free trade was also testimony to the success of the League on the ground, a point that deserves fuller treatment than it has so far received; while we still lack a comprehensive study of the Anti-Corn Law movement, there is growing evidence of its local success. Such evidence remains fragmentary. For example, League subscriptions show the overwhelming importance quantitatively of Lancashire and Yorkshire, but the subscription lists printed in *The League* reveal a far more comprehensive national support, with the pennies and shillings of the artisans and petty bourgeoisie indicative of the League's stature as a giant voluntary association for the Smilesian classes. It is clear, too, that support for the League did not merely come from the floors of provincial exchanges, but was far more likely to be organized around Nonconformist chapels, in areas as diverse as Brixton, Dalkeith, and Wrexham.[178] The League also drew on female support to an extent not yet recognized by historians of women's political

[173]   McCord, *Anti-Corn Law League*, 104–7; Kadish, *Corn Laws*, vol. 1, xlv–lii.

[174]   J. Evans, *Lancashire's Orators and Authors* (1850), 34–8, 63–7, 92–6; W. C. Bryant, 'Introduction to the American Edition', *The Political Writings of Richard Cobden* (2 vols; 2nd edn., 1868), vol. 1, i–ii.

[175]   R. F. Spall, 'Free Trade, Foreign Relations, and the Anti-Corn Law League', *International History Review*, 10 (1988), 405–32.

[176]   12 Mar. 1840, Anti-Corn Law League Letters, no. 429, Manchester Central Library.

[177]   Cobden hailed the men of intellect 'shrinking from protection'. To C. P. Grenfell, 11 Apr. 1845, Grenfell Papers, D/GR/8/30, Buckinghamshire Record Office.

[178]   S. Smith, 'Journal', *passim*, Scottish Record Office, RH4/156; Mitchell, *Dalkeith*, 38; R. Wallace, *Organise! Organise! Organise! A Study of Reform Agitations in Wales, 1840–1886* (Cardiff, 1991), 14–18.

participation, with, for example, an active Female Anti-Corn Law Association at Walsall, and female petitions in Scotland, as well as the better-known bazaars at Manchester and London.[179] Above all, after 1843 working-class interest in Repeal, diverted into Chartism after 1837, returned to the attack on monopoly. This could be seen in Manchester, Leicester, Wakefield, Bolton, and Oldham in the 1840s, while in the Potteries, in 1852, the Whig Leveson-Gower attributed his success to enthusiastic free trade working-class pressure on publicans and shopkeepers.[180] As Chartists in part recanted their opposition to free trade, so Repeal emerged at the centre of enduring popular narratives of working-class welfare and freedom.[181]

The conventional regional picture of the League also requires revision, for only in terms of finance was this a movement of northern exporters. Geographically, the pattern of support is far more diverse.[182] In the North, while Manchester and Leeds were the chief bastions of the movement, towns such as Halifax, Bradford, Bolton, and Wigan were just as active. In other regional metropolises, such as Birmingham and Nottingham, the passion of Manchester was missing, but local research reveals the prominence of the Corn Laws as a political issue in the 1830s, and the success of the League in focusing this sentiment, even if, as at Nottingham, it was at the cost of stimulating fervent protectionist opposition. In Birmingham, although the cause of free trade was overshadowed at first by currency reform and later by the Complete Suffrage Movement, by 1845 a Free Trade Association was active, contributing largely to the League's £250,000 fund, and to the Cobden Testimonial Fund. As a result, a Protectionist seat was recaptured in 1847, and the groundwork was laid for Bright's successful parliamentary transfer to Birmingham in 1857.[183] Among provincial cities, Bristol, Derby, Leicester, and Norwich also sported significant local movements.

Above all, London has been too often ignored in accounts of the League, for while, as we have seen, the City did not offer its purses to the movement's funds,

[179]　J. B. Smith Election Papers, vols 5 and 6 (Walsall); Cameron, 'Anti-Corn Law Movement', 127, 140, 201; Wallace, *Organise!*, 158 n. 2; F. K. Prochaska, *Women and Philanthropy* (Oxford, 1980), 54, 62–4; 'Eliza Ashurst', *Biographical Dictionary of Modern British Radicals. Vol. 2 1830–1870*, ed. J. O. Baylen and N. J. Gossman (Brighton, 1984), 13–15. Intriguingly, Mrs Margracia Loudon ('one of the earliest labourers in the cause, that labourer a *Woman*'), excerpts from whose *Philanthropic Economy* (1835) had been republished by the League in 1842, claimed to have converted Peel to free trade: Mrs Loudon to Cobden, 3 Jan. 1852, CP3, WSRO; cf. J. Mill to Peel, 3 July 1846, seeking a pension for Mrs Loudon, Peel Papers, Add. MS 40595 fos. 85–6.

[180]　Brown, 'Chartists and the League'; R. Boyson, *The Ashworth Cotton Enterprise* (Oxford, 1970), 206; A. T. Patterson, *Radical Leicester* (Leicester, 1954), 233, 305–7, 311 ff.; M. Winstanley, 'Oldham Radicalism and the Origins of Popular Liberalism, 1830–52', *Historical Journal*, 36 (1993), esp. 636–9; Gash, *Politics in the Age of Peel*, 176.

[181]　McCord, *Anti-Corn Law League*, 210–11; Godfrey, *Chartist Lives*, 229–31; E. Biagini, *Liberty, Retrenchment and Reform: Popular Liberalism in the Age of Gladstone, 1860–1880* (Cambridge, 1992), 97–101.

[182]　Schonhardt-Bailey, 'Lessons in Lobbying', *passim*.

[183]　D. Fraser, 'Nottingham and the Corn Laws', *Transactions of the Thoroton Society*, 70 (1966); id., 'Birmingham and the Corn Laws', *Transactions of the Birmingham Archaeological Society*, 82 (1965), 1–20; id., *Urban Politics in Victorian England* (Leicester, 1976), ch. 10.

the London meetings of the League did act as a vital national focus. There was a network of local associations in the capital which sustained popular, although not City, enthusiasm for the League, much as in the days of Wilkes, revealing the tension between the City élite, and the *menu peuple* of Bethnal Green, Camberwell, and Marylebone.[184] Here, first Place, and later colleagues like Henry Chapman and, above all, Sidney Smith had provided the League with vital metropolitan bases from which not only to launch bazaars and to win over émigrés such as Mazzini, Louis Napoleon, and General Espartero, but to win the City by-election of 1843 and to emerge as the 'great Fact' acknowledged by *The Times* in 1843.[185] The London presence of the League was even completed by the setting up of its own West End Free Trade Club, 'a union of like-minded men, thoroughly in sympathy and disposed for efficient co-operation'.[186]

Nor did the League remain simply an English urban body. In Scotland, the picture is also one of extensive popular participation, with the League encouraging the regeneration of an earlier anti-Corn Law tradition, especially vocal in the early 1830s among the working men of Glasgow. Glasgow, after Lancashire and York-shire, remained the readiest subscriber to the free trade cause, and Cobden himself emerged rapidly as a popular hero, attested to by numerous Scottish petitions in his defence on the occasion of his contretemps with Peel in 1843.[187] In Wales, too, the League acquired a considerable following in both North and South, benefiting from, but also politicizing in a new way, the forces of Welsh Dissent. As Wallace has shown, it acted both as 'a model in the techniques of political agitation', but also helped forge a new political consciousness.[188]

Nor was rural England wholly impregnable to the League's forces, even if successful agitation normally required the sympathy of an important local land-owner.[189] It received this from Earl Ducie in Gloucestershire and from Lord

---

[184]   See especially the reports of London free trade meetings in the *Sentinel*, 1843–6, a paper supporting both Repeal and complete suffrage.

[185]   S. Smith, 'Journal', *passim*. Smith was retained for the League at a salary of £350 in 1840 to canvass in London. He remained into the 1870s the key Liberal agent in the City. See, too, T. P. Thompson to H. B. Peacock, 10 and 22 May 1845, on a meeting of the London Complete Suffrage Association, where the former spoke on free trade to 'small citizens and their families', T. P. Thompson Letters, Manchester Central Library; for the Metropolitan Young Man's Anti-Monopoly Association, 1841, Ramsay MacDonald Papers, PRO 30/69/1383.

[186]   *The League*, 27 July 1844, 24 May 1845, 2 May 1846. In 1848 the Club seems to have had about two hundred members, including forty-three MPs, *The Times*, 6 Apr. 1848, but it disappeared *c.*1850–1; A. I. Dasent, *The History of St James Square* (1895), 125, 239; membership papers of Sir J. Philipart, KV (author's possession, courtesy of Peter Mandler).

[187]   Addresses, etc., CP 522–85, e.g. 574, from the handloom weavers of Perth, expressing 'heartfelt gratitude for the bold and generous efforts which you have made to cheapen the price of food and to give a fresh impulse to the sickly commerce of our country'. For the background to this episode, see Gash, *Politics in the Age of Peel*, 366–9.

[188]   See n. 178; I. G. Jones, 'The anti-Corn Law Letters of Walter Griffith', *Bulletin of the Board of Celtic Studies*, 28, pt. 1 (1978), 95–128.

[189]   For one early example of rural independence, see a meeting of Saxmundham labourers in 1839, reported by Jephson, *The Platform*, vol. 2, 330.

Clarendon in Wiltshire, although, perhaps more typically, in Northamptonshire Earl Spencer's conversion to Repeal proved a stronger stimulus to organized protectionism.[190] In Berkshire, the recently countrified City magnate C. P. Grenfell, who enjoyed close ties with the League, spurned the advances of the Maidenhead protectionists with a homily on the numbered days of class legislation.[191] Elsewhere, as among the Wiltshire villages, the League's success indicated the emergence of a more independent form of rural protest, a portent of the agricultural unionism of the 1870s.[192] These examples only qualify the picture of rural protectionism, against which League lecturers such as John Buckmaster were able to make little headway, but they provide a useful reminder that the League's message was also one of agricultural reform, and that Cobden himself acquired a lasting 'agricultural popularity'.[193] But despite some stirrings of radicalism among the labourers, and Cobden's strong appeal to the tenant farmers, the League's impact in the counties was necessarily strongest where urban penetration was greatest. This was the moral to be drawn from the League's registration campaign, which by 1846 had already delivered several seats into the movement's hands. As Prest argues, it was the fear of rural democracy that ultimately and powerfully carried Peel on the road to Repeal.[194] If timing is an obstacle to the full acceptance of Prest's ingenious argument, it may at least be admitted that the League attack on the landed interest had heightened the symbolic divisiveness of the Corn Laws to an extent that made Repeal both prudent and necessary.[195]

By 1846, therefore, the League had successfully turned free trade into a popular moral crusade, converting a 'pocket question' for the cotton lords into a symbol of new community of interest and a new understanding of the nation itself. Free trade rapidly replaced the Corn Laws as a symbol of Britishness, sanctified by royal approval, an elevation of provincial Britain that began in 1846, and was completed in the Great Exhibition of 1851.[196] It also elevated Cobden from a despised parvenu into both a fit appointment to the ministry, and, more long-lastingly, into a patriot hero to rival Wellington and Peel.[197] For Cobden, like Peel, had sacrificed personal

---

[190] Prentice, *Anti-Corn Law League*, vol. 2, 55; Clarendon to C. Bradford, 8 Nov. 1844 (draft), Clarendon Deposit, c. 525, folder 9, Bodleian Library; R. L. Greenall, 'Three 19th century Northampton Agriculturalists', *Northants Past and Present*, 7 (1988–9), 453.

[191] Draft reply to Maidenhead District Committee of the Berkshire Association for Protection of Agriculture, 7 Apr. 1844. Grenfell Papers, D/GR/8/21–3.

[192] E. Newman, 'The Anti-Corn Law League and the Wiltshire Labourer: Aspects of the Development of Nineteenth-Century Protest', in B. Holderness and M. E. Turner (eds.), *Land, Labour and Agriculture, 1700–1920* (1991), 91–107.

[193] J. C. Buckmaster (ed.), *A Village Politician: The Life-Story of John Buckley* (1897); 'Mr Cobden' in *Bagehot's Historical Essays*, 220.

[194] Prest, *Age of Cobden*, 96–7.

[195] Kemp, 'Reflections on Repeal'.

[196] For monarchy and Repeal, see *Letters of Queen Victoria, 1837–61*, ed. A. C. Benson and Viscount Esher (3 vols, 1908), vol. 2, 48–51, 87, 233. For protectionist disapprobation, see Disraeli, *Bentinck*, 45–6; A. Briggs, *Victorian People* (Harmondsworth, 1965), 50 for 1851.

[197] Read, *Peel and the Victorians*, 216; see below, Ch. 5.

fortune to the national good, and as a result emerged as a genuinely popular statesman.[198] Not only did Peel himself laud Cobden's efforts, but from many parts of Britain Cobden received the homage of the people, as well as the more tangible testimonials of his fellow cotton masters.[199] This was a movement of opinion that re-echoed throughout Europe and the colonies.[200] As we will see, the cult of Cobden was to be strongly articulated after his death, but the myth of Cobden was a contemporary one, built up in *The League* and in the accounts of Martineau, Dunckley, and Prentice.[201] Without the early death of Peel in 1850, Cobden's stature might perhaps have been even greater, but after 1850 Peel was to vie with Cobden in the working-class memory as a hero to whom the people owed prosperity and freedom. Even so, however strong the cult of Peel, it was the myth of the League, and the legacy of Cobden that cast a far longer shadow over the terrain of Victorian and Edwardian politics. But most immediately, it was the Whigs, who, having baulked the challenge of free trade in corn in December 1845, turned in July 1846 to face the implications of Repeal for commerce and the colonies.

---

[198]   In a rare witticism, Prince Albert acknowledged 'the English people have turned their affections from Richard Coeur de Lion to Richard Coeur de Coton', R. Fulford, *Prince Consort* (1949), 243. For Albert's own high estimation of Cobden in 1846, see F. Eyck, *The Prince Consort: A Political Biography* (1959), 32.

[199]   The Cobden Testimonial Fund (1845-8) raised some £76,759, committing its donors 'to an approval of my Free-Trade principles only', a unique personal and political tribute in Victorian England: H. Ashworth, *Recollections of Richard Cobden and the Anti-Corn Law League* (1877), 337-40.

[200]   e.g. *Sydney Morning Herald*, 12 July 1843, 3 Apr. 1844, 5 June 1846; '*the* man of the age', Revd J. West, editor of *Launceston Examiner*, 12 June 1850, cited in M. Roe, 'Society and Thought in Eastern Australia, 1835-1851', Ph.D. thesis, Australian National University (1960), 74; a village in Ontario was named Cobden in *c.*1850 by Jason Gould: see A. L. McCready to Jane Cobden-Unwin, 16 Jan. 1939, CP Add. MS 6043, WSRO. See Ch. 3 below for Cobden's European reputation.

[201]   See, too, J. Passmore Edwards, 'The Mission of Richard Cobden', *Howitt's Journal*, 3 (1848), 200-3.

2

The Whigs, the City, and Free Trade, 1846–1853

February 1849 must be the doomsday of all Protectionists.

Cobden to Russell, 4 July 1846, Russell Papers, PRO30/22/5B.

You cannot halt between two opinions. Free trade in all things or General Protection.

Elgin to Grey, 6 June 1848, quoted Schuyler, *Old Colonial System*, 166.

THE Whig contribution to the establishment and dominance of free trade in Victorian Britain has been relatively neglected. With the emphasis firmly upon Peel and Repeal in the 1840s, and Gladstone and budgets after 1853, the years 1846–52 have appeared as a caesura in fiscal policy.[1] Russell's Whig ministry, driven by expediency and characterized by 'timidity and maladroitness', has all too readily appeared a resumption of the confusion and mismanagement which had marked the Whigs in office before 1841.[2] This contrast between Peelite mastery of finance and Whig incompetence owed much to contemporary impressions, most influentially, perhaps, that of Gladstone, for whom the policy of the Whig governments represented a severe lapse from the path of Liberal Tory economic virtue.[3] It has been argued more recently that the Whigs at least shared many of the liberal economic ideas of the Tories, and that even if there was no distinctive Whig economic policy, the Whigs in office in the 1830s and 1840s sought to some extent to take up the strands of Liberal Tory policy.[4] More strongly, Brent has argued that the Whigs were influenced by their own distinctive brand of political economy, best seen in the Drummond Professors at Oxford—economists such as Neate and

---

[1] Cf. H. C. G. Matthew, 'Disraeli, Gladstone, and the Politics of Mid-Victorian Budgets', *Historical Journal*, 22 (1979), 615–43.
[2] D. Southgate, *The Passing of the Whigs* (1962), ch. 6, esp. 161; L. Brown, *The Board of Trade and the Free-Trade Movement, 1830–42* (Oxford, 1958), *passim*.
[3] Gladstone, 'Party as it was and as it is' (draft), 12 Apr. 1855, Gladstone Papers (hereafter GP), British Library, Add. MS. 44745, esp. 186 ff.
[4] P. Mandler, *Aristocratic Government in the Age of Reform. Whigs and Liberals, 1830–1852* (Oxford, 1990), e.g., 126, 197–9, 249–50. In retrospect, Lord John Russell described Whig policy in the 1830s as a 'gradual approach to free trade . . . in the spirit of Huskisson'. John, Earl Russell, *Recollections and Suggestions, 1813–1873* (1875), 205.

Rickards.[5] Parry has suggested that free trade lay at the centre of Liberal political rhetoric between 1846 and 1866, as a doctrine of progressive improvement through individual effort, freeing government from responsibility for economic management, while drawing to the Liberal-Whig Party the support of much public opinion.[6]

In this perspective, the years 1846–52 take on a new importance, for free trade offered to the Whigs their most hopeful opportunity to rival Peel's executive command, while harnessing the support for the policy that had been stirred by the League's popular politicians. When Russell took office in July 1846, his political designs sought to consolidate Peelite support behind the Whigs, to win over the middle-class electorate, and to accommodate the Radicals of the League in a ministry 'not for land, not for commerce, not for manufactures, but for the benefit of the whole people of the united Empire'.[7] In meeting these demands, as Russell's critics noted, to 'support John Russell meant to support free trade', for free trade was 'no longer an *experiment* but an unalterable system'.[8]

If more by accident than design, Whig economic policies also provide a vital clue in the burgeoning historical debate concerning the relative power of land, industry, and the City of London within the nineteenth-century British State.[9] Traditionally, as we have seen, Peelite finance, culminating in the repeal of the Corn Laws in 1846, has been interpreted as at least a symbolic sacrifice of the landed interest for the benefit of provincial industry.[10] Yet while Repeal vitally, if not necessarily permanently, removed protection from agriculture, it had left intact several ramparts of monopoly which surrounded the 'monied' arm of the 'gentlemanly capitalist' order. Here, Whig economic reforms were as crucial for the City and commerce as was the repeal of the Corn Laws for the landed interest. Above all, policies concerning timber, sugar, shipping, the colonies, and the Bank of England were all to affect important elements within the City of London and its nexus of financial and commercial institutions, which historians in recent years have suggested were far more vital to Britain's economic fortunes than the over-valued cotton industry of the North.[11] If Peelite finance had resolved in large part the conflict between land and industry, not the least of the achievements of the Whig government was the application of free trade policies to the City of London and to the Empire, in a manner that decisively shaped the fortunes of both in the second half of the nineteenth century. Consideration of the peculiar needs of land did not disappear

[5]   R. Brent, 'God's Providence: Liberal Political Economy as Natural Theology at Oxford, 1825–60', in M. Bentley (ed.), *Public and Private Doctrine* (Cambridge, 1993), 85–107; above, 9.

[6]   J. P. Parry, *The Rise and Fall of Liberal Government in Victorian Britain* (1993), 168–73.

[7]   *Hansard*, 3rd ser., 87, c. 1176, 16 July 1846.

[8]   First Viscount Ponsonby to Sir Charles Wood, 3 Feb. 1851, Hickleton Papers, A4/113, Borthwick Institute of Historical Research, York.

[9]   See above, 12–18.

[10]   Above, 5.

[11]   P. J. Cain and A. G. Hopkins, *British Imperialism* (2 vols, 1993), *passim*; for a vivid description of the City in these years, see D. Kynaston, *The City of London, 1815–1890: A World of its Own* (1994).

after 1846, but after Repeal agricultural protectionism depended in large part upon its allies in commerce and the empire, both for intellectual coherence and political support. On the other hand, Whig support for free trade was important not only for closing off the possibility of protectionist *revanche* for the landed interest, but for dismantling a series of buttresses of the old colonial system in a way that encouraged a new relationship between the City, the State, and free trade after 1850.

The Whigs and the legacy of Peel

The Whig ministry that came into office in July 1846 was, despite repute, not ill-equipped to benefit from the economic legacy of Peel. True, Sir Francis Baring, seen as the natural Whig Chancellor, declined to join the government. Yet in many ways this was no loss to a reforming ministry. In the years 1839–41 Baring had proved both hesitant and wayward. Although he was a master of Treasury detail, and had important family connections in the City, his suspicion of income tax made him a more enthusiastic proponent of economy than of fiscal reform.[12] Lord John Russell himself has had a reputation for being uninterested in political economy, and his conversion to free trade in the 'Edinburgh letter' of November 1845 has been seen as a '*coup d'état*' demanded by political expediency.[13] But this belies the evidence. For not only had free trade grown in intrinsic political appeal for the Whigs in the late 1830s, but Radical and Anti-Corn Law League pressure since 1837 had encouraged Whigs as well as Tories to look to total repeal.[14] In 1843 Russell had urged on Labouchère the need to outbid Peel by opposing imperial preference, and had advocated a low fixed duty on corn.[15] Russell continued to suggest a low or moderate fixed duty throughout 1844, but, as he wrote to Parkes, 'we ought to look forward to a total abolition as desirable'.[16] By the beginning of the following year, in association with Howick, he had evolved, as Peter Mandler has shown, a clear vision of future Whig policy combining free trade and social improvement.[17] This was announced to the electorate in the Edinburgh letter of November 1845, and reiterated in Russell's subsequent address to the City of London electors in July 1846.[18] If he proved reluctant to abandon a low fixed duty, he was keen to reassert the primacy of the natural order in food supply—'Is it', he wrote, 'for the good of the nation at large, we must ask, that a cabinet ever should

---

[12] For Baring's earlier career as Chancellor of the Exchequer, 1839–41, see Brown, *Board of Trade*, 69, 219–22. As a young man, Baring had attended the early meetings of the Political Economy Club, but in 1846, despite several attempts, had still not completed *The Wealth of Nations*; from his reading of Mill's *Political Economy* in 1842, he 'did not gain much'. Diaries of Sir Francis Baring, 1819–1852, *passim*, Barings' Archives, Bishopsgate, London. In the abortive Whig ministry of December 1845, Russell had initially proposed Baring as Home Secretary, not Chancellor.

[13] Gladstone, 'Party as it was', fos. 186–8; Southgate, *Passing of the Whigs*, ch. 5.

[14] See above, 25.

[15] Russell to Labouchère, 8 Dec. 1843, Russell Papers, William Perkins Library, Duke University, North Carolina.

[16] Russell to Parkes, 4 Apr. 1844, ibid.

[17] Mandler, *Aristocratic Government*, 218–35.

[18] Draft election address, Russell Papers [hereafter RP], PRO 30/22/5B, fos. 3–4.

undertake to regulate the amount, the quality of food necessary for twenty eight millions of people? Can any artificial scheme exceed in providence and forethought that natural arrangement by which sellers supply the market according to the wants of the buyers?'[19] Popular welfare might require Whig intervention in the form of factory or public health legislation, but food supply was to be left to God's providence.

Among other leading Whigs, the erratic Howick, now third Earl Grey, and Colonial Secretary, combined a strong theoretical grasp of political economy, imbibed from McCulloch, with a determination to press ahead with liberal policies. In December 1844 he had urged on Sir Charles Wood the need to abandon the Corn Laws in order to encourage agricultural investment and an improvement in the condition of the working classes. Their 'difficulties and privations', he believed, made clearer '. . . the duty of making every effort to get rid of all those restrictive laws which most undoubtedly tend more or less to depress the value of labour'.[20] Howick reiterated the primacy of free trade as the solution to the 'Condition of England' question in forthright terms to Russell a few weeks later:

It is my firm conviction that there are measures within the power of Parliament the adoption of which would in no long time work a great improvement in the condition of the labouring classes; of these the first and the foundation of every other ought in my opinion to be the sweeping away of all restrictions upon the freedom of trade except those duties which we impose simply and exclusively with a view to revenue.

It is, he concluded, 'our duty and our interest as a party to come forward very decidedly to demand free trade on the ground of justice to the working classes'.[21]

Grey's optimism as to the prospects of such a course was not uniformly shared by his Whig confrères, yet it is clear that the Cabinet as a whole were not 'the Bourbons of the fisc', ill-versed in political economy.[22] For not only did the Whigs patronize their own version of liberal political economy (Neate, for example, had been Baring's private secretary in the 1830s), but several had a close interest in economic policy. Above all, Grey's brother-in-law Sir Charles Wood, who rose to unexpected prominence as Chancellor of the Exchequer in Baring's absence, had been educated at Oriel in the heyday of Copleston and the Noetics (the intellectual leaders of political economy in Oxford), had good City contacts, and had studied monetary issues closely in the 1830s. He had chaired the Select Committee on the Banks of Issue in 1840, whose report was in some ways the progenitor of the Bank Charter Act of 1844.[23] Among other ministers, Clarendon at the Board of Trade in

[19] 'Reflexions on the present State of the Corn Laws', unfinished MS, *c.* Nov./Dec. 1845, Russell Papers, Duke University.

[20] Grey to Wood, 26 Dec. 1844, Hickleton Papers, A4/55/1.

[21] Howick (Grey) to Russell, 18 Jan. 1845, Russell Papers, Duke University.

[22] Southgate, *Whigs*, 140–2.

[23] For Wood at Oriel, see Fremantle to Wood, 12 Oct. 1883, Hickleton Papers A4/136; see, too, Wood–G. W. Norman letters in Hickleton Papers, and Norman Papers, Centre for Kentish Studies, Maidstone; on Wood and the Act of 1844, Torrens to Wood, 29 Jan. 1848 Hickleton Papers, A4/156. See, too, R. J. Moore, *Sir Charles Wood's Indian Policy, 1853–66* (Manchester, 1966), and J. A. Jowitt,

1846, if less strident in the free trade cause than his brother C. P. Villiers, had had extensive experience of commercial negotiations in the 1830s, and entertained no doubt that the Whigs and the aristocracy would stand or fall according to their adherence to 'the principles of free trade in all their bearings and consequences'.[24] Clarendon's removal from the Board of Trade to Ireland limited his influence on economic policy, but his successor Henry Labouchère, scion of a London banking family, related by marriage to the Greys and Barings, accepted the centrality of free trade to Whig policy, and had helped redirect the Whigs towards free trade on the sugar duties in 1841.[25] Among other ministers, Clanricarde, Sir George Grey, Macaulay, Minto, Morpeth, and Palmerston were also committed free traders.[26] So too was a later addition to the Cabinet, Granville, who, before his unexpected promotion to the Foreign Office in 1851, had, as Vice-President of the Board of Trade, masterminded the Great Exhibition of 1851 as a celebration of free trade, the basis of his long-lasting rapport with Manchester.[27] The majority of the Whig administration was therefore united by a belief in the priority of free trade as their goal, and while it may be plausible to argue that in some part they shared the Peelite evangelical vision of Christian political economy, in their version this component was weaker and the economic optimism greater than in the Peelite credo.

The movement of the Whigs towards an optimistic version of free trade was encouraged by two further factors, those of political necessity and bureaucratic advice. First, the Whigs were, above all, united by a determination that office should be used to advance the cause of Whiggery, avoiding any early junction with Peelites or Protectionists, but exploiting the potential of free trade to draw around the Whig aristocracy the urban middle-class electorate. This, as Brent has argued, had been clearly foreshadowed in the election of 1841.[28] The consolidation of free trade was now central to the Whigs' claim to the gratitude of the electorate, and their main hope of outflanking the Cobdenite Radicals. Russell's 'conversion' to free trade by 1845 had represented a victory for the Anti-Corn Law League, for Cobden's tactics had been designed to win over the Whigs (not Peel) to free trade.[29] It was now Russell's aim to win over free traders to the cause of the Whigs: to encapsulate, as Searle has put it, 'the triumph of Free Trade but the defeat of the Free Traders'.[30]

'Sir Charles Wood (1800–85): A Case Study in the Formation of Liberalism in Mid-Victorian England', M.Phil. thesis, University of Leeds (1980).

[24] H. E. Maxwell, *The Life and Letters of George William, Fourth Earl of Clarendon* (2 vols, 1913), vol. 1, 238–9.

[25] His speech on the sugar duties in 1839 had been separately printed; see, too, R. Brent, *Liberal Anglican Politics, 1830–1841* (Oxford, 1987), 288–92; Mandler, *Aristocratic Government*, 163.

[26] Clanricarde belonged and was landlord to the Free Trade Club at 14 St James Square.

[27] E. Fitzmaurice, *The Life of Lord Granville* (2 vols, 1905), vol. 1, 40–3.

[28] Brent, *Liberal Anglican Politics*, 295–8.

[29] Cobden to Easthope, 30 Dec. 1842, Papers of Sir John Easthope, William Perkins Library, Duke University.

[30] G. R. Searle, *Entrepreneurial Politics in Mid-Victorian Britain* (Oxford, 1993), 50.

Second, if, under Peel, the Board of Trade had receded from its primacy in the struggle for free trade, its influence was revived in the late 1840s. On a range of policies from sugar duties to shipping, detailed questions were raised beyond the technical grasp of politicians, who increasingly resorted to official advice. This was provided by a talented group of young civil servants, who, for the most part, subscribed to an optimistic view of free trade. For example, the future high priest of Victorian Cobdenism Sir Louis Mallet was at this time a junior official, as was Edgar Bowring, the son of the dogmatic free trade utilitarian Sir John.[31] As Board of Trade librarian, Bowring had been responsible for getting up 'a good economical library', and had, with Mallet, co-operated in 1849 in rebutting the protectionist arguments of Sir John Byles. In this, they were aided by another young official, Lord Hobart, whose later career was also a testament to his faith in Cobden.[32] Besides this galaxy of talent, the ultimate embodiment of late Victorian economic orthodoxy Sir Thomas Farrer was introduced in 1848, after an early career at the Bar.[33] Finally, although no Cobdenite, and in the process of freeing himself from the toils of a Recordite upbringing, much work on Whig policy (especially the Navigation Acts) was performed by Farrer's Eton friend, the young Sir Stafford Northcote.[34] It is not too much to suggest that not only the Whig implementation of free trade in the 1840s, but the whole subsequent interpretation of free trade in Victorian Britain owed its origins to this precocious group of mandarins, valuable apprentices to the Board's old free trade sorcerers, Porter and MacGregor.

On entering office in July 1846, however, the Whig appropriation of free trade began with a characteristic consideration of men, rather than measures. They faced strong pressure to include Cobden himself in or near the Cabinet. Some Whigs recoiled with predictable hauteur, but even Palmerston did not wholly dismiss the idea of a diplomatic post for Cobden.[35] Grey and Clarendon were enthusiastic, but eventually Cobden's triumphant free trade 'Grand Tour' of 1846–7 temporarily resolved the dilemma. It revived, however, in the summer of 1847. With an election imminent, and with the Radicals restive, the capture of Cobden seemed eminently prudent to Wood: 'He [Cobden] will be in a very difficult and awkward position for us. He has been elevated to a high post, complimented in every way, and of course,

[31]   B. Mallet, *Sir Louis Mallet: A Record of Public Service and Political Ideals* (1905); T. H. S. Escott, *Great Victorians* (1916), 128; Diaries of E. A. Bowring, 1841–52, William Perkins Library, Duke University.

[32]   V. H. Hobart and E. A. Bowring, *Free Trade and its So-called Sophisms: A Reply to 'Sophisms of Free Trade etc . . . examined by a Barrister'* (2nd edn., 1850). (Mallet's role in this publication is revealed in Bowring's diaries.) Mary, Lady Hobart (ed.), *Essays and Miscellaneous Writings of Vere Henry, Lord Hobart* (2 vols, 1885), esp. 'The "Mission" of Richard Cobden', vol. 2, 185–209.

[33]   T. C. Farrer (ed.), *Some Farrer Memorials: being a selection from the papers of Thomas Henry, first Lord Farrer, 1819–1899, on Various Matters* (privately printed, 1923).

[34]   A. Lang, *Life, Letters, and Diaries of Sir Stafford Northcote, first Earl of Iddesleigh* (2 vols, Edinburgh, 1890); S. Northcote, *A Short Review of the History of the Navigation Laws of England* (1844); *Parliamentary Papers*, 1847–8, 10, pt. II (431) SC (House of Lords) Navigation Laws, qq. 4716–4980; Clarendon dep. c. 525, folder 2, Correspondence with Northcote, Board of Trade, 1846.

[35]   Palmerston to Russell, 14 July 1846, RP, PRO 30/22/5B.

must take a part. You know how difficult it is for a person in such a position not to take an adverse line at times and this might be very inconvenient.'[36] Clarendon once more urged similar ideas, fearing to leave Cobden 'an outlying deer to be stalked by Peel' and attracting a 'great following in the country'.[37] On this occasion, the opposition of the Queen deterred Russell from offering Cobden the Cabinet and the Presidency of the new Poor Law Commission, while the growing distance between Cobden and the Whigs thereafter ended what was probably bound to have been, on both sides, an unconvincing and improbable coalition of men.[38] But Cobden's shadow, if not his person, was to loom large in the work of the Whig Cabinet between 1846 and 1852.

Above all, in July 1846 Cobden spelt out for Russell what he saw as the lessons of Corn Law Repeal:

Do not lose the *free trade wind*. Your countrymen can only entertain one idea at a time. There is much to do yet. All the anomalies of the tariff must be removed. All differential duties must follow corn. The absurd 50 per cent protection in the innumerable petty items in the tariff must be swept away. Sugar and coffee must be equalised. I would not give the sugar interest a longer respite than Peel has given the English agriculturists. February 1849 must be the doomsday of all protectionists.[39]

Cobden's agenda for free trade reform was, in fact, to be implemented to a very marked extent over the following six years. For Whig economic designs embodied an ambitious attempt to advance the cause of free trade in a manner that would win over to them the votes of the middle classes, while evincing their fitness, as Peter Mandler has stressed, as 'Foxite trustees' for the people.[40] This attempt by the Whigs to pick up the Peelite mantle, before either Disraeli or Gladstone became plausible contenders for it, deserves serious attention. At its heart lay necessarily that bugbear of Whig aristocratic government: budgetary policy.

Whig finance, 1846–51

Whig budgets have had a bad press from Gladstone onwards, although this has both obscured the difficulties they faced, and ignored the principles and strategy which underlay their constuction.[41] First, in the circumstances of 1846–7, with famine in Ireland and crisis in the colonial and domestic economy, it is hardly surprising that short-term considerations in part undermined the Whigs' attempt to evolve a coherent budgetary policy. The need to relieve Ireland dictated a policy of government loans (even Peel accepted their necessity), while the downturn in the

[36]   Wood to Russell, 14 Aug. 1847, RP, PRO 30/22/6E.
[37]   Clarendon to Grey, 8 and 20 Aug. 1847, Grey Papers.
[38]   F. A. Dreyer, 'The Russell Administration, 1846–1852', Ph.D. thesis, St Andrews (1962), 65–72, for further details.
[39]   Cobden to Russell, 4 July 1846, RP, PRO 30/22/5B.
[40]   Mandler, *Aristocratic Government, passim.*
[41]   Cf. S. Northcote, *Twenty Years of Financial Policy* (1862); S. Buxton, *Finance and Politics: An Historical Study, 1783–1885* (2 vols, 1888), vol. 1, ch. 6.

economy removed any chance of meeting current expenditure out of current income—the Gladstonian standard of fiscal rectitude. Sir Charles Wood was therefore faced by an unenviable task—perhaps the most severe financial crisis of the
century: the horrendous problem of Irish famine, growing demands for military
and civil expenditure, and strong pressures to provide financial relief for the
agricultural interest and for West Indian planters. Against these demands, there
arose the strident Radical call for cheap government, which the Whig economists
such as Baring were ready to endorse.[42] Herein lay the fiscal and political dilemma
for Wood—how to satisfy traditional Whig interests while expanding Whig support among the shopocracy and middle classes. Wood ('successful only in relation
to the problems he faced', as the *DNB* noted) was ultimately unable to resolve this
dilemma, yet the Whig budgets of 1848–51 were not without reforming intent and
political astuteness.

The first Whig budget, that of 1847, was essentially an Irish budget and a time-
marker. A shortfall in revenue ruled out bold measures, and famine ruled out
Wood's wish to apply income tax to Irish landlords.[43] Its main interest lay in the
clear intention of Russell and Wood to rely upon income tax as what Northcote
later termed 'a permanent and necessary support', whether to cover short-term
needs (in this case Ireland and defence expenditure), or, in future, fiscal reform
through the abolition and reduction of duties.[44] Fiscal opportunity opened, in
Russell's sanguine mind at least, in late 1847, when he urged on Wood the need for
tariff revision and social reform. By raising a further £6m from direct taxes, Russell
wished to abolish window and soap duties, as well as those on timber and copper
ore, while increasing expenditure on defence and education. He gave pride of place
to the abolition of the soap tax, as an appeal both to the sanitary crusaders and the
Smithian orthodox, as 'the only necessity of life mentioned by Adam Smith, which
yet remains taxed'.[45] Yet there was also an equalitarian intent, through the adjustment of income tax and insurance premiums, to benefit the professional classes, but
not 'Jones Loyd, Rothschild, or Swan & Edgar'.[46]

None of this met any enthusiasm from Wood, too well aware of both falling
revenue and rising expenditure to contemplate Russell's optimistic plans for fiscal
reform.[47] Wood pointed out the indispensability of the taxes the Radicals wished to
reduce, and the insuperable obstacles to the raising of income tax or the abolition of
the soap duty.[48] By September he was resisting demands for further expenditure in

[42]   F. Baring to C. Wood, 24 Dec. 1848, Hickleton Papers, A4/54.
[43]   Monteagle to Russell, n.d., end of 1846, RP, PRO 30/22/5G, f. 179; Clarendon to Russell, 20
Jan. 1847, RP, PRO 30/22/6A, fos. 187–8; Wood to Sir Francis Baring, 30 Dec. 1846 (copy); Russell
to Wood, 3 Jan. 1847, Hickleton Papers, A4/54.
[44]   Northcote, *Financial Policy*, 104. This course was anathema to Sir Francis Baring.
[45]   Russell to Wood, 24 Aug. 1847, Hickleton Papers, A4/56.
[46]   Ibid. 21 Aug. 1847.
[47]   For rising defence demands, see M. S. Partridge, 'The Russell Cabinet and National Defence,
1846–52', *History*, 72 (1987), 231–50.
[48]   Wood to Russell, 20 and 23 Aug. 1847, RP, PRO 30/22/6E.

Ireland, and was already forecasting 'a good handsome deficit'.[49] Three months later he was contemplating raising the recently reduced duty on Canadian timber in a desperate search for sources of revenue other than income tax.[50] Rising military expenditure, with war in South Africa, the demands of Canada, and those of the West Indies ultimately ruled out tariff revision, while parliamentary and public opinion ruled out increased income tax.

This was the background to the notorious series of four budgets in 1848, in the face of a rising deficit and resulting in resort to the reserves and Exchequer Bills, wherein lay the gravamen of the Gladstonian indictment of Whig finance and the apparent deathbed of the Whigs' fiscal ambitions. Above all, the Whigs were now faced by a widespread Radical economy campaign, both within Parliament and outside, a movement which in turn revived the demand for parliamentary reform.[51] This campaign permanently shaped Liberal and Radical thinking on financial issues, as several historians have shown, while sharpening the Cobdenite attack on aristocratic extravagance, and the desire to remove 'the fetters on our industry'.[52] For the advanced Liverpool Financial Reformers, led by Gladstone's merchant brother Robertson, those fetters included all customs and excise duties, for which direct taxes were to be substituted.[53] This was an aspiration that continued to enthuse a small mid-Victorian group of fiscal reformers.[54] But in 1848 the campaign for financial reform soon ran out of steam, having failed to ignite the popular movement that the Radicals sought to create. This failure stemmed in part from the inability of the Radicals to order their own priorities between parliamentary and financial reform, and the incoherence of their ideas on taxation. But, equally, it revealed that Radical dissatisfaction with Whig finance was easily exaggerated, and that however constrained by circumstance, Wood retained a clear sense of the underlying political objective of Whig finance, the conciliation of the middle classes.

Unlike Russell, however, Wood saw that this aspiration would require not only peace and a return to good trade, but lower taxes and reduced expenditure:

Everything convinces me that the question of the middle classes is taxation; they are all for peace and order, against the lower orders, do not care much, I think, for the franchise or

---

[49]   Wood to Clarendon, 25 Sept. 1847, Treasury Letter Book II, fo. 79, Hickleton Papers, A4/185; Wood to Grey, 2 Sept. 1847, Grey Papers.

[50]   Wood to Grey, n.d., *c*.30 Dec. 1847; Grey, Journal, 31 Dec. 1847, Grey Papers.

[51]   W. N. Calkins, 'A Victorian Free Trade Lobby', *Economic History Review*, 2nd ser., 13 (1960–1), 90–104; N. C. Edsall, 'A Failed National Movement: The Parliamentary and Financial Reform Association, 1848–54', *Bulletin of the Institute of Historical Research*, 49 (1976), 108–31; R. E. Quinault, '1848 and Parliamentary Reform', *Historical Journal*, 31 (1988), 831–51; Searle, *Entrepreneurial Politics*, 50–74.

[52]   Matthew, 'Budgets'; P. R. Ghosh, 'Disraelian Conservatism: a Financial Approach', *EHR*, 99 (1984), 268–96; Cobden to Robertson Gladstone, 7 Jan. 1850, Glynne–Gladstone Papers, 579.

[53]   Searle, *Entrepreneurial Politics*, 59.

[54]   For one example, A. Alison, *To the Electors: Universal Free Trade* (1852); for Alison, see B. Hilton, *The Age of Atonement: The Influence of Evangelicalism on Social and Economic Thought, 1785–1865* (Oxford, 1988), 326. See, too, below, 116.

anything of that kind but are raging for a revision of taxation . . . They hate the income tax, being in distress—and we are now finding the evils of direct taxation, which not only pinches but shews *where* it pinches.

The moral was clear: '. . . we must keep our fingers out of the people's pockets and try to keep down our expenditure. This is the desideratum of those classes whom we must retain at present.'[55] The hallmark of Whig finance was, therefore, to be in the short term—for 1848 and 1849—a search for economy, with a detailed review of all government expenditure in the autumn of 1848. This resulted in substantial cuts in military spending, together with savings on excise collection, education, and the royal household.[56] Wood also continued his internecine strife with Grey in an effort (largely fruitless) to cut down the demands of the Colonial Office.[57] By early 1849 the result of this was the prospect of a small budgetary surplus, the restoration of Whig credibility among the Radicals, and the gradual revival of Wood in public estimation.[58] Wood's 'low-spending, anaemic Peelism', as Parry has described it, had much to commend it; even Cobden was prepared to recognize the progress of retrenchment.[59]

Government parsimony and the return of economic prosperity, moreover, promised in 1850 a substantial surplus, which gave rise to a lively debate on the Whigs' future budgetary strategy. Wood and Russell kept up their joint front against Baring's continued assault on income tax (which prosperity now made less irksome to the middle classes), and saw in the surplus the possibility of tariff revision. For Russell, this meant resisting the idea of sops to the landed interest, a possibility canvassed by a number of landed Whigs, who had not yet abandoned all idea of a return to a fixed duty on corn. In Russell's view this would only serve to 'revive the Corn Law league and its agitation combined with projects for the abolition of the Church immediately and of the Throne prospectively . . . it would resume a struggle the cessation of which has mainly contributed to our stability during the heavings of the Earthquake of Paris'. Instead, he revived his pet topic, the soap duty.[60] As before, he decried it as 'against all sanitary principles', whose

---

[55]   Wood to Grey, 24 Apr. 1848, Grey Papers. This view was shared by the Whig whip, Tufnell. See Tufnell to Russell, 7 Mar. 1848, RP, PRO 30/22/7B f. 34. For middle-class opinion, see A. Howe, *The Cotton Masters 1830–1860* (Oxford Historical Monographs: Oxford, 1984), 232–3; Searle, *Entrepreneurial Politics*, 51–74.

[56]   Royal expenditure had been an early object of the Liverpool Financial Reformers, Robertson to W. E. Gladstone, 22 Mar. 1848, Glynne–Gladstone Papers, 661; Searle, *Entrepreneurial Politics* , 66.

[57]   For details of this economy campaign, see Wood to Grey, 19 May 1849; Grey Journal, 6 Dec. 1848, Grey Papers; Russell to Wood, 17 Dec. 1848, Hickleton Papers, A4/56. For Wood and the Colonial Office, see Wood to Grey, 9 Apr. 1847, 19 May 1849, Grey Papers.

[58]   *Greville Memoirs*, vol. 6, 182–4, [8 August 1849].

[59]   Parry, *Liberal Government*, 173–4; Searle, *Entrepreneurial Politics*, 65; *Speeches on Questions of Public Policy by Richard Cobden*, ed. J. Bright and J. E. Thorold Rogers (single vol. edn., 1878), 254 [8 Mar. 1850].

[60]   Russell to Duke of Bedford, 18 Dec. 1849, in G. P. Gooch (ed.), *The Later Correspondence of Lord John Russell, 1840–1878* (2 vols, 1925), vol. 1, 197–8; Russell to Wood, 4 and 19 Jan. 1850, Hickleton Papers, A4/56.

abolition 'would be a declaration on behalf of the great body of the people, relieving consumers of all classes instead of relieving one such class'.[61] Russell hereby sought to reaffirm the policy of the 1845 Edinburgh letter associating free trade and social reform, and seeking a Whig middle ground between protectionism and radicalism.

Russell's proposals once more placed Wood in a quandary, for while the latter was sympathetic to the need for fiscal reforms, he knew that their cost outran the surplus available. Somewhat to Russell's surprise, Wood favoured not one bold gesture, but a number of smaller fiscal concessions, including a measure of relief to land. As a result, the budget of 1850 saw the abolition of the excise on bricks and an adjustment of the stamp duties. The latter was largely a measure of Treasury tidying-up, but the former was an element of reform dear to the Radicals, promising cheaper cottages for the poor, and, Wood believed, appealing to the sanitary movement and to farmers.[62] He therefore offered a prudent fiscal reform, a measure of progress, although it fell short of the major 'experiments' in tariff revision that the Radicals demanded.

Wood's failure to satisfy Radical demands for fiscal reform and for cheap government contributed to the Whigs' problem over the renewal of income tax in 1851. This led to the resignation of the government on 21 February 1851, and, despite their temporary restoration to office until 20 February 1852, overshadowed the last year of Whig finance. The debate over income tax and the turmoil of the ministry have been allowed to obscure a wide-ranging discussion within the Whig Party on future fiscal policy. Four main views competed within the ministry. On the Radical wing, James Wilson, whose views were perhaps the closest to those of the Liverpool Financial Reformers, urged strongly the retention of income tax, with the surplus generated to be devoted to the abolition of remaining duties.[63] On the economist wing of the party, Sir Francis Baring, in particular, urged the reduction of income tax and the necessity of concessions to property-owners. Between these extreme positions, most opinion cohered around two strategies. Russell, Sir George Grey, Lansdowne, and Clarendon, worried about growing protectionist strength in the countryside, favoured the retention of income tax, but relief for the landed interest by the transfer of some local charges to the Exchequer, a policy that had for a long time appealed to Russell as a centralizing measure.[64] Interestingly, Wood, who in 1850 favoured relief to the landed interest, now strongly anathematized Russell's proposals as an attack on local self-government, raising the spectre of rule not by the gentry, but by 'prefects and the bureaucratic'. Wood himself emphasized the

[61]   Russell to Wood, 4 and 19 Jan., 24 Feb. 1850, Hickleton Papers, A4/56.
[62]   For the making of this budget, see Russell to Wood, 19 Jan., 24 and 26 Feb. 1850, Hickleton Papers, A4/56; Wood to Russell, n.d., early Feb. 1850, RP, PRO 30/22/8C, fos. 355–6.
[63]   Wilson to Grey, 17 Dec. 1850, Grey Papers.
[64]   Mandler, *Aristocratic Government*, 270; for these views, see Russell to Wood, 28 Dec. 1850, 1 Jan. 1851, Hickleton Papers A4/56; George Grey to Russell, 27 Dec. 1850, 2 Jan. 1851; Lansdowne to Russell, 19 Nov. 1850, RP, PRO 30/22/8G; Russell to Sir George Grey, 26 and 31 Dec. 1850, Sir George Grey Papers, vol. III, Barings' Archives.

need for popular reforms, above all the abolition of the window tax, with further remissions on timber and coffee, although with a renewed house tax to make up half the revenue lost from windows. He urged relief to the many—the consumers—not to the few—the property-owners—as the key to popularity and electoral success, for 'better . . . a really popular budget than [by any] attempt to please people who cannot be pleased'.[65]

In the event, Wood's budget on 17 February 1851, based on these proposals, fell with the government, only to be substantially reintroduced on 4 April, following a detailed canvass of opinion among Wood's colleagues.[66] Despite considerable Cabinet pressure for the abolition of only half the window duty, Wood stuck to his guns, defending the switch to a house duty as far more acceptable to the Radicals (De Lacy Evans, Cobden, Brown) and to most Whigs. For, despite the unfavourable reception given to Wood's budget, it met most Radical desiderata. William Brown supported the house tax as 'just and equitable', while Baines rejected the clamour against the budget as 'unjust and vulgar'. He saw Wood's budget as fully consistent with previous budgets since 1841 and 1842 in upholding income tax and reducing other duties: 'There can also be no doubt that most of us gain more in the cost of living under free trade and low duties than we lose by Income Tax.'[67] Wood's budgets, although dominated by short-term considerations, reaffirmed the priority that had been attached to fiscal issues by the Whigs in 1841. By combining the furtherance of free trade and fiscal reform, as did the budgets of 1850 and 1851, the Whigs looked once more to finance to restore the electoral alliance between their landed and urban supporters. Arguably, Wood, like Baines, allowed his vision to be too strongly slanted by his experience of the West Riding, but this combination undoubtedly held out the best hope of Whig popularity, enabling them to consolidate their hold on the middle ground between the Radicals and protectionists. It will, as Morpeth (by then seventh Earl of Carlisle) noted, 'keep with us the bulk of the Liberal Free traders, who are our real strength in the country'.[68] Many Radical objectives remained unfulfilled—above all retrenchment had some way to go, and the abolition of the tea duty remained a central popular demand—but by reducing expenditure, and by retaining income tax as a shield for fiscal reform, the Whigs had staked some claim to the Peelite mantle, advancing consumer welfare, economic prosperity, and administrative reform. This was a fiscal *via media*, which had much in common with Gladstone's budget of 1853, which deployed some of Wood's arguments, and to whose defence Wood publicly rallied.[69]

---

[65] Wood to Russell, 31 Dec. 1850, RP, PRO 30/22/8G.

[66] 'The Budget of 1851', Hickleton Papers, A4/188; G. C. Lewis to Russell, 2 Mar. 1851, RP, PRO 30/22/9A.

[67] Brown to Wood, 21 Mar. 1851; Baines to Wood, 26 Feb. 1851; also Ellice to Wood, 21 Feb. and 21 Mar. 1851, Hickleton Papers, A4/78, A4/160, A4/103A (transcripts).

[68] 'Budget of 1851', Hickleton Papers, A4/188.

[69] Searle, *Entrepreneurial Politics*, 79, 82. But for Wood's private doubts about the budget, see *Gladstone Diaries* (*GD*), vol. 4, 11–15, Mar. 1853.

The Whigs, the City, and gentlemanly capitalism

Whig budgetary policy was subject not only to the strictures of Gladstone, the Radicals, and the Protectionists, but also suffered in the City of London from unfavourable comparison with Peel's handling of finance.[70] To some extent, the Whigs appeared insensitive to City opinion, both on technical questions of government borrowing, but also on wider issues such as that of railway finance, in whose complexities they were notably reluctant to intervene, although they were under some City pressure to do so.[71] Moreover, despite the Whigs' strong power-base in the City in the 1840s, symbolized by Russell's election in 1841, and his return at the head of the poll in 1847, their relationship with its gentlemanly capitalists was, at best, ambivalent. Thus Clarendon, after a long talk with Lionel Rothschild, reported the latter's view that 'he and other monied and mercantile men are always maltreated by Whig ministers far more so than by the Tories, that their advice is looked upon as insincere and their opinions dictated by their own interests'.[72] Rothschild remained a leading supporter of the Whigs; many other City men were not only to share his suspicions of the Whigs as financiers, but were to rue the consequences of the party's policies directed towards achieving Cobden's 'doomsday of the Protectionists', and to removing from the back of the liberal state the copestone of monopoly which had so limited the Whigs' freedom of action in the 1830s.[73]

At the centre of Whig policy, therefore, lay the determination to abandon imperial preference, the umbrella under which the vested interests of sugar, shipping, and timber had long sheltered. This policy had already been signalled in 1841, when the reduction of sugar duties had been the focus of their attempt to re-create the Liberal electoral alliance of Anglicans, Dissenters, the Irish, and the Radicals, on a free trade basis. On their return to office, this intent was put into immediate effect, for in July 1846 Russell's Sugar Bill proposed the equalization of the duties on foreign and colonial sugar. Equalization was to take place gradually (otherwise, Russell was advised, the benefits would be for speculators, not consumers[74]), but would be completed by 1851. Although Peel himself had already significantly reduced imperial preference, the Whigs resumed this policy as one signalling a clear breach with the Liberal Tory past, seeking to distinguish themselves from Peelite tenderness to colonial interests without forfeiting the support of anti-slavery opinion.[75]

Whig radicalism on this issue had been strongly voiced by Clarendon, when in 1840 he had urged the unilateral abolition of preference as a more desirable experi-

---

[70] See, for example, the views of C. P. Villiers reported in C. S. Parker, *Sir Robert Peel from his Private Papers* (3 vols, 1891–9), vol. 3, 352.

[71] James Pattison to Russell, 12 Jan. 1847, RP, PRO 30/22/6A f. 132.

[72] Clarendon to Wood, 9 May 1847, Hickleton Papers, A4/57.

[73] See above 25.

[74] Antrobus to Russell, 10 July 1846, RP, PRO 30/22/5B.

[75] For Tory perplexities on the sugar duties, see e.g. *GD*, vol. 3, 10 July 1846.

ment than Peel's early strategy of negotiation with Spain and Brazil. For, as Clarendon wrote to Sir John Easthope:

if we prove that under the Tropics as elsewhere the freeman is a cheaper productive instrument than the slave, slavery and the Trade will become extinct. This I consider can only be effected by giving to the West Indians free commerce in all commodities with all the world, by removing from them all the restrictions that our own vicious system has imposed and by withdrawing from them in return that monopoly which experience shows to be equal[ly] prejudicial to the extent and economy of their cultivation.[76]

Despite strong pressures from Whig families dependent on West Indian incomes, and from strong City interests organized in the West India Committee,[77] Russell now persisted in this policy, announcing the Whigs' intention to restore the 'natural interests of commerce'. He declared: 'Freedom ought to be infused into every part, and that the circle by which these interests were protected ought to be broken.'[78] Colonial interest groups, like those of industry and agriculture, were to be dethroned in favour of a self-regulating market economy, in which government would respond to the needs of the many (the consumers) by removing the privileges of the few. In the West Indies, once the artificial incentive of monopoly was removed, low prices and increased production would result from modern technology, capital investment, and efficient management. Low prices would guarantee consumer welfare—for increased consumption of sugar was now an index of the amelioration of the condition of the working-classes[79]—while increased consumption at lower duties would maximize state revenue. The Whig policy of equalization could therefore, in theory, promote the interests of the planters, the consumers, the slaves, and the Exchequer.

In the short term, however, this was by no means the case, for the Sugar Act of 1846 was followed by widespread distress in the West Indies and Mauritius, culminating in the failure of numerous colonial sugar firms in the commercial crisis of 1847–8.[80] This ruin of 'a great number of wealthy and substantial merchants' (including, for example, the politically well-connected firm of Reid, Irving and Co., headed by Sir John Rae Reid, Bank of England director and MP for Dover, 1832–47) had been correctly predicted by the Protectionists.[81] For them, the sugar

---

[76] Clarendon to Sir John Easthope, 19 June 1842, Easthope Papers.

[77] Grantley Berkeley to Russell, 25 July 1846; Ferguson to Russell, 27 July 1846; Labouchère to Russell, n.d., 1846, enclosing J. J. Travers to Sir G. Larpent, RP, PRO 30/22/5B; *Reports of the Acting Committee . . . of West India Planters and Merchants*, 1848–9; M. J. Higgins ['Jacob Omnium'] *Is Cheap Sugar the Triumph of Free Trade?* (1848); D. Hall, *A Brief History of the West India Committee* (St Lawrence, 1971).

[78] *Hansard*, 3rd ser., 87, esp. c. 1314–15, 1320, 20 July 1846.

[79] For the defence of Whig policy along these lines, see Wood, *Hansard*, 3rd ser., 88, cc. 55–77, 27 July 1846, 97, cc. 42–71, 3 Feb. 1848. For some cultural implications, H. Mintz, *Sweetness and Power* (New York, 1985), 174 ff.

[80] D. Morier Evans, *The Commercial Crisis, 1847–1848* (2nd edn., 1849, reprinted 1969), for full details; A. C. Howe, 'Free Trade and the City of London, *c*.1820–1870', *History*, 77 (1992), 401–2.

[81] *Hansard*, 3rd ser., 88, c. 42, 27 July 1846 (Bentinck).

question was distinct from the 'ordinary and regular principles applicable to free trade', and state intervention in the form of preference was justified on moral grounds—those of justice to former slaves and to planters.[82] This was inadmissible by the Whigs, who were rather inclined to see in the commercial failures of 1847–8 a purging of the inefficient and possibly the immoral, as the providential order rooted out the unjust and the speculators. Protectionist pressure, however, moved the Whigs towards some moderation of their policy, for example, permission to use molasses in breweries, the lengthening of the period of equalization, and additional aid for immigrant labour.[83] This was justified on the grounds of expediency, while the Whigs held out strongly against any return to the old system. 'That', Clarendon wrote, 'would be retaxing the whole community for the benefit or the supposed benefit of a particular class . . . it would be a complete triumph to the Protectionists and beyond all doubt lead again to a Corn Law agitation.'[84] Radicals such as James Wilson held out against this degree of relief as endangering both the cause of free trade and the Whigs' credibility among the middle-class reformers.[85] But the Whig compromise was not ill-judged, sufficient to gain the support of most Peelites, who did not favour any further measure of protection.[86] Tactical concessions thus defused a strong Protectionist counter-attack, while not obviating the policy of equalization and the restoration of the natural economic order, nor providing any long-term compensation for the planters for the 'years of mismanagement and evils arising from protection'.[87] The rights of the community were, as Clarendon had urged, upheld against those of a class, and free trade in the West Indies hastened the liquidation of many gentlemanly capitalists who had survived under the preferential regime.

What this crisis revealed, most notably, was the continuing strong presence of the West Indian interest, which had far from lost its political voice in the Reform Act of 1832.[88] In a real sense, this interest group lay at the centre of Protectionist

[82]   For Protectionist tactics, see R. Stewart, *The Politics of Protection. Lord Derby and the Protectionist Party, 1841–52* (Cambridge, 1971), 130–3.

[83]   The Select Committee on Sugar and Coffee Planting (*Parl. Papers*, 1847–8, 36) provided few voices to support Whig policy, even among former Whig MPs, although several endorsed free trade as the correct solution for the problems of the West Indies *in principle*. For studies of Whig policy and its impact, see P. D. Curtin, 'The British Sugar Duties and West Indian Prosperity', *Journal of Economic History*, 14 (1954), 157–64; W. A. Green, *British Slave Emancipation: the Sugar Colonies and the Great Experiment, 1830–1865* (Oxford, 1976); N. Deerr, *The History of Sugar* (2 vols, 1949–50). For the concession to brewers, see Clarendon dep. c. 547, B. Greene to J. Macgregor (Board of Trade), 17 Oct. 1846.

[84]   Clarendon to Wilson, 15 Jan. 1848, Wilson Papers, Duke University; see, too, Grey to Wood, 2 Jan. 1848, 2 Feb. 1848, Hickleton Papers, A/55/1.

[85]   Wilson to Grey, 12 Jan. 1848, Grey Papers; Grey to Wood, 2 Jan. 1848, 20 Apr. 1848, Hickleton Papers, A4/55/1.

[86]   Gladstone to Lord Harris (Governor of Trinidad), 20 June 1848, Gladstone Letters, Duke University.

[87]   Clarendon to Wilson, 3 June 1848, Wilson Papers.

[88]   B. Higman, 'The London West Indian Interest, 1807–1833', *Historical Studies*, 13 (1967), 1–19; cf. J. A. Thomas, *The House of Commons, 1832–1901* (Cardiff, 1939), 4–5; Stewart, *Politics of Protection*, 72, n. 1.

power and tactics in 1847–8, for example, in supplying the evidence for Bentinck's Committee on Coffee and Sugar Planting.[89] But the conventional image of that West Indian interest—of absentee proprietors, West Country gentlemen such as Sir Christopher Codrington, or impoverished resident proprietors—is belied by the evidence of this committee. For the West Indian interest by the late 1840s had effectively become a City of London interest. After emancipation in 1834 much City capital had been invested in the West Indies and Mauritius in a positive attempt to meet the growing British demand for sugar, but also as a by-product of the difficulties of West Indian planters, whose growing debts in the City resulted in the forfeiture of mortgaged estates.[90] As a result, James Borthwick explained:

the very nature and composition of the body called the West Indian Body in London places it in some degree antagonistic to that of the resident proprietors and the absentee proprietor too. The merchant in the City of London is the representative of capital. Capital has neither humanity not patriotism . . . the man who represents capital goes into that market of the world where capital returns the best interest, he does not care what becomes of the West Indies nor what becomes of England *quoad* his position as a capitalist.[91]

It was as a result of this development that City firms were now implicated in the crisis precipitated by the Sugar Act of 1846. Many were ruined, while others bolstered the Protectionist forces that gathered strongly in the City of London around men such as the merchant banker Thomas Baring. Yet, ironically, the new economic regime under free trade also encouraged the process whereby the sugar industry was controlled from London. For in London in 1854 an Encumbered Estates Court was set up which facilitated the transfer of West Indian estates to City ownership. This City sugar interest was to re-emerge in the later nineteenth century as the leading dissentient from free trade orthodoxy.[92] The Whig policy of free trade, therefore, removed the political props of the sugar industry, both heightening immediate commercial crisis, but promoting the long-term reconstruction of a major City interest. At the same time, free trade in sugar was proclaimed as a policy geared to the general interests of the state and society, the tax-gatherer, and the working-class consumer.[93]

The Whig assault on imperial preference also threatened the timber duties, and the Canadian merchants in the City who had benefited considerably from them. These duties had long been the *bête noire* of Whig-Radical reformers such as Poulett Thomson, Henry Warburton, and, outside Parliament, G. W.

---

[89] See notes 77 and 83 above. For the West Indian activities of one City firm, see Richard Wilson's interesting account, *Greene, King & Co* (1988), 32–59.

[90] R. A. Lobdell, 'Patterns of Investment and Sources of Credit in the British West Indian Sugar Industry, 1838–1897', *Journal of Caribbean History*, 4 (1972), 31–53.

[91] *Parl. Papers*, 1847–8, 25, SC Sugar Planting, q. 12956.

[92] See esp. R. W. Beachey, *The British West Indies Sugar Industry in the late 19th century* (Oxford, 1957). See, too, Ch. 6 below.

[93] *Greville Memoirs*, vol. 6, 61 [14 May 1848]: 'Graham said about the West Indians that the Old Proprietors must be ruined . . . The people of this country had tasted cheap sugar, and would not now go back to dear.'

Norman.[94] In his retrospective account of Whig policy, Lord John Russell also singled out the 'timber interest' as one of the 'powerful colonial interests' which had obstructed Whig reform.[95] Whig proposals for diminished preference in 1840 had been followed by reductions by Peel in 1843 and 1844, but after 1846 the Whigs were to treat this issue in a wavering and inconsistent fashion until 1851.

Two main factors help account for this waywardness. First, Canada, as we have seen, had already borne the brunt of the Peelite equivocation with regard to the Corn Laws.[96] As a result, the years 1847–9 were ones of severe trade dislocation, whose force was brought home to the Whigs by men with strong Canadian connections, such as 'Bear' Ellice. Ellice, for example, wrote to Russell, so 'satisfying our conscience, for not stating these opinions in the House of Commons', to the following effect:

It is perfectly true that mercantile affairs in Canada are in the same distressing condition, with those at home, and in other colonies which have been dependent on fictitious credit and protection; and [which] have been suddenly exposed to the blight occasioned by the recent Revolution in our fiscal and financial policy, and it is true alas that the whole trade of Canada is engrossed by the British, and that they are suffering in proportion from these causes.[97]

Elgin, the Governor-General in Canada, and Grey's brother-in-law, also emphasized in his despatches the link between Canadian distress and British commercial policy.[98] Distress was in turn seen as the source of growing Canadian sentiment in favour of annexation with the United States. It therefore seemed preferable to the Whig Cabinet to delay reform of the timber duties in the short term, avoiding the appearance of unfair measures, even if this meant retaining the 'rag of protection'.[99] But the second strong recommendation for delay, as we have seen, was Wood's growing desire to retain existing revenue duties, of which timber was a lucrative one.[100] Wood's reluctance to abandon the timber duties may also have been increased by Grey's unwillingness to reduce Canadian expenditure, for neither Wood nor Russell shared Grey's alarmist propensity to see any demand for cuts as equivalent to severing the ties between Britain and Canada.[101]

Grey himself, as a sound political economist, was prepared to agree that British policy had distorted the allocation of capital in Canada, with regard to corn and timber, and that the British Government had some responsibility to restore a

---

[94] Brown, *Board of Trade, passim*; J. Potter, 'The British Timber Duties, 1815–60', *Economica*, 22 (1955), 122–36; 'A Merchant' [G. W. Norman], 'Hints on the Timber Trade' (1821), Norman Papers, Z4. The Norman family were engaged in the Baltic timber trade.

[95] Russell, *Recollections*, 210.

[96] Above, 18.

[97] Ellice to Russell, 30 May 1849, RP, PRO 30/22/7F.

[98] Grey to Wood, 18 Apr. 1849, Hickleton Papers, A4/55/1; D. L. Burn, 'Canada and the Repeal of the Corn Laws', *The Cambridge Historical Journal*, 2 (1928), 265; Elgin to Russell, 10 Dec. 1849, RP, PRO 30/22/8C.

[99] Russell to Grey, 7 Dec. 1848, 1 Jan. 1849, Grey Papers.

[100] Wood to Grey 30 Dec. 1847, ibid.

[101] Grey to Wood, 18 Apr. 1849, Hickleton Papers, A4/55/1.

'natural order' of economic development. He was, therefore, ready to promote Canadian railways, with a visionary scheme whereby a £5m loan would be funded by the receipts from timber duties. He wrote:

Our timber duties are the last remaining example of a system of the very worst protection, and I have curious evidence of the extreme injury instead of benefit which they have caused to New Brunswick. It is a protection which we should hereafter find it very hard to defend with any consistency, and which it would nevertheless be very imprudent politically to remove, unless for some such purpose as this.[102]

For good measure, Grey threw in a sinking fund to be raised by land sales alongside the railway, and military colonies as 'an admirable kind of emigration'. The realism of Russell and Wood seem to have dug the grave of this imaginative scheme, although privately Grey continued to promote Canadian railways and their finance, and to urge similar schemes on Russell as the alternative to American annexation.[103] However, for the most part, the Whigs aimed to solve Canadian economic problems in more pedestrian ways, by commercial negotiations with the United States over tariff duties and fisheries, which were to culminate in the Reciprocity Act of 1854.[104] Moreover, the return of prosperity in Canada after 1849 allowed the Whigs to contemplate with some equanimity the renewal of their attack on the timber interest in 1851, although its completion was left to Gladstone, while Canadian economic development was left to private enterprise.[105]

In attacking imperial preference for sugar and timber, the Whigs had therefore had a decisive impact on two vested interest groups which lay very much at the heart of the City in the 1840s. The results of their policy, above all on sugar, were notable in the commercial crisis of 1847–8, in which many West Indian firms failed. That crisis itself may not be attributed solely to Whig policy (the Protectionist charge), although Whig ministers did not ease the financial situation until late in the day.[106] Importantly, the crisis threw into relief not so much Whig policy, as the behaviour of the 'banking interest', above all the discount policy of the Bank of England. Most City voices in 1847 ascribed the crisis not to Whig ineptitude, nor to the Sugar Act of 1846, but to Peel's Bank Charter Act of 1844. This had been widely opposed at its inception, even within the Bank of England,[107] and the crisis confirmed City fears about its impact, to the extent that it was said that by April

---

[102] Grey to Russell, 18 Nov. 1848, RP, PRO 30/22/7D.

[103] Grey to Russell, 21 Nov. 1850, 4 Mar. 1851, RP, PRO 30/22/8F and 9B.

[104] D. C. Masters, *The Reciprocity Treaty of 1854* (1937; new edn., 1963); R. E. Ankli, 'The Reciprocity Treaty of 1854', *Canadian Journal of Economics*, 4 (1971), 1–20.

[105] D. C. M. Platt and J. Adelman, 'London Merchant Banking in the First Phase of Heavy Borrowing: The Grand Trunk Railway of Canada', *Journal of Imperial and Commonwealth History*, 18 (1990), 208–27.

[106] Arguably, Whig calls on the City for loans for Irish relief had both depleted funds available and pushed up the interest rate, the cost of business survival.

[107] Peel pushed through the Act with the aid of Governor Cotton 'without much support from his colleagues'. Peel to Wood, 31 Aug. 1847, Hickleton Papers, A4/122.

1847 the Act had only three defenders left in the City.[108] Widespread criticism of the Act was voiced in evidence to the Secret Committee on Commercial Distress, while the provincial call for free trade in banking was also revived.[109] That the Bank Charter Act survived in this climate of hostility owed much to the Whigs' determination to uphold and strengthen it against Protectionist and Radical attempts to undermine it.

Whig resolve, in turn, owed much to Wood's own consistency, for he shared paternity for the Bank Charter Act and endorsed its underlying doctrine. The Whigs as a whole had supported the 1844 Act, in a cross-bench alliance against City opinion.[110] Russell believed that it had not, by 1847, had a fair trial, and that it might well work in the future if the management of the Bank were to be strengthened, for example, by a longer term of office for the Governor, and more constant communication with the government of the day.[111] In the event, Whig suspension of the Act in October 1847 both halted the commercial panic and saved the Act.[112] In the aftermath, the Whigs were careful defenders of the Act in Parliament, appointing, for example, Sir Francis Baring as Chairman of the Secret Committee. Important steps were also taken to ensure an inflow of new talent into the Bank, encouraging service as directors by leading City magnates, rather than the hereditary succession by young and often obscure merchants.[113] The Whig defence of the Bank Charter Act, and their encouragement of the reshaping of Bank policy and personnel were therefore vital contributions to securing the Peelite monetary consensus.[114] Whig policy had bolstered the Treasury–Bank relationship, which, together with the withdrawal of imperial preference and the purgative effects of the crisis of 1847, amounted to a substantial, if unintended, transformation by the state of the interests that lay embedded in the structure of the City of London itself. Such a transformation was to be taken still further by Whig policies towards shipping and the empire.

The Whigs, shipping, and the empire

The Whig assault on monopoly and preference with regard to sugar and timber, as well as the repeal of the Corn Laws, immediately called into question the future of the Navigation Acts, hitherto the occasional rather than persistent target of Radical

---

[108] T. Spring Rice to Wood, 25 Apr. 1847, ibid., A4/130.

[109] Howe, 'City of London', 399; F. W. Fetter, *Development of British Monetary Orthodoxy, 1799–1875* (Camb. Mass., 1965); L. White, *Free Banking in Britain, Theory, Experience, and Debate, 1800–1845* (Cambridge, 1984).

[110] Fetter, *Monetary Orthodoxy*, 194; Kynaston, *City of London*, 129.

[111] Russell to Wood, 29 May 1847, Hickleton Papers, A4/56.

[112] Wood to Baring, 27 Oct. 1847, Hickleton Papers, A4/54.

[113] G. W. Norman to Wood, 23 and 28 Aug., 16 Sept. 1847; S. J. Loyd to Wood, 21 Aug. 1847, Hickleton Papers, A4/129 and A4/134. For details, see Howe, 'City of London', 406, and id., 'From "Old Corruption" to "New Probity": The Bank of England and its Directors in the Age of Reform', *Financial History Review*, 1 (1994), 23–41.

[114] Peel acknowledged this: Peel to Wood, 15 Aug. 1848, Hickleton Papers, A4/122.

reformers. Yet, as recent research has stressed, the Acts were no mere antiquarian survival, but in very real ways constrained the British shipping industry.[115] In particular, they confined to British ships not only the coasting and fishery trades, but large sections of the import trade, notably from the colonies, but also with important restrictions affecting Africa, Asia, America, and Europe. In addition, British-registered ships had to be British built, providing a legal monopoly for British shipbuilders, while the employment of foreign seamen was severely limited. Support for the Navigation Laws was deeply rooted not only in the economic interests of shipowners, builders, and seamen, but also in conceptions of the British past. These linked national security and power with the Navigation Acts, whose virtues even Adam Smith had famously recognized.[116] Their repeal therefore constituted an important and decisive test of the Whigs' free trade credentials, more especially as the prospect unleashed a strong Protectionist counter-attack, and set in train a series of parliamentary battles which served to tarnish the Whigs' eventual victory.[117] Even so, this was a vital complement to the repeal of the Corn Laws. It was also with comparative dispatch that Whigs were ready to jettison this fundamental pillar of the old colonial system, which Peel had investigated in 1844, but had declined to reform.[118] In face of Peelite inaction, Whig progress deserves the revaluation that it has recently begun to receive.

Despite the attraction of repealing the Navigation Acts, the Whigs were well aware of the formidable obstacles they faced.[119] In January 1847 Clarendon concurred with Grey (the two ministers with the strongest departmental interests at stake): 'The Navigation Laws want repealing, but the question will be almost as difficult as getting rid of the Corn Laws, for in the minds of many they are an institution, a bulwark, bound up with Church and State, and as Ricardo [J. L.] says the fortieth article of the national Creed.'[120] At this point, Whig policy was confined to the suspension of the Acts with regard to the shipping of corn, but few doubted the party's ulterior intent of repeal. Suspension opened the way for the Radicals to press the theoretical case for reform, which lay squarely on the grounds of the restoration of the natural order in commerce.[121] As the leading campaigner J. L. Ricardo, the stockbroker nephew of David, made plain: 'No code of laws which human wisdom could devise could operate so well as the natural laws which regulate trade and commerce; and every attempt to interfere with the natural course

---

[115] S. Palmer, *Politics, Shipping and the Repeal of the Navigation Laws* (Manchester, 1990), esp. chs. 3 and 4.

[116] Palmer, *Shipping*, ch. 4; R. L. Schulyer, *The Fall of the Old Colonial System* (Oxford, 1945), ch. 5; B. Semmel, *The Rise of Free Trade Imperialism* (Cambridge, 1970), 198–202; Howe, 'City of London', 403.

[117] Stewart, *Politics of Protection*, passim.

[118] *Parl. Papers*, 1844, 8 (545), SC British Shipping.

[119] Palmer, *Shipping*, 66–75.

[120] Clarendon to Grey, 9 Jan. 1847, Grey Papers.

[121] The Liverpool MP William Brown also pressed suspension for cotton, urging 'every relaxation however slight helps to show the impolicy of maintaining them', to Sir C. Wood, 22 May 1847, Hickleton Papers, A4/78.

of things by legislative means was certain to produce waste and extravagance of various kinds.'[122] The case for repeal was endorsed by most of the evidence produced by a Select Committee in 1847, with some pressures exerted by provincial merchants and manufacturers, but with few signs of any out-of-doors League-style campaign.[123]

Other factors also favoured action. On the diplomatic front, the *Zollverein* had for some time pointed to the Navigation Laws as an obstacle to progress in Anglo-*Zollverein* commercial negotiations. In Clapham's classic account, only recently superseded, repeal of the Acts was essentially the by-product of this diplomacy.[124] Yet, if not the *primum mobile* of Whig action, the *Zollverein* provided, as Wood urged, the strongest ground on which to proceed.[125] Even stronger pressures now came from the colonies, which, once deprived of the benefits of colonial preference, were quick to urge the removal of metropolitan monopolies.[126] Repeal of the Navigation Acts therefore acquired strong momentum as the logical culmination of Whig policy, which had already removed differential duties in the colonies, and had moved to equalize the sugar and timber duties at home.[127]

But these factors predisposing the Whigs to repeal still left open the question of timing and presentation. Here, the attraction of repeal waxed, as, in the difficult conditions of 1846–7, the Whigs' inability to satisfy Radical and Peelite fiscal demands waned. Hence, Wood urged:

All this [his review of the financial situation] renders the Navigation Laws a better question to raise, for if we disappoint our people in point of taxation, it may be as well to turn their attention to the remaining piece of antiquated legislation which ought to be swept away. Indeed some of the absurdities resulting from the existing law will hardly bear to be stated.[128]

Pertinently too for Wood, repeal of the Acts was to be costless (financially), and would raise no strong, Whig landed opposition. In addition to its diversionary value, Wood considered the case to be strong not only on diplomatic grounds, and by reason of the Acts' open absurdities, but because of what he saw as the impact on the shipbuilding trades at home: 'I believe that the principle [*sic*] effect of them has been to produce a very general combination amongst all persons connected with shipbuilding and which will be put down by altering these laws and by nothing

---

[122]   *Hansard*, 3rd ser., 89, c. 1011, 9 Feb. 1847.
[123]   *Parl. Papers*, 1847, 10, SC Navigation Laws, *passim*.
[124]   J. H. Clapham, 'The Last Years of the Navigation Acts', *English Historical Review*, 25 (1910), 480–501, 687–707; id., '*Zollverein* Negotiations, 1828–1865', in *Cambridge History of British Foreign Policy* (3 vols, Cambridge, 1922–3), vol. 2, 466–87, are nice reminders of Clapham's early career as a diplomatic, not an economic, historian.
[125]   Wood to Russell 1 Sept. 1847, RP, PRO 30/22/6F.
[126]   Report of the Montreal Board of Trade, 14 Aug. 1846, Clarendon dep. c. 547; *The Canadian Economist: Free Trade Journal and Weekly Commercial News* (Montreal), May 1846–Apr. 1847. Burn, 'Canada and Repeal'. This aspect is well covered in Schulyer, *Old Colonial System*, ch. 5.
[127]   See below, 61 and above, 50.
[128]   Wood to Russell, 20 Aug. 1847, RP, PRO 30/22/6E.

else.'[129] Repeal also held the attraction that it would bring the Peelites firmly over to the Whig side, while sharply dividing both from the Protectionists in the coming session.[130] In the event, the issue came close to dislodging the Whigs from office, even though it had held out the strongest prospect of refurbishing their image as a party of radical reform among the middle-class electorate.

By October 1847, therefore, the Whig Cabinet was broadly agreed on the need to repeal the Navigation Acts, although the details remained to be decided.[131] Herein lay the rub. For the details revealed deep divisions within the party as to the extent and means of repeal, and opened the way for renewed parliamentary investigation, and a major Protectionist revival which came near to toppling the Whigs in 1849.[132] On the extent of repeal, Grey, Clarendon, and Labouchère favoured virtually complete abrogation (reserving only the coasting trades and perhaps the colonial fisheries to British monopoly), but Wood was by no means sure that Britain should abandon the monopoly of colonial trade.[133] The crux of the issue became whether to proceed by treaty and reciprocity (by a short bill allowing the Queen in council to grant reciprocal rights of carrying goods in national vessels), or whether to proceed by unilateral action. The example of the Corn Laws and the sugar duties was urged in favour of the latter: 'It would be most absurd', Grey wrote, 'to go back to the old plan of negotiation which has so uniformly failed.' Rather, he argued:

in all these commercial questions, the sound policy is not to ask for concessions from other states as the condition upon which we will consent to do what our own interest prescribes to us at any rate, but on the contrary, to adopt ourselves a liberal system, convinced that whatever other nations may do, this is what is best for ourselves, while they will be far more liable to follow our example if we abstain from any injury to them . . . and show by our conduct that we are convinced that all these restrictions are really most injurious to those who impose them.[134]

This model statement of the unilateral free trade case met the approval of Labouchère (now at the Board of Trade), but progress was delayed by the appointment of a House of Lords Committee ('wholly unnecessary' in Grey's view), which reported in March 1848. In June Labouchère secured agreement to the general principle of repeal, but the doubts, especially of Palmerston and Auckland, remained strong, and the bill was delayed for the session.[135] In December the Foreign Office conducted their own inquiry as to the likely response of foreign

[129]   Ibid., 1 Sept. 1847, RP, PRO 30/22/6F.
[130]   Ibid., 20 Aug. 1847, RP, PRO 30/22/6E.
[131]   Grey Journal, 13 Oct. 1847, Grey Papers.
[132]   Palmer, *Shipping*, chs. 6–8.
[133]   Wood to Russell, 23 Aug. 1847, RP, PRO 30/22/6E.
[134]   Grey to Labouchère. 19 Sept. 1847 (copy), Grey papers.
[135]   Bowring Diary, 14 July 1848: 'This is rather too bad, as this was to be the great measure of the session . . . I suppose Lord John thinks that as long as the Free Trade question is not disposed of, there is a bone of contention left between the Peelites and Protectionists, which will prevent their uniting against him.'

nations,[136] which served little purpose save that of delay, and the provision of ammunition for the Protectionist counter-attack. This in turn provided Palmerston and Auckland with further arguments for delay on the grounds that public opinion was against the policy.[137] What ultimately decided the Whigs to go ahead (retaining a dispensing power to reimpose the laws in relation to particular countries) was not so much the promise of continental reciprocity resulting from Palmerston's inquiry, but legal opinion that they had no option but to proceed by direct legislation and not by treaty, and the confidence of Labouchère in the strength of their case on technical as well as political grounds.[138] In 1849, therefore, when Labouchère's bill was reintroduced, the Whigs steeled their parliamentary nerves, called doubting peers home from abroad, and ultimately won a narrow parliamentary majority in June.[139]

Rather than providing an affirmation of Whig reforming ability, the campaign to repeal the Navigation Laws provoked a rallying of Protectionist forces. This is interesting in itself, for it reveals at the heart of the Protectionist campaign not simply the squirearchy valorized in Disraeli's *Lord George Bentinck*, but the shipping interest of the City of London—those most likely to suffer immediate losses.[140] More widely, the campaign united the City with some provincial banking and commercial interests, alongside the optimistically protectionist gentry, and much university opinion. It was a powerful combination, within and without Parliament—the basis of a potential Protectionist ministry, geared to resist repeal of the Navigation Acts and to reintroduce a moderate fixed duty on corn. As Vincent has urged, this raises the question 'not why Free Trade passed in 1846 but why Protection was not restored in 1849'.[141] In part the answer lay, again as Vincent suggests, in the renewed spectres of European Revolution and British Chartism in 1848. But it also partly lay in the Whigs' own determination to use repeal of the Navigation Laws to draw a clear line between their attachment to free trade and the dangers of a Tory return to protection. In this way they sought to draw to themselves the support both of the Peelites and the urban free trade electorate. Certainly, the Protectionist counter-attack and the Whigs' own divisions deprived

---

[136] *Parl. Papers*, 1849, 51, Correspondence with Foreign States; Palmer, *Shipping*, 139–40.

[137] Labouchère to Russell, 21 Apr. 1848 reporting Auckland's views; Palmerston to Russell, 14 Apr. 1849, RP, PRO 30/22/7B, fo. 326, and 7F, fos. 181–3.

[138] Labouchère to Russell, 14 Feb., 21 Apr., and 18 Sept. 1848; 29 Sept. 1849, RP, PRO 30/22/7A, fos. 68–70; 7B, fo. 326; 7D, fos. 168–9; 8A, fo. 270.

[139] Carrington to Russell, 7 May 1849, RP, PRO 30/22/7F; first Viscount Ponsonby to Wood, 3 Feb. 1851, Hickleton Papers, A4/113, recalling his voting against Free Trade in 1846, but in favour of repeal of the Navigation Acts in 1849, announcing that 'I cannot wish you success in the support of Free Trade'; *Greville Memoirs*, vol. 6, 176 [11 May 1849]; Grey Journal, 18 Apr., 7 and 8 May 1849, Grey Papers; Palmer, *Shipping*, 162.

[140] For the wider context, see A. D. Macintyre, 'Lord George Bentinck and the Protectionists: A Lost Cause?', *TRHS*, 5th ser., 39 (1989); for the City, see Howe, 'City of London', 403–4; Palmer, *Shipping, passim*.

[141] Stewart, *Politics of Protection*, e.g. 141–6; J. Vincent (ed.), *Disraeli, Derby and the Conservative Party: The Political Journals of Lord Stanley, 1849–69* (Hassocks, 1978), xiii–xiv, 2–9.

them of some of the benefits of repeal, but they drew comfort from the fact that the Peelites had been clearly separated from Protectionists, which 'gives great advantage to the government'.[142]

Other compensations were also available to the Whigs, for the repeal of the Navigation Acts went hand in hand with Labouchère's setting up of the mercantile marine department of the Board of Trade, while a review of post office shipping contracts led to the definition of the later nineteenth-century relationship between the state and the shipping interest.[143] By removing protection from vested shipping interests, and by promoting marine efficiency, the Whigs could justly claim to have advanced the wider interests of the City, the economy, and the nation. As a result, by 1852 the evident prosperity of shipping in the wake of repeal was recognized, even by the Protectionists, as an obstacle to the continuance of their cause. There was, therefore, to be little resistance in 1854 when the Peelite Cardwell introduced the Coasting Trade Bill, ending the reservation of the coasting trade for British-registered vessels, so completing the abolition of centuries-old protection for British shipping.[144] After 1854 grumbling protectionist voices were still heard in shipping circles, but, indicatively, one of the leading City dissentients in 1849, W. S. Lindsay, was by 1860 a close ally of Cobden and a strong advocate of the view that repeal had in fact laid the foundations of the 'golden age' of British shipping, thereafter a powerful bulwark of the case for free trade in Britain.[145]

In their abandonment of imperial preference and their repeal of the Navigation Acts, the Whigs had moved decisively beyond Peelite prescriptions for the 'old colonial system'. But to what extent had they, under the guidance of Russell and Grey, created a new and durable 'free trade empire'?[146] Two points in the Whig policy call for particular attention: imperial tariffs and systematic colonization. The first signal of the new imperial policy, with the adjustment of sugar duties in July 1846, was the rapidly passed and little discussed Colonial Possessions Act of August 1846. By this Act, Great Britain abandoned all rights to impose differential duties in the colonies (although omitting to ensure that tariffs might not be imposed against Britain). This was presented as a necessary act of equity, as Britain abandoned colonial preference, but Grey still conceived of the empire as an economic whole, with a unitary policy of fiscal free trade: 'The common interest of all parts

---

[142] Russell to Clarendon, 18 June 1849, cited in Dreyer, 'Russell Administration', 154.
[143] Labouchère to Russell, Jan. 1848; 14 Feb. 1848, RP, PRO 30/22/7A, fos. 1–2, 69–70: Labouchère to Grey, 18 Nov. 1849, Grey Papers. See, too, R. Prouty, *The Transformation of the Board of Trade 1830–1855* (1957), 88 ff. For free traders, communications were vital: 'It is our interest irrespective of all other nations on the earth, to make our postal charges cheap and communications easy. It is one of the most important instruments for promoting our extended commerce', W. Brown to Sir C. Wood, 1 Jan. 1848, Hickleton Papers, A4/78.
[144] Palmer, *Shipping*, 177.
[145] Stanley to G. F. Young, 13 Feb. 1852, Young Papers, British Library, Add. MS 46712; W. S. Lindsay, *Our Merchant Shipping: Its Present State Considered* (1860).
[146] Semmel, *Free Trade Imperialism*; W. P. Morrell, *British Colonial Policy in the Age of Peel and Russell* (Oxford, new imp., 1996).

of that extended Empire requires that its commercial policy should be the same throughout its numerous dependencies, nor is this less important than before, because our policy is now directed to the removal—instead of, as formerly, to the maintenance of artificial restrictions upon trade.'[147] In line with this conception of empire, the Australian Customs Act of 1850 prohibited the imposition of differential duties within the Australian colonies, and Grey had resisted the suggestion of Canadian retaliatory duties against the United States.[148] Thus, his administration of the Colonial Office found an essential part of its *raison d'être* in the mutual abandonment of tariffs (save for revenue) by metropolis and colony. He continued tenaciously to defend his 'free trade empire' into the 1890s, but, as we will see, it proved increasingly difficult for Whigs and Liberals to reconcile the grant of colonial autonomy with the imposition of imperial free trade.[149]

Grey's own vision of empire, however, owed much to the influence of Wakefield's ideas upon systematic colonization, and on entering the Colonial Office in 1846 he was immediately confronted with the menacing shape of the importunate New Zealand Company. Reconstructed in the late 1830s under Wakefieldian ideas of colonization,[150] this Company had become a leech on the Treasury in the 1840s, and in 1844 Stanley had reluctantly agreed to a grant of £100,000. Grey's accession to office was widely regarded by the Company as paving the way to both an open purse and to a Wakefieldian oasis after the years in the Stanleyite desert. It was to be gravely disappointed. First, Grey's own evaluation of Wakefield's ideas had altered with his more optimistic view of the scope for the employment of capital and labour at home after the repeal of the Corn Laws.[151] Second, in the light of the financial difficulties faced by the Whigs (and the more urgent demands on the Colonial Office), the case for casting more money into the fathomless pit of the New Zealand Company seemed weak. Third, the company itself, if Radical and Wakefieldian in origins, had soon become the prey of City speculators—above all, the protectionist shipping interest. As a result, while the Whigs honoured Stanley's pledges and had to satisfy the strong Radical interest in the colonies (particularly that of Charles Buller until his death in 1848[152]), Russell, Wood, and Grey closed

[147]   Grey, *The Colonial Policy of Lord John Russell's Administration* (2 vols, 1853; reprint, 1970), vol. 1, 281–2; J. Ward, 'The Colonial Policy of Lord John Russell's Administration', *Historical Studies. Australia and New Zealand*, 9 (1960), 244–62, esp. 252.

[148]   C. D. Allin, *Australasian Preferential Tariffs and Imperial Free Trade* (Minneapolis, 1929), 38–40; Grey to Elgin, 15 Feb. 1851, in A. G. Doughty (ed.), *The Elgin–Grey Papers, 1846–52* (4 vols, Ottawa, 1937), vol. 2, 806–7.

[149]   Earl Grey, *The Commercial Policy of the British Colonies and the McKinley Tariff* (1892); E. Porritt, *Fiscal and Diplomatic Freedom of the British Overseas Dominions* (Oxford, 1922); D. B. Swinfen, *Imperial Control of Colonial Legislation, 1813–1865* (Oxford, 1970), 105–11; below, 108.

[150]   Semmel, *Free Trade Imperialism*, 169–75; J. S. Marais, *The Colonization of New Zealand* (1927); P. Turnbull, *Fatal Success: A History of the New Zealand Company* (Auckland, 1989).

[151]   See, for example, Grey to Wood, 26 Dec. 1844, Hickleton Papers, A4/55/1.

[152]   Semmel, *Free Trade Imperialism*, 118 ff; Grey to Wood, 22 Nov. 1852, Hickleton Papers, A4/55/1, *re* Whig policy to the Company in 1847: 'the real explanation of which is that we could not afford to have C. Buller resign on this question'. Buller's death in 1848 eased the Whigs' dilemma.

the purse strings against the clamant company. Russell strongly deprecated exposing the state (and the taxpayer) to the demands of speculators, and had no wish to rescue bankrupt City companies.[153]

Whig policy, therefore, was based on the abandonment, not the consolidation, of state colonization—the desire to free the state from the demands of vested interest groups, although accepting the need to defend and administer existing colonies. Russell, in particular, put forward a consistent Whig defence of empire, based on free trade, not preference, yet clearly distinct from the policy of the Cobdenite reformers. In his view, the case for empire included a favourable, but not protected market for British goods, valuable military bases, a sense of kinship with Canada and Australia in time of war, and their contribution to Britain's world power and prestige. For such benefits, Britain should willingly bear the additional expenditure for the defence of the colonies ('compensation for subjection'), while holding open the possibility of imperial representation in the House of Commons in return for a colonial military contribution.[154] Russell's ideas represented the epitome of the mid-Victorian assessment of the costs and benefits of empire; the consensus on empire disappeared from the forefront of political debate until its revival by Disraeli in the 1870s.

Free trade and the end of Whig politics

The Whig appropriation of free trade between 1846 and 1852 contains a dual interest. On the one hand, free trade had become central to the evolution of a strategy for Whig political survival. On the other, Whig policy held vital ramifications for a variety of economic interests which constituted leading segments of the City of London in the 1840s. There was, of course, no actual Whig policy for the City, but the unintended consequences of the party's decisions were arguably of more lasting importance than their immediate political results. Whig advocacy of free trade in sugar, timber, shipping, and the colonies, together with the dramatic effects of the commercial crisis of 1847, had led to a major reconstruction of the City, in which many old interests tied into the protectionist regime were uprooted. The 'doomsday of the Protectionists' advocated by Cobden in 1846 had arrived, with the liquidation of many of the interests of rentiers and gentlemanly capitalists.[155] The Whig policy of free trade had, then, been carried against the interests of many in the City, for whom preference and protection were more palatable, both practically and ideologically.[156] Arguably, if free trade under Peel had provided the basis for the modernization of the aristocracy, the Whigs had created the conditions for the transmutation of the City into the shape that modern historians recognize,

---

[153] Russell to Grey, 1 and 7 Apr. 1847; Grey to Buller, 23 Feb. 1847 (copy); Wood to Grey, 4 Apr. 1847 and 29 Mar. 1850, Grey Papers.
[154] Russell to Grey, 19 Aug. 1849, Grey Papers; Russell, *Recollections*, 198.
[155] Some, of course, survived, for example the Hudson's Bay Co.
[156] Howe, 'City of London', 391–410.

but whose origins have been ill-defined. The City of London was not the hidden motor behind Britain's adoption of free trade, but by removing City interests from dependence on the state, the Whigs had laid the basis for its emergence as a bastion of later nineteenth-century free trade policies. This did not, however, surrender the state to the City, as historians and sociologists sometimes misleadingly imply. Rather, by freeing the state from the vested interests of land and the City, Peel and the Whigs had established the ideology of free trade as a guarantee of a neutral political order, part of the Victorian social contract that would survive into the twentieth century.[157]

On the other hand, free trade provided no recipe for Whig survival. Here, their intent seems clear in that by the late 1830s the Whigs had put the issue at the centre of their electoral platform. By the early 1840s they had been drawn to an increasingly optimistic interpretation of free trade, and the possibility of economic progress through the restoration of the natural order. This order would maximize the power of the state, increase the wealth of the middle classes, improve the welfare of the working classes, and, possibly, aid the survival of the landowners.[158] As the guardians of the natural (but not simply the territorial) order, the Whigs stood to gain politically from the attachment of the middle classes, the defusion of working-class discontent, and the removal of protected economic interest groups from the back of the state. Strengthened by the reduction of demands on it, the state would be controlled by Whig politicians, but would be responsive to the guidance of enlightened bureaucrats, mindful of the working-class needs for cheap food and healthy dwellings, and accountable to an electorate to be selectively expanded.[159]

Arguably, this project was largely successful—and formed the basis of the Gladstonian domestic order. But for the Whigs free trade did not supply a strong enough bond to overcome the wider sources of party disintegration, compounded by the vagaries of Russell's leadership.[160] Ultimately, torn between Russellite 'radicalism', Wood's 'Peelism', and Palmerston's opposition to both, the Whig government fell apart, the occasion provided by Russell's Militia Bill, whose defeat in February 1852 allowed the Protectionists back into office.[161] The issue of the militia was itself an important one, for it not only allowed Palmerston to take revenge on

---

[157] For this idea, see R. McKibbin, 'Why was there no Marxism in Great Britain?', *English Historical Review*, 99 (1984), 322–3; E. Biagini, *Liberty, Retrenchment, and Reform. Popular Liberalism in the Age of Gladstone, 1860–1880* (Cambridge, 1992), 93–138.

[158] Clarendon to Wilson, 7 May 1850, Wilson Papers, Duke University. Clarendon was worried in 1850 about the short-term impact of free trade on agriculture (including his own estates), but 'My faith, however, in the principles of free trade and my conviction of their ultimate triumph are not one atom shaken by any reverse of fortune that may happen to myself.'

[159] R. Quinault, '1848 and Parliamentary Reform', *Historical Journal*, 31 (1988), 831–51. In 1852 Russell canvassed the idea of special representation for 'great commercial bodies'. Wood to Russell, 4 Aug. 1852, Russell to Wood, 6 Aug. 1852, Hickleton Papers, A4/56; Memorandum on Reform, 12 Aug. 1851; Wilson to Russell, 16 Nov. 1851, RP, PRO 30/22/9E, 68 ff; 9H, fos. 127–8.

[160] Southgate, *Passing of the Whigs*, 210–27; J. Prest, *Lord John Russell* (1972), esp. 303–41.

[161] Mandler, *Aristocratic Government*, ch. 7; Parry, *Liberal Government*, 169 ff.

Russell for his dismissal from office in 1851, but revealed the growing divisions within the forces of Radicalism.[162] On the one hand, Palmerston's exploitation of foreign policy had won him the support of Radicals such as Roebuck and Walmsley; on the other hand, it alienated further the Manchester School, because after 1846 Cobden's 'political history' was, as Morley wrote, 'one long antagonism to the ideas which were concentrated in Lord Palmerston'.[163] Cobden's (and Peel's) hopes that free trade would lead to a more peaceful world society seemed essentially threatened by a minister who appeared to delight in intervention overseas and in the intricacies of balance of power diplomacy, and who sought through the panics induced by French invasion scares to increase military expenditure, so dashing the fiscal hopes of the financial reformers.[164]

Nevertheless, in February 1852 the more immediate issue with the accession of the Derby administration was the future of free trade itself, for with the Whigs in disarray, the opportunity for protectionist revenge seemingly beckoned.[165] The threat was more apparent than real, yet provided some prospect that the Whigs might reunite in order finally 'to consign protection to the grave', while in Manchester the Anti-Corn Law League was speedily revived.[166] Given the growing disunity of the Radicals, it did so only in order to defend 'the vast social benefits' of free trade, not to advocate any wider political objects upon which the Leaguers themselves were now divided and impotent.[167] Against this background, the general election of July 1852 proved largely decisive in confirming the attachment of urban, and considerable portions of rural, England to free trade, despite a verdict marred by an unusual degree of bribery and corruption.[168] It remained only for Parliament itself to confirm this result, but it did so in a manner that made evident the slim prospects for Whig political renewal.[169]

---

[162] M. Taylor, *The Decline of British Radicalism* (Oxford, 1995), 215–19.

[163] Taylor, *Radicalism*, 149–57; J. Morley, *The Life of Richard Cobden* (2 vols, 1881), vol. 2, 6; 'Cobden', Morley wrote to Gladstone, 'was sometimes reckless in his aversion to Lord Palmerston', *GD*, vol. 10, 152 n., 24 Oct. 1881.

[164] Above, 45; Taylor, *Radicalism*, 215.

[165] Stewart, *Politics of Protection*, 194–5.

[166] J. Wilson to Grey, 29 Feb. 1852, Grey Papers; Bowring Diaries, 12 Mar.; H. Ashworth, *Recollections of Richard Cobden MP and the Anti-Corn Law League* (1877), 341–67.

[167] Ashworth, *Cobden*, 350; Cobden to J. B. Smith, 4 Mar. 1852, Smith Papers; Howe, *Cotton Masters*, 233–4, 237–8.

[168] For a variety of judgements on the election, see Denison to Russell, 15 July 1852, reporting 'one voice among the artisans and labourers . . . we have received the greatest benefits from Free Trade', Lady Theresa Lewis, C. Wood to Russell, both 19 July 1852, PRO 30/22/10C, fos. 172–3, 191–6, 215–20; J. Wilson to Grey, 25 July 1852, Grey Papers; Villiers to G. Wilson, July 1852, Wilson Papers, M20/19, Manchester Central Library; *Greville Memoirs*, 6, 345–8 [23 July 1852].

[169] With the death of Wellington, Parkes wrote that even the Tories were preparing for the 'burial of protection and the Old Duke in a common Mausoleum', to Wood, 14 Oct. 1852, Hickleton Papers, A4/67; Sir George Grey believed the election left commercial policy in doubt: Grey, 'Memorandum, 1845–66', fos. 58–66, Sir George Grey Papers, Barings' Archives; others believed it desirable on constitutional grounds that Parliament, not the electorate, should be seen to give the final verdict on free trade.

For, while Cobden and the Manchester School sought in November 1852 a bold parliamentary assertion of free trade principles, this seemed the only remaining bond that united them with the Whigs, a party now stigmatized by Cobden as 'incapable of doing any good for the country'.[170] The Whigs themselves, while equally anxious to declare their free trade credentials, remained divided. Most, with the support of some Peelites, were ready to back C. P. Villiers's declaration that the policy had been 'wise, just, and beneficial'.[171] Unsurprisingly, this was resisted by Disraeli and the Protectionists, but, to the discomfiture of many Whigs and Radicals, it was Palmerston who now seized the centre ground, with a compromise resolution, which supplanted that of Villiers.[172] It was the passing of this resolution on 26 November which, as Gladstone wrote, ended 'the great controversy of Free Trade'.[173] On this occasion Palmerston himself proclaimed what became the distinctive mid-Victorian understanding of free trade at home— as a policy of neutrality between classes and the state, and, as such, the bastion of political and social stability. What remained to be worked out were the implications of free trade for the international order, a process through which Palmerston's own ascendancy would be assured.[174]

The road to that ascendancy was also made easier by the divisions among the Whigs, which were accentuated by their attempts to shape a coalition to succeed the Derby government. For, on the one hand, keen free traders such as Grey, while valorizing the Whig contribution to financial reform, held back from further political change, as proposed by Russell, and wished now to consolidate a 'party of order' around the landed interest as a bulwark against 'democracy'.[175] For this group, a Derbyite government ready to accept free trade was preferable to a Whig government exposed to Radical influence. On the other hand, moderate Whigs such as Wood saw equally little future in a Whig–Radical alliance, and, lamenting the end of the 'Whig position', were ready to drift into the Aberdeen coalition of Whigs and Peelites, ultimately formed on the defeat of the Derby government in December

---

[170]   To T. Thomasson, 27 Sept. 1852, Cobden–Thomasson Letters, BLPES. Cobden now looked with favour upon non-Protectionist Tory government, to Bright, 30 Aug. 1852, CP, Add. MS 43649.
[171]   *Hansard*, 3rd ser., 123, cc. 351–81; *Free Trade Speeches of C. P. Villiers*, vol. 2, 427–73; for the complex machinations behind this resolution, see Sir Charles Wood, Political Journals, vol. 1, 1845–55, 'Formation of the Aberdeen Coalition', fo. 142, copy (by Lord Northbrook) in Northbrook Papers, Barings' Archives.
[172]   *Hansard*, 3rd. ser., 123, cc. 451–61, 23 Nov. 1852; see, too, Palmerston to Wood, 19 (bis) Nov. 1852, Hickleton Papers, A4/63.
[173]   *GD*, vol. 4, 471 [26 Nov. 1852].
[174]   *Hansard*, 3rd. ser., 123, c. 451 ff, 23 Nov. 1852. Here, Palmerston declared free trade as 'the great principle of domestic policy', above party politics, and hence 'of utmost importance to our relations with any foreign country in the world' (c. 461).
[175]   Grey, responding to events in Europe in 1848, initially advocated further parliamentary and social reform. By 1852 he was disillusioned with democracy, and Russell. With free trade secure, he believed, 'Whig views upon other matters [being] *now* in fact those to which the great body of the country gentlemen have been compelled to come round'. Whig survival now required 'no party connection with the Manchester School'. Grey to Wood, 10 Apr. 1849, 17 and 21 Nov. 1852, Hickleton Papers, A4/55; Grey to Russell, 17 Feb. and 3 Mar. 1851 (copies), Grey Papers.

1852.[176] This coalition, with Gladstone in harness as Chancellor of the Exchequer, now represented for them the best guarantee against both Derbyite Conservatism and Cobdenite Radicalism.

The likelihood of a return to protection had already been expunged by Disraeli's budget of December 1852, preparing the way for the lasting consolidation of the free trade finance of the 1840s in Gladstone's celebrated budget of 1853.[177] In this, he succeeded where the Whigs had failed, by appealing to the urban middle classes and escaping from the debilitating aristocratic embrace. As Gladstone himself now recognized, on such issues as public economy and colonial policy, the Peelites were 'much more in harmony with the strong or advanced Liberal party than the Whigs'.[178] He not only increased taxation (by means of succession duties) on the landed interest, but achieved goals which Wood had earlier set himself, applying income tax to Ireland, and reducing a whole range of duties, including those on tea, soap, and timber. The reduction on tea, for example, had been a distant aspiration for the Whigs, but Gladstone was now able to satisfy the mixed pressures brought to bear by Liverpool financial reformers, by Manchester merchants, and by City of London financiers.[179] Overall, whereas the Whigs had achieved the remission of duties to the value of £2.45 m between 1847 and 1851, Gladstone in one swoop removed duties to a value of £1.5 m, completing 'the final extinction of the Class Interests connected with the West Indies, the Timber and the Shipping Trades'.[180]

In this way, Gladstonian finance won the somewhat reluctant support of the Whigs, including Wood, while largely satisfying the urban Radicals, the basis of Gladstone's long-lasting rapport with the mid-Victorian bourgeoisie.[181] As the residuary legatee of Peelite-Whig finance, Gladstone was widely seen as having completed the work of fiscal reform begun in 1820, 'the abandonment of all Class Monopolies', and the establishment of a tariff largely for revenue alone, although

---

[176] Wilson to Grey, 19 Feb. 1852; cf. Wood to Grey, 5 Nov. 1852, 'the Whig position is gone', and 27 Dec. 1852, Grey Papers. Aberdeen's strong free trade credentials have been neglected by most historians. His goal in 1852 was 'conservative progress', but at a more rapid pace than Peel had achieved. Aberdeen to Russell, 16 Sept. 1852, RP, PRO 30/22/10E, fos. 44–5. For the formation of the Aberdeen coalition, see J. B. Conacher, *The Aberdeen Coalition, 1852–55* (Cambridge, 1968).

[177] 'The League may be dissolved when you wish', Cobden wrote to Wilson, 4 Dec. 1852, Wilson Papers, M20/19; Morley, *Cobden*, vol. 2, 125; Ghosh, 'Disraelian Conservatism'.

[178] Gladstone, 'Party as it was', fo. 199; for the budget, see Intro, *GD*, vol. 3, xl; Matthew, 'Budgets'; Searle, *Entrepreneurial Politics*, 79–85; Conacher, *Aberdeen Coalition*.

[179] G. R. Porter to Clarendon, 9 Dec. 1846, Clarendon dep. c. 547; A. Redford, *Manchester Merchants and Foreign Trade. Vol. I 1794–1858, Vol. II 1850–1939* (Manchester, 1934 and 1956), vol. I, 149–51; petition from merchants and traders in the City of London, *re* tea trade, 14 Mar. 1853, copy in Barings' Archives, Guildhall, HC2. 41.2.

[180] T. Tooke and W. Newmarch, *A History of Prices and of the State of the Circulation from 1793 to the Present Time* (6 vols, 1838–57), vol. 5, 482.

[181] Searle, *Entrepreneurial Politics*, 85–6; Robertson Gladstone, reflecting Liverpool opinion, had hailed his brother's appointment as Chancellor of the Exchequer as the return of 'the liberal spirit of Free Trade'. To W. E. Gladstone, 1 Jan. 1853, Glynne–Gladstone Papers, 663.

some elements of protection remained to be purged in his later budgets.[182] He thus emerged as the most prominent architect of the mid-Victorian fiscal consensus, seeking the lowest amount of government expenditure consistent with national safety, the minimum number of revenue-raising duties, and low, if possible no, income tax.[183] This policy was designed both to ensure some balance of taxation between social classes (that is, between direct and indirect taxation), and also to reduce taxation to the minimum. The intention was to leave the maximium amount of income to 'fructify' in the pockets of the people, and to remove from the hands of the state resources which in the past had led both to warmongering and corruption. This alliance between free trade and cheap government appealed widely across the political spectrum, from the Peelites to the Chartists. It therefore faced relatively few and slight challenges, although some critics believed that Britain was an undertaxed nation in the early 1850s, while others sought to alter the balance of taxation between social groups, most drastically those Radicals who wished to abolish all indirect taxation (and with it all customs houses) in favour of universal free trade and reliance upon direct taxation alone.[184] But this vision was soon marginalized by the success of Gladstone's budgetary strategy, whose combination of retrenchment, a minimal role for the state, and a pacific foreign policy ensured its survival into the 1890s.

Gladstone's 1853 budget was accompanied by an important, yet neglected consolidation of customs regulations, made possible by a tariff which had now shrunk from over 1,000 items in 1841 to only 360.[185] This legislation had been made politically desirable by a strong campaign for customs reform led by City of London merchants, the successors of the petitioners of 1820, for whom the impedimenta of a centuries-old customs system, including many residues of patronage and corruption, constrained unfairly the dynamism and smooth running of British overseas trade.[186] Their campaign for reform had drawn widespread support from both Leaguers and protectionists within the City of London, and from merchants

---

[182]   Tooke and Newmarch, *History of Prices*, vol. 5, 469–71, 480.

[183]   Matthew, 'Budgets', *passim*.

[184]   G. W. Norman, *An Examination of Some Prevailing Opinions as to the Pressure of Taxation in this, and other Countries* (1st edn. 1850); interestingly, Poulett Scrope concurred with Norman, but found himself constrained publicly by 'the certainty of disgusting a popular constituency by trying to persuade them they are not over-taxed', to Norman, 4 Mar. 1850, Norman Papers, U310/C48; Norman also urged this argument upon the Whig Chancellor, to Wood, 11 Mar. 1851, Hickleton Papers, A4/129; see above 46 for the movement for customs abolition and universal free trade.

[185]   The Customs Acts Consolidation Act; Tooke and Newmarch, *History of Prices*, vol. 5, 444–5. This simplification perhaps accounts for the disappearance of *Clement's Customs Guide*, published 1842–54.

[186]   *Committee of London Merchants for Reform of the Board of Customs. Digest of Proceedings* (1852); *Customs Reform: Final Report of the City Committee* (1854); *Parl. Papers*, 1851, 11; 1852, 8; 1852–53, 99, Select Committee on Customs. This was also an item of unfinished Peelite business, Peel noting in 1844, 'I think that the Customs are hardly sufficiently alive to the importance of freeing the import of goods from the control & meddling of Customs House officers.' To Gladstone, 26 Nov. 1844, Peel Papers, Add. MS 40470, fo. 268.

throughout Britain.[187] It was given added impetus by strong mercantile resentment of Sir Thomas Fremantle's campaign against what he believed were irregularities within the London dock companies.[188] This stimulated an unusual outburst of metropolitan middle-class self-assertiveness, with the supposedly 'gentlemanly' City proclaiming its belief that 'trade, shipping, and manufacture are the sources not only of the greatness and prosperity but of the stability of the state', and that the aristocracy, for whom the Board of Customs was a mere creature of patronage, could no longer 'govern a commercial country by feudal institutions'.[189] It was a message to which Gladstone proved sympathetic, and with James Wilson as financial secretary to the Treasury, a new customs code was drawn up.[190] This effectively removed mercantile grievances, ensuring efficiency within a service vital to the daily pursuits of the City and its merchants, and in a manner fully consonant with the Peelite-Gladstonian ethic of good government.[191]

Customs reform, therefore, while only a subordinate part of fiscal policy, represented an important complement to the budget of 1853, and its consolidation of free trade within the domestic political and social order. What still remained uncertain in 1853 was the extent to which the now unsullied example of British free trade would inspire imitation abroad, providing, as Sir Robert's son Frederick Peel put it, 'new securities of international tranquillity and . . . the bonds of peace between different countries'.[192] The Prussian minister Bunsen had also looked to Gladstone to 'try some combined attack upon the brocaded walls of Protection', but it was at this point that the Whig-Peelite free trade inheritance provoked considerable disagreement among those who were to wrestle with its implications for Britain's position in the world.[193]

---

[187] T. A. Mitchell, Russian merchant and MP Bridport, 1841–75, was its president, Sidney Smith, former agent of the Anti-Corn Law League, was for a time its secretary, S. Smith, 'Journal', *passim*.

[188] Fremantle to Wood, 10 and 25 Sept. 1850, 18 and 20 Nov. 1851, Hickleton Papers, A4/136; Fremantle to Russell, 14 Feb. 1852, RP, PRO 30/22/10B, fo. 131; Bowring Diaries, 11 May 1853. Joseph Parkes considered this the one issue that had damaged Wood as Chancellor, to Wood, 24 Oct. 1852, Hickleton Papers, A4/67.

[189] *Committee of London Merchants*, 175.

[190] GD, vol. 4, 505–20 [11 Mar.–23 Apr. 1853]; E. I. Barrington, *The Servant of All: Pages from the Family, Social, And Political Life of My Father James Wilson* (2 vols, 1927), vol. 1, 223–34; *Hansard*, 3rd ser., vol. 126, cc. 65–205, 21 Apr. 1853.

[191] Interestingly, several of the London merchants active on this occasion were also involved in the Administrative Reform Association shortly afterwards.

[192] *Hansard*, 3rd ser., 123, c. 445, 23 Nov. 1852.

[193] Bunsen to Cobden, 2 Feb. 1853, CP3, WSRO.

3

The Age of Cobden and Palmerston: Britain, Europe, and Free Trade, 1846–1865

> Now what excites the special curiosity and interest of the world in us is that,
> considered as we are to be the head of all the commercial nations of the earth, we
> have been seen, after years of experience of the Protective System, to abandon it
> for that of Free Trade.
>
> C. P. Villiers, 31 Jan. 1850, Free Trade Speeches, ii. 382.

> and Europe mourns, A common loss, Free-trade's prophetic son.
>
> J. A. Wade, On the death of Richard Cobden, c.1865 CP 281, WSRO.

THE repeal of the Corn Laws, as we have seen, offered to the world 'the example of liberality' in commercial policy, but also marked a profound breach with the earlier Tory tradition of freer trade and empire. The Whigs, despite their own search for reciprocity in commercial negotiations in the 1830s, had, under pressure from the Radicals, advanced towards unilateral free trade in their opposition to Peelite policy in the early 1840s, and in office had sustained their attack upon imperial preference and the Navigation Laws. Typically, Grey had urged 'without reserve the principle of meeting hostile tariffs with free imports', and believed that Peel himself 'completely adopted our principle and threw overboard the policy of insisting upon reciprocity. [He] made all his great Commercial Reforms without the slightest regard as to whether foreign nations met us in the same spirit or not.'[1]

Yet after 1846 free traders could not affect complete indifference to the implications of their nostrums for Britain's foreign policy, although their responses would prove keenly divergent. On the one hand, Cobden, emblem and eponym of free trade, had, through his pamphleteering in the 1830s and through the propaganda of the League, expounded a series of ideas explicitly rejecting 'balance of power' diplomacy in favour of 'non-intervention in the political affairs of other nations'.[2]

---

[1] Grey to Elgin, 15 Feb. 1851, *Elgin–Grey Papers*, vol. 2, 806–7.

[2] This summary draws upon *The Political Writings of Richard Cobden* (2 vols, 1867; 1878, ed. L. Mallet); *Speeches on Public Policy*, and Cobden's extensive but unpublished correspondence. Useful attempts to summarize Cobden's ideas may be found in L. Mallet, *Free Exchange* (1891); J. E. Thorold Rogers, *Cobden and Modern Political Opinion* (1873); J. Morley, *The Life of Richard Cobden* (2 vols, 1881); J. MacCunn, *Six Radical Thinkers* (1907); J. A. Hobson, *Richard Cobden: The International Man* (1918); W. H. Dawson, *Richard Cobden and Foreign Policy* (1926); P. J. Cain, 'Capitalism, War, and Internationalism in the Thought of Richard Cobden', *British Journal of International Studies*, 5 (1979), 229–47; N. C. Edsall, *Richard Cobden, Independent Radical* (1986). W. Hinde, *Richard Cobden. A Victorian*

In Cobden's early theory of international relations, traditional aristocratic diplomacy was to be superseded by the spontaneous pursuit of the common good by the peoples of Europe, inspired by British example. Under the motto, 'no foreign politics', Cobden valorized contacts (cultural as well as commercial) between peoples as a substitute for traditional diplomacy, in the belief that international trade would provide the basis for a pacific world order. Chambers of Commerce might then replace the diplomatic corps in upholding this new regime. Pressing his vision to its utopian or quasi-anarchist limits, Cobden foresaw a Europe without states, not so much a federation, as a Europe of municipalities within an international division of labour. In this vision, the democracy that would liberate the peoples of Europe was integrally linked to free trade, just as surely as protection cohabited with aristocracy. By the repeal of the Corn Laws, albeit by a landed Parliament, Cobden believed Britain would be taking the first step in leading the world back to the paths of international morality, from which her false example of protection had led it astray. Hence, his famous prediction in January 1846, the basis of many later protectionist attacks, that 'if you [Britain] abolish the Corn-law honestly, and adopt Free Trade in its simplicity, there will not be a tariff in Europe that will not be changed in less than five years to follow your example'.[3]

Cobden's ideas on foreign policy shared much in common with the views of those influenced by both Benthamite and Quaker pacifist thought, and some of his precepts, as well as his deepening suspicion of Palmerston, were not dissimilar from those who came to opposite conclusions, for example, the Russophobic David Urquhart.[4] They place him securely among the foremost of A. J. P. Taylor's 'Trouble Makers', the Radical critics of British foreign policy.[5] This tradition was emphatically one of 'Little England', in that Britain's power was conceived as that of an economic engine, rather than based on territorial aggrandisement, imperial conquest, or diplomatic prowess.

Yet, in Victorian Britain, for the most part, Cobden remained an 'outsider', whose ideas on foreign affairs led him into an abiding anatagonism towards the leading practitioner of the 'old' diplomacy, Palmerston.[6] As Foreign Secretary

Outsider (1986) provides a good personal portrait. See, too, D. Read, *Cobden and Bright, A Victorian Political Partnership* (1967) and P. Cain, 'Introduction', *The Political and Economic Works of Richard Cobden* (6 vols, 1995).

[3] *Speeches*, 185.

[4] F. H. Hinsley, *Power and the Pursuit of Peace* (1963); M. Howard, *War and the Liberal Conscience* (Oxford, 1978); P. Brock, *Pacifism in Europe to 1914* (1972); S. Conway, 'Bentham, the Benthamites, and the 19th Century British Peace Movement', *Utilitas*, 2 (1990), 221–43; id., 'John Bowring and the 19th Century Peace Movement', *Historical Research*, 64 (1991), 344–58; id., 'The Politicisation of the 19th Century Peace Society', *Historical Research*, 66 (1993), 267–83; M. Taylor, 'The Old Radicalism and the New: David Urquhart and the politics of opposition, 1832–1867', in E. F. Biagini and A. J. Reid (eds.), *Currents of Radicalism* (Cambridge, 1991), 23–43.

[5] A. J. P. Taylor, *The Trouble Makers: Dissent over Foreign Policy, 1792–1939* (1957).

[6] K. Bourne, *Palmerston: the Early Years, 1784–1841* (1982); D. G. Southgate, *The Most English Minister* (1966); J. Ridley, *Palmerston* (1970).

(1830–4, 1835–41, 1846–51) and as Prime Minister (1855–8, 1859–65), Palmerston conspicuously vaunted his defence of the interests of England, lambasting Cobden and the futility of 'Manchester man's' foreign policy, the 'complete denial of all that he [Palmerston] had ever stood for'.[7] Palmerston himself, schooled in Smithian political economy, undoubtedly shared with Cobden a belief in the potential association between commerce and peace, but deplored and rejected the wider Radical vision of international relations. For, as the late Kenneth Bourne put it: 'The successful defence of the "vital political interest" which Cobden spurned was the prerequisite of the international trade and communication which he [Cobden] equated with international peace.'[8] Such defence required not only goodwill, in which Cobden traded, but constant diplomatic watchfulness, and ready expenditure on arms, permitting both the threat of force, and, on occasion, its use.[9] The Palmerstonian emphasis on the primacy of politics has therefore been seen as the basis of the mid-Victorian 'free trade empire', with its gunboat diplomacy, territorial annexations, and rhetoric of British paramountcy.[10] But any such forceful promotion of trade was abhorrent to Cobden, rejecting wars 'got up' as part of the old diplomacy, which he persistently excoriated for its chimerical pursuit of the 'balance of power' and its dependence upon the nefarious influences of the court, the services, and the aristocracy, rather than upon the virtuous will of the people. Despite their often close agreement in substance, Cobden therefore remained Palmerston's most powerful and effective critic, and consistency in this respect kept him from accepting office in 1859.[11]

These very different understandings of the relationship between free trade and British foreign policy, as well as the ambiguous relationship between Palmerston and Cobden, have strongly, but paradoxically influenced subsequent debate. On the one hand, for those who emphasize their overt antagonism, Cobden has often been seen as a mere visionary whose ideas scarcely mattered, rejected both in Victorian Britain, where his views on war isolated him from the throngs of the Palmerstonian bourgeoisie, and in Europe where, by the 1870s, the resurgence of protectionism became a central plank in the fair trade critique of 'Cobdenism' and 'One-sided Free Trade'.[12] At the same time, Palmerston, for many the epitome of British foreign policy in the nineteenth century, has been shown to have been widely acclaimed, even by Radicals, as a far more effective embodiment of the interests of England, including those of its cotton lords, than the 'outsider' Cobden.[13]

---

[7] K. Bourne, *The Foreign Policy of Victorian England, 1830–1902* (Oxford, 1970), 86.

[8] Bourne, *Foreign Policy*, 86, and doc. 29, 255.

[9] For one interesting episode recently brought to light, see R. Braithwaite, 'Palmerston and the Nuñez', *Journal of Imperial and Commonwealth History*, 23 (1995), 395–426.

[10] R. Hyam, *Britain's Imperial Century, 1815–1914* (2nd edn., 1993) provides a good overview.

[11] E. D. Steele, *Palmerston and Liberalism, 1855–65* (Cambridge, 1991), 95; Cobden to Ashworth, 10 July 1859, Cobden Papers (hereafter CP), British Library Add. MS 43653, fo. 305.

[12] N. McCord, 'Cobden and Bright in Politics, 1846–1857', in R. Robson (ed.), *Ideas and Institutions of Victorian Britain: Essays in Honour of George Kitson-Clark* (1966), 61–85; for Europe, see below, 172.

[13] M. Taylor, *The Decline of British Radicalism* (Oxford, 1995), esp. 280–4; V. A. C. Gatrell, 'The Commercial Middle Class in Manchester *c.*1820–1857', unpublished Ph.D. thesis, University of

On the other hand, in so far as free trade was a foremost 'interest of mid-Victorian England' to which both Cobden and Palmerston were self-consciously directed, the differences between their outlooks have sometimes been elided. In the 1840s the German protectionist Friedrich List saw in free trade merely a neo-mercantilist strategy for British domination of the world, while for later German protectionists, such as Fuchs, Cobden 'well knew how to cloak the special interests of England in the garb of a philanthropic cosmopolitanism'.[14] In a similar vein, it has often been held that 'free trade' merely imparted a new 'informal' character and a new ideological dynamic to British imperial expansion in the nineteenth century.[15] Nor has the deeply rooted conflict between Cobden's and Palmerston's visions of free trade within the international order troubled more recent theorists of 'hegemonic stability', who see in free trade the ideology and practice by which British dominance of the world economy was transformed into a stable international system, an order in which free trade was both a benefit for England and a public good for the world. In the light of this interpretation, it is tempting to see Cobden not as the 'outsider', but as the unconscious agent of the Victorian state.[16] It is this unresolved relationship between Palmerstonian *Weltpolitik* and Cobden's Radical vision of Europe that this chapter sets out to explore.[17] For whether free trade would be the prelude to a peaceful international order, or merely a means to cheaper government and increased exports, remained a central conundrum in the age of Cobden and Palmerston.

Cobden, free trade, and Europe, 1846–51

For Cobden, the repeal of the Corn Laws in 1846 contained an implicit challenge to demonstrate that free trade was not a policy for the benefit of England alone, as contintental protectionists claimed, but a policy of universal application. It was in order to expedite this process that Cobden, spurning office with the Whigs, embarked in July 1846 on a tour of the Continent, ready to propagate the message of

---

Cambridge (1971), contains a valuable discussion of the erosion of 'Cobdenite panaceas' within Manchester in the 1850s.

[14] F. List, *The National System of Political Economy* (1844; Eng. edn., S. S. Lloyd, 1885); W. O. Henderson, *Friedrich List: Economist and Visionary* (1983); R. Szporluk, *Communism and Nationalism: Karl Marx versus Frederick List* (Oxford, 1988); K. Tribe, *Strategies of Economic Order* (Cambridge, 1995), ch. 3; C. J. Fuchs, *The Trade Policy of Great Britain and her Colonies since 1860* (1905), 18. Fuchs' important study was first published in 1893 as part of the Verein für Sozialpolitik's series, *Die Handelspolitik der wichtgeren Kulturstaaten in den letzen Jahrzehnten* (Leipzig, 1892–3) (hereafter, *Handelspolitik*).

[15] J. A. Gallagher and R. Robinson, 'The Imperialism of Free Trade', *EcHR*, 2nd ser., 6 (1953–4), 1–15; cf. O. MacDonagh, 'The Anti-Imperialism of Free Trade', *EcHR*, 2nd ser., 14 (1961–2), 489–501; B. Semmel, *The Rise of Free Trade Imperialism* (Cambridge, 1970); id., *The Liberal Demons of Empire* (1994).

[16] P. K. O'Brien and G. A. Pigman, 'Free Trade, British Hegemony, and the International Economic Order', *Review of International Studies*, 18 (1992), 100.

[17] This chapter therefore for the most part excludes the Empire. This is well covered in D. C. M. Platt, *Finance, Trade and Politics in British Foreign Policy, 1815–1914* (Oxford, 1968), and there is an extensive subsequent literature on this theme, well surveyed in Hyam, *Britain's Imperial Century*.

the Anti-Corn Law League to the benighted nations of Europe.[18] Here was Cobden's form of 'counter-diplomacy', based, as he put it, on 'an instinctive monomania against this system of foreign interference, protocolling, diplomatising etc.', and designed on the contrary 'to try to prevent the Foreign Office from undoing the good which the Board of Trade has done to the people'.[19] By 1846 Cobden's own advocacy of free trade was already well known in Europe, particularly in France, where Bastiat had recently celebrated the achievements of *Cobden et la Ligue* (1845).[20] The Corn Law battle had been widely and enthusiastically followed in most European nations, including Hungary and Russia.[21] Independently of Cobden's own endeavours, the European free traders had called a Congress for 1847 at Brussels, an event celebrated by ridicule in the early writings of Marx and Engels.[22] The groundwork was therefore already in place for Cobden's own attempt to stimulate the adoption of free trade in Europe by moral exhortation. If this proved abortive in the immediate term, cut short above all by the Revolutions of 1848, his crusade not only evoked considerable local enthusiasm, but left a lasting imprint on the European free trade movement. It helped create and sustain a progressive and secular intelligentsia, 'une Pléiade de bons citoyens et d'hommes éclairés', at the centre of European liberal politics, a group later duly enrolled as honorary members of the Cobden Club.[23] Their influence was central to domestic support for free trade on the Continent and to the reception of Britain's more traditional commercial diplomacy.[24]

[18] Mrs Salis Schwabe, *Richard Cobden: Notes sur ses Voyages, Correspondances et Souvenirs* (Paris, 1879); English edn. with additional material: *Reminiscences of Richard Cobden*, preface by Lord Farrer (1895); Cobden to Schwabe, 12 July 1846, 'I will be an ambassador from the Free Traders of England to the governments of the great nations of the continent', Schwabe, *Reminiscences*, 2. The account which follows draws on Cobden's manuscript travel diaries, CP, Add. MS 43674. These have now been published as *The European Diaries of Richard Cobden, 1846–1849*, ed. M. Taylor (Aldershot, 1994). For convenience I have added page references to this timely edition (hereafter *Diaries*).

[19] Cobden to Bright, 24 Oct. 1846, CP, Add. MS 43649, fo. 62.

[20] Bastiat to Cobden, 9 Feb. 1846, CP 215, WSRO.

[21] E. H. Haraszti, 'Contemporary Hungarian Reactions to the Anti-Corn Law Movement', *Acta Historica*, 8 (1961), 381–403. In Russia, when staying with Alexander Potemkin, Cobden discovered in this 'pleasant, intellectual society' that 'The ladies were all *au courant* with the proceedings of our League and had read our speeches and sympathised with our movement' (21 Sept. 1847, *Diaries*, 199). Regrettably, A. J. P. Taylor was diverted from the study of European reactions to the Anti-Corn Law League upon which he apparently began research in Vienna in 1928: *A. J. P. Taylor. Letters to Eva, 1969–83*, ed. E. Haraszti Taylor (1991), 1. For other immediate responses to Repeal, see *The Times*, 7 Feb. (France), 9 Mar. and 6 July (Russia), 17 Mar. (Spain).

[22] *Karl Marx and Friedrich Engels: Collected Works* (vol. 6, 1976), 274–8, 282–90.

[23] M. Chevalier to J. Wilson, 9 Aug. 1847, in E. I. Barrington, *The Servant of All: Pages from the Family, Social, And Political Life of My Father James Wilson* (2 vols, 1927), vol. 1, 281; below, 120. Interestingly, the term 'Cobdenisme' was already used in France in 1847, *Journal des Économistes*, 65 (Apr. 1847), 117, but appears only later in English, for example in J. M. Stuart, 'Italy', in *Free Trade and the European Treaties of Commerce* (Cobden Club, 1875), 98; cf. *OED*, 1887. See below, 112.

[24] For the European background, see C. P. Kindleberger, 'The Rise of Free Trade in Western Europe, 1820–1865', *Journal of Economic History*, 35 (1975), 20–55; P. Bairoch, *Commerce extérieur et développement économique de l'Europe au XIXe siècle* (Paris, 1965), and id., 'European Trade Policy, 1815–1914', in P. Mathias and S. Pollard (eds.), *The Cambridge Economic History of Europe. Vol. VIII*

Cobden's political aims in his European tour combined an appeal to the peoples of Europe with an attempt to convert their rulers to the benefits of free trade.[25] Audiences with Louis Philippe and Carlo Alberto, Metternich and Nesselrode, Pio Nono and the King of Naples, were complemented by public banquets, civic rather than state occasions, a suitable reflection of Cobden's belief in Europe as a congeries of tariff-less cities. With little initial faith in monarchs or princes, Cobden laid emphasis on the press and opinion, widely distributing copies of Bastiat's works, speaking to influential ministers and customs officials, and addressing merchants, journalists, and local economic societies. His underlying message emphasized the benefits of free trade in terms of revenue (especially through the ending of smuggling), of prosperity in removing the distortion of the economy encouraged by monopoly seeking agrarians and industrialists, and in terms of peace, for only through the principles of free trade would Europe avoid the wars fostered by its self-interested rulers.[26] Here, essentially, was the message of Adam Smith purveyed to Europe not as an abstract truth, nor as the calico bagman's philosophy, nor as the hegemonic policy of Europe's first industrial nation, but as a source of economic and moral benefits 'for humanity and civilization'.[27] Its reception is therefore worth brief discussion.

In France, the foundations for a free trade movement were well laid, with a burgeoning academic tradition of liberal political economy and a *journal de combat* in the organ of the Society of Economists, the *Journal des Économistes*, itself modelled on the literary efforts of the Anti-Corn Law League.[28] The French State was also well aware of the benefits to be gained from lower tariffs, even if negotiations with Britain in the 1830s and 1840s had proved fruitless.[29] Protectionist resistance remained deep rooted and well organized, with particularly strong vested interests in iron and timber, and with Louis Philippe himself among the monopolists, as Cobden soon discovered.[30] The opposition parties too, both of the Left and the

The Industrial Economies: The Development of Economic and Social Policies (Cambridge, 1989), 1–160. For a good overview of British influence, see K. Fielden, 'The Rise and Fall of Free Trade', in C. J. Bartlett (ed.), *Britain Pre-eminent: Studies of Britain's World Influence in the Nineteenth Century* (1969), 76–100.

[25] Schwabe, *Reminiscences*, 2.

[26] Cobden also on occasion advertised the benefits of Whig colonial policy, e.g. in his speech at Bordeaux, *Banquet offert à M. Cobden, 1 Sept. 1846* (Bordeaux, 1846), 15.

[27] C. J. Garnier, *Richard Cobden, Les Ligueurs et la Ligue. Précis histoire de la dernière révolution économique et financière de l'Angleterre* (Paris, 1846); Cobden's speeches *passim*, e.g. at Madrid, 14 Oct. 1846, reported in Schwabe, *Cobden*, 14.

[28] M. Lutfalla, 'Aux origines du libéralisme économique en France', *Revue d'Histoire Économique et Sociale*, 4 (1972), 494–517; L. Le Van-Mesle, 'La Promotion de l'économie politique en France, 1815–81', *Revue d'Histoire Moderne et Contemporaine*, 27 (1980), 270–94; Y. Breton and M. Lutfalla (eds.), *L'Économie politique en France au XIXe siècle* (Paris, 1991).

[29] L. Brown, *The Board of Trade and the Free-Trade Movement, 1830–42* (Oxford, 1958) 118–27; B. M. Ratcliffe, 'Great Britain and Tariff Reform in France, 1831–36', in W. H. Chaloner and B. M. Ratcliffe (eds.), *Trade and Transport History. Essays in Honour of T. S. Willan* (Manchester, 1977), 98–135.

[30] S. B. Clough, *France: A History of National Economics, 1789–1939* (1964 edn.), 137–41, 212–13; Cobden Diary, 6 Aug. 1847, *Diaries*, 45. Fonteyraud had forewarned Cobden of the power of the

Right, were arguably even more hostile or indifferent to free trade than the government itself, thus confining the power base of the free traders to the liberal intelligentsia (and some merchants) of Paris, and to the most obvious beneficiaries of free trade: the wine growers of Bordeaux, the silk manufacturers of Lyons, and the merchants of Marseilles. Certainly, with only a dozen or so active advocates of free trade in the Chamber, progress towards this goal depended on the enthusiasm of men such as Adolphe-Jerome Blanqui and Bastiat, inspired by the apparent success of the Anti-Corn Law League in England, and aiming to create a comparable impact on and through public opinion.[31]

Cobden's presence in itself embodied a cause and proclaimed a strategy, serving as the centrepiece in the efforts of the liberal economists to stimulate a French free trade movement on the lines of the League, and also to influence the elections of 1846.[32] He addressed the Paris branch of the Association pour le Libre Échange on 18 August as the prelude to its first national meeting on 28 August, before moving to Bordeaux, the leading provincial centre of free trade opinion.[33] His visit also coincided with the launch, on the lines of *The League*, of *Le Libre Échange*, designed to foster free trade opinion. This campaign failed to impress Cobden ('They are mere children in France in working their constitutional reforms', he told his brother), but, supported by numerous petitions, it culminated in a parliamentary bill to abolish fifteen prohibitive duties and place 298 items on the free list.[34] This moderate reform was killed off by the overwhelming protectionist lobby in the Chamber by late 1847, and, as the July Monarchy collapsed, the hopes of the free traders went with it.[35] The last issue of *Le Libre Échange* appeared in April 1848. Despite the adherence of such luminaries as Sainte-Beuve, Tocqueville, and Lamartine, the drift of the Second Republic liberal economists, aristocrats, and merchants towards free trade was soon submerged not only by socialistic 'National Workshops', but by the old-fashioned protectionism of Thiers and his followers.

'sylvocrats' and the 'sidérocrates', n.d., *c.*June 1846; see, too, Anisson-Duperon to Cobden, 9 July 1846, CP 2, WSRO.

[31] A. J. Tudesq, *Les Grands Notables en France (1840–49)* (2 vols, Paris, 1964), vol. 2, 607–20; Breton and Lutfalla, *L'Économie politique*, chs. 2 and 3; D. Russell, *Frédéric Bastiat and the Free Trade Movement in France and England, 1840–1850* (Geneva, 1959); L. Bruel, *Bastiat et le Libre-Échange* (Paris, 1931); W. Walton, *France at the Crystal Palace* (Berkeley, 1992); Bastiat to Cobden, *passim*, CP 215, WSRO; *De la liberté du commerce et de la protection de l'industrie. Lettres échangés entre MM Blanqui et Émile de Girardin, 1846–47* (Paris, 1847).

[32] Russell, *Bastiat*, 75 ff.; Bastiat's Association pour le Libre Échange had been set up at Bordeaux in Feb. 1846; *The Economist*, 22 Aug. 1846; *Journal des Économistes* (hereafter *JDE*), *passim*. For a sceptical view of Cobden's presence, see Ashburton to Croker, 20 Aug. 1846, in *The Croker Papers*, ed. L. J. Jennings (3 vols, 1885), vol. 3, 79.

[33] *JDE*, 57 (Aug. 1846), 82–101; Cobden Diary, 18 Aug. 1846, *Diaries*, 48. Other local associations were formed at Le Havre, Lyons, and Marseilles, where Cobden spoke privately on 28 Dec. 1846 on his journey from Spain to Italy.

[34] Cobden to Frederick Cobden, 4 Sept. 1846, CP, Add. MS 50750; *Programme de Réforme Douanière proposé par l'Association pour le Libérté des Échanges* (Paris, 1847); L. Amé, *Étude sur les tarifs de douane et sur les traités de commerce* (Paris, 1876), vol. 1, 250.

[35] H. Say to Cobden, 19 Feb., 5 Mar. 1848, CP 2, WSRO.

Cobden's address to Europe on liberty and protection in March 1848 read more as an epitaph than a clarion-call.[36]

Nevertheless, this campaign for a liberal French tariff was not unimportant. First, it had indirectly served the ends of British diplomacy in moving French opinion towards unilateral tariff reform and away from the possibility bruited in the 1840s of a customs union between Belgium and France, a scheme prompted by fear of Prussia's absorbing Belgium within the *Zollverein*, but one bound to meet stern British opposition.[37] Second, even if a strong protectionist counter-attack had been launched, Cobden's visit had lastingly boosted the morale and determination of the French free traders.[38] Third, the main legacy of this stimulus in the short term was felt not on the French tariff, but in the wave of speculation on European federation and universal peace which accompanied the Second Republic. This was strongly inspired by the secular free trade economists, who, alongside the Anglo-American religious pacifists, participated in the discussions of peace and disarmament at the Paris Peace Congress of 1849, attended too by Cobden and Chevalier.[39] The United States of Europe and peace remained democratic and republican causes, but after 1848 the most influential friends of free trade were to be found in the senate of the Empire, not in the *ateliers* of the Republic.

For, paradoxically, the revolution of 1848, which ended the hopes of the French free traders in the short term, did more than Cobden's visit to strengthen free trade in the future. In its wake, free trade was reinterpreted as the indispensable basis of social peace and economic modernization. Blanqui and others argued that economic crisis was endemic in protected trades, encouraging 'socialism' in industrial towns. Increasingly, French free traders saw in their policy a means to improve working-class living standards, while avoiding the dangers of socialism and of protectionism.[40] Protectionism meant high costs of production, a high cost of living, and wealth concentrated in the hands of the few. By contrast, working men as consumers would benefit from the growth of factory production, with mass

---

[36] Printed in *JDE*, 76 (Mar.) 1848. Interestingly, Thiers' views found an audience among the English protectionists: *Speech of M. Thiers on the Commercial Policy of France and in opposition to the introduction of Free Trade into France, 27 June 1851*, trans. M. de Saint Felix (London, 1852); Malmesbury to Disraeli, 17 July 1851, Disraeli Papers, dep. Hughenden 99, Bodleian Library, Oxford. See, too, J. Bright, *Hansard*, 3rd ser., 123 cc. 431–2, 23 Nov. 1852.

[37] D. Pinkney, *The Decisive Years in France* (Princeton, 1986), 140; T. Juste, *L'Union Douanière Franco-Belge. Le Comte de Muelenaere, 1794–1862* (1869); Lord Clarendon was kept abreast of the importance of these schemes, and the interlinked issue of railways, by James Henderson, e.g. 30 Mar. 1844, Clarendon dep. c. 547. See, too, A. de Ridder, *Les Projets d'union douanière franco-belge* (1933); H. T. Deschamps, *La Belgique devant la France de Juillet* (1956), esp. 338–48.

[38] e.g. Voisin to Cobden, 24 Aug. 1847, CP 2, WSRO; 'his [Cobden's] portrait is to be seen in almost every French village', according to D. Le Marchant to Sir F. Baring, 18 Oct. 1846, in Baring/Wood letters, Hickleton Papers, A4/54; L. Reybaud, 'Économistes Contemporains: Richard Cobden et l'École de Manchester', *Revue des Deux Mondes*, 3 (1860), 257–312, esp. 303.

[39] P. Renouvin, *L'Idée de fédération européenne dans la pensée politique du XIXe siécle* (Oxford, 1949); Cobden Diary, 16–31 Aug. 1849, *Diaries*, 207–11.

[40] e.g. Bastiat to Cobden, 20 Apr. 1847, CP 215, WSRO.

consumption and a rising standard of living as the means to social stability.[41] Above all in these years, the ideas of Chevalier took shape, based on the identity of protection with poverty and free trade with welfare, with the general interest of state and society in man as consumer. As a Saint-Simonian pacifist rather than a free trader, Chevalier attended the Paris Peace Congress of 1849, but from 1850 he became the most effective French advocate of free trade, ready to search for a practical policy of tariff reductions which the Cobden–Chevalier Treaty of 1860 would realize, but whose genesis may be traced back to his meeting with Cobden at the Paris banquet of 1846.[42]

In 1846 Cobden believed such tariff reductions should result from popular opinion and governmental self-interest, not from diplomatic negotiations. Hence, in moving from France to Spain, where British efforts to negotiate a commercial treaty had failed in the early 1840s, he urged on the government the financial benefits of ending smuggling, and the political benefit of harnessing growing public sentiment in favour of reform.[43] He had found such opinion at public dinners in Madrid, Seville, Cadiz, and Málaga, while meetings at some of Spain's long-established economic societies showed signs of their turning in a free trade direction.[44] Politicians such as Narváez agreed that Britain's unilateral action had removed one outstanding objection to free trade in Spain, namely that the ending of protection would be to act primarily in Britain's interests. On the other hand, in a case that Cobden did not press, Britain's numerous bondholders retained a strong interest in the Spanish government's fiscal prosperity, and had for a long time been advocates of financial reform in Spain.[45] But any government that moved decisively to financial reconstruction faced massive obstacles from protectionists, who included a newly powerful group of Catalan textile industrialists, as well as from those who were anti-governmental on any ground. Here, Cobden encountered the prevalent immobilism of Spanish politics which was continually to frustrate the efforts of British diplomats, for the 'sprinkling of free trade tendencies' in Spain in the 1840s were not the making of an Anti-Corn Law League.[46] As Cobden, in an

---

[41]   See, especially, Y. Charbit, 'Ideas on Population as Part of Social Thought: The French Free Traders (1848–1870)', unpublished D.Phil. thesis, University of Oxford (1973). I am grateful to Professor P. Mathias for drawing my attention to this thesis.

[42]   A. L. Dunham, *The Anglo-French Treaty of Commerce of 1860* (Ann Arbor, 1930), 28–39; Breton and Lutfalla, *L'Économie politique*, ch. 4; J. Walch, *Michel Chevalier, économiste Saint-Simonien* (Paris, 1975); J. B. Duroselle, 'Michel Chevalier et le libre-échange avant 1860', *Bulletin de la Societe d'Histoire Moderne et Contemporaine*, 19 (1956). Some English free traders had long aspired to the fusion of free trade and Saint-Simon which Chevalier embodied. See T. P. Thompson to J. Bowring, 26 Feb. 1833, quoted in C. P. Castorina, 'Richard Cobden and the Intellectual Development and Influence of the Manchester School of Economics', unpublished Ph.D. thesis, University of Manchester (1976), 139.

[43]   J. B. Williams, *British Commercial Policy and Trade Expansion, 1750–1850* (Oxford, 1972), 161.

[44]   For Cobden in Spain, see *The Economist*, 24 Oct., 21 and 28 Nov. 1846; Schwabe, *Cobden*, 1–49. For the founding of the Cadiz free trade association, Bulwer to Palmerston, 28 Nov. 1846, FO 185/218.

[45]   Platt, *Finance, Trade*, 35–7; J. Henderson to Clarendon, 15 Sept. 1846, Clarendon dep. c. 547. Henderson did press this case, see Bulwer to Palmerston, 12 Dec. 1846, FO 185/218.

[46]   Schwabe, quoted in *Greville Diary*, 5, 21 Jan. 1847. Castorina, 'Cobden', ch. 4 (5) has a useful discussion of 'Cobdenites' in Spain.

unusually laconic vein, noted, 'The spirit is awakened—how soon will it sleep again?'[47]

Much greater encouragement awaited Cobden in Italy, for not only did he discover the depth of the Italian tradition of free trade political economy, but he met a number of enthusiastic statesmen ready to embrace it as the key to national progress, men such as Potenziani, 'full of progress, & political economy', as voiced in a new journal *Il Contemporaneo*.[48] In Rome itself Cobden unexpectedly found 'the most cheering proof of the widespread sympathy for free-trade principles which I had seen in the course of all my travels'.[49] He found that not only was Pio Nono favourable to free trade, but the King of Naples was not ignorant of it, and General Pepe, the leader of the 1821 uprising, proclaimed it as 'the practical teaching of the Gospel'. Tuscany lived up to its past, a model even for Britain, with Florence's Academia Georgophili, 'a little Parliament where the most important branches of politics—as for instance all that touches upon political economy—can be publicly discussed'.[50] In Bologna, Turin, and Milan, Cobden came fully into the mainstream of the discussion of economics and the Risorgimento, meeting many of its leading political and academic participants: Cavour, Minghetti, Pettiti, Cattaneo, Balbo, and Scialoja. In these liberal circles, Cobden found a due appreciation of Britain's industrialization and her exemplary lead in repealing the Corn Laws, while parts of Italy confirmed his view of the benefits of agrarian specialization, for he found 'no class in the rural districts here [Tuscany] so depressed as our agricultural labourers'.[51] He also found in Carlo Alberto a monarch professing to share his principles, an indication that free trade might after all come from above rather than below. Certainly, Cobden was widely welcomed as a symbol of the economic and political progress which the northern Italian capitalist class sought to achieve through unification, and the Risorgimento generation from Cavour to Minghetti freely acknowledged his inspiration.[52]

[47] Cobden Diary, 13 Nov. 1846, *Diaries*, 74. To Frederick he noted, 'I hope I am doing good by indoctrinating individuals. I confess I can't see any *tangible* result from my labours.' (Cadiz, 6 Nov. 1846) CP, Add. MS 50750, fos. 29–30.

[48] Cobden Diary, 25 Jan. 1847, *Diaries*, 95; see, too, V. Schiavo, 'L'Esperienza Torinese di Richard Cobden', *Il Risorgimento*, 36(1), Feb. 1984, 18–34; id., 'La Visita di Richard Cobden a Milano nel 1847', ibid. 38(1), Feb. 1986, 28–40; id., 'Richard Cobden in Italia', ibid. 41(1) Feb. 1989, 51–76.

[49] Cobden Diary, 10 Feb. 1847, *Diaries*, 98–9. For Cobden's papal interview, see J. Freeborn (consul) to Palmerston, 15 Mar. 1847, FO 43/41.

[50] Cobden Diary, 2 May 1847, *Diaries*, 125. To Bowring, Cobden likewise noted this society was 'doing good service for political economy. It is a kind of tribune where everything may be discussed.' 3 May 1847, CP15. For the speeches on this occasion by Ridolfi, Lambruschini, and Cobden, see A. Moreno, *Scritti di Pubblica Economia* (Arezzo, 1899), 225–36. For the tradition, see, e.g. J. M. Stuart, *Free Trade in Tuscany* (Cobden Club, 1876). See, too, G. B. Hamilton to Palmerston, 3 May 1847, no. 5, FO 79/41.

[51] Cobden Diary, 9 May 1847, *Diaries*, 127; see, too, M. Minghetti, *Della Riforma delle leggi frumentarie in Inghilterra e degli effeti che possono derivarne al Commercio Italiano* (Bologna, 1846).

[52] G. Natali, *Riccardo Cobden in Italia* (Imola, 1930); D. Carina, speech at Royal Tuscan Academy of Arts, 30 Apr. 1865, copy translation, CP 290, WSRO; Pettiti to Cobden, 28 Mar. 1846, CP2, WSRO; E. Martinego to T. Fisher Unwin, 12 Jan. 1903, CP 982, WSRO. Garibaldi became an honorary member of the Cobden Club in 1868. For the background, see G. Are, 'Economic Liberalism in Italy,

Yet, as Cobden moved from Milan, by way of Venice and Trieste, to Vienna, he encountered a conspicuous contrast, the devotion of the Habsburg lands to the protectionist ideas of Friedrich List, whose influence in Central and Eastern Europe was persistently to hem in the advance of free trade.[53] Cobden discovered that in Hungary the patriotic party of Kossuth urged the wearing of the products of 'national industry': 'The spirit of Dr List & the Irish repealers was invoked to defend Hungarian nationality & this prevented the patriots seeing how absurd it was to attempt to establish manufactures before they had made roads.'[54] The Hungarian Diet itself was divided. Kossuth-style liberals, hostile to the Austrian policy of high tariffs and customs union with Germany, urged protection to national industry. But landowners, led by Szechenyi, favoured agricultural exports as the basis of progress, had closely followed the activities of the League, and welcomed Repeal in 1846.[55] In Austria itself Cobden found protectionism favoured by the public, by university professors, and, less usually, by the British Ambassador, Ponsonby. Interestingly, Cobden seems not to have met the British agent Blackwell, an advocate of Magyar independence and of free trade, who, lacking the ambassadorial support that Sir Robert Gordon had provided before 1847, bypassed Ponsonby in his continuing efforts to undermine List's doctrines.[56] Here at least would have been due occasion for Cobden's inveterate dislike of the old school of diplomacy, of which he fondly believed Metternich to be the last of a dying breed. Several future commercial diplomats were to find the resources of the Austrian old guard by no means exhausted.

But it was in the German states that the depth of the conflict between List and the free traders was brought home to Cobden. The influence of List in southern Germany was strong, with cotton manufacturers and their bankers favouring protection, while the consumers lacked union and spokesmen. Yet the likely expansion of the *Zollverein* to include the agrarian states of Hanover, Oldeburgh, and Mecklenburgh, would favour low duties, while the majority of the Prussian Diet were said to favour free trade. The *Zollverein* itself had become far more protectionist by the 1840s than its originators had intended, but, even so, it faced pres-

1845–1915', *Journal of Italian History*, 1 (1978); S. Woolf, *A History of Italy, 1700–1860: The Social Constraints of Political Change* (1979); G. Gioli, 'The diffusion of the economic thought of Adam Smith in Italy, 1776–1876', in H. Mizuta and C. Sugiyama, *Adam Smith: International Perpspectives* (1993); C. M. Lovett, *Carlo Cattaneo and the Politics of the Risorgimento, 1820–1860* (The Hague, 1972), esp. 22–7, 33; K. R. Greenfield, *Economics and Liberalism in the Risorgimento* (Baltimore, 1934), 242–3, 270.

[53]   Cobden had met List in June 1846 in London, but no record of their exchanges survives. Henderson, *List*, 123. List's *National Economy* had been translated into Magyar in 1843, while List's tour in the Habsburg lands in 1844 aptly prefigures that of Cobden in its aims and methods, ibid. 109 ff.

[54]   Cobden Diary, 30 June 1847, *Diaries*, 145.

[55]   Haraszti, 'Hungarian Reactions', *passim*. A Magyar Cobden Society was still active in 1922, CP 807, WSRO.

[56]   For Blackwell's letters to Gordon, see *South Eastern Affairs*, 1–4, 1931–4.

sures for higher tariffs from Listian-inspired millowners and ironmasters from southern Germany, the Rhine, and Upper Silesia.[57] It had therefore become the object of much Palmerstonian suspicion, for while the *Zollverein* in principle was calculated to achieve good, it was 'dashed and mixed up with evil', and appeared 'a league formed for the purpose of excluding by high duties the importation of British manufactures into Germany'.[58] Anglo-German relations were further complicated by the Navigation Acts, against which Prussia threatened differential duties, and by the nascent aspiration for a German navy and navigation code.[59] On the other hand, immediate fears of Prussian designs to expand the *Zollverein* to include not only Hanover, but also the Low Countries, had been stilled by the Anglo-Hanover Treaty of July 1844, and by the limited Belgian-*Zollverein* Treaty of September 1844.[60]

After July 1846 Palmerstonian policy in Germany was still directed against the expansion of the *Zollverein*, while looking towards the reciprocal benefits that the British example of Repeal held out.[61] Cobdenite hopes lay in stimulating domestic pressure for this liberalization of the *Zollverein* tariff, building on the desire for freer trade in the primarily agrarian north German provinces, and in Hanseatic cities, states Prussia wished to attract into the *Zollverein*. Cobden looked to enlightened Prussian ministers and officials such as Eichhorn and Dieterici, to the creation of public opinion favouring free trade through men like the old Etonian but naturalized Prussian John Prince Smith, and through papers like *Deutscher Freihafen*.[62] His visit undoubtedly stimulated the progressive liberal free traders, who in May 1847 founded an association in Berlin, while he also found in Hamburg a well-established free trade tradition, even if this smacked more of the self-interest and particularism of a leading port than of his own universalist moral and social vision.[63]

While, therefore, free trade ideas had gained ground under British impetus, the Revolution of 1848 in Germany, as elsewhere, was to be more marked for its

---

[57]   The effective rate of protection had increased through fixed duties at a time of falling prices. Henderson, *List*, 99 ff.; id., *The Zollverein* (1959 edn.), 183–6.

[58]   Palmerston's Memorandum on Relations with Germany, 16 Sept. 1847 in Bourne, *Foreign Policy*, doc. 43. For Palmerston's urging free trade upon Prussia, Palmerston to Bunsen, 14 June 1847, cited in J. H. Clapham, '*Zollverein* Negotiations, 1828–1865', in *Cambridge History of British Foreign Policy 1783–1914* (3 vols, Cambridge, 1922–3), vol. 2, 473.

[59]   Diary, 27 July 1847; *Diaries*, 164; Clapham, '*Zollverein* Negotiations', 471–3; Henderson, *List*, 96–8.

[60]   Henderson, *List*, 94–6; id., *Zollverein*, 161–70.

[61]   Palmerston to Howard, no. 10, 14 Aug. 1850 (draft), FO 64/312.

[62]   W. O. Henderson, 'Prince Smith and Free Trade in Germany' in Henderson, *Britain and Industrial Europe, 1750–1870* (Leicester, 1972), 167–78; J. Becker, *Das Deutsche Manchestertum. Eine Studie zur Geschichte des wirtschaftspolitischen Individualismus* (Karlsruhe, 1907); for one German admirer of Cobden, see A. Kretzschmar, *Richard Cobden, der Apostel der Handelsfreiheit, und die jüngste staatsökonomische Revolution in Grossbritannien* (Grimma, 1846).

[63]   For Cobden's Hamburg visit, see J. Ward, *Experiences of a Diplomatist* (1872), 74. For an interesting comparison between Hamburg and Manchester, see J. Breuilly, *Labour and Liberalism in Mid-Nineteenth Century Europe* (Manchester, 1992), 197–227.

protectionist proclivities.[64] More decisively, the Revolution re-awoke a wider discussion of the economic unity of Germany, where, in a way that was unfamiliar in
Britain since the Acts of Union, free trade entailed strategic choices for states
engaged in a battle for nationhood.[65] Tariffs had become an uppermost issue in the
battle for supremacy in Germany between Prussia and Austria in the years 1848–
53. On the part of Prussia, the main stimulus towards liberalization of the tariff
came from her desire to undermine Austrian attempts to build her own version of
Mitteleuropa based on high tariffs and prohibition.[66] The latter was a prospect
eminently distasteful to Palmerston, but the Austro-Prussian conflict induced a
sense of impotence in some British diplomats, unable after 1846 to throw their
weight into the scales of commercial diplomacy. From Paris, Cowley thus wrote to
his protectionist Minister, Malmesbury:

If we had anything to offer in return for advantages we asked, the case might be different, but
as Peel chose to give everything and ask for nothing in return the balance is quite against us.
The North of Germany is liberally inclined and will make a fight for a liberal tariff. I cannot
conceive a greater misfortune for us, than Austria succeeding in putting herself at the head
of the Customs Union. I believe that both commercially and politically it would be a serious
blow to our interests. If Prussia remains true to herself for once, she can prevent this, but
who can reckon on such a vacillating King and government?[67]

But on this occasion Cowley's misgivings were unfounded. Prussia's influence
within the *Zollverein* led to the defeat of an Austro-German customs union, and
Hanover and Oldeburgh's adhesion to the former in 1851 confirmed its shift in a
liberal direction.[68] British diplomatic support for 'enlightened policy' was able to
build on Cobdenite inspiration for German free trade opinion, particularly in
Prussia, while the repeal of the Navigation Acts in 1849 finally removed an important source of Prussian anxiety.[69] Yet Prussia's policy primarily depended upon the
support of enlightened bureaucrats like Delbrück, for whom free trade was above
all a national, state-building, policy, and who acted in defiance of large reservoirs of
protectionist sentiment, among artisans, manufacturers, and *Junkers*. Thus, while
the supporters of free trade remained, as Henderson depicted them, a highly

[64]   According to H. Best, *Interessenpolitik und nationale Integration 1848–9* (Gottingen, 1980), 149,
91% of petitions to the Frankfurt Assembly were protectionist in character. I am grateful to Frank
Trentmann for this reference.
[65]   Henderson, *Zollverein*, passim; H. Böhme, *The Foundations of the German Empire: Selected
Documents* (Oxford, 1971); H. Kiesewetter, 'Economic Preconditions for Germany's Nation-Building in
the Nineteenth Century', in H. Schulze (ed.), *Nation-Building in Central Europe* (Leamington, 1989),
81–105; R. A. Austensen, 'Austria and the "Struggle for Supremacy in Germany", 1848–64', *Journal of
Modern History*, 52 (1980), 195–225; id., 'The Making of Austria's Prussian Policy, 1848–52', *Historical
Journal*, 27 (1984), 861–76.
[66]   Henderson, *Zollverein*, 196–213.
[67]   Cowley to Malmesbury, 1 July 1852, Cowley Papers, FO 519/209.
[68]   Henderson, *Zollverein*, 202–28.
[69]   Bunsen, the Prussian Minister in London, remained a keen and lasting admirer of Cobden,
Memoirs by his wife, Frances (1868), vol. 2, 206, 230, 417, 516, 526.

disparate and potentially easily divided group, the repeal of the Corn Laws and the British model of free trade had helped both to undermine List's influence and to win important recruits, such as Julius Faucher, who helped ensure that free trade ideas were firmly in the ascendant in the Germany of the 1860s.[70]

Nowhere was the importance of the state rather than public opinion more obvious than in Russia. Here, so Cobden learnt, a policy of high protection had been adopted in the 1820s, largely at the instance of powerful interest groups. Customs officials opposed high duties, as did the nobility; their leading proponents were, rather, the manufacturers of Moscow, and their bankers, who were active at the centre of power, but whose influence threatened the loss of all customs revenue in the near future, according to the English partner of Thomson Bonar. Interestingly, however, several English merchants, engaged in cotton-spinning or iron-works, including the fabulously wealthy City merchant Giles Loder and the iron manufacturer Francis Baird, benefited from protective duties.[71] Unsurprisingly, Cobden found that the intelligentsia's desire for reduced duties was outweighed by political support for infant industries, but this did not preclude some modest tariff liberalization in the 1840s and 1850s.[72]

On his return from Russia, Cobden took ship from Hamburg and thus completed his 'Grand Tour' without visiting Belgium, the country where free trade perhaps found its most vocal support, and Cobden his greatest admirers.[73] A Belgian Free Trade Association, on the French model, had been set up in July 1846,[74] and in September 1847 it summoned the citizens of all nations to a congress of economists on free trade and peace.[75] This first World Congress of Economists met without Cobden, but with a swathe of his epigoni from the League, including T. P. Thompson, Sir John Bowring, William Brown, William Ewart, and James Wilson. It complemented *par excellence* Cobden's message that free trade was a doctrine of wealth, progress, and liberty, a surer means to improve mankind than the schemes of the utopian socialists, or of the protectionists. Some delegates

---

[70] Henderson, *Industrial Europe*, 173; see, too, L. Krieger, *The German Idea of Freedom* (1957), 407–13; W. M. Haller, 'Regional and National Free-Trade Associations in Germany, 1859–1879', *European Studies Review*, 6 (1976), 275–96; V. Hentschel, *Die Deutsche Freihändler und der volkwirtschaftliche Kongress 1858 bis 1885* (Stuttgart, 1975). Further details of Anglo-German relations are now available in J. R. Davis, 'Trade, Politics, Perspectives, and the Question of a British Commercial Policy towards the German States, 1848–1866', unpublished Ph.D. thesis, University of Glasgow (1994).

[71] In the 1860s Horace Rumbold noted of the English community, 'they have adopted Russian modes of thinking and acting and are as a body retrograde monopolists who have steadfastly opposed and continue to oppose every improvement in the matter of Trade', Rumbold to Clarendon, 14 July 1869, Clarendon dep. c. 482.

[72] Williams, *Commercial Policy*, 174–5; Cobden Diary, 15 Sept. 1847, *Diaries*, 197; A. Bou[w]towski to Cobden, 14/24 Aug. 1847, CP 2, WSRO; S. Yakobson, 'Richard Cobden's Sojourn in Russia, 1847', *Oxford Slavonic Papers*, NS 7 (1974), 60–74; W. T. Pintner, *Russian Economic Policy under Nicholas I* (Ithaca, New York, 1967), 239–40; below, 89.

[73] For Cobden's knowledge of events in Belgium, see his Diary, 11 Mar. and 29 July 1847, *Diaries*, 110, 165; for his admirers, see below, 143.

[74] Bastiat to Cobden, 23 July 1846, CP 215, WSRO.

[75] Its proceedings may be best followed in *Journal des Économistes*.

dissented, among them a little-known 'Marx, homme de lettres, economiste, à Bruxelles', but Britain's minister to Belgium Lord Howard de Walden warmly approved proceedings, which, he wrote:

can hardly fail to operate favourably in conveying at once and distinctly to the Intelligent Classes of Society the opinion of enlightened and practical statesmen of different countries on the extreme benefits which would result to the community in general of all nations from the abandonment of the restrictive system in matters of commerce, on which the favoured few alone prosper.[76]

As Marx's criticisms indicated, here was an effective embodiment of liberal bourgeois opinion, which would successfully dent the landed-cum-clerical protectionist regime in Belgium and Europe as a whole in the coming generation.[77] In Belgium itself the change was swift, from the 'apogee of protectionism' in 1844, through gradual reciprocal tariff reductions between 1845 and 1851, and culminating in a free trade regime in 1852–3.[78] *L'Économiste Belge*, under de Molinari, built on the earlier work of the Free Trade Association, emerged as a strongly free trade, pacific journal, closely identified with Cobdenite goals.[79]

Cobden's 'Grand Tour' therefore provides many clues as to the rise and fall of free trade in Europe over the next generation, but as an ideological crusade, designed to stimulate the unilateral adoption of liberal policies, its rewards were meagre. It failed directly to inspire any commercial negotiations or immediate tariff reductions, and evoked few signs that free trade would result spontaneously from the peoples of Europe. More depressingly still, the French invasion scares at home in 1847–8 soon redirected Cobden's attention back to the domestic need to reduce public expenditure, as he now considered 'the struggle against arms to be the real free trade battle'.[80] Moreover, on the Continent the 'notes of liberty' chimed discordantly for the 'mission of Cobden', and the Revolutions of 1848 soon divided liberal sentiment, with opposition to free trade from the democratic Left as well as the protectionist Right.[81] Cobden was therefore confirmed in his belief in the need to cut the military taproot of protection, seeking to reduce national expenditure, to

---

[76]   De Walden to Palmerston, no. 27, 21 Sept. 1847, FO 10/133.

[77]   *JDE*, 71 (Oct. 1847), 250–76; Marx, *Collected Works*, vol. 6, 282–90 (from *Northern Star*, 9 Oct. 1847, a speech undelivered at the Congress).

[78]   E. Mahaim, 'La Politique commerciale de la Belgique', in *Handelspolitik*, I (1892), 197–238; de Walden to Palmerston, no. 92, 25 July 1851, FO10/159; de Walden to Granville, no. 31, 21 Feb. 1852, FO 10/164; E. H. Kossmann, *The Low Countries, 1780–1940* (Oxford, 1978), 232–3.

[79]   W. H. van der Linden, *The International Peace Movement, 1815–1874* (Amsterdam, 1987), 492–3. Its foundation in 1855 alongside the Société Belge d'Économie Politique prepared the way for the Congress on Customs Reform at Brussels in 1856, a sequel to 1847 but in even more discouraging circumstances. See, too, C. van der Maeren 'Progress of Free Trade in Belgium', *The Economist*, 22 Jan. 1876, 126–7.

[80]   To George Wilson, 17 Jan. 1848, Wilson Papers, M20/14.

[81]   Cf. J. Passmore Edwards, 'The Mission of Richard Cobden', *Howitt's Journal*, 3 (1848), 200–3; in the early part of 1848 Cobden drew some comfort from the fact that none of the new governments was protectionist, and that all included men who had sat down to dinner with him on his European tour, *The Times*, 6 Apr. 1848.

stop loans for foreign armaments, and to encourage popular support for peace, a cause more likely than free trade to prosper in the wake of the 1848 Revolutions. He attributed the Revolutions themselves to the crushing impact of armaments on the European economies and on popular welfare.[82]

Against this background, Cobden combined his fiscal campaign with the search for peace, pressing in the House of Commons his motion in favour of arbitration treaties between nations in June 1849. On this occasion he distanced himself from ideas of a 'Congress of Nations', while urging the case for 'a kind of common law among nations', an important stimulus to the movement for a code of international law, which his followers, such as Leone Levi and Henry Richard would take up.[83] Shortly after, in August 1849, Cobden's attendance at the Paris Peace Congress signalled not only his growing alliance with religious pacifism, but part of his campaign to stop the sinews of war in the form of loans. He hoped, as did Chevalier, that free trade would make converts through peace, while he attempted to disprove the belief that war itself might benefit trade.[84] This represented an important attempt to broaden the European basis for free trade, by identifying it with popular movements including Mazzinians and republicans, and with the federal ideas of Europe which Hugo and others articulated in 1848–9.[85] This potent mixture of free trade, peace, and a 'United States of Europe' remained an important ideal on the European Left in the next generation, providing an alternative model of Europe to that of the Concert of the Great Powers. Nevertheless, with the reassertion of control by the old order after 1848, this merely served to emphasize Cobden's growing distance from the centre of policy-making, and the growing dependence of his free trade goals on the support of governments rather than peoples.

Moreover, despite Cobden's growing distrust of the 'Palmerston system', British policy-makers had by no means entirely neglected the interests of free trade. Cobden's tour itself received, with few exceptions, the willing endorsement of British diplomats abroad, and there is some evidence that they made formal attempts to preach the benefits of free trade.[86] There was also a desire and readiness

---

[82] L. J. Carter, 'The Development of Cobden's Thought on International Relations, particularly with reference to his role in the mid-nineteenth-century peace movement', unpublished Ph.D. thesis, University of Cambridge (1970), ch. 4.

[83] Cobden, *Speeches*, 389–98; van der Linden, *Peace Movement*, 911–29; C. Phelps, *The Anglo-American Peace Movement in the Mid-Nineteenth Century* (1930), chs. 3–5; L. Appleton, *Memoirs of Henry Richard: Apostle of Peace* (1889).

[84] Cobden, 'Loans and Standing Armaments', *Westminster Review*, 52 (1849); D. Nicholls, 'Richard Cobden and the International Peace Movement, 1848–1853', *Journal of British Studies*, 30 (1991), 351–76.

[85] Above, 77.

[86] Cobden to Frederick Cobden 15 July 1847, CP 28, WSRO; Platt, *Finance, Trade*, 143; 'Statement on Import Duties for Foreign Governments', 7 Feb. 1851, FO 83/126; correspondence with Portugal and Spain, including 'steps taken by Lord Howden' to induce Spain to adopt 'a more liberal system of commercial policy', FO to BT, 28 Dec. 1850, FO 83/249; Palmerston held the Foreign Office's Spanish correspondence to be 'an instructive lesson in political economy', *Hansard*, 3rd ser., cxv, c. 677, 27 Mar. 1851; Bulwer to Sir J. Easthope, 12 Oct. 1847, Easthope Papers; E. A. Bowring Diaries, 29 Aug., 4 and 13 Nov. 1846; 9 Jan. 1850.

to engage in limited diplomatic spadework with European states, in pursuit of a vision of prosperity that the British example propagated by Cobden had placed before the European public. Here, much was achieved by Cobden's arch-antagonist Palmerston, with regard, for example, to the implications of repeal of the Navigation Acts, and the opportunity it offered to clear up several outstanding commercial difficulties. A modified convention with the *Zollverein*, and a commercial treaty with Tuscany in 1847 were followed by commercial treaties with Sardinia (on 27 February 1851) and Belgium (on 27 October 1851).[87] Tariff reforms and reductions were also unilaterally adopted in Sardinia, Switzerland, Holland, Portugal, Spain, Austria, the *Zollverein*, Belgium, France, and Russia, changes which, in the opinion of the statistician William Newmarch, made 'the adoption of Free Trade in them as a simple question of time'.[88] Significantly, Palmerston's successor at the Foreign Office, Granville, was also ready to endorse the reduction of foreign tariffs as a specific aim of British diplomacy (albeit 'only when fitting opportunities occur'), and had already, as we have seen, joined in celebrating the Great Exhibition of 1851 as a part of the Cobdenite mission of commerce and peace.[89] Against the old congresses of princes, the Exhibition took its place as a symbol of the new era in commerce and diplomacy, which Cobden—but also the Whigs—had launched since 1846.[90]

Cobden versus Palmerston, 1852–9

Although in many ways the 1851 Exhibition provided a compelling demonstration of free trade optimism, the 1850s saw the eclipse of many Cobdenite nostrums. Where some experts such as Newmarch saw evidence of the success of unilateral free trade, with Britain drawing other nations in her train, others were by no means convinced that tariff alterations abroad had benefited Britain, or held that relatively minor changes in European tariffs lent only the merest glimmer of accuracy to Cobdenite prophecies of crumbling tariff walls.[91] Already by 1850 some Manchester Conservative cotton masters were ready to proclaim free trade a failure as an

---

[87]   Henderson, *Zollverein*, 174; Williams, *Commercial Policy*, 217, 186; de Walden to Malmesbury (no. 3), 6 Mar. 1852, FO 10/164.

[88]   T. Tooke and W. Newmarch, *A History of Prices and of the State of the Circulation from 1793 to the Present Time* (6 vols, 1838–57), vol. 5, 482.

[89]   Quoted in Bourne, *Foreign Policy*, 312. For Granville, see above, 42. The Great Exhibition proved in many ways the best advertisement for the Cobdenite world-view, complete with royal endorsement. The internationalist as opposed to the imperial dimension to these exhibitions is neglected in their most recent history, P. Greenhalgh, *Ephemeral Vistas* (Manchester, 1988). For Chevalier's vision, see especially *Exposition Universelle de 1867 à Paris. Rapports de Jury Internationale* (13 vols, Paris, 1868), vol. 1, 1–33.

[90]   Bunsen, *Memoirs*, vol. 2, 243; H. Bosanquet, *Free Trade and Peace in the Nineteenth Century* (Kristiania, 1924), 75; for a protectionist view, see *Derby Diary*, ed. J. Vincent, 63 [1 May 1851].

[91]   Statistics were copiously provided, as by the former Board of Trade official and then MP for Glasgow, J. MacGregor, *Commercial Tariffs and Regulations, Resources and Trade, pt 23, Appendix* (1850), esp. 52–70; and on the reciprocitarian/protectionist side, by the MP for North Warwickshire, C. N. Newdegate, *A Collection of the Customs Tariffs of All Nations* (1855).

economic prescription, and, in increasing numbers in the 1850s, Manchester Whig-Liberals were to look enthusiastically to Palmerston for the advance of British commercial interests, especially beyond Europe.[92] This was an audience that Palmerston was successfully to cultivate, for few among provincial business-men were yet willing to endorse the Cobdenite ideal of 'no foreign politics'. Similarly, in the metropolis few gentlemanly capitalists were ready to forego loans to foreign governments, and even those who admired Cobden's advocacy of free trade recoiled from his later 'crotchets'.[93] Palmerston himself readily reiterated his enduring beliefs in the importance of commerce and its potentially beneficial results, without in any way altering his contempt for Cobdenite ideals, nor wishing to depart from the policy of promoting free trade by British example rather than by tariff-bargaining, which had guided Peel in 1846 and the Whigs in the late 1840s.

Significantly, therefore, it was from the protectionists in the minority Derby government of 1852 that there issued the first comprehensive challenge to the unilateral free trade model of 1846. For this government came close to an Anglo-French commercial agreement, which, had it succeeded, might well have over-shadowed that of 1860 in subsequent historiography.[94] Yet this diplomatic exercise was above all designed to highlight the deficiencies of unilateral free trade, and to mark out the benefits of commercial reciprocity. Building on the intellectual foun-dations of Torrens, Disraeli and Malmesbury sought to advertise the limitations of Peelite free trade by securing substantial French concessions on British coal, linen yarns, and cottons, in return for reciprocal reductions on silks, wine, and brandy.[95] They sought thereby to exploit Louis Napoleon's desire for good relations with England and negotiated determinedly throughout most of 1852. But ultimately neither side was ready to make concessions substantial enough to attract the other before the fall of the Derby government.[96]

Anglo-French negotiations continued after the Tories left office, with, for

[92] Gatrell, 'Commercial Middle Class', *passim*. W. R. Callender, jun., for example, attacked the belief that increased imports of grain into Britain would be followed by increased exports, a delusion, he believed, that Cobden's European Tour had encouraged: 'Free Trade and Our Cotton Manufactures', *Blackwood's Magazine*, Aug. 1850, 123–40, esp. 128.

[93] *City Press*, 8 Apr. 1865, 2; G. W. Norman, *Papers on Various Subjects* (1869), 55.

[94] R. Stewart, *The Politics of Protection. Lord Derby and the Protectionist Party, 1841–52* (Cambridge, 1971), 208; W. F. Monypenny and G. W. Buckle, *The Life of Benjamin Disraeli, Earl of Beaconsfield* (6 vols, 1910–20), vol. 3, 396–7; Malmesbury to Disraeli, 28 Dec. 1851–24 Sept. 1852, Disraeli Papers, dep. Hughenden 99, Bodleian Library, Oxford; Cowley–Malmesbury Correspondence, 1852, Cowley Papers, FO 519/196 and 209. Even so, the early moves for a Convention began under the Whigs, E. A. Bowring Diaries, 5 and 6 Feb. 1851; FO 881/551, Correspondence respecting the Negotiation of a Commercial Convention with France, 1849–1855 [6 May 1855].

[95] Malmesbury to Disraeli, 24 Sept. 1852, Disraeli Papers, dep. Hughenden 99, Bodleian Library; for provincial pressure, A. Redford, *Manchester Merchants and Foreign Trade* (2 vols, 1934 and 1956), vol. 2, 6; see, too, *Parl. Papers*, 1852, 17 (495), Select Committee on Wine Duties; W. Whitmore, *The Wine Duties* (1853), urging reduction as part of the completion of free trade; A. Briggs, *Wine for Sale: Victoria Wine and the Liquor Trade, 1860–1984* (1988), 18–40, for the 1850s debate.

[96] E. Hertslet, memo of 'Attempts since 1830 to accomplish commercial arrangements with France', 3 Mar. 1860, FO 97/207.

example, the Board of Trade preparing for the French Emperor a review of the practical results of free trade in England.[97] At the Exchequer, too, Gladstone remained open to French proposals, but preferred, as in respect of Prussia, to advance the cause of free trade by the example of his 1853 budget reforms.[98] Clarendon, at the Foreign Office in the Aberdeen coalition, also reaffirmed the Whig-Peelite policy of unilateral free trade, urging that 'a change in the Commercial Policy of France could not be effected with reference to the wants, or the wishes, or the policy of any Foreign state, but could only be the result of conviction on the part of the French Government and nation that the adoption of a different system was of essential importance to the future well-being of the Empire'.[99] The freer trade convictions of the French Emperor's advisers did indeed grow in the mid-1850s, while, against the background of the Treaty of Paris in 1856, official and unofficial attempts were made to hasten the French advance to a liberal tariff, and even to add free trade to the agenda of the Paris negotiations.[100] But this was an advance that was halted internally by the forces of French protectionism, and diplomatically by Palmerston's firm attachment to unilateralism.[101] Clarendon himself remained keen on the search for an agreement with France, which was politically attractive, but fiscal exigencies in the wake of the Crimean War postponed this issue until 1859–60.[102]

The continuance of Whig-Peelite unilateralism therefore remained the keynote of British commercial diplomacy in Europe for the remainder of the 1850s. But this 'abstentionism' did not preclude the settling of various issues of concern to free traders and merchants, for example the Sound Dues question, vital for Baltic shipowners, and the conclusion of a treaty of friendship and commerce—including most-favoured nation status—with Switzerland in 1855.[103] Britain also continued

---

[97]   Memo by E. A. Bowring, BT 1/553A/1277/60; for a second, more convincing, edition, Bowring to Russell, 18 Feb. 1860, Russell Papers (hereafter RP), PRO 30/22/28 fos. 319–21.

[98]   Gladstone to Cowley, 21 Feb. and 17 May 1853, to Bunsen, 6 Apr. 1853, GP Add. MS 44528, fos. 101, 138–9, 127; Bunsen to Gladstone, 30 Mar., 8 and 19 Apr. 1853, GP, Add. MS 44111, fos. 317–22; Davis, 'Trade', 198–213.

[99]   Clarendon to Waleski, 7 Sept. 1853 in Hertslet, 'Attempts', FO 97/207, 318 ff.

[100]   Interestingly, McGregor, the former Board of Trade official, and MP for Glasgow 1847–57, apparently met the Emperor in 1856 to urge free trade, Cowley to Clarendon, 15 May 1856, Clarendon dep. c. 52, F. Leveson Gower to Clarendon, 3 June 1856, Clarendon dep. c. 54; (in 1857 McGregor was to abscond from debt to Boulogne, whence he applied for the Chiltern Hundreds and soon after died). See, too, M. Chevalier to Cobden, 2 Feb. 1856, CP, Add. MS 43647, fos. 63–4; Chevalier to Clarendon, 7 June 1856, Clarendon dep. c. 52, fo. 288, and Apr. 1856, Clarendon dep. c. 54, fos. 199–200; Dunham, *Anglo-French Treaty*, 21–4. The Manchester Chamber of Commerce also pressed for Anglo-French commercial negotiations in 1856, Tooke and Newmarch, *History of Prices*, vol. 5, 397–9.

[101]   Palmerston to Clarendon, 8 Apr. 1856, Clarendon dep. c. 49. Gladstone, pressed by Sheffield merchants, also defended 'non-diplomatic free trade', Tooke and Newmarch, *History of Prices*, 397–9.

[102]   Clarendon to Palmerston, 6 Apr. 1856, Clarendon dep. c. 135 (favouring a declaration of the Congress in favour of free trade in food and raw materials); G. C. Lewis to Clarendon, 14 Mar. 1856, 9 and 15 Jan. 1857, dep. c. 40, and c. 70; Steele, *Palmerston*, 250–1.

[103]   C. E. Hill, *The Danish Sound Dues Question and the Command of the Baltic* (Durham, NC, 1926), 241–68; A. G. Imlah, *Britain and Switzerland, 1845–60* (1966), 111–15.

her post-Crimean attempts to make Russia 'a great and thoroughly European power' by means of economic modernization.[104] She thus not only took a benign interest in the emancipation of the Russian serfs, but urged forward a commercial treaty, with Palmerston pressing the Russian ambassador that 'to secure a good understanding with England they ought to liberalise their commercial system'. With some delay, the Anglo-Russian Commercial Treaty was signed in January 1859.[105] This decade also saw the conclusion of a number of extra-European treaties, for example with Morocco in 1856, in which almost all restrictions on imports were removed and tariffs fixed at 10 per cent.[106] Chile, China, Japan, Persia, and Siam also concluded commercial treaties, all signals of Palmerstonian tenderness for British interests abroad, and a degree of activism from within the Commercial Department at the Board of Trade.[107] Symbolically, it was therefore Palmerston, not Cobden, who was called upon to celebrate free trade, urging the power of British example above diplomatic persuasion, at the Free Trade Hall in Manchester in November 1856.[108] Cobden himself, in the wake of the Crimean War, had relapsed from the active promotion of free trade abroad, fearing that this would be counter-productive in Europe and unsuccessful in Britain. He wrote to his leading Belgian supporter, Corr van der Maeren (formerly Michael Corr of Co. Meath):

I am bound moreover to tell you that the public mind in England grows weary of any question which it has been discussing for a great number of years and which it believes to have been fully disposed of. It would be very difficult to bring people to entertain the topic of Free Trade in reference to other countries with which they have no right to interfere.[109]

Cobden's apparent renunciation of the apostolate of free trade reflected his growing isolation in the 1850s, as Europe turned from tariffs to war, and as Britain became embroiled in his twin bugbears, the Eastern Question and territorial acquisitions in Asia. Above all, the Crimean War and British military engagement in China, symbolized in the *Arrow* incident of 1857, highlighted the sharp distinction between the world-view of Cobdenite non-intervention and that of Palmerstonian

---

[104] Clarendon to Palmerston, no. 117, 20 Apr. 1856, reporting his conversation with Orloff, FO 27/1169.

[105] Steele, *Palmerston*, 249; Wodehouse to Clarendon, 11, 18, and 25 Apr. 1857, Clarendon dep. c. 71, fos. 447–52, 458–69, 488–93; Clarendon to Wodehouse, no. 765, 4 Nov. 1857, FO 65/490; Wodehouse to Clarendon, no. 506, 14 Nov. 1857, FO 65/499; G. de Bernhardt, *Handbook of Commercial Treaties* (1912), 743–52.

[106] F. R. Flournoy, *British Policy towards Morocco in the Age of Palmerston* (1935), 165–81; Steele, *Palmerston*, 57–8.

[107] Steele, *Palmerston*, 199, 340 ff; Gatrell, 'Commercial Middle Class'; Hyam, *Britain's Imperial Century*, 100–1; L. Levi, *The History of British Commerce* (2nd edn., 1880), 379–99.

[108] *Manchester Guardian*, 7 Nov. 1856, 3; A. Taylor, 'Palmerston and Radicalism, 1846–1865', *Journal of British Studies*, 33 (1994), 178.

[109] Cobden to van der Maeren, Nov. 1856; Cobden to T. Winkworth, 17 Nov. 1856. CP 127, WSRO. He did nevertheless endorse the English appeal made by Maeren's International Association for Customs Reforms. International Association (1857); see, too, Maeren to Mrs Cobden 20 Apr. (misdated 1862) on the native roots of free trade in Belgium. CP 127, WSRO. For Maeren, see Henderson, *Industrial Europe*, 156, 183–4.

'gunboat diplomacy', however misleading that term. On the one hand, Cobden vigorously assailed the operations of the old diplomacy, the covert influence of the court and the services, while, on the other, the 'Feargus O'Connor of the middle classes' held before the nation the 'John Bullish' ideal of British power and influence.[110] This reassertion of the old diplomacy, as Cobden saw it, destroyed the pacific potential of increasing trade, in which he had naïvely seen the basis of a new world order. As is well known, Palmerston's successful pursuit of 'the interests of England' also rallied to his side the flourishing Liberal bourgeoisie, including many of Cobden's erstwhile supporters, who both during the Crimean War and in the election of 1857, following the *Arrow* incident, abandoned the Manchester School.[111] Yet Cobden's political isolation in Palmerstonian Britain should not conceal several ways in which the Palmerstonian practice of war, paradoxically, advanced Cobdenite principles of peace.

First, although the Crimean War may not be considered a free trade war, in the sense that its conduct was far more determined by expediency than by theory, through the abandonment of privateering and curtailment of the right of capture at sea, British policy approximated far more than in the past to the Cobdenite apophthegm of 'free ships making free goods'. As Olive Anderson has shown, this policy suited Britain's economic interests as the 'the Great Emporium of the Commerce of the World', and did not preclude old-fashioned blockade and seizure of contraband designed to stifle Russia's war effort.[112] On the other hand, as Semmel has argued, British policy also promoted Cobdenite ethics of war, a half-way house to the ideal of commercial peace in time of war, and a symbolic abandonment of traditional naval policy which the free traders had long sought.[113] The Declaration of Paris in 1856, which made permanent these wartime changes, represented the culmination of the liberal association between peace and commerce.[114] For many now feared that Clarendon had gone too far towards the abandonment of British rights, and even against the background of the American Civil War the Cobdenites were subsequently unable to press successfully their campaign for the complete abandonment of commercial blockade and the immunity of mercantile shipping in wartime.[115]

---

[110]   *Speeches*, 310–49, 370–88, but also the sources in note 2 above.

[111]   Gatrell, 'Commercial Middle Class'; A. Howe, *The Cotton Masters 1830–1860* (Oxford Historical Monographs: Oxford, 1984), 215–49; Taylor, *Radicalism*, 280–4; 'the most warlike returns have come from the most popular constituencies', Cobden to Richard, 13 Apr. 1857, in Hobson, *Cobden*, 208.

[112]   O. Anderson, *A Liberal State at War: English Politics and Economics during the Crimean War* (1967), 248–74. See, too, Cardwell Memo on Commercial Policy towards Russia, 29 Oct. 1854, Granville Papers, PRO 30/29/23/4, fos. 181–8.

[113]   B. Semmel, *Liberalism and Naval Strategy: Ideology, Interest, and Sea Power during the Pax Britannica* (1986), 51–67.

[114]   Yet Cobden lamented to Gladstone that 'the great revolution at Paris seems never to have been realized in the public mind', 10 June 1857, GP, Add. MS 44135, fos. 7–8.

[115]   Semmel, *Naval Strategy*, 68–83; Howe, *Cotton Masters*, 245.

Second, the Treaty of Paris of 1856 in another respect vindicated a Cobdenite world-view. For, in Protocol 23 the making of peace paid deference for the first time to the demands of the peace societies for arbitration. This Protocol owed much to pressure from Quaker pacifists, Cobden's closest allies in the 1850s, but also a great deal to the British plenipotentiary Lord Clarendon, who, as we have seen, was one of the most committed of Whig free traders.[116] It upheld the desirability of mediation between states before resort to war. In practice, this enjoyed little immediate success, but its value lay in its existence, setting out an ideal of international conduct, if not a machinery of enforcement. This would encourage and energize the peace movement in the 1860s and 1870s, and provide the basis for Gladstone's willingness to resolve the *Alabama* dispute by means of arbitration.[117]

Third, however much Gladstonian finance was in retreat during the war, the experience of war finance highlighted the potential appeal of Cobdenite fiscal ideas, above all, to the 'People's William'. Gladstone's domestic ambitions turned increasingly to the desirability of stringent, but not inflexible constraints upon governmental expenditure, while his growing recognition of the complexity of Britain's foreign relations drew him closer to Cobden's international ideas.[118] This intermingling of fiscal and international goals was to provide the domestic basis for the Cobden–Chevalier Treaty of 1860, the culmination of what Overstone christened 'Gladstone-Cobdenism'.[119] At the same time, despite Cobden's apparent isolation in the 1850s, a growing number of Radicals, including, for example, the Urquhartites, shared his condemnation of Palmerstonian policy, and, as Miles Taylor has shown, it was hostility to Palmerston, rather than admiration for him, that brought together the 'Liberal' Party in 1859.[120]

It was against this background in the late 1850s, with the prospect of a further resort to war in Europe, this time over Italy, that Cobden himself reassessed his own approach to international relations. Belatedly, but effectively, events had eroded his belief in the unilateral spread of free trade. His ideal of the millennium set out in 1846 had all but crumbled, as war between nations supplanted his vision of peace and world community. It was arguably at this point that he and his followers moved decisively from an Enlightenment cosmopolitan world-view to an acceptance of the necessity of relations between nation-states, based on sovereign

---

[116] G. B. Henderson, 'The Pacifists of the 1850s', *Journal of Modern History*, 9 (1937), 314–41; Lord Richard Grosvenor to Clarendon, 27 Mar. 1856; J. Sturge to Clarendon, 1 June 1856, Clarendon dep. c. 54, fos. 177–82, 221.

[117] Bourne, *Foreign Policy*, 84; Henderson, 'Pacifists of the 1850s'; M. M. Robson, 'Liberals and "Vital Interests": The Debate on International Arbitration, 1815–72', *Bulletin of the Institute of Historical Research*, 32 (1959), 38–55.

[118] *The Gladstone Diaries (GD)*, vol. 5, xxv–xxxiii; Gladstone to Cobden, 12 Oct. 1859, GP, Add. MS 44135, fos. 29–30.

[119] Overstone to Granville, 20 Jan. 1871, *Overstone*, vol. 3, 1205–6.

[120] Locally, *Memoir on Transactions in Central America* (Manchester Free Trade and Foreign Affairs Committee, Apr. 1857); nationally, Taylor, 'The Old Radicalism and the New', 39–41.

peoples.[121] This shift from cosmopolitanism to internationalism had been encouraged by Cobden's growing appreciation of the importance of national interests, which protectionists had hitherto claimed as their own, but which Cobden now integrated into his vision of a liberal international order, based on the self-interest of nations. In place of his vision of the 1830s and 1840s, in which economic principles would be a sufficient guide to political relations, Cobden revalued commercial treaties as 'peace bonds between nations' rather than pacts between rulers. They hence required a legitimacy hitherto lacking in the old reciprocity regime, and helped reconcile the potential conflict between the theory of the free market and the doctrine of national sovereignty. Treaties offered the 'binding together of nations', the basis of 'a great international compact' which would supply a source of human culture rising above what was increasingly termed 'chauvinism'.[122] While retaining his distrust of governments and diplomatists, Cobden believed that free trade treaties could establish lasting ties between peoples as nations, by supplying their mutual wants.[123] It was against this background that Cobden himself, hitherto the Radical exponent of 'no foreign politics', and the 'enemy of protocols' was ready to negotiate, on Palmerston's behalf, the Cobden Treaty of 1860.

The Anglo-French Commercial Treaty and the re-ordering of British policy, 1859–65

The Anglo-French Commercial (Cobden–Chevalier) Treaty, signed at Paris on 23 January 1860, embodied an agreement whereby Britain was to make substantial reductions of her duties on silks, wine, and spirits, and to renounce any restrictions on the export of coal. In return, France agreed to abolish prohibitory duties and to admit British goods at maximum duties of 25 per cent within five years, with immediate reductions on coal, iron, and machine tools.[124] For many of the treaty's critics, this represented an abrogation of free trade principles, and a lamentable return to the reciprocity regime, abandoned by Peel in 1846. In other ways, how-

---

[121]   For this transition, see, too, E. J. Hobsbawm, 'Working-class Internationalism', and G. Claeys, 'Reciprocal Dependence', in F. van Holtoon and M. van der Linden (eds.), *Internationalism in the Labour Movement* (Leiden, 1988), esp. 12–16; for Cobden's case, see Carter, 'Cobden's Thought', chs. 6 and 7, and P. N. Farrar, 'Richard Cobden: Educationist, Economist and Statesman', unpublished Ph.D. thesis, University of Sheffield (1987), ch. 20. See, too, A. Wandrucz, 'Liberal Internationalism', unpublished Ph.D. thesis, University of London (1952) and S. C. Neff, *Friends But No Allies: Economic Liberalism and the Law of Nations* (New York, 1990), 44–8.

[122]   For a typical expression of this outlook by one of Cobden's disciples, see M. E. Grant Duff, *Miscellanies, Political and Literary* (1878), 94–111.

[123]   Dunham, *Anglo-French Treaty*, 52. Cobden's ideas in this way moved from a simple association between commerce and peace to a view of 'regulatory liberalism', that is, rules governing exchange between nations, more often associated with the post-1945 international order. For this perspective, see R. O. Keohane, 'International Liberalism Reconsidered', in J. Dunn (ed.), *The Economic Limits to Modern Politics* (Cambridge, 1990), 165–94.

[124]   Dunham, *Anglo-French Treaty*, *passim*. The terms of the treaty were the subject of a subsequent convention negotiated by Cobden, not without some disquiet on the FO's part. See, e.g., Hammond to Russell, 12 and 24 Sept., 3 and 10 Oct., RP, PRO 30/22/28. The text is printed in Levi, *British Commerce*, 428–33.

ever, the treaty is best considered as the completion of the intermittent commercial negotiations between France and Britain since the 1830s, which had attempted to widen French markets for British goods, and which were now brought to a successful head in the unusual political and diplomatic circumstances of 1859–60. But, for the Cobdenites, the treaty was more than this, for, they argued, it was, on Britain's part, as unilateral an extension of the benefits of free trade as was the repeal of the Corn Laws, for it offered the benefits which France gained to all nations.[125] Typically, Bright wrote:

> There could really never have been any difference of opinion respecting the Treaty among those who desire the extension of free trade principles if the very name of treaty had not furnished a ready means of misrepresentation. Taken with the traditional meaning a treaty of commerce implies exclusive dealing and bargaining between the two countries; but I need hardly assure you, with whom I struggled for seven years for the principles of unrestricted freedom of commerce that I should be the last man to identify myself with so retrograde a policy. All that England has done in this case has been to carry out in practice, towards all the world, in respect of some remaining items of our tariff, that principle of free trade which we have so loudly professed and which we had previously applied to our important articles of production.[126]

On France's side the departure from tradition was far more dramatic. For although Nye has argued that in many respects the French tariff was more liberal than the British one, the ending of the prohibitory regime accomplished a long-sought goal of the French free traders, seeking for France the economic benefits that they believed free trade had given to Britain.[127] More importantly, France intended to negotiate further treaties with European powers whose benefits would be transmitted to Britain by virtue of the most-favoured nation clause in the Cobden Treaty. By this means, as the Board of Trade official Mallet put it, 'we secured the alliance and co-operation of France in breaking down the whole of the prohibitory laws of Europe'.[128] The high tariff walls of continental Europe would fall in domino fashion. By December 1860 Mallet was thus expectantly watching Franco-Belgian negotiations, a signal that 'the whole fabric [of protection] is coming down and it matters little what falls first'.[129] By February 1861 Franco-Prussian

---

[125] In Palmerston's view, the treaty form of agreement was primarily 'the choice of the French Government', 'a sop to the Emperor', Steele, *Palmerston*, 33–4, 97.

[126] Bright to President of the (Manchester) Chamber of Commerce, 19 Feb. (1860), Letter 32, Bright Collection, Princeton University Library.

[127] J. V. Nye, 'The Myth of Free Trade Britain and Fortress France: Tariffs and Trade in the Nineteenth Century', *Journal of Economic History*, 51 (1991), 23–46; cf. D. A. Irwin, 'Free Trade and Protection in Nineteenth-Century Britain and France Revisited' and J. V. Nye, 'Reply to Irwin on Free Trade', in ibid. 53 (1993), 146–58; see, too, Breton and Lutfalla, *L'Économie politique*, ch. 11.

[128] L. Mallet, 'Commercial Treaty with Austria', memo. 1866, p. 9, PRO CAB1/1; Cobden to Gladstone, 16 Jan. 1860, GP, Add. MS 44135, fo. 191; Cobden to Parkes, 11 Feb. 1860, quoted in Edsall, *Cobden*, 341: 'The effect of the treaty will be felt all over the world. It will raise the topic of "international tariffs" into practical importance with all the governments of Europe.'

[129] Mallet to Cobden, 28 Dec. 1860, CP, Add. MS 43666, fo. 117.

discussions had been convened, and with Bowring active in Turin, 'there seems a general Treaty-mongering all over Europe'.[130] This 'tariff round' produced French treaties with Belgium (1 March 1861), Prussia[/*Zollverein*] (August 1862), Italy (17 January 1863), Switzerland (30 June 1864), and Austria (December 1866). From such treaties, England derived considerable benefit through the most-favoured nation clause of the Cobden–Chevalier Treaty, the clause that now became the lynchpin of the new European economic order.[131] With the treaty as the cornerstone of the 'low tariff bloc' over the next twenty years, Europe arguably achieved its nearest approach to a liberal trading regime until after the Second World War.[132]

The treaty therefore in many ways promoted European economic expansion, and contained substantial benefits for English exporters, so much so that for one critic it represented 'a mere capitulation and surrender for the benefit of Manchester'.[133] Even so, this was not primarily an exporters' treaty, but one whose major recommendations were political and diplomatic. The political advantages of a commercial treaty with France had long been recognized, but the idea of an entente cordiale gained powerful reinforcement in 1859–60, as the Italian question threatened to divide Britain and France.[134] For, while no simple palliative for French expansion,[135] it helped draw Britain and France together at a time when mutual suspicion was intense following not only the Orsini incident in 1858, but the war scare of 1859, which had precipitated the raising of a volunteer movement. It was primarily to avert the danger of war that Cobden and Gladstone were ready to depart from the principle of unilateral free trade. Thus Cobden claimed: 'Mon unique objet . . . est d'encourager la paix et de favoriser les sentiments bienvaillants entre les deux pays', while Cowley reported to Clarendon that Gladstone 'does not [delude] himself as to the results of the Treaty and that he considers it more as a political move to render France more dependent upon us and therefore less likely to quarrel with us than as a commercial advantage'.[136] Gladstone himself held

---

[130]   Ibid., 6 Feb. 1861, CP Add. MS 44366, fo. 129. Bowring's later career has been little studied, but his renewed advocacy of free trade went some way to restore his credentials after the *Arrow* incident. In June 1860 he had assured Dobrée, the Governor of the Bank of England, that 'the Emperor is bent upon maintaining Peace, & that the Tariff will be much more advantageous to England than is calculated upon'. Dobrée Diary, 19 June 1860, Bank of England Archives. For his Italian visit, Bowring to Russell, 18 Dec. 1860, RP, PRO 30/22/73.

[131]   For example, duties on cotton piece goods came down to 10%, on gloves to 5%, and on steel bars from 13 to 9 francs. K. B. Clayton, 'Anglo-French Commercial Relations, 1860–1882', unpublished MA thesis, Manchester University (1954), 58.

[132]   Dunham, *Anglo-French Treaty*, 98–100; H. Lack, *The French Treaty and Tariff of 1860* (1861); W. O. Henderson, *The Genesis of the Common Market* (1962), 64–88.

[133]   Cited in Clayton, 'Commercial Relations', 76. In the same vein, Du Cane on Gladstone's 1860 budget as 'simply and essentially a Manchester budget', *Hansard*, 3rd ser., 156, c. 1449, 21 Feb. 1860.

[134]   A. Iliasu, 'The Cobden-Chevalier Commercial Treaty of 1860', *Historical Journal*, 14 (1971), 65–98.

[135]   Clarendon was opposed to it on these grounds.

[136]   Cobden to Chevalier, 31 Oct. 1859 in Schwabe, *Cobden*, 339; Cowley to Clarendon, 15 Jan. 1860, Clarendon dep. c. 536; Cobden to Gladstone, 11 Nov. 1859, GP Add. MS 44135, fos. 44–5; Cobden to Arlès-Dufour, 25 Dec. 1859, CP, Add. MS 43666, fos. 214–15.

strongly in retrospect, that 'there were only two alternatives, one of them the French Treaty & the other war with France'.[137]

Nevertheless, even in this diplomatic context, the treaty undoubtedly had ulterior domestic recommendations. Above all, it coincided neatly with Gladstone's attempts to put Peelite fiscal reform back at the centre of politics after the unorthodox practices of Crimean War finance, and as a restraint on expensive Palmerstonian defence policies.[138] In this respect Gladstone was never ready to go as far as Cobden wished in refusing to provide finance for war preparations, but the treaty was directly tied to budgetary and political considerations. For it greatly advanced the Peelite–Gladstonian policy of a revenue tariff with few items, now reduced from several hundred to a mere forty-eight, and so deliberately erected a long-term obstacle to increased governmental expenditure, save by means of direct taxation. This was made plain by Gladstone's budget of 1860, for the loss of revenue of £2m as a result of the treaty was to be covered in part by using the (windfall) terminable annuities, but also by raising income tax to 10*d*. In this package Gladstone neatly balanced the military demands of Palmerston with the pacific ideals of Cobden, while advancing his own fiscal and political ambitions. He thus provided funds for fortifications, but also in 1861 secured the abolition of the paper duties, to the satisfaction of both his moderate and Radical allies, if to the chagrin of the Whigs.[139]

For Cobden himself, in addition to the immediate pacific influence of the treaty, its benefits lay in taking up the stillborn policy of 1846–7, accepting now that free trade was a goal which might be furthered by emperors, acting on behalf of peoples, especially in states in which vested interests held inordinate sway. Interestingly, Chevalier won Cobden over to the treaty as an instrument by emphasizing Napoleon III's authority to bypass the Chamber in treaty negotiations. In doing so, the Emperor could claim a popular legitimacy which the interest-ridden Chamber lacked, an argument that appealed to Gladstone, but did not entirely remove the taunt of the 'despotic' origins of the treaty.[140] Cobden himself emphasized the overriding moral and political advantages that:

a complete revolution in the Commercial system of France will confer on Europe, and the world, *in proving that the Emperor has renounced the policy of war & conquest & that instead of*

---

[137]   Gladstone to Mundella, 5 Feb. 1894, GP, Add. MS 44258; Gladstone, 'The History of 1852–60 and Greville's Journals', *English Historical Review*, 2 (1887), 296–302.

[138]   Cobden to Russell, 23 Dec. 1859, 2 July 1860 in G. P. Gooch (ed.), *The Later Correspondence of Lord John Russell, 1840–1878* (2 vols, 1925), vol. 2, 250–2, 262–4; J. Morley, *The Life of William Ewart Gladstone* (3 vols, 1903), vol. 2, 42–68; H. C. G. Matthew, 'Disraeli, Gladstone, and the Politics of Mid-Victorian Budgets', *Historical Journal*, 22 (1979); A. Hawkins, 'Gladstone and the Politics of Finance during the 1850s', *Victorian Studies*, 26 (1983), 287–320.

[139]   Matthew, 'Budgets', *passim*; Lord Acton, briefly an MP, welcomed the budget 'for the confirmation it contains of my view that he [Gladstone] is not inclined to democracy and class legislation, but tries to carry out the true principles of economy'. Cited D. Mathew, *Lord Acton and his Times* (1968), 111.

[140]   *Hansard*, 3rd ser., 156, c. 836, 10 Feb. 1860, noting the 'union of the nations' rather than of governments; cf. L. Wolowski, cited in Clayton, 'Commercial Relations', ch. 2.

the sword of the great Napoleon, he will wield the pen of Sir Robert Peel. The moral effect of this would restore confidence to the commerce of the World.[141]

Cobden also shared Chevalier's view of the treaty as part of a Saint-Simonian-style project for the modernization of the French economy, while welcoming its impact as a boost to the European peace movement, as greeted by Arlès-Dufour in France and as urged upon Samuel Morley in the City of London.[142] Treaties as peace bonds were, despite the regressive complement of Palmerstonian forts, an important moral boost to the ideal of a liberal international order.[143]

The process of negotiation itself, with Cobden rather than the British Ambassador Lord Cowley uppermost, also in large part offered a model of a new diplomacy, a treaty negotiated between peoples, represented by Cobden—'a simple citizen'—and Napoleon, and not between old-style diplomats; a foreign policy without a Foreign Office, and almost a vindication of Cobden's 1830s ideal of contacts between peoples replacing the traditional diplomatic structure. This impression was furthered by the Commissions which sat at Paris, intimately involving scores of British businessmen, 'the most eminent and intelligent of our manufacturers'.[144] Here was a form of entrepreneurial diplomacy of which Cobden had always dreamt, and in which he saw a model for the future, depending on:

the will of the trading and industrious classes. Have they intelligence and self-respect enough to compel our courtly and aristocratic classes to adapt their ideas of foreign policy to the wants and interests of the age or will they allow the Foreign Office still to foster all the prejudices and personal predilections which flourished in the regime 60 years ago?.[145]

For Cobden, the treaty embodied not the diplomatic advantage of two Great Powers, but 'a victory for humanity'.[146] It was the diplomatic recognition of the new order made possible by material progress, with the vast expansion of trade and shipping, unprecedented improvements in postal and telegraphic communications, huge capital outflows, and with the possibility of a more united Europe symbolized

---

[141] Cobden to H. Ashworth, 2 Jan. 1860 (original emphasis), CP, Add. MS 43654, fo. 2.

[142] Cobden Diaries, 1860–1, *passim*, e.g. 10 June, 12 Oct. 1860, 26 Jan. 1861, CP, Add. MS 43675; Arlès-Dufour to Cobden, 21 Jan., 17 Nov. 1860, 13 Sept., 11 Oct. 1861, CP 216, WSRO; Cobden to Arlès-Dufour, 19 Feb., 19 Sept. 1861, CP, Add. MS 43666; Cobden to Morley, 29 Jan., 25 Mar. 1861, CP, Add. MS 43670, fos. 101, 118; G. R. Searle, *Entrepreneurial Politics in Mid-Victorian Britain* (Oxford, 1993), 131, 169.

[143] *Hansard*, 3rd ser., 156, c. 1527, 21 Feb. 1860 (Grant Duff); ibid., c. 549, 15 Mar. 1860 (Taunton, formerly, Labouchère); Cobden, speech at Rochdale, 1861, in Schwabe, *Cobden*, 352–3; Layard congratulated Cobden on 'this enormous advance in the international policy of European nations', 30 Dec. 1860, CP 6, WSRO.

[144] Cobden to Hammond (FO), (copy), 22 Sept. 1860, CP 6, WSRO. For their evidence, Conseil Supérieur de l'Agriculture, du Commerce et de l'Industrie, *Enquête. Traité de Commerce avec l'Angleterre* (6 vols, Paris, 1860).

[145] Cobden to W. Hargreaves, 31 Oct. 1860, CP, Add. MS 43655. For one lasting Cobdenite disciple recruited in 1860, see W. H. C. Armytage, *A. J. Mundella, 1825–1897: The Liberal Background to the Labour Movement* (1951), 30–2.

[146] Cobden to T. Thomasson, 2 June 1861. Cobden–Thomasson Letters, BLPES.

by projects such as the Channel Tunnel, which Cobden's friends Chevalier and Watkin would later launch.

Cobdenite new diplomacy, however, worked only with the support of the old; the attempt at a treaty early on received the support of Russell and the neutrality of Palmerston, while its successful completion was welcomed for its material and diplomatic advantages, as we have seen.[147] Cowley himself for the most part worked harmoniously with Cobden, although he was surprised by the successful outcome of the negotiations. Traditionalists, even the free trader Clarendon, suspicious of some aspects of the treaty, were also only slowly won over to this initiative.[148] Nevertheless, public and parliamentary opinion rallied strongly to the treaty, as did the leading commercial bodies, such that by the end of February Clarendon saw it 'growing in favour thro'out the country . . . many manufacturers believe they can smash the corresponding interests in France—several constituencies would have made short work with their representatives if they had indulged in party or personal politics'.[149]

Yet the treaty by no means went without influential opposition, for it was open to attack from both flanks. On the one hand, it occasioned a flurry of Tory opposition, purporting to find in it merely an inferior version of that negotiated by Pitt's government in 1786.[150] Under this umbrella, several threatened interests were able to shelter. Opposition was notable among the shipping interest, faced by the ending of its recently revived hopes for the restoration of reciprocity.[151] Similarly, among producers, the silk and ribbon manufacturers of Macclesfield and Coventry, as well as the remaining Spitalsfield weavers, were more aware of the treaty's benefits for Manchester than for themselves.[152] Thus, there threatened a wider 'combination of the anti-French party, Ribbon manufacturers, Distillers, Licensed Victuallers, Wine merchants' with the Tory opposition.[153] Nevertheless, although at one point it seemed the Tories might launch an assault on the treaty, their hopes of office

[147] Russell recalled: 'Though we [he and Palmerston] were not fond of treaties of commerce, we thought it would be of great advantage to both countries', q. 3081, SC, Trade with Foreign Nations, *Parl. Papers*, 1864, 7.

[148] C. P. Villiers was also among its critics, Steele, *Palmerston*, 97 ff; H. E. Maxwell, *The Life and Letters of George William, Fourth Earl of Clarendon* (2 vols, 1913), vol. 2, 205–17.

[149] Clarendon to Duchess of Manchester, 27 Feb. 1860, in A. L. Kennedy (ed.), *'My Dear Duchess'* (1956), 97; Steele, *Palmerston*, 95–9; T. A. Jenkins (ed.), *The Parliamentary Diaries of Sir John Trelawney, 1858–1865* (Camden 4th ser., vol. 40, Royal Historical Society, 1990), 96, 106, 108; Clayton, 'Commercial Relations', ch. 2; A. C. Howe, 'Free Trade and the City of London *c*.1820–1870', *History*, 77 (1992), 407.

[150] Mallet, Cobden's adjutant, considered the 1786 Treaty as 'in some respects more liberal than this', to Cobden, 28 Dec. 1860, CP, Add. MS 43666, fo. 121. The publication of *The Journal and Correspondence of William, Lord Auckland* (4 vols, 1861–2) proved timely.

[151] W. S. Lindsay, *History of Merchant Shipping and Ancient Commerce* (vol. 3, 1876), ch. 14; id., *Our Merchant Shipping: Its Present State Considered* (1860).

[152] For example, the silk manufacturers of Macclesfield saw the treaty as 'one-sided as regards English silk trade', a foretaste of the later 'Fair Trade' critique. Brocklehurst to BT, 7 Feb. 1860. BT 33/4 Correspondence relative to the French Treaty. Silk and Cotton.

[153] Dunham, *Anglo-French Treaty*, 115 n., citing H. [?J.] B. Smith to Chevalier, 21 Feb. 1860.

encouraged them not to antagonize France by opposition, especially when they could expect little support in the Commons.[154]

On the other hand, the treaty faced Liberal and Whig opposition, partly from those who feared the growing ascendancy of Gladstone and the rising power of France, but primarily from political economists, who dogmatically proclaimed any treaty to be at variance with free trade, and a departure from the doctrine of non-intervention. Such, for example, was the view of Overstone, McCulloch, his pupil Earl Grey, the old Whig-Leaguer C. P. Villiers, and of Bonamy Price, the Drummond Professor at Oxford. Opposition was not based solely on dogma, with, for example, the Bank of England and Lord Clarendon worried by the fiscal consequences of the lowering of duties, which contained the hidden threat of increased direct taxation, even of a graduated income tax.[155]

Undoubtedly, public reactions to the treaty were strongly geared to perceptions of its economic costs and benefits, although, as we have seen, this was far from the primary goal of either Cobden, Gladstone, or even Palmerston. Moreover, the implications of the treaty, 'really a great European operation', as Gladstone put it, could not be ignored if it was to be, as the secretary of the English Commission wrote, 'the starting-point for a general system of reductions in the import tariffs of the continent'.[156] This was a recipe for European economic progress which emphatically identified Britain's welfare with Europe, rather than with the Palmerstonian swing towards the empire, which Steele has recently described.[157] Mallet, in the wake of the Indian Mutiny of 1857, mistrusted the economic health of Eastern markets, and wrote to Cobden, 'on the whole, I am confirmed in my opinion that the wise thing for us to do is to expand our European trade in every possible manner'.[158] To his surprise, it was in Mallet, a Board of Trade mandarin who had flourished under Whig patronage, that Cobden now found his closest fellow spirit, ready even to join his campaign to infuse commercial values into the Foreign Office machine.[159] Above all, the two men shared a vision of free trade as the ally of political progress in Europe, with the breakdown of monopoly at the behest of public opinion as the sign of liberal democracy, itself the ultimate guarantor of a peaceful international order.[160]

Moreover, it was this optimistic vision of Europe that inspired what Gaston has termed 'the forward school' in British commercial diplomacy, a school closely allied to the Manchester School through men such as Mallet, and which exercised a

---

[154] *Trelawney Diaries*, 108 (8 Mar. 1860); Cowley to Clarendon, 15 Jan. 1860, Clarendon dep. c. 536; Steele, *Palmerston*, 95–101.

[155] Howe, 'City of London', 407; Kennedy (ed.), *'My Dear Duchess'*, 97–8.

[156] Morley, *Gladstone*, vol. 2, 22; Lack, *French Treaty*, 17.

[157] Steele, *Palmerston*, 206 and 343 ff.

[158] Mallet to Cobden, 21 Sept. 1861, CP, Add. MS 43666, fo. 140.

[159] Ibid., 10 Oct. 1861, CP, Add. MS 43666, fo. 147; Cobden to Bright, 4 Sept. 1861, CP, Add. MS 43651, fo. 256.

[160] For Mallet's thinking, see esp. B. Mallet, *Sir Louis Mallet: A Record of Public Service and Political Ideals* (1905), and L. Mallet, *Free Exchange* (ed. B. Mallet, 1891).

strong and neglected influence in Britain's relations with Europe between 1860 and 1865.[161] For the 1860 Treaty not only initiated the wider European search for commercial treaties, but prompted Britain herself to renegotiate her own commercial treaties as part of the new European order, temporarily, at least, countervailing the Palmerstonian swing to the East. Here, Russell, that ever mutable politician, revealing in his keenness for Europe his deep Foxite origins, now set in train a series of negotiations which resulted in the substantial restructuring of Britain's commercial relations.[162] In doing so, Russell was sensitive to commercial opinion, for which the Board of Trade, now headed by the old Leaguer, Milner Gibson, became an effective conduit, but also responded to the Cobdenite optimism that he had occasionally felt in the 1840s. Commercial confidence would be both the result of peace and a contributor to it, forming an essential element in the 'happiness of nations'. Treaties themselves became the most eligible and tangible ties between nations.[163] So completely did Russell now identify himself with liberal economics that by 1865 he urged the abolition of income tax as completing the work begun by Peel in 1842.[164]

More immediately, by June 1860 Russell had commissioned the drafting of treaties with Spain, Portugal, and Austria, and by April 1861 had made formal overtures to all leading European countries.[165] These first bore fruit in Belgium, where, as we have seen, the current of doctrinal free trade ran high in the 1850s, although with the Belgian ministry dependent upon the votes of cotton-spinning deputies, Britain paid a higher indirect cost, calculated by the capitalization of the Scheldt Dues, than was anticipated.[166] Russell's diplomacy encapsulated the traditional desire for friendly relations with the Low Countries, with a strong and independent Belgium, with the aim of keeping in power the Belgian Liberals, 'interested as we are in the good example in regard to order, progress and prosperity afforded by this people under a Constitutional Ministry'.[167] A treaty also helped allay mutual suspicions aroused by the fortification of Antwerp, in which Cobden

---

[161] J. W. T. Gaston, 'Trade and the late Victorian Foreign Office', *International History Review*, 4 (1982), 317–38; id., 'Policy-Making and Free-Trade Diplomacy: Britain's Commercial Relations with Western Europe, 1869–1886', unpublished Ph.D. thesis, University of Saskatchewan (1975).

[162] A. Iliasu, 'The Role of Free Trade Treaties in British Foreign Policy, 1859–1871', unpublished Ph.D. thesis, University of London (1965). For the Foxites and Europe, see L. G. Mitchell, *Holland House* (1980). In the 1820s, Russell had written extensively on the history of Europe, and returned to this theme in his inaugural presidential address to the Royal Historical Society, *TRHS*, 2 (1872), 9–14.

[163] Iliasu, 'Treaties', 209–14.

[164] Russell to Palmerston, 6 Apr. 1865 in S. Walpole, *The Life of Lord John Russell* (2 vols, 1889), vol. 2, 405.

[165] Iliasu, 'Treaties', ch. 4, *passim*; 'Memorandum on Commercial Relations between the U.K. and Portugal' [1860], FO 881/1414.

[166] Russell to Howard de Walden, 31 Dec. 1861, 4 Feb. and 13 May 1862, RP, PRO 30/22/14C; de Walden to Russell, 29 Apr., 6 May, 9 and 24 Aug., 20 Sept. 1861, 3 Jan., 7 Feb., 14 Mar., 7 Apr., 16 May, 8 July, 15, 18, and 24 Aug. 1862, RP, PRO 30/22/46; M. E. Grant Duff, *Studies in European Politics* (Edinburgh, 1866), 356–7.

[167] De Walden to Russell, 7 Apr. 1862, PRO 30/22/46, fo. 237.

himself had become embroiled.[168] But given Belgium's strong free trade credentials, refurbished by Cobdenite allies such as Molinari and van der Maeren, the
Treaty of July 1862 was both logical and exemplary.

In Italy, where 'Piedmont's ostentatious devotion to Free Trade . . . endeared
Italian nationalism to the middle classes', both Gladstone and Russell were keen to
consolidate Italy's progress to nationhood by both a liberal tariff and a treaty with
Britain.[169] Gladstone, for example, warned strongly against the emergence of a
protectionist tariff in the new Italy, for thereby 'class will be set against class and
classes against the community. If parts of the people are taught by vicious commercial laws to prey upon the rest, such a system must retard and impair the
union . . . and slacken the growth of the new kingdom in wealth and power'.[170]
Rather, he urged for Italy the same moral, political, and economic benefits which
the Anglo-French Treaty proffered, 'for the blessings which increase of trade
usually brings with it; peace, security, goodwill'. He went on: 'Public feeling, I am
thankful to say, is warm in the Italian cause; but it will be confirmed and quickened
by finding that it is not to deprive itself of those advantages which follow in the
basis of a sound commercial treaty.'[171] Anglo-Italian negotiations waited upon the
Italo-French Treaty of 1863 negotiated by Cobden's old admirer Minghetti, which
lowered existing duties and converted them to an *ad valorem* basis. This treaty
favoured Italy's specialization in agriculture, but in the August 1863 Anglo-Italian
Treaty Britain resisted further reductions in her wine duties on fiscal grounds. The
treaty therefore replicated that with France, granting most-favoured nation status
with regard to imports, exports, and shipping.[172] British opinion had held out
strong hopes of the Italian market, but the procedures of the Foreign Office
('unfortunately free trade is not one of the traditions of the Foreign Office', as
W. E. Forster put it) occasioned some displeasure, contributing to the setting up of
the Select Committee on Foreign Trade in 1864.[173] But in the case of Italy, at least
the hopes of 1846–7 had to some extent been fulfilled.

This was also to be so in Germany, where the strength of Listian doctrines
encountered by Cobden in the 1840s had been much diminished. Above all, the
progress of liberal opinion had coincided with Bismarck's consolidation of Prussian
hegemony in Germany through the use of lower tariffs.[174] Not only did the
Cobden–Chevalier Treaty therefore lead to a vital Franco-Prussian Treaty in

[168]   *L'Économiste Belge*, 24 May 1862; cf. S. van der Weyer, *Richard Cobden, Roi des Belges* (Bruxelles,
1862; London, 1863).
[169]   Bourne, *Foreign Policy*, 98; 'Customs Union in Italy' [1859], FO 881/837.
[170]   To James Lacaita, 1 Dec. 1860, GP, Add. MS 44233, fo. 156.
[171]   Ibid., fos. 155–62, cited in part in P. Bolchini, 'Anglo-Italian Economic Relations (1861–1883)',
unpublished Ph.D. thesis, University of London (1967), 23, n. 2.
[172]   L. S. West to Russell, 6 and 25 Jan. 1863; Sir James Hudson to Russell, 28 Mar. 1863, RP, PRO
30/22/70.
[173]   *Hansard*, 3rd ser., 169, c. 422, 17 Feb. 1863; Bolchini, 'Anglo-Italian Economic Relations', 28;
Iliasu, 'Treaties', ch. 4.
[174]   See above 82 and n. 65.

March 1862, but Britain's commercial relations with Germany were revised in the Anglo-*Zollverein* Treaty of 1865. This resulted from close co-operation between the Foreign Office and the Prussian free traders, Delbrück and Philipsborn.[175] It conformed to the emergent pattern of extending the provisions of the 1860 Treaty, a pattern that was also now followed with regard to the British colonies. Herein lay a substantial bone of contention for the future, but for the next thirty years 'the Treaty remained the groundwork of Anglo-German commercial relations'.[176]

This treaty contained broader implications, for Prussia had assumed considerable importance in Russell's thinking, not only as holding the key to the success of free trade in Germany, but because of the likely impact of her example on both Austria and Russia. In the early 1860s Austria had not entirely abandoned her own attempts to influence Germany as a whole, in particular to draw the southern German states back into her protectionist orbit, to undermine Prussia's influence in Germany, and to bind both Venetia and Hungary permanently to her. The dream of an Austro-German customs union, an economic *Mitteleuropa* surrounded by vast tariff walls had not entirely dissipated.[177] Nevertheless, Austria's failure to prevent the Franco-Prussian treaty of 1862 and her decisive exclusion from the *Zollverein* in 1865 not only secured the triumph of 'Cobdenism' in Germany, but heightened the desirability of Austria's coming to terms with a free trade Western Europe.[178] This added impetus to a long series of negotiations with Austria, whereby Britain had sought to ensure that the Habsburg Empire would at last form part of 'the ever-widening circle of commercial civilization and contribute their share to the commonwealth of Europe'.[179]

In Austria British diplomats aimed at far more than a simple most-favoured nation treaty; rather, they sought a 'radical Tariff reform' which would end decades of Austrian protection—a financial reconstruction that would free government finance from monopolists, and benefit Europe as a whole.[180] In this, they faced the strong opposition both of vested interests and of dogmatic protectionists, and

[175] Napier to Russell, 26 Nov. 1864, RP, PRO 30/22/82; Napier to Layard, 31 July and 2 Aug. 1865, Layard Papers, Add. MS 39116, fos. 206–13, 221–2, the latter reporting that Bismarck would sign the treaty if it gave no trouble, but was otherwise 'engaged altogether in the congenial occupation of pursuing chamois and persecuting Austrians and Liberals'.

[176] Presciently, Russell noted 'The Colonial article in the draft treaty gives us some trouble—as we leave the colonies pretty free to make their own tariff. We should be very glad to have that article omitted.' Russell to Napier, 8 Mar. 1865, RP, PRO 30/22/113; Clapham, '*Zollverein* Negotiations, 1828–1865', 479–80; Iliasu, 'Treaties', 346 ff.; below, 180, 220.

[177] D. C. Long, 'Efforts to secure an Austro-German Customs Union', *University of Michigan Historical Essays* (ed. A. E. R. Boak), 11 (1937), 45–74; Henderson, *Zollverein*, 286–303; Morier to Russell, 19 Nov. 1864, RP, PRO 30/22/82.

[178] Clarendon to Russell, 29 Sept. 1864, reporting interview with Rechberg, RP, PRO 30/22/25; cf. Napier to Russell, 17 Feb. 1865, RP, PRO 30/22/82; Bonar to Russell, 15 Feb. 1865, RP, PRO 30/22/43, fo. 199.

[179] Mallet memo. 'Commercial Treaty with Austria', PRO CAB 1/1 [1866]; K. F. Helleiner, *Free Trade and Frustration: Anglo-Austrian Negotiations 1860–70* (Toronto, 1973), for a detailed account.

[180] Mallet, 'Commercial Treaty with Austria', CAB 1/1; Morier to Layard, 3 May 1865 (copy), Box 33, Papers of Sir Robert Morier, Balliol College, Oxford.

negotiations in the early 1860s had made little progress.[181] In an attempt to press them further, British businessmen and the Association of Chambers of Commerce sent their own free trade mission to Austria, with the financier and MP Somerset Beaumont launching himself as the new Cobden. Such amateur commercial diplomacy alienated the professionals, but, with the support of Clarendon, it helped pave the way for a Commission of Inquiry in which Morier and Mallet were well placed to press for free trade, although they also feared the Commission as an outlet for the Austrian protectionists.[182] The failure of Austria's *Zollverein* diplomacy, however, provided the necessary spur for successful treaty negotiation, for, as von Hock the deputy minister of finance concluded:

Austria for the most serious political, fiscal and economic reasons, cannot isolate herself from the general movement towards Free Trade, which has spread from the West of Europe right up to her own borders, without inviting the enmity of those States, without suffering grievous losses of customs revenue, without harming her trade, and without surrendering her industry to the monopoly power of a few.[183]

This policy led first to a treaty with the *Zollverein* itself. But with Gagern, head of the Austrian Commercial Section, now ready to see free trade as 'a life and death question for Austria', and with Russell urging a treaty as the means to financial stability and the retention of Great Power status for Austria, negotiations began in earnest in November 1865, and reached a preliminary conclusion on 16 December 1865.[184]

This agreement embodied, for Gladstone, the entire abandonment by Austria of 'her tenacious adherence' to the protective system, in which Britain played the part not of 'haggler', but of 'auxiliary' to the 'Government of a foreign State, to enable it more easily to overcome the prejudices and to enlighten the ignorance of its own people' as to the mutual benefits of commercial treaties.[185] Britain's role as enlightened auxiliary included a readiness, as in 1860 with regard to France, to make budgetary changes favourable to Austria. In this case the timber duties, long the target of financial reformers, were finally expunged from the tariff in Gladstone's 1866 budget, while the duty on wine in bottles was equalized with that imported in casks, a boon to Austrian (as well as the French) exporters.[186] The mutual adjust-

---

[181] 'There is no great element of promise about this proposal', Gladstone agreed with Russell, 13 Feb. 1865, *GD*, vol. 6, 334.

[182] Napier to Morier, 17 July, Layard to Morier, 14 June and 26 July 1865, Morier Papers, Box 33; Clarendon to Russell, 29 Sept. (Vienna); 9 Dec. 1864, RP, PRO 30/22/26, 177 ff., 182–5.

[183] 3 Mar. 1864, quoted (and trans.) in Helleiner, *Frustration*, 54.

[184] Iliasu, 'Treaties', ch. 6; *Hansard*, 3rd ser., 183, cc. 376–82, 3 May 1866. The same economic and diplomatic logic also led to negotiations with France, D. C. Long, 'The Austro-French Treaty of 1866', *American Historical Review*, 41 (1936).

[185] *Hansard*, 3rd ser., 183, c. 377, 3 May 1866.

[186] For Gladstone's memorandum on the timber duties, and Cabinet responses to it, see Layard papers, Add. MS 39117, fos. 94–151 [12–16 Sept. 1865]. See, too, Gladstone, *GD*, vol. 6, 383 [12 Sept. 1865]. Only the Duke of Somerset opposed this concession. It was, however, decided to retain the registration duty on corn, whose abolition had been urged as a boon to Austria, for example, by Morier, on which occasion Gladstone was surprised to find himself at odds 'with a man on the grounds that he

ment of the Austrian tariff was to prove the occasion of protracted negotiation, but the agreement of 1865 expressed for Mallet and the leading free traders 'the soundest principles of political economy as well as the highest grounds of international morality'.[187] In the Austrian Commercial Treaty, Mallet saw the model of the future, whereby Britain was able to co-operate in the reconstruction of European tariffs, and in which tariffs and customs were admitted to be 'a measure of international taxation and [is] therefore a proper subject for international regulation'. Such treaties, he hoped, would become 'part of the common law of Europe'.[188] In many ways, Mallet's ideas here foreshadowed the regulatory liberal ideas of the post-1945 international order, expressing an ideal of European co-operation which many liberal intellectuals shared in the early 1860s, but which were shortly to run into the sands in the face of the Austro-Prussian War of 1866. Not only did this stultify liberal hopes in general, but more immediately it put paid to an early resolution of the supplementary commercial negotiations between Britain and Austria. These were eventually concluded only in 1869, an interval that was to forfeit much of the goodwill and idealism of 1865.[189]

The optimism of the free traders in the mid-1860s was, however, considerable, and extended to those geographical areas in which free trade had normally promised least. First, in 1865–6 encouraging reports from Spain were made both by the British minister Crampton and by the Newcastle chemical manufacturer Allhusen, although, as in the late 1840s, hopes raised proved premature.[190] Second, it seemed possible that Russia, the 'last stronghold of the pure protective system', might succumb to Western commercial example and diplomatic pressure.[191] For the Anglo-Austrian Treaty of 1865 had strongly emphasized that 'the principal states of Europe [combined] into a commercial coalition based on the principles of free trade, from which the great Empire of Russia alone yet keeps aloof'.[192] Here, it was

---

goes further in the matter of Free Trade than myself', to Morier, 20 Nov. 1865, Morier Papers, Box 33. Austria also sought to make the treaty conditional upon raising a substantial loan, although eventually this was floated in Paris, not London. Layard to Bloomfield, 9 and 13 Sept. 1865, Layard Papers, Add. MS 39117, fos. 59–61, 110ff.; Gladstone to Layard, 16 Aug. 1865, ibid., Add. MS 38991, fos. 375–6; L. B. Steefel, 'The Rothschilds and the Austrian Loan of 1865', *Journal of Modern History*, 7 (1936).

[187] For Austria's 'last moment' conditions, see *GD*, vol. 6, 396–7 [13 Nov. 1865]; Mallet to Derby, 30 July 1866, Derby Papers, 12/3/11, Liverpool Record Office.

[188] Mallet, 'Commercial Treaty with Austria', CAB 1/1, copy sent to Layard, 9 Feb. 1866, Layard Papers, Add. MS 39118, fo. 264.

[189] The war, Mallet feared, 'will be deplorable for all friends of progress and freedom'. To Layard, 26 June 1866, Layard Papers, Add. MS 39120, fo. 462; below, 109. For the long negotiations, see Mallet Papers, Austrian Tariff Commission, BL Add. MS 38814–15.

[190] The wine duties on Britain's part entrenched protectionism on Spain's precluded progress. See, *inter alia*, Crampton to Layard, 7 July 1865, Add. MS 39116, fo. 36; Mallet to Layard, 24 Jan. 1866, Add. MS 39118, fos. 147–9; Allhusen to Layard, 14 Apr. 1866, Add. MS 39119, fo. 439.

[191] Gladstone, *Hansard*, 3rd ser., 183, c. 379, 3 May 1866; J. S. Lumley, and A. Buchanan to Layard, both 28 Feb. 1866, Layard Papers, Add. MS 39118, fos. 476–7, 379–80; T. Mitchell to Layard, 14 Mar. 1866, ibid., Add. MS 39119, fo. 154. See, too, Grant Duff, *European Politics*, 109.

[192] 'Memorandum on the Trade between Great Britain and Russia', 4 Dec. 1865, in K. Bourne and D. C. Watt (eds.), *British Documents on Foreign Affairs [hereafter BDFA]: Part 1 Series A. Russia, 1859–1914* (ed. D. C. Lieven, 6 vols, 1983), vol. 1, 92–119.

hoped that Prussia and Britain might combine in an assault upon the Russian tariff, with the German Commercial Congress in 1864 having promoted the idea of a *Zollverein*–Russian Treaty. British diplomats actively canvassed the merits of free trade in Moscow and St Petersburg, aided in part by the visit of a delegation from the British Association of Chambers of Commerce, although this threatened to be counter-productive when the future fair trader Sampson Lloyd urged that each country should decide its own course of policy.[193] This indeed seemed to be the case, for as Thomas Michell, the British attaché at St Petersburg, was only too aware, and as Cobden had discovered in 1847, the aim of Russian policy since 1823 had been to become an exporting, not an importing, economy. It thus sheltered its manufactures behind high tariffs, while its exports of grain to Western Europe expanded, as they did substantially in the wake of the repeal of the Corn Laws.[194] Here was a still largely mercantilist policy, sustained by Russian merchants and manufacturers, against which her enlightened press, the example of the West, and the best propagandist efforts of Michell, Lumley, and others, had only a small liberalizing effect on the Russian tariff in the later 1860s.[195] Even so, by 1871 Buchanan, the British Ambassador, welcomed in Russia's muted advances, a tendency to 'improve their international relations', although this fell short of concluding commercial treaties.[196]

Finally, the substantial progress in Britain's European commercial policy since 1860 was consolidated by institutional change at home, with the creation in 1865 of the Commercial Department of the Foreign Office.[197] This was welcomed by Cobden as an attempt to educate diplomatists in commercial policy, although it perpetuated the damaging division of responsibility between the Board of Trade and the Foreign Office, which businessmen had striven to end.[198] It also side-stepped the aims of Cobden's closest allies, including Mallet, as well as Forster, representing the Association of Chambers of Commerce, who had urged a strengthened Board of Trade.[199] That idea served only to arouse fears of undue governmental intervention in trade, smacking of the departed mercantilist era, or, as Morier put it, 'the blight of the economical fallacy that Free Trade implies

---

[193]   For this episode, Mitchell to Layard, 19 July 1865, Layard Papers, Add. MS 39116, fos. 114–16.
[194]   S. E. Fairlie, 'The Anglo-Russian Grain Trade, 1815–1861', unpublished Ph.D. thesis, University of London (1959), esp. ch. 5.
[195]   'By dint of persevering . . . the wedge may at least be driven into some faulty joint of the rotten Protectionist armour in which the Muscovites place such faith', Lumley to Layard, 28 Feb. 1866, Layard Papers, Add. MS 39118, fos. 476–7; see, too, *The Times*, 10 Apr. 1868.
[196]   Buchanan to Granville, 14 Nov. 1871 in *BDFA: Russia*, vol. 1, 231–2. For Michell's important contribution to free trade in Russia, see Buchanan to Clarendon, recommending a CB, 11 Aug. 1869, Clarendon dep. c. 482, fos. 131–42. In 1871 a trademarks declaration was added to the 1859 Anglo-Russian Treaty.
[197]   This is well treated in Iliasu, 'Treaties', ch. 5; see, too, R. A. Jones, *The Nineteenth-Century Foreign Office* (1971), 86–8.
[198]   Searle, *Entrepreneurial Politics*, 171–4, 193–5.
[199]   Mallet to Cobden, 10 Oct. 1861, CP, Add. MS 43666, fo. 147.

having no commercial policy'.[200] The impact of the creation of the Commercial Department was also partly vitiated in the eyes of the Cobdenites by the failure to appoint Mallet (with 'the whole tariff map of Europe at his fingers' ends and the knowledge of men and things') as its head, and the fear that it might become a 'black hole' within the Foreign Office.[201] This remained to be seen, although Mallet's early reports were predictably gloomy.[202]

Yet this pessimism was not in 1865 entirely justified, for since the Anglo–French treaty of 1860, Britain had played a strongly constructive role in European diplomacy, with ministers such as Russell, Milner Gibson, and Layard seizing advantage of a European-wide movement towards free trade to endorse, if only partially and belatedly, the Cobdenite vision of international commercial relations.[203] Thus, Layard, a Foreign Office minister earlier associated with the Administrative Reform Association and advocacy of 'business principles', reported 'Commerce for the present driving out *haute politique* . . . we are thinking principally of tariffs, trade marks . . . and Treaties of Commerce'.[204] Given this 'mania for commercial treaties', it proved only mildly ironical for Disraeli to observe 'the extraordinary behaviour of the free trade party in patronising artificial agreements of exchange'.[205] For Cobden's disciples, in Britain and Europe, any departure from the principle of unilateral free trade since 1860 had been amply vindicated by the alluring prospect of 'the final inauguration of free trade in Europe by 1870', bringing in its train the moral and social benefits which Cobden had promised in the 1840s.[206]

'Cobden's name is great: & will be greater'[207]

Among the moral benefits of free trade which Cobden had consistently propagated for twenty years were its foreign relations, with amity between nations leading towards universal peace. If this seemed chimerical in the age of Palmerston, with disarmament vastly overshadowed by the bellicosity of the 1850s, both the Peace of Paris and the 1860 Treaty in some ways boosted the cause of peace, while the course

---

[200] Morier to Lady Salisbury, 5 Nov. 1867, Morier Papers, Box 33.

[201] Ibid.; Layard to Hammond, 1 Nov. 1864, Layard Papers, Add. MS 38959, fo. 71.

[202] Mallet to Cobden, 2 Feb. and 12 Mar. 1865. CP, Add. MS 43666, fos. 191, 196.

[203] For Milner Gibson, see *The Times*, 25 Jan. 1865, cited in Steele, *Palmerston*, 205. It should also be noted that important progress had been achieved with regard to French shipping duties, with W. S. Lindsay playing Cobden's role in minor key, see Lindsay, *History of Merchant Shipping*, vol. 3, 437–54; Levi, *British Commerce*, 522.

[204] Layard to Morier, 25 Jan. 1865[6], Morier Papers, Box 33. For Layard's earlier career, see Searle, *Entrepreneurial Politics*, 90 ff.

[205] Russell to Layard, n.d. [*c.*June] 1865, Layard Papers, Add. MS 38991, fo. 215; *Hansard*, 3rd ser., 169, c. 439, 17 Feb. 1863.

[206] Morier to Lady Salisbury, 5 Nov. 1867, a disquisition on 'the principles of commercial policy of the British Empire', Morier Papers, Box 33. For the Board of Trade's more mundane agenda, see memo on European Tariffs, Dec. 1864, FO 881/1321. But even the Board of Customs official Oglivy believed 'the great principles of Free Trade and of International Commercial Union are daily gaining ground in Europe and are exercising a most beneficial and moral influence over the destinies of nations', restraining to some extent war fever in Europe in 1866. To Mrs Cobden, 31 May 1866, CP Add. MS 6027.

[207] *GD*, vol. 6, 347, 7 Apr. 1865.

of the Risorgimento provided, in Cobden's eyes, a modest victory for non-intervention. The Cobdenites also gathered a few crumbs of comfort from the Polish crisis of 1863.[208] But it was in the Schleswig-Holstein crisis of 1864 that Cobdenites sensed a significant turning-point in British foreign policy, with what appeared to be the long-awaited eclipse of Palmerstonian diplomacy. For, in this crisis Palmerstonian hints of intervention were revealed as 'pure bluff', and this conspicuous failure on a European scene now dominated by Bismarck was greeted by Cobden as 'a revolution . . . in our foreign policy . . . our Foreign Office will never again attempt to involve us in any European entanglements for the Balance of Power . . . Non-intervention is the policy of all future governments in this country.'[209] Bright also welcomed the end of Britain's fixation with the balance of power, and the start of a healthier preoccupation with political reform at home.[210]

If these judgements were for the most part premature, the death of Cobden in April 1865 permitted considerable optimism among his most loyal followers. The Radical critique of foreign policy, the analysis of the social composition of the Foreign Office, the debunking of the balance of power, the setting out of a framework for pacific settlement of international disputes had all been established in a lasting fashion. Cobden's career had served firmly to root the 'idealist' tradition in foreign policy, the staple of the subsequent ideas of Hobson, Brailsford, Ponsonby, and 'the League of Nations generation', whose admiration of Cobden was to be unstinted.[211] Cobden had also more immediately inspired 'the forward school' in British commercial diplomacy, a small group of votaries, dedicated to realizing the goal of a free-trading and democratic Europe. The most self-conscious of these disciples was Mallet, with his intense belief in commercial treaties not as the small change of diplomacy, but as 'peace bonds between nations', signalling the victory of progressive opinion over vested interests and reactionary ideas. Low tariffs and most-favoured nation clauses would become elements in a 'great international compact'.[212] This vision was shared by numerous Liberal and Radical politicians, such as Henry Richard and Grant Duff, who traced back to Cobden the ideal of a free-trading, pacific, and even a federal Europe. In this mood of liberal optimism, many of Cobden's hopes in free trade, peace, and public opinion seemed near fulfilment.[213]

---

[208]   Morley, *Cobden*, vol. 2, 404.
[209]   Cobden to Chevalier, 5 Nov. 1864, in ibid. 450. For 'Mancunian' influence in this crisis, see K. A. P. Sandiford, 'The British Cabinet and the Schleswig-Holstein Crisis, 1863–4', *History* 58 (1973), 360–83.
[210]   J. E. T. Rogers (ed.), *Speeches on Questions of Public Policy by John Bright* (1869), 331–2 (Birmingham, 18 Jan. 1865). For Radical self-deception in this view, see J. P. Parry, *The Rise and Fall of Liberal Government in Victorian Britain* (1993), 190–1.
[211]   See below, 302–3.
[212]   Above, 98. For similar ideas, see Mallet's friend, Grant Duff, *Miscellanies*, 94–113.
[213]   In 1865, amidst British signs of liberal optimism, an Anglo-French Working-Men's Exhibition celebrated free trade and peace at the Crystal Palace, while the foundation-stone of the new Blackfriars' Bridge in July 1865 contrasted profound peace 'when the former restrictions of commerce have been removed, and by the adoption of free trade, those separate interests which divided nations have been

This liberal vision was not a British peculiarity, but the cynosure of a generation of European intellectuals, statesman, diplomats, and democrats as diverse as Chevalier, Bunsen, Napoleon III, and Mazzini. Ideas of free trade, democracy, and peace had been promoted in a series of temporary leagues and associations, which built on J. B. Say's lesser-known law, 'that the theory of markets will necessarily scatter the seeds of concord and peace'.[214] Most of such seeds fell on stony ground, for example the idea promoted in 1866 of a European Congress for tariff reform, which was stopped in its tracks by the Austro-Prussian War.[215] But other movements, such as Passy's Ligue Internationale et Permanent de la Paix, set up in 1867, acted as an impressive testament to the body of continental liberal, pacifist sentiment, broadly in line with 'the spirit of Cobden'.[216] Other important organs of opinion acquired a sensible appeal, for example the International Social Science Association, active between 1862 and 1865, described by Goldman as 'a liberal forum . . . an amalgamation of constitutionalism, republicanism, anti-clericalism, and above all, free trade'.[217] Similar ideas also suffused more pedestrian associations, such as those for decimalization, or even an international currency, as an appropriate sequel to free trade, 'a new step in the *rapprochement* of nations and the spread of civilization'.[218]

For most of these groups Cobden remained a beacon, one of the few British statesmen who left his name undarkened on the European horizon. He was appreciated above all as 'the international man', the antithesis both of Palmerston's John Bullish image and of continental 'chauvinisme'.[219] For Bunsen, Cobden in 1860 had become 'the first diplomatist of the world', but he also acted as a model for Emile Ollivier, the creator of Napoleon's liberal empire, for whom 'To be Cobden would be greater and would suit me better than to be Robert Peel.'[220] As a European

---

happily bridged over'. Farrar, 'Richard Cobden', ch. 19; R. Coningsby to Mrs Cobden, 28 July 1865, CP Add. MS 6025; D. Nevill, *My Own Times* (1912), 279–80.

[214] Quoted in E. Silberner, *The Problem of War in Nineteenth-Century Economic Thought* (Princeton, 1946), 83.

[215] This idea was floated in Britain by the Newcastle businessman Allhusen, closely involved in Anglo-Austrian negotiations and a member of the Newcastle committee of the Association Internationale pour la Suppression des Douanes, set up in Belgium in 1863; the Congress proposal had also been endorsed by Chevalier. Allhusen to Layard, 23 Apr. 1866; Layard to Cowley, 25 Apr. 1866, Layard Papers, Add. MS 39119, fos. 499, 502, 541; Allhusen to Layard, 9 and 11 May 1866, ibid., Add. MS 39120, fos. 83, 108.

[216] For Passy's debt to Cobden, see 'Notes by F. Passy', for Mrs J. Cobden-Unwin, *c*.1907, in CP 301, WSRO. See, too, E. Potonié's Ligue du Bien Public, *c*.1858–9, in S. E. Cooper, *Patriotic Pacifism. Waging War on War in Europe, 1815–1914* (New York, 1991), 206, 213.

[217] L. Goldmann, 'The Social Science Association', *Past and Present*, 114 (1987), 153.

[218] F. S. L. Lyons, *Internationalism in Europe, 1815–1914* (1963); Henderson, *Common Market*, 56–63; Searle, *Entrepreneurial Politics*, 174–6; W. S. Jevons, *The Papers and Correspondence of W. S. Jevons*, ed. R. D. C. Black (7 vols, 1972–81), vol. 7, 75.

[219] Thus, McCullagh Torrens in an early appreciation sought to 'portray him rather as a European statesman', to Mrs Cobden, 26 Sept. 1865, CP Add. MS 43677; 'Richard Cobden', *British Quarterly Review*, 43 (Jan. 1866); below, 146–7.

[220] Bunsen, *Memoirs*, 11, 526; E. Ollivier, *Journal, 1846–60*, ed. T. Zeldin and A. Troisier de Diaz (1961), vol. 1, 424. See, too, Hobson, *Cobden*, 272–7.

statesman, Cobden was lamented in many of those cities in which he had been fêted in 1846: Paris, Madrid, Milan, Turin, and Berlin.[221] For European liberals in the later 1860s, 'Mr Cobden's name signifies more in the world at large than that of any English statesman . . . an emblem . . . which is still rampant and zealous and successful.'[222]

Britain remained, therefore, the leading focus of attention for European free traders, whose aspirations were, if anything, to be increased by the death of Palmerston in October 1865. But three blemishes clouded the Cobdenite world-view, shadows whose growth would ultimately dim and dissipate those aspirations in Britain, Europe, and the Empire. First, the territorial expansion of Britain under Palmerston had created in the East a magnet which threatened her European vocation. This not only presaged Britain's future as Disraeli's 'Asiatic power', but also portended the growing expenditure, corruption, and military influence most feared by Cobdenites such as Bright and Mallet.[223]

Second, the dismantling of imperial regulation by the Whigs in the 1840s now turned upon free trade itself in the self-governing colonies. Thus, in Canada rising tariffs in the later 1850s culminated in the Galt Tariff of 1859, for even if this was primarily fiscal in intent, it was associated with a growing protectionist rhetoric, and embodied a strong, if incidental, protection to native industry.[224] Against this, the Colonial Office and British commercial bodies could only impotently protest.[225] Followed too by the ending of the Elgin Reciprocity Treaty in 1866, Canada had established the preconditions for her 'National Policy' in the 1870s. In a similar vein, in the Antipodes a 'democratic' protectionist movement in Victoria asserted

[221]   Uniquely for an Englishman, Cobden earned his place in the *Panthéon des Illustres Françaises au XIXième siècle*, ed. V. Frond (vol. 16, Paris, n.d., 1865?); Frond also published separately but unprofitably his homage *À Richard Cobden* (Paris, 1865); D. Carino, Royal Tuscan Academy of Arts and Manufactures, 30 Apr. 1865, CP 280; *L'Économiste Belge*, 8 Apr. 1865 (for whom Cobden embodied the spirit of the age, 'les qualités diverses d'une génération à la fois positive et ardente, pacifique et audacieuse'); for Cobden held up as an example to Berlin artisans, F. von Holtzendorff, *Richard Cobden. Ein Vortrag, gehalten im Berliner Handwerkerverein* (Berlin, 1866); CP 762, Bound vol. from Free Traders of Spain in honour of Cobden, presented to Mrs Cobden, 4 June 1866, CP 762, WSRO; in Vienna, a street was named after Cobden, C. Helm to Mrs Cobden, 3 May 1865, CP 772, WSRO.

[222]   Faucher to Morier, 7 July 1869, Morier Papers, Box 34. See, too, Castorina, 'Richard Cobden', ch. 4 (3). For adverse European views of Palmerston, see Steele, *Palmerston*, 275.

[223]   e.g. Morier to Lady Salisbury, 5 Nov. 1867, Morier papers, Box 33. This followed Cobden's own fears concerning British policy in China and Japan, e.g. Cobden to E. Alexander, 30 Nov. 1863, Cobden–Alexander letters, Bodleian Library, MS Don. e. 123. See, too, M. Taylor, 'Imperium et Libertas?: Rethinking the Radical critique of imperialism during the nineteenth century', *Journal of Imperial and Commonwealth History*, 19 (1991), 1–23.

[224]   The Galt Tariff did not become a major focus of debate, but its retrogressive nature was noted by the *Morning Star*, 17 Jan. 1860; see, too, Cobden to Gladstone, 25 Feb. 1862, GP, Add. MS 44136, fo. 178.

[225]   B. Forster, *A Conjunction of Interests: Business, Politics and Tariffs, 1825–1879* (Toronto, 1986); D. B. Swinfen, *Imperial Control of Colonial Legislation*; E. Porritt, *Fiscal and Diplomatic Freedom of the British Overseas Dominions* (Oxford, 1922); id., *Sixty Years' of Protection in Canada, 1846–1907* (1908, MacMillans for the Cobden Club); Redford, *Manchester Merchants*, vol. 2, 101; F. D. Munsell, *The Unfortunate Duke: Henry Pelham, Fifth Duke of Newcastle, 1811–1864* (Columbia, Missouri, 1985), 256.

itself against 'those who regulate the fiscal policy of Downing St . . . who at this time [1866] appear to have no other God to worship than an utter free trade policy'.[226] But however much 'the Manchester idea' seemed 'to pervade the mind of Edward Cardwell', the British Government was impotent to prevent the Victorian Tariff of 1866, which signalled a protectionist trend in Australia against which only New South Wales stood firm under the influence of the 'Cobden of Australia', Henry Parkes.[227]

If, at the periphery, colonial autonomy endangered the free trade empire, in Europe Prussian autocracy proved a more immediate and substantial threat. Above all, the Austro-Prussian War of 1866 not only marked a decisive failure of arbitration in what Gladstone saw as an ideal opportunity, but war in Europe presaged growing military budgets, always the death-knell of free traders' hopes. Even so, in the short term the war of 1866 was not entirely nugatory in its impact, for it spurred on some free traders to more urgent efforts to achieve a tariff-free Europe.[228] In the wake of war and nationalism, the British diplomat Morier revived the earlier idea of turning the Paris Exhibition of 1867 into a European Congress devoted to international co-operation on tariffs.[229] He appealed, with his usual self-dramatization, 'pas comme agent diplomatique . . . mais comme Européen . . . comme disciple de Cobden et croyant zélé de l'église internationale' to Benedetti, the French Ambassador at Berlin, to organize this event. Such a Congress, under Napoleon III's presidency would, he urged, provide a powerful counter to the growth of militarism, and would substitute international dependence for national independence, 'removing artificial and mischievous obstructions to free exchange of products . . . and [framing] a general European compact of co-operation in this great cause'.[230] This failed to draw Napoleon III, for whom, in the wake of Sadowa, army reform seemed more urgent than tariff reform.

By 1866, therefore, the power of the Prussian army, under the direction of Bismarck, seemed the most potent solvent of Cobdenite aspirations cherished in Europe since 1846. Oddly, Bismarck himself had not escaped the indirect influence of Cobden's ideas in Germany[231] but his ideals in politics, as Morier pungently and prophetically declared, were hardly congruent with Cobden's philosophy:

---

[226] For this and the following quotation, see *Victorian Hansard*, 1866, 17 Apr. and 3 May, cited from La Nauze Papers, Box 2 Folder 6, Archives of Business and Labour, Australian National University. For the background, see S. Macintrye, *A Colonial Liberalism* (Melbourne, 1991).

[227] G. D. Patterson, *The Tariff in the Australian Colonies, 1860–1900* (Melbourne, 1968). Parkes had recognized the employment benefits of tariffs, but a meeting with Cobden in Sussex in the early 1860s recalled him to the ranks of the faithful. A. W. Martin, *Henry Parkes: A Biography* (Melbourne, 1980), 196; J. A. La Nauze, ' "That fatal, that mischievous passage": Henry Parkes and Protection, 1859–1866', *Australian Quarterly*, 19 (1947), 52–61.

[228] Mallet thus believed Britain should stand ready to 'come in again with a real power of intervention, whenever these Tariff questions in Europe are again matters of interest and as I believe they will be, of necessity'. To Layard, 12 June 1866, Layard Papers, Add. MS 39120, fo. 331.

[229] See above, 107.

[230] R. Wemyss, *Memoirs and Letters of the Rt. Hon. Sir Robert Morier* (2 vols, 1911), vol. 2, 92–7.

[231] G. S. Graham, 'Cobden's Influence on Bismarck', *Queen's Quarterly*, 38 (1931), 433–43.

when our great-grandchildren have to get up the history of the nineteenth century, they will to a certainty find Cobden labelled as the representative of the one doctrine—exchange of cotton goods and Christian love internationalism—and Bismarck as the representative of the opposite doctrine—exchange of hard knocks and blood and iron internationalism.[232]

Morier's prescience was often greater than his diplomatic judgement. In Bismarck's Europe the future was bleak for the 'gospel of St Cobden'. In Gladstone's Britain it would be less easily renounced.

[232] Wemyss, *Morier*, vol. 2, 140.

4

Free Trade and Liberal Politics, 1866–1886

The name and character of Mr Cobden, and the main ideas and views which he laboured so anxiously and so powerfully to spread, are elevated much above the level of mere party combinations, however just and honorable, and attach themselves directly to the common interests of mankind. They are entitled to universal acceptance, and if unhappily they are in fact embraced with few exceptions by the members of one party only, that circumstance is to be regarded with satisfaction in the interests of that party, but with the hope that others may gradually be brought within their influence.

Gladstone to T. B. Potter, 18 July 1866[1]

Take the last half-century. There have been various policies, commanding general assent; free trade—? Here Sir Orlando gave a kindly wave of his hand, showing that on behalf of his companion he was willing to place at the heart of the list a policy which had not always commanded his assent.

A. Trollope, *The Prime Minister* (1876), ch. 20.

COBDENITE foreign policy, Gladstonian fiscal politics, and Palmerstonian 'free trade imperialism' had all merged in the 'Age of Equipoise' as essential, if sometimes discordant, elements in a domestic political consensus. In this context, free trade had become almost 'an unspoken assumption', as protectionism retreated to the margins of politics after 1860. 'Not for one generation, but for the best part of two', Morley was to recall, 'his [Cobden's] political thought supplied both parties, more or less sincerely, with working principles and fighting watchwords, and was accepted as the system by which the strength of the nation could be secured.'[2] Thus, as Searle and others have shown, while some of the Radical entrepreneurial ambitions of the 1840s class politics had receded, the central goals of the free traders in fiscal and foreign policy had become the orthodoxy of the mid-Victorian state, ensuring the abandonment of privilege, extravagance, and corruption at home, and the promotion of commerce and free trade abroad.[3]

Yet if the world seemed safe for free trade in 1865, it soon faced vital challenges. Gladstonian fiscal politics were slowly to be undermined by rising public expendi-

---

[1] Cobden Papers, British Library (hereafter CP), Add. MS 43678, fo. 52.
[2] J. Morley, *Recollections* (2 vols, 1917), vol. 1, 143.
[3] G. R. Searle, *Entrepreneurial Politics in Mid-Victorian Britain* (Oxford, 1993), *passim*; A. Howe, *The Cotton Masters 1830–1860* (Oxford Historical Monographs: Oxford, 1984), 229–47.

ture, while still facing the Radical demand for the further abolition of indirect taxation. Implicit in the popular demand for 'the free breakfast table' was the threat, long suspected by Gladstone's critics, of heavier direct taxation on the propertied classes.[4] Some of the latter, not surprisingly, preferred to end the regime of 'free imports' by increasing customs duties, nor were they disquieted by the indirectly protective effects which some duties, as on spirits, might confer. Cobdenite foreign policy also receded, with 'free trade, peace, and goodwill' challenged abroad by Bismarck's war machine and tariff barriers, and at home by the demand for an aggressive commercial diplomacy, deploying the tools of reciprocity treaties and retaliatory tariffs. Even the ramshackle Palmerstonian empire came under threat, from both the continuing Radical demand for its liquidation, but also from the new call for its closer integration within an imperial *Zollverein*, or a federated Anglo-Saxon commonwealth. Most of these challenges to free trade began as straws in the wind in the 1860s, but gradually merged into a well-orchestrated 'fair trade' campaign in the late 1870s and early 1880s, before achieving considerable respectability in their articulation before the 1886 Royal Commission on the Depression in Trade and Industry.[5] In this context Cobden himself became an anti-hero, whose predictions of an era of peace and free trade in Europe were widely attacked.[6] As a result, 'Cobdenism', a term which first gained widespread currency in the 1880s, was much more the construction of its enemies than of its friends.[7]

Such friends abounded in Gladstonian Britain, for the cult of Cobden was deep rooted and well organized. Above all, through the Cobden Club, Cobden's ideas were to be reworked extensively over the next two decades in ways that helped transform the gospel of the industrial bourgeoisie of the 1840s into a vital compo-

---

[4] See above, 98.

[5] B. H. Brown, *The Tariff Reform Movement in Great Britain, 1881–1895* (New York, 1943) remains the standard account. See, too, S. H. Zebel, 'Fair Trade: An English Reaction to the Breakdown of the Cobden Treaty System', *Journal of Modern History*, 12 (1940), 161–85.

[6] 'It is a lamentable fact that the name of Cobden is now seldom quoted in any controversy on the question [free trade], except by some adversary, who triumphantly points to the refutation of one of his too sanguine prophecies', S. Buxton, *Finance and Politics: An Historical Study, 1783–1885* (2 vols, 1888), vol. 1, 145.

[7] 'Cobdenisme' was coined in France in the 1840s; *The Morning Herald* spoke of 'Cobdenisms', 31 Mar. 1846, cited in D. Read, *Peel and the Victorians* (1987), 207; Overstone assailed 'Gladstone-Cobdenism' in 1871 (to Granville, 20 Jan. 1871, see D. P. O'Brien, *The Correspondence of Lord Overstone* (3 vols, Cambridge, 1971), vol. 3, 1205–6), while 'Cobdenism' seems to have been first used singly by J. M. Stuart in the Cobden Club's *European Treaties of Commerce* (1875), 98. See, too, *Worcester Journal*, 20 June 1885. The first attribution in *OED* is to W. J. Harris, *National Review*, Nov. 1887, 311. For Harris, a leading Protectionist author, see J. R. Fisher, 'Public Opinion and Agriculture, 1875–1900', unpublished Ph.D. thesis, University of Hull (1972), 240 ff. G. Saintsbury more positively noted, '*Manchesterthum* and Cobden must always be closely connected; indeed Cobdenism would be perhaps a more correct and certainly a less invidious name for the thing', *Manchester* (1887), 154–5. 'Cobdenic' was first used, hostilely, by the disillusioned League lecturer Alexander Somerville in 1853 (see above, 6), but approvingly by Morier and others in the 1860s and 1870s.

nent of popular Liberalism, a 'living force in the public issues of the present hour', as the *Quarterly Review* noted in 1882.[8] Cobden's posthumous reputation, moreover, saw the idol of the Manchester School transmuted into a popular 'hero', the successor of Cromwell, Wilberforce, and Cobbett.[9] In these ways, Cobdenism did not become a frozen ideology inherited from the League, but a revitalized creed, whose renewed dissemination helped decisively to inoculate the late-Victorian electorate against the threats of fair trade and tariff reform. Free trade had become an essential part of popular identity, the firmest link between the 'old' Radicalism and 'new' Liberalism.[10]

This diffusion of the Cobdenite variant within Liberal politics needs, however, to be understood against a much broader attachment of Victorian opinion to free trade. First, if Cobden supplanted Peel as a popular symbol of free trade, the Peelite model remained influential, particularly among 'the statesmen in disguise', the Victorian bureaucracy. Here Peelite–Gladstonian finance, the guarantee of the minimal and 'knaveproof' state, became the central tenet of institutional loyalties, inherited by Treasury officials such as Lingen, Hamilton, Mowatt, and Murray.[11] In this, little separated the Treasury from the Board of Trade, although the latter was in some ways attached, as in the 1830s, to a more strident version of free trade, with men such as Calcraft, Hobart, Farrer, and Giffen all self-confessed Cobdenites.[12] Central to the aims of this group was the desire to limit government finance to a few indirect taxes of a non-protectionist nature. This identity of aims linking Peel, Gladstone, and Cobden, was well put by Mallet at the Board of Trade: 'It was, I believe, Cobden who put the thought into my head that the only effectual method of forcing governments to economy was to cut off irrevocably some important fiscal resource.' In this, Mallet detected 'the financial genius of Peel & Gladstone. The latter has not I think originated any great principle. He has merely ably carried on Peel's policy.'[13] By 1870 this group looked with some satisfaction upon the success of Peelite–Gladstonian finance, for a mere five duties (spirits, sugar, tea, tobacco, and wine) now raised some 95 per cent of all customs revenue, a proportion that remained largely constant, even after the abolition of the sugar

---

[8]   Vol. 153, 553.

[9]   E. Biagini, *Liberty, Retrenchment and Reform: Popular Liberalism in the Age of Gladstone, 1860–1880* (Cambridge, 1992), 42; M. Finn, *After Chartism: Class and Nation in English Radical Politics, 1848–1874* (Cambridge, 1993), 238, 258, 311.

[10]   See, too, A. Howe, 'Towards "The Hungry Forties": Free Trade in Britain, *c.*1880–1906', in E. Biagini (ed.), *Citizenship and Community* (Cambridge, 1996), 193–218; E. Biagini and A. J. Reid (eds.), *Currents of Radicalism* (Cambridge, 1991), *passim*; P. Joyce, *Visions of the People* (Cambridge, 1991) for thoughts on language, free trade, and radical continuity, esp. 61–70, 287.

[11]   H. Roseveare, *The Treasury: The Evolution of a British Institution* (1969), ch. 7.

[12]   See *DNB* and Calcraft Family Papers, Dorset Record Office, D86/F25; T. C. Farrer (ed.), *Some Farrer Memorials* (privately printed, 1923), and Farrer Papers, Surrey Record Office; Giffen Papers, BLPES; above 43 for Hobart.

[13]   Original emphasis, Mallet to Grant Duff, 4 Nov. 1868, Grant Duff Papers, MS Eur F234/37, India Office Library.

duty in 1874.[14] As recently as 1869 the corn registration duty imposed after Repeal had itself been abolished. This had represented for J. S. Mill 'the last remaining shred of protectionism' within the British tariff.[15] The total number of tariff duties had thus diminished from about a thousand in 1842 to a score or so in 1870; by the 1890s, they were confined to cocoa, coffee, chicory, tea, tobacco, wine, beer, spirits, and playing cards.[16] One of Gladstone's vital allies in this process of fiscal reform, the Peelite Sir Thomas Fremantle, on retiring from the Board of Customs in 1873, thus recounted the success of his own efforts to 'advance the commercial interests of this country, by carrying out in detail constant and extensive reductions and abolitions of import duties, and during my chairmanship at the Customs relief has been afforded to the Taxpayer by reductions and abolitions of duties to the extent of £19,623,046 per annum'.[17]

Despite this marked success, for some the minimal state had yet to be realized, with their targets variously set on the sugar and tea duties, the 'free breakfast table', and the further reform of customs administration.[18] Here, a free trade policy conjoined relief for the working-class consumer with the prospective abolition of hostile tariffs abroad and the avoidance of what Mallet feared as 'national isolation'. But, as we will see, the ramifications of fiscal free trade for foreign policy were complex, for the fewer the import duties that remained, the more reluctant were the Treasury and the Customs to abandon them by means of commercial negotiations. On the other hand, the links between free trade and the minimal state were highly prized, not least for limiting the ability of the state to intervene in the domestic economy, an ideal clearly expressed by this generation of civil servants and epitomized for general consumption in works such as Farrer's *The State in its relation to Trade* (1883). Heterodox opinions were rarely to challenge this free trade monopoly of official wisdom before Chamberlain's tenure of the Colonial Office in the 1890s.[19]

Nor was academic and expert opinion any less uniform than the views of the civil servants it had helped shape. As the studies of Kadish and others have shown, free trade ideas were both vigorously and tenaciously propounded by economists in

[14]   *Statistical Abstract of the UK, 1866–1880* (1881 [C.- 2935]), 12.

[15]   J. S. Mill to Lalande, 2 May 1869, in *The Collected Works of J. S. Mill*, ed. F. E. L. Priestley, et al. (33 vols, Toronto, 1963–91), vol. 17, 1595–6; cf. J. Prest, 'A Large or a Small Amount? Revenue and the Nineteenth-Century Corn Laws', *HJ*, 39 (1996), 467–78.

[16]   Numbers vary according to subdivisions of tariffs; Levi, with subdivisions, notes 53 duties in 1875; cf. 1,098 in 1844, 396 in 1855, 133 in 1865, and 65 in 1869; *The History of British Commerce* (2nd edn., 1880), 491, 417 n.; *Statistical Abstract of the UK* (1894), 26–7; with subdivisions, 40 duties were in operation in 1894.

[17]   Fremantle to Gladstone, 26 Nov. 1873, GP, Add. MS 44139, fo. 299. For policy details, see extensive Fremantle papers, Buckinghamshire Record Office.

[18]   Mallet to Grant Duff, 4 Nov. 1868; L. G. Rylands (ed.), *Correspondence and Speeches of Mr Peter Rylands MP* (2 vols, 1890), letters 35, 38, 52, 101 [1869–71].

[19]   For one exception among Colonial Governors, Sir Anthony Musgrave's *Economic Fallacies: Free Trade v. Protection* (Adelaide, 1875). This earned a swift reproof from Kimberley, the Colonial Secretary. See C. D. W. Goodwin, *Economic Inquiry in Australia* (Durham, NC, 1966), 541–2.

Victorian Oxbridge and in the newer metropolitan and provincial universities.[20] At times, they assumed strongly 'Cobdenite' expression, notably through Thorold Rogers, at both Oxford and King's College, London, where he found a fellow spirit in Leone Levi, Professor of Commerce and Commercial Law.[21] At Cambridge in the 1870s, Henry Fawcett supplied a popular and orthodox defence of free trade to counter emerging fair trade arguments.[22] From the universities there also issued a succession of free trade evangelists, such as Toynbee, Leadam, and de Gibbins. From such lecturers free trade loyalties would extend deeply into working-class education through the university extension movement.[23] Deviant notes (until the challenge of the historical economists of Birmingham, Cambridge, and the LSE in the early twentieth century) were rare, the most damaging sounded by J. S. Mill's support for infant industries, which Cobden believed had done more harm than the remainder of Mill's writings had done good.[24] Outside the universities, the Political Economy Club, bringing together civil servants, dons, and City bankers, also remained an important and influential bastion of orthodoxy, despite its inclusion of occasional heretics such as H. R. Grenfell.[25]

The formation of popular opinion followed very similar lines. Since the 1840s, school textbooks had been strongly liberal in economic teaching, and this showed no tendency to waver later.[26] Mechanics' institutes, mutual improvement societies, and working men's clubs also saw few effective challenges to free trade views, as any Chartist leanings towards protectionism were eradicated from working-class political economy.[27] Equally, by the 1860s trade unions and the co-operative societies were bulwarks of Cobdenite and Gladstonian views.[28] If this working-class free trade tradition had its origins in the Paineite Radical critique of the state, by the 1860s its characteristic beliefs in low taxes, retrenchment, and peace—'the moral economy of free trade'—left it virtually indistinguishable from Gladstonian

[20] A. Kadish, *The Oxford Economists in the Late Nineteenth Century* (Oxford Historical Monographs: Oxford, 1982); id., *Apostle Arnold: The Life and Times of Arnold Toynbee* (Durham, NC, 1984); id., *Historians, Economics, and Economic History* (1990); A. Kadish and K. Tribe (eds.), *The Market for Political Economy: The Advent of Economics in British University Culture, 1850–1905* (1993).

[21] Kadish, *Historians*, 3–34; F. J. C. Hearnshaw, *The Centenary History of King's College, London* (1929), 243–6, 310.

[22] P. Deane, 'Henry Fawcett: The Plain Man's Economist', in L. Goldmann (ed.), *The Blind Victorian. Henry Fawcett and British Liberalism* (Cambridge, 1989), esp. 98, 102–5.

[23] Kadish, *Historians*, 72–5, 77–87.

[24] For Cobden reported by Mallet, M. Grant Duff, *Notes from a Diary, 1889–91* (2 vols, 1901), vol. 1, 99–100 [28 June 1889]. Mill's views were 'greatly shaken' by subsequent experience; letter to A. Michie, 7 Dec. 1868, in *Works*, vol. 16, 1515.

[25] *Minutes, Proceedings etc.* (1921); Goldmann (ed.), *The Blind Victorian*, 181.

[26] Above 32; J. R. Shackleton, 'Jane Marcet and Harriet Martineau: Pioneers of Economic Education', *History of Education*, 19 (1990), 283–97.

[27] e.g. Kadish and Tribe, *Political Economy*, 93–4, for the East End Adam Smith Club, *c.*1879. Popular critics of free trade struggled to avoid the peril of reaction which they saw behind the reciprocity movement in the late 1860s. See, e.g., *National Reformer*, 3 and 10 Oct., 5 and 19 Dec. 1869.

[28] E. Biagini, 'British Trade Unions and Popular Political Economy, 1860–80', *Historical Journal*, 30 (1987), 811–40; id., *Liberty, Retrenchment and Reform*, esp. 142 for Cobden as a co-operative hero.

Liberalism, as Biagini has shown.[29] Only the most enthusiastic fiscal reformers such as Charles Tennant looked forward to the total abolition of customs houses, 'this shameful system which is robbing the working-classes of 2/3 of their wages of labour'.[30] But for Tennant, as for other popular Radicals such as Noble and Holyoake, it was Cobden, rather than Peel, who 'more than any other helped tear down Protection and Monopoly and to set up Liberty and Free Trade', and working men were increasingly keen to appropriate Cobden as their own, not their employers', exemplar.[31]

The secular religion of free trade therefore took root at both élite and popular levels. But within the context of Liberal politics, the economic, moral, and political ideas of Cobden became the property of the Cobden Club, an intellectual colony loosely modelled on the Fox Club of the early nineteenth century. As an ideological lobbying group, proclaimed in 1866 as 'henceforth an English institution',[32] its activities helped reinforce the 'Cobdenic' message at a time when it was coming under threat both at home and abroad. It is the diffusion of this popular message, and its construction as an ideological system against which to judge Liberal fiscal, foreign, and social policies, that will be the primary concern of this chapter.

'The Church of Cobden': The Cobden Club, 1866–76[33]

The importance of the Cobden Club as the epicentre of Liberal values remains difficult to gauge. For while German protectionists (and some British ones) believed its influence to be all-powerful within the Gladstonian Cabinet,[34] to many at home it seemed little more than the private worship of Cobden by a hard core of devotees led by the none too respected Thomas Bayley Potter.[35] Modern opinion implies assent to the latter view, for the Club has been almost completely ignored

---

[29] Biagini, *Liberty*, 93–138; see, too, Finn, *After Chartism*, 238, for the Reform League lamenting Cobden's death at its first meeting.

[30] C. Tennant, *The People's Blue Book* (4th edn., 1872), 136; see, too, in somewhat less Radical vein, S. M. Peto, *Taxation: Its Levy and Expenditure: Past and Present* (1863), 399. From Liverpool, *The Financial Reformer* (1858–1906) continued to preach its gospel of strict economy and direct taxation.

[31] Tennant, *The People's Blue Book* (4th edn., 1872), 457–8; for Noble, see *DNB*, and G. H. Perris (later, secretary Cobden Club), preface, J. Noble, *Facts for Politicians* (rev. edn., 1892); *The Papers and Correspondence of W. S. Jevons*, ed. R. D. C. Black (7 vols, 1972–81), vol. 3, 269, for the defence of Cobden by a Manchester housepainter in 1866. Frederic Harrison had in 1863 noted the importance of Cobden and Bright as leaders of the London working men, Harrison to Cobden, 26 Feb. 1863, CP, Add. MS 52416, fos. 11–12.

[32] *Morning Star*, 23 July 1866.

[33] The phrase is Maine's, *Pall Mall Gazette*, 10 Jan. 1872.

[34] C. J. Fuchs, *The Trade Policy of Great Britain and her Colonies Since 1860* (1905), 178–88; Anon., *Der Cobden-Club* (Berlin, 1881); cf. E. Nasse, 'Der Cobdenclub und die deutsche Waarenausfuhr', *Jahrbücher für Nationalökonomie und Statistik*, new ser. 4 (1882), 409–60; Morley, *Recollections*, vol. 1, 167; E. Somes Saxton, *Home Trade v. Foreign Trade. A Tract for the Times* (Workman's Association for the Defence of British Industry, 1886). Saxton was the grandson of the protectionist shipowner of the 1840s, Joseph Somes.

[35] For Granville, 'the foolometer', to Gladstone, 9 Feb. 1884, in A. Ramm (ed.), *The Political Correspondence of Mr Gladstone and Lord Granville, 1876–1886* (2 vols, Oxford, 1962) (hereafter *GG Corr. 1876–86*), vol. 2, 155; 'The Thomas Potter Club', for the 'glorification and social advancement of

by historians of Liberalism and the Liberal Party.[36] Yet the following sections will attempt to reveal the centrality of the Club between 1866 and 1886 in defining the ideological context of Liberal policy-making, and its not insignificant impact on party electoral fortunes in the short and long terms.

The origins of the Cobden Club lay in a suggestion by Thorold Rogers to Thomas Bayley Potter in March 1866, following a conversation between Bright and Rogers.[37] Bright himself played little part in the Club whose value he doubted, but Potter, Cobden's successor as MP for Rochdale, enthusiastically took up Rogers's suggestion.[38] Following his active part in the Union and Emancipation Society, Potter had already sought J. S. Mill's help in setting up a Political Science Association, on the lines of the Social Science Association, and the Cobden Club now took on this model, as a 'public arena for the discussion of general principles and their appplication'.[39] In the bracing atmosphere of parliamentary reform, Potter successfully canvassed support among Liberal MPs, while Gladstone took the chair at the first dinner of the Club on 21 July 1866.[40] Regular committee meetings began in February 1867, with Potter's co-adjutants at this point including Lord Houghton, Viscount Amberley, W. E. Baxter, Thomas Bazley, and Henry Fawcett.[41] By March 1867, 350 members had enrolled and an outline of the Club's future

---

the respectable member for Rochdale and for the enlargement of his acquaintance with the nobility and gentry of Great Britain and the Continent', *The World*, 18 July 1887.

[36] *A History of the Cobden Club* was published in 1939. See, too, Brown, *Tariff Reform Movement*, 4 ff., H. J. Hanham, *Elections and Party Management: Politics in the time of Disraeli and Gladstone* (1959; 1978 edn., Hassocks), 101, and H. Perkin, 'Land Reform and Class Conflict', in J. Butt and I. F. Clarke (eds.), *The Victorians and Social Protest* (Newton Abbot, 1973), esp. 200–1. A. Ramm confuses the Cobden Club with the Political Economy Club, *Sir Robert Morier: Envoy and Ambassador in the Age of Imperialism, 1876–1893* (Oxford, 1973), 4 n. 1, as does J. W. T. Gaston, 'The Free Trade Diplomacy Debate and the Victorian European Common Market Initiative', *Canadian Journal of History*, 22 (1987), 67.

[37] Cobden Club Minute Books (hereafter CCM), vol. 1, flyleaf, Cobden Papers, 1185, WSRO; *Rochdale Observer*, 30 Mar. 1890. The Club did not aspire to become a permanent social centre, but was first housed in the Reform Club and later by the National Liberal Club (CCM, 10 July 1873, 12 July 1884). It is noted in T. H. S. Escott, *Club Makers and Club Members* (1914), 232; G. J. Ivey (ed.), *Clubs of the World* (2nd edn., 1880), 25.

[38] R. A. J. Walling (ed.), *The Diaries of John Bright* (1930), 318: 'I do not see the use of the Club, and I feel too sad at the loss I have sustained to enable me to enjoy evenings of gossip and almost of frivolity in connexion with any institution bearing his name' (1 Apr. 1868). See, too, Bright to Potter, 3 Apr. 1874, 'You are its life and soul . . . I have not been able to see how it could be permanently sustained and made useful as you wish it to be.' T. B. Potter Letters, Manchester Central Library.

[39] Mill to Potter, 17 Mar. 1864, Potter Letters, printed in Mill, *Works*, vol. 15, 683; J. Thompson to Potter, 7 Mar. 1864, Potter Letters. Bright proved less keen: 'Unfortunately these societies become the field in which men smitten with personal vanity disport themselves, & they run to frivolity & waste. The 'Social Science Congress' is a striking case in point, and I know not that any real good has yet come from its labours.' Bright to Potter, 21 Mar. 1864, Bright Papers, William Perkins Library, Duke University.

[40] *The Gladstone Diaries* (GD), vol. 6, 453 [21 July 1866]: '. . . It was really a true and fine theme'; Potter to Gladstone, 28 June, 17 July, 1 Aug. 1866, GP, Add. MS 44282, fos. 7, 11–14.

[41] *The Amberley Papers*, ed. B. and H. R. Russell (2 vols, 1937, new edn., 1966), vol. 1, 521, [misdated] 15 July 1866; vol. 2, 11.

prepared.[42] Political dinners were to provide its most obvious public face well into the Edwardian period, the occasion for the rallying of the faithful and a rousing restatement of the Cobdenite faith by Liberal leaders, including Gladstone, Chamberlain, Morley, and Churchill.[43] But such a 'mere annual orgie' [*sic*] was insufficient for genuine devotees, and the Club soon extended its aspirations beyond propaganda by dinner to the forging of 'an instrument for diffusing good opinions'.[44] Initially, this took the form of distributing the edition of Cobden's *Political Writings* initiated by Mrs Cobden and to which free traders such as Grant Duff looked in the expectation that 'his general political reputation will rise considerably . . . and his body of doctrine, if not exempt from heresy, will be found far more wide-ranging and complete than it is often thought to be'.[45] This was soon followed by an exemplary essay by Louis Mallet, the 'intellectual director' of the Club, setting out 'the chief lines on which should be built, for some time to come, the policy of this nation'.[46] In 1870 Bright and Thorold Rogers published through the Club their two-volume edition of Cobden's speeches, providing for some 'the most unanswerable arguments in favour of the great principle of freedom of trade and industry', but the occasion of some tension between Mrs Cobden and the Club.[47] More widely, by April 1869 a literary subcommittee was actively organizing essay competitions and publishing a variety of free trade works, ranging from the weighty and influential *Systems of Land Tenure in Various Countries* (ed. J. W. Probyn, 1870) to pungent tracts like that of 'A Disciple of Richard Cobden' (the diplomat R. B. D. Morier), *Letters on Commercial Treaties, Free Trade and Internationalism* (1870).

The primary impetus behind the Club at this point was not so much a Whig-like veneration of a past leader, nor was its purpose that of a metropolitan base for free trade MPs and provincial fellow spirits which the Free Trade Club of the 1840s had briefly provided. Rather, it sought to cement the perceived change in the Liberal Party with regard to Cobden's political views, and to develop those beliefs as the

---

[42] 'How much you must be gratified by the proceedings of the Cobden Club. There could not have been a better plan devised for keeping his memory fresh in the recollections of his country and at the same time perpetuating his opinions', wrote F. W. Chesson to Mrs Cobden, 6 Mar. 1867, CP, Add. MS 6031, WSRO.

[43] Cf. the view that the Club 'has continued to establish for itself a reputation for good eating and gourmandizing which would have astounded the Apostle of Free Trade and Peace', *The City Lantern* (Manchester), 24 May 1878.

[44] Mill to Chadwick, 9 Jan. 1868, in *Works*, vol. 16, 1350. Mallet was highly critical of the Club's start, condemning it as 'a gigantic failure, and worse, a fraud' in September 1866; by January 1867 he feared 'it is a blind business; no-one seems to have an idea what it is to do or be and the list contains names as little identified with Cobden as possible', Mallet to Morier, 1 Sept. 1866 and 16 Jan. 1867 [misdated 1866], Morier Papers, box 33.

[45] M. E. Grant Duff, *Studies in European Politics* (Edinburgh, 1866), 373.

[46] L. Mallet, *The Political Opinions of Richard Cobden* (1869), which had first appeared in the *North British Review*, Mar. 1867; Mallet to Grant Duff, 24 Aug. 1866, Grant Duff Papers, MS Eur. F 234/37; *Cobden Club Report*, 1882; Grant Duff, *The Teachings of Richard Cobden* (1871), 8.

[47] Levi, *British Commerce* [19]; Mrs Cobden, incomplete to n.d. *c.*1870, CP, Add. MS 6030, WSRO.

touchstone for Liberal policy at home, while also fostering free trade as an international creed.[48] In some ways, therefore, it matched Cobden's own aspiration in the 1830s for Smithian societies, devoted to 'the spread of liberal and just views of political science', at home and abroad.[49] The Club published numerous free trade tracts by foreign authors such as David Wells, Jules Simon, and Erwin Nasse, although the Franco-Prussian War put an end to more ambitious schemes for an International Free Trade Congress, which Dilke and Mallet had proposed in 1870.[50] The Club's impact was also restricted by a desire not to embarrass the Liberal government on issues of current policy. For example, in 1869 it rejected Goldwin Smith's suggestion that it should lay the *Alabama* case before some eminent jurist.[51] This left the Club to concentrate on the elucidation of future policy, above all the extension of Cobden's own unclear ideas on land reform, which remained a constant preoccupation for the next twenty years. The Club's importance in this period lies primarily in its contribution to Liberal ideology and the sustenance of the central beliefs of the Manchester School. If Gladstone was later to see himself as 'fundamentally a "Peel–Cobden man" ', Potter's vocation was to ensure that through the Club the mid-Victorian Liberal Party comprised 'Cobden–Gladstone men'.[52]

How well did Potter succeed? The first clue is provided by membership of the Club itself, even if this is in most cases only passive testimony of ideological commitment. Analysis of its composition suggests, above all, six types of member.[53] First, and central to the Club's *raison d'être*, one quarter of all members in 1875 were honorary members (204), qualified by 'some public service in the cause of free trade'.[54] Of these, the largest number (56) was drawn from the United States, with 36 from France, 26 from Germany and the Habsburg Empire, 37 from the remainder of Western Europe, 14 from Iberia, 8 from Northern Europe, 8 from Russia, and 5 from the British Colonies.[55] Partly as a result of Goldwin Smith's ties with the Club, America assumed an early importance, which was sustained by the enthusiasm for free trade of men such as D. A. Wells, although the vicissitudes of the policy in the United States produced more frustration than progress, and some

---

[48] J. E. T. Rogers, *The Free Trade Policy of the Liberal Party* (Manchester, 1868); Mallet to Duff, 30 Nov. 1868, Grant Duff Papers, MS Eur. F 234/37.

[49] *Political Writings*, 14. In like vein, on Cobden's death, van der Maeren had urged, instead of monuments, international institutions to spread Cobden's principles, *L'Économiste Belge*, 8 Apr. 1865.

[50] CCM, 11 Mar., 13 and 27 May, 10 and 17 June, 1, 7, 22 July 1870; Mill to Dilke, 28 Feb. 1870, *Works*, vol. 17, 1703. Mallet also ascribed the failure to the absorption of Cobden's followers by the Liberal Government, to Corr van der Maeren, 18 Nov. 1872 (copy), CP, Add. MS 43677, fo. 173.

[51] CCM, 17 Nov. 1869; 19 Apr. 1872; cf. Goldwin Smith to Potter, 1 Nov. 1869, CP, Add. MS 43677, fo. 166.

[52] H. C. G. Matthew, *The Liberal Imperialists* (Oxford Historical Monographs: Oxford, 1973), vii; Searle, *Entrepreneurial Politics*, 148–9.

[53] This analysis is based on *Cobden Club. List of Members* (1875), published with the Annual Report.

[54] CCM, 2 Feb. 1872.

[55] Also represented were Serbia (1), Brazil (2), Mexico (1), and Egypt (1). Nine honorary members were British, including Gladstone and C. P. Villiers.

honorary members, having reneged on the cause, had to be quietly dropped.[56] The rising tide of protectionism in the British colonies also made it imperative for the Club to keep open some channels for free trade ideas, and a considerable amount of attention was devoted to men such as Henry Parkes and the free traders of New South Wales.[57]

In the 1870s it was the European links of the Club that assumed greatest importance, bringing together a free trade intelligentsia of considerable distinction, including Michel Chevalier, de Molinari, Frederic Passy, Corr van der Maeren (the 'Cobden of Belgium'), E. Lavaleye, J. Faucher, and Marco Minghetti. As we have seen in Chapter 3, these illuminati were the stalwarts of other international bodies, such as the International Social Science Association of 1862–6, and free trade was an essential part of their vision of Europe, both in terms of domestic and international policy.[58] Yet the preponderance of French free traders is significant, a good index of the relative strength of free trade internationalism in the Europe of the 1870s. The Cobdenite credentials of some of these members was, of course, suspect, but basic criteria were upheld too, and Potter's idiosyncratic attempt to enrol Bismarck in 1876 was prevented.[59]

The second leading body of members was drawn from the ranks of the parliamentary Liberal Party—there were 103 in 1875. Interestingly, such members were recruited from all sections of the party. Adopting Parry's notion of Whig-Liberals, we find men such as Amberley, Houghton, Sir Henry James, and J. G. Dodson alongside Radicals and Dissenters such as J. J. Colman, J. G. McMinnies, and Samuel Morley.[60] We find both the residues of the evangelical free trade *mentalité*, and also the archetypal secular free traders such as Fawcett and Sir M. E. Grant Duff. The Celtic fringe was well represented, with twenty-nine MPs, the majority from Scotland, and a good number (nine) from Ireland. The membership included many former MPs, including a number recently defeated in the 1874 election, such

[56] D. A. Wells, *The Creed of Free Trade* (1875). He later vetted American members. See, too, Wells to L. Mallet, 11 Sept. 1885, Mallet Papers (in private hands); F. B. Joyner, *David Ames Wells, Champion of Free Trade* (Cedar Rapids, Iowa, 1939). Potter returned in optimistic vein after a trip to the United States in 1879 which had aroused much protectionist suspicion: Potter to Gladstone, 1 Dec. 1879, GP, Add. MS 44282; cf. E. P. Crapol, *America for the Americans: Economic Nationalism and Anglophobia in the late Nineteenth Century* (Westport, Conn., 1973), 28–38.

[57] Cobden Club to Henry Parkes, 18 Nov. 1873: 11, 13 Feb., 6 Mar., 9 May, 8 June, 1874; 9 June 1875: 23 July, 16 Sept. 1876; 1 Aug. 1877; 18 Aug. 1880, Parkes Papers, Mitchell Library, Sydney.

[58] Above, 107.

[59] R. Wemyss, *Memoirs and Letters of the Rt. Hon. Sir Robert Morier* (2 vols, 1911), vol. 2, 140–2. But Morier's strict principles would also have barred all English members save half a dozen. J. Faucher, one of the most active free traders in Germany and once Cobden's secretary, advised on candidates. In 1869 he thus held Otto Michaelis properly debarred, as 'guilty of imposing new taxes in the eyes of the people', Faucher to Morier, 12 June 1869. Morier Papers, Box 34. Michaelis was acceptable in 1871. For Faucher, see V. Hentschel, *Die Deutsche Freihändler* (Stuttgart, 1975), esp. 18, 68.

[60] J. Parry, *Democracy and Religion: Gladstone and the Liberal Party, 1867–1875* (Cambridge, 1986). The Club also collected the remnants of the Reform Party of the 1840s and 1850s, MPs such as G. Hadfield, J. A. Hardcastle, J. Otway, and G. Thompson: see M. Taylor, *The Decline of British Radicalism* (Oxford, 1995), Appendix 1, 351–5.

as the financier Somerset Beaumont, the Radical wire-manufacturer Peter Rylands, and the farmers' friend James Howard. Many young aspiring Liberal MPs also joined the Club, for example the brewer Edward North Buxton, the shipowner F. H. Evans, and the Glasgow merchant Stephen Mason. As a political training-ground, the Club offered some of the advantages that the Eighty Club would later provide.[61]

The third leading group comprised provincial businessmen, most obviously the relicts of the Anti-Corn Law League, drawn heavily from the textile industries, but with representatives of iron and steel, engineering, chemicals, brewing, and banking. Hereditary free trade allegiances marked families such as the Ashtons, Armitages, Buckleys, Cheethams, Masons, Platts, and Rylands in Lancashire, with Behrens, Illingworths, and Willans from Yorkshire.[62] Others such as E. K. Muspratt and C. Allhusen had been actively involved in the commercial diplomacy of the 1860s.[63] More up-to-date industrial types are notable, with the new model employers of the 1860s, Bass and Brassey, and self-conscious business politicians such as J. Whitwell, soon to be President of the Association of Chambers of Commerce. Also significant were the representatives of the communications revolution of the mid-century, the cosmopolitan capitalists such as Watkin and Peto in railway-building, and Pender in telegraphy.[64] The presence of City of London businessmen was greater than in the 1840s, with, for example, the merchant bankers George Goschen, Lionel and Nathan de Rothschild, the private banker Sir John Lubbock, the Australian merchants Alexander and William McArthur, and the City watch-seller, Sir John Bennett. The stockjobber George Webb Medley would become a leading light in the 1880s.[65]

The fourth group comprised academics, lawyers, and civil servants, part of the metropolitan intelligentsia with its Oxbridge outposts. Prominent academic Liberals included G. C. Brodrick, a leading writer for the Club and later Warden of Merton College, Oxford, the historian Sir John Acton, the Oxford mathematician H. J. S. Smith, and the Eton schoolmaster Oscar Browning.[66] Political economists

[61] Membership of the Club proved a distinct asset to Francis Channing when seeking a seat in East Northamptonshire in 1885, F. W. Channing, *Memories of Midland Politics* (1918), 7.

[62] For these families, See Howe, *Cotton Masters, passim*; for Willans, see F. W. Hirst, *In The Golden Days* (1947), 49 ff.

[63] E. K. Muspratt, *My Life and Work* (1917); above, 96, 103.

[64] Pender's presence well illustrates Thomas Hardy's perception of the telegraph, 'a machine which beyond everything may be said to symbolize cosmopolitan views and the intellectual and moral kinship of all mankind'. *A Laodicean* (1881), ch. 2; according to F. W. Chesson, in 1851 Cobden had urged Prince Albert that the profits of the Great Exhibition should go to an Atlantic telegraph, Chesson to Mrs Cobden, 29 Aug. 1865, CP, Add. MS 6031, WSRO.

[65] G. W. Medley, *Pamphlets and Addresses* (1899); Medley (1826–99), like the free trade publicist Mongredien, was also a well-known chessplayer, an association of ideas worth further exploration. Webb Medley prizes for economics are still awarded at Oxford.

[66] The Club included 17 of the academic Liberals who met at the Freemason's Tavern in 1864, 21 who belonged to the Century Club (1866–80), and 13 to the Radical Club (1871), C. Harvie, *The Lights of Liberalism: University Liberals and the Challenge of Democracy, 1860–86* (1976), 246–56, 261–2.

were represented not only by Thorold Rogers, but by Cliffe Leslie, and his successor as Professor of Political Economy at Queen's College, Belfast William Graham, as well as a former Professor of Political Economy at Dublin J. A. Lawson, later Solicitor-General for Ireland.[67] Among lawyers and legal reformers were Serjeant J. Simon, C. H. Hopwood, J. W. Probyn, and Sir Edward Sullivan.[68] Civil servants were fewer, but included the Cobdenite diplomats Morier, Mallet, and Odo Russell, as well as the Board of Trade official Sir Henry Lack, and Sir John Lambert from the Local Government Board.[69]

Fifth, one can single out extra-parliamentary Radicals, including publishers and editors such as A. W. Paulton, and Henry Rawson (of the *Morning Star*), as well as the suffrage activists James Beal and Edmond Beales, the tax abolitionist Thomas Briggs, London municipal reformer Mark Marsden, and the Italophiles W. H. Ashurst and William Shaen.[70] Thomas Briggs, for example, set up a Free Trade League in 1874 to campaign for the 'free breakfast table', repealing all taxes on food and so completing the work of 1846.[71] Here, there was an important overlap with groups such as the London Financial Reform Union, the Travelling Tax Abolition Committee, and the Workmen's Peace Association, keeping open useful channels of communication with the world of plebeian radicalism.[72]

Finally, the Cobden Club attracted, in a way the Anti-Corn Law League had never done, significant representation from the landed interest itself, with thirty-one peers among its members in 1875, including Clarendon, Ducie, Devonshire, and Westminster. The landed gentry were represented by former MPs J. S. Trelawney and Charles Colvile (who had 2,000 acres in Derbyshire), and C. S. Roundell of Yorkshire. In this category, too, we should include those who were intimately connected with the landed interest, for example the agriculturist James Caird, the nurseryman and corn merchant Augustus Mongredien, and Charles Wren Hoskyns, a leading writer on agriculture.

Such diverse groups were clearly drawn towards the Cobden Club by the esteem in which they, like Gladstone, had held its eponymous hero, 'perhaps', as Mill put it, 'the most perfectly honest man among all English politicians'.[73] To that extent,

---

[67] J. S. Mill had been a founding member.

[68] Perkin, 'Land Reform', 200–1.

[69] Lack served at the Board of Trade 1852–76, later at the Patents Office (1876–97). Author of *The French Treaty* (1861); see PRO BT 191 for official papers. Several officials were prominent in the Club only on leaving public service, for example two later chairmen, Farrer and Welby.

[70] For Beales, see Finn, *After Chartism*, 256; J. O. Baylen and N. J. Gossman, *Biographical Dictionary of Modern British Radicals, vol. 2 1830–1870* (Brighton, 1984).

[71] T. Briggs, *The Peacemaker: Free Trade, Free Labour, Free Thought, or Direct Taxation the True Principle of Political Economy* (1877), 2nd edn., *Poverty, Taxation and the Remedy* (1884); *The Beehive*, 29 Mar., 29 Oct. 1873, 31 Jan., 14 Mar. 1874. Briggs (1808–92) was later a keen follower of Henry George: *Financial Reformer*, May, 1892, 70–1.

[72] This level of politics has been well reconstructed in Biagini, *Liberty, Retrenchment and Reform*.

[73] Mill to W. E. Hickson, 24 Apr. 1865, *Works*, vol. 16, 1037. In 1875 25 members had also been subscribers of £200 or more to the Cobden Fund of 1860; H. Ashworth, *Recollections of Richard Cobden MP and the Anti-Corn Law League* (1877), 369–72. John Bright's closeness to Cobden, however, acted as a deterrent to participation. Above, 117.

they shared 'no common bond except a general notion that Cobden was a useful member of society, without knowing exactly why'.[74] Yet such admiration was not evenly distributed within the Liberal Party, for the balance of the Club's member-ship pulled it towards the Radical-Dissenting nexus, with which Potter himself was identified in the early 1870s.[75] This is confirmed by parliamentary divisions over foreign policy. For example, Henry Richard's motion in favour of a permanent system of arbitration in 1873 was supported by thirty-eight Club members (out of a total of eighty-eight MPs) but opposed by seventeen (out of ninety-eight).[76] Over the Eastern Question in 1878 the Club supplied ten out of the thirty-seven Whigs, but thirty-eight out of the seventy-four Radicals, as identified by Jenkins.[77] Sim-ilarly, looking at the range of pressure group activities in which the Club's members were predominantly involved, it can be seen that the weight is strongly towards Radicalism and Dissent, with thirty-one belonging to the Jamaica Committee, twenty-nine to the Howard Association, twenty-five to the Free Land League, twenty-two to the Anti-Contagious Diseases Act Association, and twenty to the International Arbitration and Peace Association, all readily, if loosely, affiliated with 'Cobdenic principles'.[78]

Even so, the Club should not be seen as a Radical political association in origin, but as a missionary organ devoted to the dissemination of Cobden's ideas, opinions that the Anti-Corn Law League had found 'so unpopular and difficult to inculcate upon the nation', but which were now 'universally held'.[79] As such, its goals were both propagandist and educational, for the early work of the Club included the creation of a network of university prizes, encouraging the youth of America, the empire, and Britain to discourse upon the Cobdenite message. It was an educational effort that reaped considerable dividends, drawing out a stream of the talented into the cause, for example the future Australian politician B. R. Wise, the political economist J. S. Nicholson, and the civil servant Charles Troup, winners of the Oxford and Cambridge Cobden prizes.[80] The Club also supported the university extension movement, providing the literary backup for courses of free trade lectures in large towns, although by 1886 the Club's pamphlets had ceased fully to satisfy a new generation of extension lecturers.[81] Other prizes were regularly offered to working men's colleges and trade unions, while the Club's literature was donated to a wide range of public libraries and academic

[74] Mallet to Thorold Rogers, 21 Dec. 1878, Thorold Rogers Papers, 471, Bodleian Library, Oxford.

[75] T. A. Jenkins, *Gladstone, Whiggery, and the Liberal Party, 1874–1886* (Oxford, 1988), 34, 36.

[76] *Hansard*, 3rd ser., 217, cc. 52–73, 8 July 1873.

[77] Jenkins, *Gladstone, Whiggery*, appendix, 295–306.

[78] H. L. Malchow, *Agitators and Promoters in the Age of Gladstone and Disraeli* (1983). Also promi-nent among overlapping interests were the Commons Preservation Society (19), the Sunday Society (17), and the Sunday Prohibition Association (16).

[79] R. N. Philips to Mrs Cobden, 20 Jan. 1867, CP, Add. MS 6028, WSRO.

[80] Troup's essay was published in 1884, *The Future of Free Trade*; he became permanent under-secretary at the Home Office, 1908–22. F. W. Hirst was among future prizewinners, Edwin Cannan among losers. See, too, Kadish, *Historians*, 79, 125, 129, 161, 170, 185, 187, 194.

[81] CCM, 24 Apr. 1874, 16 June 1875, 23 Jan., and 6 Feb. 1886.

institutions.[82] It thus both encouraged and made available to the serious-minded Victorian reader a comprehensive elaboration and defence of free trade.

Besides these stimuli to Cobdenite studies, the Club's main impact lay in the energetic diffusion of free trade literature for propagandist purposes. There were, for example, close links in the early years with the Financial Reform Association,[83] the National Reform Union, and the National Liberal Federation, ensuring that local party organizations were kept fully supplied with the Club's literature. Illustrative too of the degree to which free trade had lost some of its religious aura, one may note the Club's close ties with Bradlaugh, whose National Secular Societies were important channels for disseminating free trade literature in Britain and America.[84] These were the vital arteries along which the lifeblood of Cobdenism was to flow, gaining an audience far in excess of that reached by the Anti-Corn Law League in the 1840s.[85] Herein lay the real vocation of the Club, the major part of whose expenditure was initially to go on publications designed to reach the Liberal activists. For example, in the early years of the Club, 1866–75, it distributed 133,854 copies of tracts and books, at a cost of £5,518. Heading the list were 15,000 copies each of the proceedings at the Cobden Club dinner in 1873 and 1874, followed by 10,000 each of 'The Commercial Policy of France', Grant Duff on 'The Teachings of Cobden', and Lord Hobart on 'The Mission of Cobden'.

These titles in themselves also announce the main themes of Cobdenite propaganda, the insistence on the centrality of Cobden's political legacy in directing the Gladstonian Liberal Party, and in particular its foreign policy. Four themes were uppermost in the first decade of the Club's existence. First, the most doctrinaire of Cobdenites wished to reiterate the link between internationalism and free trade, upholding the need to convert the world as a whole to the Cobdenite creed, and the considerable optimism, sustained against much evidence to the contrary, in the prospects of free trade in Europe, the British Empire, and the United States. The Club watched attentively the progress of commercial negotiations with Europe, and the changes in American fiscal policy. At this level, Mallet and the 'forward school' in foreign policy saw the Club as a valuable adjunct against the traditionalists of the Foreign Office, and, ideally, it would have formed 'a kind of private Foreign Office for commercial questions'.[86]

---

[82]   Jevons's 'List of Selected Books in Political Economy' from *Monthly Notes of the Library Association of the UK*, 3, 1882, included several Cobden Club publications, *Papers and Correspondence*, vol. 7, 101–7.

[83]   W. N. Calkins, 'A Victorian Free Trade Lobby', *Economic History Review*, 2nd ser., 13 (1960–1), 90–104; CCM, *passim*, e.g. 30 June 1877, 27 July 1878, 2 June 1883.

[84]   CCM, 31 Jan. and 28 Feb. 1891, in which Annie Besant reported to the Club that 'Free thinkers in America are Free Trade almost to a man.'

[85]   Potter believed the Club 'reaches some quarters at home and abroad which other organisations fail to do'. To Gladstone, 9 Apr. 1886, GP, Add. MS 44282.

[86]   Mallet to Morier, 23 June 1878, Morier Papers, Box 44. The *Cobden Club Essays*, 2nd ser., 1871–2, had, for example, a 'special object' with regard to commercial negotiations with Germany: see Mallet to Rogers, 5 Nov. 1871, Rogers Papers, 465.

Second, land law reform predominated among novel directions of Cobdenite thought, above all in the comparative study of continental land systems with a view to reform at home, the encouragement of peasant farming, and the reform of the law of landlord and tenant. Here, the Club effectively took up the 'Free Trade in Land' campaign which had foundered after the Anti-Corn Law League, and built on the revival of this theme following Cobden's controversy in 1863 with the editor of *The Times* J. T. Delane.[87] The 'Cobden Affair' had, Mill acknowledged, 'for the first time in the country turned people's minds to the question of small properties in land—a thing I tried hard to do, seventeen years ago'.[88] Potter tried more successfully to keep this issue alive, in collaboration with groups such as the Land Tenure Reform Association, Land Law Reform League, and Commons Preservation Society.[89] On this issue, too, the Club was able to take advantage of its European and diplomatic contacts in producing an important and pioneering set of essays, *Systems of Land Tenure in Various Countries*. This initially helped popularize the comparative and historical method in England (despite the Club's supposed association with 'cosmopolitical economic science'), but was also reprinted in 1881 at the request of Gladstone in order to influence Liberal debate on this issue.[90] On the other hand, the land question led to an early rift between the Club and Mill, whose 'socialistic views' on land were wholly antithetical to those of the Club's mentor, Mallet: 'all who have any faith in the great principle of Free Exchange should take their stand against Mill's false science . . . Cobden's whole [preaching] was to remove the false distinction between land and other property. Mill begins by reasserting the distinction in its most naked form.'[91]

Third, but to a lesser extent, the Club focused on British fiscal policy, and in particular on the need for retrenchment in local and national expenditure.[92] The

[87] *Mr Cobden and 'The Times'* (Manchester, 1864); J. Morley, *The Life of Richard Cobden* (2 vols, 1881), vol. 2, 420–39.

[88] Mill to T. Hare, 27 Jan. 1864, in *Works*, vol. 15, 918–19.

[89] George Shaw-Lefevre (Lord Eversley), E. N. Buxton, Dilke, Fawcett, Farrer, Granville, Harcourt, Duke of Westminster, and Sir John Lubbock supported both land reform groups. For the links between repeal of the Corn Laws, free trade, and the Commons, see Eversley, *Commons, Forests and Footpaths of England and Wales* (rev. edn., 1910), 171. See, too, Potter to P. Rylands, 9 Dec. 1872 in L. G. Rylands (ed.), *Correspondence of Peter Rylands*, vol. 1, 214–15.

[90] Morier was also active in this publication, partly to bring into the open his own report on land tenure which he characteristically believed had been deliberately hidden away in an obscure Blue Book by his enemies at the FO. Morier also advocated 'agitation à [l'] outrance for a simple system of land registration and the transfer of land by public registration instead of our simply awful present private system of land conveyancing . . . England, you know, is the country of Free Trade. I support Free exchange. The commodity called Land is not reckoned Trade.' Morier to Mallet, 31 Jan. 1870; and see Morier to Mallet, 9 Feb. 1881, Morier Papers, Boxes 44 and 45; CCM, 5 Feb. 1881; a facsimile of Gladstone's letter to Potter, 31 Jan. 1881 was included in the second edition; see, too, Gladstone to Lord Elcho, 31 Jan. 1881, in *GD*, vol. 10, 15. For the work's impact, see S. Collini, D. Winch, and J. Burrow, *That Noble Science of Politics* (Cambridge, 1983), 263–5.

[91] Mallet to Thorold Rogers, 5 Nov. 1873, Thorold Rogers Papers, 466. See, too, C. Dewey, 'The Rehabilitation of the Peasant Proprietor', *History of Political Economy*, 6 (1974), 38–9.

[92] *Local Government and Taxation* (1875); 2nd ser., 1882.

diminution of indirect taxation, for example, was seen as the way in which Britain could remain the workshop of the world and beat off American economic competition. Loosening the bonds on industry would also make Britain a better place for the artisan to live in.[93] During Gladstone's government of 1868–74, with its considerable success in fiscal reform, this was a less urgent cause. It did, nevertheless, provide a suitable theme on which the Club's appeal merged with that of Liverpool's financial reformers and London's plebeian radicals.[94]

Finally, the Club's concern lay, naturally, with Cobden himself, not so much as the subject of a personality cult, but with an important political evaluation of his legacy and its relevance, by influential interpreters such as Mallet and Thorold Rogers. As we have seen, not only were Cobden's own works made readily available, but essays such as that of Mallet supplied 'the very expressed essence of Mr Cobden's thought'. Thorold Rogers, a self-conscious disciple, was influential as a pioneer economic historian, as well as a Radical MP, providing a clear elucidation of his mentor's political legacy in *Cobden and Modern Political Opinion* (1873).[95] This intellectual reassessment provided a Cobden rooted not simply in the Lancashire terrain of the League, but ready to assume the proportions of 'International Man', a perspective to be consolidated later by the publication of Morley's biography in 1881.

With these themes of foreign and fiscal policy, land reform, and Cobden himself successfully established as the core of the Club's identity, its funds were exhausted by 1876, the year in which it joined with the Political Economy Club in celebrating the centenary of the publication of Smith's *The Wealth of Nations*.[96] At this point the Club had reached not only an intellectual (as well as financial) hiatus, but a political turning-point. Its direction and impact in its second decade were to be significantly different.

The 'good old cause': the Cobden Club, 1876–86

The centenary of the publication of *The Wealth of Nations* was greeted in Britain with a mixture of complacency and unease.[97] For satisfaction in possessing 'the greatest, the most stable, and the most lucrative commerce which the world has ever seen' coincided with perceptions of growing depression in trade since 1873, and a sense of pessimism induced by the coal famine of 1871–3, the spectre of Britain's resources on which her greatness was based, diminishing much more rapidly than

[93]   See Grant Duff, *Teachings of Richard Cobden*, 9–10, for a typical statement.
[94]   Biagini, *Liberty, Retrenchment and Reform*; id., 'Debate on Taxation', in Biagini and Reid, *Currents of Radicalism* (Cambridge, 1991); Calkins, 'Free Trade Lobby'.
[95]   Grant Duff, *Teachings of Richard Cobden*, 8; Kadish, *Historians*, 23–4.
[96]   *Revised Report of the Proceedings at the dinner of 31 May 1876 held in celebration of the Hundreth Year of the Publication of the 'Wealth of Nations'* (Political Economy Club, 1876).
[97]   G. M. Koot, *English Historical Economics, 1870–1926. The Rise of Economic History and Neomercantilism* (Cambridge, 1987), 13.

expected.[98] The awareness of depression grew perceptibly in the later 1870s, and began to expose free trade to growing criticism, with a revival of protectionist agitation reflected in Parliament and the press.[99] This was exacerbated by the trend of events abroad, which considerably muted Cobdenite optimism with regard to the prospects of international free trade. In America, it was argued, the Club's efforts had become counter-productive, while in Europe the renewed stirrings of protectionist bodies in France and Germany induced a cautionary note. In 1875 the Club was already on the defensive, as 'war and protection' threatened the 'impending collapse of the tariff system', with little hope of active diplomacy to counteract this tendency in public opinion.[100] Prospects in the empire were no more encouraging, with only New South Wales held out as 'a brilliant exception' to the colonial drift to protection.[101] In this depressing context, the dispatch of Cobden Club literature to Japan, and of Lord Houghton to visit the Emperor of the Brazils 'with a view to interesting him in the Free Trade question' were at best tepid morale boosters.[102]

Nor was the domestic political context any more favourable, as the Cobdenite message appeared to wither in the years of Disraeli's government. For Peter Rylands, Disraeli himself was a 'model anti-Richard Cobden politician', and legislation such as the Cattle Diseases Bill was clearly anti-Cobdenite.[103] Similarly, the rising spirit of war in England seemed symptomatic of a wider revulsion against Liberal values, the most worrying feature of which was the new questioning of free trade itself. The late 1860s had seen some talk of reciprocity, but it was in 1877 that the Club first took seriously the reports of growing protectionist sentiment among the working classes, while Mallet questioned the economic orthodoxy of the Association of Chambers of Commerce.[104] At A. J. Mundella's suggestion, this prompted the publication of Mallet's important tract on reciprocity, but also led to the call for a new League-style crusade against protectionism at home and abroad.[105] This was unduly alarmist, for the Conservative Party was not yet ready

[98]   *The Economist*, 3 June 1876; S. B. Saul, *The Myth of the Great Depression, 1873–1896* (1969).
[99]   Brown, *Tariff Reform Movement*, 8 ff; Fisher, 'Public Opinion', 232–54, 327–37.
[100]   *Free Trade and the European Treaties of Commerce* (Cobden Club, 1875), which includes a report of discussion of treaties of commerce and public opinion at the Political Economy Society in Paris, 6 Aug. 1875.
[101]   CCM, 7 July 1877.
[102]   CCM, 23 June 1877; 29 May 1880. Significantly, among the Club's favourite authors, works of Fawcett and Mongredien were translated into Japanese in the 1880s. C. Sugiyama and H. Mizuta (eds.), *Enlightenment and Beyond: Political Economy comes to Japan* (1988), Appendix 2.
[103]   CCM, General Meeting, 6 July 1878; see, too, J. Spain, 'Free Trade, Protectionism and "The Food of the People": Liberal Opposition to the Cattle Diseases Bill, 1878', in Biagini (ed.), *Citizenship and Community*, 168–92.
[104]   CCM, 24 Nov. 1877 (C. Hudson, Bolton); 2 Mar. 1878 (H. S. Scudamore on Lt. Armitt, leader of the War Party at Hyde Park); Mallet in discussion.
[105]   CCM, 15 Dec. 1877, 6 July 1878 (T. Briggs); *Reciprocity. A Letter to T. B. Potter MP.* (17 Mar. 1879), reprinted in Mallet, *Free Exchange* (1891). See, too, W. H. C. Armytage, *A. J. Mundella, 1825–1897* (1951), 82, 195–6; Mallet to Rogers, 15 Dec. 1878, Thorold Rogers Papers, 470.

to revert to protectionism.[106] Yet the Club's advocacy of free trade became more strident, as it moved away from Mallet's vision of a centre for foreign policy studies towards a more Radical concept of its place in domestic politics.

Above all, the Club—'the fountainhead of pure doctrine'—had to meet the political and ideological challenge posed by the emerging fair trade movement in its attempts to rally the growing discontents of agriculture and industry.[107] First, against the growing evidence of agricultural depression, it sought to reinforce its appeal to the farming interest. The claims of tenants were strongly advocated by W. E. Bear in a Club pamphlet in 1876, occasioning a swift defence of the rights of landlords from the pen of the Duke of Argyll.[108] This was a good reflection of the broader divisions of Victorian opinion, but for the Club it illustrated the difficulty, as Peter Rylands noted, of moving beyond the clear guidance offered by Cobden.[109] It also raised the question of political impetus, with some fearing that Argyll would turn the Club in a Tory direction, while others welcomed the impetus given by land reform to the alliance between rural and urban radicalism. The Club had no wish to dish its aristocrats, but it now looked increasingly to influence the views of the tenant farmers and agricultural labourers through members such as the farmers' friend James Howard, and through growing links with the Agricultural Labourers' Union.[110]

The Club's message remained a moderate one, paying tribute to Cobden's belief in the virtues of peasant proprietors, while rebutting the idea that agrarian depression was the result of free trade. In order to boost land reform, the Club commissioned from Brodrick a major investigation of the land laws, refurbishing its strong links with academic Liberals. Cobdenites such as George Shaw-Lefevre became leading proponents of land reform nationally, proclaiming the benefits of small estates as a remedy in England as well as Ireland, and combining Radical language with a policy which, with the growing discussion of land nationalization in the late 1870s and early 1880s, might appear socially conservative. Tenurial reform, economic efficiency, and proper cultivation of the land were pressed as the appropriate alternatives to reciprocity and protection.[111]

---

[106] Bright thought 'Free Trade needs no defenders and is in no danger'. He rather feared that free trade advocacy would 'tend to excite a feeling in some minds that we were apprehensive of danger to the good old cause'. To Potter, 2 Dec. 1879, Potter Letters.

[107] Gladstone to Potter, 29 Aug. 1881, *GD*, vol. 10, 116.

[108] W. E. Bear, *Landlord and Tenant* (1876); cf. Argyll, *Contracts between Landlords and Tenants* (1877). For a detailed account, see J. W. Mason, 'The Duke of Argyll and the Land Question in late nineteenth-century Britain', *Victorian Studies*, 21 (1977–8), 149–70 esp. 155–6.

[109] CCM, 7 July 1877.

[110] CCM, 2 Mar. 1878; cf. Potter lamenting that 'we have so many landowners' in the Club. To Rogers, 8 Apr. 1877, Rogers Papers, 545.

[111] Fisher, 'Public Opinion', 466 ff. For typical statements, see Lord Carrington, *Agricultural Depression. Speech to Tenants of South Bucks* (1879); Cobden Club, *What Protection does for the Farmer* (1881); I. S. Leadam, *Farmer's Grievances and How to Remedy Them* (Manchester, 1880); id., *Speech on Agricultural Topics* (Altrincham, 1885). For Leadam, see Kadish, *Historians*, 77.

But depression and fair trade cries were by no means confined to rural England, with growing worries that 'most of the dangers which threaten our commercial supremacy are due to the slight knowledge which the working-classes and their leaders have of Political Economy'.[112] To meet this challenge to 'Cobdenic principles', the Club sought to reinforce the general case for free trade. This was most successfully put into a popular form in the writings of the corn merchant Augustus Mongredien, above all in his tract *Free Trade and English Commerce* (1879). Mongredien's style, it was felt, was calculated to do more 'good among the general readers' than Fawcett's more 'abtruse' views.[113] This popularizing campaign supplemented the Club's general policy of disseminating Cobden's own works, and the number of tracts published increased significantly in an attempt to educate the public mind at a time of protectionist revival.

The first stirrings of fair trade in the late 1870s had stimulated a swift response, almost before the so-called 'Policy of Self-Help' had been formulated by W. F. Ecroyd. Nevertheless, 'Ecroydism' became a distinct strand in the 1880 general election, and drew forth a wider defence of free trade. For example, Hartington, victorious against Ecroyd in north-east Lancashire, paid considerable attention to his opponent's protectionist policies.[114] At Bradford, the industrial 'storm-centre' of fair trade, the progressive Liberal Arnold Toynbee, enthusiastically defended free trade, upholding the rights of the community above those of uncompetitive industries. Toynbee also joined E. T. Cook in campaigning in the Oxfordshire countryside in the election of 1880, on grounds very similiar to those of more old-fashioned Liberals.[115] The impact of this free trade crusade in the election of 1880 should not of course be exaggerated, although it was certainly an issue of some importance.[116] It is significant because it both organized the Cobdenites behind the Liberal revival, and energized the intellectuals behind free trade. Nevertheless, by June 1880 the Club regarded the protectionist threat as dead, killed off by the revival of trade and the election of a Liberal Cabinet, twelve of whose fourteen members were also members of the Club.

But victory in 1880 did not induce complacency. The fair trade movement grew rather than receded as a threat, with the election of Farrer Ecroyd as MP for Preston in May 1881, despite the Club's aiding the efforts of the Manchester-based National Reform Union against him.[117] The Conservative Party itself now took

---

[112]   *Capital and Labour*, cited in *Hundreth Year of 'Wealth of Nations'*, 85–6.

[113]   CCM, 17 May 1879. Fawcett's *Free Trade and Protection* (1878) was a response to the revival of protectionism in Europe and Britain. By 1884 it had sold *c*.6,000 copies, many distributed by the Club. See Deane, 'Henry Fawcett', in Goldmann (ed.), *The Blind Victorian*, 103.

[114]   B. Holland, *The Life of Spencer Compton, Eighth Duke of Devonshire* (2 vols, 1911), vol. 1, 266–9; Spencer Compton, *Speeches* (1880).

[115]   Brown, *Tariff Reform Movement*, 11; Kadish, *Arnold Toynbee*, 73–7, 96.

[116]   R. Shannon, *The Age of Disraeli* (1992), 378ff.

[117]   Brown, *Tariff Reform Movement*, 18–25; CCM, 14 and 21 May 1881. For the first stirrings of fair trade in Preston, see A. Howe, 'Edward Hermon', in D. J. Jeremy (ed.), *Dictionary of Business Biography* (5 vols., 1984–6), vol. 3, 178–81.

a greater interest in reported working-class support for protectionism in the industrial North, just as in August 1881 the National Fair Trade League was formed.[118] Significantly, T. B. Potter at this time began to cultivate links with the TUC through Thomas Burt, Henry Broadhurst, and George Howell, in order to counter the 'fallacies of protection' among the working classes.[119] More widely, the apparent prospering of fair trade unleashed a major popular crusade to sustain free trade, in which Gladstone himself was to join, with a wide-ranging defence of its economic and moral benefits at Leeds in October 1881.[120] The Club set up a special publications fund, drawing on such lordly stalwarts of free trade as the Dukes of Devonshire and Westminster, as well as the new model employer Brassey and the Radical cotton-spinner Thomasson, with also a sizeable sum from the City stock-broker G. W. Medley. This fund supported publications such as George Potter's *The working man's view of free trade*, as well as Medley's *Reciprocity Craze*. Such tracts were issued in hundreds of thousands, not tens, and the Club had at last found the genuine threat to free trade against which it could campaign with conviction and effectiveness. Although it may be argued that fair trade did not represent a powerful threat to free trade in 1881, this was in part due to the speed with which the Cobdenites rallied to the defence of the latter. The redirection of its efforts towards the working class represented a significant change of strategy, which contributed towards the depth of attachment of the working class to free trade in late-Victorian Britain.

Above all, it was the combined threat of the revival of protectionism with the enfranchisement of the agricultural labourer in the Reform Act of 1884 which induced a free trade propaganda drive of immense proportions. For, in late 1884 low corn prices after the harvest had produced a strong cry for a duty on foreign corn in many parts of the country. In particular, the defeat of Lord William Compton in the South Warwickshire election of 1884 by the fair trader S. S. Lloyd alerted the Club to the imminent threat of democracy and protectionism, a combination that it believed had already been used to destroy free trade abroad. The Club now therefore worked closely with the Liberal Party, after Schnadhorst had written to Potter in November that 'It looks as if we shall have to fight the battle of free trade over again. I view with considerable apprehension the ignorance on this question of the labourers who will soon have the vote.'[121] The Club also found an invaluable ally in Joseph Arch, ready himself to help educate the labouring popu-

---

[118] Report of R. G. C. Mowbray on opinion in Lancashire, to W. H. Smith, 10 Aug. 1881, in Hambledon Papers, PS 7/1/80. I am most grateful to Dr Lucy Brown for referring me to this source. Even so, Stafford Northcote prepared to say in the East Riding, 'some things which will not be palatable to our Neo-Protectionists', to E. Stanhope, 17 Sept. 1881, Stanhope Papers, Kent Archives Office. (Margaret Hall kindly provided me with this reference.)

[119] CCM, 25 May, 23 July, 1881. He also seems to have had links with the editor of *Lloyd's Dispatch*.

[120] W. E. Gladstone, *Speeches delivered at Leeds, 7 and 8 Oct. 1881* (1881); see, too, Gladstone, 'Free Trade, Railways, and the Growth of Commerce', *Nineteenth Century*, 7 (1880), 367–8; GD, vol. 10, xxxvii, and 127, Gladstone to Halifax, 18 Sept. 1881.

[121] CCM, 22 Nov. 1884.

lation in free trade principles, with his own tract for the Club to distribute.[122] The issue of free trade was also given extensive coverage in the *English Labourers' Chronicle*, as well as in the urban popular press.[123]

The general election of 1885 was to see the culmination of the Club's propagandist efforts, with an additional publication fund, and the production in millions of a fresh range of leaflets (including fifty thousand in Welsh), specifically designed for the new electorate.[124] A close working relationship with the publishers Cassell and Co. ensured an uninterrupted flow of free trade tracts, which Liberal agents and activists distributed effectively over the nation.[125] Some individuals suffered as a result, for example the Gloucestershire labourer William Scaysbrook, 'a village Cobden' unable to withstand 'a tyrant of the field' Sir Peter van Nolten Pole, who dismissed him for distributing Cobden Club leaflets.[126] But this vast educational effort helped significantly to diffuse the old free trade message to the newly enfranchised rural labourers, an important contribution towards making free trade safe within the new political dispensation.[127] For example, together with the issue of smallholdings free trade played a leading part in the return of A. B. Winterbottom for east Gloucestershire, ending forty-three years of unbroken Tory rule.[128] Indeed, what appeared to be the dispassionate political virtue of the rural electorate in supporting free trade earned it the lasting gratitude of the Liberal Party, and for Gladstone the agricultural labourers now appeared an important bulwark of his free trade achievement of the 1860s, providentially just as it was being questioned by some of its original middle-class and Peelite supporters, and with some popular fair trade success in the borough elections in 1885.[129]

This proved to be the high-water mark of electoral Cobdenism. For not only did

[122]   J. Arch, *Free Trade vs Protection* (1880), and id., *Cobden Club Leaflet*, xviii.

[123]   Fisher, 'Public Opinion'; N. Scotland, 'The National Agricultural Labourers' Union and the Demand for a Stake in the Soil, 1872–96', in Biagini (ed.), *Citizenship and Community*, 151–67. While most of the Club's efforts were directed to the countryside in 1885, it did not neglect urban areas such as Tower Hamlets, where the sugar bounties had created support for fair trade. E.g. CCM, 16 Feb. 1884.

[124]   Potter to Gladstone, 7 Dec. 1884, GP, Add. MS 44282. The Welsh leaflets occasioned some doubts, particularly the inclusion of references to disestablishment, which, as Henry Richard noted 'was not necessarily Cobdenic': CCM, 4 July 1885.

[125]   CCM, 6 Feb. 1886, on occasions 'the entire power of the great house of Cassell and Co. had been devoted . . . to the services of the Cobden Club'.

[126]   *Cheltenham Free Press*, 24 Oct. 1885; CCM, 23 Jan. 1886.

[127]   'Is it too soon to congratulate you on the pluck of the agricultural labourers of the Southern and Midland Counties. I do hope and think that our ten million of leaflets for the Cobden Club have borne fruit.' Potter to Gladstone, 5 Dec. 1885, GP, Add. MS 44282. For an editorial in this vein, 'The triumph of Hodge', *Cheltenham Free Press*, 12 Dec. 1885. For the check to fair trade nationally, see Zebel, 'Fair Trade', 172.

[128]   N. Scotland, 'The Decline and Collapse of the National Agricultural Labourers' Union in Gloucestershire, 1887–96, Pt. II', *Gloucestershire History*, 1988, 16 ff.

[129]   Gladstone blamed the Liberals' urban losses primarily on fair trade in 1885. *GD*, vol. 11, 435–6 [26 and 27 Nov. 1885]. See, too, ibid. 423 [6 Nov. 1885]. One League scion, T. T. Greg had announced himself a 'convinced but unwilling free trader', ready to accept a 5s. duty on corn'. To L. R. Phelps, 19 Aug. 1881, Phelps Papers, Oriel College, Oxford.

some Cobdenites in 1885 already fear that political partisanship threatened free trade,[130] but in 1886 divisions over Ireland reduced the Club to political impotence. Ireland posed a manifold problem for English free traders. First, for some, the trend of Irish legislation since 1880, for example judicial rents, had represented the abandonment of the principles of free contract and free exchange, upon which men such as Mallet rested their free trade beliefs. For them, free trade was above all a market philosophy based on free exchange and individual property rights. Yet Gladstone's Irish policy presaged 'still further outrages on all economical and financial laws'.[131] Second, the prospect of Ireland under Home Rule posed the direct threat of the reimposition of protective tariffs. For in Ireland, far more so than England, there had developed since the 1830s an economic case for protection, and its protagonist Isaac Butt, then Professor of Political Economy at Trinity College, Dublin, had emerged in the 1870s as the leader of the Home Government party.[132] By the 1880s, protectionism had entered strongly into Parnell's idea of the new Ireland, although this was by no means fully shared by all his followers.[133] For many, the case for Home Rule was based on the idea that English political interest had distorted Ireland's natural economic development, so that Home Rule would restore to Ireland her natural advantages. Many Home Rulers therefore remained Cobdenites, and even after 1886 discussed co-operation with the Club.[134] Even so, the case for greater government intervention in Ireland to compensate for past disadvantages led inevitably to the case for 'native industries', with its Listian complexion of protection, a cause that was anathema to English free traders.[135] In his Home Rule Bill of 1886 Gladstone himself retained control of customs by the Imperial Parliament, and sought to show, as Colin Matthew has argued, that 'the recognition of national identity need not mean protection and cartelization'.[136] But this was not sufficient to assuage the doubts of those free traders such as Mallet and

---

[130]　For adverse comments on the Club's partisanship, see *Saturday Review*, *The Economist*, and *Worcester Journal*, all 20 June 1885, following the Club Dinner of 13 June, addressed by Dilke and Chamberlain.

[131]　See especially Mallet to Farrer, 1 Feb. 1886, on Irish policy since 1880: 'Mr Gladstone . . . began by relegating Political Economy to Saturn. What a retribution has already fallen upon [him]', Farrer Papers, Surrey Record Office.

[132]　R. D. Collison Black, *Economic Thought and the Irish Question, 1817–1870* (Cambridge, 1960), 139–44. In 1874 Bright noted 'the absence of political economical knowledge in Ireland is remarkable': to Potter, 15 Mar. 1874, Potter Letters. But, see T. Boylan and T. P. Foley, 'The Teaching of Economics at the Queen's Colleges in Ireland (Belfast, Cork and Galway)', in Kadish and Tribe (eds.), *Political Economy*, 111–36.

[133]　L. Kennedy, 'The Economic Thought of the Nation's Lost Leader, Charles Stuart Parnell', in *Parnell in Perspective*, ed. G. Boyce and A. O'Day (1991), 171–200.

[134]　J. G. S. MacNeill, *English Interference with Irish Industries* (1886); CCM, 7 July 1890, J. McCarthy to R. Gowing, 24 May 1890 (copy).

[135]　R. Dennis, *Industrial Ireland. A Practical and Non-Political View of 'Ireland for the Irish'* (1887). Mallet predicted 'this measure [Home Rule] will end in the creation of a Socialist republic in Ireland'. To Farrer, 7 Apr. 1886, Farrer Papers.

[136]　'Intro', *GD*, vol. 12, xliii; C. O'Brien, *Parnell and His Party, 1880–1890* (Oxford, 1957), 109–14; A. O'Day, *Parnell and the First Home Rule Episode* (1986), 88–90, 101–2, 188.

Northbrook, who were already fearful of the collectivist trend of English legislation, while it increased the anxieties of some Radicals, including both Bright and Chamberlain.[137]

As a result of these cumulative doubts, the issue of Home Rule severely weakened the Club politically, for after 1886 many of its Unionists, including stalwarts such as Mallet, ceased to play an energetic part in the Club's affairs.[138] The majority of members, on the other hand, appear to have followed Potter in favouring Home Rule, but this produced further dissent from loyal Cobdenites such as Watkin, who complained that the Club was now a 'Gladstone Club'.[139] Even on issues more directly related to free trade, such as sugar bounties and the gold standard, the Club now found itself bitterly divided.[140] After 1886 there was, therefore, some truth in the view expressed by Mallet that only Potter held the Club together, that 'after him, it must fall to pieces, for its members have no cohesion and no common rallying-point'.[141] This pessimism was not unfounded, but it was greatly exaggerated. The membership of the Club certainly declined, having fallen by 1899 to only 497, of whom 263 were overseas members. Even so, as we will see, experts such as Farrer continued to exert an important influence on technical policy discussions, while the Club's international presence was still marked. But after 1886, it ceased to be of any electoral significance, and lost the high Liberal profile it had previously enjoyed.[142]

How then may we evaluate the part played by the Club in its first two decades? Was it, as Mallet lamented, 'a good instrument, not well used'?[143] Clearly, its range was more restricted than some intellectual groupings, whose contributions to Liberalism have recently been highlighted by historians, for example the National Association for the Promotion of Social Science, on which, as we have seen, the Club had been in part modelled.[144] On the other hand, its active promotion of Liberal ideology deserves attention alongside comparable intellectual pressure

[137]   Mallet to Farrer, 20 and 26 Jan. 1886, Farrer Papers; Northbrook feared that if Ireland were free fiscally, 'how could we prevent protective duties being put on to exclude English goods', 11 Dec. 1885, cited in J. Vincent (ed.), *The Later Derby Diaries. Home Rule, Liberal Unionism and Aristocratic Life in late Victorian England* (privately printed, Bristol, 1981), 443; for Radical reactions in Birmingham, see G. D. Goodlad, 'Gladstone and his Rivals', in Biagini and Reid (eds.), *Currents of Radicalism*, 166.

[138]   Mallet now dismissed the Club as 'a set of windbags whose heads are full of socialism, particularism, suspicion etc. & who do everything with a party purpose': to Farrer, 25 Jan. 1886, Farrer Papers.

[139]   CCM, 10 July 1886; see, too, Watkin to Bright, 8 Dec. 1887, linking Home Rule with protection, Watkin Papers, Manchester Central Library. Interestingly, the Club at this juncture first elected women members, including Florence Nightingale and Cobden's daughter Ellen Millicent, the wife of Walter Sickert: CCM, 10 and 24 July 1886.

[140]   Below, 202, 206; British intervention in Egypt had also proved divisive, CCM 11 Mar. and 22 July 1882; 24 Mar. 1883.

[141]   Mallet to Potter, 8 Mar. 1889, in CCM, 9 Mar. 1889. The Club was already labelled by some 'The T. B. Potter Club': see Cobden Club scrapbook, in possession of Mr Charles Smedley.

[142]   See below, 262 for the Club's revival in the early 20th century.

[143]   Mallet to Morier, 23 June 1878, Morier Papers, Box 44.

[144]   Above, 117.

groups such as the Liberty and Property Defence League.[145] The Club's aim was not that of high theory, but of applied political argument. Its activities were both educational and political in function, comparable in an earlier generation to the Society for the Diffusion of Useful Knowledge and the Anti-Corn Law League, and in themselves they belie the frequent assumption that free trade's political strength lay in silence. Free trade in later Victorian Britain rested not on 'unspoken assumptions', but on a carefully articulated defence, in which considerable energy and money were devoted to the promulgation of its tenets, and vast amounts of literature descended upon the electorate. Here, the Club helped meet the widely felt need for political education, especially in the countryside after the Education Act of 1870.[146] The major pamphlets of the Club also undoubtedly influenced policy debate, above all on commercial diplomacy and the land question.[147] But in assessing the economic component of popular Liberalism in mid-Victorian England, the outpourings of Mongredien and Medley need to be taken as seriously as those of Fawcett and Farrer. This literature may not have altered the results of elections, but if propaganda is ever of electoral significance it was vital that the free traders remained alert and active, and effectively outgunned the fair trade movement in the early 1880s.[148] In order to do so, free trade did not remain a static creed inherited from the 1840s, but in the 1870s and 1880s it was reworked, to take account of events and of changes in economic method, in ways that renewed its currency and ensured its longevity.

It is paramount to note that the defence of free trade did not involve the simple dusting-off of the mouldering pamphlets of the 1840s and yellowing copies of *The League*. First, and above all, where the League had affirmed its belief in the benefits of free trade on dogmatic grounds, the Cobdenites were amply able to demonstrate statistically that free trade meant prosperity, both in absolute terms and relative to other nations. To this end the Club took a keen interest in the writings of Robert Giffen, whose statistical defence of the benefits of free trade now offered an invaluable extension of Cobdenite principle beyond dogma.[149] A whole range of data, however crude by later standards, was able to show that real wages had risen, that pauperism had fallen, and that trade had boomed since the repeal of the Corn Laws.[150] It was this statistical message that was turned into common truths in the

---

[145]   N. Soldon, 'Laissez-Faire as Dogma: the Liberty and Property Defence League, 1882–1914', in K. D. Brown (ed.), *Essays in Anti-Labour History* (1974), 208–33; E. Bristow, 'The Liberty and Property Defence League and Individualism', *Historical Journal*, 18 (1975), 761–89.

[146]   R. Jefferies, *Hodge and His Masters* (1880; 1979 edn.), 276, 286.

[147]   For critical notice, see Ritchie, *Hansard*, 3rd ser., 266, cc. 1728–39 (12 Aug. 1881).

[148]   For positive evaluations of the Club's literature, see CCM, 27 Mar. 1886; and *Mining Journal*, 7 Feb. 1885.

[149]   Giffen's leading papers were brought together in *Economic Enquiries and Studies* (2 vols, 1904); for an appreciation of their value, see C. P. Villiers to Bright, 3 Jan. 1884, Bright Papers, Add. MS 43386. Giffen also contributed lengthy letters to the press, e.g. *The Times*, 27 Nov., 12, 26, and 31 Dec. 1884, the last reaching four columns. For a modern reappraisal of free trade and national income, see D. N. McCloskey, *Enterprise and Trade in Victorian Britain: Essays in Historical Economics* (1981), 155–72.

[150]   e.g T. Brassey, *Work and Wages, practically illustrated* (1872, 4th edn., 1873); id., *Foreign Work and English Wages considered with reference to the depression of trade* (1879).

popular works of Mongredien and Medley. But the free traders had also to confront the depression of the late 1870s. Here, a plausible case was assembled, based on the ineradicability of the trade cycle, the over-extensive growth of earlier years and the failure of depression to erode the general benefits of prosperity.[151] This case was reinforced by international comparisons, above all with the United States, which was the only strongly protectionist nation, but which had seen its shipping decline, was marked by vast pools of unemployment, and where the fortunes of the few had been made at the expense of the many.[152]

Second, the least successful claim made by the League in the 1840s was its promise that free trade would promote working-class welfare, an argument that made uneven headway against the fear of unemployment and lowered wages.[153] The Club's leading claim now purported to show that 'the working classes had more steadily benefited from free trade than any other class'.[154] Here, Giffen's statistics, embracing wages and consumption patterns, usefully underpinned the argument for the distributional benefits of free trade for the working classes in town and country. The contrast between working-class immiseration before 1846 with the popular affluence of the 1870s was sustained not only by the statistical case, but by the testimony of oral history, as old labourers, Radicals such as Holyoake, and former Chartists lent their weight to the case for improvement.[155] This case was further supported by international comparisons, and the condition of the working classes in Germany under tariffs was now frequently adduced in favour of British free trade.[156]

Third, the free traders had to counter not the old arguments of protection, but the new ones, that free trade had failed as an international policy, that it was one-sided, and threatened Britain's long-term prosperity in an age of growing international rivalry.[157] But here the case of the fair traders for reciprocity or retaliation was soon met by the claim that retaliation was erroneous in theory and unworkable in practice.[158] If retaliation meant that Britain should tax the imports of protectionist countries, her food and raw materials would immediately be hit, jeopardizing the gains of free trade, while if it sparked off a cycle of competitive retaliation, Britain, as the world's leading export economy, would have most to lose. This case against retaliation, built up by Bonamy Price, Farrer, and Fawcett at the academic level,

---

[151] Interestingly, the language of evangelical political economy revived at this time, attributing depression to declining commercial morality. See J. Garnett and A. C. Howe, 'Churchmen and Cotton Masters', in D. J. Jeremy (ed.), *Religion and Business in Modern Britain* (1988).

[152] e.g. W. E. Baxter, *United States' Protection versus British Free Trade* (Cobden Club Leaflet 33, c.1884). See, too, W. Rathbone, *Protection and Communism: Effects of the American Tariff upon Wages* (1884).

[153] L. Brown, 'The Chartists and the Anti-Corn Law League', in A. Briggs (ed.), *Chartist Studies* (1959), 342–71.

[154] CCM, 26 May 1883; see, too, 5 May and 9 June 1883.

[155] C. Godfrey, *Chartist Lives* (New York, 1987), 329–31; G. J. Holyoake, *Robbing a Thousand Peters to pay one Paul* (Cobden Club Leaflet, c.1885).

[156] *The Results of Protection in Germany* (Cobden Club Leaflet 3, c.1884).

[157] Brown, *Tariff Reform Movement*, 8; Zebel, 'Fair Trade', 161–85.

[158] For a curt dismissal, see *The Oxford Handbook of Political Economy* (2nd edn., Oxford, 1885), 30.

was soon effectively deployed for popular consumption by Sydney and Edward Buxton, Thorold Rogers, and Holyoake. At a theoretical level, few new arguments were necessary to make this case, but in the face of the fair traders' emphasis on the balance of trade, the free traders did for the first time place growing emphasis on 'invisibles' (shipping, insurance, financial services) within the balance of payments.[159] Renewed attention was also paid to rejecting the Millian heresy, namely, support for infant industries, whose harm was not confined to distorting the allocation of capital and labour, but brought in its train the assemblage of interest groups within the polity.[160] Corruption and log-rolling on a massive scale would ensue, as in the United States.[161]

This was, of course, not an argument confined to new countries, but to (non-revenue) tariffs wherever they appeared. For the benefits of free trade for the working classes were not only economic, but political and social. From the 1870s one of the most insistent arguments in favour of free trade was its centrality if states were to remain free from the power of interest groups, from 'protectionist political cliques', and from 'selfish industrial demands'. The lesson of Repeal in the 1840s in dissociating the interests of land from politics was now invoked to instil the desire to avoid 'associat[ing] with politics the selfish interests of trade classes'.[162] Free trade was a guarantee both of the livelihood and the political independence of the people, and of the right of the community to be defended against the over-mighty trading classes, which was the central pillar in the Victorian social contract in which the state remained a limited and neutral force to be invoked with caution.[163]

If this defence of free trade essentially refurbished the 'good old cause', it also significantly altered its direction. For while, ideologically, the Cobden Club, as a broad church, is difficult to pinpoint exactly, it found itself increasingly mobilized behind the Radical version of Cobden, as proclaimed by Chamberlain in 1883.[164] This was not a predetermined direction, for, as Maine had sensed in 1872, the Club faced a dilemma between Cobden's own inconsistent objects—the minimum power of the state and 'the deposition of the privileged classes', an object increasingly to be achieved through state power wielded by the growing electorate.[165] This conflict, already apparent in the 1870s, was posed with increasing sharpness in the 1880s, and, as we have seen, was central to free traders' perceptions of Irish legislation. It also lay behind the string of resignations from the Club which followed the election

---

[159]   See esp. Medley, 'England under Free Trade' (1881), 63–5, in G. W. Medley, *Pamphlets and Addresses* (1899); see, too, John Noble, *Free Trade versus Protection* (Cobden Club Leaflet 28, *c.*1884).

[160]   See above, 115.

[161]   *Protection in New Countries* (Cobden Club Leaflet 46, *c.*1885–6).

[162]   J. Slagg, *Free Trade and Tariffs* (National Reform Union, 1881).

[163]   R. McKibbin, 'Why was there no Marxism in Great Britain?', *EHR* 99 (1984), 297–331; Biagini, *Liberty, Retrenchment and Reform*, 93–138.

[164]   *Cobden Club Report*, 1883. For the *Saturday Review*, 20 June 1885, it had become 'exclusively a Radical Association'.

[165]   *Pall Mall Gazette*, 10 Jan. 1872.

of the French socialist Clemenceau as an honorary member, and the choice of Chamberlain as speaker at the annual dinner in 1883. Such signs of the Club's increasingly radical vocation saw the departure of such stalwarts as Cartwright, Clarendon, Goschen, Morier, Lords Arthur and Odo Russell.[166]

This rift brought sharply into Cobdenite focus the wider later nineteenth-century conflict between individualism and collectivism. Free traders such as Mallet believed that the distinctive character of Cobden's economic policy 'was the belief that the social problem (by which I mean the reconciliation of the interests of property with those of the proletariat) was to be solved by Peace and Free Trade in the largest sense, of Free Exchange, between all nations . . . and by the steady adoption of the principles of personal liberty and personal responsibility'.[167] Thus, although Mallet's early ideas had derived in part from the Ricardians and above all from the optimistic Bastiat, he shared in some ways the view of free trade propounded by those whom Hilton has seen as sharing a 'market way of thinking', an economic mode typical of evangelical retributive theology. This, for example, closely links Mallet with the Peelite Duke of Argyll, in whose 'pure strain of individualism' Hilton detects 'a throwback to the first half of the nineteenth century'.[168] Mallet himself later devoted his retirement to exposing the errors of the Ricardians and Mill, and refining his own views of personal responsibility and private property in ways that took a strong anti-socialist cast.[169] This increasingly distanced him and his individualist confrères from Liberals such as Chamberlain, who, they believed, wished to invoke the power of the state, not the exertions of the individual, to right the balance between property and poverty. Mallet's understanding of free trade therefore took him towards the social philosophy of the Liberty and Property Defence League, as it did other prominent Cobden Club members such as Grant Duff, Watkin, and T. L. Mackay, as well as more Radical free traders like J. H. Levy.[170] For example, Grant Duff was still able to argue that with no armies and no tariffs, free exchange could lead to a property-owning democracy in Europe.[171] Here, then, was the tail-end of the 'old' evangelical retributive theology and the 'old' individualist Liberalism, typically but mistakenly assailed as 'Cobdenite' by the Fabians and progressives of the 1880s and 1890s.[172]

By the 1880s this individualistic outlook was that of a minority, even within the

---

[166] CCM, 11 Mar. 1882, 2, 9, 16 June, 28 July 1883.

[167] Mallet to T. B. Potter, 10 June 1883, enclosed in Mallet to Lord Odo Russell, Ampthill Papers, FO 918/54.

[168] B. Hilton, *The Age of Atonement: The Influence of Evangelicalism on Social and Economic Thought, 1785–1865* (Oxford, 1988), 261, 363.

[169] L. Mallet, *Free Exchange*, pt. 2; B. Mallet, *Sir Lonis Mallet* (1905), ch. 4.

[170] M. W. Taylor, *Men vs the State. Herbert Spencer and Late Victorian Individualism* (Oxford, 1992); Soldon, 'Laissez-Faire'; J. W. Mason, 'Thomas Mackay: The Anti-Socialist Philosophy of the Charity Organisation Society', in K. D. Brown (ed.), *Essays in Anti-Labour History*, 290–316.

[171] Liberty and Property Defence League, *Annual Report* (1894–5).

[172] See below, 192.

Cobden Club: as one of Mallet's contemporaries noted, 'the kind of Cobdenism you preach is very unlike the Cobdenism that passes current in the world'.[173] Rather, most of the Club's members had fused their beliefs with those of the emerging 'New Liberal' and the old popular Radical traditions, emphasizing the popular entitlement to cheap food and moving towards a view of the duty of government to ensure the people's welfare.[174] This in some ways equates with what Hilton has suggested was a *rights* way of thinking about free trade, a *political* mode, emphasizing less the rights of property enshrined within the market approach, than the consumer's right to cheap food via free imports, and the community's right to be freed from the oppressive power of vested interests.[175] In practice, rights and market approaches to free trade overlapped, but from the 1880s the contradiction within Cobden's thought which Maine detected took most Liberals towards the view that the state might intervene beneficially. This did not necessarily mean a large state, but it did mean land reform, with several free traders ready to move from individual proprietorship to endorse land nationalization.[176]

Fiscal reform also remained central—both the reduction of expenditure, especially on arms, and the removal of unequal burdens on consumers through increased land taxes and death duties (including local ones), a cause which ultimately Harcourt was to acknowledge in the 1894 budget.[177] This would make possible the popular fiscal goal of the 'free breakfast table' long advocated by Bright and taken up by advanced Radicals such as Sidney Webb in the 1890s. The Cobdenites also had other ambitions, for example the adjustment of railway rates, which, it was held, favoured foreign goods at the expense of British for the benefit of the railway companies, rather than the producers or consumers. But increasingly the central goal of the free traders was to be the advocacy of direct rather than indirect taxation, the goal of Cobden's financial reform allies in the 1840s, even if this now re-opened the way to greater state expenditure. For these Liberals, the state, rather than representing as in the past a form of aristocratic power and privilege, contained the democratic potential to guarantee popular welfare. For the individualists, this opened up the prospect, which they had already perceived in Ireland in the early 1880s, of the spoliation of the rich by the poor. But for those who would be christened New Liberals, the way was open from Gladstonian tax-minimalism to Lloyd George's supertax, a route linking free trade and popular welfare, clearly, if

---

[173]   Quoted B. Mallet, *Mallet*, 35.

[174]   Interestingly, Grant Duff noted if, as Mallet believed, the choice lay 'between Rousseau and Smith, Jacobinism and Cobdenism', it was difficult to think Lord Kimberley 'a terrible comet in Rousseau's host'. To Mallet, 11 Feb. 1886, Grant Duff Papers, MS Eur. F 234/43.

[175]   Hilton, *Atonement*, 261.

[176]   e.g. Walter Wren, MP for Wallingford, 1880–5; A. Lupton to T. Rogers, 1 Aug. 1884, Thorold Rogers Papers, 455.

[177]   *Death Duties* (Cobden Club Leaflet 38); A. Offer, *Property and Politics 1870–1914* (Cambridge, 1981), 205–6.

incompletely, signposted in the writings of T. H. Green, Arnold Toynbee, B. R. Wise, L. Atherley-Jones, and 'Brougham Villiers' (F. J. Shaw).[178]

The Cobden Club's defence of free trade, less and less Cobdenite in the eyes of its more Whiggish and individualist members, therefore provided in the longer term a series of ideological bridges between the Manchester School and the Edwardian progressives.[179] In the mid-1880s it offered a Radical programme with a popular appeal, designed to attract urban and rural workers to the Liberal Party, while avoiding both the increasing sterility of the individualist message of free exchange and the potent fears still aroused by the collectivist message of state intervention, for at this point such intervention was still seen by the Cobdenites as far more likely to favour the classes than the masses. In this, the Club was not far removed from the 'Unauthorised Programme' of Chamberlain, while remaining far more acceptable to the party leaders. Thus, Farrer, the strongly Cobdenite Board of Trade official, distanced himself from the 'use which wealth and Toryism make of the political economy', and claimed to see nothing in Chamberlain's proposals 'contrary to the best political economy'.[180] To that extent, the message preached by the Cobden Club was not that of free exchange and individualism, but of radical democracy and community welfare. In this way, alongside other means of dissemination, it played its part in promoting the attachment of the working class, in town and country, to the Victorian Liberal state, helping to defend the masses against the classes, and the British people against the militarism, high taxation, and statism of continental Europe. Within the Liberal Party in the mid-1880s this still reinforced Gladstonianism, providing an alternative both to the growing influence of Henry George within Radical circles, and to Chamberlain's 'three acres and a cow'. It sustained the old Radical goal of cheap government and non-intervention, but also provided moral, economic, and political arguments, which remained central to Liberalism when it later faced the threat of tariff reform. Certainly, the Cobdenite current within Radicalism had in the 1870s and 1880s been sustained and renewed with lasting effect.[181]

Besides this major achievement of the Cobdenites, other impacts were perhaps transient, yet discernible. First, within Europe, through its very existence and its honorary members, the Club did help sustain the case for free trade and internationalism. 'You would be amazed', Potter wrote to Gladstone from Rome,

---

[178]   M. Freeden, *The New Liberalism: An Ideology of Social Reform* (Oxford, 1978), esp. 32–60; below, 192–4.

[179]   By 1883 Mallet even regretted his suggestion of Morley as Cobden's biographer, for 'several utterances . . . seem to make it impossible to regard him as a Cobdenite'. To Potter, 10 June 1883 in Ampthill Papers, FO 918/54.

[180]   Farrer to Chamberlain, 31 Oct. 1885, Chamberlain Papers, JC 5/30/1, Birmingham University Library.

[181]   Chamberlain in his speech to the Club dinner of 1883, for example, strongly played up the theme of Cobden's radicalism. *Report*, 1883.

'at the respect people have for the Cobden Club. I only wished we deserved it but we are doing some good.'[182] Such admiration was not universal, and the Club had strongly to fend off implausible accusations that it was spending vast sums of money spreading its doctrines in Germany, in which the Liberal MP William Cartwright became heavily embroiled.[183] The Club's dinners, 'audit days of International Economy', also provided a platform for foreign statesmen that was not readily open to them at home, and in this way helped to promote tariff liberalization.[184] The Club's writings, too, were of some importance in influencing debate through the honorary members.[185] Some Liberals believed that British businessmen would be better off funding free trade propaganda in Europe ('doing what Bismarck and Co. are credited with supposing the Cobden Club & the terrible Cartwright to be doing') rather than urging imperial expansion, but the Cobden Club had soon found the international defence of free trade beyond its resources.[186]

Second, within the British Empire, the Club helped keep alive the free trade message in adverse conditions. Particular attention was paid to Australia, especially New South Wales where politicians such as Henry Parkes and George Reid remained strongly committed Cobdenites.[187] The Club also claimed successfully to have influenced colonial policy. For example, it saw the repeal of the Indian cotton duties in 1882 as a victory, since several of its members, including Mallet and Baring, were leading officials associated with India, although the power of the

---

[182] 25 Nov., 1874, GP, Add. MS 44282, fo. 68.

[183] 'Trade Mission to Berlin', Cartwright Papers, Box 1, Northants RO. Cartwright, 'the Cobden Club's apostle', it was held in the press, had visited Germany in order to use corrupt means to advance free trade policies. See *Deutschen Volkswirtschaftlichen Correspondenz* (Berlin), 15 Feb. and 22 Mar. 1879. Odo Russell, the British Ambassador in Berlin, advised Cartwright to maintain a dignified silence, for 'Bismarck's object is to present the free traders and the Cobden Club to Germany in the light of the Jesuits and the Vatican or the socialists . . . that is as the enemies of the Fatherland—and you as the propagator of these doctrines of the Devil are to be stamped out by him as St Michael stamps out Beelzebub.' Russell to Cartwright, 3 Mar. 1879, Cartwright Papers, Box 20. Bismarck's tactics paid off and the Cobden Club thus played a small part in Germany's return to protection in 1879. For a positive continental view of the Club, see K. von Scherzer, *The Times*, 9 Oct. 1875.

[184] Bunsen, Cobden Club, *Annual Report*, 1875; Morier had thus hoped in 1882 that the Spanish free trader Moret Y. Prendergast's presence at the dinner would further his aim of an Anglo-Spanish commercial treaty. Morier to Mallet, 17 June 1882, Morier Papers, Box 45. Morier believed the dinners were 'more thought of abroad than they are in England': to Derby, 20 June 1882, Papers of the 15th Earl of Derby, 920 DER (15)/20, Liverpool Record Office.

[185] For example, the library of the Italian politician Minghetti included an extensive collection of Cobden Club literature, although this failed to inhibit his pragmatic accommodation of growing protectionist pressures in the 1880s. M. Gavelli (ed.), *Catalogo del Fondo Marco Minghetti* (Bologna, 1986). In 1877 the *Journal des Débats* viewed the Club's publications as 'un arsenal . . . des armes précieuses', according to Lyons: FO 881/3438/279c.

[186] Grant Duff to Mallet, 22 Nov. 1885, Grant Duff Papers, MS Eur F234/43; 'Intro', *GD*, vol. 13, xliii for the failure to create an effective 'Free Trade International'.

[187] CCM, 10 May 1879 reporting the Governor of South Australia, Jervois, as anxious to distribute Cobden Club literature; A. W. Martin, *Henry Parkes: A Biography* (Melbourne, 1980); W. G. McMinn, *George Reid* (Melbourne, 1989); D. Currie was also supplied with literature for Cape Colony. CCM, 8 May 1880.

Manchester cotton interest was scarcely negligible.[188] In fact, the Club won a considerable following in India, not so much for its message, as for its organizational example; some historians have therefore plausibly suggested that it formed a model for the Indian Congress movement in the 1880s.[189] T. B. Potter also kept up sustained pressure with regard to the fiscal regime of the Crown Colonies, above all Malta and Ceylon, pressure to which the Conservative Colonial Secretary Carnarvon proved to some extent amenable.[190]

Third, the Club's members promoted, if with diminishing impact, the ideal of Cobdenite foreign policy, particularly the goal of an active commercial diplomacy. In the late 1870s they had, therefore, drawn attention to the wine duties as the means to a renewal of the commercial treaty system, the only fiscal duties whose remission by Britain might encourage reciprocal concessions. Here, undoubtedly, William Cartwright, one of the Club's most active members, did some good by his persistence in pressing the case for the reform of the wine duties in the 1870s, eventually gaining and chairing a select committee in 1879. Cartwright's report fully endorsed the Mallet-type free trade case, that any sacrifice of the revenue would be more than compensated for by the general boost to trade, and the additional guarantees of peace, inherent in commercial treaties.[191] As we will see, this gave a strong, if ultimately insufficient, fillip to Liberal commercial policy in the early 1880s. In all these ways, therefore, the Club fulfilled Mallet's ideal of a 'private FO', but, as we have also seen, its achievements were far wider in party and popular political spheres.

The Cult of Cobden, 1866–86

The Cobden Club's devotion to its hero should not be viewed in isolation from the Liberal Party, nor from a wider appreciation of the benefits of free trade which Cobden's career symbolized. As several recent studies have reiterated, Liberalism throve upon the images of its leaders, with Gladstone most famously celebrated as the 'People's William', and John Bright as the 'plain man's hero' or 'the tribune of

---

[188]   CCM, 4 Mar., 29 Apr. 1876; 20 July 1877; Annual Report, 29 July 1882; Annual Meeting, 28 July 1883; A. Redford, *Manchester Merchants and Foreign Trade* (2 vols, 1934 and 1956), vol. 2, 21–31; I. Klein, 'English Free Traders and Indian Tariffs, 1874–96', *Modern Asian Studies*, 5 (1971), 251–71. In 1885 Grant Duff thus wrote from India to Mallet: 'Yes, thank God! The interest of Manchester will prevent the idiotic cotton duties being re-imposed here', 26 June, Grant Duff Papers, MS Eur. F 234/43. Henry Fawcett, however, opposed repeal, S. Niyogi, 'Fawcett and the Indian Cotton Duties', *Quarterly Review of Historical Studies*, 18 (1978–9), 230–5.

[189]   S. Maccoby, *English Radicalism 1853–86* (1938), 378, citing *Bombay Times*, 10 Aug. 1885. Grant Duff, however, lamented the 'defilement' brought through association with the Club's Indian expert, William Wedderburn. To Mallet, 8 July 1886, Grant Duff Papers, MS Eur. F 234/43. See, too, Grant Duff to Mallet 14 Apr. 1883, F 234/41.

[190]   Food duties on bread and rice were the particular objects of Potter's campaign to abolish the 'whole paltry fabric of impediment to free trade in the Eastern Seas'. Potter to Carnarvon, 14 Feb. 1877, Carnarvon Papers, PRO 30/6/21.

[191]   *Parl. Papers*, 1878–9, 14, SC, Wine Duties; for Cartwright's campaign for, and handling of, this committee, see his diaries, Cartwright Papers, Box 6/13.

the people'.[192] John Bright himself remained the authentic guardian of the League covenant between the 1840s and the 1880s, giving his imprimatur to popular accounts of the Corn Law struggle, and defending free trade in numerous speeches and public letters.[193] If Bright survived as the living embodiment of free trade, Cobden's untimely death in 1865 stimulated the early, yet long-lasting appropriation of his career to public uses not only by the Cobden Club, but in multifarious forms of popular representation. To a large extent, what became the democratic appropriation of Cobden acted as the antidote to Cobdenism, assailed by protectionists and by socialists.[194] This use of Cobden culminated in the Edwardian defence of free trade which exploited to the full the Cobden Centenary of 1904, besides which the centenaries of Gladstone (1909) and Bright (1911) were but pale imitations. Cobden's career lent itself in some ways far more easily than that of Bright to Radical celebration, for he died as he had lived—an outsider, untainted by political compromise, absorption into the 'official class', or support for Unionism. Cobden, an Anglican, lacked Bright's close identification with the puritan strand in British political culture, but this itself slowly faded in resonance in late nineteenth-century Britain.

Cobden's place in popular memory was emphatically linked to the struggle for the repeal of the Corn Laws, with subordinate attention paid to his municipal, pacific, and diplomatic endeavours. Only in 1891 did his friend Edward Watkin celebrate the former in *Alderman Cobden of Manchester*, while the latter awaited full treatment until Hobson's *Richard Cobden: The International Man* in 1918. The repeal of the Corn Laws, on the other hand, had been a focal point of popular histories of Britain since the 1840s, led by Martineau and Charles Knight, and continued in the works of Molesworth and McCarthy, as well as in such popular histories of free trade as that of Mongredien.[195] In these accounts, Repeal constituted one of the central narratives of the people's struggle for their liberties. Constitutional narratives have recently become the focus of much post-modernist attention, but the battle for Repeal arguably provided an even more important theme in the people's history, for this tale of the deliverance of the people from aristocratic oppression was vital in the making of Liberalism and democracy.[196] In

---

[192]   Biagini, *Liberty Retrenchment and Reform*, *passim*; G. D. Goodlad, 'Gladstone and His Rivals' in Biagini and Reid, *Currents of Radicalism*, 163–83; P. Joyce, *Democratic Subjects* (Cambridge, 1994).

[193]   *Diaries of John Bright*, 469, approving 'Great Movements and How to Make Them'; preface, W. N. Molesworth, *The History of England from the year 1830* (3 vols, 1871–3; new edn. 1874); preface, A. Mongredien, *Free Trade and English Commerce* (1881 edn.); H. J. Leech (ed.), *Public Letters of John Bright* (1885), *passim*.

[194]   For this ambiguity, see F. Trentmann, 'Wealth versus Welfare: The British Left between Free Trade and National Economics before the First World War', *Historical Research*, 70 (1997), 70–98.

[195]   Above, n. 193; J. McCarthy, *A History of Our Own Times* (4 vols, 1880), esp. vol. 1, 324–59, vol. 3, 226–60, 405–7.

[196]   Cf. J. Vernon, *Politics and the People: A Study in English Political Culture, c.1815–1867* (Cambridge, 1993).

such a tale, the image of Cobden was writ largest, although Peel, Bright, C. P. Villiers, and of course Gladstone, retained their popular stature.[197]

This cult of Cobden was articulated above all by his representation as a popular hero in sculpture and print.[198] Busts and statues of him were not, of course, to outnumber those of Queen Victoria or Peel, but the handful that were unveiled served to enshrine his importance as a cultural symbol within the political icono- graphy of Victorian Britain.[199] Interestingly, it was Cobden 'the international man' who was first commemorated, with a bust presented by the Belgian Society of Political Economy to the Chamber of Commerce at Verviers, 'le Manchester du continent' in January 1866. The occasion was used to emphasize the support of local industrialists for free trade, and coincided with efforts to create a European federation of Chambers of Commerce for the suppression of customs.[200] Manches- ter followed in April 1867, with a bronze statue unveiled by the old Leaguer George Wilson, and in Salford in June a marble statue was unveiled by C. P. Villiers.[201] Both statues, with their opening ceremonial processions of local politicians, trades, friendly, and co-operative societies, typified the cultural aspirations of the provin- cial élite, combining civic virtue and rugged independence.[202] Yet the subtext underlying the statues as political symbols was made clear at Manchester, where surplus funds collected were devoted to endowing the Cobden Chair of Political Economy, whose duties were to include evening lectures for primary school teach- ers.[203] In London, Cobden not only joined the national cultural heroes in Westmin- ster Abbey, but was commemorated in Camden Town by the Radical shopkeepers of the St Pancras Vestry, although they needed to draw on the deeper purse of Napoleon III in order to complete the statue unveiled in June 1868.[204] These

---

[197] Read, *Peel and the Victorians*; Joyce, *Democratic Subjects*; Villiers enjoyed a strong popular reputation in Wolverhampton during his long career as its MP; his part in Repeal was revived in *The Free Trade Speeches of C. P. Villiers*, ed. 'A Member of the Cobden Club' (2 vols, 1883); 'C. P. Villiers', *Westminster Review*, 1883; A. Bisset, *Notes on the Anti-Corn Law Struggle* (1884), 86–177. The links between Gladstone, Cobden, and free trade are well illustrated in T. Archer, *Gladstone and his Contem- poraries: Fifty Years of Social and Political Progress* (4 vols, 1883).

[198] Additionally, Cobden gave his name to co-operative mills at Sabden (1866), a bridge (1883 in Southampton, erected by the National Liberal Land Company, chaired by Thorold Rogers), as well as pubs, as at Newcastle and Midhurst, and a coffee-house in Birmingham (1883). The first illustrates part of the notable process whereby Cobden was associated with the co-operative movement, and found a strong admirer in the long-lived G. J. Holyoake.

[199] In addition to the public statues discussed below, Parian-ware busts of Cobden were produced in considerable numbers; similarly, numerous photographs and prints were commonly available.

[200] *Journal des Économistes*, 1866, 157–8, 437–56.

[201] Villiers, *Free Trade Speeches*, xciii.

[202] B. Read, *Victorian Sculpture* (1982), 112–13.

[203] *The Times*, 6 Mar. 1866; 23 Apr. 1867. Jevons first held this chair, but his lectures created some local controversy, with his views on strikes deemed 'by no means consonant with that enlarged and generous sympathy with the masses which pre-eminently distinguished the illustrious reformer whose memory and services this lectureship was designed to commemorate', by 'A Cobdenite', 19 Oct. 1866. Jevons, *Papers and Correspondence*, vol. 3, 129–31; vol. 1, 207.

[204] The requisition for the bust in the Abbey was supported by Dickens, Disraeli, Jowett, Maurice, and Tennyson: 19 May 1866, CP 792, WSRO; List of Subscribers, Metropolitan Memorial, CP 789,

sculptures were all primarily memorials to a past career, asserting the claims of Cobden to a permanent place in the national memory alongside those of other favourites of the 'Age of Equipoise': Peel, Wellington, Prince Albert, and Cromwell.[205] Appropriately, they fulfilled Cobden's call for the Victorian middle class to find its own cultural heroes to supplant public admiration for the feudal past.[206]

The context for later statues erected at Bradford and Stockport was significantly different. First, that at Bradford in 1877 coincided with both the stirrings of the fair trade movement in the city, together with the recrudescence of the Eastern Question and the threat of war.[207] Its unveiling thereby acquired a new ideological purpose, the reaffirmation of the Cobdenite message in bad times. This was driven home by Bright himself in two speeches, celebrating Cobden as the benefactor of the people at home and the benefits of a tariff-free and therefore pacific Europe.[208] The second statue, at Stockport, Cobden's first parliamentary seat, fulfilled in 1886 an intention announced in 1865, when £1,000 had been raised. It was belatedly completed in the face of the protectionist revival, which had seen Cobden's old seat fall to the fair trader L. J. Jennings in 1885 and 1886.[209] 'No Trade's Fair that is not Free', announced the mottoes on the triumphal arch that greeted the statue's arrival, and the Marquess of Ripon, with Cobden's Radical daughter Jane at his side, drove home the message of the dangers held out by any return to protective duties.[210]

Statues announced a judgement on character and achievement as well as the appropriation of public space for political ends. Yet, as Gladstone noted in 1866, 'it

WSRO. The subscribers, it was claimed, embraced 'all from the wealthy merchant and well-to-do tradesman to the industrious mechanic and poor working-man'. H. Mitchener to Mrs Cobden, 19 Aug. 1866. F. W. Chesson reported 'These St Pancras men are all Cobdenites to the backbone. They are thoroughly warm, disinterested admirers of the great man who has gone', to Mrs Cobden, 2 Sept. 1865: CP Add. MS 6031, WSRO. The statue itself records Napoleon III as the 'principal contributor': *The Times*, 13 June and 19 Dec. 1868 (1,000 francs from Napoleon); E. Gleichen, *London's Open-Air Statuary* (1928), 192. A copy of Woolner's Westminster bust was presented to Napoleon III and kept at Versailles.

[205]   Busts were also presented to the Reform Club, to Rochdale Town Hall, and, by Bright, to the Brighton Art Gallery: Potter to Gladstone, 10 June 1868, GP, Add. MS 44282; *The Times*, 23 Apr. 1874.

[206]   Howe, *Cotton Masters*, 253, 309; Arlès Dufour thus felt that even Cobden should be commemorated alongside warriors and kings 'for the sake of the principle which triumphed under him'. To Bright, 5 Apr. and 24 May 1865, Bright Papers, Add. MS 43383, fos. 144, 145.

[207]   Interestingly, it was funded by the estate of an American partner of a Bradford firm, G. H. Booth of Firth, Booth and Co., stuff merchants: R. Gowing, *Richard Cobden* (1885), 86; A. H. Robinson, *Bradford's Public Statues* (Bradford, n.d., *c*.1983).

[208]   *Speeches of the Rt Hon. John Bright MP on the occasion of the inauguration of the Cobden Memorial* (1877).

[209]   For his view of Cobden, see L. J. Jennings, 'The Manchester School', *Quarterly Review*, 153 (1882), 152–82.

[210]   *The Cobden Statue* (Stockport Museums and Art Gallery Service, 1986); Mayor of Stockport, Joseph Leigh to Jane Cobden, 25 Nov. 1886 CP 971, WSRO; *The Times*, 29 Nov. 1886: *Cheshire County News*, 29 Nov. 1886. Leigh was also the defeated candidate in 1885 and 1886.

is not upon bronze and marble that the renown of such a man as this depends'.[211]
The printed word was far more important as a means by which Cobden's significance was brought home to a national audience. As we have seen, this was one of the
primary purposes of the Cobden Club, but independent of it there emerged a
sizeable devotional literature, of the type which, Collini has suggested, imparted
and strengthened the Victorian creed of individualism.[212] This began with Thorold
Rogers's funeral oration, whose paean to Cobden's selfless devotion to public
causes, based on perseverance, energy, religion, manliness, and simplicity, was
widely echoed throughout the world.[213] The rush of early biographies promoted
diverse views of Cobden, designed to model his career in particular images. For the
influential Congregationalist divine Newman Hall, Cobden was, above all, an exemplar of a human instrument ordained to accomplish God's work through a life of
practical benevolence, bringing food to the people, and encouraging good order,
social elevation, and peace.[214] This was re-echoed locally by the Manchester
Unitarian revivalist preacher, J. H. Hopps, for whom Cobden was 'a modern
prophet . . . in this man's life also God manifested himself to the English people'.[215]
In more mundane vein, for John MacGilchrist, Cobden's life was less a spur to
salvation than a recruiting sign for the army of political progress, hopefully an
inspiration to young men to reject political stagnation and imbibe Cobden's 'high
ideal of citizenship'. MacGilchrist, an old Anti-Corn Law League hand, now
asserted Cobden's claims to be considered at least as radical as the Chartists,
creating a link between the Radicalism of the 1840s and the new movement for
parliamentary reform.[216] Immediately after the Second Reform Act, Cobden was
placed firmly as an architect of English freedom, his career that of a patriot,
showing 'how we may build up in England a constitution which shall lie four-
square on justice, truth, mercy and purity'.[217]

Other biographies underlined the pertinence of Cobden's career for the 'people',
for example A. T. Scott, for whom 'no statesman that this country has ever
produced can be said to have a greater claim to be called the representative of the
working classes as Mr Cobden', 'the champion of the working men'.[218] For Joseph

[211] *The Times*, 23 July 1866.
[212] S. Collini, 'Manly Fellows: Fawcett, Stephen, and the Liberal Temper', in Goldmann (ed.), *The Blind Victorian*, 41–59.
[213] J. E. T. Rogers, *A Sermon preached at West Lavington Church, Sunday, 9 April 1865* (1865); in Australia, Revd J. C. Woods, *In memory of Richard Cobden. A sermon* (Adelaide, 1865); *Sydney Morning Herald*, 18 June 1865.
[214] C. Newman Hall, *Richard Cobden, MP* (1865); id., *Newman Hall: An Autobiography* (1898), 99–100.
[215] *A Lecture in memory of Richard Cobden who 'gave the people bread'* (n.d., *c*.1867).
[216] J. MacGilchrist, *Richard Cobden: The Apostle of Free Trade, His Political Career and Public Services. A Biography* (1865), esp. vi, 135, 153.
[217] Revd H. W. Parkinson, *Richard Cobden* (Rochdale, 1868), 18.
[218] A. T. Scott, *In Memoriam: The Life and Labours of Richard Cobden* (1865).

Johnson, a Manchester publicist of 'self-effort', Cobden was 'the champion of the rights of the Industrious Classes'.[219] For Thomas Bullock, he was not only 'our greatest Political Economist', but 'the natural leader of the people of England', a position based on his contribution to the human race, a 'universal man, whose career had increased the material prosperity of Europe', and whose scheme of 'a congress of nations' would ensure peace for posterity.[220] Interestingly, Bullock was one of the most influential of Victorian educators, with a crop of school textbooks to his name, in which the free trade battles were always strongly emphasized, and who believed above all in improving literature as the antidote to vice and delin-quency.[221] His Cobden was 'a study for young men', which might 'start into life a Richard Cobden of the future', and aimed 'to inspire our youth with a sense of the worth of manly courage, tempered with a becoming modesty; of the pricelessness of untainted virtue . . . industry, labour, truth . . . of the necessity and nobility of a spirit of self-dependence'. Through such men, Bullock urged, England might 'avoid effeminacy, voluptuousness and ruin', and so perpetuate her 'greatness and glory'.[222]

If Bullock stressed Cobden's manliness, it was 'his dual soul' which struck the journalist Frederick Edge as being 'feminine in creative energy, masculine in resolution, endurance and judgement'.[223] Edge portrayed Cobden at home, in the fastnesses of rural Sussex. As a result, Cobden's political message was integrated with the English past; he was transmuted into an authentic voice of England's lost yeomanry, whose qualities he embodied and whose standing he promised to restore through land reform, a policy that would also reinvigorate the empire and enable Britain to rival the United States in future prosperity.[224]

Finally, Cobden's internationalism was by no means forgotten, with the *British Quarterly Review* portraying him as 'the comparative anatomist of modern civilisa-tion', who 'not only believed in the worth of international sympathy as a humaniz-ing sentiment, but in the policy and wisdom of international knowledge as indispensable to a full reciprocity of benefits'.[225] This was a conscious attempt by the MP MacCullagh Torrens to balance portraits such as that by MacGilchrist with

---

[219] Joseph Johnson, *Life of Richard Cobden: Apostle of Free Trade and Champion of the Rights of the Industrious Classes* (Manchester, 1865).

[220] T. Bullock, *Richard Cobden. (A study for Young Men)* (1866).

[221] e.g., *Illustrated School History of England* (1877), 240–51; *The History of Modern Europe* (1863 and 1871), 315–16; *Juvenile Delinquency* (1848).

[222] Bullock, *Richard Cobden*, esp. 47.

[223] F. M. E[dge], *Richard Cobden at home. A fireside sketch* (1868). Edge was a journalist and writer on Anglo-American affairs. Hilton, in Goldmann, *The Blind Victorian*, 70, notes 'the feminine ideal of peaceful improvement' as characteristic in the third quarter of the nineteenth century; 'the heart of a woman, the intellect of a man' was the verdict of [McCullagh Torrens], 'Richard Cobden', *British Quarterly Review*, 43 (1866), 12.

[224] Equally, as English correspondent of the *Chicago Tribune*, Edge sought for that city's recently formed Free Trade League a bust of Cobden, which 'would possess a talismanic power in the Empress City of the West'. To Mrs Cobden, 12 Mar. 1866, CP Add. MS 6027, WSRO.

[225] 'Richard Cobden', 4.

Cobden 'as a European statesman'.[226] Interestingly, in this context the London International School, which Cobden had helped found in 1864 as part of the new international order heralded by the 1860 Treaty, now appealed in part as a memorial to him.[227] In this vein, too, Fox-Bourne (at the time a war office clerk, later a prominent journalist), celebrated Cobden as the exemplar of British commercial prosperity, while Leone Levi held Cobden up to students of commerce and commercial law as a model whose life would encourage 'future labourers in the never-ending struggle for progress', inspired by the essential message that 'the free intercourse of nations is the handmaid of peace and prosperity'. Suitably, he preferred International Cobden Lectureships as fitter memorials than statues and obelisks, 'at best silent instructors'.[228]

These early biographies of Cobden created an image that served to perpetuate the relevance of his career, both in form and substance, stressing 'the tribute which popular memory pays to the longevity of good in a man's works', by contrast with the evanescence of 'performances . . . which attract more attention and win more praise at the time', a scarcely veiled comparison with Palmerston.[229] In this respect, too, Mrs Cobden proved to be a zealous (and jealous) custodian of her husband's fame and memory. For, as we have seen, she soon organized, with the help of F. W. Chesson (also secretary to the Jamaica Committee), the publication of Cobden's *Political Writings*, in English and American editions.[230] Their distribution among politicians and former Leaguers in itself proved a valuable stimulus to the revitalization of Cobden's leading principles.[231] His reputation was also well served by a generation of authors and journalists who had been active in the 1840s, often closely associated with the Anti-Corn Law League. For the League had, as MacGilchrist noted, created a body of journalists who looked up to Cobden as their great master, and who in the 1850s and 1860s were at the centre of the literature of improvement created for the working man: thus '[they] were enabled to communicate to those to whom they discharged the duty of political and economic instruction, many personal traits and incidents of Cobden's public life'.[232] For example, one of Cobden's obituarists, J. E. Ritchie, had been active in the League struggle in East Anglia and

---

[226] Torrens to Mrs Cobden, 26 Sept. 1865, Cobden Papers, Add. MS 43677. Above, 107.

[227] P. N. Farrar, 'Richard Cobden: Educationist, Economist and Statesman', unpublished Ph.D. thesis, University of Sheffield (1952), ch. 20; W. A. C. Stewart and W. P. McCann, *The Educational Innovators* (1967), 317–26. For its subscribers, International Education Society Ltd., BT 31/992/1506c, PRO; J. A. Emerton (English International College) to Mrs Cobden, 4 and 29 Nov. 1866, CP, Add. MS 6027, WSRO.

[228] H. R. Fox-Bourne, *English Merchants* (2 vols, 1866), vol. 2, 365–84; L. Levi, *On Richard Cobden: An Introductory Lecture (King's College, London, 12 Oct. 1865)* (1865).

[229] Torrens, 'Richard Cobden', *British Quarterly Review*, 43 (Jan. 1866) 2.

[230] Above, 118; interestingly, too, among Cobden's allies, the shipowner W. S. Lindsay also intended a biographical study; see W. S. Lindsay, *Incidents in the Life of Richard Cobden* (1869), CP 289, WSRO; Lindsay Papers, National Maritime Musuem, LND3/1, fos. 285–324.

[231] e.g., J. Hickin and J. Falvey to Mrs Cobden, 26 and 28 Jan. 1866, CP Add. MS 6027, WSRO.

[232] MacGilchrist, *Richard Cobden*, 274.

in the Anti-State Church Association, before taking up journalism in London, largely in association with Cassell, a publisher whose grand idea, he recalled, was to 'elevate morally and socially and intellectually the people of whose cause he was ever an ardent champion and true friend'.[233]

Through this devotional literature, Cobden was situated at the centre of a Radical tradition of continuing pertinence for the working man, and ripe for revival at particular moments in Liberal politics.[234] Thus, in 1877 the 'A' of the 'ABC' of the League, Henry Ashworth, published his highly informative memoir of Cobden.[235] He not only placed 'on record many of the details of a struggle of national importance, the remembrance of which is in danger of passing away', but also brought out their significance in the context of the Anglo-French commercial negotiations of the 1870s and the threat of retaliation.[236] Against the background of Disraelian foreign policy and the Bulgarian atrocities, it was Cobden's work for peace and arbitration that was highlighted in the Penny Biography published by G. Dyer in 1877.[237] This note was also struck by Henry Richard's article on Cobden for the ninth edition of the *Encyclopaedia Britannica* in 1877, a vignette that Morley read 'with entire sympathy and admiration', in a political context that he found 'almost unbearably oppressive—the sight of one's country drifting to the hateful abyss'.[238] Oddly, it was an 'official' interpretation of Cobden that was the longest in coming, for an edition of his correspondence which Potter and the Cobden Club wished to publish was constantly hampered by his widow, before finally being abandoned by his daughters in 1878 in favour of Morley's biography.[239] Morley himself obstructed the publication in English of Mrs Salis Schwabe's *Souvenirs de Richard Cobden*, published, as a result, in Paris in 1879.[240] Such delay and wrangling therefore left, as the most important interpretations of Cobden's career, Mallet's 1867 essay on Cobden's political opinions (reprinted as the introduction to the one-volume edition of the *Political Writings* in 1878), and Thorold Rogers's *Cobden and Modern Public Opinion* (1873), which, as we have seen, provided Gladstonian Liberals with a clear and authoritative guide to Cobden's political pertinence. They also served as the basis for the more popular but full account of Cobden's life,

---

[233]   J. E. Ritchie, *In memory of Richard Cobden. A Biography* (1865); *British Senators* (1865), 366–82; *Christopher Crayon's Recollections* (1898); Bisset, author of *Notes of the Anti-Corn Law Struggle* had also been a League lecturer.

[234]   e.g., D. Brewster, *The Radical Party; its Principles, Objects and Leaders: Cobden, Bright, Mill* (Manchester, 1867).

[235]   Henry Ashworth, *Recollections of Richard Cobden, MP, and the Anti-Corn Law League*.

[236]   This was well appreciated by Bright, *Public Letters*, 228 (1 Apr. 1879).

[237]   See, too, 'The Cobdenic Legacy', in D. Puseley, *The Critical Review or Past and Present* (1877), 49–60, 85–7.

[238]   To Richard, 8 Apr. 1878, cited in H. R. Evans, 'Henry Richard and Cobden's Letters', *Transactions of the Hon. Soc. of Cymmrodorion*, 54–8 (1958), 81.

[239]   None has ever appeared: cf. *The Times*, 19 June 1872, 10f. See CCM, 3 Mar. 1877 *et seq.*; this episode is well covered in Evans, 'Henry Richard and Cobden's Letters'.

[240]   *Bright Diaries*, 407 [15 Apr. 1878].

written against the revival of protection, by Lewis Apjohn, and published in 1881.[241]

In 1881 Morley's *The Life of Richard Cobden*, however long delayed, more than compensated by not only setting new standards in political biography, but also allowing the depiction of a Cobden that was designed to stimulate some of the responses of the 1840s at a time when they were under threat from the fair trade movement.[242] Mallet welcomed Morley's 'exposition of policy', while Morley used his own pages in the *Fortnightly Review* to underscore the value of commercial treaties just when they were being assailed in and out of the Liberal Party.[243] More widely, with Morley himself hailed as 'the most capable exponent alive of the principles which Mr Cobden spent enforcing', his biography provided a 'manual of public spirit' which underwrote the lessons of the 1840s as a guarantee against the newly fashionable dallying with protectionism.[244] This, then, was not sheer nostalgia, nor, as critics held, the 'canonization of Cobden' in an age of growing doubt, but a Cobdenic message for the present and future. William Clarke, a Fabian in the making, acclaimed Cobden as 'the truest democrat of his time', with a progressive vision of 'the modern community [which] proclaims the equal well-being of all as its aim and motive'.[245]

Morley's biography also left a trail of more popular works in its wake. The most notable was that of Richard Gowing, the secretary of the Cobden Club, whose *Richard Cobden* (1885) appeared in Cassell's World's Workers series, in the company, *inter alia*, of Titus Salt, Dickens, Lincoln, Livingstone, Franklin, and Handel. This was a work that stressed to the full the relevance of Cobden's career to the debates of the 1880s, and even included a chapter on the Cobden Club itself. But once more the link with Cassell is important, illustrating the alliance between popular educational publishers and progressive causes. Cobden fitted naturally into this world, which emphasized the values of the autodidact and improvement through moral character. Cobden's personal 'heroism' was also the theme of other

---

[241] Lewis Apjohn, *Richard Cobden and the Free Traders* (Memorable Men of the Nineteenth Century, 4 (1883), preface, 1881).

[242] Bright looked forward to a cheap edition, 'for I can conceive of hardly anything better than that that volume should enter into scores of thousands of homes, to instruct scores of thousands of families in this country', quoted in *Rochdale Observer*, 19 Nov. 1881; for Gladstone's appreciation, letter to Morley, GD, vol. 10, 152 [24 Oct. 1881]. See, too, D. A. Hamer, *John Morley: Liberal Intellectual in Politics* (Oxford, 1968), 121–2.

[243] *Fortnightly Review*, 29 (1881), 794–800. Mallet found in the proofs of *Cobden* 'unspeakable consolation that there should be such a portraiture'. To Morier, 20 Jan. 1879, Morier Papers, Box 44.

[244] Quotations from [Spencer Walpole] 'The Life of Mr Cobden', *Edinburgh Review*, 155 (Jan. 1882), 60–91; [J. C. Morrison], 'The Life of Richard Cobden by John Morley', *MacMillan's Magazine*, 45 (Jan. 1882), 210–22; see, too, [E. C. Whitehurst], 'Richard Cobden', *Westminster Review*, new ser. 61 (Jan. 1882), 98–136; 'Richard Cobden', *London Quarterly Review*, 58 (Apr.–July 1882), 1–33; [A. J. Balfour], 'Morley's *Life of Cobden*', *Nineteenth Century*, 11 (Jan. 1882), reprinted in *Essays and Addresses* (Edinburgh, 1893), 185–223; A. N. MacNicoll, 'Richard Cobden', *Gentleman's Magazine*, 252 (1882), 424–2; [A. Allardyce], 'The Canonisation of Cobden', *Blackwood's Magazine*, 130 (Dec. 1881), 793–810; Goldwin Smith, 'Peel and Cobden', *Nineteenth Century*, xi (1882), 869–89.

[245] William Clarke, 'Richard Cobden', *British Quarterly Review*, 75 (1882), 146–79, esp. 159.

versions propagated by the Cobden Club. Frances Cooke's *An English Hero: The story of Richard Cobden* (1889), for example, was designed for 'young readers', for whom Cobden provided a model of fortitude, courage, perseverance, individual effort and energy, and devotion to noble ideals, a hero raised up by God to work for the people's welfare, for, 'Was not *he* a hero, who was true from boyhood to great aims in life, and who bravely did his duty through evil and good report?'[246] Of course, this type of literature upheld many heroes and many causes, but Cobden proved remarkably long-lived, and wide-ranging in his appeal. It was, for example, with the same message but to a very different audience that Lady Dorothy Nevill presented her Sussex neighbour's life, with its 'enduring proofs of pure morality, keen intelligence, perfect disinterestedness, undaunted courage, high patriotism, and an invincible faith in the predetermined triumph of good over evil'.[247]

Cobden's reputation found a further important means of communication in the innumerable popular lectures devoted to his career. He had modestly outlined their purport before his death. He wrote to a prospective lecturer:

I do not think it possible to impart sufficent interest to the personal topic . . . The only course would be to make it a politico-economical lecture, showing the state of our commerce and the condition of the people under the old regime of monopoly and corn laws,— particularly the periodical crises and distress and discontent of the masses—as contrasted with the enormous development of commerce, wealth, prosperity and popular contentment under the rule of free trade.[248]

Such themes became staple among Liberal and Radical lecturers from the 1860s to the 1890s and beyond.[249]

Print, statuary, and lectern provided vital means whereby the political legacy of Cobden was reinforced within popular culture, through the primacy of personal example, for the qualities of the man were implicitly inseparable from the rightness of the causes he supported. Symbolically, he was the perfect figure-head to reconcile within the Liberal creed the secular and evangelical strands from which popular political economy had developed since the 1840s. More than this, he had emerged at the centre of a narrative of English history, in which the free trade battle encapsulated the liberation of the English people from aristocratic misrule. Here was a heroic, democratic narrative in which Cobden figured as the peer of Washington, Garibaldi, and Mazzini in the making of national popular identity.[250] If, as has

---

[246]   Mundella acquired 100 copies for distribution as prizes, etc.; Armytage, *Mundella*, 327.

[247]   Lady Dorothy Nevill, 'Some Recollections of Cobden', *The Woman's World*, ed. Oscar Wilde, 2 (1888), 346–51. For Cobden as local hero, see, too, W. H. Burnett, *Midhurst Almanac, 1893*, 27–31.

[248]   To James Richardson, 26 Mar. 1864, Cobden Papers, Duke University; C. Kemp to Rogers, 2 Dec. 1871, Rogers Papers, 417.

[249]   For Cobden as the subject of National Reform Union lectures, see John Johnson Collection, Bodleian Library, 'Creeds, parties, policies', Box 21; for George Dawson's lecture on Cobden, *Biographical Lectures*, ed. G. St Clair (1886), 523–33; admission card to Canon Barker's lecture, 'Great Reformers in Church and State. Richard Cobden', Toynbee Hall, 31 Jan. 1897, CP 795, WSRO.

[250]   Interestingly, admiration for Cobden, and his memorabilia, strongly motivated one of the pioneers of people's history, Henry Willett of Brighton: see R. Samuel, *Theatres of Memory, Vol 1. Past and Present in Contemporary Culture* (1994), 20, 44.

been recently argued, John Bright was a central figure in middle-class and demo-cratic identity, Cobden proved at least an equal, and in some ways a more lasting and versatile symbol of the English people.[251]

These popular representations of Cobden complemented the literary work of the Cobden Club in reinforcing the centrality of the political lessons of the 1840s for the working man. In doing so, they helped provide a means of informing and enthusing the electorate before either the Conservative or the Liberal Parties had developed extensive propaganda machines, with the latter, for example, only begin-ning its *Liberal Magazine* in 1886. In this educational task, the Club was by no means working in isolation. As we have seen, institutionally, the Club found important allies in both the National Liberal Federation and the secular societies. Other bodies carried similar messages. For example, in the north of England the National Reform Union, the closest successor to the Anti-Corn Law League, kept the issue of free trade well before the electorate, with a series of tracts, as well as campaigns by lecturers such as Joseph Howes.[252] Above all, the Financial Reform Association, if largely superseded by the Cobden Club, acted as a gadfly on its back, urging its free trade 'junior' to renewed popular campaigning, and conducting its own lecture drives, especially on the 'free breakfast table' issue in the early 1880s.[253] Locally, it provided a Cobdenite redoubt amidst Liverpool's increasingly sectarian and Tory democratic politics. Finally, in the provinces and London a number of popular political organizations owed a direct allegiance to the Cobdenite model, for example the London Free Trade Association of 1866, the Dialectical Society, and Cobden Clubs in Leeds (1869), Blackburn (1868), Bury, Bermondsey, and Seacombe.[254]

In this way, the Cobden Club and the cult of Cobden were of vital importance at the level of popular political knowledge in transmitting the free trade values of the 1840s to the new political generation of the 1880s and beyond. The Club had been the leading means whereby Liberals had responded to the call of the *Financial Reformer* for new 'enlightenment with respect to the principles of political economy. The generation that was educated by the Anti-Corn Law League has passed and it seems as if the work of the organisation will have to be done over again

---

[251] Joyce, *Democratic Subjects*.

[252] The NRU lacks its historian, but its tracts included J. Slagg, *Free Trade and Tariffs*, J. Watts, *The Logic of Free Trade*, and J. Pim, *Our Foreign Commerce and Free Trade Policy* (1882); Joseph Howes, *Twenty-Five Years Fight with the Tories* (Leeds, 1907).

[253] *The Financial Reformer*, 1858–1906; Calkins, 'Free Trade Lobby' pays little attention to the FRA's later years, but notes its increasing presence (103). Asquith and Haldane lectured under its aegis in the early 1880s; Samuel Morley seems to have been its main financial pillar, with the Cobden Club indirectly subsidizing its work.

[254] *Address of the Free Trade Association of London to the American Free Trade League* (1866); E. Belfort Bax, *Reminiscences and Reflexions of a Mid and late Victorian* (1918; repr. New York, 1967), 227–30; *Sunday Special*, 5 Jan. 1881 (opening of the Kensal Road Cobden Club by Passmore Edwards); *Birkenhead News*, 17 Jan. 1886 (Seacombe Cobden Club); *The Beehive*, 22 Oct. 1870; *Club and Institute Journal* (Working Men's Club and Institute Union), 7 Dec. 1883, 9 Jan., and 27 Feb. 1885. I am grateful to Detlev Mares for the latter references.

before the ghost of protection is finally laid.'[255] As Colin Matthew has emphasized, this was pre-eminently the age of political rhetoric, in which the spoken word was the primary means of political communication.[256] But rhetoric acted intimately in harness with print, and although there are many uncertainties concerning the impact of political propaganda in any age, there can be little doubt that both the massive literature of the Cobden Club and the representations of Cobden in sculpture and print did have an important impact on the nature and values of late-Victorian popular political culture. An effective distribution network allowed propaganda to be carried to many homes, and if at this time politics began to leave the public sphere, the Club successfully combined print and privacy.[257] Its discussion of free trade aimed both to inform the Liberal activist and to enthuse the voters, providing simple messages, which, however, represented an intellectual challenge, and rose above the sloganizing of the party handbill, and the imaginative appeal that the Primrose League had begun to exploit. Through its direct discussion of one major issue of politics, carefully linked to Radical ideas on foreign and domestic policy, Cobdenite literature added depth to discussions in the press, and reinforced the prevalent free trade bias of working-class reading.[258] This popular appeal of Gladstone-Cobdenism for the most part successfully sapped embryonic support for fair trade in the early 1880s, and perpetuated free trade as an integral part of the rational democracy that many felt was threatened in the age of household suffrage. Almost uniquely, and against the expectation of many, in Britain the advent of democracy consolidated rather than undermined free trade.[259] But in the colonies and in Europe, democracy and nationalism had combined to challenge free trade, and with it the liberal international order, to whose interlocking vicissitudes we must now turn.

---

[255]   1 Jan. 1879, 6, and quoted in Brown, *Tariff Reform Movement*, 12.

[256]   H. C. G. Matthew, 'Rhetoric and Politics in Britain, 1860–1950', in P. J. Waller (ed.), *Politics and Social Change in Modern Britain* (1987), 34–58.

[257]   For the image of the newly enfranchised elector with his Cobden Club leaflet, 'seated comfortably at his fireside, engaged in the duty which falls to his lot as a "capable citizen" in these stirring times', see G. Whitelaw, *Co-operative Voting, the only means to Proportional Representation* (1885), 12.

[258]   C. Salmon, 'What the Working Classes Read', *Nineteenth Century*, July 1886, 114–15.

[259]   Cf. A. S. Milward, 'Tariffs as Constitutions', in S. Strange and R. Tooze (eds.), *The International Politics of Surplus Capacity: Competition for Market Shares in the World Recession* (1981), 57–66.

5

Britain and Free Trade in the Age of Gladstone, Bismarck, and Disraeli: The Hegemon's Dilemma, 1865–1886

I have never thought Cobden an oracle either on foreign or home affairs. He believed three things with all his heart. That the repeal of the Corn Laws would break the power of the landed aristocracy. That the example of England would bring about free-trade all over the world. That great wars would never be made again, being incompatible with the ideas of an industrial age. On all three points he has been wrong. The landowners are stronger than before. Europe is showing more protectionist tendencies than twenty years ago and America itself following suit—and all the world is armed to the teeth.

Lord Derby to Sir Stafford Northcote, 26 Feb. 1877.[1]

THE Liberal vision of European progress, based on free trade, peace, and democracy, so strongly propagated between 1846 and 1865, was to be steeply in decline in the next generation. In the wake of the Austro-Prussian War of 1866 and the Franco-Prussian War of 1870, the growing costs of armaments imposed heavy demands upon exchequers, for whom tariffs grew in attractiveness as sources of revenue.[2] The threat posed to free trade by escalating military budgets was, of course, one familiar to economists and politicians schooled by Smith, Mill, and Cobden, but it now evoked a candid reappraisal in the writings of Cliffe Leslie, Passy, and de Lavaleye.[3] This fiscal-military challenge was exacerbated by the onset of European-wide depression after 1873, as falling prices, declining profits, and rising unemployment drastically revised the axiom that free trade was synonymous with prosperity.[4] This revivified a protectionist tradition that had never entirely disappeared in England, and had remained vocal abroad.[5] A third challenge, but

---

[1] Iddesleigh Papers, BL, Add. MS 50022, fos. 131–2; Derby Papers, 17/2/6 (copy).

[2] For an overview of military expenditure and fiscal policy, see J. M. Hobson, 'The Military Extraction Gap and the Wary Titan: The Fiscal-Sociology of British Defence Policy 1870–1913', *Journal of European Economic History*, 22 (1993), 461–506; id., 'The Tax-Seeking State: Protectionism, Taxation and State Structures in Germany, Russia, Britain and America, 1870–1914', unpublished Ph.D. thesis, University of London (1991).

[3] E. Silberner, *The Problem of War in Nineteenth-Century Economic Thought* (Princeton, 1946) brilliantly elucidates this.

[4] P. A. Gourevitch, *Politics in Hard Times: Comparative Responses to International Economic Crises* (1986); S. B. Saul, *The Myth of the Great Depression 1873–1896* (1969).

[5] C. N. Newdegate and Lord Bateman exemplified protectionist continuity from the 1840s.

one whose contours were more slowly defined, was that of European imperial expansion, the neo-mercantilist and protectionist implications of which became clear only in the early 1880s.

The interlocking pressures of rising military expenditure, economic depression, and territorial imperialism all exposed the fragility of Britain's ability to shape the international economic order in her own free trade image.[6] Her supposed leadership of the world economic system—the hegemony attributed to Britain by late nineteenth-century German historical economists and by latter-day theorists of international relations—proved chimerical, as nation after nation imitated the American-inspired model of protection, propagated extensively by List in the 1840s, but now more enthusiastically endorsed in Germany, France, Italy, Canada, the Australian colonies, and not without its supporters in England.[7] Most simply, Britain's eclipse has been ascribed to the negligence of her aristocratic diplomatic corps, ever disdainful of trade, but whose passivity in the face of incipient protectionism in Europe, it has been claimed, now had drastic consequences.[8] For such dereliction, its critics hold, contributed significantly to the long-term decline of the British economy, as Britain stood apart from the commercial evolution of Europe. In a more complex view, Britain's apparent conservatism in foreign economic policy can be attributed to misplaced confidence in her free trade traditions, whose domestic strength was such that, as we have seen, any threatened violation of Cobdenite orthodoxy risked damaging political consequences. Against this background, historians have found it surprising that Britain both failed to attempt 'to persuade other major powers of the benefits of maintaining a world free-trade market', and that she remained indifferent to the merits of the 'new model' German industrial state, which received only belated endorsement from the tariff reformers of 1903.[9]

Yet neither failure is surprising when set against the dilemmas that Britain faced as a 'hegemonic' power.[10] For, on the one hand, there did exist the possibility of

[6]   P. K. O'Brien and G. A. Pigman, 'Free Trade, British Hegemony and the International Economic Order', *Review of International Studies*, 18 (1992), 104–10.

[7]   W. O. Henderson, *Friedrich List: Economist and Visionary* (1983); Y. Breton and M. Lutfalla, *L'Économie politique en France au XIXe siècle* (Paris, 1991), chs. 6 and 11; W. H. Dawson, *Protection in Germany* (1904); W. Lotz, *Die Ideen der deutschen Handelspolitik von 1860 bis 1891* (Leipzig, 1892); *Free Trade and the European Treaties of Commerce* (Cobden Club, 1875), esp. 95–8 (J. M. Stuart on 'economic Germanism' in Italy); G. W. Cole, *Protection as a National System Suited for Victoria: Being Extracts from List's National System of Political Economy* (Melbourne, 1860); C. D. W. Goodwin, *Economic Inquiry in Australia* (Durham, NC, 1966), 3–26; id., *Canadian Economic Thought* (Durham, NC, 1961), esp. 56–9; S. S. Lloyd (ed.), List, *The National System of Political Economy* (1885).

[8]   D. C. M. Platt, *Finance, Trade and Politics in British Foreign Policy, 1815–1914* (Oxford, 1968), esp. xx–xxix, 82–148; J. W. T. Gaston, 'Trade and the late Victorian Foreign Office', *International History Review*, 4 (1982); O'Brien and Pigman, 'Free Trade, British Hegemony'.

[9]   *The Gladstone Diaries* (*GD*), vol. 10, intro, xxxff.; E. H. H. Green, *The Crisis of Conservatism: The Politics, Economics, and Ideology of the British Conservative Party, 1880–1914* (1995).

[10]   A. Stein, 'The Hegemon's Dilemma: Britain, the United States, and the International Economic Order', *International Organisation*, 38 (1984), 355–86; R. Rogowski, *Commerce and Coalitions* (Princeton, 1989), 159–71.

ending the unilateral policy that had been in place since 1846—making her the so-called 'one-sided free trade state'—by enacting a policy of aggressive commercial diplomacy, and abandoning, if necessary, low tariffs in favour of retaliation and imperial preference.[11] Arguably, this fair trade policy offered the best chance of maximizing British power relative to that of other nations, but it also contained the danger of a zero-sum game, ending in the closure of the economic system, a world of autarkic, neo-mercantilist states.[12] For both fair traders and, later, tariff reformers, these were risks worth running if Britain were not to submit to a relative loss of power through European and American competition. The alternative Cobdenite ideal, on the other hand, accepted the inevitability of a decline of British power, given her finite natural resources, and urged a strictly non-interventionist foreign policy, a 'little England' outlook in which British power would rest on her moral stature and European trade rather than on her territorial extent and military might.[13] This policy might appear to sacrifice power, but would maximize wealth and welfare, and might, in the long term, for example by the avoidance of costly imperial entanglements, coincide with both prosperity and power.[14]

In practice, these antithetical ideals did not present themselves so starkly, although they had underlain the conflict between Cobden and Palmerston, and were to grow keenly in political and polemical definition.[15] For in the 1870s and 1880s Britain had decisively to modify her commercial policy to take account of militarism, protectionism, and, increasingly, of empire, those powerful solvents of the Cobdenite world-view. In this process of readjustment, policy-makers always operated under the legacy of the Cobdenite vision of a free trade Europe, and the model of 1860 continued to dominate Britain's European commercial diplomacy.[16] Nevertheless, the scope of that policy inevitably contracted, for, above all, the swing to the East, begun under Palmerston, exploited by Disraeli, and confirmed by the occupation of Egypt in 1882, portended an age of commercial and imperial

[11]   B. H. Brown, *The Tariff Reform Movement in Great Britain, 1881–1895* (New York, 1943); S. H. Zebel, 'Fair Trade', *Journal of Modern History*, 12 (1940).

[12]   Stein, 'Hegemon's Dilemma', 384–5.

[13]   See Cobden, 'England, Ireland, America' (1835), in *The Political Writings of Richard Cobden* (2 vols, 1867; 1878, ed. L. Mallet), 45, for America's prospective rise and Britain's fall; in 1878 Gladstone argued that the United States would supplant Britain as the workshop of the world, a view of Dutch-style decline which Granville thought avoidable, 'unless we go conquering Affganistans [sic], and civilizing Asia Minors', Granville to Gladstone, 30 Oct. 1878, A. Ramm (ed.), *GG Corr. 1876–86*, vol. 1, 84.

[14]   This 'neo-Cobdenite' perspective strongly informs P. K. O'Brien, 'The Costs and Benefits of British Imperialism', *Past and Present*, 120 (1988), 163–200.

[15]   Above, 71–2; M. Swartz, *The Politics of British Foreign Policy in the Era of Disraeli and Gladstone* (1985).

[16]   PRO T172/945, 'Commercial Diplomacy, 1860–1902'. This paper commissioned by the Treasury 'shows how useless a weapon retaliation has been in the hands of foreign nations', Diaries of Sir Edward Hamilton, Add. MS 48681, 17 Dec. 1903. Its author was the Cambridge economic historian H. O. Meredith. See W. Runciman to C. P. Trevelyan, 16 Oct. 1903, Trevelyan Papers, University of Newcastle, CPT13; see, too, P. Ashley, *Modern Tariff History* (1st edn., 1904).

diplomacy in which the Cobdenite Western vision would necessarily shrink in importance.[17] British policy in this context is better seen not as a careless and complacent abdication of 'hegemony', but as a determined attempt to reconcile the entrenched political morality of free trade with a world system dominated by Bismarckian power politics and protectionist tariffs. Even so, in the face of such a violent check to the Cobdenite advance in Europe, there came back into play in Britain the mutually contradictory forces of dogmatic hostility to commercial diplomacy, and the fair trade demand for retaliatory tariffs. It was in the strategic middle ground between 'splendid economic isolation' and tariff warfare that Cobdenite free traders sought the unspectacular, but not unsuccessful readjustment of British commercial policy in the age of Gladstone, Bismarck, and Disraeli.

The Liberals and Europe, 1866–74

The Francophile Cobdenite vision that lay at the heart of British policy in the early 1860s met its first significant challenge during the Liberal government of 1868–74. For, in several ways, Gladstone's Cabinet proved less conducive to an active commercial policy than had Palmerston's. In part, this reflected the growing complexities of the European diplomatic situation faced by the Foreign Secretary, Clarendon. To some extent, also, domestic preoccupations were uppermost in the wake of the 1867 Reform Act, even if Gladstone's own fiscal ambitions had on the whole been fulfilled.[18] After 1866 the British tariff had been largely pared to the bone, with relatively few, but highly productive duties remaining (including tea, sugar, wine, coffee), upon which the burden of state expenditure rested. In this fiscal context, Gladstone was highly sensitive to the political and social implications that would follow from any further attempts either to introduce the 'free breakfast table' or to abolish income tax.[19]

More directly, there survived among numerous Liberal free traders the belief that the 1860 Treaty had been an exceptional departure from 1840s orthodoxy. Above all, Gladstone's Chancellor Lowe spearheaded a frontal attack on Cobdenite diplomacy, and brought to the centre of the Cabinet the purely unilateral free trade view, in which Britain's commercial policy should be decided solely by reference to her own interests, not those of other governments through tariff-bargaining. Policy should be dictated by fiscal need and not by Cobden's, nor even Russell's ideal of a liberal Europe. Lowe believed commercial negotiations to be pointless, since Britain's 'minimalist' tariff had deprived her of bargaining power, while an active promotion of free trade abroad merely increased continental suspicion that free

---

[17]   As Bright reminded T. B. Potter in 1877, Cobden 'would never touch India in any shape', 4 Dec. 1877, Potter Letters; J. Morley, *The Life of Richard Cobden* (2 vols, 1881), vol. 2, 360–1; W. H. Dawson, *Richard Cobden and Foreign Policy* (1926), 193–202, 206–9.

[18]   *GD*, vol. 7, intro, xxvi–xxix.

[19]   Ibid., lxxxv–lxxxvii; E. Biagini, 'Debate on taxation', in E. Biagini and A. J. Reid, *Currents of Radicalism* (Cambridge, 1991), 134–62.

trade was a self-interested British ideal.[20] For Lowe, the Board of Trade itself represented 'a form of combination with some commercial interests to force upon the Treasury fiscal changes which on the general principles of taxation it does not appprove'.[21] Duties might be altered, but only with reference to domestic, fiscal priorities; Britain's example might guide other nations, but it was up to them to follow without further tariff incentives. This view won considerable support inside the Cabinet, in particular from Kimberley, and increasingly from Gladstone himself.[22] Influential and expert opinion reinforced these doubts—for example, that of Overstone—reviving the unilateralist hostility to treaties as a return to commercial bargaining and an abrogation of Peelite 'pure free trade'.[23]

In this context, Board of Trade officials, despite the benevolent overlordship of John Bright, and commercial activists within the Foreign Office faced increasing difficulties in their schemes for further treaties.[24] But visionary cosmopolitan optimism had by no means disappeared. In 1869, for example, J. Savile Lumley (later, first Baron Savile), the minister at Brussels, proposed to trump schemes for a Franco-Belgian customs union by a British-inspired union of Belgium and Holland, which France and the *Zollverein* might join, constituting 'a Commercial Federation . . . which would form a peaceful coalition capable of still further extension . . . as might result in the establishment of a peaceful policy throughout Europe'.[25] This diplomatic panjandrum earned a swift reproof from Clarendon, but Mallet was so emboldened by Lumley's European *Zollverein* scheme as to urge on Clarendon his earlier ideas of a free trade Europe by congress.[26] For 'it seems to

[20] For a good account of Lowe's thinking, see A. Iliasu, 'The Role of Free Trade Treaties in British Foreign Policy, 1859–1871', unpublication Ph.D. thesis, University of London (1965), ch. 7. Lowe believed that by 1862 with only 45 items on her tariff, Britain needed full fiscal liberty in order to safeguard her revenue. See, too, J. Winter, *Robert Lowe* (Toronto, 1976). Lowe's distaste for tariffs had been marked during his Australian political career in the 1840s: see S. Elliott Napier, 'Robert Lowe and his association with Australia', *Royal Australian Historical Society, Journal and Proceedings*, 18 (1932), 1–31; R. Knight, *Illiberal Liberal: Robert Lowe in New South Wales, 1842–50* (Melbourne, 1960).

[21] Lowe to Gladstone, 26 July 1869, GP, Add. MS 44301, fos. 58–9.

[22] Mallet found Kimberley 'imbued with all the false and immoral principles of the Palmerston school with the dogmatism and pedantry of Lord Overstone and Lowe superadded'. To Morier, 24 Mar. 1870, Morier Papers, Box 34. For résumés of Cabinet views, see *GD*, vol. 8, 55 [1 Nov. 1871] and FO 27/2007, 17 July 1873.

[23] Overstone to Granville, 25 Feb. and 1 Mar. 1870, Granville Papers, PRO 30/29/151; Overstone to Grey, 7 Nov. 1872, see D. P. O'Brien, *The Correspondence of Lord Overstone* (3 vols, Cambridge, 1971), vol. 3, 1231–2. Grey himself was not against a new treaty, mistaken though he considered the original one to have been, Grey to Overstone, 9 Nov. 1872; ibid. 1234–5; Bonamy Price, Drummond Professor of Political Economy at Oxford also concluded against treaties in *Contemporary Review*, 13 (1870), 321–45. Interestingly, Lowe and Overstone, whose views had clashed on limited liability, agreed in their aversion to 'Free Trade by treaty'. William Newmarch also opposed treaties, *Address on Economy and Trade* (NAPSS, 1871), 25.

[24] Bright to Clarendon, 13 May 1869, friendly pressure in Denmark; cf. Mallet to Clarendon, 24 June 1869, 27 July 1869, *re* Spain and Portugal, all in Clarendon dep. c. 499, folder 6.

[25] Lumley to Clarendon, no. 155, 14 Apr. 1869, FO 10/294.

[26] Clarendon to Lumley, 21 Apr. 1869, Clarendon dep. c. 475; Mallet to Clarendon, 21 Apr. 1869, with copies of Morier to Benedetti, 10 Oct. 1866, and Mallet to Morier, n.d., Oct. 1866; ibid., dep. c. 499, folder 6; J. Gaston, 'The Free Trade Diplomacy Debate and the Victorian European Common

me', he wrote, 'an object of great political importance that England which is still regarded with great industrial jealousy on the Continent, should in some way or other identify herself with the international arrangements which must be the order of the day in Europe if peace is to be maintained for some time to come.'[27] British suspicion of France's intentions towards Belgium, and the onset of the Franco-Prussian War, stymied this call 'to connect ourselves with the European system', but hopes for commercial treaties were not wholly abandoned. In particular, the diplomat Morier, rarely silenced by official discretion, launched, as 'a disciple of Cobden', a frontal assault on Lowe's policy, defending modern commercial treaties as part of Britain's world mission, a means of reconciling national and international interests, and a source of higher human culture.[28]

The proponents of treaties were scarcely encouraged by the eventual conclusion of the Anglo-Austrian negotiations begun a decade earlier. For the treaty agreed in December 1865 took a further four years to be implemented following the War of 1866, the *Ausgleich*, and the Austro-German Commercial Treaty eventually agreed in March 1868.[29] Mallet determinedly conducted a long series of negotiations, although even his patience waned, given his belief that the benefits of free trade were so transparent in Austria's case—as the only means to stimulate the economic growth which would overcome the disintegrating forces of nationalism—that too much haggling to reconcile protectionist manufacturers was unjustified.[30] On the other hand, Clarendon as Foreign Secretary was well placed to complete his earlier efforts to convince the Austrians of the merits of free trade. Even Lowe's fiscal policy was not unhelpful, for the budget of 1869 included the abolition of the corn registration duty, a step resisted when canvassed in 1865.[31] Eventually, therefore, the Convention giving effect to the 1865 Treaty was signed on 30 December 1869, and hailed by Gladstone as 'a supplement in miniature' to the 1860 Anglo-French Treaty.[32] At the same time, with the 'final shred of protection' now gone from the British tariff, Gladstone also held that in future 'the margin which remains open to us for any commercial treaty is very narrow'.[33]

The tightening scope for successful commercial negotiations was soon to be

Market Initiative' [hereafter 'Common Market'], *Canadian Journal of History*, 22 (1987), 68. See, too, above, 103.

[27]   Mallet to Clarendon, 21 Apr. 1869, Clarendon dep. c. 499, folder 6.

[28]   'A Disciple of Cobden' (R. Morier), *Commercial Treaties: Free Trade and Internationalism: Four Letters* (1870).

[29]   Above, 101–3; K. F. Helleiner, *Free Trade and Frustration: Anglo-Austrian Negotiations, 1860–70* (Toronto, 1973), 112–33; Iliasu, 'Free Trade Treaties', ch. 6.

[30]   Mallet to Clarendon, 17 Mar. and 21 Oct. 1869, Clarendon. dep. c. 499, folder 6.

[31]   Above, 114, cf. 102 n. 186.

[32]   A. Ramm (ed.), *The Political Correspondence of Mr Gladstone and Lord Granville, 1868–1876* [hereafter *GG Corr. 1868–76*] (Camden 3rd ser., 81 and 82, Royal Historical Society, 1952), vol. 2, 272; above, 103.

[33]   *Hansard*, 3rd ser., 190, cc. 882–3, 28 Feb. 1870.

revealed, as the Anglo-French Treaty of 1860 neared the end of its ten-year term.[34] Not only had Lowe and the unilateralist economists already challenged the desirability of treaties in principle, but British businessmen, as in the case of the Association of Chambers of Commerce, seemed, at best, indifferent to the fate of the Anglo-French Treaty. The views of both camps were re-echoed in the *The Times* and *The Economist*.[35] Inside Parliament, doubts as to the value of treaties had been expressed by MPs such as Birley of Manchester, Hermon of Preston, and Hill of Coventry, while outside it the Revivers of British Industry and the Manchester Reciprocity Association had voiced weak expressions of protectionism.[36] More dangerously, many Frenchmen, whether as republicans who were resentful of the treaty as the product of imperial diktat, or as manufacturers yet to be weaned off protection, had continued to oppose the treaty, especially with the impact of the cotton famine in the mid-1860s, and the subsequent depression.[37] In 1869 a protectionist-inspired *enquête* into the treaty was already under way, a cause furthered by the Franco-Prussian war, which created both the need for a rapid increase in revenue and the opportunity for the resurgence of protectionist interests held in check by the Second Empire. By 1871 Thiers ('je suis un ancien Protectioniste . . . Je reste Protectioniste'[38]) openly played to these groups in denouncing the treaty, but emphasized diplomatically the need for revenue as a reason for modifying, not abandoning, it.[39]

---

[34]   Under its original terms, the treaty lasted for ten years, but remained in force on an annual basis thereafter until 12 months after its denunciation. Its renegotiation was delayed by the Franco-Prussian War but began in earnest in March 1871. The treaty was denounced by France on 15 March 1872, and was therefore due to expire 15 March 1873. A. L. Dunham, *The Anglo-French Treaty of Commerce of 1860* (Ann Arbor, 1930), 100, 312.

[35]   J. W. T. Gaston, 'Policy-Making and Free-Trade Diplomacy: Britain's Commercial Relations with Western Europe, 1869–1886', unpublished Ph.D. thesis, University of Saskatchewan (1975), 129; K. B. Clayton, 'Anglo-French Commercial Relations 1860–1882', unpublished MA thesis, Manchester University (1954), 76–9.

[36]   Association of the Revivers of British Industry, handbills and broadsheets, 1868–9, British Library; Brown, *Tariff Reform Movement*, 5–7; (Manchester) Reciprocity Association to Lord Derby, 6 Oct. 1869, 20 Jan. 1870, Derby Papers; 'A Manchester Merchant', *An Inquiry into the commercial position of Great Britain and the causes of the present ruinous and alarming state of our maufacturing interests* (Manchester, 1869).

[37]   Dunham, *Anglo-French Treaty*, 295 ff; Clayton, 'Commercial Relations', 81 ff; M. S. Smith, *Tariff Reform in France, 1860–1900* (Ithaca, 1980), 34–9; A. Devers, 'La Politique Commerciale de la France depuis 1860', *Handelspolitik*, 146. The constitutional changes of 1869 removed the imperial power of treaty-making, leading Lyons to speculate (rightly) to Clarendon, 3 Dec. 1869 that 'I am afraid we shall never again, either in political or commercial affairs, have as good times as we had under the personal power of the Emperor.' Newton, *Lord Lyons: A Record of British Diplomacy* (2 vols, 1913), vol. 1, 240, also quoted Gaston. Lyons, the British Ambassador in Paris advised inaction in the face of this opposition.

[38]   Gaston, 'Free-Trade Diplomacy', 124.

[39]   For his economic ideas, see esp. R. Schnerb, 'La Politique Fiscale de Thiers', *Revue Historique*, 201 and 202 (1949). Fiscal motives were particularly emphasized by the French diplomat, Gavard; see *Diplomate à Londres. Lettres et Notes, 1871–77* (Paris, 1895), 119–23; Gavard to Chichester Fortescue, 9 Sept. 1872, in Granville Papers, PRO 30/29/56.

Oddly, Thiers retained the confidence of British free traders, for whom a renewed treaty represented a welcome confirmation of French free trade sentiment.[40] But, more typically in Britain, the suggestion of any backsliding from the provisions of 1860 met the hostility of the Chambers of Commerce and firm resistance from the Foreign Office.[41] In this dilemma, Gladstone, in many ways the key architect of the 1860 Treaty, seemed increasingly drawn to the arguments of its opponents. Influenced perhaps by the need to bolster British revenue to satisfy the military alarmists of 1870–1, and so sympathetic to Lowe's fiscal arguments, Gladstone found the future of the treaty 'one of the most nicely balanced questions within my recollection'. Yet the delicate calculations that favoured the deal in 1860 now told against it, for: 'It is difficult to move backwards in a case where the forward aspect of our measure was the ground for adopting it.'[42] Above all, Gladstone regretted that 'the treaty of 1860, which I looked to as the great instrument of further & more effectual progress, is to be made by the French government the starting-point of a backward movement'.[43] In particular, he was wary lest during tariff negotiations gains would be retained by some industries, but at the expense of the whole, 'the interests of society'.[44] This was a potent fear, for the morality of free trade lay, above all, in its ability to depose, not to empower, vested interest groups. In these circumstances, Gladstone was drawn back to his reasoning in the mid-1840s: 'is it not our safest course to fall back upon our old basis namely that the cause of freedom in commerce will, as a rule, be most effectively advanced by leaving each nation to consider the subject in the light of its interests alone?'[45]

The political and diplomatic, if not the economic, advantages of the renewal of the treaty were strongly pressed by Bright, by his successor at the Board of Trade Chichester Fortescue, and by W. E. Forster, supported by Mallet at the Board of

---

[40] Bright hoped to keep the support of Thiers, cf. his finance minister, Pouyer Quertier, 'the Newdegate of the French Protectionists', finding proof of the progress of Free Trade in France in the former's attempts to 'keep alive the Treaty with England': Bright to Granville, 5 Sept. 1871, Granville Papers, PRO 30/29/52, cf. Bright to T. B. Potter, 29 Oct. 1872, Potter Letters.

[41] Granville took the opportunity at the Cobden Club dinner in June 1871 to warn that the government would not agree to a new treaty on a 'retrograde principle'. *Report, 1871*, 17. He described himself and Gladstone as 'strong Edmund Potterites' (the leading Manchester calico printer and erstwhile President of its Chamber of Commerce) in resisting concessions to Thiers. Granville to Bright, 21 Sept. 1871 (copy), Granville Papers, PRO 30/29/52; *The Times*, 14 July 1871; A. Redford, *Manchester Merchants and Foreign Trade* (2 vols, 1934 and 1956), vol. 2, 51; Gaston, 'Free-Trade Diplomacy', 126; the London Committee for the Maintenance of the Anglo-French Treaty sought to avoid tariff increases, FO 146/1615 CP, Correspondence, Aug. 1871–Mar. 1872, no. 29, in Enfield to Lyons, 180, 28 June 1872.

[42] Gladstone to Fortescue, in *GD*, vol. 8, 25 [24 Aug. 1871].

[43] Gladstone to Bright, 1 Nov. 1871, *GD*, vol. 8, 55. See, too, to Chevalier, 24 Jan. 1872, ibid. 101.

[44] Ramm (ed.), *GG Corr. 1868–76*, vol. 2, 257 [10 Sept. 1871]. The main point at issue in 1871–3 was the French desire to impose duties on raw materials, with compensatory duties on imports made from such materials.

[45] 'Memorandum by Mr Gladstone. French Treaty. 3–9 Oct. 1871', printed in Ramm (ed.), *GG Corr. 1868–76*, vol. 2, 272.

Trade, and by Lyons, the British Ambassador in Paris.[46] Gladstone himself was prepared to recognize the 'special circumstances of France, and the claims growing out of them'.[47] As a result, after the denunciation of the treaty by France in March 1872, Britain continued to negotiate, and in November signed a new treaty which gave up few of the gains of 1860.[48] Despite some adverse comment in Britain, it won the qualified approval of *The Economist*, and was hailed as a victory by the French free traders.[49] But it never came into effect, for the fall of Thiers in May 1873 led to the abandonment of the new French tariff; a new treaty was agreed in July 1873 which, in effect, restored that of 1860, with the additional benefit of the exemption of British goods from the French shipping duties: the *surtaxes de pavillon*.[50]

The 1873 Treaty created at best a balance of the discontented. It was acceded to primarily at the request of France, yet was to last only until 1877 when France's other commercial treaties expired. Thus, while the French protectionist agitations of the early 1870s had been checked, they had also gained a breathing-space.[51] On the British side, the hopes of the Treasury and Customs for fiscal autonomy had given way before the political arguments of the diplomats, with Lowe isolated, not ascendant.[52] On the other hand, Gladstone had moved decidedly towards the view that treaties had proved largely fruitless, had jeopardized, if not surrendered, Britain's fiscal freedom, and had unduly compromised Britain in France's domestic politics, disadvantages that outweighed the benefits of proffering an example for others to follow, and an impetus to peace.[53] Disillusioned by four years of commercial haggling, the simplicity of most-favoured nation status now seemed a desirable

---

[46] See esp. Bright, Forster, and Fortescue to Granville, 1871–3 in Granville Papers, PRO 30/29/52 and 56; Gaston, 'Free-Trade Diplomacy', 122–56; Clayton, 'Commercial Relations', ch. 5. At Cabinet on 24 Oct. 1871 only Forster, Fortescue, and Halifax favoured going on with negotiations, with Kimberley, Granville, Lowe, Gladstone, and Argyll against. *GD*, vol. 8, 50; see, too, ibid. 55, Gladstone to Bright, 1 Nov. 1871; Bright to T. B. Potter, 29 Oct. 1872, Potter Letters. Bright's voice remained influential despite his departure from the Cabinet.

[47] To Hammond, 24 Aug. 1872, in *GD*, vol. 8, 199–200.

[48] The treaty was based on most-favoured nation treatment, not on reciprocal tariff concessions, but this permitted the imposition of the new French tariffs under the law of 26 July 1872. It was, for Kimberley, 'a discreditable muddle', 'A Journal of Events during the Gladstone Ministry, 1868–1874, by John, first Earl of Kimberley', ed. E. Drus, Royal Historical Society, *Camden Miscellany 21*, Camden Third ser., 90 (1958), 34 [10 Oct. 1872]. The treaty also evoked unfavourable comment in Germany: see O. Russell to Granville, no. 28C, 27 Nov. 1872, FO 64/750.

[49] Clayton, 'Commercial Relations': chs. 5 and 6; Gaston, 'Free-Trade Diplomacy', 150–8; Redford, *Manchester Merchants*, vol. 2, 51. Under the treaty, a joint commission was set up to agree the level of compensatory duties; these were set at such a low level as to be genuinely compensatory, rather than protective, and so failed to win the Assembly's approval.

[50] Dunham, *Anglo-French Treaty*, 316–17. For the latter, Clayton, 'Commercial Relations', 156–9; W. S. Lindsay, *History of Merchant Shipping and Ancient Commerce*, vol. 3 (1876), 456–60; *Hertslet's Commercial Treaties*, 14 (1880), 340–6.

[51] Smith, *Tariff Reform in France*; H. Lebovics, *The Alliance of Iron and Wheat in the French Third Republic, 1860–1914* (Baton Rouge, 1988); E. O. Golob, *The Méline Tariff: French Agriculture and Nationalist Economic Policy* (New York, 1944).

[52] Lowe had complained pointedly to Gladstone about his not being consulted by the FO, 7 Oct. 1872. GP, Add. MS 44302, fo. 92.

[53] Iliasu, 'Free Trade Treaties', 405–7.

escape from the 'compromises and expedients' that many felt to be enshrined in the 1860 Treaty. Official British hostility to future treaties, as expounded by Lyons to the French, did not offer much promise of a substantial rebuilding of the Cobden treaty system on modified terms.[54]

As a result, the 1873 Treaty appeared to 'the forward school' very much a *pis aller*, at best a cynical manœuvre, which concealed the absence of a genuine free trade foreign policy.[55] This view was confirmed by Britain's neglect of the opportunity to take up negotiations with Germany.[56] Such a move, Cobdenite diplomatists had hoped, would have led to a new Anglo-German Commercial Treaty, so stiffening the hands of continental free traders in the face of rising protectionist sentiment, and would have lent official weight to the otherwise impotent exhortations of the Cobden Club.[57] Equally disillusioning was the failure to make any progress in treaty negotiations with Spain and Portugal.[58]

The fears of the Cobdenites had also been greatly amplified by the dramatic weakening of their official position. In 1872 their bureaucratic power centre, the Board of Trade, found itself shorn of its Commercial Division, with its business transferred to the recently created Commercial Department of the Foreign Office. This administrative switch had been advocated by Lowe, hoping thereby to emasculate the Board whose tariff diplomacy he saw as a persistent threat to fiscal stability.[59] Such a reorganization had originally been pressed by Mallet, Morier,

[54]   Lyons to Granville, no. 283, 15 July 1873, FO 27/2007.

[55]   Mallet to Morier, 13 Feb., 26 May 1873, Morier Papers, Box 36. For the wider Cobdenite programme at this time, especially free trade as an antidote to communism, see Mallet, Memo. 19 Aug. 1871, FO 146/1615.

[56]   Odo Russell to Granville, 9 Mar. 1872, 4C, with copy of W. A. White to Russell, 8 Mar. 1872, FO 64/750; FO to Russell, Feb. 1873 (draft), and 4 June 1873, FO 64/779; Odo Russell to W. A. White, 27 Oct. 1872, FO 364/7; L. Mallet to O. Russell, 20 Aug. 1871, FO 918/54; B. Mallet, *Sir Louis Mallet* (1905), 89 ff. The case for a treaty rested on deeming British spirit duties protectionist, *GD*, vol. 8, 25 [24 Aug. 1871]. See, too, J. Faucher, 'A New Commercial Treaty between Great Britain and Germany', *Cobden Club Essays*, 2nd ser., 1871–2, 261–339. This failure was later seen as a critical turning-point. Thus, in 1878 the diplomat White lamented 'Protection is in high favour in the Wilhelm Strasse . . . if Granville had taken our advice in 1871 . . . all this decline of Free Trade principles in Germany might have been prevented.' To W. Cartwright, 24 Apr. 1878, Cartwright Papers, 20/560; cf. White to Cartwright, 23 Feb. 1872, ibid. 20/375.

[57]   Chichester Fortescue to Granville, 28 Mar. 1872, on a commercial treaty with Germany as desired 'by the best German free traders . . . as the only means of promoting the cause in Germany and Europe generally'. PRO 30/29/56. See, too, Odo Russell to Granville, 2, 15 Mar., 21 June, 8 Nov. 1873, Granville Papers, PRO 30/29/93.

[58]   Granville had received Cabinet approval for an most-favoured nation but not a tariff treaty with Spain in Nov. 1872, *GD*, vol. 8, 236 [15 Nov. 1872]. For various efforts with regard to Spain, see *BDFA Pt. I, ser. F*, vol. 26, Spain, 1846–96, esp. docs. 19 and 22. For earlier lack of progress in Spain, see Clarendon to Layard, 20 Dec. 1869, Clarendon dep. c. 475; Lyons to Clarendon, 8 and 27 Feb. 1870, Clarendon dep. c. 477, where concessions to Spain were seen as a factor likely to alienate French wine-growers, the mainstay of free trade in France; *Hansard*, 3rd ser., 197, c. 1425, 8 July 1869; 201, c. 1940, 13 June 1870.

[59]   Gaston, 'Trade and the Foreign Office', 325; Gladstone to Fortescue, 3 Jan. 1871[?2], Strabie Papers, DDSh CP3/324, Somerset Record Office; Fortescue to Morier, 26 Jan.1872 ('He thinks too that having got rid of Mallet & the Commercial Department here he will hear no more of commercial treaties.'), Morier Papers, Box 44.

and 'the forward school', who had hoped to gain a *point d'appui* within the Foreign Office from which to turn it more effectively to the tasks of commercial diplomacy.[60] But in 1872 it was more a case of the Board of Trade divesting itself of responsibility for commercial treaties, which the Foreign Office reluctantly took over.[61] As in 1864, Mallet stood out as the Board official best qualified to turn the new department into an active organ of commercial diplomacy. But by 1872 he had irremediably alienated the Foreign Office, and, increasingly depressed by the prospects for free trade, he willingly acquiesced in his transfer to the India Office.[62] This left the Commercial Department to be run by Charles Kennedy, recommended in the eyes of his superiors by 'his having devoted particular attention to political economy for which he obtained distinction at the university', but also a man without the 'uncontrollable crotchets' which had so marked, and marred, Mallet's career.[63] It is tempting to see in Mallet's discomforture the devaluing of commercial diplomacy, and, as Gaston suggests, the reassertion of traditional anti-mercantile prejudices in officials such as Lister and Tenterden.[64] Yet the changes of 1872 were in some ways the natural corollary of those of 1864, completing the Foreign Office's commercial armoury, and the early years of the Commercial Department were by no means unsuccessful; even the Chambers of Commerce were temporarily appeased.[65]

It is, moreover, too much to see in this official reorganization and the Anglo-French Treaty of 1873 the end of an enlightened Liberal international policy, which, the free traders had hoped, would help restore harmony, peace, and prosperity to Europe.[66] For while commercial treaties had made little headway (Lowe, for example, did block progress with Spain[67]), their benefits were still recognized by

---

[60] Above, 104; Morier to Mallet, 10 Feb. 1870, Morier Papers, Box 44; R. A. Jones, *The Nineteenth-Century Foreign Office* (1971), 87–9; Mallet to Cartwright, 25 Nov. 1871, Cartwright Papers, 20/372.

[61] Jones, *Foreign Office*, 88–9. Cf. Gaston, 'Trade and the Foreign Office', 325–7. Farrer, for example, welcomed the ending of the Board's commercial role.

[62] Granville to Fortescue, 6 Jan. 1871 [2], Strabie Papers, CP3/121.

[63] Jones, *Foreign Office*, 89; Tenterden to Sanderson, 5 Oct. 1875, cited in Gaston, 'Trade and the Foreign Office', 326.

[64] 'Trade and the Foreign Office', 328 ff. This was to some extent Mallet's own view, although more subtly he bemoaned the absence of 'any breath of international feeling or sympathy with the Free trade movement abroad', Mallet to Bright, 16 Apr. 1872, Bright Papers, Add. MS 44383, fos. 197–8.

[65] A. R. Ilseric and P. F. B. Liddle, *Parliament of Commerce* (1960), 24; C. M. Kennedy: 'The Commercial Department and the FO considered in relation to the Board of Trade & the proposed Ministry of Commerce', memo, 26 Jan. 1883, Kennedy Papers, FO 800/4, fos. 78–93.

[66] Mallet was thoroughly disillusioned by March 1870: 'Seriously I am nearly desperate. The utter contempt with which this Government treats all international questions, the evident determination of Lowe to strangle out Cobden's work, Bright's collapse, Forster's fiasco and Gladstone's entire absence of control and sagacity point to one result. It is now, I firmly believe inevitable, the entire ruin of our international policy and the loss of all our European prestige.' Cited in R. Wemyss, *Memoirs and Letters of the Rt. Hon. Sir Robert Morier* (2 vols, 1911), vol. 2, 138. For an earlier expression of Mallet's disillusionment, see M. Bentley, *The Climax of Liberal Politics* (1987), 64.

[67] Lowe's positive contribution to free trade diplomacy lay mainly in his support for the use in Foreign Office examinations of Smith's *Wealth of Nations*, Mill's *Political Economy*, Vattel and Wheatstone's *Elements of International Law*, all texts central to the Cobdenite canon. See Lowe to Granville, n.d., 1870, Granville Papers, PRO 30/29/66.

many, for example Odo Russell at Berlin, as valuable instruments, 'peace bonds', all the more necessary in Bismarckian Europe.[68] There also remained a substantial body of Liberal and Radical opinion which continued to link low tariffs with reduced armaments, peace, and the 'free breakfast table'.[69] These causes by no means receded from the centre of Liberal policy-making back into the penumbra of the peace societies and Radical clubs from which they had emerged in the 1840s. For in substantive ways, Liberal policy between 1868 and 1874 fulfilled wider Cobdenite aspirations. Clarendon's impressive drive for European disarmament in 1869–70, non-intervention in the Franco-Prussian War, military reforms and reduced armaments expenditure, and, above all, Gladstone's agreement to the arbitration of the *Alabama* claims in 1871, all signalled departures from Palmerstonian orthodoxy.[70] Thus, in the *Alabama* arbitration, for the first time, a Great Power was prepared to limit the definition of her 'vital interests' in order to allow a procedure in international disputes long advocated by Liberals, and which boosted considerably the morale of the peace movement after the bitter blow of the Franco-Prussian War.[71] That war had, in turn, revivified the 1848 ideal of European federation, the idea of a 'United States of Europe' hitherto confined to journals such as *Le Cosmopolite* and *Les États Unis de l'Europe*, but now propagated by the Regius Professor of Modern History at Cambridge, better known for his subsequent reincarnation as the prophet of empire, J. R. Seeley.[72] Here, undoubtedly, were steps forward for 'Cobdenic policy', broadly conceived, however poor the immediate prospects of commercial treaties.[73]

Other Radical objectives were also keenly pressed, for example the attempt, foreshadowing the later efforts in the early twentieth century, to assert parliamentary control of foreign policy, including treaty-making.[74] Henry Richard revived Cobden's search for disarmament with a morale-boosting parliamentary division in favour of international arbitration in 1873, and with a continental tour, a pacifist

---

[68] Cited in Gaston, 'Free-Trade Diplomacy', 40–3; Odo Russell to Granville, 9 Mar. 1872 FO 64/750.

[69] Biagini, 'Debate on Taxation'; its foreign policy equivalent still requires study. For some European linkages, see esp. van der Linden, *The International Peace Movement 1815–1874* (Amsterdam, 1987), *passim*.

[70] e.g., Clarendon to Loftus, 2, 9, and 16 Mar. 1870, Clarendon Papers, FO 361/1; Newton, *Lord Lyons*, ch. 7; R. Millman, *British Policy and the Coming of the Franco-Prussian War* (Oxford, 1965), 153–9.

[71] Robson, 'Liberals and "Vital Interests": The Debate on International Arbitration, 1815–72', *Bulletin of the Institute of Historical Research*, 32 (1959), 38–55; Granville at Cobden Club Dinner, 24 June 1871, *Report* (1871), 18.

[72] Van der Linden, *Peace Movement*, 724, 889, 912; Seeley, 'United States of Europe', *MacMillan's Magazine* (1871), 436–48. Seeley's early lectures at Cambridge emphasized the history of Britain as part of the European system.

[73] See, e.g., F. Seebohm, *On International Reform* (1871).

[74] This became the hobby-horse of Peter Rylands ('the chief prosecutor of the FO'), but alienated experts such as Morier and Mallet. A. Russell to Morier, 22 Mar. 1870, Morier Papers, Box 34; *Hansard*, 3rd ser., 214, cc. 448–59, 14 Feb. 1873. The issue was something of a cleft stick for Cobdenites, allowing protectionists and 'non-diplomatic' free traders to unite in opposition to commercial treaties.

version of Cobden's 1846 free trade tour, which strengthened the links between British and continental liberal opinion.[75] However disappointed men such as Mallet were with the Liberal Cabinet of 1868–74, Gladstone's policy had striven consistently to reconcile an elevated international morality with diplomatic realism. The weakness of this Liberal vision of international relations was not that it fell short of Cobdenite prescriptions, but that in the aftermath of the Franco-Prussian War—a war between European neighbours in which arbitration proved fruitless and the Concert of Europe impotent—it was already out of date and had raised expectations it could not fulfil.[76] This not only alienated Whigs and Liberal intellectuals, but also offered to Disraeli the chance to seize the mantle of Palmerston, and, surprisingly, to do so with the support of some of Cobden's disciples.[77]

Cobdenism and Conservatism, 1874–80

The Cobdenite strand in Gladstone's international vision was to re-emerge strongly in his onslaught on 'Beaconsfieldism' as an affront to the public conscience of Europe.[78] Yet, oddly, Beaconsfieldism itself had in the mid-1870s briefly promoted the ends of Cobdenism, much as the minority Conservative government of 1852 had almost pre-empted the Cobden Treaty of 1860.[79] For, as Gaston has argued, there was a remarkably visionary attempt by Disraeli's government to promote the idea of a 'European common market' in the mid-1870s.[80] At this time, both growing expenditure on armaments in Europe and fears of rising import duties encouraged Kennedy at the Foreign Office to embark on a new round of tariff negotiations, aimed at securing new commercial treaties and minimal tariff increases. At the Exchequer, Northcote, 'the disciple of Peel & Gladstone & their agent in all their Free trade reforms', was sympathetic, although as President of the

---

[75] Above, 84–5; *Hansard*, 3rd ser., 217, cc. 52–73, 8 July 1873; C. S. Miall, *The Life of Henry Richard MP* (1889), 206–45; L. Appleton, *Memoirs of Henry Richard* (1889), 131–2; Appleton's belief that 'no man was more gratified than the Prime Minister himself' is, however, scarcely borne out by the PM's jaundiced diary entry: 'Spoke on Mr Richard: beaten again: so much the worse for the beaters.' *GD*, vol. 8, 353 [8 July 1873].

[76] A. J. P. Taylor, *The Trouble Makers: Dissent over Foreign Policy 1792–1939* (1957), ch. 3; D. Schreuder, 'Gladstone as "Troublemaker": Liberal Foreign Policy and the German Annexation of Alsace-Lorraine, 1870–71', *Journal of British Studies*, 17 (1977–8), 106–35; in 1870 Gladstone felt strongly the absence of 'the action of a common or public or European opinion', to which he would later appeal over the Eastern Question: J. Morley, *The Life of William Ewart Gladstone* (3 vols, 1903), vol. 2, 318; below, 176.

[77] Parry, *The Rise and Fall of Liberal Government in Victorian Britain* (1993), 292; Wemyss, *Morier*, vol. 2, 290–4 (Morier to Jowett, 16 Nov. 1873); R. T. Shannon, *Gladstone and the Bulgarian Agitation, 1876* (1963), esp. 211–15.

[78] See below, 175–6.

[79] See above, 87. Derby, the Foreign Secretary, was noted in his earlier career for his 'liberal internationalism' and his strong commercial support: J. Vincent (ed.), *Disraeli, Derby and the Conservative Party* (Hassocks, 1978), 143; Millman, *British Policy*, 227; for his later tenure of the Foreign Office, see J. Vincent (ed.), *The Diaries of Edward Henry Stanley, 15th Earl of Derby, 1869–1878* (Camden 5th ser., 4, Royal Historical Society, 1994).

[80] Gaston, 'Common Market', 59–82.

Board of Trade in 1866, Mallet had found him indoctrinated by his brother-in-law, Farrer, and 'full of wrong ideas'.[81] Northcote's first budget in 1874 was notable for relieving taxation on the working classes, with the abolition of the sugar duty, a deliberate attempt 'to satisfy the free traders and the democracy', while tacitly accepting the permanence of income tax, however much its burden might be adjusted to relieve the middle classes.[82] More dramatically, Northcote revived the idea put forward by Allhusen, Morier, and Mallet in the mid-1860s for nothing less than a European congress in order to establish a common tariff.[83] Northcote recognized this as 'a great and difficult task', but since Britain appeared to lack bargaining counters in Europe, and as many of the treaties negotiated in the years 1860–5 were now coming up for renewal, the idea of a tariff conference proffered a means of influence to Britain: 'The principles of an "European Tariff" ', Northcote urged Derby, 'might be conceivably settled in such a manner as to leave each nation free to impose higher or lower rates according to its financial necessities.'[84] This 'undoubtedly novel and brilliant scheme' seemed far too likely to fail for the Foreign Office mandarins to take it up with any enthusiasm, and there seems no evidence that the Foreign Secretary Derby seriously promoted the tariff conference scheme.[85]

On the other hand, the idea of a European tariff congress, in line with Northcote's personal 'hankering', was proposed by France—then involved in concurrent negotiations with Italy—when in late 1875 negotiations for the renewal of the Cobden Treaty were resumed. There was now floated in the chancelleries of Europe the vision, realized in the Treaties of Rome of 1957, of 'the eventual establishment, on a free trade basis, of international commercial arrangements of a general character'.[86] Northcote himself enigmatically reported to the House of

---

[81]   Mallet to Rogers, 21 Dec. 1878, Rogers Papers, 471 for the first quotation. Above, 43 for Mallet as Northcote's colleague at the Board of Trade in the 1840s; 'a free trader and a liberal in almost everything at the Board of Trade', according to Granville, to Russell, 4 Jan. 1852 (copy), Granville Papers, PRO 30/29/20/2; S. Northcote, *Financial Policy* for the Peelite legacy; for his stint at the Board of Trade, see Mallet to Morier, 1 Sept. 1866, Morier Papers, Box 33.

[82]   P. Smith, *Disraelian Conservatism and Social Reform* (1967), 207. Northcote's financial policy deserves more attention, but see S. Buxton, *Finance and Politics* (2 vols, 1888), vol. 2, chs. 27–33; A. Lang, *Life, Letters, and Diaries of Sir Stafford Northcote, First Earl of Iddesleigh* (2 vols, 1890), vol. 2, 52–97. Northcote also hoped abolition of the sugar duty would encourage France to reduce her sugar bounties: Northcote to Derby, 6 Mar. and 4 Apr. 1874; (copy), Salisbury to Northcote, 2 Feb. 1874, Derby Papers, 16/2/6. For some of the complexities of the sugar duties, see J. B. Smith, *Free Trade in Sugar* (1871).

[83]   Above, 107. Cf. Gaston, 'Common Market', 66–7, 74; Northcote's 1847 memorandum on 'Commercial Treaties' does not to my mind imply an international tariff union, but the multiplication of bilateral treaties, Iddesleigh Papers, Add. MS 50043, fo. 12 ff.

[84]   Northcote to Derby, 28 Sept. 1875, Derby Papers, 16/2/6; Gaston, 'Common Market', 62. Northcote also consulted Mallet, 11 Oct. 1875, Iddlesleigh Papers, Add. MS 50052, fo. 136.

[85]   Cf. Gaston, 'Common Market', 77, citing Derby to Lyons, 11 Dec. 1875, but this is a comment on a French proposal. Tenterden at the FO feared the 'contrast of the success of Cobden and the failure of the Conference': to Derby, 5 Oct. 1875, Derby Papers, 16/2/10.

[86]   Lyons to Derby, 365 Comm., 12 Dec. 1875, reporting conversation with Decazes, the French Foreign Minister, in FO 881/2735 (CP). See, too, Lyons to Derby, 23 Comm., 24 Jan. 1876 and Derby to Lyons, 28 Comm., 16 Feb. 1876 in FO 881/3011.

Commons his support for 'a large and comprehensive understanding come to by the Powers of Europe as to some common basis for tariffs'.[87] The details of such an arrangement remained sketchy in the extreme, and it soon receded in favour of bilateral Anglo-French negotiations, although France concurrently negotiated with several other European countries.[88] The prospects of a renewal of the 1860 Treaty seemed favourable in 1877, with a relatively strong group of free traders in government in France, and Léon Say, an enthusiastic free trader, as French Ambassador in London, although their position was weakened, as Lyons noted, by the absence of a party in France devoted to free trade.[89] As negotiations proceeded, however, the French desire to adopt a new general tariff with increased specific duties held up progress, as did the fiscal exigencies of Disraeli's government, which ruled out using the wine duties as a sweetener for a new treaty, as Derby, Mallet, and the free traders urged.[90] Any opportunity for an agreement receded after the crisis of 16 May and a strong protectionist resurgence led by French industrialists. French diplomacy was now firmly directed towards negotiating on a country-by-country basis, and she gave priority to her treaty with Italy; Anglo-French negotiations wilted until the return of the Liberals to office in 1880.[91]

The failure to renegotiate the Anglo-French treaty in 1877 typified the pattern of Britain's commercial diplomacy in the next few years. For example, in Italy, with rising government expenditure and growing support for protection among industrialists, agrarians, and shipowners, Cobden's old admirer Minghetti found moderate duties an insufficient guarantee of political survival. The Government of the Left, which succeeded the Historic Right in 1876, sought in its negotiations with France to raise many import duties, and adopted a new protectionist tariff in 1878.[92] In 1875 Minghetti had already given notice to terminate the Anglo-Italian Treaty of 1863, while Luzzatti's attempt to bargain for reductions of British wine duties in

---

[87] *Hansard*, 3rd ser., 227, c. 1581, 7 Mar. 1876.

[88] Lyons to Derby, 16 Jan. and 23 Feb. 1877; Lumley to Derby, 24 Feb. 1877, FO 881/3162; Michel Chevalier reported to Bright that in this renewal everything depended upon the French government: 'If they incline to the free trade policy, the whole set of new treaties will be favourable to free trade. If not, there will be no change of importance', 7 Mar. 1876, Bright Papers, Add. MS 43383, fos. 214–15.

[89] Lyons to Derby, 1 May 1877, no. 210, in FO 881/3438; for Say, see J. Garrigues, 'Léon Say sous la troisième République', *Revue Historique*, 579 (1991); Smith, *Tariff Reform in France*, 42. Say had defended treaties against Lowe at the centenary celebration of *The Wealth of Nations*: see *Revised Report*, 24.

[90] 'The nation will lose a great deal more [than £100,000] by the recurrence of France to an exclusive commercial system', Derby to Northcote, 11 Apr. 1877, Derby Papers, 17/2/6; Mallet to Morier, 7 May 1877, Morier Papers, Box 44. Mallet here contemplated a series of adjustments involving France, Spain, Portugal, and Italy; he was even ready to hold back reductions from 'recalcitrant countries': 'a course I should not take myself, except as a temporary expedient, with a certainty of success'. See, too, Mallet to Corry, 10 May 1877; H. S. Northcote to Corry, 19 May 1877, Disraeli Papers, dep. Hughenden, 135/3. For the financial problems of the government, see Smith, *Disraelian Conservatism*, 267.

[91] Dunham, *Anglo-French Treaty*, 340 ff.; Gaston, 'Free-Trade Diplomacy', ch. 8; Clayton, 'Commercial Relations', 205–32; Smith, *Tariff Reform in France*, 47 ff.

[92] P. Bolchini, 'Anglo-Italian Economic Relations (1861–1883)', unpublished Ph.D. thesis, University of London (1967), ch. 7; Minghetti's Cobdenite credentials had already come under suspicion, T. B. Potter to Gladstone, 10 Jan. 1875, GP, Add. MS 44282.

exchange for Italian reductions of their proposed higher duties on cotton goods failed to win over either the Treasury or Manchester; as Lister laconically noted, 'The cotton spinners would not be consoled for the destruction of their trade with Italy by drinking cheaper marsala.'[93] The example of the abortive Franco-Italian treaty of 1877 proved unattractive to the Chambers of Commerce, but the Anglo-Italian Treaty of 1863 was periodically renewed pending further negotiations, all of which proved fruitless in the later 1870s, with the Conservative government wholly out of sympathy with the Government of the Left.[94]

In Germany, too, the fiscal pressures for tariffs grew strongly in the later 1870s, but the one that emerged in 1879 was given a distinct protectionist twist, within a 'financial policy of National Independence'.[95] British policy, having once more proved inflexible over her spirits duties in 1877, was reduced to one of impotent remonstrance, with little enthusiasm for J. A. Crowe's suggestion of the aggressive use of wine duties, see-sawing up and down in order to win concessions from European powers.[96] To Mallet, such a policy smacked of protectionism, although Crowe claimed to 'have met numbers of men of the liberal and free trade party who talk of reciprocity—meaning reprisals as a thing that might at a pinch be advocated whilst amongst conservatives I have found men who argue that reprisals are the true policy of this country'.[97] The alternative policy, that of persuasion, seemed to Crowe to be 'most hopeless', and indeed the amateur diplomacy of the Cobden Club through William Cartwright served only to add its members to the ranks of the *Reichsfeinde*, against whom German opinion solidified.[98] Disturbingly for Britain, there was now a greater readiness on Bismarck's part to reach mutually beneficial economic arrangements with Austria, frustrating British efforts to work towards free trade through Hungarian agrarian interests.[99] The Anglo-Austrian Treaty was denounced in January 1876, but a one-year treaty negotiated in December of that year was indefinitely renewed in November 1877 on a most-favoured nation basis, whose terms increasingly reflected the protectionist-minded German-

---

[93]   Quoted Bolchini, 'Anglo-Italian Economic Relations', 210. Lister regarded Luzzatti as a 'rank Protectionist', 6 Dec. 1878.

[94]   P. Bolchini, 'Anglo-Italian Economic Relations', ch. 7; for Franco-Italian commercial diplomacy, see W. B. Harvey, *Tariffs and International Relations in Europe, 1860–1914* (Chicago, 1938), ch. 9.

[95]   For Germany's return to Protection, Lotz, *Handelspolitik von 1860 bis 1891*; W. H. Dawson, *Protection in Germany* (1904); I. N. Lambi, *Free Trade and Protection in Germany, 1868–1879* (Wiesbaden, 1963); H. Böhme, 'Big Business, Pressure Groups and Bismarck's turn to Protectionism, 1873–79', *Historical Journal*, 10 (1967), 218–36; Hobson, 'The Tax-Seeking State', esp. 41–96; the best diplomatic analysis was that of J. A. Crowe, Crowe to Odo Russell, 28 May 1880, FO 64/965.

[96]   O. Russell to Derby, 28 July 1877, Derby Papers, 16/1/16; Treasury to FO, 19 May 1877, T12/8; Crowe to Russell, 11 Mar. 1879, Ampthill Papers, FO 918/25.

[97]   Crowe to Russell, 22 Mar. 1879, ibid.

[98]   Above, 140; 'Herr Cartwright aus London, das englische Parlaments-Mitglied, der Reise-Apostel des Cobden-Clubs', Beilage zu Nr. 13 der *Deutschen volkswirthschaftlichen Correspondenz*, Berlin, 15 Feb. 1879, in 'Trade Mission to Germany', Cartwright Papers, 1/20.

[99]   Gaston, 'Free-Trade Diplomacy', ch. 7.

Austrian *rapprochement*.[100] Russia, the remaining Great Power, threatened like Britain by rising German tariffs, still remained outside the commercial treaty system, but her own customs duties had been sharply (by one-third) increased in real terms by the demand in 1876 for their payment in gold.[101] Interestingly, in 1879 John Bright attempted to enlist the Marquess of Dufferin, the new British Ambassador, in the vain search for a more liberal Russian tariff, but this was more in order to improve Anglo-Russian political relations than to expand British commerce.[102]

Finally, therefore, British attention turned to the Iberian Peninsula, the cockpit in which free traders had fought in vain for decades. In Spain, however, the prospects for freer trade receded decisively when the tariff of 1877 discriminated against Britain, with damaging effects on her trade over the next decade.[103] This was, purportedly, retaliation for the supposed discriminatory element in British wine duties (favouring claret rather than port or sherry), duties whose adjustment by the late 1870s was seen as the only way in which Britain could boost tariff treaties.[104] Wine constituted the one major European product upon which British revenue collection was based, and for which British demand might rise substantially.[105] This case preoccupied British commercial diplomats, winning enthusiastic support from both Bulwer-Lytton and Morier, when head of mission in Portugal in 1874–6 and 1876–81, respectively. Yet at this point fiscal arguments effectively ruled out an Anglo-Portuguese commercial treaty, although Morier did succeed in negotiating favourable treaties with the Portuguese colonies of Goa and Lourenço Marques.[106]

British commercial negotiations between 1875 and 1879 therefore proved largely fruitless, at a time when Cobdenites feared 'the impending collapse of the tariff system', and which may rightly be seen as the turning-point in Europe's reversion to protectionism.[107] Most leading European governments now resorted to tariffs in

---

[100] De Bernhardt, *Handbook of Commercial Treaties* (1912), 14. This was still in force in 1912; Gaston, 'Free-Trade Diplomacy', ch. 7; White to Sanderson, 25 Oct. 1877, Derby Papers, 16/2/14; *The Economist*, 18 Oct. 1879, 'Tariffs and Treaties', 1189–90, on Bismarck's visit to Vienna. For tariffs in the wider diplomatic context, see B. Waller, *Bismarck at the Crossroads* (1974), 102–9.

[101] Harvey, *Tariffs*, ch. 4.

[102] *Diaries*, 417 [15 Feb. 1879], 419 [8 Mar. 1879].

[103] S. B. Saul, *Studies in British Overseas Trade, 1870–1914* (Liverpool, 1960), 137–41; for one complaint, Duke of Wellington's Spanish agent, *The Times*, 4 Jan. 1881.

[104] See above, 141; Derby to Northcote, 19 Aug. 1877, Iddesleigh Papers, Add. MS 50022 fos. 156–7; Northcote to Derby, 22 Aug. 1877 (wine duties and Spanish tariff), Derby Papers, 16/2/6; Morier to Cartwright, 1 Jan. 1877, Cartwright Papers, 20/492; BDFA Pt.I, ser. F, vol. 26, Spain, docs. 60, 61, 64–6.

[105] See *inter alia*, 'Wine Duties' (Aug. 1878), FO 881/3683. Mallet had prophetic faith in 'an almost inexhaustible reserve of consuming power for such an article as cheap wine'.

[106] Lytton to Derby, 3 Jan. 1876, no. 1 Comm., FO 63/1060; Ramm, *Morier*, 73–102. See, too, Gaston, 'Free-Trade Diplomacy', 270–92. Besides the wine duties, the Cattle Plague Diseases Bill of 1878 complicated this question, with Morier looking to the expansion of the Iberian cattle trade to pay for English exports. See, e.g., Morier to Cartwright, 30 June 1878, Cartwright Papers, 20/363, and above, 127.

[107] Cobden Club, *Treaties of Commerce*, 13 (Mallet), 33 (Chevalier).

the face of commercial depression and vastly increased demands for military expenditure. Fiscal need lay behind many of these attempts to raise tariffs, which were more protectionist in appearance than reality, for, as Kennedy noted, 'for the most part, they are in truth, the result of financial exigencies, and of the necessity for raising revenue by measures of indirect taxation'.[108] Yet Kennedy also urged the need for co-ordinated action in order to preserve the gains of the commercial treaty system. The failure of Britain to do this, he believed, was not simply the result of the prejudices of the Foreign Office's specialists in *haute politique*, but lay in the Disraelian Administration's relative indifference to European tariff policy: 'H. M. Govt . . . did nothing and left matters to drift.'[109]

As we have seen, the Conservative record was not so blank as this suggests, but in Britain, as in Europe as a whole, tariff revision was soon swamped in a rising tide of military expenditure. The recrudescence of the Eastern Question, against whose deleterious consequences Cobden had inveighed in the 1830s, equally alarmed his successors, with Mallet foreseeing '[twenty] years of stagnation, reaction and intolerable taxation all over Europe'.[110] In addition, the costly reassertion of British power in India and Africa broke the back of Northcote's fiscal radicalism, and rendered vain any attempt to return to the Peelite economy in which he had been reared.[111] On the other hand, Britain could not afford entirely to ignore the prospective replacement of the Cobden treaty system by a series of new European tariff treaties, in which British interests would be conspicuously and deliberately ignored.[112] This required a reassessment of British policy, although there was no serious attempt within the government to adopt the fair trade policy of retaliatory duties.[113] *Faute de mieux*, even those officials most hostile to tariff-bargaining accepted the continued necessity of commercial treaties. Thus, T. V. Lister acknowledged that 'until the world has changed very much for the better, they must, in some form or other, continue to exist'.[114] It further followed that if Britain were successfully to engage in treaty-making, wine duties were the only bargaining-counter.[115] A reluctant Northcote therefore caved in to pressure in 1879 by granting

[108] 'The Commercial Policy of European States and British Trade', 29 Jan. 1879, FO 881/3834.
[109] Memo. 26 Jan. 1883, FO 800/4, fo. 78; for the very different tone of 1865, see Layard to Morier, 25 Jan. 1865, Morier Papers, Box 33.
[110] Mallet to Grant Duff, 4 Jan. 1877, Grant Duff Papers, MS Eur. F 234/37.
[111] For one attempt, 'The Cabinet Journal of Dudley Ryder, Viscount Sandon, 11 May–10 Aug. 1878', *Bulletin of the Institute of Historical Research*, special supplement, 10 (1974), 51 [10 Aug. 1878].
[112] For a summary of the FO view, see C. M. Kennedy, 'Business of the Commercial Department', 18 Apr. 1878, FO 881/3577.
[113] See, for example, the debate on Bateman's motion in House of Lords, 29 Apr. 1879, *Hansard*, 3rd ser., 245, cc. 1356 ff.; *The Economist*, 3 May 1879; also Hertslet memo., 29 Apr. 1879 in Disraeli Papers, dep. Hughenden 56/1.
[114] T. V .L [ister], 'Commercial Treaties', 20 Mar. 1879, FO 881/3864.
[115] Kennedy memo, 10 Mar. 1879, FO 800/4, fos. 254 ff. Lister had acknowledged himself a convert to Mallet's views as early as 1875: Lister to Derby, 21 Sept. 1875, Derby Papers, 16/2/10, on which occasion he also declared 'the extension of British trade and the credit of the FO are the only things I have to care for', hardly an anti-mercantile *profession de foi*, cf. Gaston, 'Trade and the FO', 328.

a Select Committee on the Wine Duties, which, as we have seen, gave voice to the Cobdenite case that, in adjusting the duties, lost revenue would be compensated for by the boost to trade and by the guarantees for peace inherent in commercial treaties.[116] This prescription came too late for any significant redirection of Conservative policy, but Gladstone, in taking office in 1880, would once more look to the wine duties as the basis of commercial progress, a belated attempt not at the hegemonic imposition of free trade, but at propping up the toppling 'Cobden treaty system'.

If Conservative inaction had largely affected Western Europe, Disraeli's embroilment in the Eastern Question was to bring in its train some compensatory attention to South-Eastern Europe. For while the Bulgarian atrocities attracted most public interest, commercial policy took on a new importance, with several attempts to tie newly created states into the British trading regime. This was part of a concerted effort to reinforce British commercial interests in the Balkans as well as in Turkey, for an underrated dimension in the Eastern Question was the fear of Russian protectionism, a factor deeply entrenched in the mind of the Foreign Office.[117] The policy was signalled in 1876, when Britain gained most-favoured nation status from Romania, but it was followed by a tariff treaty in 1880, which gave Britain important reductions on cotton goods.[118] The treaty itself complemented that agreed in March 1879 with Serbia.[119] Here, one might see the exercise of British hegemony, with Britain, as Fuchs argued, gaining unilateral concessions as a result of 'her great political ascendancy'.[120] But the timing of the treaties suggests not so much a self-confident assertion of power, as a defensive fear of encroaching protective tariffs, and the burgeoning commercial power of Germany, Austria, and Russia. In particular, the annexation of Bosnia-Herzegovina by Austria was to be followed by the imposition of the higher Austrian tariff in 1880.[121] Conservative commercial diplomacy also to some extent compensated for the damage done by the Congress of Berlin, where Disraeli had, so Odo Russell believed, agreed to the extension of Austria to Salonica, and to the opening up of a great Eastern trade for Germany, to be followed by an Austro-German

---

[116] Above, 141; *The Economist*, 22 Mar. 1879, 330.

[117] 'Review of British Consular Reports on Trade with Turkey in Europe, Turkey in Asia and Persia, 1868–1877, with notes on Anglo-Indian trade . . . and remarks on the Commercial Policy of Russia', 30 Apr. 1878 [E. Hertslet], FO 881/3882.

[118] W. A. White to Dilke, 9 Sept. 188[0], PRO 364/7; White was surprised that such difficult negotiations had aroused so little interest at home. See, too, FO 881/3096; FO 881/4313; H. S. Edwards, *Sir William White* (1902), 179–81. In 1874 Grant Duff, finding Charles of Romania 'a little shaky about Free Trade' ensured he sat next to Mallet, 'the inheritor of Cobden's mantle', at the Orientalist Congress of 1874. *Notes from a Diary, 1873–81* (2 vols, 1898), 82 [15 Sept. 1874]; Lord Derby, *Hansard*, 3rd ser., 231, cc. 1192–3, 14 Aug. 1876.

[119] Kennedy, memo on Servian Treaty, 14 Oct. 1879, FO 800/4 fos. 184–201; FO 881/3891. Reports on Serbia's free trade leanings were less favourable by 1885, *Cobden Club, Annual Dinner and Proceedings* (1885), 12.

[120] C. J. Fuchs, *The Trade Policy of Great Britain and her Colonies since 1860* (1905), 60.

[121] Redford, *Manchester Merchants*, vol. 2, 55.

Zollverein.[122] This was a possibility that diplomats such as White in Romania were anxious to avoid, without going to the lengths of Morier's visionary idea of a Balkan customs union, with a tariff of 'pure customs duties and absolute free trade'. As Agatha Ramm succinctly put it, it was 'a dream remote from Balkan realities'.[123] More generally, however heartening the vaunted allegiance of men such as the Romanian Foreign Minister Ionesco to the Manchester School,[124] these crumbs of comfort for the Cobdenites hardly outweighed in the official mind and public opinion the far more obvious commercial failures in Western Europe.

It was, therefore, Britain's apparent inability to prevent the slide towards protectionism in Europe which led to a growing volume of criticism of British commercial policy in the late 1870s.[125] Yet such dissatisfaction derived from diverse sources and incompatible beliefs. For some, the Foreign Office remained an unnecessary commercial institution, whose interference harmed the course of trade.[126] For others, commercial treaties were at best a matter of indifference, to be tolerated as a necessary evil, so long as none of them accepted terms less favourable than those of the 1860s, even in the changed economic and fiscal climate of the 1870s. For a third group, what was needed was the far more vigorous prosecution of British interests abroad, although not all agreed that the best means towards this would be the creation of a French-style Ministry of Commerce.[127] Lastly, and most insistently, there re-emerged the plea that British policy should itself engage in retaliation, ending 'one-sided free trade', while the policy of fair trade would encourage 'genuine free trade', the case that W. F. Ecroyd pressed vigorously from 1879.[128] Together with the added voices of dissatisfied sugar refiners, and more powerfully the growing agricultural lobby for protection, economic 'heresy' was becoming

---

[122]   Tenterden to Granville, 30 Oct. 1880, Granville Papers, PRO 30/29/193. For fear of the Austro-German *Zollverein*, see *The Economist*, 18 Oct. 1879.

[123]   For Morier's schema, Morier to O. Russell, 14 June 1878, FO 918/55; A. Ramm, *Sir Robert Morier* (Oxford, 1973), 143.

[124]   '[A] great admirer of England . . . he informed me he was of the Manchester School and had always been an advocate of free trade.' St John to Derby, 9 Aug. 1876, FO 881/3096. He nevertheless sought a moderate import duty for the protection of native industry.

[125]   Commercial treaties were not the sole issue at stake. Increasingly, the bane of English officials in the FO, Treasury, and Board of Trade became the sugar bounties, an issue that gave rise to an enormous paperload—see FO 549, 1–24 (Confidential Print), for a small sample—and which had a demonstrable impact of the call for 'Fair Trade'. See below, Ch. 6.

[126]   e.g. P. Rylands, a Cobden Club member, and seen by Morier (Ramm, *Morier*, 138) as typical of the Manchester School, *Hansard*, 3rd ser., 214, cc. 454–9, 14 Feb. 1873.

[127]   J. Slagg, 'The Commercial Treaty with France', *Fortnightly Review* (1877), 389–91; Redford, *Manchester Merchants*, vol. 2, 115; Samuelson, *Hansard*, 3rd ser., 233, cc. 731–4, 6 Apr. 1877; S. Lloyd, *Hansard*, 3rd ser., 247, cc. 1919–27, 8 July 1879. For official rebuttal of this case, see Kennedy memos, 8 July 1879 and 26 Jan. 1883, FO 800/4, fos. 66–74, 78–93.

[128]   Brown, *Tariff Reform Movement*; Zebel, 'Fair Trade'; W. F. Ecroyd, *The Policy of Self-Help* (1879); Ecroyd Papers, Cuttings on Free Trade, Fair Trade and Tariff Reform, 1879–1905, Manchester Central Library, L1/2/18. Bateman urged reciprocity as 'real Free Trade', 'the coping-stone of the Free trade system', *Hansard*, 3rd ser., 245, c. 1366, 29 Apr. 1879.

an embarrassment to the Conservative Party, which even Disraeli sought to disavow.[129] Yet such divided mercantile and party opinions made any 'forward' commercial policy difficult to embrace, although, in a conciliatory gesture, Salisbury in 1879 appointed for the first time a commercial attaché for Europe.[130]

If commercial policy increasingly evoked back-bench Tory dissatisfaction, for the Cobdenites, it was the Eastern Question that heightened and made visible the potential contradictions between Britain's Great Power diplomacy and their own internationalist ideas.[131] For, on the one hand, the crisis made plain a new conception of Britain's part in the world order, as that of an irretrievably imperial power, both European and Asiatic, whose prestige made non-intervention impossible, yet whose international influence would still work for free trade and civilization. On the other hand, against 'Beaconsfieldism' there revived an oppositional 'little England' view of foreign policy, in which Britain should avoid intervention abroad and pursue material and moral progress at home.

Nowhere was the growing tension between imperial power and Cobdenite precept better expressed than in the bifurcation of policy adumbrated by formerly likeminded Cobdenites Sir Louis Mallet and Sir Robert Morier.[132] Here, in stark contrast, could be seen 'Cobden & Internationalism vs Realpolitik & Imperialism'.[133] Mallet, although now a leading India Office administrator, utterly abhorred British policy in the East, which he believed threatened the entire achievement of the Cobdenites since 1846. He thought that Britain's world power was necessarily linked to her natural resources, defined primarily by coal supply. In the coal famine of the early 1870s he already saw the limits to Britain's future material progress, and thought it 'honorable to measure our policy by our power and to reserve our strength for noble national life . . . if not of the kind John Bull has been used to admire'.[134] He saw war and territorial expansion—the hallmark of British policy under Disraeli, and Lytton (in India)—as 'a kind of fatality which is driving this

---

[129]   Above, 129. In 1879, Northcote warned Balfour of the dangers of countervailing duties as a 'weapon of diplomacy', 'If you are to engage in a commercial war, you must make up your mind for some very curious episodes': 3 May 1879, Iddesleigh Papers, Add. MS 50020, fos. 172–5. For an orthodox defence of free trade and commercial treaties, see R. Bourke, Conservative Under-Secretary for Foreign Affairs, *Hansard*, 3rd ser., 250, cc. 621–4, 13 Feb. 1880.

[130]   This itself aroused considerable scepticism at the Foreign Office: see Villiers–Lister memo for Salisbury, 12 Apr. 1879, Lister Papers, Bodleian Library, c. 1034, fo. 272; Lister to O. Russell, 29 Apr. 1879, FO 918/49.

[131]   'Of late our ministers have been too much occupied with "high politics" to have time for the furtherance of so prosaic a blessing as commercial prosperity.' See Grant Duff (Nov. 1878), *Miscellanies, Political and Literary* (1878), 113 n.

[132]   Ramm, *Morier*, 129–40, prints extensive extracts from this correspondence.

[133]   Morier to W. Cartwright, 11 Mar. 1878, Cartwright Papers, 20/557.

[134]   Mallet to Morier, 21 May 1874, Morier Papers, Box 36. Jevons's warnings in *The Coal Question* (1865) took on sharp relief during the coal famine of 1871–3. Gladstone feared the famine as 'a great public calamity: how much greater than the cattle plague which made ten times as much noise', William to Robertson Gladstone, 22 Feb. 1873, *GD*, vol. 8, 290.

country, like other historical empires, to its ruin'.[135] Were such aggrandisement to succeed:

all the aspirations of the political school to which I and you, to a great degree, have belonged, are at an end. It will be a curious page in the record of the future historian charged with the vengeance of the people, on which is written the little episode of the Free Trade movement in England.

The magnificence of the political conception to which it owed its origin, the prospect which it held out for human progress and for English greatness—and the ruin caused by the combined action of the stupidity and corruption on the part of our public men. Of course, I use the word corrupt in the indirect sense of accessibility to the influence of society and personal interest—in which the pressure of the services plays a great part.[136]

Mallet, while disclaiming a 'peace at any price policy' (more properly associated with men such as Joseph Sturge and Henry Richard), believed war in 1877–8 was wholly unjustified on grounds of policy, especially as Britain's commitments were outstripping her military resources, and a war advocated by corrupt and reactionary forces represented the false patriotism of those who sneer at Cobden, 'a very low national ideal and a vulgar concept of national greatness'.[137] Britain should thus eschew wars of honour and prestige in favour of the 'glimmering dawn of higher life', securing for all the peoples of Europe their highest interests:

by the same process—viz. by the widest possible extension according to time and circumstance of free institutions, equal civil and religious rights, and above all and before all as the foundation, Free Trade. By a resolute faith in these forces and the support of them as far as our strength permits always by moral and perhaps also in extreme cases by physical aid, I think there is a chance of our holding on our way and keeping together the little national unit called England until we really become a civilised country—but we cannot also become a great military Empire, holding down subject races by force and attempting to combine in a common system, despotic and democratic forms of government.[138]

Mallet's ideas here crystallized Cobden's own thinking on foreign policy, lending greater coherence to, without unduly distorting, his views from the 1830s, although in a very different domestic and international context.[139] Nevertheless, this was a Cobdenism whose application Morier, the self-styled 'disciple of Cobden' of 1870, disputed. For Morier, there was, for example, no congruence between democracy and free trade. Rather, free trade had receded with democracy, in Europe, the United States, and Australasia. This gave little hope for the future. Secondly, Morier upheld the resort to war as 'the motive force of all international

[135] Mallet to Morier, 7 July 1877, Morier Papers, Box 44; see, too, B. Mallet, *Mallet*, ch. 4; L. Mallet, *Free Exchange* (1891), 110–20, Letter to Lavaleye, 10 Mar. 1878.
[136] Mallet to Morier, 7 July 1877, Morier Papers, Box 44.
[137] Ibid., 24 and 26 Jan. 1878.
[138] Ibid., 26 Jan. 1878. Printed in part in Ramm, *Morier*, 130–1.
[139] 'Cobden had no time to elaborate a system . . . I have done little more than put into a connected shape ideas which they [friends and correspondents] have heard from him over & over again.' Ibid. 23 June 1878.

and diplomatic action', which could not rely upon moral influence alone. In the Eastern Question, Cobdenite non-interference, Morier believed, would have reduced Britain to impotence. In a manner reminiscent of Palmerston, he wholly disputed the Cobdenite notion of commerce replacing diplomacy, and saw in the physical resources of the British Empire not merely its domestic coal reserves, the essential instrument of British power. Against Mallet's 'little England' ideal, 'a carefully husbanded wealth created by a sound domestic policy', he counterposed material power and prestige through an active imperial policy.[140] Such a policy would still include the Cobdenite goal of free trade, but would be based on the realities of power, not on Gladstonian sensibilities.

This intriguing debate, the lines of which are still reflected in historical controversy, well illustrates how perceptibly the spectre of empire had begun to overhang the progress of free trade.[141] For Mallet, as Morier put it, 'a Cobdenite exceptionally acquainted with the imperial mechanism', empire would lead to the decline of British power; for Morier, 'an imperialist exceptionally influenced by Cobdenic ideas', empire was the indispensable condition of that power. This was a conflict that was articulated at several levels in the late 1870s. Morier, for example, in many ways typifies the drift of the intelligentsia and the City of London towards Conservative policy, a movement encouraged by the Bulgarian atrocities. At the popular level, not only did empire replace interest in international issues, but jingoism significantly overlapped with plebeian support for fair trade.[142] On the other hand, the Eastern Question had become a focal point for the definition of Cobdenite values against those of Disraelian government, with members of the Cobden Club conspicuous in the Bulgarian agitation.[143] It was against this background that Liberals and Cobdenites launched their political campaign of 1879–80 against both fair trade and 'Beaconsfieldism', and that Gladstone himself faced the need to rethink the part of free trade within Liberal foreign policy.

Gladstone, free trade, and Europe, 1880–6

Gladstone, in whose making as a Liberal free trade had formed so central a strand, and who had been the leading Cabinet proponent of the 1860 Treaty, readdressed the issue in print and in public in the years 1879–81. This itself, as Matthew has written, was a victory for the fair traders.[144] Two perspectives dominated Gladstone's thinking.[145] First, in his opposition to 'Beaconsfieldism' in the late 1870s Gladstone had formulated a new, liberal understanding of the 'Concert of

---

[140] Quoted in Ramm, *Morier*, 139, from Morier to Mallet, 20 Jan. 1879.

[141] O'Brien, 'Costs and Benefits'; cf. P. Kennedy, 'Reply', *Past and Present*, 125 (1989), 186–92, and O'Brien, ibid. 192–9.

[142] CCM, 2 Mar. 1878; H. Cunningham, 'Jingoism in 1877–78', *Victorian Studies*, 14 (1971), 451.

[143] Shannon, *Bulgarian Agitation*, 167, 206, 221, 249 (e.g. Potter, Probyn).

[144] Intro., *GD*, vol. 10, xxxi; above, 130; Gladstone, 'Free Trade, Railways, and the Growth of Commerce', *Nineteenth Century*, 7 (1880), 367–88.

[145] For their clear elucidation, see, especially, Intro., *GD*, vol. 9, xxxviii–xlvii.

Europe'. The notion of the Concert as the adjunct of balance of power diplomacy, so disdained by Cobden for its self-serving conservative uses, had acquired under Gladstone a radical cutting-edge, as the means to enforce international law, preserve peace, and relieve oppressed peoples. In this context, as Matthew has argued, Gladstone saw in free trade the partner, not the enemy, of the Concert. Britain's providential mission to hold out an example of free trade would inspire the drive towards international amity, but the Concert would supply the necessary political direction in the avoidance of war. Here, Gladstone deployed a concept of Europe drawing not only on material exchange, but on the Christian and Hellenic past, and expressing itself in a European public opinion or conscience, operating above national and local concerns. His predisposition, whatever his views on the merits of particular commercial treaties, remained firmly to act within a European community whose moral goals would be best achieved with low armaments and low taxes, the world free trade made possible. For sixty years, he later attested, his life had been 'a constant effort to do all I could for economy and for peace; not the peace of this country only but of the world'.[146]

Second, Gladstone defended free trade as a moral and economic good, to which Britain owed her prosperity, and the incorruptibility of her public life.[147] To some extent, commercial diplomacy itself might jeopardize this achievement, if it gave rise to powerful vested interests, or if it drew the state back into economic activity. Gladstone continued, therefore, to see treaties as exceptional departures from orthodoxy.[148] But if, as he believed, free trade was an absolute good, its defence required action both at home and abroad, for it was only in a free trade world that his view of international amity and the public law of Europe could operate, while few could doubt by 1880 the reality of European, American, and colonial protectionism. This therefore encouraged at least an open-minded approach towards European governments, rather than a simple Lowe-type retreat to commercial isolation.

Wider pressures also indicated the enlivening potential that free trade still held. This goal activated the important section of the Liberal Party organized in the Cobden Club, while 'coming men' such as Morley highlighted the importance of commercial treaties to Britain's international position.[149] Free trade also enjoyed continuing support among the working classes, with strong Radical pressure for the 'free breakfast table', involving lower duties on all articles of working-class consumption. This, in turn, was strongly linked to the desire to lower governmental expenditure, as Radicals still held to an ideal of a minimal state, in which some, as

---

[146]   Gladstone to Mundella, 5 Feb. 1894, GP, Add. MS 44258.
[147]   *Speeches, delivered at Leeds, 7 and 8 Oct. 1881* (1881); Intro, *GD*, vol. 10, xxx ff.
[148]   Gladstone to Rivers Wilson, 30 June 1881, *GD*, vol. 10, 88–9.
[149]   Above, 149; Morley, 'On the Policy of Commercial Treaties', *Fortnightly Review*, 29 (1881), 794–800; see, too, typically, J. A. Hardcastle, 'The Fallacies of Fair Trade', *Edinburgh Review*, 154 (1881), 562–95.

we have seen, dreamt of the complete abolition of customs houses.[150] More plausibly, others sought the reduction of armaments, with the Liberals' return to power coinciding with the formation of the International Arbitration and Peace Association, with the support of numerous MPs, and with Henry Richard reminding the Liberals of the essential tie between protectionism and militarism.[151] In this context, the Liberal government of 1880 not only bowed its head to the Cobdenite goal of peace, in accepting Henry Richard's disarmament motion in June 1880, but also turned to the reconstruction of the central pillar of the free trade edifice, the Cobden Treaty of 1860.

Gladstone himself, rather against the run of his views in the early 1870s, but reflecting the new concerns aroused by fair trade at home and protectionism abroad, was amenable to the Foreign Office's desire to adjust wine duties in order to 'make a good bargain with France', an objective that had secured the reluctant endorsement of the Inland Revenue and Board of Customs.[152] As in 1860, Gladstone was once more at the Exchequer, and his budget of 1880 provided fiscal scope for commercial negotiations by anticipating a loss of £230,000–240,000 on the wine duties in the event of a successful renewal of the Cobden Treaty.[153] 'Success' in 1880 implied no retrogression from 1860, a treaty that Gladstone still upheld as exceptional, 'an accommodation to the exigencies of the French Emperor's position'.[154] This stringent position in principle left sufficient scope for negotiation in practice, with Dilke, the Foreign Office minister in charge of the negotiations, by no means indifferent to the exigencies of the Third Republic, and with the key issue at stake the conversion of *ad valorem* duties into specific ones. Here, at least, was some room for manœuvre, which Dilke explored with initial enthusiasm but growing frustration between 1880 and 1882.[155]

For, as in the abortive discussions of 1877, any *via media* between British insistence, as a minimum, on equivalent terms to those of 1860 and the protectionist dynamics of French politics seemed unlikely.[156] In particular, whereas in 1860 Britain had agreed in principle to the conversion of *ad valorem* into specific duties, in the era of falling prices since 1873 this step seemed all too likely to increase the protective as well as the revenue impact of the new French tariff. Even so, the

[150]   Above, 116.

[151]   Malchow, *Agitators and Promoters in the Age of Gladstone and Disraeli* (1983), xvii, 242–3; IAPA *Reports*, 1881, 1882; *Hansard*, 3rd ser., 252, c. 87, 15 June 1880.

[152]   For Gladstone's ambivalence towards treaties, see e.g., *Revised Report of Proceedings . . . Hundredth Year of the Publication of the 'Wealth of Nations'* (1876), 42 ff.; 'Customs Tariffs' [T. V. Lister], Oct. 1879, FO 881/3977; 'Wine Duties' [T. V. Lister], 29 Apr. 1880, FO 881/4128; even so, Gladstone expressed 'little faith' in the success of negotiations, to Dilke, 11 May 1880, Dilke Papers, BL Add. MS 43875, fos. 7–8, printed in *GD*, vol. 9, 521–2.

[153]   *Hansard*, 3rd ser., 252, cc. 1625–31, 10 June 1880; this proposal was limited by time and lapsed; 253, c. 1239, 1 July; c. 1787, 6 July.

[154]   Ramm (ed.), *GG Corr. 1876–86*, vol. 1, 124 [4 May 1880].

[155]   D. Nicholls, *The Lost Prime Minister. A Life of Sir Charles Dilke* (1995), 92–8.

[156]   Smith, *Tariff Reform in France*, ch. 4; Dunham, *Anglo-French Treaty*, 319–50; Clayton, 'Commercial Relations', chs. 9 and 10; Gaston, 'Free-Trade Diplomacy', ch. 8.

vicissitudes of French politics offered some hope of an administration sympathetic
to free trade, with the return of Dilke's friend Gambetta to office in October 1881.
As in 1872, Lyons, the British Ambassador at Paris, also strongly favoured a tariff
treaty—even on worse terms—on political grounds, a view that 'Cobdenite' free
traders supported.[157] For others in Britain, however, the insistence upon no retrogression from the terms of the 1860 Treaty was paramount. This was true both of
fiscal free traders who believed that the British tariff should be determined solely by
domestic considerations, and of businessmen who feared they would pay the economic cost for the possible political gains of a treaty.[158] British negotiators had also
to bear in mind the likely fair trade reaction to any treaty deemed to be less
favourable than that of 1860. This particularly worried Chamberlain, Dilke's friend
and ally at the Board of Trade, for, he wrote:

The manufacturers and workpeople now dependent on the French trade will form a most
powerful re-inforcement to the sugar refiners, the shipping interest, and the advocates of
Reciprocity generally; and their individual influences will be direct, important, and capable
of early organisation; they are not unlikely to outweigh as a political force the more widespread, indirect, and less readily appreciated national interests which would be prejudiced by
any reversal of our Free Trade policy.[159]

On the other hand, the failure of negotiations might also, as Chamberlain and the
Foreign Office feared, increase the pressure for retaliatory duties in Britain.[160] To
some, including Dilke and Chamberlain, the idea of raising British wine duties—
purportedly on fiscal grounds—was not without its attractions as a retaliatory
threat, although the idea of using such a bargaining-counter was anathema to the
fiscally orthodox.[161]

In fact, the ensuing lengthy negotiations were not unproductive, with the Board
of Trade at one point calculating that new French duties would be lower on £18m
worth of British trade and higher on £9m.[162] The real sticking-point remained
textiles, and while some progress proved possible, it always seemed insufficient to
win over Manchester and Bradford, the latter already the centre of considerable fair

---

[157] Newton, *Lord Lyons*, 453 (30 Dec. 1881); Dilke to Gladstone, 28 Sept. 1881, GP, Add. MS
44149; T. Barclay, *Thirty Years: Anglo-French Reminiscences (1876–1906)* (1914), 75–6.

[158] Earl Grey, *Free Trade with France* (1881); Redford, *Manchester Merchants*, vol. 2, 53 (27 Apr.
1881); Mundella believed the public opposed any increases: memo. to Dilke, [3] May 1881, Dilke
Papers, Add. MS 43911, fos. 201–2; *Hansard*, 3rd ser., 262, cc. 119–41, 9 June 1881; *Statist*, 11 June
1881.

[159] Chamberlain to Dilke, 23 Apr. 1881, FO 27/2532, also quoted in Gaston, 'Free-Trade Diplomacy', 247 ff.; Dunham, *Anglo-French Treaty*, 343.

[160] Tenterden to Granville, 20 June 1881, Granville Papers, PRO 30/29/193; Granville to
Gladstone, 23 June 1881, Ramm (ed.), *GG Corr. 1876–86*, vol. 1, 283–84; Chamberlain to Gladstone, in
Gladstone to Dilke, 2 May 1881, Dilke Papers, Add. MS 43875, fos. 47–8; Lyons to Dilke, 14 June 1881,
Dilke Papers, Add. MS 43883.

[161] Mundella memo, [3] May 1881; Dilke memo, 4 May 1881, Dilke Papers, Add. MS 43911, fos.
201–2, 204–9. See above, 168 for J. A. Crowe's support for this.

[162] Dilke to Granville, 25 and 28 Sept. 1881, Granville Papers, PRO 30/29/121.

trade agitation. As its MP Forster warned, 'We shall be charged not merely with neglecting interests but with sacrificing them & that too by abandoning the principles of Free Trade & it would not be a charge easy to meet because it would be true.'[163] These obstacles proved insuperable, despite the work of Manchester's ablest commercial diplomats.[164] With commercial opinion therefore largely against a treaty, Gladstone regretfully faced the failure of negotiations on political grounds, but confident that 'we with our insular position can afford the loss infinitely better than France can'. Commercially, he was 'certainly of opinion that we are so strong in our command of the general market of the world—although we sometimes get a little frightened about it—as to be independent of all huckstering, a matter much more suitable for those who have not yet extricated themselves from the arid labyrinths of Protection'.[165] Diplomatically, Gladstone realized that one of the attractions of the treaty-making in 1860, the 'authority from the Continent of Europe to propagate practically the doctrine of free trade', had much diminished by the early 1880s, given the protectionist advance in Europe.

That advance had, however, much reduced the French readiness for compromise. Hence, Gambetta's return to office produced no increase in free trade's political strength, for he himself was soon under pressure from the protectionists.[166] Even the most convinced free traders in France, such as Léon Say, adopted a pragmatic approach to the treaty question.[167] More importantly, French negotiations with Belgium and Italy neared completion on terms far more favourable to French interests than those of the 1860 Treaty, offering an attractive alternative to the latter.[168] Understandably, British policy leaned reluctantly more towards the abandonment of the treaty than its watering-down. Thus, at the Foreign Office, by June 1881 Granville already considered 'Cobden's treaty was a great coup. But it was administering mercury to a very diseased liver. It would be worth a great deal to get out of the habit of administering mercury as a portion of a normal diet.'[169]

The end of the treaty required, in the view of most, some substitute in its place.[170] This entailed a lengthy debate as to the merits of most-favoured nation treatment, a status that left Britain dependent upon gains secured by third parties in tariff negotiations. Such treaties would not necessarily benefit Britain's

---

[163]   Forster to Dilke, 27 Dec. 1881, with copy, Forster to Granville, 'better no treaty than a treaty which will make Fair trade a popular cry', Dilke Papers, Add. MS 43911, fos. 298–301.

[164]   Redford, *Manchester Merchants*, vol. 2, 53; 'Henry and Sir Joseph Lee', *DBB*, vol. 4, 703–14.

[165]   Gladstone to Dilke, 2 Nov. 1881, Dilke Papers, Add. MS 43875, fos. 76–7; printed in *GD*, vol. 10, 155–6.

[166]   Smith, *Tariff Reform in France*, 186–7.

[167]   Thus, Lyons noted, Say 'will not be a martyr to his free trade principles'. To Dilke, 1 Feb. 1882, Dilke Papers, Add. MS 43883. See, too, G. Michel, *Léon Say, sa vie, ses œuvres* (Paris, 1899), esp. 352–8.

[168]   Clayton, 'Commercial Relations', 273; Devers, 'Politique Commerciale', 171 ff.

[169]   Ramm (ed.), *GG Corr. 1876–86*, vol. 1, 284 [23 June 1881]; Gladstone had earlier ruled 'Sooner no treaty with France than a bad one', Dilke Diary, 27 Apr. 1881, Dilke Papers, Add. MS 43924.

[170]   *Hansard*, 3rd ser., 267, c. 1869, 24 Mar. 1882 [Lubbock].

particular exports, the leading consideration behind the search for a new treaty in 1880–1, but would provide a minimal safeguard against discrimination.[171] Yet even the apparently simple resort to most-favoured nation status concealed two vastly complicated issues, whose later development did much to determine British trade policy. First, it was unclear whether the terms of most-favoured nation treaties also bound the British colonies; were they, as some claimed, independent economic units, or were they, as in the 1865 and 1862 treaties, part of a wider whole?[172] This had major repercussions for imperial unity, as we will see in the next chapter. Second, did most-favoured nation status rule out countervailing duties? This was an issue made topical, if not yet urgent, by the question of sugar bounties, designed to foster the promotion of sugar-beet production in Europe.[173] In the event, neither issue was resolved, although Britain gained most-favoured nation status by the legislative action of the French Assembly, confirmed by the Anglo-French Commercial Convention of February 1882.[174] After years on a life-support machine, the Anglo-French Treaty had finally expired, the apparent end of 'Cobdenite commercial liberalism', although Gladstone and others purported to believe that free trade itself was strengthened, not weakened, by the absence of treaties.[175] If this failure was a moral gain, Anglo-French trade itself seems not to have suffered, and, ironically, as Dilke claimed, by virtue of the Franco-Belgian Treaty, most-favoured nation treatment actually gave British trade better terms than those of 1860.[176] Even more ironically, what seemed to be the end of Cobdenism in Britain was greeted by French experts as 'a new and probably definitive consecration of the work of 1860'.[177]

Despite the chastening experience of the Anglo-French negotiations, treaty-making both within and outside Europe remained an important aim of British foreign policy. In March 1883 the Cabinet was ready to endorse treaties as an instrument of future policy, although Gladstone stipulated that the Foreign Office

[171] Some, e.g., Tenterden, doubted the value of most-favoured nation status: to Granville, 20 June 1881, Granville Papers, PRO 30/29/193. Cf. Kennedy, 'Remarks on the most-favoured nation article', 21 June 1880, FO 800/4, fos. 268–70; 'MFN article in commercial treaties', 17 Dec. 1881, FO 881/4557. Dilke leaned strongly in this direction by November 1881, Dilke Diary, 10 Nov. 1881, Dilke Papers, Add. MS 43924.

[172] Board of Trade (Farrer) to FO, 23 Feb. 1882, BT 12/17. This issue was made particularly pertinent by Canadian attempts to negotiate directly with France, see R. A. Shields, 'The Canadian Treaty Negotiations with France: A Study in Imperial Relations, 1878–1883', *Bulletin of the Institute of Historical Research*, 40 (1967), 186–202.

[173] BT (Farrer) to FO, 30 Jan. 1882, BT 12/17.

[174] De Bernhardt, *Commercial Treaties*, 313–19.

[175] *Hansard*, 3rd ser., 267, c. 1911, 24 Mar. 1882; see, too, Rivers Wilson to Dilke, 23 Mar. 1882, Dilke Papers, Add. MS 43912; cf. Cobdenite regret, *Manchester Guardian*, 15 May 1882.

[176] B. R. Mitchell with P. Deane, *Abstract of British Historical Statistics* (Cambridge, 1962), 323–4, shows a slight fall in export values (current prices) between the quinqennium 1876–80 and that of 1886–90, but wholesale prices were falling rapidly at this time. See, too, F. Crouzet, *Britain Ascendant* (1984), ch. 11; Dilke to Granville, 9 Nov. 1884, Granville Papers, PRO 30/29/122; S. Glynn and G. Tuckwell, *The Life of Sir Charles Dilke* (2 vols, 1917), vol. 1, 400; Clayton, 'Commercial Relations', 293.

[177] L. Amé, quoted in Smith, *Tariff Reform*, 193.

was not to act without prior Cabinet authority.[178] Treaties, in principle, were still encouraged by Dilke and Chamberlain, more enthusiastically than by Granville or Gladstone, with Childers, Gladstone's successor as Chancellor of the Exchequer, half-way between the two camps.[179] At the Foreign Office Kennedy was also keen to urge forward treaties, although in the light of events in Egypt, Gladstone opposed reopening negotiations with France. Nor were the prospects elsewhere wholly encouraging for Cobdenite evangelism, with, for example, Dufferin reporting from Russia that the best that could be hoped for was no increase in protection.[180] In Germany, there had been some exploration of Anglo-German tariffs in 1880, with a tentative British willingness to adjust duties on spirits. But the mood in Berlin was scarcely conducive to free trade negotiations, with Bismarck reportedly declaring: 'all Cobdenites and Free Traders are Nihilists.'[181] Closer Austro-German economic ties also prevented the amelioration of the Austrian tariff in Britain's favour, despite a British initiative in 1880.[182] As this economic *Mitteleuropa* took shape, and with the Cobden treaty gone, Britain was forced once more to look towards the commercial promise of the Mediterranean.[183]

Here, the prospects were not unfavourable, with Italy anxious for a treaty on grounds of general policy, although her attachment to 'bloated armaments' as a sign of national greatness, and Britain's unreadiness to adjust wine duties in her favour, ruled out any 'commercial bargain'.[184] The most-favoured nation treaty agreed in June 1883 tacitly acknowledged the Italian shift to protection, but offered political benefits—the consolidation of Anglo-Italian understanding which paved the way for the Mediterranean Accords/Treaties of 1887.[185] With regard to the Iberian peninsula, the Liberal government now proved far more ready to adjust the wine duties, for long the bugbear of the free traders, a course facilitated by the ending of the Cobden Treaty in 1882. In Portugal, the enthusiastic Morier, still anxious to demonstrate his Cobdenic principles, was well placed to exploit the wine duties when head of mission in 1876–81.[186] As we have already seen, he had successfully

---

[178]   Kennedy, 'Commercial Treaties', 11 Apr. 1883, FO 881/4779; Gladstone, *GD*, vol. 10, 412–13 [5 Mar. 1883]; Dilke Diary, 5 Mar. 1883, Dilke Papers, Add. MS 43925.

[179]   'The others do not seem to have thought about it', Granville to Gladstone, 28 Feb. 1883; Ramm (ed.), *GG Corr. 1876–86*, vol. 2, 35.

[180]   CCM, 1 May 1880.

[181]   W. A. White to W. Cartwright, 24 Mar. 1881, Cartwright Papers, 20/639. For the wider context, see R. J. S. Hoffman, *Great Britain and the German Trade Rivalry, 1875–1914* (Philadelphia, 1933); P. Kennedy, *The Rise of Anglo-German Antagonism, 1860–1914* (1980). For attempts to portray the benefits of Cobdenism in Germany, see A. Held, 'Schutzzoll und Freihandel', *Jahrbuch für Gesetzgebung, Verwaltung und Volkswirtschaft im Deutschen Reich*, vol. 3 (1879), 437–86; F. Simonson, *Richard Cobden und die Antikornzollliga* (Berlin, 1883); K. Walcker, *Richard Cobden's volkwirtschaftiche und politische Ansichten* (Hamburg, 1885).

[182]   Gaston, 'Free-Trade Diplomacy', ch. 7; FO to Sir H. Elliot, Elliot to FO, 1880, Commercial, FO 7/2000 and FO 7/1001.

[183]   Dilke Diary, 2 Aug. 1881, 13 Feb., 30 Nov. 1883, Dilke Papers, Add. MSS 43924, 43925.

[184]   Sir A. Paget to Granville, 19 May, 22 June 1880, Paget Papers, BL Add. MS 51227.

[185]   Bolchini, 'Anglo-Italian Economic Relations', 209–20.   [186]   Ramm, *Morier*, 168 ff.

negotiated colonial treaties, whose 'every step, he averred to Mallet, 'was argued in the language of your doctrines . . . [for] my business is *international* pure and simple'.[187] This preparatory work culminated in the negotiation of a most-favoured nation convention completed by his successor in May 1882, a considerable achievement after years of fruitless bargaining.[188]

More importantly still, in 1881 Morier, having become British minister at Madrid, was also ideally placed to infiltrate Spain's hitherto impenetrable protectionist labyrinth. While the vicissitudes of Spanish politics made consistent aims in diplomacy difficult, Morier met with gradual success.[189] His main strategy followed the line laid down by the Wine Duties Committee of 1879, that of adjusting wine duties in return for a more liberal Spanish tariff, in the expectation that revenue foregone would be amply compensated by trade expansion. But Spain had so far proved remarkably unreceptive to the blandishments of the free traders, producing in 1882 a protective tariff which famously provoked Chamberlain to consider retaliation.[190] British manufacturers were ready to glimpse in the Spanish market a welcome boost to trade at a time of depression, rising tariffs, and compensation for the failure of the Anglo-French negotiations. Moreover, unlike the French case, a way forward could be seen in the combination of the reduction with the reclassification of wine duties, so as to put Spain on an even footing with France, while breaking down Spain's high tariff walls.[191] The Board of Customs uttered its usual dire warnings concerning the threat to revenue, but with Childers at the Treasury willing to adjust wine duties, and with the Board of Trade favouring a treaty, Morier's energetic negotiations had by 1885 brought Britain to the verge of success.[192]

It was at this point that the dilemmas of Gladstonian finance were clearly broached. First, while tariff treaties held out the hope of long-term prosperity, they did so at the cost of a short-term fall in revenue. Such a fall in revenue was what the Liberal government could least afford, given its growing entanglements abroad, especially in Egypt, and the rising costs of armaments expenditure.[193] Second, while Radicals were eager to cut revenue (as the tap for military spending), what the

[187] Morier to Mallet, 10 Oct. 1882, Morier Papers, Box 45.
[188] This was supplementary to the Commercial Treaty of 1842. *Hertslet's Commercial Treaties*, 15 (1885), 293–5.
[189] Ramm, *Morier*, 168 ff.; *BDFA Pt. I, ser. F*, vol. 26, Spain, docs. 76, 77, 91, 98, 108, 111–12, 116, 125.
[190] D. W. R. Bahlman (ed.), *The Diary of Sir Edward Hamilton, 1880–85* (2 vols, Oxford, 1972), vol. 1, 310 [21 July 1882]; Gaston, 'Free-Trade Diplomacy', 294 ff.; Chamberlain to Dilke, 4 July 1882, Dilke Papers, Add. MS 43885, fos. 242–4.
[191] See, for example, D. Joaquin Jamar, *A Brief Review of the Treaty Negotiations between Spain and England* (1882).
[192] Ramm, *Morier*, 181–6; Gaston, 'Free-Trade Diplomacy', *passim*; Childers to Granville, 23 Apr., 4 June 1885, Granville Papers, PRO 30/29/119; *GD*, vol. 11, 56, 60 [10 and 17 Nov. 1883]. The agreement to move to a treaty was made in December 1884; Hertslet, *Commercial Treaties*, vol. 17 (1890), 1015–6.
[193] Parry, *Liberal Government*, 292. In 1884 Campbell-Bannerman expected 'Radical Economists', including Labouchère, would support increased naval expenditure, but that Henry Richard and 'the

prospective Spanish treaty offered was a 'cheap wine bottle' rather than a 'free breakfast table'. More alarmingly, the budgetary shortfall was in part to be made up by beer duties—a tax on working-class consumers—even though this was to be balanced by greater direct taxation. This left the Radicals half in agreement with Conservative critics of the budget, objecting to increased beer duties, while wine, a luxury good, escaped. In these circumstances Gladstone now sought to back out of the provisional agreement with Spain. He could not, however, avoid the increased taxes in the June 1885 budget, the defeat of which led to the fall of his government, the result, as he saw it, of an unprincipled alliance between the Tories and the Irish, 'opposed to indirect taxation generally'.[194] Gladstonian finance, torn between its search in principle for economy and low taxation, and the demand in practice for growing expenditure and increased taxation, threatened by 1885 to impose impassable fiscal obstacles to successful commercial negotiation.

Nevertheless, this setback was only temporary, for in 1886, the year of Liberal disunion, one major achievement of the Home Rule government was a successful conclusion to the Spanish negotiations.[195] The necessary reduction in wine duties was made possible by reductions in the military estimates, as Hamilton delighted to find in Harcourt a Chancellor who 'out-Gladstoned Gladstone', a 'former financial heretic converted so suddenly into an apostle of economy'.[196] In 1886, with the upward spiral of expenditure only temporarily halted, and with depression threatening government revenue, it was already possible to see the doom of the Peelite–Gladstonian fiscal model.[197] But in the short term, the old model of 1860, including cheap wine for the working man, had briefly been resuscitated as a vital element in British fiscal and foreign policy.[198]

The Anglo-Spanish treaty of 1886 illustrated the importance of 'huckstering' and of most-favoured nation treatment, for the differential duties imposed by Spain in 1877 had undoubtedly harmed British trade.[199] More importantly, those duties had acted as a warning of the hidden dangers faced by Britain in the absence of the security, however minimal at times, afforded by most-favoured nation treatment, 'the sheet-anchor of free trade'.[200] This belief, while not universally shared, had

---

peace party' would oppose yielding to a 'panic'. To Childers, 2 Oct. 1884 in Childers to Gladstone, 6 Oct. 1884, Add. MS 44130.

[194] Gladstone to Hartington, 10 June 1885, *GD*, vol. 11, 354.

[195] Hertslet, *Commercial Treaties*, vol. 17, 1020, 1026; *Annual Register*, 1886, 393–4; Redford, *Manchester Merchants*, vol. 2, 54.

[196] D. W. R. Bahlman (ed.), *The Diary of Sir Edward Walter Hamilton, 1885–1906* (Hull, 1993), 29 [25 Feb. 1886]; Gaston, 'Free-Trade Diplomacy', 312 ff.; Harcourt Papers, dep. 118 (1886 budget), Bodleian Library, Oxford.

[197] Buxton, *Finance and Politics*, vol. 2, 319.

[198] Cf. T172/858, T. J. Pittar, 23 Jan. 1905, for an adverse reassessment of this treaty.

[199] Saul, *Overseas Trade*, 137–41. British traders had lost out badly in the Spanish market 1879–86, as a result of a tariff preferential to Germany and France. In 1877 Britain contributed 31% of Spanish imports; in 1886, 13%; Gaston, 'Free-Trade Diplomacy', 16 ff.

[200] Morley, 'Commercial Treaties', 794–7.

therefore continued to guide British commercial policy, and had prevented a retreat into economic isolation in the 1880s. By 1886 Britain enjoyed most-favoured nation treatment with regard to all Western European powers, in a series of treaties which survived, in most cases, until 1914.[201] As in Spain, this certainly interrupted any uniform upward trend to high tariffs, and more generally amounted to a determined and not unsuccessful attempt to preserve the gains of commercial treaties amidst the perils of European protectionism and the fiscal demands of imperial expansion. No doubt Gladstone himself may be open to criticism for an outdated anti-huckstering complacency, but the spadework of Dilke and the Foreign Office had largely compensated for this apathy, enabling British policy to reach a necessary compromise between unilateralism and fair trade at home, in rescuing what was salvageable from the wreck of the Cobden treaty system. This had gone some way towards circumventing the objection of dogmatic free traders, such as Farrer, that the very existence of commercial treaties encouraged a belief in retaliation.[202] On the other hand, there was by 1885 little scope left for free trade schemes such as Molinari's revival of the idea of an Anglo-Dutch–Belgian customs union, capable of driving a wedge into 'the worm-eaten trunk of continental protection'.[203]

The girth of that trunk remained a vital concern to the Liberal government.[204] As a result, the Liberals remained ready to conclude new commercial treaties outside Western Europe, in particular continuing the Conservative policy of underpinning the Balkan settlement by commercial agreements designed to contain the spread of German, Austrian, and Russian protectionism.[205] Thus, Gould, the British minister at Belgrade, wrote encouragingly to Granville: '[T]he Prime Minister is looked up to by these people as the patron saint of the Slav[e]s and it is our interest to consolidate as much as possible these small states, which will otherwise soon fall a prey to their big neighbours, whose "idée fixe" is to oust us commercially from the whole of these regions.'[206] The Romanian and Serbian treaties were complemented by those with Montenegro (1882) and Greece (1886).[207] Above all, in Turkey

---

[201]   For a 'Return of Most-Favoured Nation Clauses . . . in force 1 July 1903', see *Parl. Papers*, 1904, 45 [cd. 1807].

[202]   Farrer, *Free Trade versus Fair Trade* (1885), 361, an apologetic conclusion to a work sponsored by the Cobden Club.

[203]   *The Times*, 23 Jan. 1885; cf. Lumley, above, 157. For Molinari, see Silberner, *Problem of War*, ch. 7.

[204]   Most countries gave rise to free trade concern in the 1880s, for example Switzerland, whose tariff of 1883 was seen as '. . . a distinctly retrograde step', BT to FO 18 May 1883, BT12/18, fo. 431. Belgium and Holland remained treasured exceptions, Farrer, *Free Trade*, 79–80, 276–80.

[205]   White at Belgrade feared attempts to exclude Britain from trade in the Balkans. To Cartwright, 28 Dec. 1880, Cartwright Papers, 20/609.

[206]   Gould to Granville, 1 Mar. 1881, Granville Papers, PRO 30/29/184. For Foreign Office perceptions of Bismarck's commercial designs in South-East Europe, see Tenterden to Granville, 25 Sept. and 30 Oct. 1880, ibid., PRO 30/29/193.

[207]   The latter was facilitated by the work of J. Gennadius, honorary member of the Cobden Club and Greek Minister-General in London, 1885–92; *Who Was Who*, 1929–40; he had been a keen follower of Cobden since the 1840s, *History of the Cobden Club*, 74. For treaty details, see de Bernhardt, *Commercial Treaties*, 449–57.

Britain was quite prepared to negotiate a new commercial treaty, on the basis of increased duties, secure in the knowledge that it was framed with her goods in mind, that the revenue was earmarked for English rentiers, and that 15 per cent Turkish duties were preferable to effective Russian ones of 60–70 per cent.[208] In this case, unlike that of France, higher duties were commensurable with the interests of the City and industry, as commercial policy was effectively shaped to reinforce British economic and diplomatic interests in the Balkans and the Ottoman Empire.[209]

More widely, despite Gladstone's failure to revive in a lasting manner either the Concert of Europe or the Anglo-French Treaty, the Liberal government had successfully preserved the kernel of Britain's free trade policy in the face of fair trade at home and protectionism abroad. Even the disillusioned Cobdenite Mallet could write encouragingly to Granville in 1885, of the long-term benefits secured by the 1860 Treaty, ensuring a much greater free trade area than otherwise conceivable.[210] Moreover, looking at the pattern of European trade, the fair traders' fears of Britain's imminent exclusion were by no means realized in the decade after 1886.[211] By 1892, on the Liberals' return to office, Giffen's statistics purported to show that free trade was growing in the world, not declining, and that 'the area of England's foreign trade is not in the process of being circumscribed by a wall of protectionist tariffs in foreign countries'.[212] Yet the partial success of this restructuring of the European free trade order could not conceal the growing importance of empire, whose economic and political implications remained anathema to the Cobdenites.

'Imperialism is fatal to Internationalism'[213]

The swing to the East in British foreign policy, apparent under Palmerston, and made obvious under Disraeli, became irreversible in the 1880s. As a result, British trade became increasingly dependent upon Asian and African markets. For, as D. C. M. Platt convincingly argued, the 1880s saw an overwhelming change in

---

[208] FO 881/3882, 5127, 5188, 5286; for Sir Joseph Lee and the Turkish Tariff, FO 78/3742; BT 12/18, fo. 318, 14 Apr.; fo. 813, 5 Oct. 1883. Anglo-Turkish negotiations concluded satisfactorily in June 1885, but the new tariff was not put into effect.

[209] Redford, *Manchester Merchants*, vol. 2, 79–80, 82–3; P. J. Cain and A. G. Hopkins, *British Imperialism* (2 vols, 1993), vol. 1, 400–6.

[210] Mallet to Granville, 9 Feb. 1885, Granville Papers, PRO 30/29/151. By this date Mallet's hopes, like those of other free traders, lay in America's conversion to free trade, as the commercial successor to Britain. Mallet expected this within three or four years. It took sixty. For relative satisfaction after 1886, see Redford, *Manchester Merchants*, vol. 2, 55.

[211] Hamilton in 1887 prepared a memorandum for Gladstone on free trade since 1860, showing progress more 'from general enlightenment and the example of this country than to any direct effect of the treaty of 1860 though I have no doubt that the Treaty helped to set the Free Trade ball "rolling by"', 15 Feb. 1887, GP Add. MS 44191.

[212] Giffen memo: 'The Relative Growth of Free Trade and Protection', 25 May 1892, circulated to Cabinet by Mundella, 24 Aug. 1892, but originally prepared for Hicks Beach, GP, Add. MS 44258, 282 ff.

[213] Mallet to Morier, 4 Feb. 1885, Morier Papers, Box 44; see, too, B. Mallet, *Mallet*, 174–81.

British policy towards 'semi-civilized and barbarous' areas.[214] Moreover, as Platt intriguingly put it, Britain's continuing adhesion to free trade entailed further imperial expansion—that is to say that, with the discounting of an active policy of retaliation in Europe and America, empire appeared to offer the most accessible new openings for trade.[215] Already the 1880s had seen considerable mercantile pressure for colonial expansion, with an overt appeal to offset Europe by empire.[216] Thus, in the wake of the failure of the Anglo–French negotiations of 1882, the *Statist* took comfort in the view that commercial treaties were not needed by a country 'with a vast Colonial empire'.[217] This seeming rejection of Cobdenite aspirations went still further, confirmed emphatically by the occupation of Egypt in 1882. Here was the warlike action, long feared by men such as Mallet, which finally epitomized the failure of the Cobdenite world-view: 'I look upon the Egyptian business as quite fatal. Nothing but a miracle now can save us from a return to all the old follies of alliances, balance of power, great wars, annexation etc etc. and the gradual possession of half of the African continent, if indeed, the whole fabric does not collapse before us.'[218] Providence did not supervene to release Britain from her imperial vocation, as the scramble for Africa began and the retreat from Europe accelerated. Thus, symbolically, in 1883 Britain abandoned the Channel Tunnel, commenced by the Cobdenite optimists Watkin and Chevalier in 1875, but now the victim of militarist fears of invasion and patriotic glory in isolation.[219]

In the face of this fading of 'free trade, peace and goodwill', British policy-makers were not entirely passive. First, if the moment seemed inopportune for Cobdenite evangelism in Europe, Liberal policy beyond Europe proved attentive to free trade imperatives in a number of important ways. Thus, Baring's Indian budget of 1882, with its abolition of import duties, heartened the Cobdenites, as 'the most important contribution to the Free trade policy of recent years'.[220] Commercial treaties were also used to secure trade outside Europe, even if often with political and strategic goals equally in mind, as in the case of the Anglo–Korean

---

[214]   Platt, *Finance, Trade*, 152. See, too, Platt, 'Economic Factors in British Policy during the "New Imperialism" ', *Past and Present*, 39 (1968), 120–38.

[215]   Platt, *Finance, Trade*, 147; but, as the previous section has shown, this was not the result of the exclusion of British goods.

[216]   London Chamber of Commerce to FO, 9 Apr. 1885 (on imperial federation), FO 83/864.

[217]   22 Apr. 1882, 447.

[218]   Mallet to Morier, 15 Oct. 1882, Morier Papers, Box 44; CCM, 22 July 1882. Sir Wilfrid Lawson wished the Club to condemn the bombardment, for 'peace throughout the world was a great object with Mr Cobden and should be a great object with the Club'. This was successfully opposed by Mallet, Potter, and Borlase.

[219]   For divided counsels, 1875–83, see Kennedy Papers, FO 800/4, fos. 2–53. See, too, A. Bisset, *Notes on the Anti-Corn Law Struggle* (1884), ch. 6, 'Free Trade and the Channel Tunnel', 257–305; free trade opponents of the Tunnel included Goldwin Smith, Sir John Lubbock, J. A. Hardcastle, Cyril Flower, and G. J. Holyoake: see James Knowles, *The Channel Tunnel and Public Opinion* (1883).

[220]   Mallet to Derby, 15 June 1882, Derby Papers, 920 DER(15)/20/Mallet; *Cobden Club, Annual Report, 1882*; above, 140.

treaty of 1883.[221] Elsewhere, as European interest in the periphery increased, Britain sought to update long-standing arrangements, as in the case of Morocco in 1886, and in Central and South America, with treaties with Honduras, Guatemala, Mexico, Paraguay, Uruguay, Venezuela, and Salvador all concluded or proceeding in 1886.[222] These took their place among the means by which Britain sought to maintain 'fair treatment, equal favour, and open competition overseas'.[223] On the other hand, Britain failed in her negotiations with the United States in 1884–7 to secure lower duties on British West Indian produce, although to the orthodox such an agreement, giving exclusive advantages to one part of the empire, would itself have been 'entirely at variance with a Free Trade policy'.[224]

Second, if Britain did not aspire to the model of the Bismarckian industrial state, there is some evidence of a lower key reshaping of diplomatic support for trade.[225] Dilke's tenure of office had done something to restore commercial confidence in British diplomacy, with a clear political line of responsibility for trade.[226] This did not go as far as some wanted, and it effectively scuppered the idea of a Ministry of Commerce.[227] The Royal Commission into the Depression in Trade and Industry set up by the minority Conservative government in 1885 also generated much canvassing of opinion on the wider issue of state support for trade, but views were evenly balanced between those those who urged a more interventionist role on behalf of industry and finance, and those in favour of abstention, preserving the reputation of the Foreign Office for integrity and incorruptibility.[228] Such divided opinion did not prevent all change, and, as Platt showed, the Bryce memorandum of July 1886 represented a sensible adjustment of British policy, and proved a stimulus towards a more active support for British trade, as, for example, in

---

[221] I. Nish, 'The Anglo-Korean Treaty of 1883', in I. Nish (ed.), *Aspects of Anglo-Korean Relations* (London School of Economics, 1984), 15–26. See, too, FO 881/5471, for British policy in Asia.

[222] 'Business of the Commercial Department, Feb. 1886', FO 881/5188; 'Business of the Commercial Department, July 1886', FO 881/5286. For the importance of Mexico to Manchester and Bradford, Rivers Wilson to Dilke, 18 Oct. 1881, Dilke Papers, Add. MS 43911, fo. 291; see, too, BT to FO 13 June 1883, BT 12/18, fo. 493.

[223] Platt, *Finance, Trade*, 83.

[224] Farrer to Granville, 13 Jan. 1885, cited in G. A. Pigman, 'Hegemony and Free Trade Policy: Britain, 1846–1914 and the USA, 1944–90', unpublished D.Phil. thesis, University of Oxford (1992), 225.

[225] How interventionist the Bismarckian state really was also occasioned some doubt.

[226] See Platt, *Finance, Trade*, app. This was an attempt to respond to business critics, but some of those preferred a revamped Board of Trade (e.g. Behrens, cited Chamberlain to Dilke, 7 Dec. 1880, Dilke Papers, Add. MS 43885, fo. 116). The Board acquired in 1882 a greater say in FO business, but Dilke resisted the idea of a Ministry of Commerce, although he also (wrongly) foresaw the Tories moving Kennedy to the BT as the most effective arm of commercial diplomacy. See Dilke to Granville, 2 Oct. 1882, PRO 30/29/122.

[227] For this campaign, see Ilersic and Liddle, *Parliament of Commerce*, 30–7; Redford, *Manchester Merchants*, vol. 2, 115; Chamberlain to Dilke, 28 Dec. 1882, Dilke Papers, Add. MS 43885, fo. 320; Dilke to Gladstone, memo. 23 Nov. 1882, GP, Add. MS 44149, fos. 92–3.

[228] 'Questions of Assistance to British Commercial Interests in Foreign Countries', Jan. 1887, FO 881/5266. See, too, Rosebery to Bryce, 27 Feb. 1886, FO 83/932.

China.[229] Here was a clear recognition that free trade—in the sense of open markets—required an active government role. This remained distasteful to the purists—not necessarily idle aristocrats, but to experts such as Farrer—as well as to *The Economist*, but it represented a *via media* increasingly to the taste of provincial business and the City of London.[230] Even so, for government, the key responsibility remained that of information, with the inauguration of *The Board of Trade Journal* in 1886 the prelude to a series of policies designed to improve commercial intelligence.[231] By 1886 this policy, combined with the modified pursuit of commercial treaties that we have already seen, amounted to a significant readjustment of policy, which was by no means unsuccessful. Certainly, the Foreign Office and the Board of Trade achieved considerably more than critics of *laissez-faire* and aristocratic passivity sometimes allow.

Third, a growing official and unofficial eye was kept on the tariff policy of European powers overseas. For example, French colonial policy, which had slowly moved to free trade in the 1860s, began a gradual reversal in French West Africa in the late 1870s.[232] This produced a readiness by Britain to establish protectorates, as with the Niger chiefs in 1883, guaranteeing free trade in this region.[233] As Villiers Lister wrote: '[T]he jealousy of French colonial possessions shown by the English has nothing to do with any dislike to France or to increase of French power, but is founded upon their system of Protection which ruins or prevents trade.'[234] Imperial historians have shown that this 'tariff factor' played a significant, if not overwhelming, part in Britain's readiness to make territorial acquisitions in the early 1880s, and to give diplomatic support to 'aberrations' such as the North Borneo Company, the occasion of much Liberal soul-searching.[235] By 1884 the Foreign Office was belatedly, but keenly, concerned with the threat to free trade presented by European rivals in Africa. At the Berlin West Africa Conference a strong emphasis was placed on keeping open newly colonized areas to British trade, albeit with a clear-eyed appreciation of the hollowness of the 'internationalism' of Leopold of Belgium's International Association.[236]

---

[229] Platt, *Finance, Trade*, 275–6, 403–15; Rosebery as Foreign Secretary declined to address the Cobden Club on diplomatic support for trade by legitimate means, CCM, 6, 13 Mar. 1886.

[230] Farrer, *The State in its Relation to Trade* (1883); S. R. B. Smith, 'British Nationalism, Imperialism and the City of London, 1880–1900', unpublished Ph.D. thesis, University of London (1985), *passim.*

[231] Platt, *Finance, Trade*, 111–14.

[232] A. Girault, *The Colonial Tariff Policy of France* (1916); C. W. Newbury, 'The Protectionist Revival in French Colonial Trade: The Case of Senegal', *Economic History Review*, 2nd ser., 21 (1968), 337–48; id., 'The Tariff Factor in Anglo-French West African Partition', in P. Gifford and W. R. Louis (eds.), *France and Britain in Africa* (1971).

[233] GD, vol. 11, 60 [17 Nov. 1883]; A. D. Nzemeke, *British Imperialism and African Response: The Niger Valley, 1851–1905* (Paderborn, 1982), ch. 2.

[234] Lister to Granville, 29 Mar. 1883, copy in Lister MSS, c. 1034, fos. 277–90; 'Correspondence respecting Differential Treatment of British Trade in the French Colonies', July 1884, FO 881/4992.

[235] Granville to Dilke, 21 Dec. 1881, Granville Papers, PRO 30/29/121; Dilke Diary, 13 Jan. 1882, Dilke Papers, Add. MS 43924.

[236] S. E. Crowe, *The Berlin West Africa Conference, 1884–85* (1952); S. Forster, W. J. Mommsen, and R. Robinson (eds.), *Bismarck, Europe, and Africa: The Berlin Africa Conference, 1884–1885 and the Onset*

Finally, if free trade seemed under threat in Africa, the prospects in the settled British Empire scarcely proved reassuring. It had, for example, come as a considerable shock to Gladstone to discover in 1871 both how autonomous and how protectionist the Australian colonies were, 'near the *reductio ad absurdum* of the colonial connection'.[237] Colonial protectionism, so contrary to British policy in Europe, threatened free trade Britain with being 'made fools of . . . in the face of the whole world'.[238] Yet, given the degree of autonomy granted to the colonies, the Liberals had no alternative but to pass, undebated in the Commons, the Australian Customs Duties Act of 1873. This represented a complete departure from orthodoxy, permitting the imposition of differential duties within the Australian colonies. As Kimberley regretfully recalled:

We never pretended for a moment to believe that the Australian Act was consistent with sound economical views. We passed it solely on political grounds, considering that having given the Australian colonies full control of their domestic affairs, even to the point of allowing them, as in Victoria, to lay protective duties on our goods, we could not prudently refuse them the further liberty they asked for.[239]

After this Act, British policy was effectively confined to supporting the merits of inter-colonial free trade (an Australian *Zollverein*), aided by the propagandist efforts of some colonial governors; since governors increasingly tended to voice local views, these were mostly to be heard in New South Wales, the outstanding exception as the Australian colonies sheltered behind rising tariff barriers.[240]

Canada proved no more promising, although Gladstone mistakenly believed the Canada Tea Bill of 1872 was a 'mild argument for free trade'.[241] More weightily, the 'incidental protection' of 1858-9 had steadily been transformed into the full-blown 'National Policy' of 1879. This, *The Economist* felt, 'must satisfy the most fervent Protectionist'.[242] Such a demonstration of colonial autonomy was already by the early 1880s complicating British commercial diplomacy, for it remained technically

---

of Partition (Oxford, 1988). In the late 1870s Morier had been much concerned with a 'fair field and no favour' in the Congo, although the treaty he devised was never ratified: Ramm, *Morier*, 112.

[237] Gladstone to Kimberley, 16 May 1871, *GD*, vol. 7, 496; P. Knaplund, *Gladstone and Britain's Imperial Policy* (1927), 104–21, 247–51.

[238] Gladstone to Kimberley, 29 Dec. 1871, *GD*, vol. 8, 87.

[239] Kimberley to A. Musgrave, 19 July 1875, Field Musgrave Papers, Duke University; also quoted Goodwin, *Economic Inquiry*, 541. Unusually, Farrer had shown some flexibility on this issue, for he wrote 'Have we not been too absolute concerning differential duties? Like Commercial Treaties they may be protective or may if they are made for the purpose of lowering existing Tariffs, pave the way for Free Trade. The danger is of course in the use which may at any time be made of them for Protectionist purposes.' Memo. on Australian Tariff, 1 Feb. 1872, Kimberley Papers, c. 4121, Bodleian Library, Oxford.

[240] e.g., *Speeches of Sir Hercules G. R. Robinson* (Sydney, 1879), 83.

[241] *GD*, vol. 8, 253 [3 Dec. 1872].

[242] *The Economist*, 22 Mar. 1879, 330; see, too, 19 Apr. and 3 May; Goldwin Smith, 'The Canadian Tariff', *Contemporary Review*, 40 (Sept. 1881), 378–98, defended the tariff on grounds of fiscal necessity; cf. F. Hincks, 'Canada and Mr Goldwin Smith', ibid. 825–40; E. Porritt, *Sixty Years of Protection in Canada, 1846–1907* (1908), 315 ff.; O. J. McDiarmid, *Commercial Policy in the Canadian Economy* (Cambridge, Mass., 1946), 155–79.

to Britain to negotiate with foreign powers on behalf of her colonies. Thus, the abortive Franco-Canadian negotiations of 1878–83 proved unsatisfactory to all parties, a failure not in any way softened by the provocative support given by the Canadian High Commissioner Galt to the fair trade movement in Britain.[243]

This combination between fair trade in Britain and the growth of protectionism within the British Empire had, however, spawned the influential 'new colonial policy' of the early 1880s, the possibility of an imperial *Zollverein*, against which free trade opinion was increasingly vociferous.[244] Yet the idea of closer imperial ties, including commercial ones, was not without its Liberal supporters, and, significantly, many of the most prominent Liberal backers of the Imperial Federation League, founded in 1884, including Bryce, Dilke, and Forster, had been closely involved in British commercial diplomacy.[245] Here was emerging a group of Liberal politicians, ready, like the diplomat Morier, to try to reconcile free trade and empire. On the other hand, it was to be the Conservative attempts to reconstruct the British Empire in the next generation that would more dramatically and deliberately challenge the Cobdenite order, which had, with important modifications, survived the impact of protection, militarism, and depression in Bismarckian Europe.

---

[243]　Shields, 'The Canadian Treaty Negotiations', 201.

[244]　e.g., T. H. Farrer, *Free Trade vs Fair Trade*, first published 1881, 4th edn., 1887.

[245]　Tuckwell, *Dilke*, vol. 1, 400–1; memo. [? by Pauncefote], c. 20 Apr. 1882, Dilke Papers, Add. MS 43882, fos. 227–8; but cf. Bateman [BT] to Dilke, *re* Galt's proposals, 20 Mar. 1882, Add. MS 43912. Morley 'Commercial Treaties' (1881) had added to the usual arguments in favour of commercial treaties, their attractiveness as an alternative to a 'National Imperial Customs Union', 800. See, too, T. Wemyss Reid, *The Life of W. E. Forster* (1889), 598–9.

6

'The Free Trade Fetish': Gold, Sugar, and the Empire, 1886–1903

> I do not think that there is anyone more convinced than myself of the theoretical
> soundness of Free Trade views or of the practical advantages which we have
> derived from their application . . . while I hold that also Peace or Free Trade are
> most excellent things, it may sometimes be necessary to threaten war and to risk
> war in order to preserve peace, and so it may be necessary to threaten, or even
> resort to retaliation in order to secure the development of Free Trade.
>
> Chamberlain to Strachey, 23 Jan. 1899.[1]

'FREE trade idolatry' remained, especially in the eyes of its critics, at the centre of
both Liberal politics and British foreign policy in late Victorian Britain.[2] Yet,
paradoxically, it also seemed to many commentators that Cobdenism was dead.
The most self-conscious of Cobdenites, Sir Louis Mallet, believed that the free
trade battle had ended in defeat, the cause ironically killed off by Gladstone's own
economic heresies.[3] Observers and obituarists repeatedly, if prematurely, identified
the 'last of the Cobdenites', for example in Sir Thomas Farrer of the Board of
Trade, and in Cobden's biographer Morley.[4] As Cobdenite certainty withered,
those most closely identified with mid-Victorian optimism believed themselves to
be beleaguered defenders of truth against error, with Gladstone considering himself one of a dying breed, 'fundamentally a Peel–Cobden man'.[5] Another old
faithful, Goldwin Smith, asserted the permanent validity of the principles of the
Manchester School—free trade, retrenchment, religious equality, peace, and 'common sense' government—while conscious of their rapid fading, surviving as mere
relics of a personal connection.[6] This pessimism seemed all too justified by 1896,
when celebration of the jubilee of the repeal of the Corn Laws turned all too easily

---

[1]   Strachey Papers, S/6/10, House of Lords Record Office.

[2]   For a representative view, see Lord Penzance [J. P. Wilde], 'The Free Trade Idolatry', *Nineteenth
Century*, 19 (1886), 380–95, 590–605.

[3]   Mallet to Farrer, 25 Jan., 1 Feb. 1886, Farrer Papers; Mallet to T. B. Potter, 8 Mar. 1889, in CCM,
9 Mar. 1889.

[4]   Morley wrote to J. A. Spender in 1898 to affirm his own claims against *The Westminster Gazette*'s
description of Lord Salisbury as 'the only living example of a "resolute Cobdenite" ': 'MP' [Morley] to
Spender, 11 Nov. 1898, Spender Papers, Add. MS 46391, BL. For Farrer, *The Times*, 13 Oct. 1899: 'the
only surviving unimpaired specimen of the Manchester School.'

[5]   Quoted H. C. G. Matthew, *The Liberal Imperialists* (Oxford Historical Monographs: Oxford,
1973), vii.

[6]   Goldwin Smith, 'The Manchester School', *Contemporary Review*, 67 (1895), 377–89; 'The End of
the Manchester School', *Spectator*, 12 Nov. 1898, 681–2.

into the obsequies of Cobdenism. Thus, for Gladstone, the publication of *The Jubilee of Free Trade* appeared 'an act of great gallantry for the Cobdenian faith is in all points at a heavy discount—Peace, Retrenchment, Free Trade and all the rest of it, to my great grief I must confess'.[7] This verdict was one shared by enemies and friends, as Conservatives, socialists, and Liberals applauded or lamented the 'decline of Cobdenism' and the 'demise of the Manchester School', the receding world of peace, free trade, and goodwill.[8]

Intimations of that mortality had, however, been greatly exaggerated. On the one hand, the apparent abandonment of *laissez-faire* and the rapid growth in expenditure, largely upon armaments, had been interpreted too readily by the old-style Radical individualists, such as Mallet, Goldwin Smith, Mackay, and Levy, as symptoms of a terminal disease—'collectivism' or 'state socialism'.[9] On the other hand, for budding collectivists and socialists, it was excessive attachment to *laissez-faire* and individualism that rendered the Liberal Party itself moribund, a living corpse, awaiting the arrival of the Fabian burial-party and a Shavian funeral oration.[10] Yet despite these two apparently fatal threats, Cobdenism survived by adaptation into the new organicist age. For, despite the fears of the critics, it proved possible for Liberalism to abandon *laissez-faire* while retaining and strengthening its attachment to Cobden's doctrines on free trade, taxation, war, and internationalism.[11]

Free trade, therefore, continued to embody the single most popular element in Liberal and Radical politics, both as a defence of the community and of individual welfare. It served to link Liberalism not only with old Radicalism, but formed a bond with the new socialism of Henry George, whose advocacy of land nationalization carried the welcome complement of a strong message of free trade.[12] Within

---

[7] To T. Fisher Unwin, 23 June 1896, CP 981, WSRO.

[8] S. Low, 'The Decline of Cobdenism', *Nineteenth Century*, 40 (234), 1896, 173–86; 'The Revolt against Manchesterism' was the *point de depart* for the Progressive Rainbow Circle in its first year, M. Freeden (ed.), *Minutes of the Rainbow Circle, 1894–1924*, Camden Soc. 4th ser., vol. 38 (Royal Historical Society, 1989), 17–26.

[9] M. W. Taylor, *Men vs the State. Herbert Spencer and Late Victorian Individualism* (Oxford, 1992), esp. ch. 1; T. Mackay (active as a Cobden Club writer in the mid-1880s), *A Policy of Free Exchange* (1890); anti-socialism was the predominant message of the Free Trade in Capital League (1889), and of A. E. Hake and O. E. Wesslau, *Free Trade in Capital* (1890); in like vein, the Free Trade Extension League of the 1890s, for which see John Johnson Collection, 'Free Trade and Protection', Box 3. For J. H. Levy, see E. Belfort Bax, *Reminiscences and Reflexions of a Mid-Victorian* (1918, reprint 1967), 229–30.

[10] W. Clarke, 'Political Defects of the Old Radicalism', in *William Clarke: A Collection of his Writings*, ed. H. Burrows and J. A. Hobson (1908), 71–2; cf. his earlier appreciation of Cobden, above, 149.

[11] See especially M. Freeden, *The New Liberalism: an Ideology of Social Reform* (Oxford, 1978), for ideological continuity in liberalism, although this work pays relatively little attention to the retention of free trade alongside the abandonment of *laissez-faire*. Interestingly, the Jubilee edition of Morley's *Cobden* in 1896 also prompted reflections on the permanence of Cobden's legacy, e.g., *Reynold's*, 28 June, *Daily Chronicle*, 27 June 1896.

[12] G. H. Murray, secretary of the Royal Commission on the Depression in Trade and Industry (RCDTI), wrote disarmingly to Farrer when the latter was preparing a new edition of his *Free Trade*

this emerging 'New Liberal' synthesis, proponents of progressive policies in the 1890s characteristically combined a strong belief in free trade with an advocacy of state intervention.[13] Few critics were more aware of the deficiencies of *laissez-faire* than the Webbs, yet their 'National Minimum' was urged as 'the necessary completion of the Free Trade policy', extending it beyond its existing fiscal interpretation.[14] For a self-styled Cobdenite (E. Adam) writing in 1899, free trade was now associated with land values taxation, old age pensions, and better working-class housing.[15] But, equally, old Radical goals, such as the 'free breakfast table', moved easily on to the progressive agenda, as fiscal free trade was combined with a mounting growing advocacy of increased direct taxation by Cobden Club recruits such as Asquith, Fletcher Moulton, and Murray MacDonald, politicians who bridged the worlds of Cobden and the Edwardian progressives.[16] This proto-collectivist interpretation of free trade was, of course, far from universal, for much of the rhetoric remained individualistic, identified with hostility to facets of state and municipal intervention, which some leading free traders such as Farrer and Lubbock espoused.[17] Even so, it may be claimed that, despite its lack of intellectual rigour, this represented a substantial rethinking of the political pertinence of Cobden, sufficiently plausible to transform the hero of the Liberty and Property Defence League in 1891 into the symbol of 'New Liberalism' by 1904. Above all,

---

versus Fair Trade, that George's *Protection* 'ought to do good as there are lots of people who will listen to him while they will suspect you': 26 June 1886, Farrer Papers. The Cobden Club similarly applauded George's single tax/free trade tour of Australia in 1890, while treating land nationalization as an open question, CCM, 14 June, 22 Mar. 1890; George was enthusiastically taken up by the Liverpool financial reformers, *The Financial Reformer*, Dec. 1888, Jan. 1889, June and July 1889.

[13]   Above, 138. For example, Atherley-Jones, the son of Ernest Jones, the Chartist opponent of the League, on whom see Freeden, *New Liberalism*, 145–6 and L. A. Atherley-Jones, *Looking Back* (1925); B. R. Wise, pupil of T. H. Green, friend of Toynbee and Milner, made his career in Australian politics, but his *Industrial Freedom* (1892) won the plaudits of both Farrer and Webb; thus, for Farrer it was 'just the book I would have liked to write', and for Webb it as 'a good modern statement of fiscal Free Trade . . . in England he would inevitably have developed into a refined Collectivist'. See Farrer to Wise, 11 July 1892, in CCM, 6 Aug. 1892; A. G. Austin (ed.), *The Webbs' Australian Diary, 1898* (Melbourne, 1965), 27. See, too, J. Ryan, 'B. R. Wise: An Oxford Free Trade Liberal', MA thesis, University of Sydney (1966), and id., 'Wise' in *Australian Dictionary of Biography* 12, 546–9; J. M. Robertson also moved easily from free trade to collectivism, G. A. Wells (ed.), *J. M. Robertson: Liberal, Rationalist, and Scholar* (1987).

[14]   S. and B. Webb, *Industrial Democracy* (2 vols, 1897), vol. 2, 863–72.

[15]   'A Cobdenite', *Free Trade and Social Problems*, copy in John Johnson, 'Free Trade and Protection', box 5. Adam was the unsuccessful Liberal candidate at Glasgow Central (1895) and Edinburgh West (1900).

[16]   S. Webb, 'The Moral of the Elections', *Contemporary Review*, 62 (1892), 372–87; *The Radical Programme*, manifesto of the Metropolitan Radical Association, 1897.

[17]   For their part in London politics, see J. Davis, *Reforming London* (Oxford Historical Monographs; Oxford, 1988), 119, 149–50, 152–4. This remained a staple feature of the shopkeeper mentality satirized by authors such as H. G. Wells in *Kipps* (1905): Mr Shalford's 'political creed linked Reform, which meant nothing, with Peace and Economy, which meant a sweated expenditure, and his conception of a satisfactory municipal life was "to keep down the rates."' Even so, Farrer, for example, sympathized with 'socialism' and its fiscal demands: see A. Haultain (ed.), *Goldwin Smith's Correspondence* (1913), 244 [7 July 1892].

the defence of free trade in late Victorian Britain provided the bridge whereby many Cobdenite Liberals moved from individualism towards the advocacy of collectivism, which distinguished the New Liberalism of the Edwardian period.[18]

This defence and reworking of free trade has often been missed by historians, for it took place not at the level of the towering waves of economic and social theory, but in the murky shallows of recondite policy debate. Even so, most of these policies centred, as in the past, upon the politics of agrarian production and working-class consumption. Most obviously, the fall in food prices since 1846, and more especially since 1873, seemed from the agricultural perspective to be a damning indictment of the repeal of the Corn Laws, and the final vindication of protectionist fears in the 1840s.[19] On the other hand, with Britain's rapid shift of population away from agriculture after 1850, falling food prices had become the vital guarantee of working-class welfare, which posed an insuperable obstacle to any attempt to reintroduce a measure of protection for agriculture. Alone of the major Western Powers, Britain failed to provide any protection for agriculture in the face of the Great Depression, and England's farmers and landlords failed to establish a serious political base for any agrarian *revanche* for defeat in the 1840s.[20] Only in the late 1890s did the need to guarantee Britain's food supply in wartime lend a glimmer of political respectability to the case for protection, although, as Offer has shown, the Navy, not the farmers, remained the guarantors of Britain's food supply.[21] Hence, for the most part dependence upon foreign food supply acted as an automatic barrier to agricultural protection. As Farrer typically put it: 'Our danger has been discontent under Trade Depression, which seeks expression in any fad, and Foreign and Colonial example. What has saved us is that we could not protect anything unless we protect food, and this even our farm labourers will not hear of.'[22] Free traders therefore met the case for agricultural protection with the old arguments for land law reform, as well as newer ones for technical education in the countryside, market gardening, and Danish-style co-operation.[23] They also

[18]   D. Blaazer, *The Popular Front and the Progressive Tradition: Socialists, Liberals, and the Quest for Unity, 1884–1939* (Cambridge, 1992), 26–37.

[19]   P. J. Cain and A. G. Hopkins, *British Imperialism* (2 vols, 1993), vol. 1, 110; for successful adaptation, see F. M. L. Thompson, 'An Anatomy of English Agriculture, 1870–1914', in B. A. Holderness and M. E. Turner (eds.), *Land, Labour and Agriculture* (1991), 211–40. Cobdenites were not short of recipes for agricultural prosperity, e.g., S. Morgan, 'Cobden, the Farmer's Friend', *Horticultural Times*, 8 July 1893.

[20]   J. R. Fisher, 'Public Opinion and Agriculture 1875–1900', unpublished Ph.D. thesis, University of Hull (1972), *passim*. Ironically, had Cobdenite land reform succeeded in creating a nation of peasant proprietors, support for protection would probably have been much greater. In France in the early 1890s Léon Say sought a 'nouveau Cobden' to oppose the Corn Laws advocated by the French farmers, mobilized behind Méline: G. Michel, *Léon Say, sa vie, ses œuvres* (Paris, 1899), 430–6, 449.

[21]   A. Offer, *The First World War: An Agrarian Interpretation* (Oxford, 1989), esp. 217–32.

[22]   Farrer to B. R. Wise, 11 July 1892, in CCM, 6 Aug. 1892. See, too, Mallet to Farrer, 25 Jan. 1886, Farrer Papers.

[23]   See *inter alia* G. Armitage-Smith, *The Free-trade Movement* (1st edn., 1898, reprint, 1910), ch. 5; H. de Gibbins, new edn., Mongredien, *The Free Trade Movement* (1897); Cobden Club leaflets, e.g. 58:

continued to expound regularly to popular audiences the 'progress of the working classes' since Repeal, a cause assisted by the Royal Jubilees of 1887 and 1897, with their paeans to material progress under Queen Victoria.[24] But, for the most part, conflict between free trade and protection was, as *The Economist* claimed, a paper controversy, for there was no genuine political threat to free trade.[25]

What was most unusual in late Victorian Britain was the comparative failure by the 1890s of any alternative economic prescription to free trade. In Europe since the 1870s protectionist policies had been successfully implemented on the back of coalitions of interest groups, political parties, and economic ideologies.[26] In the United States, protection had become an integral part of both fiscal policy and an ideology of economic nationalism.[27] In Canada, a 'National Policy' had fused ideas and interests into a dominant consensus, while in Australia in the 1890s Deakin, the protégé of the protectionist David Syme, was to produce his own variant of colonial Liberalism, based on tariffs and social reform.[28] In Britain, on the other hand, fair trade had failed either to produce a successful coalition of interest groups, or to win over any substantial body of intellectual or popular support.[29] Only slowly was the discontent of agrarians, manufacturers, and imperial federationists fused, under the aegis of Britain's historical economists, into the tariff reform assault on the body of Cobdenism pronounced dead a decade earlier. This failure, as we have seen, was in large part the result of the vigorous defence of free trade in the 1880s, a campaign that had tamed, but not eradicated, the threat of fair trade. Demands for reciprocity, retaliation, and a myriad of surrogates for protection continued to be voiced regularly, if thinly, into the 1890s. A resolution in favour of fair trade famously gained a majority at the National Union of Conservative Associations at Oxford in 1887, and retaliation was ripe for revival in the context of hostile foreign tariffs and

S. Morgan, *Small Fruit Farms: A Permanent Remedy for Agricultural Distress*; 59: G. J. Holyoake, *Co-operative Farming in Denmark*; 92: *Poultry-Keeping for Profit*; 93: *Apple-Growing in England*; for land reform, see F. W. Channing, *Memories of Midland Politics* (1918); for one local debate, at Halstead, Essex, see *Essex Standard*, 26 Nov. 1887.

[24] e.g., the Radical John Noble's free trade lectures supported by the Cobden Club in London, CCM, 23 June 1888, 10 May 1890; C. S. Roundell, *The Progress of the Working Classes* (Skipton, 1890), one of a series of free trade lectures for the people, delivered at Skipton, Petersham (Surrey), and Nantwich, 1889–90. Roundell was Liberal MP Grantham, 1880–5, Skipton, 1892–5; Flora Thompson, *Lark Rise to Candelford* (1949 edn.), 236; B. Mallet, *British Budgets, 1887–1913* (1913), 114–15.

[25] 'The Jubilee of Free Trade', 6 June 1896, 723–4; S. Buxton likewise believed that, despite new attacks upon it, free trade as an 'accepted maxim of tedious orthodoxy' did not require vehement advocacy, *Finance and Politics* (2 vols, 1888), vol. 1, 146.

[26] Above Ch. 5.

[27] E. P. Crapol, *America for the Americans: Economic Nationalism and Anglophobia in the late Nineteenth Century* (Westport, Conn., 1973); D. A. Lake, *Power, Protection and Free Trade: International Sources of U.S. Commercial Strategy, 1887–1939* (Cornell, 1988).

[28] B. Forster, *A Conjunction of Interests: Business, Politics and Tariffs, 1825–1879* (Toronto, 1986); S. Macintyre, *A Colonial Liberalism* (Melbourne, 1991); J. A. La Nauze, *Political Economy in Australia: Historical Studies* (Melbourne, 1949); id., *Alfred Deakin: A Biography* (2 vols, Melbourne, 1965; single vol. edn., 1979).

[29] Above, 134; B. H. Brown, *The Tariff Reform in Great Britain, 1881–1895* (New York, 1943), esp. 129–52; E. H. H. Green, *The Crisis of Conservatism* (1995), 30–5.

trade scares such as the 'Made in Germany' panic in 1896.[30] Yet, politically, retaliation seemed to hold few trumps for the Conservative Party, with Salisbury's talk of retaliation, for example, blamed for many Conservative losses in the election of 1892.[31]

Even, therefore, in the age of tariff wars in Europe, Britain rarely contemplated commercial aggression. The statistical battery compiled by Levi and Giffen, and reinforced by acolytes such as Bowley, was sufficient to convince Tory as well as Liberal Chancellors of the economic folly of fair trade prescriptions, while the still voluble Cobden Club ensured the vigilance of public opinion through its vigorous pamphlet campaigns.[32] Under Salisbury, a successful tariff bargain on the model of the 1860s was struck with Greece, negotiated by the Cobdenite Gennadius.[33] A Trade and Treaties Committee was also set up in 1890, yet it acted not as the high command of a tariff battery, but merely as a concerned spectator, as other nations engaged in damaging internecine disputes.[34] Such conflicts served to weaken rather than strengthen the case for tariffs. Thus, by the early 1890s Germany was ready to renegotiate treaties, and her commercial diplomacy had some advantages for British trade, reinforcing the case for free trade.[35] In August 1892 the Trade and Treaties Committee was disbanded, its work considered complete by the incoming Liberal government.[36] The spectre of America also loomed larger in the wake of the

---

[30] R. J. S. Hoffman, *Great Britain and the German Trade Rivalry 1875–1914* (Philadelphia, 1933); W. E. Minchinton, 'E. E. Williams: "Made in Germany" and after', *Vierteljahrschrift für Sozial- und Wirtschaftgesichtetliche*, 62. Band, Heft 2 (1975), 229–42; C. Buchheim, 'Aspects of 19th century Anglo-German Trade Rivalry Reconsidered', *Journal of European Economic History*, 10 (1981), 273–89. Other 'scares' concerned 'Prison goods' 1894/95, and 'Made in America' *c.*1899–1902. For a free trade response, see C. Furness, *The American Invasion* (1902).

[31] W. T. Stead, 'The General Election and After', *Contemporary Review*, 57 (1892), 290–1; Brown, *Tariff Reform Movement*, 79; Green, *Conservatism*, 5. The Cobden Club exploited this issue amidst continuing fears of farmers' support for grain taxes, CCM, 21 and 28 May, 18 June, 6 Aug. 1892.

[32] Sir Henry Bergne at the Foreign Office appears as the civil servant most keen on retaliation, but cf. Board of Trade orthodoxy in R. Giffen, letters and memoranda to Hicks Beach, 1886–97 in Earl of St Aldwyn Papers, PC/PP/61/ 6, 7, 7a and b, 19, Gloucestershire Record Office. For the uses and abuses of statistics, see G. M. Koot, *English Historical Economics 1870–1926* (Cambridge, 1987), 73–9; D. C. M. Platt, *Mickey Mouse Numbers in World History* (1989), 5–6, 14–18, 26–30.

[33] Mallet, *British Budgets*, 37; Gennadius to Ferguson, 17 Feb. 1890 et seq., FO 32/623; the nonagenarian Earl Grey, as in 1860, demurred, 'Protection, Free Trade, Fair Trade, Colonial Trade', *Nineteenth Century*, 31 (1892), 58. Other negotiations, for example with Spain, were also undertaken.

[34] Its reports, some printed as parliamentary papers, were not all glooomy, with the negative impact of the Méline Tariff in 1892, for example, balanced by the benefits of reduced tariffs in the treaties of Central Europe. See D. C. M. Platt, *Finance, Trade and Politics in British Foreign Policy, 1815–1914* (Oxford, 1968), 377, and FO 412/54 Further Correspondence concerning Commercial Treaties and Tariffs, 1892 (CP); FO 83/1153 Trade and Treaties Committee, 2nd Report; *Parl. Papers*, 1890–1, C. 6286, 78 [1st Report]; C. 6349 [3rd Report]; *Parl. Papers*, 1892, C. 6641, 72 [7th Report]; C. 6648 [9th Report]. A. J. Mundella chaired the Committee, see W. H. C. Armytage, *A. J. Mundella 1825–1897* (1951), 285–6.

[35] Hoffmann, *German Trade Rivalry*, 225–32; P. Ashley, *Modern Tariff History* (1st edn., 1904), 66–72; Hicks Beach, *Hansard*, 4th ser., 1 c. 112–13, 9 Feb. 1892.

[36] Sir Edward Grey to Manchester Chamber of Commerce, 18 Mar. 1893, minutes of the Tariff and Trade Committee of the Manchester Chamber, M8/3/1, Manchester Central Library. The Manches-

McKinley Tariff of 1890, but 'McKinleyism' produced little genuine threat to British trade. For, on the one hand, free traders took perverse solace in America's continuing dependence on protection, which they believed postponed, rather than accelerated, the inevitable economic supersession of Britain by America.[37] On the other hand, the veteran 'world leader' of free trade, Gladstone, proclaimed its universal benefits and anticipated the American future as the world's leading and, if suitably guided, free trade power.[38]

This provided comfort for the prescient, but far more widespread was the economic doubt embedded in the late-Victorian political mind by the reports of the Royal Commision on the Depression in Trade and Industry (RCDTI) set up by Salisbury's minority government in August 1885 and completed in December 1886.[39] While this is rightly seen as a typically masterful Salisburian attempt to divert fair trade pressures in the Tory Party into relatively innocuous channels, inevitably the Commission provided a forum for the discontented.[40] Its evidence and minority reports significantly impinged on subsequent discussions of economic policy, rather in the manner of the Select Committee on Import Duties of 1840. It was for this reason that the former Liberal ministers had refused to take part in the Commission, whose very existence seemed to question the unquestionable.[41] The RCDTI therefore had a predictably double-edged effect. On the one hand, it reinforced economic orthodoxy through its reports, in much of its evidence from an array of civil servants, industrialists, and merchants, and in the bulk of the press attention it received.[42] As George Murray, the future head of the Treasury but at this point secretary to the Commission and leading author of its report, recorded, the Commission was 'a rather non-descript body; but with a flavour of "Tariff

ter Chamber regarded the committee as more effective than a Ministry of Commerce would be, beneficially 'removing these questions from the turmoil of political discussion in Parliament, and . . . staying unnecessary agitation throughout the country': id., fos. 323–4.

[37] On America's economic rise, Hankey Thomson to O. Russell, 13 Aug. 1883, FO 918/73; R. Donald, 'McKinleyism and the Presidential Election', *Contemporary Review*, 62 (1892), 489–504; for relative indifference in Manchester, see A. Redford, *Manchester Merchants and Foreign Trade* (2 vols, 1934 and 1956), vol. 2, 94; cf. Lake, *Power, Protection, and Free Trade*, 99–102. See, too, Stanley (BT) to Farrer, 6 Aug. 1892, Farrer Papers, 96; Giffen to Hicks Beach, 26 Aug. 1891 ('Nothing will be accomplished of what the US intend', St Aldwyn papers, PC/PP/61/7; Giffen to Lubbock, 11 Oct. 1892, Lubbock Papers, Add. MS 49658, vol. 1, BL; Lubbock played a leading role in countering 'McKinleyism'. For the fair trade view, see Brown, *Tariff Reform Movement*, 76, 84, 105.

[38] *GD*, vol. 12, intro., xlii–xliii; Gladstone, 'Free Trade', *North American Review*, 150 (Jan. 1890), 1–27.

[39] *Parl. Papers*, 1884–5 (348) 71, Depression of Trade and Industry, R. Com. Memo; 1886, C. 4621 and C. 4715, 21 [1st and 2nd Reports]; C. 4715–I, 22 [2nd. Report, App.]; C. 4797 and C. 4893, 23 [3rd and Final Reports].

[40] P. T. Marsh, *The Discipline of Popular Government: Lord Salisbury's Domestic Statecraft* (Hassocks, 1978), 28, 82.

[41] Brown, *Tariff Reform Movement*, 63; J. K. Cross, one of those who declined to serve, considered, 'probably its most useful purpose will be to prove that the so-called depression is more a depression of prices than a scarcity of employment'. To Gladstone, 17 July 1885, GP Add. MS 44491, fos. 307–8.

[42] *The Economist*, 22 Jan. 1887, 101–2; *The Times*, 17 Jan. 1887; for a local example, see R. C. Lehmann in *Cheltenham Free Press*, 7 and 21 Nov. 1885.

Reform" or "Fair Trade". Northcote was a hard-shell Free Trader; and was rather glad to get me as secretary to the Commission. Between us we produced a Report which, I think, for the moment scotched the Tariff Reform movement.'[43]

On the other hand, the Commission had allowed heterodox notions to enjoy 'the oxygen of publicity', whose effects were reinforced by their endorsement in minority reports.[44] In this debate, the hitherto unshakeable pillars of the mid-Victorian state came under probing scrutiny: the gold standard, free imports, and the free trade empire. Initially, considerable attention was paid to the effects of the fall in prices since 1873 as a factor in depression. For some, the cause of this fall lay in the demonetization of silver since 1873, and the remedy lay in a bimetallic (gold and silver) standard. But the commissioners baulked at this complex and rebarbative issue, hiving it off to a separate Royal Commission into Gold and Silver. This left the burden of heterodoxy to be carried by the fair trade commissioners, whose dissent from the relative optimism of the majority report centred on their belief that 'the greatest and most permanent causes of the depression' lay in 'the action of foreign bounties and tariffs and the growing effect of directly or indirectly subsidized foreign competition'.[45] Their leading prescriptions for reform were twofold. First, a change in fiscal policy to institute both countervailing duties against foreign bounties, and retaliatory tariffs against foreign protection. Here was the full voice of the fair trade movement which had since 1879 been attempting to gain the public ear. Second, the empire re-emerged as a recipe for economic revival, with the recommendation of 'a fiscal policy . . . which will enable the various portions of the Empire to cooperate more effectually for mutual aid and defence in commercial matters'.[46] Such a policy would be based on a discriminatory tariff against foreign food imports, i.e. the adoption of the imperial preference which some of the more ardent federationists of the mid-1880s had already embraced. In summary form, this dissenting report set out the case for a 'national policy' for Britain's revival as an economic power in the late nineteenth century, and this series of nostrums, concerning money, bounties, and imperial economic unity, were to be trumpeted with increasing volume in the later 1880s in a resounding challenge to Britain's 'free trade fetish'.

Given the apparent persistence of a depression in the economy, these unorthodox remedies necessarily commanded a diverse audience among neo-mercantilist and historical economists, industrialists, landowners, farmers, imperial traders, and enthusiasts, and among sections of working-class opinion. Yet none of these remedies for depression generated a wider *Weltanschauung* able to challenge the potent

[43] 'Notes by GHM of his official career, 1880–1892', Murray MS, 1685, Blair Castle; to Farrer, Murray wrote 'I can't say I feel very much wiser on the subject than I did before we began', 29 June 1886, Farrer Papers.

[44] S. H. Zebel, 'Fair Trade', *Journal of Modern History*, 12 (1940), 175; Green, *Conservatism*, 28, 30, 55.

[45] *Parl. Papers*, 1886, C. 4893, 23, Final Report, 64, para. 122.

[46] Ibid., para. 138.

hold of free trade within the popular, political, business, academic, and administrative mind. That wider ideological challenge would come in 1903, but ironically the 'stale Cobdenism' which the tariff reformers would then attack had in fact already honed its defences, polished its armour, and modernized its ideological weaponry in the preceding technical debates over money, sugar, and the empire, to which we must now turn.[47] These anterior debates not only illuminate essential elements in the late-Victorian and Edwardian conflict between free trade and protection, but also helped load the dice more strongly against the success of Chamberlain's tariff reform campaign, even before it had been launched.

Free trade and the gold standard, 1881–98

Historians have generally assumed that British economic hegemony in the late nineteenth century was based upon the 'trinity' of free trade, the gold standard, and balanced budgets.[48] This 'religion of financial orthodoxy' forged in the post-Waterloo years through 'the Peelite politics of atonement' undoubtedly dominated the Victorian Treasury, yet its tenets were never as infallible as they have sometimes in retrospect appeared.[49] Not least, from the late 1870s the gold standard in Britain had come under strong threat from the movement for a bimetallic standard, linking silver and gold at a fixed ratio.[50] This was an international movement, with powerful support in America, Europe, and Asia, which sought by diplomatic agreement (bimetallic conferences were held in 1867, 1878, 1881, and 1892) to reverse the strong drift of European nations, led by Germany, towards the gold standard after 1873. In contrast to the British combination of free trade and the gold standard, the adoption of gold did nothing to slow down the European reversion to protectionism by the late 1870s. The early advocates of bimetallism wished, in effect, to restore the free market in monetary agents by removing the hand of the states that had suppressed the use of silver since 1873. They believed that at a time of slackness of gold production the abandonment of silver had artificially increased demand for gold, raising its price to the detriment of British trade with silver-using countries such as India, China, and Argentina. The adoption of a bimetallic standard—that is, the remonetization of silver—would therefore restore the world's supply of

---

[47]   Other technical issues also challenged orthodoxy, but generated less widespread public concern, for example trademarks and shipping subsidies. On the latter, see Platt, *Finance, Trade*, 103–4.

[48]   H. Roseveare, *The Treasury: The Evolution of a British Institution* (1969), 118; J. Tomlinson, *Problems of British Economic Policy, 1870–1945* (1981), chs. 2 and 3; S. Pollard, *Britain's Prime, Britain's Decline* (1990), 235–50.

[49]   B. Hilton, *The Age of Atonement* (Oxford, 1988), ch. 6; P. F. Clarke, 'The Treasury's Analytical Model of the Economy between the Wars', in M. Furner and B. Supple (eds.), *The State and Economic Knowledge* (Cambridge, 1990), 171–207.

[50]   E. H. H. Green, 'Rentiers versus Producers? The Political Economy of the Bimetallic Controversy, *c.*1880–1898', *English Historical Review*, 103 (1988), 588–612, cf. A. C. Howe, 'Bimetallism, *c.*1880–1898: A Controversy Re-opened?', ibid. 105 (1990), 377–391; Green, 'The Bimetallic Controversy', ibid. 673–83. See, too, M. Friedman, 'Bimetallism revisited', *Journal of Economic Perspectives*, 4 (1990), 85–104.

money, and would at least halt, and hopefully reverse, the unsettling fall in prices since 1873, the most obvious outward sign of the Great Depression.[51]

Political and diplomatic action was therefore urged as a means of restoring the natural monetary order.[52] For it did not follow that 'to question the gold standard was to question free trade'.[53] Quite the contrary: free trade, some of its firmest advocates believed, was unsustainable without the monetary stability that only a bimetallic standard could ensure. As Mallet put it:

a common standard of value with other countries [is] a measure dictated by commmon sense and a necessary complement of a Free trade policy. No one would ever have dreamed of a Free trade policy if all countries had a different standard of value shifting perpetually. Such a state of things makes foreign trade mere gambling. The object of a wise government is to remove friction and assimilate so far as possible the conditions of home and foreign trade. I think that the late Government has done more to discredit and damage the cause of Free trade than any other.[54]

Here was an argument for 'convergence' and monetary union *avant la lettre*, but one that appealed strongly to liberal internationalists and the old advocates of a free trade Europe, such as d'Eichtal and de Lavaleye, for whom bimetallism now seemed a more eligible and more hopeful means of progress than commercial treaties.[55] More widely, as an international cause, bimetallism seems on the whole to have won the support of liberal political economists, for example, in America, Japan, and Australia.[56] Most commonly, it was regarded as the most likely means to restore an open, international economy, which the Great Depression had disrupted. Despite later support from protectionists, the genesis of international

---

[51] 'If I thought that the scarcity of gold had nothing to do with it, I should be at a loss to account for the long continued depression', Mallet to Farrer, 2 [Jan.] 1886, Farrer Papers, 46.

[52] Mallet thus wrote: 'My interest in "Bimetallism" is derived from the belief that it is one of those beneficent international measures, which are essential to the steady progress of Free Trade, and which would have had an especial interest and attraction for the "International Man" ', Mallet to T. B. Potter, 8 Mar. 1889, CCM, 9 Mar. 1889.

[53] Green, 'Bimetallic Controversy', 677. For a contemporary rebuttal, Mallet to Fremantle, 26 Oct. 1885, et seq., in Welby Papers IV, fos. 135–7, BLPES.

[54] Mallet to Farrer, 25 Jan. 1886, Farrer Papers, 48.

[55] Howe, 'Bimetallism', 387–89; M. Dumoulin (ed.), *La Correspondance entre Émile de Lavaleye et Marco Minghetti (1877–1886)* (Institut Historique Belge de Rome, 1979), 48–51, 62.

[56] Generalizations on this vexed issue are most difficult. But it may be noted that the leading theorist of bimetallism in America, F. A. Walker, seems to have been a free trader, *malgré lui*, B. Newton, *The Economics of F. A. Walker* (New York, 1968), 157–9. While both leading parties in America paid deference to silver, the Democrats were its strongest advocates by 1896, as they were of free(r) trade; for Japan, see N. Tamaki, 'Economists in Parliament: The Fall of Bimetallism in Japan', in C. Sugiyama and H. Mizuta (eds.), *Enlightenment and Beyond: Political Economy comes to Japan* (1988), 223–36, with its useful account of Taguchi, 'the Adam Smith of Japan' and its leading bimetallist; C. D. W. Goodwin, *Economic Inquiry in Australia*, 197–209, makes clear the support of pastoralists and free traders, not of national economists, for bimetallism. In Europe, bimetallism in France had a liberal provenance, but was clearly linked to agricultural protection and the Méline Tariff by Y. Guyot, *The Comedy of Protection* (1906), ch. 15; for Russia, see P. Apostol, 'Un bimetalliste russe' [G. Boutmy], *Journale des Économistes* (Sept. 1897), 370–9; for Germany, see F. Stern, *Gold and Iron: Bismarck, Bleichröder, and the Building of the German Empire* (1977; 1980 edn.), 180–1.

bimetallism owed little to the ideas of the national economists or tariff reformers. 'There is', Mallet wrote, 'in some quarters, a muddle-headed notion that because Bi-metallism has been taken up by some who hold Protectionist views, that it must be opposed to Free trade. But this is so stupid that it is really not worth arguing out.'[57]

In Britain the original impetus for monetary reform came from two directions: from merchants, especially those trading in Eastern and Latin American markets, affected by the relative change in prices, and from a group of Anglo-Indian civil servants who had experienced at first hand the effects of the fall of silver prices.[58] In 1881 these groups formed the International Monetary Standard Association, under whose auspices the debate over bimetallism was generated, and from which the Bimetallic League emerged in 1886. The cause of the bimetallic standard gained credibility from the important support it won within the City of London, particularly from two former Governors of the Bank of England, H. H. Gibbs (Lord Aldenham) and H. R. Grenfell. It also benefited from the decision to separate out an inquiry into currency from the RCDTI. As a result, rather than being lost amidst the welter of debate that the latter generated, the Currency Commission allowed the bimetallic case to be voiced simply and effectively, although not to gain majority support. For the monetarily orthodox, the Commission was regarded as a great mistake, since the case for gold had been far less well defended than the case for bimetallism had been articulated.[59]

Concern for monetary orthodoxy also grew in the late 1880s and 1890s in large part from the protectionist allies that bimetallism acquired. For, despite its strong epistemological link with free trade, and its strongest political base in free trade Lancashire,[60] bimetallism was to some extent hijacked ideologically and rhetorically by protectionists, and defended by some heterodox economists, above all H. S. Foxwell, who would later support tariff reform. Its superficial identity with the cause of the producers in Lancashire contrasted with support for the gold standard by the supposed *rentiers* of the City of London. This allowed polemicists to deploy the colourful, if traditional, language of producers and industry versus *rentiers*, 'goldbugs', and idleness. Such contemporary rhetoric should not be taken seriously as a historical analysis, but it was not without its attractions for depression-hit farmers, manufacturers, and merchant bankers. Some farmers, but not many, were led by Henry Chaplin into the bimetallic fold through the promise of diminished

---

[57]   Mallet to Potter, 12 Apr. 1889, in CCM 13 Apr. 1889, a succinct riposte to E. H. H. Green, 'Bimetallic Controversy', 677. See, too, Mallet to Kimberley, 6 May 1886, Kimberley Papers, MS Eng., c. 4227.

[58]   Howe, 'Bimetallism', 385–6.

[59]   R. Giffen to M. Hicks Beach, 3 Jan. 1889, St Aldwyn Papers, PC/PP/61/20.

[60]   See, most recently, T. Wilson, 'The Battle for the Standard: the Bimetallic Movement in Manchester', *Manchester Region History Review*, 6 (1992), 49–58. Leading working-class bimetallists in Lancashire were later stalwart opponents of tariff reform. See P. F. Clarke, *Lancashire and the New Liberalism* (Cambridge, 1971), 96–9.

competition and increased prices, that is to say for reasons quite opposite to those
of men such as Mallet, who believed that bimetallism usefully distracted 'Chaplin
and co.' from their harmful pursuit of protection.[61] Many industrialists, too, while
keen to push remedies which promised to restore profits and export markets, had
no wish to go on to promote 'a national-productive base' which would see those
markets jeopardized. Indeed, the strongest rallying by industrialists (and working
men) to the bimetallic flag took place in Lancashire after 1894 when the double
standard seemed preferable to import duties as the means to restore Indian
finances. Once again, it was attractive, at least as a means to defend, not to subvert,
free trade.[62] Some City financiers favoured a double standard not because they were
opposed to 'cosmopolitical economy', but because they believed that British dominance in the world economy rested on her commodity trades, not simply on
exchange-banking, a view that recent research to some extent confirms.[63]

In view of these intellectual and 'interest group' cross-currents, bimetallism
never posed a simple challenge to liberal political economy—indeed, how could it,
when its strongest intellectual progenitors were themselves free traders? Rather,
the intricacies of the monetary debate confused free traders, as they famously
confused many.[64] The Cobden Club itself was at odds over this issue, with its
intellectual mentors Mallet and Farrer on differing sides.[65] It was, therefore, reduced to agnostic silence, although by 1895 the protectionist embrace of bimetallism drew it towards co-operation with the Gold Standard Defence Association
(GSDA) formed in that year.[66] This Association, drawn largely from London and
provincial bankers with some support from academic economists and civil servants,
concentrated its defence of the gold standard on the practical difficulties of the
institutional mechanisms required to support a bimetallic standard, and on a repudiation of the quantity theory of money upon which bimetallism was based. But
inevitably, if coincidentally, in the light of the protectionist complexion bimetallism had latterly acquired, the cause of sound finance and free trade seemed to go

---

[61]   'I thought it rather a coup to shunt Chaplin from Protection on to a cause which rests on a
perfectly sound economical basis.' Mallet to Potter, 12 Apr. 1889 in CCM 13 Apr. 1889.

[62]   Howe, 'Bimetallism', 380; Redford, *Manchester Merchants*, vol. 2, 40.

[63]   e.g., R. C. Michie, *The City of London: Continuity and Change* (1992); id., 'The City and
International Trade, 1850–1914', in D. C. M. Platt, with A. J. H. Latham and R. C. Michie, *Decline and
Recovery in Britain's Overseas Trade, 1873–1914* (1993), 21–63. One leading City bimetallist, H. R.
Grenfell, upheld free trade as an abstract truth, but believed it had only become practical politics (in the
1840s) because of the power of the 'producers'. He believed (wrongly) that it was now unsustainable for
fiscal reasons, for 'I have no belief whatever in a purely democratic country submitting to direct taxation
in lieu of indirect for one hour. I am afraid you will think me very heretical', he wrote to Mallet, 8 June
1887, Mallet Papers.

[64]   Lord Randolph Churchill ('Was I a bimetallist?' quoted Green, in 'Rentiers versus Producers?',
588; cf. 'Yes, yes—oh, rather, I assented, as one dizzily accepts the propositions of a bimetellist' (*sic*),
Somerville and Ross, *Some Experiences of an Irish R.M.* (1899), 31.

[65]   CCM, 6 and 13 Apr.; 13 July, 1889; 12 Mar., 19 Mar. 1892.

[66]   CCM, 6 Apr.; 25 May; 22 June; 6 July; 3 Aug. 1895; Gowing, secretary, Cobden Club to George
Peel, 1895–6, Gold Standard Defence Association Papers, GM/180/24/5, Royal Bank of Scotland.

together.[67] For the orthodox, this involved some intellectual contortions, for the 1844 Bank Charter Act, now seen as the lynchpin of monetary stability in England, had been based on the quantity theory of money which the bimetallists espoused.[68] The supporters of the gold standard gained a new respect for the opponents of that Act, for example Tooke, while defending it to the hilt as the symbolic and practical basis of stability, however inadequate in theory.[69] Nor could they discern any essential evil in falling prices, which for the most part ensured the material welfare of the working classes, of industry, and the City of London. As Hamilton at the Treasury urged, the opponents of bimetallism were not simply the GSDA, but 'a still more formidable set of opponents, the friends of the consuming classes, and a fight connected with prices of commodities would be as formidable as a free-trade fight'.[70] The Bimetallic League increasingly took on the cast of yet another interest group, which sought to disrupt essential economic relationships for its own sectional advantage: 'theories evolved for the purpose of defending practical jobbery', as Farrer put it.[71] The gold standard, like free trade, seemed part of the social contract upon which the Victorian state was based, with advantages not lightly to be jeopardized to assuage farmers and faddists.

The bimetallic remedy for depression also proved indigestible within party politics. For the most part, the keenest bimetallists were to be found on the Conservative benches, but the Liberal minority was always strong.[72] Conservative governments were also notably more sympathetic than Liberal ones, for whom Harcourt and Gladstone in 1892 proved adamantly orthodox, swiftly reversing the Tory instinct to flirt with this issue. The Brussels Conference of 1892 met a British stonewall, orchestrated by Harcourt, Currie, Rivers Wilson, and Fremantle.[73] Tory instinct reasserted itself in the general election of 1895, when the Conservatives

[67]　D. Kynaston, *The City of London, Vol. II: Golden Years, 1890–1914* (1995), 117–19; R. Chalmers, quoted in Green, 'Bimetallic Controversy', 677.

[68]　Thus Farrer to G. Peel, 31 Jan. 1897: 'If we depended on notes, we should—*pace* your grandfather's memory and Lord Overstone's—be in a very bad way, owing to the cramping Act of 1844', GSDA Papers, GM/180/24/5.

[69]　e.g. Farrer to Mallet, 18, 20, July, 19 Aug., 2 Oct. 1887, Mallet Papers. Nor of course did bimetallists wish to abandon the Act. See, too, D. Laidlaw, 'British Monetary Orthodoxy in the 1870s', *Oxford Economic Papers*, 40 (1988), 74–109, esp. 100–1.

[70]　'A few observations on the proposals of the American delegates', 25 July 1897, PRO T168/85. Similarly, one Lancashire trade-unionist urged the gold standard defenders to campaign against the increased prices and decreased real wages bimetallism would herald, G. F. Davies to G. Peel, 3 June 1895, GSDA Papers, GM/180/24/3; for the same point, Farrer to B. W. Currie, 1 Apr. 1895, ibid., GM/180/24/5.

[71]　Farrer to B. R. Wise, 11 July 1892, in CCM, 6 Aug. 1892.

[72]　Howe, 'Bimetallism', 389–90; Cain and Hopkins, *British Imperialism*, vol. 1, 152–3. H. R. Grenfell, a former Liberal MP, thus wrote to 3rd Earl Grey, 'there are among the Bimetallists many radicals and they are much alarmed at the alliance with Chaplin and his protectionist friends. They believe, and Gladstone and Harcourt encourage them in their belief, that bimetallism is merely a form of protection in the eyes of men like Chaplin.' 25 July 1893, Grey Papers.

[73]　Harcourt dep. 166, Harcourt Papers; C. Rivers Wilson, *Chapters from my Official Life*, ed. E. MacAlister (1916), 242–6; C. L. Currie (ed.), *Bertram Wodehouse Currie, 1827–1896: Recollections, Letters and Journals* (2 vols, Roehampton, 1901).

were strongly tempted to add bimetallism to their manifesto. The issue was strongly canvassed in Lancashire, and the new Unionist Cabinet was feared as 'a department of the Bimetallic League'.[74] But in office, with the staunchly orthodox Hicks Beach at the Exchequer (and, interestingly, with Chamberlain silent on this issue[75]) the Conservatives presided over the rapid disappearance of the issue, with no serious attempt made to reach an international agreement during the Wolcott mission of 1897.[76] Thereafter, with the upturn in the world economy after 1896, and the Indian currency question solved by the adoption of the gold-exchange standard in 1898, bimetallism was (thankfully, by most) forgotten, with only a brief reprise in 1931.

The sugar bounties, 1886–1903: producers versus consumers?

A second, equally arcane, and gladly forgotten debate in the history of European economic policy—that concerning sugar bounties—evoked a far more direct threat to free trade orthodoxy than did the search for a bimetallic standard. The discussion of bounties had rumbled through the Treasuries of Europe since the early 1860s, but it was only in the late 1880s that it assumed important political dimensions in Britain.[77] Both the fair trade movement and the RCDTI had given prominence to the apparent iniquities of sugar-bounties paid by the European powers to encourage their sugar-beet industries.[78] By 1886 it could be plausibly claimed that European sugar-beet production had been stimulated by government support, which enabled foreign producers to supply the British market at artificially low prices, and in so doing to displace British West Indian cane sugar. This change had, in turn, meant the importation of refined sugar at the expense of raw, so leading to the rapid decline of the British refinery industry.[79] The ensuing campaign against bounties demanded their end by international agreement or by unilateral British action, that is to say by prohibition of bounty-fed imports or countervailing duties, set at a level to compensate for foreign bounties. This placed free traders in a dilemma, for while, on the one hand, they abhorred artificial intervention in production (a distortion of the supply mechanism), they equally abhorred any infringement of 'free imports' into Great Britain, a distortion of the demand mechanism.

[74] T. J. Spinner, *George Goachim Goschen* (Cambridge, 1973), 182–4; memo, 5 Feb. 1896 in GSDA, GM/180/27.
[75] Chamberlain had been an original member of the Currency Commission, but showed little interest or grasp of the issue: Giffen to Hicks Beach, 20 Feb. 1890, St Aldwyn Papers, PC/PP/61/20. In 1896 he refrained from taking part in the debate, to George Peel, 20 Feb. 1896, GSDA, GM/180/24/3.
[76] Howe, 'Bimetallism', 387; T. F. Dawson, *The Life and Character of Edward Oliver Wolcott* (New York, 2 vols, 1909), vol. 1, 623–95; there is an interesting collection of Wolcott's correspondence dealing with the Mission in the Colorado Historical Society, Denver, Colorado.
[77] See, for example, above, 180.
[78] Brown, *Tariff Reform Movement*, 29–57; *Parl. Papers* 1886, C. 4797, 23, qq. 12897–13327.
[79] R. W. Beachey, *The British West Indies Sugar Industry in the late 19th century* (Oxford, 1957), 56.

British policy had, therefore, correspondingly wavered. Gladstone and officials such as Mallet had strongly opposed the introduction of bounties, and had worked for their abolition through international agreement as early as 1864.[80] Further negotiations in 1876 had ended in failure, with the Treasury strongly opposed in principle to the most obvious deterrent to bounties, that of countervailing duties. Under the influence of fair trade thinking, a Select Committee in 1879–80 had rejected this particular Treasury view, but accepted the Foreign Office argument that Britain's existing commercial treaties, especially those with Germany and Belgium, debarred the imposition of countervailing duties.[81] There the question lay dormant, until growing crisis in the West Indies and the return of a Unionist government in 1886 made the question ripe for reconsideration.[82] By July 1887, under pressure from a strong anti-bounty lobby, led by the powerful West India Committee, Britain was ready to summon a new international conference.[83] In August 1888 this led to a convention whereby the signatories agreed to outlaw bounties, with the sanction of either prohibition or countervailing duties. The British Government attempted to give effect to this agreement, with the introduction of a bill on 11 April 1889, but its second reading was at first deferred before the bill itself was withdrawn in August. Here the matter dropped, until revived by Chamberlain in the later 1890s.

This attempt at legislation, while abortive, represented a determined effort to subvert free trade orthodoxy. Above all, the Under Secretary of State at the Foreign Office, the former City financier and coffee planter Henry de Worms, sought to establish the principle of retaliatory action as one of 'the ordinary safeguards of self-preservation', and to break out of what he regarded 'the fetters we ourselves forge round our own trade interests'.[84] In this, he was supported by the influential West India lobby, as well as working-class anti-bounty groups claiming at one point the support of over 400,000 trade-unionists.[85] Interestingly, too, he secured some support from the Commercial Department of the Foreign Office, whose head, Kennedy, accepted the benefits of prohibition in reopening British refineries, in relieving the British sugar colonies, and so indirectly increasing colonial demand for British goods. This would not only help root out a false economic system, but: 'By strengthening common interests, which in late years

---

[80]   Beachey, *Sugar Industry*, 49; *Parl. Papers*, 1880, 12, Report, 4 Aug. 1880. See, too, G. A. Pigman, 'Hegemony and Free Trade Policy', unpublished D.Phil. thesis, University of Oxford (1992), ch. 6.

[81]   *Parl. Papers*, 1880, 12 [332- Sess. 2] SC Sugar Industries, qq. 708–810 [C. M. Kennedy]; for a typical free trade case against countervailing duties, see L. Levi, *The History of British Commerce* (2nd edn., 1880), 530.

[82]   Cf. the Liberal government's attempt in 1884 to negotiate a reciprocity treaty between the West Indies and the United States: above, 187; Beachey, *Sugar Industry*, 138–40.

[83]   'Sugar Bounties', 27 June 1887 [Stanley], CAB 37/20/34, PRO.

[84]   'Sugar Convention', 1 and 3 May 1888, CAB 37/21/7 and 9; 'protection, open and avowed' was the verdict of *The Economist*, 2 Mar. 1889, 271.

[85]   This claim was made in the Commons, *Hansard*, 3rd ser., 335, c. 311, 11 Apr. 1889; it was rebutted by Farrer, *The Sugar Convention* (1889), 45.

have been loosened, the policy that led to the conclusion of the Sugar Convention will unite more closely the different parts of the Empire.'[86] Advisedly, de Worms circumvented the Board of Trade and the Treasury, whose officials were still strongly averse to any change in Britain's economic policy, with, for example, Edward Hamilton at the former adamant that the Convention 'really involves a direct contravention of free trade'.[87] Yet the Convention found in de Worms a determined advocate, and it formed a central part of the Conservative government's parliamentary programme in 1889. Its subsequent failure well illustrated the obstacles to unorthodox prescriptions in late-Victorian Britain.

That failure has, in part, been attributed to the dependence of the Conservative Party on the Liberal Unionists, part of the braking system on the Tory slide to protectionism.[88] There is clearly some force in this argument, in that almost all Liberal Unionist MPs were opposed to the bill, while the young editor of the *Liberal Unionist* St Loe Strachey had two years earlier been the author of a Cobden Club pamphlet on the benefits of cheap sugar.[89] On the other hand, if the influence of the Liberal Unionists had not precluded the lengthy preparation of the Convention, why should it have prevented its ratification? Here, the explanation of failure may lie in the inadequacies of the Convention itself, but both in publicizing those inadequacies and in conducting a vigorous campaign against the Convention, the rejuvenated Cobden Club also played a notable part. This, for example, was the view of the German economist Fuchs, and of the fair traders, who increasingly raged against the Club as a symbol of 'free trade fetishism'.[90]

The Club's initial response had in fact been inhibited by the support of Mallet and others for international action against bounties.[91] It was therefore only in June 1888 that the Club inaugurated its campaign against prohibition, on the grounds partly of its fear that working-class opinion had been 'somewhat deceived' on this issue, and, above all, in the mind of Farrer, who had replaced Mallet as the Club's mentor, in order to make clear the link between bounties and protective duties, and to explain the benefits that Britain received from bounties.[92] MPs such as J. A.

[86]   'Sugar Bounties', 4 Apr. 1889, CAB 37/23/14.

[87]   Hamilton Diary, 5 Apr. 1889, Add. MS 48650, BL.

[88]   Beachey, *Sugar Industry*, 141; A. Sykes, *Tariff Reform and British Politics, 1903–1913* (Oxford, 1979), 7.

[89]   Hamilton Diary, 4 May 1889; some Tories, including Lord Randolph Churchill, were also hostile; ibid., 12 May, Add. MS 48650; *The Economist*, 13 Mar. 1889.

[90]   C. J. Fuchs, *The Trade Policy of Great Britain and her Colonies since 1860* (1905), esp. 98–9. Fuchs had contacted the Club on a visit to England in 1891, CCM, 11 Apr. 1891.

[91]   Even so, discussion of this issue in the summer of 1887 had provoked the resignation of the sugar refiner Henry Tate, CCM, 2 July 1887. Mallet's friend and colleague, T. G. Baring [Earl of Northbrook], a Club member, continued to defend an anti-bounty policy, on theoretical and practical grounds, see *Bounties and Countervailing Duties: Some Observations Addressed to Members of the Cobden Club* (1900).

[92]   For Farrer, see Cobden Club minutes, *passim*; Hamilton Diary, 12 Mar, 30 Apr. 1889, Add. MS 48650. Farrer had earlier, of course, been able to conduct his battle against bounties from within the Board of Trade, see Farrer to Chamberlain, 26 Oct. 1880, 2 Nov. 1880, Chamberlain Papers, JC2/18/1 and JC2/19/4, University of Birmingham Library.

Picton, L. Playfair, and P. Illingworth took an active part in this campaign in the House of Commons, while Farrer produced a series of pamphlets aimed at a popular audience, and a series of letters to *The Times* and *Daily News*.[93] The Club's efforts were redoubled in the spring of 1889 in order to prevent ratification of the Convention, especially in view of what they considered the failure of the Liberals to turn this into a great party question.[94] The Club kept in touch with working-class opinion through public meetings and the TUC, with foreign opinion, for example, through the President of the Bordeaux Chamber of Commerce, and with business opinion in the sugar-using trades, whose recent growth became a crucial plank in the free trade case, for it was now plausibly argued that more jobs had been created in such industries than had been lost in refining. To reinforce this point, George Mathieson, managing-director of the Hackney Confectionery Works of Clarke, Nicholls, and Coombs, wrote and subsidized the distribution of thousands of leaflets. The Club also raised a special anti-bounty publication fund, drawing on the purses of Liberal MPs such as Seale-Haynes, Dilke, Arnold Morley, and Holden.

The Club therefore had effectively organized a considerable body of opinion on this issue, but even more importantly this debate stimulated the popularization of a series of arguments which were of longer-term benefit in upholding free trade. Above all, the Cobdenites emphasized the threat that prohibition of cheap sugar posed to the working-class standard of living, and the threat to the expansion of 'new' industries, whose importance to the late-nineteenth century economic historians have rightly given credit. These appeals to both consumers and producers now supplemented the somewhat worn and less appropriate arguments that state action would divert trade from its natural channels, and that it would not in the long term secure the optimal investment of capital and labour in the West Indies.[95] These were vital, but subtle changes within the Cobdenite camp, most of whom now departed from some of the *idées fixes* of an earlier generation. Symptomatically, Mallet differed from Farrer, whom he believed upheld 'national independence', not 'international dependence' in proclaiming the benefits of cheap foreign sugar. Such a view was, for Mallet, 'wholly unworthy of anyone who understands the meaning of Free trade in its largest international sense'.[96] This was a significant distinction between the right of the consumer to 'free imports' and the right of the producer to free exchange, the former based on personality and community, the latter on private property, a distinction recalling the ideological tensions among

---

[93] Farrer, *The Sugar Convention* (1889); Gladstone found its arguments 'absolutely unanswerable' (Hamilton, 12 [13] Mar. 1889, *GD*, vol. 12, 189, 11 Mar. 1889), but the refiner George Martineau made a valiant effort in *Free Trade in Sugar: A Reply to Sir Thomas Farrer* (1889).

[94] CCM, 16 Mar. 1889; the government's weakness on this issue, demonstrated by Farrer and the Cobdenites, drew out an increasingly vigorous Liberal response, with Harcourt and Gladstone reducing de Worms and Hicks Beach to ever more desperate defences of the Convention. See, for example, the exchange in the Commons, *Hansard*, 3rd ser., 336, 21 May 1889, cc. 638–42; Brown, *Tariff Reform Movement*, 49.

[95] Above, 51.

[96] Mallet to Potter, 24 May 1889, CCM, 25 May 1889.

free traders in the early 1880s.[97] Nevertheless, this slippage from the cosmopolitan ideal enhanced the consumers' case for the defence of free trade, which had been successfully advanced in this instance against the Convention. The Club's campaign certainly both sapped the morale of the 'Conventionists' and encouraged the Liberals, above all Harcourt, to take up opposition to the bill, which was ultimately 'laughed out' of the Commons.[98] This well-orchestrated opposition was undoubtedly important as a political model, although the failure of the bill also owed much to the international complexities of the issue, not least the danger of a tariff war with France.[99]

The diplomatic campaign for effective international action against bounties was not abandoned after 1889, and was eventually to succeed, with the Convention signed at Brussels in 1902 and ratified by Great Britain in 1903. This Convention, of course, was welcomed by some 'individualist' free traders as a successful example of international action, of the type Cobdenites should advocate, and the opposition of Gladstone to sugar bounties in the 1870s was frequently and tendentiously recalled by anti-bounty activists.[100] But it was not the work of cosmopolitan free traders so much as the result of pressure from the West Indies and their powerful London lobby, coinciding with Chamberlain's search for imperial consolidation on becoming Colonial Secretary in 1895.[101] A large increase in European bounties between 1894 and 1896, along with renewed depression in the West Indies, paved the way for Chamberlain's appointment of a Royal Commission in 1896, whose report, while agreed on the harm done by bounties, was divided on remedies.[102] In the wake of the Committee's unhelpfulness, Chamberlain advocated negotiation with a view to countervailing duties, believing that inaction in 1889 had been due to 'vested interests', and that the Conservative government should recognize its duty towards its oldest colony, even at the risk of 'violent opposition' from fanatical free traders and vested industrial interests.[103] Chamberlain rightly predicted the Cobden Club's reaction, whose themes had already been well rehearsed in the 1880s, but with a Unionist government in power its influence was necessarily limited. More importantly, Chamberlain's policy scarcely raised enthusiasm within the Civil Service or the Cabinet. The Board of Customs was, in particular, reluctant to reframe the British fiscal system for the benefit of the West Indies, when it

[97]   See above, 136–8.
[98]   Hamilton Diary, 8 Jan. 1902, recalling earlier policy during the later debate on the Sugar Convention, Add. MS 48679; Brown, *Tariff Reform Movement*, 45; *The Economist*, 18 May 1889, 627.
[99]   *The Economist*, 2 Mar. 1889, 271.
[100]   Y. Guyot, 'Bounties and Free Trade', *Transactions of the National Liberal Club. Political and Economic Circle*, 4 (1901–2), 34–8; Anti-Bounty League, *Reports*, etc., 1898.
[101]   J. Amery, *The Life of Joseph Chamberlain*, vol. 4 (1951), esp. ch. 86, 'The West Indies and the Sugar War'.
[102]   Beachey, *Sugar Industry*, 150 ff; H. A. Will, 'Colonial Policy and Economic Development in the British West Indies, 1895–1903', *EcHR*, 2nd ser., 23 (1970), 129–47; *Parl. Papers*, 1898, 50 [c. 8655] Sugar Commission Report.
[103]   'Condition of the West Indies', 8 Nov. 1897 [J.C.], CAB 37/45/44.

was very doubtful whether the new policy would in fact assist those colonies.[104] The Customs arguments weighed heavily with the Chancellor Hicks Beach, who carefully assessed the claims of the 'dear' and 'cheap' sugar parties: the decline of sugar refiners was counterbalanced by the growth of fruit-growing and jam manufacture, although fruit-pickers were 'as poor as the match-makers'. As a Bristol MP, Hicks Beach counterposed the old centre of sugar-refining, whose remaining works produced 19,000 tons of sugar per annum, with the claims of the new Fry's cocoa factory, employing 2,000 hands, and using 250–300 tons of sugar per week.[105] This was an apt local reminder of the political dangers of economic tinkering.

Colonial Office opinion was by now far more favourable towards countervailing duties, going so far as to claim that they were perfectly compatible with free trade, 'if the doctrine of free trade is that the price of articles should be their natural price', and deprecating the subordination of colonial policy to the dictates of 'the sugar-eating English voter'.[106] This change of sentiment prepared the way for participation in the abortive Brussels Conference of 1898, and for Colonial Office support for the Indian Government's adoption of countervailing duties in 1899.[107] It was strongly condemned by the Liberals,[108] while Hicks Beach resisted the drift of sentiment towards duties within the government. Nevertheless, in December 1901 Britain was ready once more to participate in a new round of negotiations with a much greater likelihood of eventual success.

For, by that date the domestic debate had been transformed by the resort to a sugar duty in Hicks Beach's budget of 1901, reimposing as part of wartime taxation a tax abolished by Stafford Northcote in 1874.[109] Interestingly, the very suitability of sugar as a wartime tax had been pointed to by Primrose in 1897, and the Boer War now provided a fitting occasion, although one that Hicks Beach only reluctantly accepted, as by January 1901 the worsening of the financial situation exceeded his sense of the difficulties of taxing sugar in February 1900.[110] Although the case could be made that a sugar tax had been acceptable in the heyday of Gladstonian finance, and a stronger one that more indirect taxes were necessary in the early twentieth century, the protectionist potential of such a tax worried civil servants such as Hamilton, who feared this might portend the (Chamberlainite) 'fiscal millennium', with a return to 'good old tariff days' and the end of 'the free trade fetish'. Not only would the economic case against the tax be a strong one, but

[104]   'Correspondence on a counter-vailing duty', 7 Dec. 1897 [C.O.], CAB 37/45/52.
[105]   Hicks Beach to Chamberlain, 3 Dec. 1897, in ibid.
[106]   CO to Primrose, Board of Customs, 6 Dec. 1897, CAB 37/45/53.
[107]   'Countervailing duty on bounty-fed sugars imported into India', 2 Feb. 1899, G. Hamilton, CAB 37/49/10; Beachey, *Sugar Industry*, 166; T. G. Baring, *Bounties and Countervailing Duties.*
[108]   *Hansard*, 4th ser. 72, cc. 1199–1312, 15 June 1899; Redford, *Manchester Merchants*, vol. 2, 109.
[109]   See above, 166.
[110]   'Sugar Duty', 7 Feb. 1900 [Hicks Beach] CAB 37/52/13; cf. 'The Financial Problem', 31 Jan. 1901, [Treasury] CAB 37/56/14.

Hamilton rightly foresaw that it would help reunify the Liberal forces divided by the Boer War, providing a solid platform to unite 'poor consumers' and rather wealthier industrialists,[111] arousing solid Irish opposition, and raising the broad issue of the incidence of taxation.[112]

The sugar tax also raised important imperial and international issues, above all the spectre of its remission in the case of the West Indies, and the wholesale revolution in the fiscal system that Primrose had feared in 1897. In 1901 this was not a step for which Chamberlain was ready to base his bid for fiscal change, save as a *pis aller*[113] while pushing ahead with his diplomatic initiative against bounties, with strong support from the Foreign Office under Lansdowne.[114] Importantly, too, the existence of sugar duties now strengthened Britain's negotiating position, at least enabling her to imply readiness to enforce a penal clause against bounty-fed producers, as both Chamberlain and Sir Henry Bergne, head of the Foreign Office's commercial department, pointed out.[115] Moreover, as if to lend credibility to the claims of the Cobden Club, Cranborne at the Foreign Office foresaw action on sugar bounties as part of a larger policy of retaliation, foreshadowing Balfour's position in 1903.[116] Britain's readiness to support sanctions was therefore the crucial factor which enabled the Convention to be agreed in February 1902, although Britain was undecided whether in her case the sanction would be prohibition or countervailing duties. The Board of Trade doubted the effectiveness of the latter, and the Treasury their legitimacy, so that it was perhaps a partial victory for residual free trade sentiment that the government ultimately abandoned duties and proposed prohibition to the House of Commons in May 1903.

However, by this date the sugar convention had been overtaken by and intimately wrapped up in the wider debate on fiscal policy. Pertinently, it was on the occasion of the first reading of the Sugar Convention Bill on 28 May 1903 that Dilke smoked out Balfour's position on Chamberlainite tariff reform.[117] There is a

---

[111]   For the wealth of chocolate manufacturers, see W. D. Rubinstein, *Men of Property: the Very Wealthy in Britain since the Industrial Revolution* (1981), 69, 108, 155.

[112]   All these themes were heavily emphasized in Cobden Club leaflets between 1897 and 1903. See esp. leaflets 108–10, 112–15, 117–21, 126, 137.

[113]   If the Conference failed to reach agreement, Chamberlain had secured Cabinet approval for the remission of the sugar duty for the West Indies (Amery, *Chamberlain*, vol. 4, 253), a policy even Beach had accepted as preferable to countervailing duties. But the Convention, as signed in 1902, actually prohibited the granting of preference to the colonies.

[114]   'Brussels Sugar Conference', CAB 37/60/7; 37/60/36; 37/61/46. Lansdowne announced that in the event of the failure of the Conference, Britain would take steps to defend her interests, without actually specifying those steps, and without much confidence this ploy would work; unexpectedly it did.

[115]   'Sugar Bounties', 1 May 1901 [FO], CAB 37/57/42.

[116]   'Retaliation [in the fiscal policy of the UK]', 22 May 1901 [FO], CAB 37/57/48. This memorandum is attributed to Salisbury by Lipchitz (below n. 124), but it is derived from the Foreign Office which Salisbury had by then left, and it is signed 'C', which suggests C[ranborne]. In August 1903 Cranborne was to become 'S'[alisbury]. His later views are consistent with this memorandum, for example Cranborne to Chamberlain, 8 June 1903, cit. Amery, *Chamberlain*, vol. 5, 239, and Salisbury to Balfour, 3 and 10 Oct. 1903, 6 Sept. 1904, Balfour Papers, BL, Add. MS 49757, fos. 258, 263, 301.

[117]   *Hansard*, 4th ser., 123, cc. 141–54, 28 May 1903; R. Rempel, *Unionists Divided* (Newton Abbot, 1972), 34.

strong case for regarding the sugar debate as a stalking-horse for fiscal reform, and this was to a large extent the reaction of free traders, Unionist and Liberal. The general financing of the Boer War itself had, of course, raised the issue of future government finance, but sugar provided the single most constant and concrete instance of fiscal change. From this basis, it was possible for the free traders to reinforce their claims that prohibition would increase consumer prices, thus threatening the standard of living of the working classes, would increase the costs of industrial production, jeopardizing jobs and profits, and would increase interest group jobbery, raising the spectre of the sacrifice of the many to the interests of the few. Significantly, the Cobden Club dinner was revived in 1902 (for the first time since 1897), and acted once more as a central Liberal Party occasion, with speeches on the Sugar Convention by Spencer and Campbell-Bannerman.[118] This growing debate over ratification of the treaty occasioned an important dress rehearsal for the tariff controversy of future years, while also foreshadowing the central political alliances within the free trade camp. Several themes repay brief attention at this point.

First, the Liberals attacked the bill as one that sacrificed the people for the benefit of a small group of capitalists. The British people, the greatest consumers of sugar in the world (at 90 lb. per capita per annum) faced the burden of steeply rising sugar prices, which would deter both capital and enterprise, just in order to assist backward planters in the West Indies, or rather 'two or three capitalists who pose in this country to represent the West Indian Islands but who only represent their own interests'.[119] This was an argument that was reminiscent of the 1840s, but which drew together the Liberal appeal to progressive capitalists and working men. The case was put by interested parties such as the tea merchant Lough and the grocer Kearley among MPs, while the coal-owner Joicey, MP for Chester-le-Street, upheld that working-class interests in both jobs and welfare were threatened by a bill 'most disastrous to this country'.[120] In particular, since the Liberals believed the bill was unlikely to achieve its goals, whether assisting the West Indies or ending the operations of foreign cartels, the welfare of consumers would in vain be sacrificed to the interests of producers.

Second, the bill's provisions were politically distasteful. Its most novel feature was the power given by the Convention to a permanent commission at Brussels. This body would decide whether particular countries did offer bounties, and would authorize condign penal action. Such a bureaucratic and constitutional innovation evoked a string of arguments that are wholly familiar in Britain since she joined the Common Market in 1973, but which were unprecedented in Victorian and Edwardian politics, concerning the transfer of power over fiscal policy to an

---

[118] *The Brussels Convention and Free Trade: speeches by Earl Spencer and Sir Henry Campbell-Bannerman, Cobden Club Banquet, 8 Nov. 1902* (1903).
[119] T. Lough, *Hansard*, 4th ser. 126, c. 610, 28 July 1903. See, too, Lough, 'The Brussels Sugar Convention', *Contemporary Review*, 83 (1903), 75–85.
[120] *Hansard*, 4th ser., 126, cc. 598–611, 624–6, 707–8, 28 July 1903.

irresponsible European authority. For example, both the Conservative lawyer Gorst and the Liberal constitutional historian Bryce lamented the first time that 'we have ever subjected our legislation to foreign control'. Such dramatic constitutional implications were accompanied by domestic political fears, that the Convention embodied the subordination of policy decisions to influential interest groups, whether extra-parliamentry lobbies, with Parliament reduced to a 'body of logrollers', or subject to the sway of overmighty departments, such as the Colonial Office. Typically, the young Winston Churchill proclaimed the ideal that 'Every country [ought] to be governed from some central point of view, where all classes and all interests are proportionately represented.'[121] Certainly, this strong link between political democracy and free trade became one of the strongest platforms in the Liberal case after 1903.

Finally, in the light of still vocal calls for imperial preference and increased indirect taxation, the Sugar Convention was treated merely as the harbinger of tariff reform—with dear sugar 'the first step towards dear food' (Bowles), 'the first step towards protection' (Kearley), or the 'first action between free trade and protection' (E. Robertson)—in what was likely to be a protracted battle, or, as Churchill saw it, a 'working model' for future policy and to be resisted as such.[122] As a result, in the sugar debates the Unionist free traders were drawn towards the Liberal Party, and the debate of 29 July was the first major opportunity for the newly founded Free Food League to demonstrate its opposition to 'the protective taxation of food'.[123] On the very same day, Hamilton at the Treasury prepared for the Cabinet a brief outlining the difficulties facing a policy of imperial preference that depended upon the general taxation of foodstuffs. The debate over the Sugar Convention, therefore, was not only of great polemical importance to the free traders, but acted as a political catalyst in the organization of the anti-tariff reform camp. Arguably, too, it stiffened the resolve of the bureaucracy to resist further inroads into its free trade traditions.[124]

The intricate politics of sugar after 1886, only partially unravelled here, had raised many of the issues that fed into the wider debate over tariff reform unleashed in 1903. Hence, although politicians such as Balfour might deprecate a return to the battle cries of the 1840s, and although some historians appear to think that old 1840s pamphlets were simply dusted off by the free traders in 1903, the arguments had in fact already been subtly transmuted.[125] The Edwardian case for free trade would therefore rest upon the growing emphases on the rise of new industries

[121]　*Hansard*, 4th ser., 126, cc. 641 (Gorst), 642 (Bryce), 28 July, c. 713, (Churchill), 29 July. The issue of sovereignty had also been raised by *The Economist* in the 1889 debate: 'the Commission would deprive us of the power to regulate our tariff according to our own ideas', 13 Apr. 1889, 467.

[122]　*Hansard*, 4th ser., 126, c. 622, 28 July 1903, c. 703, 707, 716, 29 July 1903.

[123]　Rempel, *Unionists Divided*, 45.

[124]　J. W. Lipchitz, 'Sir Edward Hamilton and Tariff Reform, 1903–1905: A Study in Conscience vs. Policy', *Albion*, 4 (1972), 219–28.

[125]　Typically, M. Bentley, *The Climax of Liberal Politics* (1987), 109.

under free trade, the priority of the interests of consumers, the need to isolate the state from pressure groups, and even on free trade as a national policy, as Mallet charged. Yet, if Mallet was right to believe that internationalism, free exchange, and individual rights had been overridden, this was only a belated recognition that the Europe of empires after 1882 provided a less favourable climate for internationalism than the Europe of nations in which he and like-minded ideologues and diplomats had promoted free trade treaties in the 1860s and 1870s. Sugar itself, however vital in enhancing the appeal of free trade to working men and women, was only one part of the wider debate upon the British Empire with which the free traders had wrestled since the early 1880s, and which Chamberlain strove in 1903 to bring to the heart of British politics.

Free trade and the empire, 1886–1903

As we have seen, many free traders regarded with deep gloom the expansion of British power overseas from the 1870s. Faced with the disappointment of their internationalist aspirations, their central concern now became to resist the reconstruction of the British Empire upon the model of an imperial commercial union outlined by the fair traders after 1879, and boosted by the growing strength of imperial themes in political rhetoric and action under Disraeli. For, although Disraeli himself gave little support to fair trade, his biography of Bentinck remained a powerful incantation to the ideal of the old British Empire, never relinquished by some, and now revalued in the light of the apparent failure of the free trade Utopia of the 1840s. The fair trade ideal was given increasing precision in the 1880s, as it became entwined in a wider debate on imperial unity, and as it offered a more concrete alternative to threats of retaliatory tariffs against Europe and America. The efforts of the Fair Trade League (FTL; 1881–91) were reinforced by more specific bodies such as the Imperial Federation League (IFL; 1884–93) and the United Empire Trade League (UETL; 1891–1903), where the focus was upon the means by which the British Empire could be united both as an economic power and a political entity in the late nineteenth-century world system.[126] This growing debate upon an imperial *Zollverein* was itself lent the sanction of Chamberlain in the 1890s, while the Boer War was to spell out the possibilities and dangers of a reconstructed imperial order. If, as the free traders of the 1880s believed, 'imperialism was fatal to internationalism', the Cobdenite cause faced extinction in this lowering imperial challenge. On the other hand, the strength of the domestic attachment to free trade ensured that ultimately imperial power would be reconciled with, and constrained by, the legacy of Cobdenism.

First, it is important to recall that the notion of imperial federation was by no means synonymous with preference and exclusion. When the federation movement

---

[126] Zebel, 'Fair Trade', 182–5; Brown, *Tariff Reform Movement*, 85–128; Green, *Conservatism*, 35–41. But see, too, E. Halévy, *A History of the English People. Epilogue. Vol. 1. 1895–1905. Book III The Decline of the Unionist Party* (Penguin edn., 1940), 30–60.

had begun in the 1860s, its proponents had been colonial free traders, such as the returned Australians Westgarth and Jenkins. These men, who had been at the forefront of the creation of the Royal Colonial Institute in 1868, wished, above all, to reassert free trade within the Empire against peripheral moves in both Canada and Australia towards protection.[127] Opposition to the growth of such colonial protectionism, as we have seen, was also an important focus of Cobden Club activity, although British colonial policy had been impotent in the face of protectionist sentiment in the self-governing colonies of Canada and Victoria. Outside the Cobden Club, aspirant imperial statesmen had also defended and propagated the notion of a free trade empire. A good, if little-known example is provided by George Baden-Powell, eldest son of the Savilian Professor of Geology at Oxford and brother of the founder of the Boy Scouts. After three years of travelling in the Empire and Europe, while still an undergraduate, Powell published *New Homes for the Old Country . . . Australia and New Zealand* (1872), an argument for colonization and closer imperial ties. Having completed his undergraduate career, and winning the Chancellor's Prize at Oxford with his essay on *The Political and Social Results of the Absorption of Small Races by Large*, Powell became private secretary to Sir George Bowen, then Governor of Victoria. His first-hand knowledge of Victorian protectionism produced *Protection and Bad Times* (1879) a strong argument for free trade in young countries, a theme reiterated in numerous articles, and in *State Aid and State Interference* (1882).[128] As a result of his Australian connections and experience Powell was determined to keep before the public the example of New South Wales and the benefits of free trade: 'I believe myself strongly in the material good to be derived from all concerned in keeping tariffs low throughout the Empire. But I believe the one reliable means to this end is the intelligent appreciation of the parts of the case that are already a matter of record by the electors as well as by the statesmen of the Colonies.'[129] Powell also contributed a section on the colonies to the *Quarterly Review*, which aimed to ally Conservative opinion with the 'rapidly growing colonial sentiment'. His ideas at this point continued to emphasize the importance of free trade between all British colonies, 'the institution of unfettered commercial exchange among all English communities', although omitting to state whether this might be combined with an external tariff.[130] He became a Tory MP in 1885 and an expert on imperial trade, eventually

---

[127]   C. A. Bodelsen, *Studies in Mid-Victorian Imperialism* (Copenhagen 1924; London, 1960), 95 ff; E. Jenkins, *The Colonies and Imperial Unity* (1871).

[128]   e.g., 'The Results of Protection in Young Countries', *Fortnightly Review*, 31 (1882) 369–79, provoking from Melbourne, J. Mirams, *The Progress of Victoria. A reply to . . . by Baden Powell* (1883). For Powell, see *DNB*, *Who Was Who*, and G.Bowen, *Thirty Years of Colonial Government*, ed. S. Lane Poole (2 vols, 1889), vol. 2, 405–30.

[129]   Baden-Powell to F. S. Samuel, 29 Nov. 1881. Samuel Papers, A11 f. 27, Mitchell Library, Sydney.

[130]   Powell to Parkes, 16 July, 23 Nov. 1881, Parkes Papers.

welcoming Canadian preference in 1897 as a genuine step towards the imperial free trade he had for so long propagated.[131]

Powell is a good illustration of the growing appropriation of empire for Conservative ideology, but without an overt attempt to link this with protection and preference, although there were sufficient hints of this to deter the Cobden Club from sponsoring his writings.[132] By the early 1880s discussion of an imperial *Zollverein* associated with fair trade made increasingly obvious the distance between those ideals of empire that were consistent with free trade, and those that sought to sap its cosmopolitan character in favour of exclusive associations. Beneath a confusing rhetoric of empire, federation, and customs' unions, there may be discerned four leading models of imperial economic unity.[133]

First, there survived the old Whig–Liberal ideal of a free trade empire, deriving from colonial self-government and the abandonment of differential duties in the 1840s, that is to say, each self-governing colony setting its own revenue-only tariffs. In effect, with the waning of Wakefieldian colonial ideals, and with the impossibility of any Cobdenite abandonment of empire, this had merged into the central Liberal ideal of empire in the age of Gladstone. This had been the model for the imperial federationists of the 1860s, as it remained for Grey and the Cobden Club in the 1890s.[134]

Second, there arose in the 1880s the largely theoretical idea of an imperial customs union, in which the colonies would agree to a common revenue-only imperial tariff, the formation of which would in itself contribute substantially to a sense of political integration. This model inspired Powell, as we have seen, and Conservatives as diverse as Ashmead-Bartlett and Lord Salisbury were prepared to support the idea that 'all trade within the limits of the empire ought to be free'.[135] But this ideal proved to be a will-o'-the-wisp, conflicting both with colonial self-government and colonial fiscal necessity.[136]

Third, in the 1880s and 1890s the notion of an imperial *Zollverein* came most usually to imply free trade within the empire, combined with protective duties on foreign goods; this was the essential ideal of the FTL, its successor pressure groups, and of Chamberlain between 1896 and 1902.[137] It was a schema that proved

---

[131] 'Imperial Free Trade', *Fortnightly Review*, 61 (1897), 935–45.

[132] CCM, 6 Dec. 1879.

[133] An essay competition by the *Statist* on 'The Commercial Federation of the Empire' produced 136 entrants. The *Statist*, 2 and 9 May 1896.

[134] Grey, *The Commercial Policy of the British Colonies and the McKinley Tariff* (1892); CCM, 14 May 1892.

[135] *Hansard*, 3rd ser. 263, c. 1617, 22 July 1881; Salisbury, quoted in L. Trainor, *British Imperialism and Australian Nationalism* (Cambridge, 1994), 52.

[136] Trainor, *British Imperialism*, 53. It served, however, as a useful device to wrongstep preferentialists. See Hicks Beach, *Hansard*, 4th ser., 1, c. 111, 9 Feb. 1892.

[137] Zebel, 'Fair Trade', 182; id., 'Joseph Chamberlain and the Genesis of Tariff Reform', *Journal of British Studies*, 7 (1967–8), 131–57.

more enduring, but it posed too great a threat to colonial revenues to gain wide-spread colonial support.

Fourth, after 1902, as it became clear that the British colonies were unwilling to abandon tariffs whether for revenue or protection, imperial economic unity was redefined so as to include a measure of preference, but within a structure based on protectionist tariffs, which would be partially remitted to favour imperial goods. This was a far cry from the ideal of an imperial *Zollverein* in the 1880s, but was to be the basis of Chamberlain's advocacy of tariff reform in 1903. It was a stage that was reached only after those models of empire more consistent with the domestic morality of free trade had been progressively ruled out. Such an interplay between free trade, federation, and preference requires careful unravelling in order both to appreciate the evolution of free trade ideas of empire, and to understand the imperial genesis of tariff reform.

By the 1880s it proved impossible for Cobdenites, as for Liberals as a whole, to remain indifferent to the empire and its welfare. To some extent, this concern took the well-established form of opposition to protective duties in the self-governing and Crown colonies, for example the energetic and successful campaign against the paddy tax in Ceylon.[138] But, interestingly, the Cobden Club did not join Manchester's opposition to the Indian import duties in 1894–6, believing that they were imposed for fiscal, not protective, reasons.[139] The changing face of the British Empire in the 1880s, and the emergence of preferentialist ideas of imperial unity dictated a wider free trade engagement with the imperial debate. Significantly, as in the 1860s, free traders worked within the movement for imperial federation. As we have seen, the formation of the IFL in 1884 was by no means the work only of fair traders such as Dunraven and Vincent, but included leading free traders such as Bryce, Playfair, Samuel Morley, Cartwright, and W. E. Forster.[140] Their presence helped ensure that the League remained a 'broad church', and did not become a simple pressure group for an imperial *Zollverein*.[141] As a result, the League itself remained internally divided between those whose respective priorities were federation, defence, and trade. Among those who looked to the empire primarily as an

---

[138]   This campaign may be traced in the Cobden Club's minutes, publications, and parliamentary debates. Victory was claimed in 1892 (CCM 14 May), C. S. Salmon having been conspicuous outside the House, E. Watkin within. The Cobden Club also continued to follow the cause of free trade in Australian politics, hailing, for example, the free trade victory in New South Wales in 1894, Gowing to Parkes, 18 July 1894, Parkes Papers.

[139]   CCM, 21 July 1894; P. Harnetty, 'The Indian Cotton Duties Controversy, 1894–96', *English Historical Review*, 77 (1962).

[140]   Above, 190. Of 34 MPs supporting the League in 1884, 20 were Liberals: M. Burgess, 'The Federal Plan of the IFL 1892', in A. Bosco (ed.), *The Federal Idea: the History of Federalism from the Enlightenment to 1945* (vol. 1, 1991), 138–53.

[141]   *Report of Conference . . . 1884*; J. E. Kendle, *The Colonial and Imperial Conferences, 1887–1911* (1967), 3, reports Bryce's belief that many Liberals joined to keep the League 'out of Tory hands'. After the Liberal split of 1886, their strength clearly fell, with only 6 MPs on the committee by 1888: Matthew, *Liberal Imperialists*, 163.

economic entity, there was by no means unanimity upon the desirability of prefer-ence or protection. On the contrary, the League's greatest success, the calling of the Colonial Conference of 1887, served only to make plain the conflicting prescrip-tions for imperial economic unity, and so to put on their guard the custodians of the free trade empire.[142] Such differences were no nearer reconciliation when the League's Commercial Committee under Rawson Rawson reported in terms of the economic future of an empire united by posts and patents, not preference and protection.[143]

Despite this free trade 'success', the UETL, formed in 1891 from IFL and FTL activists, led by the fair trader Howard Vincent, kept free traders on their guard against commercial federation of the empire, with the Cobden Club closely shad-owing the new League's activities.[144] In a showpiece debate at the Conference of Chambers of Commerce of the Empire in London in 1892, G. W. Medley, one of the Club's leading members, successfully combated an imperial preference motion. The case against a *Zollverein* was forcefully and effectively argued in terms both of its impracticability, and its costs for Great Britain, asked to jeopardize three-quarters of its trade for the benefit of one quarter.[145] This was a case which official and public opinion largely endorsed.[146] Not surprisingly, as Lord Derby reported to Lady Jersey, wife of the governor of New South Wales, 'public opinion here will not stand differential duties against foreign countries for the benefit of colonists who are much better off than the average Englishman and it seems that without such duties no Imperial zollverein is possible'.[147]

Public indifference as well as internal division contributed to the collapse of the IFL in 1893, its demise engineered, some believed, by the free traders and with the death-knell sounded by the return of Gladstonian rule.[148] But its existence had revealed that Liberal free traders and leading Cobdenites such as Playfair were part of an important strand of opinion within the Liberal Party, on which the tide of Liberal imperialism would flow in the 1890s. It was, of course, tendentious for

[142] J. E. Tyler, *The Struggle for Imperial Unity, 1868–1895* (1938), ch. 15; Farrer warned Chamber-lain, his old boss, against any 'Tariff bargain with Canada—dangerous to our Free Trade policy; dangerous to the union of the Canadian provinces; dangerous in the end to the unity of the Empire . . . It will be the first step on a downward path': 11 and 15 Oct. 1887, Chamberlain Papers, JC5/30/5 and 6.

[143] Tyler, *Imperial Unity*, 186; Replies to Interrogatories issued by the Special Committee, August 1891, Imperial Federation League Papers, Add. MS 62783, BL; Rawson Rawson, *Synopsis of the Tariffs and Trade of the British Empire* (1888) and *Sequel to Synopsis of the Tariffs and Trade of the British Empire* (1889).

[144] Brown, *Tariff Reform Movement*, 115–16; CCM 21 Feb., 27 June 1891, 9 Apr. 1892; 'Commercial Federation of the Empire', Farrer Papers, 96.

[145] Medley, *Fiscal Federation of the Empire* (1892); see, too, S. R. B. Smith, 'British Nationalism Imperialism and the City of London, 1880–1900', unpublished Ph.D. theris, University of London (1985), 208–12.

[146] e.g. R. Giffen, 'Commercial Union between the U.K. and the Colonies', 9 Feb. 1891, St Aldwyn Papers, PC/PP/61/6.

[147] 15 Aug. 1891, Childs Villiers Papers, MS 2896, National Library of Australia.

[148] Tyler, *Imperial Unity*, 209; Smith, 'British Nationalism', 212–14; Kendle, *Colonial Conferences*,

Playfair to compare the IFL with the Anti-Corn Law League, but there was much
more substance in Bryce's assurance to Parkes of New South Wales that the Liberal
Party was no longer indifferent to empire, whatever the case thirty years earlier.[149]
This recrudescence of the Liberal empire of sentiment ensured that by the late
1890s all but the most unreconstructed Cobdenite could accept with Giffen that:
'We are all imperialists now because we have become accustomed to the idea of an
empire united by the bonds of affection.'[150]

Against this background, the Liberal government of 1892–5 responded to empire
with a new flexibility in the face of considerable Liberal imperial sentiment at
home, growing support for federation in Australia, especially Victoria, and rather
more in Canada and South Africa.[151] Such pressures on Great Britain were to be
orchestrated through the Ottawa Conference of 1894, which put forward colonial,
especially Canadian, aspirations for preference, alongside the narrower demands of
the Australian colonies to be free to negotiate differential tariffs with third parties.
Both Canada and the Australian colonies sought the abandonment of the Anglo-
Belgian and Anglo-*Zollverein* treaties of 1862 and 1865 respectively, which impeded reciprocal negotiations between the British colonies and the mother country,
and whose abrogation had become a central aim of the UETL. In the face of these
distasteful demands, the Colonial Secretary Ripon proved conciliatory rather than
ultra-Cobdenite.[152] He regarded Ottawa as 'a decided success', and his policy as a
whole revealed the growing flexibility of the official mind.[153] Thus, on the one hand,
the demand of the Australian colonies that they might engage in preferential trade
with other parts of the empire was conceded in the Australian Colonial Customs
Duty Act of 1895: this was part of the logic of self-government which had led to the
previous Act in 1873.[154] On the other hand, Ripon frustrated Rhodes's attempt to
introduce protection by the back door in South Africa in 1894,[155] and reasserted the
free trade case with regard to the Belgian and *Zollverein* commercial treaties,
namely that these did not impede intercolonial trade, and that preferential trade
would harm Great Britain through foreign retaliation. At the same time, colonies
might engage in separate commercial negotiation so long as Britain remained the
intermediary for their conduct. As Kimberley, reiterating his stance of 1873, ad-

[149]   Playfair, *Imperial Federation* (1892); Bryce to Parkes, 16 Jan 1895, Parkes Papers.
[150]   Giffen, 'Career and Character of Cobden', draft, *c.*1904, Giffen Papers III/22, BLPES;
Rosebery had emphasized the connection between free trade and the strength of the British Empire in
his centenary address to the Manchester Chamber of Commerce, Nov. 1897, Rosebery, *The Anti-Corn
Law League and Free Trade* (Cobden Club 1898).
[151]   Matthew, *Liberal Imperialists*, 150–94; Trainor, *British Imperialism, passim.*
[152]   Cf. E. Salmon, 'Lord Ripon met the enthusiasm of the colonies with a cold douche of
Cobdenism', in 'From Cobdenism to Chamberlain', *Fortnightly Review*, 59 (1896), 979.
[153]   L. Wolf, *Life of the first Marquess of Ripon* (2 vols, 1921), vol. 2, 211–13; L. Trainor, 'The British
Government and Imperial Economic Unity, 1890–1895', *Historical Journal*, 13 (1970), 68–84.
[154]   Trainor, 'Economic Unity'; *Hansard*, 4th ser., 31, cc. 647, 699, 1357, 7, 8, 11, 19 Mar. 1895.
[155]   Wolf, *Ripon*, vol. 2, 214–17; Brown, *Tariff Reform Movement*, 122.

vised Ripon: '[I]t is contrary, in our opinion, to the commercial interests of this country, that the colonies should impose protective duties; but for political reasons, we acquiesce.'[156]

Ripon's imperial policy was therefore not simply that of an antediluvian free trader,[157] but represented a *via media* acceptable both to the 'biographer of Cobden' to whom he appealed, and to the younger Liberals; few of the most ardent Liberal imperialists, save perhaps Buxton, were ready to endorse more ambitious schemes for commercial union.[158] Nor was Ripon's solution, recognizing colonial fiscal autonomy, but falling well short of any encouragement for preference, unattractive to expert and public opinion. For example, leading economists, while more favourable to empire than in the past, still remained generally suspicious of preference as an economic principle, despite the growing claims of the more historically-minded.[159] In the provinces, Birmingham and Sheffield remained isolated outposts of imperial preference and commercial retaliation, but the City of London's successor to the IFL, the British Empire League set up in 1896, aimed to promote trade through periodic meetings concerning communications and copyright, while also joining in the demand for the abrogation of the 1860s treaties. It remained suspect to some[160] but as the brainchild of the free trader Sir John Lubbock, it resisted the cries of the UETL, while acting as an influential conduit for City opinion and for colonial sentiment through its associated bodies. Within the Civil Service, the advice of Giffen remained the test of rectitude, with the Treasury's 'Gladstonian garrison' (the phrase was Salisbury's) intact, and even in the Colonial Office younger protectionists such as Lucas were still held in their leashes by the stoutly orthodox Meade and Round.[161]

The advent to office of Chamberlain in 1895 confronted both the public and the official mind with a different conception of political economy and an alternative prescription for empire.[162] Chamberlain's first public references to an imperial *Zollverein* were vague, linking free trade within the empire to duties against foreign countries as a 'proper subject for discussion',[163] but to insiders he announced his

---

[156]   Quoted in Trainor, 'Economic Unity', 81; see, too, R. A. M. Shields, 'Imperial Policy and the Ripon Circular of 1895', *Canadian Historical Review*, 47 (1966), 119–35.

[157]   As by E. Porritt, *Fiscal and Diplomatic Freedom of the British Overseas Dominions* (Oxford, 1922), 196.

[158]   Matthew, *Liberal Imperialists*, 164–6.

[159]   J. C. Wood, *British Economists and the Empire* (Beckenham, 1983).

[160]   See, for example, Herschell to Lubbock, 29 Aug. 1896, Avebury Papers, Add. MS 49662.

[161]   R. V. Kubicek, *The Administration of Imperialism: Joseph Chamberlain at the Colonial Office* (Durham, NC, 1969), esp. 17–18, 37–41. Herbert, Permanent Under-Secretary, 1871–92 and 1900, had also favoured protection: Trainor, *British Imperialism*, 110.

[162]   Meade thus immediately noted of his new chief, '. . . he seemed to have forgotten the good free trade principles that Farrer and Giffen instilled into him at the Board of Trade', Trainor, *British Imperialism*, 145.

[163]   Canada Club, 23 Mar. 1896; see, too, speech on 9 June 1896; C. W. Boyd (ed.), *Mr Chamberlain's Speeches* (vol. 1, 1914), 365–72.

interest in preference immediately, and hints were sufficient for Sir Thomas Farrer to launch a strong attack on the 'neo-protectionist' ideas of his former political chief at the Board of Trade.[164] Chamberlain and Salisbury were also prepared to meet the demand of the colonies, reiterated at the Colonial Conference of 1897, and of the imperial pressure groups, for the abrogation of the 1860s treaties, a clear departure from Liberal policy in 1894, from Conservative policy in 1892, and from the old Cobdenite ideal. Even so, this volte-face was not a course of which dogmatic free traders, never reconciled to those treaties, disapproved. Giffen, for example, was unconcerned by the prospect of their abrogation, advising the Cabinet in June 1897: 'Our business with the chief countries of the world will be regulated not by treaties but by the comity of nations concerned—and on broad grounds this is no terrible result to look forward to.'[165]

This abrogation of the treaties was also claimed as a victory by Vincent's UETL, with this cutting-away of a central pillar of the old Cobden system presented as a quid pro quo for Canada's unilateral granting of preference to Great Britain in April 1897. The strength of Canadian preference, drummed up by imperial enthusiasts such as George Parkin, was in Britain greeted more as a welcome Canadian step towards free trade and away from reciprocity with the United States, than as a wider spur to an imperial economic union.[166] Hence, the Colonial Conference of 1897 failed either to evoke any enthusiasm for political consolidation, or to make any headway towards an imperial *Zollverein*.[167] After 1897, with this deflation of fiscal/commercial federation, Chamberlain's main concern, as we have seen, reverted to the West Indies and his policy of 'constructive imperialism'.[168] Departmental opinion outside the Colonial Office still strongly opposed preference, as became doubly clear in 1899 with regard to the suggestion of the remission, in the Australian colonies' favour, of increased wine duties in return for reciprocal concessions.[169] This smacked to the Board of Trade of a form of tariff-bargaining, which it saw as the 'most important change in our trade policy since Sir Robert Peel's Tariff Reforms', one that would open 'the door to the

---

[164]   D. Brooks (ed.), *The Destruction of Lord Rosebery: From the Diary of Sir Edward Hamilton, 1894–1895* (1986), 264–5 [3 July 1895]; cf. Kubicek, *Colonial Office*, 155 [5 July]; Farrer, *The Neo-Protection Scheme of the Rt. Hon. Joseph Chamberlain* (Cobden Club leaflet 105, July 1896); see, too, *Australian Opinion on Mr Chamberlain's Scheme of British and Colonial Protection against Foreign Trade* (Cobden Club leaflet 107, July 1896).

[165]   Salisbury to Lascelles, 28 July 1897 in *BDFA Pt. I, ser. F*, vol. 18 Germany, doc. 329; Giffen, 'Memo. on terminating the Belgian and German Commercial Treaties', 4 June 1897, CAB 37/44/26. Earlier, Farrer had considered the treaties, which he had helped draft, contrary to colonial freedom, CCM, 27 June 1891; above, 101, 180.

[166]   *The Economist*, 24 July 1897, 1058–9; Smith, 'British Nationalism' 220; see, too, Cain and Hopkins, *British Imperialism*, vol. 1, 269. For the earlier movement for commercial union between the United States and Canada, see Brown, *Tariff Reform Movement*, 102–5; E. Wallace, *Goldwin Smith: Victorian Liberal* (Toronto, 1957), 267–77.

[167]   Kendle, *Colonial Conferences*, 30–2.

[168]   S. B. Saul, 'Constructive Imperialism', *Journal of Economic History*, 17 (1957), 173–92.

[169]   Mallet, *British Budgets*, 141.

introduction of a general system of preferential treatment of colonial produce within a short space of time'.[170] The Treasury was no less hostile, and this proposal was dropped.[171]

The debate over imperial preference and the British *Zollverein*, temporarily overshadowed by the Boer War, was vigorously revived with the approach of the Colonial Conference of 1902. The reimposition of the corn duty in 1901 as a wartime fiscal expedient acquired a powerful preferential twist, with the demand that Canada and other colonies should be exempt from the duty. This now gave a practical cast to decades of theoretical discussion of an imperial *Zollverein*.[172] The expectation of the preferential remission of the corn duty set the tone for the Colonial Conference of 1902, although the hopes of the UETL were doomed to disappointment. For Britain was by no means ready to remit the corn duty without a reciprocal reduction of colonial tariffs. Chamberlain himself was constrained from moving far beyond his own official policy ideal of free trade within the empire.[173] In fact, the single most decisive result of the Conference was to underline the colonies' attachment to high tariffs and protection, so ending the long-cherished belief that the colonies, above all Canada and the recently formed Australian federation, were prepared to work towards intra-imperial free trade. This notion of an imperial *Zollverein*—that is, of free trade within the empire—was finally shown to be unrealistic, every bit as Utopian as the idea of imperial federation in the 1880s or of a tariff-free Europe in the 1860s. Its impossibility was clearly marked out by the political dynamics of the colonies of white settlement, which left open only small hope that their tariffs might offer substantial change in a free trade direction.[174] Thus, in Canada, even the policy of preference was by 1902 advocated largely in the belief that it would not succeed.[175] In Australia the slim prospect of freer trade had receded even further after the protectionist victory in the first Australian federal election of 1901, and the subsequent budget, which free traders, despite an energetic campaign, were unable to modify in essence as opposed to detail.[176] Arguably, Chamberlain's projected imperial *Zollverein* had already been fatally flawed in

[170] A. E. Bateman, 'Wine Duties', 29 Apr. 1899, CAB/37/49/27.

[171] Kubicek, *Colonial Office*, 159–60.

[172] e.g. UETL, leaflets, 1901–2, collection in BLPES. The Canadian dimension in tariff reform is well brought out in R. Quinault, 'Joseph Chamberlain: A Reassessment' in T. R. Gourvish and A. O'Day (eds.), *Later Victorian Britain 1867–1900* (1988), 85–8.

[173] Kubicek, *Colonial Office*, 162–4; Amery, *Chamberlain*, vol. 5, ch. 94; 'Preferential trade arrangements with the Colonies', June 1902, G. W. Balfour, CAB 37/62/120.

[174] W. K. Hancock, *Survey of British Commonwealth Affairs. Vol. II Problems of Economic Policy, 1918–1939 Part I* (Oxford, 1940), 83–96, a far more wide-ranging survey than its chronological limits suggest.

[175] J. A. Colvin, 'Sir Wilfrid Laurier and the British Preferential Tariff System', *Canadian Historical Association Report* (1955), 13–23.

[176] E. Pulsford to Sir Josiah Symon, 14 Mar. 1902, G. Reid to Symon 14 Apr. 1902, Symon papers, 10/141 and 10/142, National Library of Australia; R. E. O'Connor (2 June 1902), A. Deakin (3 June), A. Downer (3 June) to Sir E. Barton, Barton Papers, MS 51/990a, 991, 992a, National Library of Australia.

Australian and Canadian politics before tariff reform itself was launched in Britain in May 1903.

The unreadiness of the colonies to reduce their own protective tariffs drove Chamberlain and the Conservative Party firmly towards preference combined with protection, the fourth and most revolutionary of the four models of imperial economic unity. Thus, before his departure for South Africa in November 1902, Chamberlain had secured Cabinet approval for the prospective remission of the corn duty in favour of the colonies.[177] This represented an important turning-point for Chamberlain—the abandonment of the ideal of a free trade empire and the promotion of the cause simply of imperial preference. Yet his ability to promote this ideal had itself been weakened by the suspicions aroused by the *Zollverein* even among those Liberals and Conservatives most sympathetic to the cause of empire.[178] In addition, the debate over the *Zollverein* had encouraged a flood of statistics which had analysed in detail the direction of British trade, and had proved, to the satisfaction of the official mind at least, the lack of economic advantages in imperial preference.[179] These were weighty disadvantages in any campaign to re-export the 'imperial project' back to the centre of British politics.

The Boer War and the 'Shade of Cobden', 1896–1903

The growing pervasiveness of empire in later-Victorian Britain challenged, but did not obliterate the wider demands of British commerce and the liberal international order. East Asia, for example, became a growing concern of policy-makers in the late 1880s and 1890s. Thus, in Japan the 1858 'Unequal' Treaty was replaced in 1894 by unconditional most-favoured nation treatment, with a conventional tariff on British goods lower than the general one. This successfully secured British commercial interests in Japan, and paved the way for harmonious diplomatic relations culminating in the Anglo-Japanese Alliance of 1902.[180] Far more contentious was the attempt to defend the 'open door' in China after 1895, for however desirable in principle, defending such a policy seemed more likely to lead to war. In growing sympathy with Cobdenite ideas, J. A. Hobson assailed the absurdity of defending free trade by force in China. More equivocally, the Cobden Club,

---

[177]   R. A. Rempel, *Unionists Divided* (Newton Abbot, 1972), 23–4; Sykes, *Tariff Reform*, 52.

[178]   Matthew, *Liberal Imperialists*, 165–8; Churchill reported his 'instinct profoundly against the *Zollverein*' to Strachey, 23 May 1902, Strachey Papers, 4/10/1.

[179]   This was throughout the position of the government's economic advisers. In retirement, Giffen, one of the leading statistical bastions of the free trade case, supported a *Zollverein* only on grounds of political, not of economic advantage. For popular consumption, L. Chiozza-Money, future 'new Liberal' MP, compiled an effective anti-Chamberlainite digest in *British Trade and the Zollverein Issue* (1902). As Platt (*Mickey Mouse Numbers*, 29) points out, since the fair/free trade debate generated many of these statistics and the way in which they were compiled, their conclusions may be questioned. See, too, the detailed studies of J. W. Root, *Tariffs and Trade* (Liverpool, 1897), *The Trade Relations of the British Empire* (Liverpool, 1903), and *Colonial Tariffs* (Liverpool, 1906).

[180]   I. H. Nish, *The Anglo-Japanese Alliance: the Diplomacy of Two Island Powers, 1894–1907* (1966), 10; Pigman, 'Hegemony and Free Trade Policy', 237–59.

obliged under the growing pressure of imperial confrontations to reassess its recent indifference to foreign affairs, upheld the duty of Britain to maintain trading rights in countries annexed by others, while showing that its own interests in 'derelict' [*sic*] countries was simply commercial. Ultimately, with war and annexation avoided, and the open door to a considerable extent preserved, the Mackay Treaty of 1902 offered some solace to British merchants, without unduly violating the Cobdenite conscience, still exercised by memories of the *Arrow* incident of 1857.[181]

Echoes of the 1850s were also revived in the growing tension between France and Britain, culminating at Fashoda in 1898, but which also encouraged attempts to rebuild an Anglo-French entente, signalled by the activities of men such as Sir Thomas Barclay, a self-styled 'disciple of Cobden', and Sir William Holland, a Manchester cotton spinner and commercial politician.[182] The Board of Trade also showed a renewed interest in commercial negotiations, under the influence of Hubert Llewellyn Smith.[183] In particular, as Germany reordered her commercial relations with Europe, Britain engaged in lengthy, if abortive, negotiations for an Anglo-German commercial treaty between 1903 and 1905, still seeking a firm basis for trade relations following the abrogation of the 1865 Treaty.[184] Encouragingly for the Cobdenites, free trade was promoted in Germany by left-wing Liberals such as Barth and Brentano, while Cobden's internationalist ideas have been identified as a strong influence on the revisionist socialism of Bernstein.[185] Intriguingly, at the other end of the European political spectrum, the Russian Emperor's interest in disarmament, if scarcely a direct exposition of Cobden's teaching, reflected the revival of the Cobdenite strand of pacifist ideas.[186]

In Britain, this recrudescence of old Cobdenite ideas had been largely provoked by the rising tide of military expenditure in the 1890s. Cobdenite analysis formed the stock-in-trade of the Increased Armaments Protest Committee, whose secretary G. H. Perris was later to become the Cobden Club's secretary, and of the

---

[181] J. A. Hobson, 'Free Trade and Foreign Policy', *Contemporary Review*, 74 (Aug. 1898), 167–80; Cobden Club, *Memorandum . . . on Future Policy* (n.d., 1898); 'Commercial Negotiations with China', July 1902, CAB 37/62/123–4.

[182] T. Barclay, *Thirty Years: Anglo-French Reminiscences (1876–1906)* (1914), 226–9; 'Sir William Holland', *DBB*, vol. 3, 303–7.

[183] For some of these changes, see Platt, *Finance, Trade*, 112–13, 378.

[184] See, e.g., 'Questions in the Commercial Department, Nov. 1900, FO 881/7426; *BDFA* Pt. I, ser. F, vol. 19 Germany, 1898–1907, var. docs.; further correspondence respecting commercial negotiations with Germany and Belgium, Mar.–Dec. 1903, FO 425/260. For Germany's new commercial policy, see K. D. Barkin, *The Controversy Over German Industrialization, 1890–1902* (Chicago, 1970), esp. 247 ff; Ashley, *Tariff History*, 77 ff.

[185] T. Barth in *Richard Cobden and the Jubilee of Free Trade* (1896), 129–64; J. J. Sheehan, *The Career of Lujo Brentano* (Chicago, 1966), esp. 124–33; for Cobdenism in the thought of E. Bernstein, see R. A. Fletcher, 'British Radicalism and German Revisionism: The Case of Eduard Bernstein', *International History Review*, 4 (1982), 339–70, esp. 353 n. 83; id., 'Cobden as Educator: The Free Trade Internationalism of Eduard Bernstein, 1899–1914', *American Historical Review*, 88 (1983), 561–78.

[186] G. J. Shaw-Lefevre, *The Shade of Cobden* (1899), 105–6; S. E. Cooper, *Patriotic Pacifism: Waging War on War in Europe, 1815–1914* (New York, 1991), 97–101, 221–2. See, too, the multi-lingual journal, *Cosmopolis*, 1896–7, with its attention to repeal of the Corn Laws, peace, and progress.

League against Aggression and Militarism.[187] Such views retained their appeal for
a younger generation, as can be seen, for example, in *Essays in Liberalism by Six
Oxford Men* (1897), in which F. W. Hirst defended an individualist social philosophy, and J. S. Phillimore vindicated a Cobdenite foreign policy.[188] By 1899 the
conduct of British foreign policy increasingly evoked the memory of Palmerstonian
panics and the 'shade of Cobden' against them. Shaw-Lefevre's book of this title
was the work of an old advocate of arbitration and public economy in the Cobden–
Gladstone tradition.[189] The Boer War itself forced the Cobden Club on to the
defensive, with the paramount need to defend fiscal orthodoxy pre-empting a
possibly divisive stance on opposition to the war.[190] Of course, this did not prevent
the pro-Boer stance of many free traders, including Jane Cobden-Unwin, the
suffragist wife of the publisher, and Club official Thomas Fisher-Unwin. The
Conciliation Committee of 1900, for example, could sport two Brights and four
Cobdens among its members. The Boer War therefore did much to revivify
Cobdenite ideas as part of the broader Radical analysis of the political and economic
ramifications of military expenditure and imperial aggrandisement. But this analysis, which bore with particular effect on fiscal policy and the dynamics of the 'new
imperialism', also prompted the transcendence of the old Liberalism and helped act
as the midwife of the new.

The fiscal implications of the Boer War were of paramount importance in the
evolution of the twentieth-century British State. As recent historians have shown,
the war made evident the extent to which government expenditure in the late-
Victorian period was running beyond the existing taxation resources, posing both
a severe short-term problem of war finance, and the longer-term one of discovering
new engines of taxation.[191] Already in the late 1880s Goschen, faced by the seeming
inelasticity of revenue on consumption goods and growing demands for state
expenditure, had questioned the viability of the Peelite–Gladstonian fiscal model of
a few, highly productive sources of revenue, and had foreshadowed the necessity of
new sources of taxation.[192] This need only became urgent in 1899, encouraging the
Board of Customs to recommend a registration duty on all food imports, while in

---

[187]   F. W. Hirst, *In the Golden Days* (1947), 199 ff.; see, e.g., *Does Trade Follow the Flag*, I.A.P.C. 6
(1896); *Empire, Trade and Armaments: An Exposure* (1896); *The Truth about the Natives*, L.A.A.M.
(1900).

[188]   I draw here on P. F. Clarke, *Liberals and Social Democrats* (Cambridge, 1978), 75–6. Yet after
1900 Phillimore became active as a Liberal imperialist in the West of Scotland, *DNB*.

[189]   Originally entitled 'Cobden and After': Shaw-Lefevre to T. Fisher-Unwin, 28 Mar 1899, CP
981, WSRO. Lefevre's Cobdenite traits are naturally well brought out by Hirst's entry in *DNB*. See,
too, F. M. G. Willson, *A Strong Supporting Cast: The Shaw Lefevres 1789–1936* (1993), esp. 177–8,
324–5.

[190]   This seems to have been the official line under the new chairman, Welby. See Welby to Jane
Cobden-Unwin, 26 June 1902, CP 1162, WSRO. Cobden Club leaflets ignored the war.

[191]   A. Friedberg, *The Weary Titan: Britain and the Experience of Relative Decline, 1895–1905*
(Princeton, 1988), ch. 3.

[192]   Mallet, *British Budgets*, 25–6, 29–31 (1889 budget); see, too, E. W. Hamilton, 'Some Remarks on
Public Finance', 24 July 1895, CAB 37/39/38.

1901 it singled out duties on corn and meat as 'great in point of elasticity and potency', a tempting lever to raise millions for the defence of empire, the development of resources, and to remedy social ills.[193] With this clear threat to the primacy of free imports since 1846, the central issue of direct versus indirect taxation became insistent. Leading free traders, while keen to decry extravagance as the source of an excessive national debt and of budgetary problems, now consistently upheld the desirability of increased direct taxes, rather than increased taxes on working-class consumption.[194] This theme had constantly underpinned the free trade campaigns against both countervailing duties and the imperial *Zollverein*, and had also increasingly led free traders to the advocacy of new direct sources of revenue, whether increased death duties or the taxation of ground values.[195] In effect, at this point, the free traders were prepared to sever the Gladstonian link between tax minimalism and free trade, accepting that increased direct taxation was the necessary price for the retention of free trade, whose historical basis had been its opposition to 'food taxes'. This revival of the fiscal debate was therefore central to the evolution of Liberal financial policy after 1899, culminating in the 'people's budget' of 1909, itself the lineal descendant of Cobden's 'national budget' of 1849.[196] But, first, the free traders turned to confront the immediate consequences of wartime finance.

The Boer War, acting as the mother of fiscal re-invention, had spawned a series of expedients which posed an obvious and cumulative threat to fiscal orthodoxy. First, the budget of 1901 saw, as we have noted, the return of sugar duties for the first time since 1874. This provided not only the basis for the Sugar Convention of 1902, but the duties themselves were widely attacked for their regressive character, for sugar, it was claimed, was now as vital an ingredient in the working-class diet as bread had been in the 1840s.[197] The 'free breakfast table', that ideal of working-class Liberalism since the 1860s, was once more under attack, but rallying to its defence now were not only the old forces of Liberalism, but the new ones of the Independent Labour Party (ILP).[198] The second unorthodox ingredient in Hicks Beach's 1901 budget was the reintroduction of the coal export duty, abolished by Peel in

---

[193] See esp. CAB 37/50/51, 'An Uniform Registration Toll' [15 Aug. 1899]; 55, 'Meat duties' [22 Aug. 1899]; 59, 'Corn duties' [30 Aug. 1899]; CAB 37/58/93 'Extension of the basis of indirect taxation', 7, 16 Oct. 1901.

[194] This had been constantly urged by 'free breakfast table' men such as J. A. Picton: e.g. Mallet, *British Budgets*, 31; *How to increase the public revenue. Memorandum by the committee of the Cobden Club* (Mar. 1902).

[195] CCM, *passim*; this theme had been taken up by new Cobdenite recruits, including Asquith, Fletcher Moulton, and Murray MacDonald; H. Cox, *The Taxation of Commodities* (Cobden Club, 1899).

[196] H. V. Emy, 'The Impact of Financial Policy on English Party Politics before 1914', *Historical Journal*, 15 (1972), 103–31; A. Offer, *Property and Politics, 1870–1914* (Cambridge, 1981), 363; J. Morley, *The Life of Richard Cobden* (2 vols, 1881), vol. 2, 33–4.

[197] Above, 211.

[198] Cobden Club leaflets, seriatim; K. Hardie, *Hansard*, 4th ser., 92 c. 734, 18 Apr. 1901. Nevertheless, the political and patriotic context of war taxation made public opposition difficult. Thus, Welby reported 'the Government are gratified with the acquiescence of the working man in the Sugar Tax. Are

1845. At a time of growing industrial discontent in the coalfields, this was probably the single most effective means of reinvigorating the alliance between aristocratic landlords, capitalist mineowners, and the industrial working class, who now joined forces to oppose the departure of the state from its position of neutrality with regard to the operation of the economy.[199] Third, and most controversially, the corn duty, abolished in 1869, was reimposed as purportedly the single most profitable expedient left in the government's fiscal armoury.[200] This was not only, as we have seen, a stimulus to imperial preference, but reintroduced the rhetoric of 'food taxes' and protection into the forefront of political debate.[201] As free traders had persistently warned during the budget debates, fiscal heterodoxy would end in a vital challenge to Britain's sixty years of free trade policy.

Such a challenge was also detected in the wider political effects of the Boer War, as public extravagance, military power, and irresponsible governance threatened to subvert the British State. For, as a number of historians have shown, there emerged from the war a powerful new understanding of the dynamics of imperialism.[202] Outstandingly, J. A. Hobson combined his own analysis of the economics of empire with a Cobdenite reappraisal of foreign policy-making. He had already built up his view of the irrationality of empire for the nation as a whole, but, as Clarke and others have shown, for Cobden's analysis of the courts, the Cabinet, the Army, and the aristocracy as the forces behind Palmerstonian expansionism, Hobson substituted a new set of parasites: the financiers, a small oligarchy of mine-owners and speculators. This sinister group usurped the power of the state to further its own ends to the detriment of the nation, whose 'true' interest in domestic reform was hidden by a 'kept press' and the jingoism of the crowds. It was this politico-economic combination that Hobson believed now imminently threatened free trade itself. For not only were the 'trading classes', the former stalwarts of free trade, effectively organized to use their influence to ensure diplomatic and military pressure to open new markets, but annexation would be accompanied by imperial preference. Thus, as free trade lost its hold on the traders and financiers, it would be abandoned for 'the political force of the commercial interests [which] must dominate her politics'.[203] The lesson that Hobson drew was that if the welfare of the

they or we in a fool's paradise? I doubt our being able to get up an effective mass meeting.' Welby to Fisher Unwin, 5 May 1901, CP 1124, WSRO.

[199] Singularly, George Harwood among the Liberals supported this duty. But there seems much evidence against Friedberg's contention that both sugar and coal duties 'faced little serious challenge'. This was true within Parliament during wartime, but not outside the Chamber. Friedberg, *Weary Titan*, 109.

[200] Hamilton Diary, 6 Feb., 20 Apr. 1902, Add. MS 48679; Friedberg, *Weary Titan*, 116.

[201] See Ch. 7 below.

[202] B. Porter, *Critics of Empire: British Radical Attitudes to Colonialism in Africa, 1895–1914* (1968); Clarke, *Liberals and Social Democrats*; P. J. Cain, 'J. A. Hobson, Cobdenism, and the Radical Theory of Economic Imperialism', *Economic History Review*, 2nd ser., 31 (1978), 565–84; P. F. Clarke, 'Hobson, Free Trade, and Imperialism' and P. J. Cain, 'Hobson's Developing Theory of Imperialism', *EcHR*, 2nd ser., 34 (1981), 308–16.

[203] J. A. Hobson, 'The Approaching Abandonment of Free Trade', *Fortnightly Review*, 71 (1902), 438.

nation, and the very existence of democracy itself were to be secured, 'a new and unexpected rally [be made] for "Manchesterism" '.[204] This analysis of the war, of economic interest, and the state was one that put free trade at the forefront of political conflict, but which realigned the 'old cause' with the policy goals of the New Liberals, a synthesis to which both individualists like Hirst, and progressives of the Rainbow Circle could subscribe.[205] As Clarke has shown, even Hirst's writings on the war, especially the essay in *Liberalism and Empire* (1900), shared Hobson's views on financial imperialism, and were far less anti-collectivist than three years earlier. At the same time, other wartime works, for example *The Heart of the Empire* edited by Charles Masterman, redirected young Liberals towards the necessity of state intervention in order to solve the 'problems of modern city life'.[206]

But, if some individualists moved towards collectivism, the predominant movement was of progressives moving back towards the 'Manchesterism' they had recently aspired to transcend. Ironically, progressives whose stance and creed had emerged from an analysis of the deficiencies of the Manchester School, had by 1902 reaffirmed its central tenet.[207] Not only did intellectuals such as Wallas abandon the Fabians over the issue of protection, but New Liberals such as L. T. Hobhouse, and ILPers, including Ramsay MacDonald, rediscovered the necessity of the link between free trade and democracy, which continental socialists had long appreciated.[208] Free trade now lay at the heart of the progressive vision, for it alone presaged the raising of revenue for social reform from direct taxation, a premiss that individualists such as Hirst and Cox shared. This, in turn, guaranteed the autonomy of the state from the power of organized capital, and made possible a foreign policy in which truly national or even international considerations would be brought to bear. This was the moral case for free trade that attracted *déclassé* intellectuals like Bertrand Russell, as well as the democratic masses to whom Hobson rather pessimistically looked in 1902 for effective defence against the 'possessing classes'.[209]

Hobson's pessimism in 1902 was in part based on his belief that the Liberals themselves would renege on free trade. He feared that alliance of imperialists of both parties to which other staunch free traders, such as the Treasury official Hamilton, looked for the dynamic reconstruction of English politics.[210] Here,

---

[204] Ibid. 444.

[205] Blaazer, *Popular Front*, 61, 72 ff.

[206] Clarke, *Liberals and Social Democrats*, 78; *The Heart of the Empire*, 1901 (published by Fisher Unwin; reprinted, Brighton, 1973, ed. B. B. Gilbert).

[207] Clarke, *Liberals and Social Democrats* brings out this revaluation of old Liberalism well, but, oddly, without emphasizing the centrality of free trade, whose merits were now freshly appreciated by progressives, e.g., Freeden (ed.), *Rainbow Circle*, 74, 75, 108, 109, 111.

[208] Above, 223. For Hobhouse's new appreciation of Cobden's ideas, see *Democracy and Reaction* (1904), chs. 1, 7, and 9. In *Liberalism* (1911) Hobhouse would reiterate that 'we want to learn our supreme lessons from the school of Cobden . . . a problem of realizing liberty' (249).

[209] Below, 266; Hobson, 'Abandonment of Free Trade', *passim*, esp. 444.

[210] Hamilton Diary, 10 June 1902, 30 Aug. 1902, Add. MS 49679 and 48680; Hamilton to Rosebery, 11 June 1903, Rosebery Papers, 10033, National Library of Scotland; Matthew, *Liberal Imperialists*, 166.

Hobson misjudged the Liberal imperialists, for, however much they seemed at times to question free trade, their unorthodoxy rarely extended as far as tariff reform. On the contrary, their concern with national efficiency actually provided new tools with which to defend free trade.[211] For they had addressed the same problems of economic development and apparent industrial decline for which the tariff reformers have acquired the questionable reputation as 'modernizers'.[212] The Liberal League pamphlets of 1902 had in particular addressed the issues of efficiency and education, which now became crucial elements in the Liberal case for free trade. Haldane, for example, concluded by 1902 that the German model of the *Zollverein* was inapplicable to the British Empire, but that the German concern with education was not. Haldane thus recalled: '[W]hat was threatening our industrial position was want of science among our manufacturers . . . the campaign in which we were engaged against the policy of Protection . . . was our opportunity for pressing the countercase for science and organisation.'[213] This case was, of course, by no means new, having been well made by Liberal imperialists—for example, Playfair—in the 1880s, but in the early twentieth century it bore restatement, and demonstration. It led, for example, to the strong Liberal imperial interest in the foundation of Imperial College in 1903.[214] Here was no complete recipe for economic revival, but at least some sign that the problem needed still to be addressed within a free trade framework, that the state, even for the free trader, might have a part to play, and that tariff reform was as likely to frustrate economic modernization as it was to undermine a healthy democracy.[215]

By 1903, therefore, it is clear that one part of both the socialist and the nascent tariff reform cases against free trade, its supposed and outdated adherence to a philosophy of individualism and *laissez-faire*, was fundamentally adrift. For, as Hobson noted, '[T]he former intellectual apprehension of Free Trade as an integral portion of the *laissez-faire* principle of government now remains little more than a discredited gospel of a doctrinaire remnant.'[216] The ideology of free trade had not only survived the successive attacks of fair traders, foreigners, faddists, and federationists, but had emerged reinvigorated from the Boer War through its interlocking with the New Liberal ideology of social reform. This identification of free trade with social reform, which appeared so clearly in the policies of the Liberal governments after 1905, however, had its origins in the early 1880s, and had been nurtured by the years of opposition to Conservative government and the flowering

---

[211] Matthew, *Liberal Imperialists*, esp. 224 ff.

[212] e.g., S. Newton and D. Porter, *Modernization Frustrated: The Politics of Industrial Decline in Britain since 1900* (1988).

[213] *Richard Burdon Haldane: an Autobiography* (1929), 151–2.

[214] W. Page (ed.), *Commerce and Industry: A Historical Review* (1919), 337.

[215] J. A. Spender, 'Free Trade and its Fruits', *Fortnightly Review*, 74 (Sept. 1903), 410–11; for a useful evaluation, see P. Alter, *The Reluctant Patron; Science and the State in Britain, 1850–1920* (Deddington, 1987), esp. 138–72.

[216] Hobson, 'Abandonment of Free Trade', 434.

of economic heterodoxy. More immediately, free trade by 1903 had been reassessed as part of a new intellectual synthesis attractive to both pro-Boers and Liberal imperialists. Ideologically, it was not commended as a return to the 1840s, but had been re-evaluated as central to economic progress, political democracy, and social welfare. The rallying of the Liberal Party to free trade after 1903 may therefore appear as the pragmatic rejoining of divided factions around a threatened Gladstonian tribal god,[217] but it had been spurred by premises fundamentally different from the outmoded Ricardian and evangelical arguments by which the nation had been drawn to the free trade cause in the 1840s.[218] Whether this new platform would successfully combat the forces of protectionism, jingoism, and the press seemed doubtful to Hobson in 1902. The next chapter will reveal the needlessness of his fears.

---

[217] See, for example, Clarke *Lancashire and New Liberalism*, 355–7, for an interpretation of the 1906 election in this direction.

[218] The Ricardian arguments were of course less outmoded, for they still influenced the single taxers. But the economic arguments of the new Liberals concerned more the notion of the natural equality of competitors and the 'mythical' freedom of contract. Freeden, *New Liberalism*, 44–5; thus Wise wrote that he had read no work of economics since 1870 which defended freedom of contract. While, therefore, the ideology of free trade was sustained by the neo-classical analysis of international trade, it had abandoned its old theories of distribution (including free exchange and individual ownership).

7

Cobden Redivivus: Free Trade and the Edwardians, 1903–1906

> In the days of Protection, producers were more powerful than consumers. Nowadays consumers are the more powerful and will remain so.
>
> Hamilton Diary, 20 Apr. 1902, Add. MS 48679.

> The great national 'match' between free traders and tariff reformers which Chamberlain had started in 1903 . . . was the more exciting because everyone took part in it, both as spectator and a player. Nobody wished or was able to think of anything else.
>
> Halévy, *History of the English People*, Epilogue, III, 206.

THE immanent threat to free trade which Hobson had discerned within the Boer War took overt political shape in the campaign for tariff reform launched by Chamberlain's Birmingham Town Hall speech of 15 May 1903. Even if this was merely a formal declaration, long after the initial skirmishes,[1] it opened the floodgates to a huge propaganda war unseen in Britain since 1886, and, arguably, since the 1840s.[2] Chamberlain and his allies were now to conduct a vigorous and vociferous war against Cobdenism, a loyalty that they believed had vitally impaired Britain's power and welfare. By contrast, Chamberlain, 'the tariff revolutionist', now put before his Birmingham audience—and would elaborate to the nation and the empire over the coming years—a policy that linked economic revival, social welfare, and imperial unity.[3] Tariffs imposed on selected imports promised to raise revenue for old age pensions, to encourage economic growth by keeping out manufactured imports, and to cement the empire together by the ties of preferential trade. These ingredients, in varying recipes, were increasingly to win over the Conservative Party and were to be widely propagated not only by Unionist politicians, but by

[1] Chamberlain, for example, had pointed to tariffs as the issue for the future at a dinner of Tory 'coming men' in 1902, W. Churchill, *My Early Life* (1930 edn.), 387.
[2] Hamilton Diary, 16 May 1903, on Chamberlain's speech as 'big with the fate of parties and perhaps of the Empire', Add. MS 48680.
[3] The phrase is that of Russell Rea, *Free Trade in Being* (1908), 236. For Chamberlain's programme, see, most recently, E. H. H. Green, *The Crisis of Conservatism* (1995), but also B. Semmel, *Imperialism and Social Reform* (1960) and A. J. Marrison, 'The Development of a Tariff Reform Policy during Joseph Chamberlain's First Campaign, May 1903–February 1904', in W. H. Chaloner and B. M. Ratcliffe (eds.), *Trade and Transport: Essays in Economic History in Honour of T. S. Willan* (Manchester, 1977), 214–41.

Chamberlain's creation the Tariff Commission (a body of experts), and by the Tariff Reform League (a body of popularizers). In sum, tariff reform represented not only an attempt to revive Britain as an imperial power, but an attempt by the 'modern' element within the Conservative Party to seize the reins of party power, and, in turn, to extend the popular foundations of Conservatism by rooting it firmly in an appeal to the working classes. This was a comprehensive challenge to the fiscal, moral, and political consensus that had cemented Victorian Britain.[4]

Here, then, lay a far more potent threat to free trade than had been presented by fair trade, bimetallism, sugar bounties, or imperial federation. Chamberlain had opened 'the great inquest' into sixty years of British politics, in which free traders were called upon not simply to restate the shibboleths of the 1840s, but to vindicate their pertinence within a new vision of democracy, welfare, and power.[5] In a very direct way this issue dominated British political life between 1903 and 1906, perhaps stimulating the most extensive popular debate in the history of British politics, with an unstoppable torrent of political information available to the electorate in meetings, speeches, tracts, leaflets, cartoons, and early political propaganda films.[6] The general election of 1906 placed the choice between free trade and tariff reform squarely before the electorate, a relatively mature democracy, called upon to deliver its verdict not only on the past, but on two very different visions of Britain's future. That election, despite its quasi-referendal or plebiscitary status, was not confined to a single issue, with, for example, both Chinese slavery and the Education Act of 1902 of considerable importance.[7] Nor was the electorate fully democratic in a numerical sense, although it has been plausibly argued that this was the first properly organized mass election since the extension of the franchise in 1884.[8] But neither consideration detracts from the vital popular ideological battle fought over free trade and tariff reform in Britain between 1903 and 1906, nor from the stunning Liberal victory, exceeding all forecasts, in winning 400 seats (a net gain of 216), with the Unionists reduced from 402 to 157 MPs, 'the most surprising [result] of any that has taken place since 1832'.[9]

---

[4]　At first this was a 'Chamberlainite' challenge, but by September, with the publication of Balfour's *Insular Free Trade* 'One of the great parties of state [was] committed to the antithesis of the policy on which we have flourished for nearly 60 years'. Hamilton Diary, 16 Sept. 1903, Add. MS 48681.

[5]　A. C. Pigou, *The Great Inquest* (1903); see, too, H. Belloc and G. K. Chesterton, *The Great Inquiry* (1903). According to R. Speaight, *Belloc* (1957), 177, only 35 copies of the latter were sold.

[6]　The Library of Congress in April 1904 produced *A Select List of References to the British Tariff Movement* (Washington) extending to 33 pp.; A. K. Russell, *Liberal Landslide: the General Election of 1906* (Newton Abbot, 1973); P. Adams, 'Tariff Reform and the Working Classes, 1903–6', unpublished M. Litt. thesis, University of Oxford (1982), 266–90; for a good collection of posters, Coll. Misc. 519, BLPES; D. Gifford, *The British Film Catalogue, 1895–1985* (Newton Abbot, 1986), films 00727, 00728, 01193, 01224.

[7]　Russell, *Landslide*, 64–94, 172 ff; S. E. Koss, 'Revival and Revivalism', in A. J. A. Morris (ed.), *Edwardian Radicalism* (1974), 75–96.

[8]　Russell, *Landslide, passim.*

[9]　Ibid. 160–1 for figures and quotation by the President of the Royal Statistical Society. Interestingly, this was Sir R. B. Martin, a leading City tariff reformer.

This ideological battle cannot properly be understood in terms of 'ancients versus moderns', as a contest between an atavistic free trade loyalty opposed to a modern, if politically immature, tariff reform policy.[10] For not only would it be as plausible to see in tariff reform an equal atavism in resurrecting the early nineteenth-century imperial system, but, as we have seen in previous chapters, the arguments on both sides had transcended the older debates conducted between cotton lords and landlords in the 1840s. Nevertheless, the Edwardian debate very deliberately evoked the conflicts of the 1840s, with, on the one side, the charge that Britain was being sacrificed on the altar of outmoded Cobdenite dogma, and, on the other, the invention of the 'hungry forties', and the powerful evocation of the threat of their return.[11] Yet the debate went much further than this, with the free traders called upon not only to look to history for their defence, but to demonstrate the continuing pertinence of their creed for economic prosperity in an era of growing foreign competition, for social welfare in an era of collectivism, and for British power in an increasingly unstable international system. In this context, free trade as a popular ideology revealed its ability to overcome the limits of party and class. Its importance has been strangely neglected, while historians have so repeatedly studied the politics of tariff reform and national efficiency.

The popular politics of free trade, however, should not obscure the continuing presence of important interest groups lurking behind policy debates. The Tariff Reform League has, for example, most often been seen as the voice of the provincial industrialists, the 'producers', erstwhile Anti-Corn Law Leaguers whose successors had taken up the traditional creed of the farmers and landlords.[12] But such producers, it is also commonly asserted, had been previously confined to the margins of British politics, penned back by the subtle operation of the City/Bank/Treasury nexus, and, for some, the power of the City of London remained a vital factor in ensuring British loyalty to free trade, to the disadvantage of industry and the nation.[13] If, in this view, the state has been seen as accessible to vested interests, more recent sociological research has suggested that it was, in fact, the state that, in

---

[10] Cf. M. Bentley, *The Climax of Liberal Politics* (1987), 109; S. Newton and D. Porter, *Modernization Frustrated: The Politics of Industrial Decline in Britain since 1900* (1988), 1–22.

[11] Below, 259; the term 'hungry forties' was coined by Cobden's daughter, Jane Cobden-Unwin in 1904. Its usage became rapid, and it is testament to the enduring success of Edwardian propaganda that even historians of a linguistic turn predate its use, *vide* P. Joyce, *Visions of the People* (1991), 189. The tariff reformers also sought historical support, urging that Britain's industrialization had been achieved under the protectionist policy abandoned in 1846.

[12] Contemporaries immediately made this point, as Hamilton shows; for modern views, see A. J. Marrison, 'Businessmen, Industries, and Tariff Reform in Great Britain, 1903–1930', *Business History*, 25 (1983), 148–78; Green, *Conservatism*, 229–38; P. J. Cain, 'The Economic Philosophy of Constructive Imperialism', in C. Navari (ed.), *British Politics and the Spirit of the Age: Political Concepts in Action* (Keele, 1996), 41–65. Chamberlain self-consciously modelled himself on Cobden as a successful business-politician.

[13] Green, *Conservatism*, 235–41; P. J. Cain and A. G. Hopkins, *British Imperialism* (2 vols, 1993), vol. 1, 214–24; G. Ingham, *Capitalism Divided: The City and Industry in British Social Development* (1984), 152–69.

Britain, as elsewhere in Europe, has manipulated interests behind the policy it favours.[14] In this case, free trade becomes the hallmark of the autonomy of the state, not the badge of its subservience to capitalist power. Yet, as J. A. Hobson urged, it was the very nature of that state which was at issue in the debate over free trade, for the Boer War had embodied the threat of the organized power of financiers and traders to pervert the instruments of the state for their own ends, ends that were now to be advanced by imperial preference and tariffs. The defence of free trade as an economic creed was therefore now indistinguishable from the defence of democracy as a political principle.

Free trade, the City, and industry

Free trade, in much tariff reform rhetoric, was commonly identified with the cause of cosmopolitan finance and the City of London. In this, the tariff reform case shared much in common with those bimetallists who also ascribed Britain's loyalty to the gold standard to the nefarious power of the City's 'gold bugs'. More distantly, this interpretation finds considerable support in those studies of Britain's economic policy that ascribe power to the City of London, and which see in adherence to free trade and the gold standard the most appropriate policy for international finance.[15] On the other hand, the Hobsonian critique of the Boer War and of the forces behind Chamberlain saw in tariff reform—but not in free trade— the threat of monopolistic finance, equally rooted in the City of London and its *rentier* interests.[16] This confusion was rife among contemporaries, with, for example, well-informed observers like Goschen finding the City 'deeply infected with Chamberlainism', while others protested its loyalty to free trade.[17] The most detailed study of City attitudes, commissioned for Chamberlain, predictably found opinions divided, with the leading financiers and importers largely opposed to tariffs, the stockbrokers and shipping interest mostly in favour, and with colonial houses divided.[18] Understandably, with regard both to the City and industry, post-

---

[14]   J. M. Hobson, 'The Tax-Seeking State', unpublished Ph.D. thesis, University of London (1991), 182–278.

[15]   See above, 199 ff.

[16]   See above, 226.

[17]   As Goschen reported to Asquith, 'The man in the street, . . . including the man in the City, is deeply infected with Chamberlainism', 8 Nov. 1903, Asquith Papers, 10, fo. 99, Bodleian Library. According to Hamilton, in 1902 Chamberlain had been 'the idol of the City', receiving its freedom. But by June 1903 he found the City noncommittal. In July he believed Nathaniel de Rothschild, Ernest Cassel ('the ablest man in the City'), and the majority of the City to favour Chamberlain. Diary, 13 Feb. 1902, 19 June, 3, 5 July 1903, Add. MS 48679 and 48681. Hamilton's views are valuable; he was the nexus between the Treasury, the Bank, and the City. For other conflicting reports on City opinion, see Goschen to Strachey, 18 June 1903, Strachey Papers S/7/4/3; L. V. to W. Harcourt, 20 Jan. and 21 Aug. 1904, Harcourt dep. 668.

[18]   W. Mock, *Imperiale Herrschaft und nationales Interesse: 'Constructive Imperialism' oder Freihandel in Gross Britannien vor dem Ersten Weltkrieg* (Stuttgart, 1982), 393–7. For stockbrokers, see, too, Loulou to Sir William Harcourt, 20 Jan. 1904, Harcourt dep. 668. For City accountants, see *The Accountant* (Nov. 1904), 1316, 1400–7, 1464, 1491–1500. For an informed recent discussion, see D. Kynaston, *The City of London, Vol. II: Golden Years, 1890–1914* (1995), 375–85.

modern historians have become wary of linking fiscal views and economic interests.[19]

Discarding such caution, it seems plausible to argue that a restatement of the economic case against tariff reform proved impotent in the face of the strong drift of the City towards Conservatism since the 1880s.[20] Leading City figures, such as Goschen, Rea, Harvey, Schuster, Tritton, Huth Jackson, and Avebury, all rehearsed the classical position on finance, the value of capital exports and services to the economy as a whole, and so forcefully rejected the deeply rooted view of the City as a parasite upon national industry which the Tariff Reform League now exploited, as had both Cobbettites and bimetallists in the past.[21] The City also, as Marrison has shown, conspicuously failed to support either the Tariff Reform Commission, or the Tariff Reform League.[22] On the other hand, the City free traders had little political success in their attempt to revive the Liberal cause in the City of London, with their candidate Felix Schuster soundly beaten against the tariff reform financier Gibbs in January 1906; on Gibbs's resignation, Gibson Bowles was equally convincingly defeated by Balfour in February 1906.[23] At this point, indeed, it seemed that the message from the City to the nation was one distinctly hostile to free trade.[24] More spectacularly, while the Unionist free trader Sir Edward Clarke was returned in January 1906, five months later he was to be unceremoniously driven from his seat by tariff reform pressure, to be replaced by Sir Frederick Banbury.[25] The City continued to act as the venue for important Liberal and Unionist free trade meetings, but, with Balfour and Banbury as its MPs, the City was scarcely a paragon of free trade virtue.[26]

If, therefore, the City of London was politically aligned with tariff reform, it may well be that its elections were not indicative of the City's views *qua* financial power, and that its real influence was exercised informally through the City/Bank/Treas-

[19]   F. Trentmann, 'The Transformation of Fiscal Reform', *Historical Journal*, 39 (1996), 1005–48.
[20]   Y. Cassis, *Les Banquiers de la City à l'époque Edouardienne* (Geneva, 1984), 357–64; Kynaston, *City of London*, vol. 2, 415–16, 501.
[21]   F. Huth Jackson, 'The "Draft on London" and Tariff Reform', *Economic Journal*, 15 (1904); *Journal of the Institute of Bankers'*, 25 (1904), 55–83, et seq.; 'Protection and the Stock Exchange', *New Liberal Review*, 6 (1903), 311–19; R. D. Denman, 'The City and the Tariff Question', *Westminster Gazette* [hereafter *WG*], 23 June 1903.
[22]   Marrison, 'Businessmen'; id., 'British Businessmen and the Scientific Tariff: A Study of Joseph Chamberlain's Tariff Commission, 1903–21', Ph.D. thesis, University of Hull (1980), ch. 3. For a comprehensive study, see A. Marrison, *British Businessmen and Protection 1903–1932* (Oxford, 1996).
[23]   *WG*, 12, 23, 25 June; 15, 23 July 1903; 16 June, 1904; 20 Oct. 1905. Huth Jackson to A. Elliot, 28 Nov. 1903, EP 19493. The free traders had considerable difficulty fielding a candidate, with Schuster arousing some doubts, for 'he looks an alien' as Goschen [*sic*] noted. To Avebury (Sir John Lubbock) 4 July 1905. For a time Curzon was an interesting runner as a cross-party candidate; Avebury to Curzon, 4 July 1905 (copy); B. Stuart, Sir J. H. Puleston to Avebury, 14 and 21 Dec. 1905, Avebury Papers, Add. MS 49672.
[24]   Goschen to Avebury, 19 and 23 Jan. 1906, Avebury Papers, Add. MS 49674.
[25]   R. Rempel, *Unionists Divided* (Newton Abbot, 1972), 171–4; A. Sykes, *Tariff Reform and British Politics, 1903–1913* (Oxford, 1979), 149–50.
[26]   For later attempts to sustain free trade in the City, see below 287.

ury nexus.[27] In this context, we may note that the Governor of the Bank of England strongly put forward free trade views at a Mansion House meeting in June 1904, that the Treasury undoubtedly enjoyed close official and social ties with the City and the Bank, and that the Treasury's orthodoxy on free trade was notorious.[28] So outspoken was its Permanent Secretary Sir Francis Mowatt that he was circumvented by Balfour, while his successors Hamilton and Murray were certainly opposed to tariffs. Nevertheless, their attachment to free trade owed little, if anything, to their affinity with City opinion. Rather, they shared the view often reiterated in the past by Board of Trade officials such as Farrer and Giffen that Britain's wealth and welfare depended upon her foreign trade.[29] This conclusion was vindicated by the official statistics collected by the Unionist government's fiscal inquiry in 1903.[30] Such statistics may in part be regarded as a partisan selection, but they were not out of keeping with the run of data produced and interpreted by non-governmental economists and statisticians such as Bowley.[31] They also accorded with the opinions of academic economists in their famous letter to *The Times* in August 1903, and the advice given to the government by Marshall in the same year.[32] Such expert views added legitimacy to the official case against tariffs,

---

[27] Interestingly, one leading City figure, A. S. Harvey, of Glyn, Mills, had been a Treasury official.

[28] *WG*, 18 June 1904; H. Roseveare, *The Treasury: The Evolution of a British Institution* (1969), 186, 222.

[29] Giffen himself reiterated this conclusion for Chamberlain's benefit in 1903: 'Only a free trade country or rather a free imports country can be the centre of the world's international commerce, as we are, which brings us enormous business and gain . . . I fear you are rather overlooking this aspect of the question.' To Chamberlain, 26 Oct. 1903, Chamberlain Papers, JC 18/18/64.

[30] Hamilton Diary, 30 June 1903, Add. MS 48681; the Treasury favoured inquiry as the opportunity to vindicate free trade. For the resulting statistics, compiled by Llewellyn Smith and Hopwood at the Board of Trade, see *Parl. Papers*, 1903, 67 [Cd. 1761]. Hopwood at the Board of Trade found himself uncomfortably placed between the statistical demands of Chamberlain, Ritchie, and his chief, Gerald Balfour. 'Poor Commercial Department,' he lamented, 'would that Giffen were with us! He would have revelled in this. As he said once, "The debate was very interesting and *all* the arguments were my own." ', Hopwood to G. Balfour, 26 June 1903, Balfour of Whittingehame Papers, M118/4, Scottish Record Office. Balfour, however, pronounced himself 'more than happy' with Hopwood's efforts: to Hopwood, 18 Sept. 1903, Southborough Papers 9, Bodleian Library. Chamberlain's Tariff Reform Commission, under the former director of the LSE Hewins, was in effect a 'Ministry of Commerce' in waiting, reflecting Chamberlain's deeply engrained suspicion of governmental policy-makers. For its workings, see Hewins, *Apologia of an Imperialist* (2 vols, 1929); Marrison, 'Scientific Tariff'. Interestingly, the Foreign Office also produced a survey of tariff wars, whose evidence was equally damning with regard to Balfour's retaliatory ideas: see 'Tariff Wars between certain European States', *Parl. Papers*, 1904, 95 [Cd. 1938].

[31] A. W. Bowley, *A Short Account of England's Foreign Trade in the Nineteenth Century* (1905); G. M. Koot, *English Historical Economics 1870–1926* (Cambridge, 1987), 79; H. O. Meredith to C. P. Trevelyan, 20 Sept. 1903, Trevelyan Papers, CPT 13. See, too, Bowley Papers, Box B, Pt. 2, Coll. Misc. 772, BLPES.

[32] A. W. Coats, 'Political Economy and the Tariff Reform Campaign of 1903', *Journal of Law and Economics*, 11 (1968), 181–229; J. C. Wood, *British Economists and Empire* (Beckenham, 1983), 121–32. Marshall, while forced to rethink many of his earlier assumptions concerning free trade, provided telling arguments against tariff reform in a memorandum for the Chancellor of the Exchequer C. T. Ritchie in 1903. A revised version was first published in 1908 and reprinted in J. M. Keynes (ed.), *Official Papers of Alfred Marshall* (1926).

enabling the Treasury and bureaucracy as a whole to defend their beau ideal, that of the state freed from the pressure of vested interest groups, the Peelite–Gladstonian ideal that had shaped the mid-Victorian generation of civil servants and their successors.[33]

Moreover, while Chamberlain and others were right to detect bureaucratic hostility to tariffs, this was by no means complete. For example, influential civil servants such as Bergne at the Foreign Office, Hopwood at the Board of Trade, and Pittar at the Board of Customs were more openly favourable to fiscal change.[34] Even Hamilton and Murray were professionally ready to implement tariffs, however remote they hoped this possibility would be.[35] Hamilton also worked well with Austen Chamberlain at the Exchequer after 1903, even if he welcomed the latter's difficulties over tobacco and silk duties in the budget of 1904 as a useful cautionary 'taste of the trouble and difficulty in which he will be landed by protectionist concessions'.[36] But most interestingly, despite the omnipotence that is often ascribed to the Treasury, its officials were in fact increasingly conscious of their impotence in the face of their political masters. In the longer run, therefore, they were unlikely to form a more effective bastion against tariffs than they did against equally inimicable policies such as pensions, wage boards, and the budget of 1909.[37] As the 1930s were to show, even a far more rigidly defined 'Treasury view' was no guarantee against its abandonment.[38] The Edwardian Treasury was primarily defending a tradition of bureaucratic autonomy ('the knaveproof state'), as well as a policy it believed had brought prosperity to the nation and people; it was not acting as the rearguard of 'cosmopolitan finance', whose forces increasingly leant away from free trade and towards protection, as the necessary price of avoiding socialism.

Nor does the evidence suggest that in supporting free trade City financiers and the Treasury were separating themselves from the interests of industry. For however self-consciously tariff reformers claimed to represent the producers, the majority of industrialists failed to line up behind their standard. The extent to which businessmen had abandoned economic orthodoxy is open to further investiga-

---

[33]   Intriguingly, in 1898 Hamilton believed that excessive orthodoxy itself threatened the financial system he so admired. To Harcourt, 15 Aug. 1898, Harcourt MSS dep. 66, fos. 127–9. For civil servants and free trade, see above, 206 (Farrer), and below, 262 (Welby).

[34]   For Bergne, see Trentmann, 'Fiscal Reform'; for Hopwood, see e.g. Bryce to Hopwood, 10 Feb. 1904, Southborough Papers 10. Hamilton reported Pittar as 'not too strongly tarred with the free trade brush'. The tobacco duty in Austen Chamberlain's 1904 budget, with its 'whiff of protectionism', had been Pittar's idea. Diary, 7 Apr. 1904, Add. MS 48682.

[35]   Diary, 18 and 30 June 1903 (assuring Chamberlain of support if he won), 14 July, 13 Aug., 23 Sept. 1903; 16 Oct. 1904, Add. MSS 48681, 48682.

[36]   Diary, 5 May 1904. The experience of the Sugar Convention was equally discouraging, Diary, 24 Nov. 1904, Add. MS 48682.

[37]   Reflecting on 40 years in the Treasury, Murray felt '. . . that our influence and effective utility has gone down by about as much as our real capacity has gone up. This is not the day of the Treasury.' Murray to Asquith, 12 Oct. 1907, Asquith Papers 19. Hamilton predicted the ultimate success of protection: Diary, 16 Oct. 1904, Add. MS 48682.

[38]   P. F. Clarke, 'The Treasury's Model', in M. Furner and B. Supple (eds.), *The State and Economic Knowledge* (Cambridge, 1990).

tion—the long tradition of a minority interest in retaliation, was, arguably, amplified in the early twentieth century, and Chambers of Commerce, picking up from the 1880s, were ready to back up demands for a modification of free trade. Yet even at its peak, this movement was never able to alter the policy of the Association of Chambers of Commerce, whose free traders were strong and influential enough to outmanœuvre the tariff reformers.[39] Moreover, as Trentmann has suggested, the ideological variant of fiscal reform pursued by Chamberlain, emphasizing imperial preference rather than retaliation, to some extent turned business opinion back towards free trade.[40] Certainly, whatever arguments were brought to bear by the tariff reformers pleading the cause of 'dying' industries in the face of foreign competition,[41] free traders were able to articulate equally plausible recipes for industrial progress, both within particular industries and for the economy as a whole.[42]

Thus, in many industries, the free trade case was powerfully voiced by representative figures and groups. For example, cotton employers, including many erstwhile bimetallists, joined with operatives in an emphatic free trade declaration in July 1903.[43] The woollen industry, contrary to worsted's flirting with fair trade in the 1880s, was also strongly opposed to tariffs.[44] Shipbuilders, and shipowners, despite some defections, also rallied strongly. For despite the tradition of greater state encouragement for shipping abroad through subsidies and bounties, despite growing fears of American 'combines', and despite the movement for preferential colonial arrangements, British shipping had retained its undoubted international pre-eminence.[45] In other industries that were supposed 'ruined' by tariff reformers,

---

[39] *Chambers of Commerce Journal, 1903–5*, passim. The Association's leading free traders included Lord Avebury, a City banker, and Sir William Holland, a leading cotton spinner.

[40] Trentmann, 'Fiscal Reform'.

[41] Green, *Conservatism*, 223–30; Semmel, *Imperialism and Social Reform*, 87, 94.

[42] See, *inter alia*, H. Cox (ed.), *British Industries under Free Trade* (1903); Swire Smith *et al.*, *Protection and Industry* (1904). Business opinion was of course well represented in the Liberal Party, whose captains of industry orchestrated their own anti-tariff campaign: *WG*, 2 July 1903; below, 247.

[43] (Cotton Employers' Parliamentary Association and United Textile Factory Workers' Association), *The Cotton Trade and Protection. Remarkable Condemnation* (Manchester, 1903). For Robert Barclay, one of the leading bimetallists, see Manchester Chamber of Commerce *Monthly Record*, Feb. 1904, 67–9; he spurned the support given to tariff reform by London financiers ignorant of productive industries. Political support was lent by the Duke of Devonshire: Rawtenstall speech, 12 Nov. 1904 (printed as *Great Free Trade League Demonstration* (1904)). Interestingly, this consensus was only seriously challenged in 1909–10 when tariff reform made much greater headway in Lancashire than it had previously. See P. F. Clarke, *Lancashire and the New Liberalism* (Cambridge, 1971), 98–100 and id., 'The End of Laissez-Faire and the Politics of Cotton', *Historical Journal*, 15 (1972), 493–512. The Tariff Reform Commission's report on cotton was countered by S. J. Chapman, *A Reply to the Report of the Tariff Commission on the Cotton Industry* (Free Trade League, 1905); see, too, C. W. Macara to Chapman, 16 June 1905, in Harcourt MSS, add. dep. 70. Even so, Loulou Harcourt sensed some protectionism in the Manchester Reform Club: to Sir William Harcourt, 21 Oct. 1903, Harcourt dep. 668.

[44] Bradford Chamber of Commerce, *Annual Reports*, 1903–6; J. H. Clapham, 'Protection and the Wool Trade', *Independent Review*, Jan. 1904, 641–50.

[45] A. Taylor, 'carrying, banking and other services . . . really gave to the maritime Empire of England its true position in the world's commerce', *Chamber of Commerce Journal*, Mar. 1905; id.,

such as tinplate and steel, however great the impact of foreign competition, leading voices attested to its modernizing, rather than its destructive impact on the industries concerned.[46] 'Infant industries', such as motor cars, also disclaimed the proffered shelter of tariffs.[47] In the trade press, every editorial in favour of tariffs was matched by a plea for continued free trade.

Similarly, with regard to the economy as a whole, against the tariff reform claim of 'modernization', free trade businessmen were convincingly able to argue that tariffs led to corruption, log-rolling, and inefficiency, and that only within the competitive environment of international markets would industrial progress be achieved. For those free traders who admitted the distortions of the international economy produced by trusts, bounties, and monopolies, the solution lay not in retaliation and tariff wars, but in maintaining an international economic order free from such distortions that would collapse either under the weight of their own weaknesses, or through domestic political pressures.[48] 'Trusts' that represented improved efficiency were therefore clearly distinguished from 'trusts' that exploited natural or artificial monopolies.[49] Free traders were also ready to urge non-tariff support for trade, whether in the form of producers' self-help, as in the case of the British Cotton-Growing Association, which was set up, with Colonial Office aid, in 1903, or through state regulation designed to promote equality of competition, as in the case of the Liberals' Merchant Shipping Act of 1906.[50] Liberal captains of industry were also in the forefront of attempts to promote scientific education and infrastructural investment by the state.[51] Even so, free imports remained central to an industrial prescription for the British economy which few were yet ready to abandon for the uncertainties of the German industrial state or the American corporate economy.

To a large extent, therefore, Hobson's prediction that the political power of

Sidelights on Protection (1905); Taylor, a Unionist free trader, won Toxteth with Liberal support in January 1906, and left the Unionists in Feb.; Rea, *Free Trade*, esp. 193; Furness, *Free Trader*, 7 Aug. 1903; J. M. Denny, 'Protection and Special Trades, III: Shipbuilding', *Independent Review* (Dec. 1903), 456–64. For worries about American shipping, see Hamilton Diary, 11 Apr., 1 and 16 May, 1 July 1902, Add. MS 48679, and CAB 37/62/126, 128 [Morgan Shipping Combination]; Kynaston, *City of London*, vol. 2, 350–1. For recent views, see D. C. M. Platt *et al.*, *Decline and Recovery in Britain's Overseas Trade, 1873–1914* (1993), 150.

[46]   W. E. Minchinton, *The British Tinplate Industry* (Oxford, 1957), 85–6; G. Tweedale, *Sheffield Steel and America* (Cambridge, 1987), 180–1; *WG*, 25 July 1903; *Free Trader*, *passim*.

[47]   *Free Trader*, Apr. 1905.

[48]   For trusts, see *WG*, 24 June, 9 July, 4 Aug. 1903.

[49]   R. Donald, 'Trusts and British Trade', *Transactions of the National Liberal Club. Political Economy Circle*, 4 (1901); H. W. Macrosty, *The Trust Movement in British Industry* (1907), the classic account. While it is tempting to believe that tariffs appealed to 'modern' forms of industry, in practice free trade appealed both to small businessmen who felt themselves victims of monopoly and to pioneer corporate capitalists such as Brunner and Holland.

[50]   A. Emmott, 'Trade within the Empire', *British Empire Review*, Apr. 1903, 280–2; var. in Emmott papers, Box 14, Nuffield College, Oxford; *Hansard*, 4th ser., 133, cc. 1367–1404 [27 Apr. 1904]; B. B. Gilbert, *David Lloyd George: A Political Life: The Architect of Change, 1863–1912* (1987), 326.

[51]   See below, 247.

commerce would align itself decisively with tariff reform proved inaccurate. The producers most likely to support tariffs remained the agricultural interest, however illogically in view of the limited benefits that colonial preference offered to them; the 'broad-acred' rushed to the tariff reform platform. Purportedly, at eight meetings alone were ranked five dukes, two duchesses, three marquises, forty-five earls and viscounts, and seventeen countesses, with a joint acreage of 3,146,284.[52] This enthusiasm was not universal, and, in particular, the remnants of the old Whig aristocracy—Spencers, Russells, Cavendishes, Elliots, and Lambtons—remained loyal to free trade, with not a little foreboding that dear bread would lead to the popular insurrection which a century of concessions to democracy had averted.[53] Sir John Sinclair, owner of 78,000 acres, descendant of 'agricultural Sir John' (a protectionist), and grandfather of the future free trade Liberal leader Archibald Sinclair, compiled a volume of 600 pages in favour of free trade.[54] In the House of Lords, before the headlong rush to the last ditch, 'old' peers such as Beauchamp, Jersey, and Portsmouth, as well as more recent creations such as Goschen, Farrer, Avebury, and Brassey, provided a distinguished defence of free trade, which the Tory managers were unable to suppress as they did the debate in the Commons.[55] Landed support for tariffs appears at first sight more symptomatic of a desire to avenge the repeal of the Corn Laws, with Chamberlain now giving an effective lead to decades of smouldering protectionism.[56] Ostensibly, the cause of imperial preference, which seemed to hinge on the exchange of British manufactured goods in return for imperial food supplies, offered no immediate agrarian revival. Such agrarian and imperial tariff reform hopes were further dashed in 1905 when the Royal Commission on Food Supply, set up with a flourish in 1903, failed to recommend dependence upon home or imperial supplies of grain.[57] Nevertheless, many tariff reformers were ready to urge sacrifice upon the nation for the cause of empire, a community whose good they elevated above that of Britain alone.[58] The imperial dimension in the debate was one that the free traders could not afford to ignore, for potentially their opponents believed it to be their strongest asset.[59]

[52] *Morning Leader*, 9 Jan. 1904; for a detailed analysis, see Green, *Conservatism*, 207–22.

[53] Interestingly, despite the presence of several prominent tariff reformers amidst his circle of plutocratic friends, Edward VII 'would never consent to taxing of people's food', according to Hamilton: Diary, 8 July, 18 Dec. 1903, Add. MS 48681; S. Lee, *King Edward VII: A Biography* (2 vols, 1925–7), vol. 2, 173. For a cautionary tale, see J. St Loe Strachey, *The Great Bread Riots* (1885, rep. 1903).

[54] This was privately circulated for the use of MPs, the Press, trade union leaders, etc.; Sinclair to Lubbock, 20 July 1904, Avebury Papers, Add. MS 49681C.

[55] A. D. Elliot, *The Life of George Joachim Goschen, First Viscount, 1831–1907* (2 vols, 1911), vol. 2, 266–70.

[56] Hamilton Diary, 23 Oct. 1904 on Earl of Cadogan, Add. MS 48682.

[57] *Free Trader*, Sept. 1905, 'Imperial Preference and Food Supplies'; A. Offer, *The First World War: An Agrarian Interpretation* (Oxford, 1989), 224–5.

[58] E. Salmon, 'From Cobdenism to Chamberlain', *Fortnightly Review*, 59 (1896), 984; Cain, 'The Economic Philosophy of Constructive Imperialism'.

[59] Russell, *Landslide*, 90; 'It is the imperial idea which stirs the enthusiasm and quickens the pulse', urged Austen Chamberlain to Gerald Balfour, 20 Dec. 1903, Balfour Papers, PRO 30/60/45.

Free trade, preference, and the empire

The empire offered to tariff reform not only an element of idealism, but was integral to its whole economic and political vision. Its credibility as a policy prescription therefore rested in large part upon its acceptability to the colonies themselves. Certainly, free traders were aware that their cause needed to be defended as strongly in Montreal and Melbourne as in Manchester, while federationists in the colonies were anxious to cement their links with Chamberlain's imperial campaign. This was seen, for example, in the case of the British Empire League in Canada, but, by and large, Canadian opinion was to disappoint the tariff reformers. Under Laurier Canada adopted a far less active imperial policy than suited the federationists, content to allow other colonies to follow its lead in offering Britain preference, but by no means ready to restrict preference to the empire, nor anxious to cultivate closer political ties.[60] The meeting of the Imperial Chambers of Commerce in Montreal in 1903 also failed to endorse preference, largely through the efforts of the British free traders, led by Sir William Holland.[61] Laurier's own lukewarmness, Campbell-Bannerman noted astutely, 'has dealt Joe his shrewdest blow yet'.[62] Even when Laurier found himself forced to compromise with protectionist manufacturers, this offered little comfort to the tariff reformers, for, if anything, Canadian opinion was tending towards reciprocity with the United States.[63] This itself won the support of some free traders, including the veteran Goldwin Smith, while some influential visionaries still looked towards the distant Anglo-Saxon dream, an American–Canadian–British alliance on a free trade basis.[64] More encouragingly for the tariff reformers, Minto, the Governor-General in Canada and elder brother of Arthur Elliot, a leading Unionist free trader, was a Chamberlainite. He found himself receiving a host of 'globetrotters', whose reports powerfully reinforced the case against preference, for example, Edwin Montagu and Bron Herbert.[65] Their conclusions were reinforced in one of J. A. Hobson's

---

[60] For a summary of Laurier's position, see *Canadian Annual Review of Public Affairs, 1907* (Toronto, 1908), *passim*. Laurier's victory in the Canadian election of 1896 had been seen as one for free trade; he had even merited a Cobden Club gold medal.

[61] *Chambers of Commerce Journal*, Jan. 1904, 'Inter-imperial relations', 'Canada and the Congress' *et al.*; ibid., Dec. 1905.

[62] To Herbert Gladstone, 22 Aug. 1903, Herbert Gladstone Papers, [hereafter HGP], Add. MS 45988, fo. 50, British Library.

[63] Goldwin Smith to Rosebery, 12 Feb., 28 Aug. 1904, Rosebery Papers, 10117; id. to Bryce, 11 Aug., 6 Nov. 1903, 5 Jan. 1905, Bryce Papers 16, Bodleian Library; id. to Rosebery, 16 Dec. 1903 in A. Haultain (ed.), *Goldwin Smith's Correspondence* (1913), 403.

[64] E. Wallace, *Goldwin Smith*, 278–89; for the Anglo-Saxon dream, see A. Carnegie to Rosebery, 12 June 1903, Rosebery Papers, 10117.

[65] E. S. Montagu and Bron Herbert, *Canada and the Empire: An Examination of Trade Preference* (1904). Minto to A. Elliot, 10 Sept., 1 Oct., 31 Jan. 1904, Minto Papers 12372, National Library of Scotland; to Madeleine Elliot, 10 Dec. 1903, EP 19483; visiting Canada in 1902, Elliot found 'no free traders' in Canadian politics. Diary, 11 Sept. 1902, EP 19526; see, too, George Peel, reported in Hamilton Diary 30 Sept. 1903 (Add. MS 48681), in A. Elliot to Minto, n.d. [Jan.] 1904, EP 19476, and Peel, 'Canada and the Empire', *Independent Review* (Jan. 1904), 611–28.

neglected works, *Canada To-day*, a damning study of North American tariff politics and of Laurier's preferential policy.[66] Interestingly, too, there was emerging in Canada a school of New Liberal thought, which combined rejection of imperial preference with the advocacy of a greater state role in economy and society.[67]

It was, therefore, to be Antipodean politicians who came to the forefront as Chamberlain's allies. In New Zealand the Prime Minister Seddon proved an enthusiastic recruit, but, above all, the Australian Premier Deakin was to become deeply entangled in the tariff reform cause in the watershed years 1903–8.[68] Significantly, in the Australian election of 1903, which followed Chamberlain's conversion to tariff reform, Deakin was ready to identify his own long-standing adherence to an ideal of imperial federation with Chamberlain's campaign, proclaiming the identity of Australian national ideas with those of British imperialists.[69] Deakin welcomed Chamberlain's announcement as a boost for the ministerialist party, for even those Australians hostile to imperial federation were attracted by preference, while others favourable to federation were drawn away from free trade. Above all, the leading advocate of free trade in Australia, B. R. Wise, now fulfilled Dilke's prophecy of 1892, by becoming the leading spokesman of the Australian Preferential League, as many free traders were drawn towards Deakin's ideal.[70] Ironically, it was the orthodox protectionists who were most suspicious of preference, fearing that this might mean the dilution of protection. Skilfully, Deakin moved to reassure them, advocating imperial preference and 'new protection', in an election full of interest and portents for British politics.

This election saw both the final flowering of the Anglo-Australian free trade ideal which stretched back to the debates of the 1840s, and the endorsement of Deakin's 'new protection', while eroding decisively the middle ground between them. George Reid, the leader of the New South Wales free traders, and long-standing Cobdenite, led the cause with an impressive statement of faith, *Australia and the Fiscal Problem*, a collection of essays aimed almost as much at British opinion as at the electors of Victoria and New South Wales.[71] The Australian free traders strongly rejected preference, advocating a revenue tariff for Australia as the best means to imperial union, regarding Chamberlain's policies as militaristic and aggressive, and illustrating the liberating impact of free trade for the rising Australian nation with the artistry of Julian Ashton. Besides this idealism, from the early economic experience of the federation was adduced the crippling impact of protec-

[66] J. A. Hobson, *Canada To-day* (1906), published by T. Fisher Unwin.
[67] A. Shortt, *Imperial Trade Preference* (1904); B. Ferguson, *Remaking Liberalism: the Intellectual Legacy of Adam Shortt, O. D. Skelton, W. C. Clark, and W. A. Mackintosh, 1890–1925* (Montreal, 1993).
[68] J. Amery, *The Life of Joseph Chamberlain* (vol. 5, 1969), 331–2; J. A. La Nauze, *Alfred Deakin: A Biography* (1979), esp. 475–514.
[69] La Nauze, *Alfred Deakin*, 331.
[70] CCM, 18 June 1892; Wise, *Australia and Preferential Trade* (Preferential Trade League of Australia, 1904).
[71] Published London, 1903; W. G. McMinn, *George Reid* (Melbourne, 1989), 201–3.

tion, as Australia faced the rising competition of free trade Argentina.[72] There is some support for the free traders' view that the election saw a rising tide of free trade in hitherto strongly protectionist Victoria, and for the view that Australians remained indifferent to Chamberlain's proposals. Yet, even more crucially for the future, it was Labour in Australia, not the free traders, which was the beneficiary of protectionism's weakening in the 1903 election.[73] Australian Cobdenites might hail the 'noble object' of 'a British Free Trade Empire', but this became an unlikely result as Deakin drew Labour towards the vista of 'new protection'.[74]

After the Australian election of 1903, the close interplay between free trade and tariff reform in England and Australia continued up to the British general election of 1906, and culminated in the 1907 Colonial Conference. Deakin, as Premier, leader of the opposition, and 'Australian Correspondent' of the *Morning Post*, remained the advocate of imperial preference. His support was valuable to the Chamberlainite cause at home, which in turn increasingly looked to Deakin as the focus for its wider imperial aspirations. In England B. R. Wise—contemplating a transfer to English politics—moved firmly into the tariff reform camp, speaking widely in favour of preference and noisily severing his ties with the Cobden Club.[75] He had now become the advocate of 'democratic imperialism' and 'belief in England' against 'colourless cosmopolitanism'.[76] Other Australians in London also worked enthusiastically in the tariff reform camp—Philip Mennell as editor of *The British Australasian*,[77] and Sir J. A. Cockburn, the former agent-general for South Australia, who, while dismayed to find himself classed as a Conservative, spoke widely in Chamberlain's favour, stood as a tariff reform candidate in 1904, and joined the Tariff Reform Commission with a watching brief for Australian interests.[78] Australian protectionists attempted to bring Chamberlain to Australia in 1904–5, and, failing that, visited him in England to assure him of Australian support.[79] The Australian experience of several British notables was also mobilized

[72]   W. Bateman, *Protection in the Commonwealth. How it burdens the primary producer; and a comparison with the Argentine Republic* (Melbourne, 1902); id., *Cloud of Depression in the Commonwealth of Australia* (Melbourne, 1903); E. T. Doxat to A. R. Blackson, 18 Feb. and 18 Aug. 1903; to G. Fairbairn, 13 May 1903, Letterbooks, Dalgety Papers, W8/29, Archives of Business and Labour, Australian National University.

[73]   La Nauze, *Alfred Deakin*, 319–22.

[74]   E. Pulsford, *Commerce and the Empire* (1903) preface (Sydney, Sept. 1903).

[75]   Chamberlain to Wise, 15 May, 6 June, 20 June, 1905, Wise Papers, MS 1327, Mitchell Library, Sydney; Wise, *Free Trade and Imperial Preference. A Correspondence* [with Perris, secretary, Cobden Club] (Letchworth, 1905).

[76]   Wise to Deakin, 14 June 1906, Deakin Papers, 1/1494, National Library of Australia, Canberra. But he did not rule out the hope that the Liberal imperialists in Britain might yet emerge as an Australian-style Liberal protectionist party.

[77]   P. Mennell to Deakin, e.g., 19 June, 12 Sept., 8 Oct., 25 Dec. 1903, 15 Jan., 19 Feb. 1904, Deakin Papers, 1/873–5, 891, 921, 943–4, 950–1, 970–4; 'Mennell', *ADB*, 10, 484.

[78]   'Cockburn', *ADB*, 8, 42–4; Cockburn to Deakin, 25 Sept. 1903, 26 Feb., 1 Dec. 1904, 14 July 1905, Deakin Papers, 1/902, 976, 1070, 1179.

[79]   F. G. [Joseph] to Sir E. Barton, 1 Jan. 1904, Barton Papers, MS 51/1334; O. C. Beale to Deakin, 4 Oct. 1904, 2 June 1906, Deakin Papers, 1/1040–2, 1519–20.

behind Chamberlain—for example, Australia's second Governor-General Lord Tennyson, and the talented imperial observer and author, Richard Jebb.[80]

Nevertheless, the strong link between Chamberlain and the colonies ultimately worked to the disadvantage of the tariff reform cause, especially in view of the unshakeable practice of protectionism in the colonies, which offered only the slightest glimmer of economic benefits to be derived from imperial preference. In August 1905 the Associated Chambers of Commerce warned that 'the value of such preferences [offered by South Africa, New Zealand, and Canada] is becoming more and more overshadowed by the increasing burden of duties and by irksome restrictions upon trade', a tendency confirmed by the South African Tariff of 1905, considered by some 'practically fatal to the commercial connection with this country'.[81] Nor had the tariff reformers successfully addressed the issue of India—that is to say, was tariff reform a policy for the white self-governing colonies only, or could India look forward to a preferential tariff behind which she could build up her textile industries?[82] For many, the colonial model of economic policy and political order, whether in the shape of Australia's Labour and 'new protection', or Canada's 'little gang of railroad men, bankers, lumber men, and manufacturing monopolists' (Hobson), impressed itself upon free traders as one to be avoided rather than imitated.[83]

In these unfavourable circumstances, even imperial enthusiasts began to work towards schemes for civil intelligence within the empire, rather than for economic unity.[84] For example, the scheme that was eventually put before the Colonial Conference in 1907, the brainchild of the jurist Frederick Pollock, had been previously canvassed in Canada by Pollock and the imperial activist Drage, and by pen in Australia.[85] It was, in essence, a free trader's scheme, which sought to bring

---

[80] Tennyson to Deakin, 14 July 1904, Deakin Papers, 1/1016; for Jebb, see J. J. Eddy and D. M. Schreuder (eds.), *The Rise of Colonial Nationalism* (1989). Interestingly, on the free trade side, C. H. Chomley, author of one of the most able of contemporary works, *Protection in Canada and Australasia* (1904) decided against accepting R. L. Outhwaite's invitation to campaign against protection in England. See Chomley to Deakin, 6 Sept. 1905, Deakin Papers, 1/1194: 'I am an Australian before I am a free trader.' He did, however, revise for the Free Trade Union/Cobden Club, Farrer's *Free Trade versus Fair Trade* (1904). For Chomley, see *ADB*, 7, 642–3.

[81] *Chambers of Commerce Journal*, Aug. and Oct. 1905. For apathy in South Africa, see Hamilton Diary, 7 Jan. 1905, Add. MS 48683.

[82] Hamilton Diary, 9 Jan. 1904, Add. MS 48681; E. Sassoon, 'India and Tariff Reform', *Nineteenth Century*, 55 (1904), 444–8; below, 292–4.

[83] Working-class opinion in England was widely cited in Australia for its resistance to protection. See, especially, M. Hirsch, *Social Conditions: Materials for Comparison between New South Wales, & Victoria, Great Britain, the United States and Foreign Countries* (Melbourne, 1901), with extensive testimonies in favour of free trade, 124–31; Hobson, *Canada To-day*, 46–7.

[84] G. S. Clarke, for example, Governor of Victoria, to A. Elliot, 6 June 1903, EP 19493; to Deakin, 13 Apr. 1907, Deakin Papers, 1/1410.

[85] J. E. Kendle, *The Colonial and Imperial Conferences 1887–1911* (1967), 56–79; Hobson, *Canada*, 100; Pollock to Wise, 11 July 1905, Wise Papers, MS 1327; G. Drage to Deakin, 23 Nov. 1904, 28 Aug., 5 Oct. 1905, Deakin Papers, 1/1063, 1189, 1235; Wise to Deakin, 26 July 1905, ibid. 1/1184; Pollock to Deakin, 6 Oct. 1905, 21 Aug. 1906, ibid. 1/1238, 1502; Glynn Diaries, 16 Apr. 1905 (Pollock to

together mutually hostile camps. While it hardly met the wilder hopes of the ardent imperial federationists, it was endorsed both by free traders in Britain and by preferentialists in Australia. It represented a small crumb of comfort for imperialists wearying of years of leagues and committees, but did little to impair the essential Liberal vision of an empire of sentiment, suitably adjusted to new considerations of defence and administrative organization, while avoiding the pitfalls so conspicuous within the 'old colonial system'. It was this image of 'free trade imperialism' that was promoted as the essential antidote to Chamberlainite 'protectionist imperialism'.[86] It both built on the more positive Liberal approach to empire developed in the 1890s, but also seemed a surer guarantee of peace within the international order, the Manchester perspective to which progressive loyalties had been revived, and from which the Gladstonian generation, still strong within the party of Morley, Harcourt, and Bryce, had rarely departed. It was the shibboleths of these Gladstone–Cobden men that now found themselves at the heart of domestic as well as imperial political debate.

Free trade and party politics

The centrality given to free trade and Cobdenism by the tariff reform assault offered to the divided Liberal Party the ideal issue around which the scars of the Boer War could be progressively healed. Not only had the pro-Boer case revived the tenets of 'Manchesterism', but now the hopes of a Liberal/Unionist fusion were finally abandoned, as the Liberal imperialists rallied to free trade and reconciled themselves to Campbell-Bannerman's, not Rosebery's, leadership.[87] Free trade proved not only a serviceable ideological cement within the party, but with the fragmentation of the Unionists under the impact of tariff reform it opened a bridge back towards co-operation with the Liberals for former Liberal Unionists. It also provided an additional stimulus and the ideological veneer for the renewed Lib–Lab alliance signalled by the Gladstone–MacDonald Pact in early 1903.[88] In these circumstances, free trade became as vital to the Liberal adaptation to 'mass politics' as was tariff reform to that of the Conservatives.

The potential electoral appeal of free trade had already been heralded by the campaign against the bread tax in 1902. This had brought home to the Liberal Party the opportunities for unity which Tory finance offered, and which Tory Party managers most feared.[89] For while the bread tax could claim a figleaf of

Glynn, 16 Feb. 1905), National Library of Australia; Drage to Barton, 25 Nov. 1904, Barton Papers, 1353a; Deakin to Tennyson, 7 Feb. 1905, Tennyson Papers, A5011, fos. 115–18, Mitchell Library, Sydney.

[86] *WG*, 4 June 1904, 2 ('The Manchester School and the Empire'); W. R. Scott, *Free Trade in Relation to the Future of Britain and her Colonies* (1903); see, too, J. S. Nicholson, *A Project of Empire* (1909).

[87] D. A. Hamer, *Liberal Politics in the Age of Gladstone and Rosebery* (Oxford, 1972), 312–14; H. C. G. Matthew, *The Liberal Imperialists* (Oxford, 1973), 102–19, 292.

[88] F. Bealey and H. Pelling, *Labour and Politics, 1900–1906* (1958).

[89] Middleton, cited C. T. Ritchie, memo, 'Colonial Preference', 15 Nov. 1902, CAB 37/63/155.

Gladstonian rectitude, it was politically inept.[90] It raised an immediate outcry against the 'dear loaf' and 'bread taxes', powerfully reviving the rhetoric of the 1840s. This threat to working-class living standards stirred the free trade sympathies of organized labour and served as the vehicle for a forceful campaign conducted by the Cobden Club's secretary Harold Cox.[91] The benefits for the Liberal Party were underlined when, in the Bury by-election in May 1902, the Liberal George Toulmin overturned a Tory majority of 850 in a campaign fought largely on the bread tax.[92] Quickly and emphatically, leading Liberals rediscovered their links with Lancashire, and their acquaintance with the Manchester School, with a carefully orchestrated anti-Corn Law demonstration in Manchester (15 May), complete with the endorsement of Cobden's daughter Jane, and the ILP's Mrs Pankhurst.[93] Here, the catchwords of the 1840s were rediscovered, but were suitably readjusted to meet the needs of a radically transformed electorate. Cobdenites, supporters of Labour, and Liberals aimed above all to put free trade at the heart of popular political argument, taking up the campaign against fair trade in the 1880s. By June 1903, Henry Fowler calculated that in twelve by-elections an aggregate Conservative majority of 20,000 had become a Liberal one of 3,496, while Woolwich had been won by Labour's Will Crooks, in elections largely fought on the bread tax. Free trade had emphatically emerged not as an 'outworn shibboleth of the 1840s', but as 'a national necessity in 1903'.[94]

Ironically, the bread tax proved short-lived, but its abolition by the former fair trader Ritchie in the budget of 1903 proved merely to be the spur to Chamberlain's tariff reform campaign.[95] This had immediate repercussions for party politics. For it ended the possibility of the synthesis of national efficiency and social welfare offered by the Liberal League, as opposition to Chamberlain's tariff platform rallied the Liberal imperialists decisively to the defence of free trade as the central Liberal goal. Despite their occasional toying with tariff reform, most Liberal imperialists now firmly rejected this course.[96] Haldane, for example, did so after

[90]   Hamilton Diary, *passim*, esp. 18 and 29 Oct., 18 and 27 Nov. 1902, Add. MS 48680.

[91]   Parliamentary Committee of the TUC, minutes, 30 Apr., 26 and 27 May 1902 (microfilm, BLPES); Brighouse Industrial Society Ltd. to C. P. Trevelyan, 11 June 1902, CPT9; Brighouse Liberal Association, 8 July 1902, CPT10; Cox, influenced by Edward Carpenter, had worked as a co-operator/ agricultural labourer in the mid-1880s, had been the Radical co-author with Sidney Webb in the 1890s (on the Eight-Hour Day), and now advocated a Radical brand of free trade before becoming, after 1906, a stalwart of individualism and anti-socialism, a distinctive rather than typical political odyssey. See *DNB* and D. Proctor (ed.), *The Autobiography of G. Lowes Dickinson* (1973), 69, 72.

[92]   *Bury Times*, Apr.–June 1902, *passim*.

[93]   Asquith to Spencer, 1 May 1902, Spencer Papers, BL [temporary no. K470]; *The Corn Tax. Speeches by Spencer and Asquith* (LPD, 1902); *Manchester Guardian*, 16 May 1902; *Bury Times*, 17 May 1902.

[94]   G. Haw, *The Life Story of Will Crooks, MP. From Workhouse to Westminster* (1917), 186–94; *Hansard*, 4th ser., 123, c. 376 (Sir H. H. Fowler), cc. 390–1 (T. Taylor), 9 June 1903.

[95]   The Cobden Club dinner designed to celebrate 'one of the greatest triumphs for free trade for many years' over the Corn Tax turned into an anti-Chamberlain protest, H. Cox to Spencer, 15, 19, and 25 May 1903, Spencer Papers, K377.

[96]   Among exceptions was T. A. Brassey, who resigned from the Liberal Party; see Brassey to H. Gladstone, 5 Aug. 1903, HGP, Add. MS 46061, fo. 5; Matthew, *Liberal Imperialists*, 101, 166. Samuel

careful study of its most compelling case, William Ashley's *The Tariff Problem* (1903). On the other hand, Chamberlain's imperial claims provided the opportunity for a restatement of the Liberal imperial vision, in which the leading malcontent Rosebery was prepared to join, while resisting the bid for the Liberal leadership urged on him by his more dogged supporters.[97] Asquith rallied enthusiastically to the free trade cause, becoming Chamberlain's chief platform opponent and editing Bastiat's *Sophisms*, while his wife Margot sought to bring the two wings of the party together socially. While some Liberal Leaguers viewed the future with despondency, the party's by-election victories in 1904 solidified Campbell-Bannerman's leadership. Free trade offered him the transcendant theme, which the Liberals had lacked since 1886, but which he now deployed to admirable, unifying, effect.[98] Finally, in December 1905 the threat to free trade provided the ideological façade behind which the anti-Campbell-Bannerman 'Relugas Compact' was broken, and Asquith, Haldane, and Grey agreed to serve under the former's leadership.[99] In opposition, free trade offered to the Liberals ideological unity and organizational concentration; in office, it brought administrative power; and in the general election of 1906 it led to an overwhelming victory at the polls, 'the biggest thing that has happened at home since 1832' in the words of Chirol, *The Times*'s foreign correspondent.[100]

Yet such an outcome was by no means assured in 1903, and the Liberal victory was based not on the instinctive stirrings of the stale residues of Cobdenism, but on a carefully organized and ideologically renewed Cobdenism, whose reshaping we have already detected in late-Victorian Britain. This creed was designed not only to draw back to the Liberal Party the strong body of Unionist free traders in the constituencies, but to enthuse the abstentionist and divided Liberal electors, and to retain within the fold working men who would otherwise have been drawn to the growing attractions of labour representation. However much the fiscal controversy appeared to revert to the battles of the 1840s, Liberal leaders were therefore keen to defend free trade 'as a concrete and living policy'.[101] As Loulou Harcourt urged, '[O]ne's facts, figures, and arguments must be essentially modern.'[102] This involved a number of ideological strands, as well as the repudiation of the tariff reform case based on the statistics of British decline. While it is impossible here to rehearse the

Storey, who prominently supported tariffs as a Liberal in 1903, had been a pro-Boer but also a member of RCDTI. Many Liberal Leaguers joined the Cobden Club and the FTU in 1903–4.

[97] Crewe to Rosebery, 29 May 1903, Rosebery Papers, 10117; Hamilton Diary, *passim*; Matthew, *Liberal Imperialists*, 100 ff.; Freeman-Thomas to Emmott, 12 May 1904, Emmott Papers, Box 3, fos. 249–50.

[98] J. Wilson, *CB: a Life of Sir Henry Campbell-Bannerman* (1973), 407–20.

[99] S. Koss, *Asquith* (1976, 1985 edn.), 64–73; Grey to Asquith, 26 Dec. 1905, Asquith Papers 10, fo. 190.

[100] Quoted in S. Koss, *The Rise and Fall of the Political Press in Britain* (vol. 2, 1984), 65.

[101] H. H. Asquith, *Trade and the Empire* (1903), prefatory note.

[102] To Sir William Harcourt, 16 July 1903, Harcourt dep. 667, fo. 185.

complexities of the debate as a whole, five nodal points of rhetorical argument may aptly illustrate the whole.[103]

First, the Liberal free traders refuted the economic case for tariff reform, rejecting the idea of the decline of Great Britain's trade, save in so far as other countries were bound within the international division of labour to exploit their own comparative advantages. Free trade itself was seen to have maximized Britain's prosperity in the past, in terms of low import prices, cheap exports, and high real wages. Here, the recipes of classical political economy were therefore not defended as an academic dogma, but as a necessary bastion of Britain's role in the world economy. Within that economy, it was accepted that some trades (hopefully the sweated, unskilled ones) might leave Britain, but that such losses would be more than compensated by the new wealth created by skilled industries and by the service sector.[104] Whereas tariffs would raise prices, lower real wages, diminish employment, and shield inefficiency, free trade continued to promise a high growth of exports and Britain's centrality to the world network of goods and services.[105]

Nevertheless, Liberal politicians were well aware that a defence resting largely on past benefits exposed them to the reiterated charge of Cobdenite complacency, and a strong substratum of debate in the party focused on alternative policies, which for the most part outlined a growing interventionist role for the state in education, commercial diplomacy, and in the economic infrastructure, including the possibility of nationalization.[106] In particular, a group of Liberal businessmen, led by Brunner, pushed strongly for 'a policy of wholesome progress', centring on 'cheaper carriage', with state ownership of canals, and subsidies for trunk roads.[107] The spectre of nationalization appeared as a political liability to Campbell-Bannerman, but infrastructural investment appealed to many provincial business-

---

[103] This summary is distilled from private correspondence, the press, periodicals, pamphlets by Liberal MPs, and *Hansard*, 1903–6. For representative views, see Asquith, *Trade and Empire*, R. B. Haldane, *Army Reform and other Addresses* (1907), Rea, *Free Trade*, J. M. Robertson, *Trade and Tariffs* (1908), the Eighty Club, *The Liberal View* (1904), Liberal Publications Department, *Pamphlets and Leaflets*, 1903–6, W. S. Churchill, *Why I am a Free Trader* (1905). For a good appreciation of the economic issues, see P. J. Cain, 'Political Economy in Edwardian England: the Tariff Reform Controversy', in A. O'Day (ed.), *Edwardian Britain: Conflict and Stability, 1900–1914* (1979), 35–59.

[104] For the case of the Leeds flax industry, virtually disappeared by 1901, but replaced, often in the same factories, by the ready-made clothing industry, see R. Shuddick to C. P. Trevelyan, 25 May 1901, Trevelyan Papers, CPT7; Rea, *Free Trade*, 26, 209. Many free traders were active in the Anti-Sweating League, *Reports*, 1908, etc.

[105] McKenna expressed this view well, noting that manufacturing was giving way to trading and shipping, 'We are the merchants and carriers of the world'. *Hansard*, 4th ser., 123, c. 545, 10 June 1903.

[106] See, for example, the policies set out by Sydney Buxton in the *Free Trader*, 2/31, 4 Mar. 1904.

[107] J. Harris, *Unemployment and Politics: A Study in English Social Policy, 1886–1914* (Oxford, 1972), 215 ff.; *WG*, 20 Aug. 1903; Brunner to H. Gladstone, 29 Dec. 1904, enclosing Runciman to Brunner, 16 Dec. 1904, HGP, Add. MS 46062, fos. 57–61; Sydney Buxton to H. Gladstone, 22 Jan. 1904, HGP, Add. MS 46012, fo. 11–12; Campbell-Bannerman to H. Gladstone, 23 Dec. 1904, 2 and 3 Jan. 1905, HGP Add. MS 45988, fos. 137–42; Brunner to Campbell-Bannerman, 15 and 16 Nov. 1903, Campbell-Bannerman Papers, Add. MS 41237, fos. 203–4; see, too, H. Thompson, *The Canals of Britain* (Cobden Club, 1902).

men.[108] Most Liberals were also able to agree upon the need for improved scientific and technical knowledge. Thus, as we have seen, the founding of Imperial College in 1903 was turned to Liberal political advantage, signalled as 'the true remedy' for economic weakness.[109] For free traders, it was Germany's higher education system, not her regressive political order, that deserved imitation. Similarly, the Liberals joined an emerging cross-party consensus in favour of a more active diplomatic support of commerce and a reorganized Board of Trade, administrative changes that fell far short of retaliation, the big revolver held out by the tariff reformers as the remedy for unfair foreign competition and hostile tariffs.[110] Positive Liberal prescriptions looked, therefore, to an enhanced role for the state, but within the framework of the classical mechanism of international trade, decisively rejecting any concept of national economy dear to the tariff reformers.

The second node of argument drew upon the Liberals' own recently refurbished defence of empire in order to attack the notion of imperial preference as a policy that threatened more to disrupt than to unite the colonies. Here, the parts played by Rosebery, Asquith, Grey, and even the ageing but still influential Dilke, in the free trade campaign were particularly valuable, emphasizing an empire of sentiment as ultimately more lasting than an empire of material interest, noting the absence of enthusiasm for free trade within the colonies, and asserting the incompatibility of British and colonial interests. Preferential tariffs could only lead to endless and politically damaging bargaining, and so hasten the decline of the British Empire, which, on the Roman model, the Edwardians most feared.[111] Typically, the *Westminster Gazette* abjured preference as a policy of imperial disruption: '[I]t removes Imperialism from the safe foundation of freedom and sentiment and involves it in the material conflicts of trading interests and class interests within the Colonies themselves and between the Colonies and the Mother-Country.'[112] The Liberals pointedly saw no advantages in sacrificing the mother country for putative and, at best, smaller benefits to the colonies. Those advantages included the absence of international friction which tariffs might generate, and the importance of good relations with Europe and America which tariffs might

---

[108]   Manchester Chamber of Commerce, *Monthly Record*, 15 Jan. 1904; *Chambers of Commerce Journal*, Jan. 1905. The Liberal imperialist Munro-Ferguson pressed the Scottish interest in state forests, *Independent Review*, May 1904, 542–52.

[109]   Above, 228; *WG*, 29 June and 25 Aug. 1903; H. Spender to Gladstone, 9 July 1903, HGP, Add. MS 46660, fos. 245–6. Haldane and Rosebery were most closely linked with this 'Charlottenburg' scheme; P. Alter, *The Reluctant Patron: Science and the State in Britain, 1850–1920* (Deddington, 1987), 152–72.

[110]   The government declined to act on the Jersey Committee's recommendation that the Board of Trade become a Ministry of Commerce and Industry, but more minor changes followed; *Parl. Papers*, 1904, 78 [Cd. 2121]; D. C. M. Platt, *Finance, Trade and Politics in British Foreign Policy, 1815–1914* (Oxford, 1968), 377 ff.

[111]   The tariff reformers readily cited Rome, but so too did the Liberals and progressives, e.g., M. Freeden (ed.), *Minutes of the Rainbow Circle 1894–1924*, Cambden 4th ser., vol. 38 (Royal Historical Society, 1989), 71; G. Harwood, *Hansard*, 4th ser., 123, c. 196, 28 May 1903.

[112]   *WG*, 30 May 1903; 4 June 1904.

jeopardize.[113] Free trade could appear at once patriotic, as in the case of Belloc, and genuinely cosmopolitan. 'I like the stranger & the foreigner', as Margot Asquith confided.[114]

Third, whereas tariffs promised additional revenue, the Liberals were, as we have seen, increasingly ready to revise the Gladstonian doctrine of taxation. That doctrine, with its emphasis on revenue taxes and a minimal degree of direct taxation, leaving a substantial reserve for times of conflict, had survived the Boer War in some disarray.[115] The Liberals were still able to level the charge of incompetent management and extravagance at Tory finance, claiming that substantial economy was still possible. But, on the other hand, new demands on the state purse were to receive growing recognition, and, equally, if expenditure was to require new taxation, taxes on land values and graduated income taxes were vastly preferable to regressive food taxes.[116] If anything supplied the need for a positive Liberal policy, it was the combination of financial and land reform, above all the taxation of land values, to which over 280 MPs were committed in 1906.[117] Fears of such 'socialist finance' were already present in Tory rhetoric in 1906, although they were to grow vastly in scale by 1910.[118] On the other hand, land reform, in its varying guises, remained a central element in Liberal appeal in both town and country, promising not only revenue, but agricultural holdings, cheaper costs of industrial production, a solution to urban overcrowding, as well as greater access to fields and mountains for town-dwellers.[119]

Land reform therefore remained central to the Liberals' fourth preoccupation, that of popular welfare. For the most part, welfare depended upon the classical mechanism of trade, which promised the continuance of high real wages, and a high and stable level of employment. Here, the Liberals deployed to maximum effect

---

[113]   C. P. Trevelyan, Notes for Free Trade speeches, Autumn campaign, 1903, CPT41, Trevelyan Papers; Brunner, cited in Russell, *Landslide*, 69–70.

[114]   Russell, *Landslide*, 69, 194–5; M. Asquith to Betty Balfour, 19 Jan. 1906, Balfour of Whittingehame Papers, 333. For the issue of alien immigration and free trade, see J. A. Garrard, *The English and Immigration* (1971), 139 ff.

[115]   See above, 225.

[116]   e.g. Loulou Harcourt to A. G. Gardiner, 28 Nov. 1904, Gardiner Papers, 1/16, BLPES.

[117]   '[W]hen they talk of avoiding "mere negativism" and having an alternative to Joe's policy, they seem to think of nothing but the rating of site values', complained Runciman. To Brunner, 16 Dec. 1904 enclosed in Brunner to Gladstone, 29 Dec. 1904, HGP, Add. MS 46062, fos. 57–61. For this theme, see A. Offer, *Property and Politics 1870–1914* (Cambridge, 1981); for two enthusiastic land reformers, see A. J. A. Morris, *C. P. Trevelyan, 1870–1958. Portrait of a Radical* (Belfast, 1977) and in Scotland, J. D. White, e.g. *Economic Ideals* (1903), *Land and Labour* (1904), *The Farmer's Friends* (Glasgow, 1904). See, too, Loulou Harcourt to Sir William, 17 Oct. 1903, Harcourt dep. 667. Land reform featured in 68% of Liberal election addresses (England only) and land value taxation in 52%. Russell, *Landslide*, 65.

[118]   The Governor of the Bank of England in Oct. 1907 hoped 'the Socialistic government will not vote a division of our Capital amongst themselves!', W. M. Campbell to E. W. Hamilton, 3 Oct. 1907, Hamilton Papers, Add. MS 48628.

[119]   e.g., C. P. Trevelyan, 'Land Reform vs Protection', *Independent Review*, 1 (1903–4), 542–54; The Garden City movement was also seen as anti-protectionist: e.g. Capt. J. W. Petavel, *Decentralisation or Protection to end Great Britain's Perils* (1902); see, too, G. L. Bernstein, *Liberalism and Liberal Politics in Edwardian England* (1986), 58–9.

both the statistical record of working-class prosperity under free trade, especially in comparison with other countries, and historical lessons of the 'hungry forties', the 'bad old days' of protection and the 'small loaf'.[120] Too often, this has been seen as the only theme of Liberal propaganda, but there is no doubt that the party's most effective line of attack on tariff reform was the threat that it posed to the working-class standard of living, the preponderant appeal to working men and women as consumers. Here was the culmination of the public rhetoric of affluence which free traders had consistently exploited against fair trade, the sugar bounties, and the fiscal expedients of the Boer War.

Even so, this left the Liberals exposed to the charge that poverty and unemployment had grown since 1846 and, especially since the 1880s, had coexisted with plenty, with the statistics of Booth and Rowntree frequently canvassed against the 'optimist' case. This was also an essential element in the socialist critique of free trade. Sidney Webb, for example, while still a free trader, provocatively claimed that the policy had created 'the Hooligan . . . the physically undeveloped, mentally undisciplined town youth'.[121] Socialists and tariff reformers were both to stigmatize the Liberal Party for its continued support for *laissez-faire* policies. Against such charges, the Liberals riposted partly that tariff reform would increase working-class poverty, but, more constructively, that the emerging progressive synthesis made available a galaxy of social reforms compatible with free trade. As Churchill, making his first appearance at the National Liberal Federation, announced: '[W]e want a government and a policy which will think that the condition of a slum in an English city as not less worthy of the attention of statesmen and of Parliament than a jungle in Somaliland.'[122] Licensing reform remained the leading issue of social reform for many Liberals, but election addresses in 1906 also urged poor law reform and pensions (69 per cent), unemployment legislation (41 per cent), and housing (36 per cent).[123] For Lord Crewe, therefore, the Liberal Party in 1906 was on trial as 'an engine for social reforms'.[124] It is, of course, true that front bench commitment to such reforms was by no means cast-iron, but there is much evidence to suggest that these issues mobilized the electorate, and that many Liberal candidates stressed the Radical potential of free trade, which the Liberals would eventually exploit in office.[125] 'Progressivism' was not an ingredient added to the Liberal platform after 1908, but was already integral to it in 1906.[126]

Finally, if the Liberal case accepted a part for the state in welfare (distribution),

[120]   These themes are well known, for example, the cartoons of horseflesh-eating German workers.
[121]   'The Policy of the National Minimum', *Independent Review*, July 1904, 168.
[122]   NLF, *Proceedings*, 12–14 May 1904; H. Samuel, in *The Liberal View*.
[123]   Russell, *Landslide*, 65.
[124]   Quoted in ibid. 33.
[125]   Cf. H. Emy, *Liberals, Radicals, and Social Politics, 1892–1914* (Cambridge, 1973), 141; Morris, Trevelyan, 55–6; Clarke, *Lancashire and New Liberalism*, 376.
[126]   Clarke, for example, notes but underplays the novelty of the Liberal platform in 1906, drawing too marked a distinction between free trade/old Liberalism in 1906 and progressive/'new' Liberalism in 1910, *Lancashire and New Liberalism*, e.g., 373, 375–6, 398.

it precluded any interference in essential economic relationships (production). Here, the Victorian social compact retained its validity, ensuring freedom of wage-bargaining as well as freedom of capital. In particular, it was the political dangers of tariffs that were highlighted, their tendency to encourage the mobilization of interest groups turning the state into a lobbying mechanism, and the power that they delivered into the hands of well-organized groups of capitalists. This became one of the most potent themes of Liberal rhetoric, voiced pungently by both the former Tory Churchill and the former socialist Burns. Churchill foresaw a new Tory party arising, '. . . like perhaps the Republican party in the United States of America—rich, materialist and secular—whose opinions will turn on tariffs, and will cause the lobbies to be crowded with the touts of protected industries'.[127] Burns also rejected the American model: '[I]ts future under the rule of the Trust and Capitalist is making it a despotism of monopoly, where money is king.'[128] Here was the strongest moral case for free trade, repeatedly urged by Liberals as diverse as Rosebery, Hirst, Gooch, and Rea. These political fears also provided an important argument against more plausible forms of anti-dumping legislation, which had, in the eyes of some Liberals, a strong justification in theory as a response to trusts and cartels.[129] Yet it was believed that the implementation of such a policy was beyond the administrative capability of the state, or would merely serve to reintroduce business interests into public life, and so threaten parliamentary government itself.[130]

The Liberal defence of free trade therefore combined a theory of international trade, a doctrine of empire, a prescription for revenue and welfare, together with a concept of the Liberal democratic state.[131] In this defence, the continuity with the 1840s and 1880s is clear, but so too are the novel elements. The Cobdenism of the Edwardian Liberals embraced an enlarged view for the state in welfare and distribution, while reaffirming the Cobdenite theory of trade, progress, and international relations.[132] While arguing effectively for the contemporary pertinence of Cobdenite ideas against the tariff reform charge of 'stale Cobdenite nostrums', this Liberal case was also able to countercharge that tariff reform itself was based on a regressive model of political and economic development, which portended a return to an outmoded concept of empire, to a revived regime of monopoly, and, above all, to the

[127] *Hansard*, 4th ser., 123, c. 194, 28 May 1903.

[128] Burns, 'Labour and Free Trade', *Independent Review*, Nov. 1903, 208–22; see, too, id., 'Political Dangers of Protection', in H. W. Massingham (ed.), *Labour and Protection* (1903), 1–37.

[129] See above, 238. Individualistic free traders such as Levy and Guyot supported action against cartels as they had against bounties, and as some had against the gold standard, i.e. as artificial hindrances to the natural order and free exchange; *Transactions, National Liberal Club. Political Economy Circle*, 4 (9 Apr. 1902), 34–8; 5, Pt. 1, 51st Dinner, 10 Feb. 1904.

[130] For the administrative case, see Haldane to Ashley, 20 Sept. 1903, Haldane Papers, 5906, National Library of Scotland.

[131] For free trade and foreign policy, see below, 295 ff.

[132] For a typical statement, see H. Samuel, 'The Cobden Centenary and Modern Liberalism', *Nineteenth Century* (June 1904), 898–909.

freshly stigmatized 'hungry forties'. Here, the Liberals turned history back upon the tariff reformers, accepting the ideological simplicity of the battle between free trade and protection, while the tariff reformers struggled to give exact content to their own message, or to vindicate its superior historical or prescriptive validity. Above all, the Liberal leadership determinedly avoided the niceties of a discussion of countervailing duties, or the implications of trusts, or the threat of nationalization, in favour of the cardinal economic and moral benefits of free trade, thus forging a clear political platform with the maximum electoral appeal.[133]

This, then, was the rhetorical kernel of the Liberal case against tariff reform, a case taken up with swiftness in May 1903 and pursued with vigour until January 1906. Free trade rapidly became the chief theme in Liberal Party publications and the essential complement of organizational renewal within the party, proving especially attractive to the Women's National Liberal Federation and to the Women's Liberal Federation.[134] It provided the motif of the newly formed League of Young Liberals, of the Young Scots, and the centrepiece of older bodies, for instance, the National Reform Union and the Eighty Club.[135] Here was an ideological enthusiasm which transcended sectional claims and which the Liberals kept squarely at the centre of their extended electoral campaign between 1903 and 1906.[136]

But free trade had never simply been a Liberal doctrine, and the campaign looked beyond the party faithful to the cultivation of those Unionists who were prepared to abandon the Conservative Party in order to defend free trade, as well as to Labour. For, as is well known, Chamberlain's tariff campaign had met strong but diffuse opposition within the Unionist Party, as it fragmented into 'free fooders', 'whole hoggers', and Balfourites, and with many individual MPs oscillating in their allegiances.[137] The Unionist Free Food League, formed in July 1903, served to act as a rallying point for the parliamentary party, and as a propagator of free trade ideas, but the 'free fooders' were unable to defend the Liberal Unionist Party machinery against the Chamberlainite attack.[138] It therefore proved short-

---

[133] F. Coetzee, *For Party or Country* (Oxford, 1990), 59; Morris, *Trevelyan*, 54. Free trade also had the advantage of obscuring the Irish Question, Arthur Elliot Diary, 30 Mar. 1905, EP 19527.

[134] A. K. Russell, 'Laying the Charges for the Landslide', in Morris (ed.), *Edwardian Radicalism*, 62–74.

[135] Russell, *Landslide*, 40 ff; the *Young Scot, passim*; for the appeal to youth of free trade, W. M. Crook to L. Harcourt, 21 June 1904, dep. 437; for the '80' Club, e.g. *The Liberal View* (1904); the NRU employed 37 free trade lecturers in 1903. Harcourt to Gladstone, Add. MS 46060, fo. 37. For one NRU activist, see F. W. Hirst, *Alexander Gordon Cuming Harvey: A Memoir* (1925); see, too, NRU material in John Johnson Collection, 'Creeds, parties, policies', Box 21.

[136] Of the 22m leaflets sold by the Liberal Publications Department in the 1906 election campaign, 9m dealt with the fiscal question, 6.6m with the Tory record, and 2.3m with Chinese Labour. HGP, Add. MS 46017, fo. 144.

[137] Sykes, *Tariff Reform*; Rempel, *Unionists Divided*; N. Blewett, 'Free Fooders, Balfourites, Whole Hoggers: Factionalism within the Unionist Party, 1906–1910', *Historical Journal*, 11 (1968), 95–124; D. Dutton, *'His Majesty's Loyal Opposition'* (Liverpool, 1992).

[138] Rempel, *Unionists Divided, passim*; Sykes, *Tariff Reform*, 92–3; Devonshire to Elliot, 2 July 1904 et seq., EP 19473; Elliot Diary, 29 June 1904, EP 19527.

lived, replaced in April 1905 by the Unionist Free Trade Club, more restricted in its ambitions, and serving primarily as a beacon for those Unionists, such as the Duke of Devonshire and Balfour of Burleigh, who expected a rallying of the faithful after the electoral defeat of tariff reform, and who were correspondingly reluctant to throw in their lot with the Liberal Party.[139] Such moderate counsels were insufficient for several leading Unionist free traders who formed the eye-catching handful of 'converts' to the Liberal Party, most famously Churchill, but also important assets such as Jack Seely, Dickson-Poynder, Ivor Guest, and the Wimborne House set.[140]

Nevertheless, this left unresolved the fate of those MPs who remained as loyal Unionist free traders, and the important reward to be recouped from the cultivation of the votes of Unionist free traders in the constituencies.[141] The former occupied much time, but ultimately the Liberal leadership, holding the trump cards, was disinclined to waive the expectations of its own candidates in favour of Unionist ones, save in a small number of seats where the Unionist free traders were firmly entrenched.[142] Unionist free trade votes offered the more substantial prize and, as we will see, provided an important stimulus to the creation by the Liberals of the ostensibly non-party Free Trade Union.[143] Equally importantly, the very existence of free trade Unionism, with its coterie of distinguished followers, widened both the respectability and the ideological defences of free trade. In particular, the Duke of Devonshire was considered to retain a strong personal following, while the ideology of the free trade Unionists advertised a range of arguments which served to expand the appeal of free trade, and which the Unionist Free Traders themselves believed acted to attract the 'pick of the businessmen of England'.[144]

Many of the compelling arguments of the Unionist free traders were of course economic ones, shared by like-minded Liberals, and deployed by recognized financial experts such as Goschen and Lubbock.[145] But, more distinctively, free

[139] The Unionist free traders have been extensively studied; the account here is therefore correspondingly exiguous. See, illustratively, Devonshire to Elliot, 27 Jan. 1905, EP 19494; on the UFTC, Devonshire to Hicks Beach, 12 Jan. 1905 and Beach to Devonshire, 14 Jan. 1905 (copy) in St Aldwyn Papers, PCC/89 and 21.

[140] Rempel, *Unionists Divided*, appendix III, 228. Wimborne House acted as one of London's last political townhouses. Lady Wimborne's son, Ivor Guest, left the Liberal Unionists for the Liberals in April 1904, successfully contesting Cardiff in 1906; Winston Churchill was her nephew. Lady Wimborne herself was exercised more by ritualism than by protectionism: E. Villiers to H. Gladstone, 26 Oct. 1905, HGP, Add. MS 46063.

[141] For one such MP, A. Taylor (East Toxteth), H. James to H. Gladstone, 2 Feb. 1904, HGP, Add. MS 46018.

[142] Rempel, *Unionists Divided*, 151; 7 only, 3 in University seats.

[143] Below, 256 ff.

[144] Strachey to Elliot, 19 Jan. 1905, EP 19494; for the Duke's importance to free trade, Hamilton Diary, *passim*, e.g. 28 Jan. 1904, Add. MS 48681.

[145] For the leading statements of the Free Food case, see Unionist Free Food League, *The Case against Protective Taxation of Food and Raw Materials* (1903), and Leaflets and Pamphlets (59), seriatim, 1903–4. For a review of this case, see Rempel, *Unionists Divided*, 109–14; Elliot, *Goschen*, vol. 2, 254, 267, 270.

trade undoubtedly appealed to the Liberal Unionists of 1886, politicians who had always differentiated themselves from the historic Tory Party, and felt some loyalty to their pre-Home Rule Gladstonianism. This was true, for example, of Arthur Elliot and Lady Frances Balfour. It was a year that loomed largely in their minds as a precedent for their own political actions in 1903–6, although other Unionist free traders were always reluctant to elevate the policy to a status equal or superior to that of the Union with Ireland.[146] Second, many Unionist free traders traced their ideas back to the Tory tradition of Peel and Huskisson. Typically, they denied that free trade in Britain was Cobdenite in origin; as we have seen, books such as Thursfield's *Peel* served as apt reminders of the Tory free trade tradition.[147] They tended readily to identify tariff reform with the anti-Peelite Tories and the old colonial system, while valorizing the mid-Victorian years of peace and low expenditure.[148] Indicatively, the traces of the Peelite administrative mind are plentiful in the Unionist free trade camp, represented, for example, by Sir Edgar Vincent and Lord Northbrook.

Third, free trade Unionism was often highly individualistic in character. Those Cobdenites who had left the Cobden Club in the 1880s now returned to defend the essentials of their doctrine—men such as Goschen, Grant Duff, and Strachey. Here was the strand of old 'Manchesterism', of empirical and Spencerian individualism which, while labelled Cobdenite, represented not the Radical doctrine of Cobden, but the late nineteenth-century Conservative reformulation of those ideas.[149] This world-view retained some Liberal defenders, for example the somewhat maverick secretary of the National Liberal Club's Political and Economic Circle J. H. Levy, but by 1900 the main body of individualist thought was subsumed within Unionism. It was a strand of opinion that was also forcefully expressed in bodies such as the Navy League, amongst whose activists were, for instance, 'free fooders' Yerburgh and Gibson Bowles.[150] Finally, there were the eccentrics and the high Tories, men like Hugh Cecil for whom individualism was more a family habit or religious dogma than a Cobdenite principle, but whose antipathy to tariff reform was also based on its threat to the landed Toryism of the

[146]   On this point, for example, Elliot and Pollock differed from Devonshire.

[147]   Above, 7. G. H. Murray, of the Treasury, likewise reminded Rosebery: 'Whatever Cobden's share in Tariff reform may have been, the man who passed the measure was not Cobden but Peel. You never hear anything of the latter from present day Tories, though they talk a good deal about the former.' 5 Oct. 1903, Rosebery Papers, 10049. Interestingly, Balfour of Burleigh believed Cobden's arguments had converted Peel: Balfour to W. Long, 18 Dec. 1907 (copy), Balfour of Burleigh Papers, TD 93/55/58.

[148]   Elliot to Ritchie, 2 Sept. 1903, EP 19493; Elliot Diary, 7 Oct. 1903; 13 Dec. 1904, EP 19526, 19527. See, too, C. B. Roylance Kent, 'The Fiscal Question: History's Argument', *MacMillan's Magazine* (Sept. 1903). Kent, also a proponent of the referendum, was secretary of the Liverpool Free Food League.

[149]   Above, 137; Taylor, *Men vs the State. Herbert Spencer and Late Victorian Individualism* (Oxford, 1992).

[150]   Coetzee, *For Party or Country*, 22–5, 72–7.

Hotel Cecil.[151] This body of Unionist free trade ideas, propagated above all in Strachey's *Spectator*, lent diversity to the free trade cause, and, although its political effectiveness would be eroded rapidly after 1906, it undoubtedly maximized the appeal of free trade in the election of 1906.

While free trade therefore opened up a profitable vein within the Unionist party for the Liberals to exploit, they did not neglect their more usual allies, the labour movement and the Irish parties, as the Gladstonian coalition was reconstructed. In Ireland, for the most part, free trade remained subordinate to Home Rule, although many free trade Unionists dwelt uneasily on the fear that Chamberlain would prove a renegade on the Union, as on free trade, in order to fulfil his protectionist aims. For, amidst a welter of conflicting Irish economic ideas, the strand of protectionism was undoubtedly thickening, with strong trade union-backed moves to defend native industry, and with Arthur Griffiths modelling Sinn Fein upon the ideas of List, Hungary, and national economy.[152] Nevertheless, this aspiration was hardly consistent with the tariff reformers' imperial framework, and most urban Irishmen, fed by a consistent hostility to indirect taxation, were not yet ready to abandon free trade.[153] More strongly, in Ulster, although tariff reform gained significant support, the cause of free trade brought the small farmers' movement, led by T. W. Russell, solidly behind the Liberals. In these circumstances, one leading Ulster Unionist plausibly complained, the Liberals had sought to 'place . . . a tariff extinguisher over the Home Rule issue'.[154]

The support of organized Labour was for the most part equally straightforward. For the Labour Representation Committee's (LRC) aim was primarily Labour representation, not to replace the capitalist economy, and no issue was more likely than free trade both to enthuse the working-class voter and to draw Liberal votes to Labour candidates within the framework of the Lib–Lab pact of 1903. In the event, the electoral cyclone of 1906 was to bring into the Commons fifty-three Lib–Lab and Labour MPs, almost all of whom were unwaveringly committed to free trade.[155] Nevertheless, the solidity of popular support for free trade was to surprise some Liberals and most tariff reformers, given their rooted beliefs in the outmoded

[151]   Blanche Dugdale, *Family Homespun* (1940); W. H. Greenleaf, *The British Political Tradition. Vol. I. The Ideological Heritage* (1983), 281–93. His brother Robert highlighted the threat of political corruption in his own free trade beliefs, e.g., to Lady Frances Balfour, 12 Oct. 1903, Balfour of Whittingehame Papers, 329.

[152]   F. S. L. Lyons, *Ireland since the Famine* (1971, 1982 edn.), 253–4.

[153]   By 1910, however, the Irish peasantry were reportedly 'food taxers to a man'. Even so, the tariff reform belief that the curse of Cobden was worse than the curse of Cromwell seems not to have been widely shared. Green, *Conservatism*, 298. See, too, J. Campbell, 'Ireland and the Fiscal Controversy', *New Liberal Review*, 38 (Mar. 1904), 168–86.

[154]   Cited in Russell, *Landslide*, 124. Russell provides a useful account of Irish politics upon which I draw here.

[155]   *Free Trader*, 15 Oct. 1909, 287–8. The 'socialist' fringe of the SDF remained suitably suspicious of free trade. For the predicament of the Left, see F. Trentmann, 'Wealth versus Welfare: The British Left between Free Trade and National Economics before the First World War', *Historical Research*, 70 (1997), 70–98.

cosmopolitan essence of free trade and inherent appeal of tariff reform for the working class. To some extent, tariff reformers took comfort in the view that Cobdenism merely provided shibboleths, unthinking claptrap for the masses but eradicable by Chamberlainite enlightenment.[156] This view has often been shared by historians, but popular support for free trade deserves a more complex explanation than it has customarily received.

Free trade and popular politics

While free trade held a unique ability both to reinvigorate the old Gladstonian party and to cement the new progressive alliance, it remained, as Unionist support confirmed, in some ways the doctrine above party that Cobden had proclaimed in the 1840s. It was therefore in order to capitalize upon this supra-party appeal that in July 1903 the Liberals created alongside their existing machinery an ostensibly non-partisan body, the Free Trade Union (FTU).[157] Under Herbert Gladstone's direction, this little-known counterpart to the Tariff Reform League (TRL) was designed to exploit the cardinal importance of free trade to the electoral benefit of the Liberal Party. The FTU appears to have originated in a suggestion of the veteran Liberal the Marquess of Ripon, who on 29 May 1903 urged on Gladstone the need for an extra-parliamentary body to fight Chamberlain's policy on economical rather than political grounds:

I should suggest that a *non-party* League or Association should be formed at once which might embrace Free Traders and Economists of all kinds. There is, of course, the old Cobden Club but it has been of late years rather ridiculous and I would not base my new Association upon it. What is, of course, needed above all things is a new Cobden, but that is an article not easy to find. The truth is that economical questions have been very little thought of for some time; our free trade policy was supposed to be unassailable and people have troubled themselves very little about the arguments by which it can be defended. The work of the forties has to be done over again.[158]

Ripon perhaps exaggerated the economical ignorance of the public, but Gladstone responded enthusiatically to his suggestion, sharing his view of the need for a strong agitating body, with a countrywide organization.[159] With the support of the ex-Cabinet, he therefore set about the formation of this body, securing a committee headed by the wealthy Arnold Morley and, as secretary, the progressive intellectual L. T. Hobhouse.[160] Importantly, too, the FTU gained the support of

---

[156]   W. S. Lilley, *On Shibboleths* (1892); Lilley, with C. S. Devas, later edited J. B. Byles's celebrated protectionist tract, *Sophisms of Free-Trade and Popular Political Economy Examined* (1904; 1st edn. 1849).

[157]   Sykes, *Tariff Reform*, 64; Bernstein, *Liberalism*, 54–5; *WG*, 13, 14, 18 July 1903.

[158]   Ripon to Gladstone, 29 May 1903, HGP, Add. MS 46018, fos. 24–6. For Ripon, see above 144, 218.

[159]   Gladstone to Campbell-Bannerman, 1 June 1903, Campbell-Bannerman Papers, Add. MS 41216, fos. 276–7. Gladstone had already initiated a provisional committee, L. V. Harcourt to Gladstone, 22 May 1903, HGP, Add. MS 45997.

[160]   Vaughan Nash, private secretary to Campbell-Bannerman and future secretary of the post-war Reconstruction Committee, and W. H. Perkin, clerk to George Peel at the Gold Standard

the Liberal imperialists, and emerged as a central organization devoted to combating the fiscal policy of Chamberlain and Balfour, largely 'by argument and concrete illustration'.[161] Funds seem to have been raised with some success, with appeals to scions of old Leaguers, such as William Agnew, alongside more novel and more questionable breeds; for example, there was a disputed £2,000 from the South African randlord J. B. Robinson via Loulou Harcourt.[162] By September 1903 the FTU had promises amounting to £20,000, but, with expenditure running at £2,000 per month, it feared the greater resources of the TRL, seeking to raise £50,000 over four years, and 'in addition they must have much larger private funds'.[163] Information on the FTU's early finances are scanty, but its funds proved sufficient to sustain its dual educational and electoral campaigns, proving well able to match the TRL as a propagandist pressure group.

Besides the constraints of finance, two controversial issues initially hampered the work of the FTU, namely, the degree to which it was to be a party organ, and the extent of its national organization. The first was decided relatively quickly. The FTU welcomed all free traders, acting as an umbrella organization, whose handle was firmly held by Gladstone, but with Unionists and Labour welcome under its shelter.[164] The second problem continued to bedevil the Union, for Gladstone and Hobhouse felt themselves at variance with the Committee in their desire for a network of branches, on the lines of the Anti-Corn Law League, creating an organizational tie between the country and the council.[165] This division centred upon timing; was the FTU's work to be merely educational, with a view to an early election, say in April 1904? Or was it to look to the longer term, in which case a radical rethink was necessary, creating a system of branches and individual membership, so 'that a more national and democratic or at least popular character should be given to our organisation'?[166] Since these questions were unanswerable, and the Liberals were to spend almost three years expecting an imminent dissolution, a *via media* inevitably emerged, with no fully fledged national organization, but the encouragement of spontaneous local free trade bodies. This solution had the advantages of avoiding close identification with the Liberal Party and so attracting Unionist free traders, and it relieved the financial burden on the FTU.[167] But it meant that the only element of nation-wide organization was provided by a federal

---

Association, had also been possibles, as had Halford Mackinder, before succeeding Hewins as director of the LSE.

[161] Draft manifesto, n.d. [June, 1903], HGP, Add. MS 46060, fos. 224–9.

[162] Gladstone to Campbell-Bannerman, 24 July, 1903, Campbell-Bannerman Papers, Add. MS 41216, fos. 312–17.

[163] 'Memo on the position and prospects of the FTU', 13 Jan. 1904, HGP, Add. MS 46106, fos. 127–9; Coetzee, *For Party or Country*, 145, for the comparative funds of the FTU and the TRL.

[164] Russell, *Landslide*, 40–1.

[165] L. T. Hobhouse to Gladstone, 30 Oct. 1903, HGP, Add. MS 46061, fos. 52–3; Gladstone to Asquith, 11 Jan. 1904, Asquith MS 10, fos. 130–1.

[166] Hobhouse to Gladstone, 11 Dec. 1903, HGP, Add. MS 46061, fos. 65–6.

[167] FTU, minutes etc., 13 Jan. 1904; 9 May 1904, HGP, Add. MS 46106, fos. 125–40.

co-ordinating commitee headed by the Duke of Devonshire, linking the Cobden Club, the FTU, and the Unionist Free Trade League, and publishing a circular letter.[168]

Without a national democratic organization, the FTU and Hobhouse had to settle for educational and electoral work. The intellectual flagship of the FTU was its weekly (from June 1904, monthly) journal the *Free Trader*, the first number of which appeared in July 1903. Edited by Hobhouse, with the help of the 'new' Liberal Chiozza-Money,[169] and with contributions from such luminaries as Hobson, Sydney Buxton, and the economist Armitage-Smith, the *Free Trader* was aimed at a select audience: 'nine tenths of its value lies in one tenth of its circulation', keeping 'serious students' and MPs informed of events, arguments, and fallacies. Here were the ready-made contents for a thousand free trade speeches. Hobhouse also supervised the production of numerous FTU pamphlets, fuller discussions of controversial topics, and, more importantly, a series of leaflets, twenty-five million of which had been distributed by January 1904. This educational work vitally reinforced the free trade case, rebutting the arguments of the TRL, putting forward detailed studies of industries, highlighting the benefits of free trade for capital and labour, and with a eye not only to the past, but also to the future growth of the economy under free trade. This was necessarily a centrist position, but it was one that aptly fused elements of the 'new' and the 'old' Liberalisms. It owed as much to Hobhouse as to Cobden.[170]

The second part of the FTU's work was electoral, with the replication of the Anti-Corn Law League's dissemination of free trade missionaries, going among the people, and countering the efforts of the TRL, especially in by-elections.[171] This work supplemented the campaigns of local Liberal parties by organizing its own meetings in the constituencies, both large-scale events and, more typically, street-corner affairs, with intensive house-to-house leafleting. For this electoral work, the FTU put together an impressive body of speakers, relying in particular on men with good working-class credentials, particularly co-operative leaders such as Holyoake, Henry Vivian, and James Rowlands, but also well-known Lib–Lab activists such as Henry Broadhurst, F. W. Soutter, and the leader of the Norfolk agricultural labourers George Edwards.[172] The Union also very effectively de-

---

[168]   Edited by E. G. Brunker; *History of the Cobden Club*, 51; few other details are available. Arthur Elliot helped create this Free Trade Federation: Diary 16 Nov. 1905, EP 19528, and see EP 19552, fos. 110, 113–19. See, too, McKenna to Elliot, 26 Nov. 1905, EP 19494.

[169]   Money combined knowledge of business and the press as editor of *Commercial Intelligence* with progressive social views. Harcourt to Gladstone, 22 May, Money to Harcourt, 29 June 1903, HGP, Add. MS 45997, fos. 31–3; Harris, *Unemployment and Politics*, 232.

[170]   See esp. editorial 11 Mar. 1904, along the lines of Hobhouse, *Democracy and Reaction* (1904), 1–12, 211–27.

[171]   McKenna to Gladstone, 14 Jan. 1904; 6 and 13 Jan. 1905, HGP, Add. MS 46061, fos. 119–20, 46062, fos. 70, 76–7.

[172]   F. W. Soutter, *Fights for Freedom* (1925), 23–108; G. Edwards, *From Crow-Scaring to Westminster: an Autobiography* (1922; rep. 1957), 96–7.

ployed veterans of the 1840s, living embodiments of the 'hungry forties', such as 'Th' Owld Chartist' William Chadwick.[173]

This 'populist' campaign served two main purposes, well revealed in the by-elections contested between May 1903 and December 1905. First, it emphasized the extent of working-class support for free trade as a non-party cause, with the Liberals to some extent holding back their official machinery in by-elections.[174] The FTU, on the other hand, was able to call both on its own resources and upon those of local Radical and trade union organizations. Secondly, this campaign did much to lend the mantle of both quasi-biblical and historicist respectability to the free trade cause. The central motif of the Union became the evocation of the past, the 'hungry forties' from which Cobden and Bright had providentially delivered the English people. It was not accidental that contemporaries saw Cobden embodied in Zangwill's *The Mantle of Elijah*. At a time both of revivalism in Wales and the activation of the Nonconformist conscience in England, the heroes of the League enjoyed a renewed popularity, while the argument from the past proved enormously influential in a deeply historically minded age.[175] Above all, if, at the intellectual level, the case for free trade clearly rested on a modern refutation of tariff reform, its appeal was also deeply rooted in popular memory, albeit a memory in large part reconstructed in the previous generation. The power of this memory was reinforced and legitimated by the survival of witnesses from the 1840s. This idea of recalling the experience of that decade was first canvassed by Rosebery, but had been widely followed locally, and provided the context for the invention of the term the 'hungry forties' by Jane Cobden Unwin in 1904. Under this name, Cobden's daughter published a vivid collection of folk memories, which proved immensely successful in articulating common perceptions of the past. To the old cry of 'dear bread', the new concept of the 'hungry forties' proved a propaganda stroke of genius.[176]

While appealing to the past, the FTU also appeared forward-looking, in its creation of the Women's Free Trade Union (WFTU). Women had played a prominent, but informal part in the Anti-Corn Law League, but by the 1900s not only were separate organizations more widespread, but free trade had peculiar claims to being 'a woman's question'. It put at the centre of politics the issue of

---

[173] *In memoriam William Chadwick* (Luton, 1908), 14; J. Bellamy and J. Saville (eds.), *Dictionary of Labour Biography*, vol. 7 (1984), 53–5; R. H. Davies to Gladstone, 9 Jan. 1904, on the Gateshead by-election. HGP, Add. MS 46023. At Cambridge, J. C. Buckmaster, author of *A Village Politician* (see above 36), campaigned for his Liberal son S. O. Buckmaster, the future Lord Chancellor, as 'an old Chartist who has suffered but remained faithful to his convictions which are now becoming popular'. To J. Burns, *c*.27 Dec. 1905, Burns Papers, Add. MS 46298, BL.

[174] Hudson to Gladstone, 1 Jan. 1904, HGP, Add. MS. 46021, fos. 31–3.

[175] C. E. Playne, *The Pre-War Mind in Britain: A Historical Review* (1928); S. L. Hynes, *The Edwardian Turn of Mind* (Princeton, 1968).

[176] This brochure also carried a commentary on 'The England of the Letters' by the progressive thinker 'Brougham Villiers' [F. J. Shaw], which brought home the moral of oppression under protection.

household expenditure, summoning wives and mothers to the defence of their domestic budgets, as well as men to the defence of their wages. This campaign was organized by a committee drawn largely, but not exclusively, from Liberal circles, 'a very Radical lot', as one Unionist wife thought on joining them.[177] Its leading figures soon included Mary, the American wife of Loulou Harcourt, Mrs Bamford Slack, to whom the Liberal by-election victory at Mid-Herts was largely ascribed by the Tories in 1904, and Lady Frances Balfour, the Liberal Unionist and suffragist daughter of the Peelite Duke of Argyll, who, with due filial piety, added free trade to the causes she stridently supported, albeit sometimes uncomfortably within her Balfour family circle.[178] The WFTU keenly recruited Unionists and anti-suffragists, for example Miss Una Birch (later Lady Richard Pope-Hennessey), and became an efficient organizational body, largely through the administrative efforts of Miss Ivy Pretious, the protégée of the positivist Frederic Harrison.[179] Despite the amorous attentions of both Reginald McKenna and Bertrand Russell, Miss Pretious, 'the epitome of the independent new woman', survived not only to become Lady Tennyson, but to organize an impressive array of lectures nationally by women free traders, urging women to influence men's votes, and a series of leaflets dealing with free trade as 'a woman's question'.[180] With a salary of some £800, Ivy Pretious was probably one of the best-paid women workers of Edwardian Britain. Under her guidance, the WFTU was demonstrative of the wider resonances that the free trade cause acquired and articulated at that time, and did much to refute the jibe of 'stale Cobdenism' that was repeatedly thrown out by the tariff reformers.

The impact of the FTU and the WFTU was of considerable importance to the Liberal Party in keeping the issue of free trade before the electorate, especially in the series of by-election campaigns between 1903 and 1906. Here, it proved more than a match for the TRL, prompting Tory charges that they faced two electoral armies.[181] Its concentration on this single issue undoubtedly helped keep the focus of the electorate on free trade, while the Liberal Party organizations dealt extensively with the secondary issues of Chinese slavery and the Education Act of 1902.

[177]   Madeleine Elliot to Una Birch, 28 Dec. 1904, EP 19494; Mrs Herbert Gladstone acted as its chairman, 1904–6, Gladstone–Glynne Papers, 1899; C. E. Mallet, *Herbert Gladstone: A Memoir* (1932), 199.

[178]   Mary to Loulou Harcourt, 14, 17, 19 Nov. 1904; 5 Aug. 1905; 23 Apr. 1906, Harcourt dep. add. 269; Mary to Lady Elizabeth Harcourt, 2, 6 Apr. 1904, Harcourt dep. 647; Lady Frances Balfour Diaries, 1903–6, Balfour of Whittingehame Papers, 417–20; Frances Balfour, *Ne Obliviscaris: Dinna Forget* (2 vols, 1930), vol. 2, 367–9, 398, 401–8.

[179]   M. Vogeler, *Frederic Harrison* (Oxford, 1984), 250–1, 267–8, 313, 373, 385; Hallam Tennyson, *The Haunted Mind: An Autobiography* (1984), 5–9; *The Times*, 10 Apr. 1958; Mary to L. V. Harcourt, 27 Apr. 1909, Harcourt dep. add. 269; See, too, C. Hazlehurst and C. Woodland (eds.), *A Liberal Chronicle. Journal and Papers of J. A. Pease, 1st Lord Gainford, 1908–1910* (1994), 31–2, 248.

[180]   C. Moorehead, *Bertrand Russell* (1992), 143; N. Griffin (ed.), *The Selected Letters of Bertrand Russell. Vol. 1. The Private Years, 1884–1914* (1992), 281, 315; Soutter, *Fights for Freedom*, 28, 106–8; John Johnson Collection, 'Free Trade and Protection', Box 6 for WFTU leaflets.

[181]   Sandars, quoted in Russell, *Landslide*, 41.

Through the primacy of free trade, the Liberals hoped to bury issues such as Home Rule, while drawing the maximum support from Unionist free traders and from working men.[182] Nevertheless, both relations with the Unionists and with labour required careful attention if the full electoral harvest of free trade was to be reaped.

In the constituencies, therefore, one of the purposes of the FTU had been to encourage the formation of local free trade bodies drawing together Liberal, Labour, and Unionist free traders.[183] These were never great in number, but by 1906 they had emerged in Wales (Cardiff, Penarth), in the North of England (Newcastle, Halifax, Bradford, Manchester, Liverpool), in the Midlands (Nottingham, Oxford, Birmingham), in London and the Home Counties (Ealing, Thames Valley, Surrey, East Grinstead, Hampstead, Chelsea, Deptford, East London), and in Ulster.[184] Some of these were distinctly Unionist in creation, for example that at Surrey, whose mainspring was St Loe Strachey, but for the most part they sought ostensibly to avoid party, while encouraging extensive discussion of the fiscal question and voting for free trade candidates.[185] For example, the North of England Free Trade Association was headed by the Liberal Unionist Thomas Hodgkin, Quaker, banker, and historian, who reluctantly abandoned the sixteenth century for the twentieth, while the Chelsea association brought together men as diverse as Balfour of Burleigh, the industrialist Hugh Bell, the future principal of Ruskin College H. S. Furniss, the civil servant Francis Mowatt, and the historian G. M. Trevelyan.[186] The most important of these regional bodies was undoubtedly the Free Trade League formed in Manchester, essentially a Unionist free trade body, seeking to emulate Manchester's earlier League, and drawing similarly on the leading employers in the textile trades, for example Tom Garnett and Edward Tootal Broadhurst.[187] Among the smaller, but influential bodies the Oxford Free Trade League sought to ally town and gown against tariffs, while at Cambridge there emerged a University Free Trade Association, organized by Arthur Elliot and Horace Darwin, with the help of Pigou and Keynes.[188] These local associations

---

[182] Elliot Diary, 30 Mar. 1905, EP 19527, for a dinner at Haldane's (Elliot, Asquith, Morley, Grey, Strachey) to 'talk over the best line for Free Traders to adopt at present as regards Local Government in Ireland'.

[183] Above, 257; Gladstone to James, 7 Jan. 1904, James to Gladstone, 9 Jan. 1904, et seq., HGP, Add. MS 46018.

[184] For details of these bodies, see esp. Elliot Papers, 19552.

[185] The Surrey Association thus supported the Liberal candidate in the Chertsey Division by-election of July 1904. Strachey to Gladstone, 26 June 1904, HGP, Add. MS 46061, fos. 248–51.

[186] North of England FTA, var. printed papers, EP 19552; Louise Creighton, *Life and Letters of Thomas Hodgkin* (2nd edn. 1918), 259–61, 282, 329; *WG*, 17 June 1904; E. L. Horniman to Balfour of Burleigh, 16 Feb. 1906, Balfour of Burleigh Papers, TD 93/55/62; H. S. Furniss, *Memories of Sixty Years* (1931), 73 ff.

[187] Clarke, *Lancashire and New Liberalism*, *passim*; printed ephemera, Manchester Central Library; Churchill described the Free Trade League as 'much the most powerful body which has been created during the present struggle', to Elliot, 28 Oct. 1904, EP 19493.

[188] Printed reports etc., EP 19552; A. W. Hall to L. R. Phelps, 24 Dec. 1903, G. E. Underhill to Phelps, 2 Oct., 19 and 21 Nov. 1903, Phelps Papers, Oriel College, Oxford. The Oxford free traders

were vital contributors to the free trade effort in particular constituencies, for example Manchester North-West and Cambridge, but more generally strove to isolate the tariff reformers and to highlight the non-party appeal of free trade. Nevertheless, their influence was probably greater upon formerly Unionist voters and recent Liberal abstentionists than on the working-class vote, and only the East London People's League against Protection took an avowedly 'populist' stance.[189]

The successful defence of free trade required more than these *ad hoc* organizations, especially if the working-class vote was to be mobilized. This was vital, for, as the Liberal T. R. Buchanan put it, 'Our best hope is that the working men will as a body keep firm. The middle classes who were Cobden's standby have been corrupted by Joe's imperialism.'[190] Keeping working men firm had to some extent been achieved by the FTU and the federated free trade bodies, but it also required more direct appeals to organized labour. In this context, perhaps surprisingly, the 'faintly ridiculous' Cobden Club scorned by Ripon in 1903 emerged briefly as a factor of some importance in articulating working-class support for the issue. Not only did its secretary Harold Cox seek a high profile for the Club in the press, but with the Lib–Lab MP Fred Maddison as organizing secretary among the working classes, he appealed for support to the labour movement, hoping to turn to advantage the Club's rediscovered non-party character.[191] In particular, Cox had maintained close links with co-operative bodies, valued allies in the defence of working-class consumption, and had organized numerous expressions of working-class opinion in favour of free trade, with an impressive endorsement of the Club's policy by 940 labour leaders in September 1903.[192] Nevertheless, Cox's 'fighting campaign' was much to the dislike of the Club's president, the old Gladstonian civil servant Lord Welby, who by December 1903 had become highly critical of what he considered Cox's independence, tactlessness, and egotism. As a result, Cox resigned, after which the Club—in any case short of funds—played a far more restrained part in the free trade campaign.[193] It contributed some important state-

---

employed G. W. Gough as 'a specialist duellist to disable any Chamberlainite lecturer that comes near the place', according to C. E. Montague to L. T. Hobhouse, 7 Dec. 1905, C. P. Scott Papers, *Manchester Guardian* archive, 126/148, University of Manchester John Rylands Library.

[189] *Free Trader*, 6 May 1904. Its secretary Sheridan Jones, a well-known land reformer and co-operator: 'Labour and the Crown Lands', *Independent Review*, Feb. 1905. For a collection of its leaflets, BLPES.

[190] Buchanan to Elliot, 4 Oct. 1903, EP 19493.

[191] Welby to Gladstone, 10 Jan. 1904, HGP, Add. MS 46061, fos. 111–12. Cox similarly attempted to gain Unionist free trade support: Cox to E. Vincent, 11 June 1902, 30 June 1903, D'Abernon Papers, Add. MS 48939, BL. By 1903 the Club had lost many of its Radical political associations and now emphasized its purely free trade credentials.

[192] For details, see esp. *Free Trader*, 11 Sept. 1903; *WG*, 19, 27 June, 6, 21 July, 31 Aug. 1903.

[193] They had earlier clashed over whether Cox should fight a by-election in Sheffield, Welby fearing the damage that the defeat of the secretary of the Club would do in a stronghold of protectionism. Welby to Gladstone, 20 June 1903, HGP, Add. MS 46060, fo. 213. On Cox's resignation, Welby to Gladstone, 15 Dec. 1903, 10 Jan. 1904, 21 Feb. 1904, Welby looking forward to a quieter life with Cox's departure; 'Poor dear Cox was able and active but a great trial. I never came across such a vain man', HGP, Add.

ments, for example its refutation of Chamberlain in *Fact versus Fiction* (1903), but its 1905 volume *The Burden of Armaments* was more symptomatic of its future direction, emphasizing the need to retrench expenditure and to avoid an arms race, themes that had long preoccupied men such as Welby, Shaw-Lefevre, and Hirst. Indicatively, Cox was succeeded by the Rainbow Circle Progressive G. H. Perris (secretary 1903–5), a leading early twentieth-century pacifist, whose growing disillusionment with Liberal foreign policy led him to join the Labour Party in 1910.[194]

In two further ways the Cobden Club exploited the 'advantages of a historic past and a historic name'.[195] First, in 1904 it orchestrated the enthusiastic and polemical nation-wide celebration of the centenary of Cobden's birth, partly in response to what was resented as the derisive treatment of Cobden by the tariff reform movement.[196] This included an effusion of publications and a great Alexandra Palace demonstration, addressed by Campbell-Bannerman, Churchill, and Lloyd George. A series of public meetings—at least sixty-three in number—were held throughout Britain (with others in America, Europe, and the Empire) largely under Liberal auspices, but with Unionist participation, and with several organized by co-operative societies, and trade and labour councils.[197] These meetings were designed not only to revive Cobdenite responses, but also re-evoked the Victorian cult of Cobden in Edwardian progressive garb, playing down Cobden's anti-imperialism, but reincarnating the 'people's' champion of the 1840s as the 'pioneer of the great Labour movement of to-day'.[198] It was here that the free trade campaign, if it could not resurrect Cobden, was at least able through his commemoration to place him at the heart of the public battle, as a far more appealing hero than Chamberlain.[199] In this context, too, the theme of the 'hungry forties' reinforced Cobden's claim to have delivered the people from aristocratic oppression, claims reinforced further by the republication of his writings and other tracts from the 1840s, such as Ebenezer Elliott's *Corn Law Rhymes*.[200]

MS 46061, fos. 73–4, 111–12, 166–7. For later activity, see *Cobden Club Circular*, July 1905–Oct. 1906 [copy in Nuffield College Library].

[194] H. Josephson (ed.), *Biographical Dictionary of Modern Peace Leaders* (Westport, Conn., 1985), 744–6; A. J. A. Morris, *Radicalism Against War, 1906–1914. The Advocacy of Peace and Retrenchment* (1972), 177–8.

[195] Spencer Walpole to C. P. Trevelyan, 11 July 1903, Trevelyan Papers, CPT13.

[196] For printed ephemera, see John Johnson Collection, 'Free Trade and Protection', Box 1.

[197] e.g., Elliot at Newbury, Diary, 8 and 9 June 1904, EP 19527; cf. the Duke of Devonshire's demurral, to Welby, 3 June 1904, CP 1204; Cobden Centenary Calendar, copy in John Johnson Collection.

[198] e.g., *New Age*, 2 June 1904, 346; *Reynold's Newspaper*, 5 June 1904; *WG*, 3 June; *Borders' County Advertiser*, 1 June; *Young Scot*, 9 June 1904.

[199] For the motif of Cobden versus Chamberlain, see, e.g., *New Age*, 9 June 1904, 'Cobden's rise is Chamberlain's fall', 354.

[200] *The Political Writings of Richard Cobden*, ed. R. E. Welby (2 vols, 1903); the *Rhymes* were designed for use at public meetings, 'the stirring notes of the Poet of the People may serve to kindle in these latter days something of that enthusiasm which they aroused so powerfully seventy years ago', Thomas Fisher Unwin, publisher's note, John Johnson Collection, 'Free Trade and Protection', box 7.

Second, the cult of Cobden and the work of the Cobden Club went hand in hand with the activities of the Cobden family, and above all the Fisher Unwin press. For Jane Cobden-Unwin and her husband Thomas Fisher-Unwin, an active Cobden Club member, leading avant-garde publisher, keen Liberal, and friend of the oppressed, quite self-consciously appropriated the Cobdenite legacy. Not only was Dunford House, Cobden's home in West Sussex, turned into a much-visited (by Anarchists as well as Liberals) shrine, but, as we have seen, Jane Cobden-Unwin's *Hungry Forties* created a central popular symbolic understanding of the free trade debate, whose lessons for new Liberals were underlined in a coda by the progressive 'Brougham Villiers'.[201] It should also be noted that Francis Hirst, for many the twentieth century's most unreconstructed Cobdenite, had also married into the Cobden family.[202] But it was, above all, through the Unwin press, then at its peak, that the free trade cause benefited from an invigorating strand of Radical and Cobdenite literature.[203] The press was responsible for a vast outpouring of serious and popular writings on free trade, some suitably and delicately embossed with 'big loaves'. In this way the link between Cassell and the Cobden Club in the 1880s was replicated. As *The Young Scot* appreciated, 'Messrs Fisher Unwin deserve the gratitude of all Free Traders for the magnificent way in which, as publishers, they are fighting the people's battle.'[204]

Much of this literature was widely known in the Edwardian labour movement, but that movement also generated its own defence of free trade as an essential component of working-class welfare. This had already been voiced in opposition to Tory fiscal policy between 1899 and 1902, but crystallized into an orchestrated defence of the 'free breakfast table' in 1903. At the national level, the Parliamentary Committee of the TUC, which had campaigned against the corn duty in 1902, began a series of leaflets, condemning Chamberlain's fiscal proposals.[205] In this propagandist work it was joined by the LRC and the General Federation of Trades Unions in a 'united Labour Manifesto', which added to the defence of free trade the goal of the redistribution of wealth, a message in no way distasteful to the Liberal Party, which pirated this leaflet to MacDonald's alarm.[206] MacDonald himself was soon able to report (to the protectionist Australian Labour Party) 'the almost

[201]   For reactions to *The Hungry Forties* see, e.g., G. W. Kitchin, Dean of Durham, 'nothing so eloquent as the "voice of the people" unspoilt by town influences' and the veteran co-operator Holyoake who appreciated its 'excellent real rustic ring', CP 154, WSRO.

[202]   See F. W. Hirst, *In the Golden Days* (1947), 220 ff.

[203]   In the 1906 election, 51 candidates had had works published by the Unwin press; 40 were returned, of whom F. E. Smith was the only Tory. Undated memo, CP 1104, f. 68, WSRO. For a good account of these years at the press, see Stanley Unwin, *The Truth about a Publisher* (1960), 79–111.

[204]   *Young Scot*, 2/4 (Jan. 1905), 52; see, too, 1/4 (Feb. 1904), 49; Campbell-Bannerman to T. Fisher Unwin, 15 Feb. 1906, CP 982, WSRO.

[205]   Trades Union Congress, Parliamentary Committee, minutes (microfilm), 30 Apr., 26 and 27 May 1902; 16, 17 June, 10 and 11 Nov., 15 and 16 Dec. 1903; 19 Jan., 3 Feb., 20, 21, 22 Mar. 1904.

[206]   Minutes, letters, and other papers concerning the LRC/Labour Party, 1900–12, fos. 218–19, 22 Jan. 1904, Coll. Misc. 196, BLPES.

unanimous opposition of organised Labour' to Chamberlain's proposals.[207] For Labour, free trade remained, as Mill had taught, the indispensable basis of national wealth.[208] In the interests of Labour, leaders such as Henderson, Kelley, and Shackleton were ready to appear on free trade platforms. Such co-operation was distasteful to some elements of the ILP, but that body itself campaigned actively against the bread tax of 1902, while Chamberlain's proposals became the first object of attack for its newly created literature department in 1903. Under Snowden's direction, the ILP was keen to keep some ideological distinctiveness, but was nevertheless emphatic in upholding free trade as the minimum condition of socialist progress, a lesson that their continental counterparts had long understood.[209] The Social Democratic Federation's Will Thorne was accordingly anxious to line up the Socialist International against Chamberlain.[210]

The Co-operative movement also responded enthusiatically not only to the leading consumer issue of low prices, but to the threat of international ill-will and the growth of militarism that tariffs portended. Henry Vivian, J. C. Gray, William Maxwell, and Fred Maddison became leading opponents of tariffs, and Co-operative Congresses repeatedly rallied to the 'free breakfast table', with 'the spirit of Villiers, of Cobden and of Bright . . . in the hearts of millions of men'.[211] Less numerously, the members of the Women's Co-operative Guild under Margaret Llewelyn Davies also campaigned strongly, stalwart opponents of dearer bread allied with the moral benefits of free trade.[212]

At the root of working-class enthusiasm lay, above all, the defence of the collective gains of two generations of working-class political activity. For, however strong the socialist dislike for the *laissez-faire* element that they identified with the 'Manchester School', organized labour saw in free trade the best defence of high wages, cheap prices, and political autonomy for the working class, gains not to be lightly cast aside in favour of the ILP's socialist or Chamberlain's fiscal millennium. Free trade encapsulated not only material benefits, but also a notion of justice dearly won from an oppressive aristocracy. Here was a cause that generated, more than any other issue, a sense of working-class identity, able to bring together oppressed agricultural labourers alongside the best-paid industrial workers and their wives. Chamberlain affected to believe that Cobdenite/Radical meetings gave 'a totally

[207] Ibid., fos. 277–9, 16 Nov. 1904.

[208] *The Bogey of Foreign Imports: the Labour Party point of view* (LRC Leaflet 9).

[209] Minutes of the National Administrative Council, 26 and 27 May 1902; 22 May, 11 June, 24 and 26 Sept., 11 Nov. 1903, ILP1/4, ILP Archives, BLPES; P. Snowden, *Mr Chamberlain's Bubble* (1903); *Facts for the Workers about Protection, Free Trade, and Monopoly* (ILP Tracts for the Times 3; 1903).

[210] Minutes, TUC Parliamentary Committee, 15 Dec. 1903.

[211] *The Co-operative Union. 35th Annual Congress 1903 (Doncaster)* (Manchester, 1903), 314–18; *The Scottish Co-operator*, 18 Dec. 1903.

[212] 'What Co-operative women think', *Free Trader*, 23 Oct. 1903. The WCG represented 380 bodies and 19,000 'splendid women'. M. Llewelyn Davies to C. P. Trevelyan, 18 Mar. 1905, Trevelyan Papers, CPT15. For one WCG meeting, with Unionist, Liberal, and socialist support, see *MG*, 12 Nov. 1903.

wrong impression as to the opinions of the working-classes', yet the tariff reform movement's own attempts to organize working-class opinion were, outside the West Midlands, a conspicuous failure.[213] On the other hand, there is considerable evidence to suggest an enthusiastic popular response to free trade, ranging from the cottages of Hampshire, the villas of suburban London, to the bothies of Aberdeenshire.[214] Against the Chamberlainite appeal to empire, to producers, and to protection, the election of 1906 was emphatically to demonstrate that 'democracy', even in its limited pre-1918 form, was ideally suited to embrace free trade, the distinctive creed of the 'unorganized consumers' and household voters of Edwardian Britain.

The people's battle: free trade, intellect, and democracy in Edwardian Britain

However plausible the arguments and ideological basis of tariff reform, designed to supply the Conservative Party with a form of *Sammlungspolitik* worthy of its European Right counterparts, the election of 1906, with its massive popular endorsement of free trade, was also a testament to the vitality of a Liberal ideology and practice that had successfully transformed the creed of the early Victorian cotton masters into the collective choice of Edwardian democracy. Free trade in 1906 had attained this position of electoral dominance not as 'old' liberal political economy, the stale creed of Cobdenism mistakenly assailed by the tariff reformers, but as part of a vigorous restatement of Liberal principles, including the people's right to cheap food, to freedom from oppression by vested interests, and to a foreign policy that combined national safety through the Navy with the avoidance of tariff wars and imperial entanglements. This defence of free trade contained within it an important international policy, but, more emphatically, the electoral verdict of 1906 reasserted a domestic political morality, from whose Cobdenite–Gladstonian roots had grown a progressive vision of popular welfare and democracy.

In some ways, this Edwardian ascendancy of free trade and Liberalism was surprising, in the light of the tariff reformers' own expectations, of historians' subsequent reconstruction of their compelling ideological case, and of the pessimism of those progessives who feared that the forces of reaction, jingoism, plutocracy, and the 'Yellow Press' would subvert the fragile democracy of early twentieth-century Britain.[215] In part, this disparity between protectionist expectation and Cobdenite result owes something to the tendency to overrate the coherence of the tariff reform case. But it also derives from the temptation to share the tariff reform indictment of free trade as mere 'Cobdenite cosmopolitanism', signifying the dominance within policy-making of the interests of international

---

[213] Amery, *Chamberlain*, vol. 5, 315; P. Adams, 'Tariff Reform and the Working Classes'; K. D. Brown, 'The Trade Union Tariff Reform Association, 1904–1913', *Journal of British Studies*, 11 (1970), 142–53.

[214] Press reports, *passim*, by-elections, 1903–6; Russell, *Landslide*.

[215] Hobhouse, *Democracy and Reaction*, 46–55, 76; A. J. Lee, *The Origins of the Popular Press, 1855–1914* (1976), esp. 181–97.

financiers, and the elevation of those interests at the expense of national and imperial interests.[216] Yet, as we have seen, the financiers of the City of London were to be found veering towards the tariff reform camp, rather than towards free trade, while business, divided throughout, failed to rally enthusiastically to Chamberlain, especially as imperial preference offered fewer temptations than protection, retaliation, or free trade. The somewhat voiceless and neglected mass of shopkeepers and small manufacturers seem also, by and large, to have rallied to free trade, if more to the conservative creed of public economy than to the New Liberal aspiration to welfare and democracy. More generally, an interesting, if not fully convincing, 'public choice' case has been made, purporting to show that the results of the 1906 election strongly conform to the economic interests of constituents, defined by their involvement in international trade, and that, if anything, the limits to the suffrage diminished the scale of the free trade victory in 1906.[217] This election provides a model test case of trade policy that was determined by direct democratic voting, and not by the impact of interest groups, but also one in which the bulk of the electors voted as 'cosmopolitans' and 'producers'.

This outcome also suggests the failure of the attempt by the tariff reformers to appropriate the rhetoric of nationalism against cosmopolitanism.[218] The link between protection and nationalism worked well in 'new' countries seeking to create national identities, such as Canada and Australia, as it did too in recently unified Germany, where Bismarck was able to emphasize the almost palpably disloyal threat posed by 'Manchesterism'.[219] However, it made far less sense in Britain, whose recent history had emphasized free trade as central both to the providential mission of Britain in the nineteenth-century world and as a calculable gain to the welfare of the British people. Free trade, as Miles Taylor has shown, had traditionally been able to clothe itself in the image of John Bull, and in 1906 the issue was often portrayed as a British ideal to be defended against threats subversive of British traditions.[220] Far from appearing anti-British, free trade itself was a vital element in national identity, part of the definition of the people as the nation. Paradoxically, Cobdenism appealed both as an expression of 'cosmopolitanism' and of patriotic 'little England' sentiment.

[216] This to some extent impairs the analysis in Semmel, *Imperialism and Social Reform*, Green, *Conservatism*, and Cain and Hopkins, *British Imperialism*, vol. 1, 202–24.

[217] D. A. Irwin, 'The Political Economy of Free Trade: Voting in the British General Election of 1906', *Journal of Law and Economics*, 37 (1994), 75–108.

[218] For a typical example, the tariff reform poster advertising a 'Free Imports' meeting, with Mr Johann Schmidt of the Cobden Club, and a speaker, Mr Schwetter, Coll. Misc. 519/90, BLPES.

[219] Above, 181. See, too, J. Becker, *Das Deutsche Manchestertum. Eine Studie zur Geschichte des wirtschaftpolitischen Individualismus* (Karlsruhe, 1907).

[220] M. Taylor, 'John Bull and the Iconography of Public Opinion in England, c.1712–1929', *Past and Present*, 134 (1992), 122–3, neatly shows how in the January election of 1910, the free trade John Bull remained more credible, despite tariff reform attempts to use this imagery. Oddly, Taylor neglects 1903–6, but see, for example, 'Wake Up! John Bull', *Review of Reviews*, July and Aug. 1903. The Liberals seem also to have benefited from the racialist feelings roused by the issue of Chinese slavery, associated with the Conservatives, G. Wallas, *Human Nature in Politics* (2nd edn., 1910), 107–8.

In these ways, the ideology of free trade provided a vital element in sustaining Liberalism as a dynamic and cohesive force in Edwardian Britain. It did so not as an adventitious survival, but as part of the continuous reapplication and reinterpretation of free trade ideas and policies in late-Victorian Britain, which had built the central bridge between Gladstonianism and New Liberalism.[221] Above all, having acted primarily as a defence of consumer interests in the narrow debates concerning money, sugar, and the empire, in the aftermath of the Boer War free trade re-emerged strongly as the systemic idea which united those threatened not only by tariffs, but by Chinese slavery, landlords, brewers, and the Church of England, the threats, as Hobhouse saw them, of 'aggrandisement, war, compulsory enlistment, lavish expenditure, Protection, arbitrary government, class legislation'.[222] The strength of New Liberalism lay not in its transcendance of Cobdenism, but, as we have seen, in its ability to dissociate free trade from *laissez-faire*, making possible a coherent intellectual synthesis sustaining a range of 'new' social policies, and helping to revive a popular democratic alliance between Liberals, intellectuals, and working men and women.

That intellectual synthesis owed much to the progressives, who had rediscovered the merits of 'Manchesterism' during the Boer War. But their continued contributions throughout the campaign did much to sustain the intellectual momentum of free trade, especially through weekly journals such as the *Speaker* and the *Independent Review*, with a constant flow of articles from the pens of Hobhouse, Hobson, Russell, and Trevelyan.[223] This undoubtedly helped sustain the Liberal Party's claim to be the party of ideas and to thwart the aim of the tariff reformers to displace the intellectual authority of 'old political economy'. That campaign, as Ewan Green has shown, embraced a comprehensive attempt to build a neo-mercantilist vision of state and society, recruiting economists such as Ashley, Hewins, Foxwell, and Cunningham, in an attempt to emulate the German 'socialists of the chair' in their extirpation of 'Manchesterism' in Bismarckian Germany.[224] Yet, however neat and logical this vision, it was one largely repudiated by the experts. This is clear not only from the well-known letter of fourteen leading economists to *The Times* in 1903, and from the policy advice of Marshall, but also from the detailed recent research into the 'market for political economy', which illustrates the academic isolation of the tariff reformers, within their redoubt of Birmingham, with some outlying support in Cambridge, Oxford, and the LSE.[225] In Cambridge many economists and Apostles, including Pigou, Keynes, Lowes Dickinson, and

---

[221] Cf., typically, Sykes, *Tariff Reform*, 62: 'The opposition to tariff reform . . . came not from "new Liberalism" . . . but from traditional free traders on traditional free trade grounds.'

[222] Hobhouse, *Democracy and Reaction*, 55.

[223] Cf. on the Unionist side, the *Edinburgh Review*, edited by Arthur Elliot, which provided an important defence of free trade.

[224] Green, *Conservatism, passim.*

[225] Above, 235; A. Kadish and K. Tribe (eds.), *The Market for Political Economy* (1993), *passim*; A. Kadish, *Historians, Economics, and Economic History* (1990), 216–18, 226–8.

H. O. (HOM) Meredith, were active free traders, as was their mentor Oscar Browning, a veteran, among other avocations, of the Cobden Club.[226] For this group, free trade seemed a necessary part of the vision of freedom and civilization propounded in the ethics of George Moore.[227] In Oxford, more staidly, Phelps and Underhill led the resistance to the 'historicist and protectionist tide', but with greater success in the university than the city.[228] At the LSE Hewin's advocacy of tariff reform led to his departure as director, while Hobhouse, Wallas, and, above all, Cannan voiced strong support for free trade, which was ultimately more influential, not least upon the young economists of the 1920s.[229]

Besides these economic experts, many scions of the intellectual aristocracy identified by Noel Annan were also remarkable in their adherence to free trade—ranging from the Darwin brothers (Horace and Leonard) to E. M. Forster, who canvassed for his Liberal friend Francis Acland in North Yorkshire in 1906.[230] Bertrand Russell wrote prominently and spoke avidly on behalf of free trade, as did the historian G. M. Trevelyan.[231] Among leading novelists, George Meredith and Thomas Hardy were notably sympathetic, while Julian Sturgis, the literary son of a partner in Barings, was drawn to publish in 1904 critical notes on Balfour.[232] The popular Zionist novelist Isaac Zangwill also brought powerful literary support to free trade as a progressive cause. Belloc, Chesterton, Buchan, and A. E. W. Mason all campaigned for free trade, the latter to the extent of becoming MP for Coventry in 1906, while J. M. Barrie, the son of a Scottish handloom weaver, followed the

---

[226] Dickinson was much involved in setting up the economics tripos at Cambridge in 1904, with the aim of attracting those aspiring to a career in the 'higher branches of business'. *Chambers of Commerce Journal*, Apr. 1904. In 1885, when 'full of Henry George', Dickinson had worked on the co-operative farm started by Harold Cox in Surrey: D. Proctor (ed.), *The Autobiography of Goldsworthy Lowes Dickinson* (1973), 69; above, 245 n. 91.

[227] P. Levy, *Moore: G. E. Moore and the Cambridge Apostles* (Oxford edn., 1981).

[228] A. C. Howe, 'Intellect and Civic Responsibility: Dons and Citizens in 19th-century Oxford', in R. C. Whiting (ed.), *Oxford: Studies in the History of a University Town since 1800* (Manchester, 1993), 39.

[229] R. Dahrendorf, *A History of the LSE* (1995), 79–80, 109; L. Robbins, *Autobiography of an Economist* (1971), 83–6, 93. Compton Mackenzie, *Sinister Street* (1913; Penguin edn., 1960) for the Oxford Union, 435–7; the *Free Trader*, 3/60 (Dec. 1905) recorded the Oxford Union regretting by 266 votes to 161 the Conservative identification with tariff reform; a Cambridge Union vote favourable to Chamberlain in November 1903 was reversed in June 1904: Kadish, *Historians*, 217.

[230] N. Annan, 'The Intellectual Aristocracy', in J. H. Plumb (ed.), *Essays in Social History* (1955), 241–87; ephemera, Cambridge FTA in EP 19552; A. Acland, *A Devon Family* (1981), 143; P. N. Firbank, *E. M. Forster: A Life* (one-vol. edn. Oxford, 1979).

[231] R. A. Rempel, 'Conflicts and Change in Liberal Theory and Practice, 1890–1918: The Case of Bertrand Russell', in P. J. Waller (ed.), *Politics and Social Change in Modern Britain* (1987), 117–39; *The Collected Papers of Bertrand Russell. Vol. 12 Contemplation and Action, 1902–1914*, ed. R. A. Rempel et al. (1985); P. F. Clarke, 'Bertrand Russell and the Dimensions of Edwardian Liberalism', in M. Moran and C. Spadoni, *Intellect and Social Conscience* (Hamilton, Ontario, 1984), 207–21; D. Cannadine, *G. M. Trevelyan. A Life in History* (1992), 61, 75.

[232] C. L. Cline (ed.), *The Letters of George Meredith* (3 vols, Oxford, 1970), vol. 3, 1545; J. R. Sturgis, *The Prime Minister's Pamphlet: A Study and Some Thoughts* (1903), 25 pp.; Sturgis to Elliot, 21 Dec. 1903, EP 19493.

creation of Peter Pan with a less memorable anti-Chamberlain satire, *Josephine*.[233]
To some extent these literary efforts were challenged by those of the new Fabian
aristocracy of intellect, with Shaw at times strident against free trade, but this
provided little comfort for tariff reformers seeking to combat socialism. Ultimately,
if the success of tariff reform was predicated upon its intellectual assumptions, then
the challenge of the historical economists to Cobdenite orthodoxy was a battle for
intellectual authority which the tariff reformers conspicuously lost.

If free trade won 'the battle of ideas', it is important to understand that this was
no abstract battle fought in the pages of academic journals, but that ideas were
effectively carried to the electorate in a campaign in which many intellectuals
themselves were ready to immerse themselves, whether Keynes on the street
corners of Cambridge, Forster on the moors of North Yorkshire, or Russell amidst
the villas of Surrey. Their presence, defending 'sane internationalism' or 'flashing
Free Trade verities', served to highlight the appeal of free trade to the rational
calculations of voters, against what was perceived as the irrational appeal of Joe's
tycoonery and imperialism. Thus, Pigou, the Cambridge founder of 'welfare economics', graduated from being the Cobden Prizeman in 1901 and the debating
vanquisher of Howard Vincent of the United Empire Trade League, to a classical
defence of free trade, and to speaking tours and popular tracts in its favour.[234] In
this way, the Millite link between the intellectuals and the people had been
reinvigorated on the most fundamental issue of public morality.[235]

Even so, as Edwardian intellectuals became increasingly preoccupied with 'human nature in politics', the appeal of free trade was not simply confined to rational
economic calculation. For by 1906 increasing attention was paid to imaginative
electoral propaganda, with considerable use of cartoons, songs, posters, magic
lanterns, and films.[236] Here, not only did tariff reform fail, according to Wallas, 'to
secure even a tolerably good tune', but free trade acquired the best jokes, deployed
in a pictorial campaign of brilliance.[237] Above all, in Francis Carruthers Gould, a
fervent Liberal, the free traders possessed the most effective and successful car-
toonist of the age.[238] With Chamberlain as his favourite subject, he devoted himself

[233]   Russell, *Landslide*, 61; Sir Arthur Conan-Doyle stood as a tariff reformer; D. Mackail, *The Story
of J. M. B.* (1941; 1949 edn.), 387.
[234]   *The Great Inquest: an examination of Mr Chamberlain's Fiscal Proposals* (reprinted from the *Pilot*,
1903); *The Riddle of the Tariff* (1903); J. Saltmarsh and P. Wilkinson, *Arthur Cecil Pigou, 1877–1959*
(Cambridge, 1960). See, too, Kadish, *Historians*, 191–6, 217–19.
[235]   For this theme, but not this context, see S. Collini, *Public Moralists: Political Thought and
Intellectual Life in Britain, 1850–1930* (Oxford, 1991).
[236]   Adams, 'Tariff Reform and the Working Classes'. For the changing political media, see A. L.
Lowell, *The Government of England* (2 vols, 1908), vol. 2, 61.
[237]   Wallas, *Human Nature*, 85; for songs, see 'The Mid-Devon Election', *New Liberal Review*, 38
(1904), 46–50.
[238]   As Unionists admitted, e.g. Lady Dorothy Nevill, *My Own Times* (1912), 13–14: 'His gifted
pencil generally carries far greater conviction than the impassioned harangues of most politicians.' For
Gould's views of the use of the pictorial form cf. appeals to the intellect, see unpublished autobiography,
esp. vol. 12, fos. 317–333, vol. 16, fo. 386, HLRO.

by word and line to the campaign against tariff reform both in the *Westminster Gazette* and in his own *Picture Politics*. Not only were his own cartoons widely reproduced, but he inspired many imitators, with, for example, the *Morning Leader* in 1904 issuing its own collection of 'Fiscal Cartoons', which it vaunted to be worth '23 volumes of any Political Educator'. Interestingly, too, the *Morning Leader* reproduced many *Punch* cartoons of the 1840s in favour of free trade.[239] Together with more serious matter, these also provided the content of the numerous magic lantern shows organized by the FTU up and down the country.[240]

If humour favoured free trade, so too did history. For not the least of the ironies of the free trade/tariff reform debate was that, while the latter assailed the abstract nature of classical political economy, utilizing the critiques of the historical economists in Germany, in England history was successfully appropriated by the free traders, most formidably, as we have seen, in Jane Cobden Unwin's invention of the 'hungry forties'. In part, this might be seen as an appeal to atavistic elements in the popular mind (perhaps 2–3 per cent of electors had been 14 and above in the 1840s) but it also represented an appeal to the collective memory of the people, with Cobden himself, as an emblematic figure whose career had been constantly reconstructed, achieving a pertinence for the Edwardians which the careers of both Gladstone and Bright lacked. Admittedly, this was an appeal to an immediate past rather than to remote yet powerful Radical myths of Anglo-Saxon England, but it was none the less an effective form of political argument. The struggle in the 1840s of rich against poor, privilege against industry, monopolists versus the people, the oppressed against the tyrannical, were all themes with a strong echo in the Edwardian Radical critique of plutocracy and corruption.[241] Against the forces of wealth, luxury, and indolence, free traders appealed to a democratic state, the embodiment of the co-operative action of individuals, not the organ of class interests. Democracy and free trade were intertwined as parts of the Liberal state, a rational, organic, and historic whole.

The success of free trade was all the more impressive in 1906 for the weight of the press was against it—all the penny morning papers were in the Unionist camp by January 1906, while the circulation of the three leading Liberal halfpenny papers, the *Daily News*, the *Daily Chronicle*, and the *Morning Leader*, scarcely matched that of the tariff reform *Daily Mail*.[242] This dominance was, as Russell suggests, to some extent undermined by the exposure of Unionist divisions, while, as Spender pointed out, not all newspaper readers were voters.[243] The Liberals also, of course, benefited from provincial press support, in particular C. P. Scott's *Manchester Guardian*, from the progressive journalists in the London press, includ-

---

[239] Cf., on the tariff reform side, Harry Furniss, *Our Joe* (1903).

[240] Some scripts for the FTU were written by the former Treasury official, Sir Francis Mowatt; for films, see above n. 6.

[241] G. R. Searle, *Corruption in British Politics, 1895–1930* (Oxford, 1987), 52–99.

[242] Russell, *Landslide*, 137; Koss, *Political Press*, vol. 2, 38 ff.

[243] Russell, *Landslide*, 143; Spender, quoted in Lee, *Popular Press*, 186.

ing Gardiner, Massingham, Cook, Masterman, and Donald, and, perhaps above all, from the powerful defence of free trade provided by Spender's *Westminster Gazette*. But in combating the tariff reform dominance of the press, the Liberal victory in 1906 also owed much to the grassroots campaigns organized by the Liberal Party, by the FTU and WFTU, to the literary work of the FTU and the progressive journals, and to the forces of organized labour, all of which sustained enthusiasm for free trade against Chamberlain's undoubted personal popularity.[244] As a result, in 1906 not only did free trade sweep the country electorally, but the turnout (83.7 per cent) was much greater than in the past and this campaign probably did more than most to reach individual voters, and non-voters, above all wives and mothers in what some termed the first 'women's election'.[245] Thus, while some 5.5 million males voted in 1906, Graham Wallas calculated that the debate had genuinely involved 10 million people.[246] This degree of popular involvement lends force to the perception of 1906 as 'the people's battle', not only in the sense that Joyce has stressed the longevity of the language of the people, but in terms of the inclusiveness of the political nation.[247]

The election of 1906 was the nearest approximation to popular sovereignty and the general will possible in a polity without universal suffrage or the referendum. At a time of growing concern about the forces of irrationality and 'improperty', democratic theorists drew distinct comfort from the reaffirmation of free trade and Liberal values in 1906.[248] This may not have cheered Fabians, who discerned too much 'conservatism' within the Liberal victory, but it had ensured the end of the wilder tariff reform visions of trade wars and world empire.[249] Moreover, as Beatrice Webb recognized, this wave of popular Liberalism was 'progressive in its direction and all the active factors are collectivist'.[250] The policy of the status quo was no longer tenable, and from the springboard of 1906 would follow the policies of social reform, and the struggle of 'the peers against the people', designed to reconcile the domestic morality of free trade with the pursuit of social welfare, economic progress, and international power.[251] The defence of free trade had itself evoked 'a new concept of the power of democracy', which led directly to the triumph of New Liberalism in the elections of 1910, and which would survive,

---

[244] A. Richmond, 'Why Free Trade Wins', *Westminster Review* (Feb., 1906), 115–23.
[245] Russell, *Landslide*, 177.
[246] Wallas, *Human Nature*, 245.
[247] Joyce, *Visions of the People*, 308–10.
[248] Hobson, *The Crisis of Liberalism* (1909, reprint ed. P. F. Clarke, Hassocks, 1974); A. F. J. Lee, 'A Study of the Social and Economic Thought of J. A. Hobson', unpublished Ph.D. thesis, University of London (1970), ch. 8, esp. 460, 492, 517, 544–8, 620, 631–4, 640; Lowell, *Government of England*, vol. 2, 516.
[249] N. and J. MacKenzie (eds.), *The Diary of Beatrice Webb* (4 vols, 1982–5), vol. 3, 23 [28 Jan. 1906].
[250] *Beatrice Webb Diary*, vol. 3, 25 [9 Feb. 1906].
[251] 'The Responsibility of the Government' (27 Jan.), 'Liberal Finance' (10 Feb.), 'The Government and Social Reform' (3 Mar. 1906), *The Speaker*; 'Victory and What to do with it', *Contemporary Review*, 89 (1906); 'The Government and its Opportunities', *Independent Review*, Jan. 1906.

under conditions of much wider suffrage, to help Labour to office in 1923 and 1929.[252] Only in the National Crisis of 1931 would free trade be dethroned from the electoral ascendancy which it had achieved in 1906. That ascendancy itself was not the result of the fortuitous survival of distant memories of the 1840s, nor of the temporary reinvigoration of 'old' Cobdenism, but of the successive reinterpretations of free trade as an understanding of history, morality, wealth, and welfare within the 'wise and shrewd democracy' of Liberal England.[253]

[252] H. W. Massingham, 'Victory and what to do with it', *Contemporary Review*, 89 (Feb. 1906), 267–73. For keen insights into the Edwardian understanding of democracy, see P. F. Clarke, *Liberals and Social Democrats* (Cambridge, 1978), esp. 134–45.

[253] W. Churchill, *Cobden Club Dinner, Report 1907*, 7.

8

The Cobdenite Moment and its Legacy

War is a passing quarrel & drifts away with its passions & tragedies; but economical controversies are notoriously long-lived.

Winston Churchill to Sir Edward Clarke, 6 Apr. 1905.[1]

Cobden's ideas—in a form strangely different from anything which could have been in his day unless as a poet's dream—have again their chance, and on them depends civilisation.

Manchester Guardian, 19 July 1928.

DANGERFIELD'S paradox, that the moment of the Liberals' greatest triumph was also that of their greatest vulnerability, was to prove peculiarly true with regard to free trade.[2] For not only did the First World War lead to the imposition of protective duties, but by 1923 the Labour Party had stolen the mantle of free trade, and by 1931 the rump of the Liberal Party was about to enter the protectionist embrace of the National Government. In 1932 the cause of tariff reform, so convincingly defeated in 1906, finally triumphed, with the abandonment of the gold standard in 1931, followed rapidly by the imposition of import duties and the systematic introduction of imperial preference. Free trade, the erstwhile symbol of British power, was relegated to the margins of British politics, the quirk of the Cobdenite few, no longer the faith of a nation. After 1945 the desirability of free trade re-emerged not as the emanation of domestic political morality, but as a diplomatic goal of the newly hegemonic American economic power. This goal was in part inspired by a distantly Cobdenite belief that free trade would lead to peace, a view imported into American commercial diplomacy by Cordell Hull, but it also embodied a predominant belief in the necessity of political understanding between nations, and a regulated code of economic behaviour.[3] Within post-war Britain's new 'Butskellite' consensus, Cobdenism was an eccentricity, at best an underground trickle of ideas, occasionally seeping through the potholes of the LSE, the Institute of Economic Affairs, and such pressure groups as Keep Britain Out

---

[1]   Papers of Sir Edward Clarke, courtesy of Mr Peter Clarke.

[2]   G. Dangerfield, *The Strange Death of Liberal England* (1935, 1966 edn.), 22.

[3]   N. de Marchi, ' "League of Nations" Economists and the Ideal of Peaceful Change in the decade of the 'Thirties' in C. D. Goodwin (ed.), *Economics and National Security: A History of their Interaction* (Annual Supplement to vol. 23, *History of Political Economy*, Duke University Press, Durham, NC 1991), 143–78; J. B. Condliffe, *The Commerce of Nations* (1951); G. A. Pigman, 'Hegemony and Free Trade Policy', unpublished D.Phil. thesis, University of Oxford (1992), ch. 5; Cordell Hull to Jane Cobden-Unwin, 20 June 1933, CP, Add. MS 52416.

and the Cheap Food League, into the margins of political life, before finding its outlet in the ideological reservoir drawn upon by the Conservative Party in the 1970s.[4]

In its later phases, this narrow ideological stream owed much to its Cobdenite sources, although it was reinforced by a torrent of Viennese liberal economics through von Hayek, and drew on a pool of professional neo-classical economists, such as Lionel Robbins. Ideologically, individuals such as F. W. Hirst, the archetype of 'stern and unbending Cobdenism', served to connect the world of Gladstone and Morley with that of Peter Thorneycroft and Sir Keith Joseph, in espousing an early anti-Keynesian creed which proved 'the herald and forerunner of a libertarian revival'.[5] Organizational continuity with the nineteenth- and early twentieth-century free trade tradition was provided by institutions such as the Free Trade Union (FTU) and the Cobden Club, which maintained a vestigial existence.[6] More loosely, the label 'Cobdenite' has been regularly applied to an understanding of twentieth-century Britain, whether to describe the collective views of economists, the beliefs of political leaders, or the state of public opinion on foreign policy in the 1930s.[7] Yet between 1906 and 1931 many of the central intellectual premisses of the Cobdenite world-view were shattered.[8] That disintegration is beyond the purview of this book, but it remains here to consider both the forms, and the limits, of the transmission of the nineteenth-century, primarily Cobdenite, tradition of free trade.

That tradition, as it has appeared in this book, was one that embraced a fiscal policy of low and few revenue-raising tariffs (combined with varying degrees of direct taxation), a political order that emphasized free trade as a popular right to cheap food combined with an avoidance of oppression by vested interests, whether of land or capital, and a foreign policy that strove for the lowest level of armaments expenditure consistent with national safety, an empire based on sentiment, and a predisposition to the promotion of international intercourse by trade, culture, and 'goodwill'. This *Weltanschauung*, which had achieved definition in the Anti-Corn

[4] The *Free Trader*, 1945–72; records of the Free Trade Union [later League] and Cobden Club, 1945–83, kindly made available to me by Mr Charles Smedley; S. W. Alexander, *Save the Pound—Save the People* (1978); R. Cockett, *Thinking the Unthinkable* (1994), esp. 122–58.

[5] D. Abel, in *F. W. Hirst: By his Friends* (1958), 90. For this Liberal–Conservative interchange, see publications of the Design for Freedom Committee, *c.*1945–8; J. Biffen, 'Peter Thorneycroft', *Guardian*, 6 June 1994.

[6] After 1958 the FTU and the Cobden Club were largely kept alive through the efforts of S. W. Alexander and Oliver Smedley. The FTU, anxious to avoid confusion with trade unions, became the Free Trade League in 1962.

[7] P. Williamson, *National Crisis and National Government* (1992), 68; M. Ceadel, *Thinking about Peace and War* (Oxford, 1987), 179. Rhodes Boyson's Conservatism professedly owed much to the influence of Cobden: *Guardian*, 16 June 1987.

[8] The dissolution of liberal political economy is the subject of the research of Frank Trentmann, of Harvard University, formerly of the LSE; for a foretaste of its results, see 'The Strange Death of Free Trade: The Erosion of the "Liberal Consensus" in Britain, *c.*1903–32', in E. Biagini (ed.), *Citizenship and Community* (Cambridge, 1996), 219–50.

Law movement in the 1840s, had been infused into popular Liberalism in the age of Gladstone, had been modified and reasserted in the age of tariffs, empire, and collectivism, and had emerged with a still central political pertinence in the 1900s, as part of the New Liberal vision of welfare and democracy. Its apogee was symbolically achieved when the Cobden Club, after decades of failure, succeeded in 1908 in calling an International Free Trade Congress, immediately following a Universal Peace Congress. This served to highlight free trade as 'an international policy', and in a very minor key provided a forum which the Second International had long provided for socialism.[9] As a gathering, it brought together politicians and economists from Britain, Europe, India, Australia, and the United States; organizationally, it had been masterminded by men as diverse as the model Gladstonian civil servant Welby, the Liberal plutocrat Mond, and the New Liberal intellectual J. A. Hobson.[10] Here was further evidence that free trade, considered the most unbending of doctrines, had in fact proved itself one of the most versatile and resilient. Even so, this was a malleability that would survive with the greatest difficulty in the age of Lloyd George, economic blockade, and total war.

Free Trade and Fiscal Politics, 1906–32

Despite Bevin's well-known quip that 'Gladstone ruled at the Treasury from 1860 until 1930', this was true only in the sense that the 'Treasury view' continued to emphasize balanced budgets, sound finance, and a vigorous scrutiny of public expenditure.[11] Before 1914 the Liberals had already breached several nostrums of Peelite–Gladstonian finance, for example by the introduction of differentiated and graduated income tax, proposals long resisted by Gladstone, but increasingly urged by many free traders since the late 1890s, and, above all, by the 'people's budget' with its supertax, increased death duties, and ill-fated taxation of land values.[12] After decades of rising demands for both defence and civil expenditure, the crisis of the fiscal regime, long predicted by Treasury officials, had arrived to haunt the Liberal government in the arms race preceding the First World War. Any notion of a Cobdenite state, with a small army, 'single standard' navy, and cheap government, with a few revenue-raising duties, was now wholly Utopian. Despite the

[9]   *Report of the Proceedings of the International Free Trade Congress* (1908); *The Nation*, 1 Aug. 1908, 'Democracy and the Peace Movement', and 8 Aug. 1908, 'Free Trade as an International Policy'. A second congress followed at Antwerp in Aug. 1910, and an International Free Trade League was set up in October. War pre-empted the third congress at Amsterdam in Sept. 1914. See (Free Trade) International Consultative Committee, report (c.1910) CP 1127 WSRO; *Concord* (Oct. 1910), 119–20; *The Burden of Protection* (1911); A. Heringa, *Free Trade and Protection in Holland* (1914).

[10]   *Proceedings*; IFTC, Special Committee, Minutes, Mar.–June 1908, CP 1189, WSRO.

[11]   H. Roseveare, *The Treasury* (1969), 235–67; P. F. Clarke, 'The Treasury's Model' in M. Furner and B. Supple (eds.), *The State and Economic Knowledge* (Cambridge, 1990).

[12]   Herein lay 'the open and unqualified adoption of the theory that taxation should be used for the purpose of social regeneration': B. Mallet, *British Budgets 1887–1913* (1913), 299; B. K. Murray, 'The Politics of the "People's Budget"', *Historical Journal*, 16 (1973), 555–70; id., *The 'People's Budget' 1909–1910* (Oxford, 1980); A. Offer, *Property and Politics 1870–1914* (Cambridge, 1981), 317–27; 'Liberal Finance, 1905–1912', PRO T171/2.

warnings of the Cobden Club, the escalation of defence expenditure, as well the desire for social reform, had proved both a stimulus to fiscal innovation and to the vigorous restatement of anti-war Radicalism.[13]

The fiscal new departure of 1908–9 was not, however, in any obvious economic sense a threat to free trade. For, while the Cobden–Gladstone fiscal model had hoped to enforce limited governmental expenditure by abolishing engines of taxation, Cobden himself, from the late 1840s, had accepted the eligibility of direct taxation over indirect taxation, even holding out the distant prospect of the abolition of customs houses. In the context of the fiscal crisis of the British state in the early twentieth century, faced by rising public expenditure, new sources of finance could only come from tariffs, including food taxes, or from direct taxation. The whole tenor of the defence of free trade against fair trade and tariff reform had highlighted the Cobdenite preference for direct taxation, such that the 'people's budget' of 1909, despite some residual Liberal qualms, was widely trumpeted as the saviour of free trade finance.[14] Even Liberal businessmen were for some time unworried by Lloyd George's finance, although the budget of 1914 awoke new alarms, provoking some MPs, the 'Holt Cave', into 'a combined remonstrance by business men and some survivors of the Cobden–Bright school of thought against the ill-considered and socialistic tendencies of the government'.[15] Despite this backlash, Liberal budgetary policy remained within the sphere of orthodoxy, as preached in 1906. Liberal policies had successfully pursued traditional Radical goals, with reductions of duties on tea (1906), sugar (1908), and cocoa (1911).[16] The coal export duty had been promptly abolished in 1906, and while some disquiet had initially been occasioned by the failure to abandon the Sugar Convention, this was eventually jettisoned in 1912.[17] Above all, Liberal finance had hit the oft-missed Cobdenite target, the land. For, as Offer has argued, the 'people's budget' was the culmination of Cobdenism, giving effect to the long-postponed Radical assault on the landed interest.[18] Here, the Edwardian period had seen a vigorous efflorescence of Henry George's combination of free trade and the single tax, in which Cobdenite themes had been central. For example, stalwarts of the land values taxation such as Verinder, Chomley, and Neilson were also vigorous proponents of free trade in

---

[13] A. Friedberg, *The Weary Titan: Britain and the Experience of Relative Decline, 1895–1905* (Princeton, 1988), 89–134; A. J. A. Morris, *Radicalism Against War 1906–1914* (1972), *passim*.

[14] In addition to sources in note 12 above, see J. R. Hay, 'British Government Finance, 1906–1914', unpublished D.Phil. thesis, University of Oxford (1970), 266 ff.; J. Harris, *Unemployment and Politics* (Oxford, 1972), 269–72.

[15] D. J. Dutton (ed.), *Odyssey of an Edwardian Liberal: The Political Diary of Richard Dunning Holt* (Record Society of Lancashire and Cheshire, vol. 129; Gloucester, 1989), 31 [19 July 1914]; B. K. Murray, ' "Battered and Shattered": Lloyd George and the 1914 Budget Fiasco', *Albion*, 23 (1991), 483–507.

[16] In 1913 only 25 articles were liable for customs duties: J. H. Higginson, *Tariffs at Work* (1913), 5.

[17] Mallet, *British Budgets*, 261; F. S. L. Lyons, *Internationalism in Europe 1815–1914* (1963), 103–10; Hay, 'Government Finance', 14–41, 266–74; Pigman, 'Hegemony and Free Trade Policy', ch. 4 (E).

[18] Offer, *Property and Politics*, 363.

Britain, America, and Australia.[19] This attack on 'rent' neatly appealed both to those who still wished to break up estates into peasant holdings, and the growing numbers who supported land nationalization. Both camps sought to lend the authority of Cobden to their cause, with his daughters enlisted on both sides.[20] In this way Lloyd George summoned up memories both of Chartism and of the Anti-Corn Law League, while carrying forward the progressive policy best able to unite Liberal and Labour activists locally and, hopefully, to appeal to the electorate nationally.[21]

Free trade, direct taxation, and land reform were central to the New Liberal message of social reform, carried in the cry of 'the peers versus the people' in the elections of 1910.[22] For, to a very large degree, those elections, especially that of January, were fought against tariff reform, which was now official Unionist policy, as it had not been in 1906. The Liberals were able to utilize the machinery constructed for the defence of free trade in 1903–6 against the continuing efforts of the Tariff Reform League, whose own financial resources, local dynamism, and rhetorical power had grown considerably since 1906.[23] Even so, the Free Trade Union, and the Women's FTU, continued to recruit a large body of well-paid lecturers, serving as a vast educational and propaganda arm of the Liberal Party. The *Free Trader* effectively voiced arguments and publicized local and national efforts, setting up, for example, on the model of *The League*, the Free Trade Fighting Fund of 1910.[24] Regional associations, above all at Manchester but also in the other cities and universities, remained active, as did the Cobden Club, and a newly formed City of London Free Trade Committee.[25] Even after 1910 free trade continued to be the leading theme of Liberal crusades, and remained central to the

[19]   Offer, *Property and Politics*, 363 ff.; Verinder, *Free Trade and Land Values* (1910; rep. Ipswich, 1916); for Neilson, see Thomas Hodgkin to Violet [Hodgkin], 11 June 1908, in L. Creighton, *Hodgkin*, 282; for Chomley, see above, 243 n. 80.

[20]   *Richard Cobden and the Land Tax* (English League for the Taxation of Land Values, 1909); Jane Cobden-Unwin, *The Land Hunger* (1910); Anne Cobden-Sanderson, *Richard Cobden and the Land of the People* (ILP, c.1909); K. Hardie, 'In Cobden's Country', *Labour Leader*, 2 July 1909.

[21]   For a useful summary, see G. R. Searle, *The Liberal Party: Triumph and Disintegration, 1886–1929* (1992), 82–95; H. V. Emy, 'The Land Campaign: Lloyd George as Social Reformer', in A. J. P. Taylor (ed.), *Lloyd George: Twelve Essays* (1971), 35–68.

[22]   P. F. Clarke, *Lancashire and the New Liberalism* (Cambridge, 1971), *passim*; for one MP, see A. J. A. Morris, *C. P. Trevelyan 1870–1958* (Belfast, 1977), 83–4.

[23]   J. A. Hobson, 'The General Election of 1910', *Sociological Review*, 3 (1910), esp. 111; F. Coetzee, *For Party or Country* (Oxford, 1990), 118–19; E. H. H. Green, *The Crisis of Conservatism* (1995), 263, 268 ff.

[24]   The *Free Trader*, issued by the Joint Literature Committee of the Cobden Club and FTU, Dec. 1907–Oct. 1908; revived on lines of 1903–6 in Dec. 1908, published regularly until July 1914; N. Blewett, *The Peers, the Parties, and the People: The British General Elections of 1910* (1972), 277, 331–5. Among the new generation of FTU lecturers were the future Professor of Economic History at the LSE, T. S. Ashton, and John Hilton, acquiring the skills to which he attributed his later success as a popular broadcaster: E. Nixon, *John Hilton* (1946), 46.

[25]   J. M. Keynes to C. P. Trevelyan, 14 Dec. 1909, Trevelyan Papers, CPT 23; Cobden Club Minutes, 1911–14, CP 1190, WSRO; H. Darwin to A. Elliot, 28 Apr. 1908, EP 19496; Clarke, *Lancashire*, esp. 274–310; below, 287.

identity of the party before 1914.[26] In an obvious sense, free trade was still the leading domestic issue which differentiated Liberals from Unionists, especially given the latter's growing commitment to social reform, which recent historians have stressed. Ultimately, but vitally, free trade and the primacy of direct taxation separated New Liberals from Radical Conservatives.

Yet Liberal fiscal policy was not without its political costs. Above all, it proved the Achilles' heel of the broad free trade coalition that had swept the Liberals to victory in 1906. For while, on the one hand, Lloyd George's budget of 1909 did revivify free trade finance, on the other, as Harcourt had warned '[it] will ensure the triumph of Tariff Reform'.[27] Here, above all, the spectre of socialism—the punitive taxation of the rich, aroused by fiscal change in 1907–8, lent substance by OAPs in 1908, and magnified by the 'people's budget'—served to detach from free trade some of its firmest advocates. This was, of course, the reverse side of the coin that had carried free trade into the collectivist camp, but whose ultimate consequences were only now made clear. Free traders hostile to Liberal policy had already lent much support to moves to form centre parties and anti-socialist groups, with Strachey in particular charging the Liberals with 'killing free trade in the name of free trade', aided and abetted by the Cobden Club.[28] But it was the 'people's budget' that now terminally divided the Unionist free traders.[29] In the battle between socialism and property, most Unionist free traders abandoned free trade, with former stalwarts such as Hugh Cecil fuelling the firebrand of anti-socialism, to be wielded by the diehards in the constitutional crisis of 1909–11.

Only a minority of Unionists remained resolutely behind free trade, some, such as Balfour of Burleigh, believing that tariff reform and protection represented a greater threat to society than did Liberal 'socialism', others preferring 'socialism for the poor' to 'socialism for the rich', and yet others genuinely accepting the Liberal case for the budget and upholding their own consistency as free traders, on the model of Peel after 1846.[30] In the wake of the demise of the Unionist Free Trade

---

[26]   e.g., Sir John Simon's 'free trade tour' of 1913 (Glasgow, Newcastle, Liverpool, and Birmingham), Simon to T. Fisher-Unwin, 17 Sept. 1913, CP 154; *The Times*, 12 Sept., 7, 13, 21, 29 Nov. 1913.

[27]   To Runciman, 24 Mar. 1909, quoted in R. Douglas, ' "God gave the land to the people" ', in A. J. A. Morris (ed.), *Edwardian Radicalism* (1974), 154. In a similar vein, Munro-Ferguson to Rosebery, 11 June 1908, Rosebery Papers 10020.

[28]   A. Sykes, *Tariff Reform and British Politics, 1903–1913* (Oxford, 1979), esp. 145–75; 'Mr Asquith and the Cobden Club', *Spectator* (8 Aug. 1908), 184–5; Strachey to A. Elliot, 23 July 1907, 20 Jan. 1908; Cromer to A. Elliot, 13 July 1908, EP 19496. Hugh Cecil felt himself disabled from defending free trade by Liberal finance, 'various schemes—and the threat of others which are to us almost as abhorrent as Protection'. To J. E. Seely, 22 June 1907, Mottistone Papers, 1, fos. 162–4, Nuffield College. See, too, Green, *Conservatism*, 154–6.

[29]   R. Rempel, *Unionists Divided* (Newton Abbot, 1972), 192–200; Sykes, *Tariff Reform*, esp. 185–90.

[30]   Balfour of Burleigh to Robert Cecil, 5 Dec. 1909 (copy), Balfour of Burleigh Papers, TD 93/55/38; Frances Balfour, *A Memoir of Lord Balfour of Burleigh* (1925), 128–33; F. B. Jevons (Vice-Chancellor, Durham), 7 Feb. 1910; James, 12 Dec. 1909; W. R. Malcolm, 2 Nov. 1909; F. Pollock, 28 Jan. 1908 and 9 Feb. 1910, all to A. Elliot, EP 19496, 19497. The latter two were strongly critical of the renegades: 'they presume we should vote for Tariff Reform for fear of what they call socialism . . . which seems to mean

Club in February 1910, these free traders were ready to throw in their lot with the FTU, providing a welcome shot of wealth and talent.[31] Even so, after 1910, free trade continued to forfeit Unionist support, especially as the prospect of Home Rule grew. For example, in 1911 Sir Louis Mallet's son Bernard, civil servant and chronicler of budgets, declined to preside over a free trade meeting, as he 'should have to make a strong attack on the Government for their socialistic and anti-free exchange policy and say Home Rule [is] so great a danger to the safety of the nation that he would urge them to vote Protectionist to avoid the greater evil'.[32] Free trade had therefore become much more a Liberal monopoly by 1914, although the continuance of Tory collectivism, the ending of the Irish issue after 1921, and the overt protectionism of the Tory Party by 1923, made for some 'Tory individualist' drift back towards the Asquithian Liberals. Even so, this was restrained by a persistent fear of socialism, while the impact of the First World War had reduced the political and moral significance of free trade.[33]

Despite the disquiet of some Liberals by 1914, it was only with the changes in economic policy during the First World War that fundamental Cobdenite fiscal values were threatened. First, in 1915 the McKenna duties on luxury goods (e.g., motor cars and clocks) aimed to restrict imports in order to free shipping space and, only to a minor extent, to raise revenue (£1m in a budget of £100m). This was clearly protective, with Lloyd George enjoying the irony of McKenna, one of the stalwarts of the FTU, giving 'away the whole principle of Free Trade'.[34] Even so, this was acceptable to most free traders, as a wartime emergency measure to be immediately reversed with peace. Yet for others it appeared as the harbinger of protection *per se*.[35] Adamantine free traders such as Hirst found any relapse from fiscal free trade difficult to swallow, and, combined with the threat of conscription, free trade and free (military) service became intertwined.[36] Second, the resolutions of the Paris Economic Conference of 1916, with their policy of temporarily and permanently excluding enemy trade, proved wholly unacceptable to a wider body

anything which conflicts with the grim and ruthless individualism of the old Manchester School, of which Harold Cox is the present representative' (Malcolm); '. . . no sympathy with their fussing over fossilized individualism and calling it the defence of personal liberty and responsibility' (Pollock).

[31]   Not only the major figures such as Balfour of Burleigh and Arthur Elliot, but E. G. Brunker also moved to FTU, and became its stalwart organizer until his death in 1951. As a student at TCD Brunker had come under the influence of the free trade economist C. F. Bastable. *The Free Trader* (May–June 1951), 351–4.

[32]   Mallet to Strachey, 15 Nov. 1911, Strachey MSS, 10/5/40.

[33]   M. Bentley, *The Liberal Mind, 1914–1929* (1977), 87–9; below, 281.

[34]   T. Wilson, (ed.), *The Political Diaries of C. P. Scott, 1911–1928* (1970), 158 (11–15 Nov. 1915); 257 (26 Jan. 1917). See, too, Lloyd George reported by Walter Long, in Hewins, *Apologia of an Imperialist* (2 vols, 1929), vol. 2, 52 (16 Sept. 1915). For the impact of war, see R. Soutou, *Les buts de guerre économique de la Première Guerre mondiale* (Paris, 1989), esp. 205–8, 193–229, 233–79.

[35]   Tariff reformers had urged luxury taxes (cars, pianos, and champagne) before 1914. *Hansard*, 5th ser., 26, c. 86, 22 May 1911 [James Hope].

[36]   In 1916 Hirst was linked with a short-lived Voluntary Service and Free Trade Association. See M. Freeden, *Liberalism Divided* (1986), 25, and *C. P. Scott Diaries*, 124–6.

of Liberal opinion, and seemingly vindicated the belief that 'Protection trod upon Conscription'.[37] Third, Balfour of Burleigh's 'Reconstruction' Committee in January 1917 endorsed imperial preference, a policy ultimately supported by the War Cabinet (against Treasury advice) in July 1918, although action was postponed until after the war.[38] Predictably, Balfour's Report was condemned by the FTU, from which Balfour now resigned.[39] Fourth, wartime and immediate post-war policy produced numerous fiscal and commercial expedients—Indian cotton duties, defence of 'key industries', the Dyestuffs Act of 1920—which, as in the Boer War, presaged the wholesale abandonment of free trade, and undermined the early assumption that peace would restore its normalcy.[40] Such fears were confirmed in Austen Chamberlain's budget of 1919, retaining the McKenna duties while introducing an element of imperial preference, and by the attempts at the post-war safeguarding of industries, ultimately embodied in the Act of 1921.[41]

The economic consequences of these departures from fiscal orthodoxy were probably small, for less than 1 per cent of the workforce was employed in safeguarded or protected industries at their peak.[42] Ideologically, the fiscal consequences of the First World War vitally, if not terminally, impaired the pre-war renewal of Liberalism. First, resistance to wartime heterodoxy had served to narrow free trade back into a strident, individualist, *laissez-faire* critique of the state and the economy. As John Turner has suggested, free trade was 'no longer the major focus of discussion about redistribution of wealth, social policy, or state intervention in the economy', but 'had become a technical matter'.[43] As such, its narrowness was to deprive it of a popular audience when the real departure from orthodoxy took place in 1931–2.

Second, wartime and post-war fiscal policy ingrained more deeply the ideological and political division between the Asquithians and Lloyd George's coalition Liberals. The former became even more distinctly and resolutely attached to free trade—Elibank wanted them to become a Free Trade Party—on grounds of

[37] J. A. Hobson, 'The New Protection', *War and Peace*, 3 (Apr. 1916), 104–5; id., *The New Protectionism* (1916); 'City Correspondent', *War and Peace*, 3 (July 1916), 158; *C. P. Scott Diaries*, 191–2, 257; Bentley, *Liberal Mind*, 40–1; R. Bunselmeyer, *The Cost of War. British Economic War Aims and the Origins of Reparations* (Hamden, Conn., 1975); Soutou, *Les buts de guerre*, 233–71.

[38] I. M. Drummond, *British Economic Policy and the Empire, 1919–1939* (1972), 55 ff.; Soutou, *Les buts de guerre*, 273–9.

[39] 'Imperial Preference' (FTU, 15 Mar. 1917); Balfour of Burleigh to FTU, 22 Mar. 1917; C. Mallet to Balfour of Burleigh, 24 Mar. 1917, Balfour of Burleigh Papers, TD 93/55/118.

[40] In 1915 Asquith had feared that the government dyestuffs scheme would lead to protection after the war: E. David (ed.), *Inside Asquith's Cabinet: From the Diaries of Charles Hobhouse* (Newton Abbot, 1977), 228 (16 Mar. 1915).

[41] R. K. Snyder, *The Tariff Problem in Great Britain, 1918–1923* (Stanford, 1944), *passim*; Chamberlain wrote to his sister Hilda: 'It was a satisfaction to stand where Father had so often stood to propose a definite preferential policy', 4 May 1919: R. C. Self (ed.), *The Austen Chamberlain Diary Letters* (Camden Fifth ser., Royal Historical Society, 1995), 114.

[42] B. Eichengreen, 'The Eternal Fiscal Question: Free Trade and Protection in Britain, 1860–1929', in F. Capie (ed.), *Protectionism in the World Economy* (Aldershot, 1992), 181.

[43] J. Turner, *British Politics and the Great War* (1992), 337–8.

principle, and as their most likely electoral asset, as the election of 1923 would demonstrate.[44] Thereafter, for many, like the Liverpool shipowner Richard Holt and the economist and press baron Walter Layton, free trade was an essential part of the meaning and purpose of Liberalism, of which groups like the FTU remained a valued bastion.[45] Yet by 1923 such free trade Liberalism, having effectively lost many of its social democratic features of 1906–14, had returned to an ideology of individual rights, economy, and sound finance, to the recovery of the innocence it had lost in the aftermath of the Boer War. Even so, free trade remained a distinct electoral asset to the Liberal Party, especially in campaigning against the protectionist diehards in the Conservative Party in the election of 1929.[46]

In some ways it was those strident and dogmatic overtones amplified in the 1920s that have perhaps influenced historical interpretations of free trade ever since. For example, F. W. Hirst, sacked as editor of *The Economist* in 1916, became genuinely influential as a prolific Cobdenite publicist, a foil for Keynes, and a considerable historian. In a sense, one suspects that that part of the Liberal mind that has been labelled 'Cobdenite' derives from Hirst's views, rather than Cobden's. A Cobden Club prizeman at Oxford, in 1903 Hirst had produced his timely anthology *The Manchester School*, followed by numerous writings in support of economy and peace, views reiterated in *The Economist* under his charge (1907–16), in the *Outlook* (1916–21), and in a long series of essays enshrining the morality of free trade, public economy, and peace, not least in his tract *From Adam Smith to Philip Snowden: A History of Free Trade in Great Britain* (1925). In 1931 Hirst's *Gladstone as a Financier and Economist*, was written at the instance of Sir Henry Neville Gladstone, merchant banker and financial expert, in order to publicize the need for economy during the Labour Government of 1929–31.[47] Finally, in 1935 Hirst's *Liberty and Tyranny* and *Economic Liberty* served as beacons for the anti-Keynesian attack on the state and bureaucracy, the road to serfdom that Hayek would more influentially denounce in 1944.[48]

Nevertheless, at the start of the 1920s that road looked far more attractive (and necessary) to the considerable body of Liberal opinion close to Lloyd George and Keynes, which favoured a more interventionist, state-centred approach to welfare

---

[44]   Bentley, *Liberal Mind*, 47 ff., 87–9, 155 ff.

[45]   *Holt Diary*, 77, 84–7, 92, 100; Freeden, *Liberalism Divided*, 122–4.

[46]   M. Dawson, ' "The Old Time Religion": Liberalism in Devon and Cornwall, 1910–31', *Historical Journal*, 38 (1995), 425–37.

[47]   Published in 1931. I am grateful to Colin Matthew for this point. See, too, F. W. Hirst, *Sir H. N. Gladstone* (1941). Appropriately, H. N. Gladstone in October 1931 unveiled a tablet to Cobden in West Lavington church, dispensing the 'pure milk of Gladstonian free trade': *The Times*, 5 Oct. 1931. Yet earlier in the year W. E. Gladstone's former secretary Kilbracken (J. A. Godley) speculated that Gladstone himself would have been 'unfaithful to free trade' in 1931. To G. H. Murray, 8 Apr. 1931, Murray Papers 1676, Blair Castle.

[48]   Abel, in *Hirst: By his Friends*, 89–91; W. H. Greenleaf, *The British Political Tradition. Vol. 2: The Ideological Heritage* (1983), 97–100. I am also grateful to Pat Thompson for his recollections of Hirst in the 1940s.

and the economy. But this progress was itself soon interrupted, with the post-war reaction against the state, and in the 1920s it was the 'new' Manchester School associated with Ernest Simon that proved more fashionable. This sought a new balance between the state and individual liberty, a half-way house between Edwardian Liberalism and the creed of Cobden and Bright.[49] Liberal summer schools, the shadow of Keynes, and the impact of world economic crisis led some of this group to the verge of the protectionist abyss, with Ted Scott, editor of the *Manchester Guardian*, confessing to Hobson: 'I find very great difficulty in accepting the theoretical Free Trade case with the confidence I felt in 1906.'[50] By 1931 many Liberals, led by Keynes, were ready to resort to tariffs, yet few were in fact ready to abandon the theoretical case for free trade, which was restated vigorously and influentially by Robbins, Layton, and Beveridge.[51]

In this welter of ideological contortions, free trade proved a withering root upon which to build consistent Liberal political purpose. Those erstwhile Asquithian Liberals, who had continued their drift rightwards into the National Government in 1931, were unable to brake the Conservative rush to protectionism.[52] For, it soon became clear that the dynamic purpose of the National Government was the abandonment of Cobdenite politics.[53] This proved unstoppable. First, the Abnormal Duties Act of 1931, although presented as an emergency measure akin to the wartime McKenna duties, served only as the bell-wether of protection, with the Import Duties Act of 1932 presented by Neville Chamberlain as the symbolic repudiation of the Cobdenism that his father had fought in vain. Joe's paternity was similarly acknowledged in the introduction of imperial preference following the Ottawa Conference of 1932. These measures followed the election of 1931, in which the National Government had won a 'doctor's mandate' to cure the British 'national' crisis. From within the National Government the New Liberal Samuel and the ethical socialist Snowden deployed the progressive arguments for free trade, but, ironically, these were now swept away in the torrent of anti-socialism, which concealed less the defence of the individual than a more subtle Conservative argument for state intervention.[54] Within Parliament, the echoes of the 1840s and 1903 reverberated strongly in the case against protection, while outside there

---

[49] Freeden, *Liberalism Divided*, 80–3, 129 ff.

[50] Quoted in ibid. 123.

[51] P. F. Clarke, *The Keynesian Revolution in the Making, 1924–1936* (Oxford, 1988), 197–225; L. Robbins, 'Economic Notes on Some Arguments for Protection', *Economica*, 11 (1930), 45–62; W. H. Beveridge (and Committee of Economists), *Tariffs: The Case Examined* (1931); J. Harris, *William Beveridge: A Biography* (Oxford, 1977), 316–24; Freeden, *Liberalism Divided*, 122–4; and, graphically, Low, *Evening Standard*, 10 Mar. 1931.

[52] Williamson, *National Crisis*, 394 ff.

[53] B. Wasserstein, *Herbert Samuel: A Political Life* (Oxford, 1992), 332 ff. Other Asquithians, for example Maclean, were equally unhappy with tariffs: 'Sir Donald Maclean', *DNB*. Blanche Dugdale noted the ironies: 'Simon advocating Tariffs and Winston demanding Food Taxes', to Robert Cecil, 15 Sept. 1931, quoted in Bentley, *Liberal Mind*, 115; A. Thorpe, *The General Election of 1931* (Oxford, 1991), 212, 240–5.

[54] Williamson, *National Crisis*, 509, 529–30.

emerged some intriguing possibilities, the most nostalgic of which was J. A. Spender's call for a new Anti-Corn Law League.[55] As a second best, Hirst set up a Liberal Free Trade Committee, which cast a few lambent Cobdenite beams in the dark years of 'England under protection'.[56] Out of the ashes of free trade some looked to the phoenix of a 'new' Liberal party in alliance with Labour; Sir Archibald Sinclair, descendant of 'agricultural Sir John', held aloft the flag of unrepentant free trade, while, in the wilderness, Lloyd George, more chameleon than wizard, temporarily rediscovered the Cobdenism he had disdained in power.[57] Briefly, free trade was restored as a central unifying device for Liberalism, a suitable ideological figleaf for the remnant of a party.

The Labour Party, in seeking to replace the Liberal Party, sought also to become the legatee of the pre-war electoral strength of free trade, reaffirmed in the election of 1923.[58] How far the Labour Party had itself become the ideological standard-bearer of Cobdenism remains an intriguing question. Hirst impishly suggested that Cobden had replaced Marx in Labour doctrine; Trentmann has recently explored the ambiguity of the British Left before 1914, torn between free trade and 'national economics'.[59] This ambivalence persisted after 1918, with Labour strongly opposed to all protective tariffs, as part of the 'definite teachings of economic science', yet ready to affirm the right of each nation to pursue its own course of economic development.[60] In post-war Britain, circumstances dictated that Labour politicians held closely to free trade, drawn in that direction by their internationalism, their hostility to armaments expenditure, their continuing attachment to the 'free breakfast table', their co-operative allies, and by the interests of many working-class consumers.[61] In electoral competition with the Liberals, Labour was anxious to emphasize its superior credentials as a party of free trade, untainted by the 'protectionism' of the coalition government, and ready to exploit free trade in order to widen its appeal to women, the middle classes, and agricultural labourers, groups whose support it needed if it was to become a national party.[62] In office, dependence

[55]   Lloyd George to Frances Stevenson, 31 Dec. 1931, *My Darling Pussy: The Letters of Lloyd George and Frances Stevenson*, ed. A. J. P. Taylor (1975), 171.

[56]   F. W. Hirst, *A Brief Autobiographical History of the Liberal Free Trade Committee, 1931–1946* (Heyshott, 1947); C. J. L. Brock, *Quotas: A Plea for Economic Liberty* (1934); C. Asquith, *The Failure of Protection* (1934); F. W. Hirst, *The First Year under Protection* (1932), copy in Beveridge Papers, IIb (1931), BLPES. I am most grateful to Philip Williamson for providing me with a copy of Hirst's diary.

[57]   *C. P. Scott Diaries*, 257; cf. J. Campbell, *Lloyd George: The Goat in the Wilderness, 1922–31* (1977), 302–3; Williamson, *National Crisis*, 447.

[58]   M. Cowling, *The Impact of Labour, 1920–24* (Cambridge, 1971), 329–30; Snyder, *Tariff Problem*, ch. 8. For the free trade views of Labour pre-war MPs, see *Free Trader*, 15 Oct. 1909, 287–8.

[59]   Hirst, *From Adam Smith to Philip Snowden: A History of Free Trade in Great Britain* (1925), 75; Trentmann, 'Wealth versus Welfare', *Historical Research* 70 (1997), 70–98.

[60]   Labour Party, Advisory Committee on Finance and Commerce, minutes, 5 Jan. 1921, in Middleton Papers, JSM/FIN, Labour Party archives, National Museum of Labour History, Manchester.

[61]   For a few pertinent points in this neglected area, see R. Lyman, *The First Labour Government* (1957), 53–4.

[62]   *Labour Organiser*, 35 (Oct. 1923), 16–19; 36 (Nov. 1923), 1–3; 39 (Feb. 1924), 12–13.

upon the support of the Liberal Party solidified its free trade instincts, while Snowden's 1924 budget won the plaudits of the Webbs as well as of Liberals.[63] The dismantling of wartime protection, the curtailment of arms expenditure, and the rebuilding of a prosperous international order seemed more urgent priorities than any half-baked proposals for a tariff-driven 'socialism in one country'. Fiscally, too, the capital levy offered a far more attractive means than did tariffs to increase national revenue within a free trade framework.[64]

In all this, Labour's hostility to protection owed much to the schooling of its new MPs in classical economics, for example the future Labour Board of Trade Minister William Graham, and Mary Hamilton, for both of whom the 1906 election had been a formative experience.[65] At the same time, Labour's recruits from the Liberals, men such as Hobson, Arnold, Ponsonby, Trevelyan, and Wedgwood were influential policy-makers.[66] For example, with Hobson installed as chairman of its advisory committee on Trade Policy, the party was quite content for the secretary of the Cobden Club F. J. Shaw ('Brougham Villiers') to prepare its case against protection in *Tariffs and the Worker*.[67] In the 1923 election Labour propaganda deliberately exploited the legacy of food taxes and the echoes of the Edwardian battle, with leaflets that were in many ways the lineal descendants of the Cobden Club pamphlets of the 1880s. In the context of recent inflation and of growing unemployment ('tariffs no remedy'), such devices continued to exercise a strong residual hold on the popular mind.[68]

As a result, organized labour, including most trade unions, and the working-class electorate, was before 1931 (and after) unwilling to endorse a policy of protection. Like the Edwardian Liberals, the Labour Party proved in this respect to be an admirable consumers' party. Only very hesitantly and incompletely did it adopt a 'producers' approach to issues of protection, unemployment, and tariffs: in the election of 1931, 93 per cent of Labour candidates defended free trade against protection.[69] Even in 1932 the party's preference for free trade rather than protection remained clear, and Labour leaders, while disowning 'old views' of free trade, deployed arguments derived from them. Thus, Attlee denounced the Imports Duties Bill of 1932 as 'calculated to corrupt political life, to raise up a host of vested

[63] N. and J. MacKenzie (eds.), *The Diary of Beatrice Webb* (4 vols, 1982–8), vol. 4, 24–5 [2 May 1924].

[64] R. C. Whiting, 'The Labour Party, Capitalism, and the National Debt, 1918–1924', in P. J. Waller (ed.), *Politics and Social Change in Modern Britain* (1987), 140–60.

[65] T. N. Graham, *Willie Graham* (1948), 29–35; M. A. Hamilton, *Remembering My Good Friends* (1944), 43, 64, 80.

[66] C. A. Cline, *Recruits to Labour* (Syracuse, 1963), 43–67.

[67] Minutes, Advisory Committee on Trade Policy and Finance, 1 and 22 July, 7 Aug., 25 Sept., 29 Oct. 1919, Middleton Papers, JSM/FIN.

[68] Labour Party Archives, 1923 election ephemera; constituency files for Bury, Newport, Stockton, Carlisle, North Camberwell; NJC, Facts for Speakers, seriatim; *The Labour Woman*, 1 Dec. 1923; J. R. MacDonald, *Labour's Policy vs Protection. The Real Issue of the General Election* (1923).

[69] Thorpe, *General Election of 1931*, 220.

interests, and so far from helping the recovery of the world, will lead to economic warfare in the future'.[70] For the most part, too, in the 1930s plans for 'socialist' foreign trade followed 'free trade principles', while, not undesignedly, the first casualty of imperial preference in 1932 had been Labour's Anglo-Russian trade agreement of 1924.[71] In this context, as Blaazer has suggested, even Labour's socialist Left found it difficult to move beyond the Edwardian progressive tradition.[72]

Free trade dethroned: the City and industry, 1906–31

By contrast with Labour, employers after 1906 were increasingly drawn to support for tariffs. The pace of this movement is difficult to judge, but there is some evidence that even the most resolutely free trade industries were by 1910 ready to accept tariffs, especially if the alternative was to be socialism. Peter Clarke, for example, has drawn attention to the growing success of the Cotton Trade Tariff Reform Association. Research by Marrison reveals the attractiveness of tariffs for employers in the iron and steel industries, while, more recently, Trentmann has surveyed the rapid crumbling of free trade loyalties during the First World War. By 1916, for example, the Manchester Chamber of Commerce was bitterly divided on this issue, with the bulk of its directors driven to resign.[73] To some extent, this disillusion with free trade was temporary, and support picked up after 1919 as part of the general swing away from state control in the economy.[74] But even Manchester was never to see a return to pre-1914 Cobdenite certainties, while, increasingly, businessmen organized to lobby for tariffs, for example, in the Empire Industries Association.[75] By the late 1920s cotton manufacturers were ready in growing numbers to join such lobbies, and by 1931 only the residual hostility of L. B. Lee prevented the Federation of British Industry from endorsing this cause.[76] In that same year the free trade edifice of Manchester finally crumbled, with the Chamber of Commerce endorsing the protectionism of the National Government, and joining the scramble for sectional benefits: 'Nobody seemed to realize what a historic debate it was—the body from which John Bright and Richard Cobden started the

---

[70]   *Hansard*, 5th ser., 261, c. 305, 4 Feb. 1932.

[71]   E. Durbin, *New Jerusalems: The Labour Party and the Economics of Democratic Socialism* (1985), esp. 251–6.

[72]   D. Blaazer, *The Popular Front and the Progressive Tradition* (Cambridge, 1992), 157.

[73]   P. F. Clarke, 'The End of Laissez-Faire and the Politics of Cotton', *Historical Journal*, 15 (1972); A. J. Marrison, 'Businessmen and Tariff Reform' *Business History*, 25 (1983); id., *British Business and Protection, 1903–1932* (Oxford, 1996); F. Trentmann, 'The Transformation of Fiscal Reform', *Historical Journal*, 39 (1996); A. Redford, *Manchester Merchants and Foreign Trade* (2 vols, 1934 and 1956), vol. 2, 203–7; F. W. Hirst, *'The Manchester Martyrs'* (1916).

[74]   Redford, *Manchester Merchants*, vol. 2, 214–19; National Union of Merchants and Manufacturers, ephemera, *c.*1920 in John Johnson Collection, 'Free Trade and Protection', box 8.

[75]   F. Capie, *Depression and Protectionism: Britain between the Wars* (1983); T. Rooth, *British Protectionism and the International Economy: Overseas Commercial Policy in the 1930s* (Cambridge, 1993); R. Davenport-Hines, *Dudley Docker: The Life and Times of a Trade Warrior* (Cambridge, 1984).

[76]   'L. B. Lee', *DBB*, vol. 3, 715–25.

movement for Free Trade which first captured Lancashire and then England, this same body some seventy [*sic*] years later discussing how the plums of protection should be shared out.'[77] Shortly after, imperial preference was endorsed. Protection and the empire, abandoned in the 1840s and vociferously resisted in 1906, had once again become central to the nation's industrial salvation.

By 1931 this was also a prescription that the City was ready to endorse. For, however much City of London financiers had sought in the 1920s to rebuild the pre-war international economic order, by August 1931 tariffs seemed preferable to socialism. Here, the financiers followed logically in the steps of their Edwardian predecessors, for, as we have seen, by 1906 a number of City figures had endorsed tariffs as a revenue-raising instrument, and by 1910 the spectre of socialism had pushed the City strongly into the tariff reform camp: in the January election the City was reduced to putting up the industrialist Sir Hugh Bell as its candidate, only to be humiliatingly defeated.[78] There is here a clue that tariffs were a matter of indifference so long as the international flow of capital and services remained unimpeded. Arguably, this continued to be the City's primary concern after 1918: the restoration of the world's network of payments and services under the umbrella of the gold standard. This financial internationalism dominated British policy-making in the 1920s, and received the grudging support of industry, if largely for the lack of any politically acceptable alternative.[79] Free trade groups drawing on the City continued to agitate, but City efforts to convert Europe to a broader free trade stance rang hollow. For example, Sir George Paish's imitation of Cobden's 1846 tour of Europe in 1926 on behalf of the Universal Free Trade Committee fell on deaf ears, as did Morrison Bell's late-1920s crusade against tariff walls.[80]

More importantly, the monetary orthodoxy of the City exacerbated tensions with industry, especially as the vaunted return to the pre-war international order seemed remote, in a world of closing markets, declining trade, and falling prices. Economic heterodoxy—above all protection and imperial preference—grew in appeal. British efforts, orchestrated through the League of Nations to shore up the international economic order, not only fell foul of industry, but began to lose the support of the Conservative Party in the late 1920s, and, eventually, the City itself

---

[77]   *Lancashire and Whitehall: The Diary of Sir Raymond Streat, vol. one, 1931–1939*, ed. M. W. Dupree (Manchester, 1987), 120 [14 Dec. 1931].

[78]   For free trade in the City, see C. Stewart, 15 Apr. 1908, and E. G. Brunker, 28 May 1909, to A. Elliot, EP 19496 and 19497. The City of London Free Trade committee was set up in Apr. 1909 and a manifesto issued in July: *Free Trader*, 15 July 1909, 188–90; see, too, F. W. Hirst, 'The City and Tariff Reform', *Free Trader*, May 1910, 124; H. G. Hutchinson, *Life of Sir John Lubbock* (2 vols, 1914), vol. 2, 267–8, 275, 302, 315; H. Bell, *In Defence of Free Trade and Sound Finance* (Electoral addresses, London, 1910; Newcastle, 1910). In Jan. 1910 the tariff reformers Balfour and Banbury both gained over 17,000 votes, Bell gained 4,623. The former were returned unopposed in Dec. 1910.

[79]   R. W. D. Boyce, *British Capitalism at the Crossroads, 1919–1932* (Cambridge, 1987) unravels this in a masterly detailed account.

[80]   Sir George Paish, 'My Memoirs', 95 ff., 113, 117–25, Coll. Misc. 621, BLPES; *The World Free Trader*, Mar. 1925; C. Morrison Bell, *Tariff Walls: A European Crusade* (1930).

urged a new trade policy, based on the empire.[81] Briefly, Labour's internationalist pursuit of freer trade through a 'tariff truce' coincided with the City's defence of the fiscal *ancien régime*. Yet this could only be a temporary marriage of convenience, which ended in precipitate divorce as the economic crisis of 1931 engulfed the Labour government. The City was now ready to swallow, indeed to urge, revenue tariffs, to abandon the gold standard as a necessary part of the price for the avoidance of socialism, and to embrace imperial preference as the best guarantee for a return on its capital investments in the colonies.[82]

The revival, decline, and fall of the Liberal empire, 1906–32

Tariff reform, on Joseph Chamberlain's model of imperial preference, ultimately triumphed with the fiscal legislation of 1932, introduced by his son Neville. The Liberal ideal of empire, revivified against Joe's challenge, had been finally expunged from British politics. Its durability had always been questionable, in the face of the fiscal autonomy granted to the colonies in 1846 as part of the logic of political economy. By 1906 that autonomy had been vastly reinforced by the dynamic of colonial nationalism, although the tariff reformers still aspired to some form of federal imperial organization, at least in the spheres of trade and defence. Against this, the Liberal 'sunset of empire' after 1906 had been based on a strong reaffirmation of the Whig–Liberal free trade ideal of Grey, Russell, and Gladstone: an empire run by Morley, Elgin, Crewe, and Harcourt was unlikely to depart fundamentally from the defence of colonial autonomy combined with the maximum of free trade which self-government permitted. More positive ideals inspired the formation of the Liberal Colonial Club in 1906, with its emphasis on imperialism and social reform, in part a rebuttal of accusations of Liberal indifference to empire.[83] Yet the divergence between Liberal and tariff reform ideals of empire remained vast, lending sharp point to the Colonial Conference which met in London in 1907.

In the Chamberlainite-Balfour 'blueprint', this Conference would have provided the stepping-stone to an empire based on firm economic ties, which Chamberlain had canvassed since the mid-1890s, and which Balfour had endorsed by 1904. After Chamberlain's defeat in 1906, it was possible for some tariff reformers, for example the Australian Liberal Cockburn, never happy in Tory circles, to believe that it would now be far easier for British Liberals to adopt new fiscal and imperial policies, and that Lloyd George would prove a better and more congenial ally than Chamberlain.[84] More commonly, many tariff reformers, singing to keep up their

[81]   Williamson, *National Crisis*, 68–70; Boyce, *British Capitalism*, 253–5.

[82]   Boyce, *British Capitalism*; Williamson, *National Crisis*; P. J. Cain, 'Colonies and Capital: Some Aspects of Anglo-Colonial Financial Relations after 1850', in F. M. L. Thompson, *Landowners, Capitalists, and Entrepreneurs* (Oxford, 1994), 213–33, esp. 230–3.

[83]   *The Times*, e.g. 19 and 20 July 1906, 7 Mar. and 23 Apr. 1907, 17 July 1908, 23 Feb. 1909, 1 Nov. 1913, 11 July 1914. See, too, *The Canadian Reciprocity Agreement* (Liberal Colonial Club, 1911).

[84]   Cockburn to Deakin, 19 Jan. 1906, 3 Aug. 1906, Deakin Papers, 1303–4; Wise to Deakin, 6 Apr. 1905, Deakin Papers, 1132; above, 242.

spirits, looked forward to the Conference with some expectation, hoping that after Chamberlain's stroke in July 1906, Deakin, the Australian Premier, would resuscitate their cause, and, less plausibly, would enter British politics to do so.[85] It was thus as the standard-bearer of the hopes of English tariff reformers that Deakin attended this Conference, and, as La Nauze has shown, his activities in London were conducted with as much intent to influence British public opinion as to inform the detailed work of the Conference sittings.[86]

What was his degree of success? Chamberlain drew solace from Deakin's presence, a welcome morale-booster at a time of deep depression for the English tariff reformers.[87] Yet, of course, Deakin's presence equally galvanized a victorious, but far from complacent free trade movement. J. A. Spender, editor of the *Westminster Gazette*, reminded Deakin that the protectionist cause in Britain was a Conservative one:

If protection wins, the Liberal and radical parties go under for years and the country will be governed by the Conservative party, the House of Lords and the manufacturing interests . . . This is a matter of life and death to us politically, and if we don't speak out when you are here, we shall never recover the ground when you are gone.[88]

Interestingly, the tariff reformers did win some by-elections at this time, and it is possible that Deakin, through his widely publicized speech at the Baltic Exchange, helped win over Balfour as well as opinion in the City of London and beyond.[89]

Yet Deakin's success must be measured not only by his impact on the domestic political scene, but also by the degree to which he advanced the wider cause of imperial preference at and outside the Conference. Within the Conference this was a cause impossible of success, given the newly refurbished free trade credentials of the Liberal Party in 1906, and even more so after the detachment of Canada and South Africa from the cause.[90] More disappointing for Deakin, one suspects, was

---

[85]   Chamberlain, 26 Apr. 1906; Milner, 25 Feb. 1907; H. A. Gwynne, 9 May 1907; G. Parker, 6 Feb. 1907; R. Lethbridge, 9 Apr. 1907; Duke of Sutherland, 26 Apr. 1907, all to Deakin, Deakin Papers, 1540/1/1390, 1640-4, 1663-5, 1389, 1395, 1452; J. A. La Nauze, *Alfred Deakin: A Biography* (1979), ch. 22; W. K. Hancock, *Survey of British Commonwealth Affairs. Volume 2: Problems of Economic Policy 1918–1939 Part I*, 81–91.

[86]   La Nauze, *Deakin*, ch. 22. The Colonial Office civil servant Hopwood noted that Deakin 'behaves like a garrulous Howard Vincent . . . He has become an active henchman for the Tariff Reform League and is going to stump the country'. To Bryce, 12 May 1907, Bryce Papers, 81.

[87]   Chamberlain, 16 May 1907; R. Jebb, 19 May 1907; L. S. Amery, 7 June 1907, to Deakin, Deakin Papers, 1540/1/1536, 1562, 1579.

[88]   Spender to Deakin, 17 May 1907, Deakin Papers, 1540/1/1543, quoted in part in La Nauze, *Deakin*, 497 n. For examples of free trade responses, see E. Pulsford, *The Colonial Conference of 1907: Empire Commerce* (1907); *What Colonial Preference Means* (Cobden Club, 1907); W. R. Malcolm, *Bond of Empire* (1907). See, too, J. D. Startt, *Journalists for Empire: The Imperial Debate in the Edwardian Stately Press, 1903–1913* (Westport, 1991), 20–4, 53–9, 155–61.

[89]   Deakin Diary, 15 May 1907, Deakin Papers, 1540/2/27; *The Needs of Empire* (pub. *The Planet*, 1907); Startt, *Journalists for Empire*, 162–75, sees the Conference as a notable fillip for tariff reform, Sykes, *Tariff Reform*, 133–4, merely a temporary one.

[90]   La Nauze, *Deakin*, 500–1; Amery to Deakin, 7 May 1907, Deakin Papers, 1540/1/1518. Laurier, back in Canada, 'descanted, to Bryce, on the difficulties in which he had been placed in England by the

the failure to win over leading British imperialists to the cause of preference. For example, two notable friends of Australian defence within the empire, Brassey and Clarke, were adamant against preference. This, Brassey wrote to Tennyson, would necessarily mean a food tax, 'a burden on our workers and our poor', while colonial manufacturers 'would insist on protection'.[91] Clarke, Governor of Victoria (1901–4), secretary of the Committee for Imperial Defence (1904–6), and now Governor of Bombay, advised Deakin that as an imperialist of thirty years' standing he was unable to back tariff reform and preference: 'Nothing is better calculated to promote mutual irritation than haggling over the terms of preference followed by an arrangement certain to give dissatisfaction to both parties.'[92] Preference for Clarke was a solvent, not a cement, of imperial ties, and this objection to intra-imperial haggling remained strongly expressed throughout the 1920s and early 1930s. Ultimately, Deakin's role in 1907 seems to have hardened existing divisions of opinion within the British Empire rather than to have advanced the cause of tariff reform and imperial preference.

Nor did the course of Australian politics on Deakin's return do much to further Anglo-Australian co-operation, for while the Conference had furthered schemes for civil intelligence along the lines of the Pollock scheme, political, and economic co-operation remained distant.[93] Deakin remained an enthusiast for imperial preference. He met only lukewarm interest in Australia, but on his return there, he ensured that protection, duly stepped up, was accompanied by a measure of unilateral preference.[94] This was opposed by the remaining free trade imperialists in Australia, who fought a penultimate stand on this issue—for example, Bruce Smith, who lamented the end of Liberalism in Australia.[95] But the new protection scheme of Deakin, followed by the fusion of free traders and protectionists in the Deakin government of 1909, killed off a coherent and organized Australian free trade movement, and did nothing to further the wider cause of imperial federation.

Despite this, the tariff reformers in Britain, able to make play with both Canadian and Australian preference, kept alive the issue of imperial preference, although the Liberal victories in the elections of 1910 were to render their efforts marginal to the discussions at the Imperial Conference of 1911. Even so, shortly after the Conference the tariff reformers gleaned comfort from the defeat in the

Protectionist Jingoes trying to make party capital and preferentialism out of him and Canada', Bryce to Hopwood, 10 Mar. 1908, Southborough Papers 7.

[91]   Brassey to Tennyson, 1 Mar. 1907, Tennyson Papers, A5011, fos. 133–7, Mitchell Library, Sydney.

[92]   Clarke to Deakin, 13 Apr., 13 Dec. 1907, Deakin Papers, 1540/1/1410, 1830. See, too, Clarke to Tennyson, 11 Feb. 1907, Tennyson Papers.

[93]   Above, 243–4.

[94]   La Nauze, *Deakin*, 425–6. The Act passed on 23 Oct. 1907. Bryce doubted whether Deakin represented general sentiment in Australia. To Hopwood, 6 May 1907, Southborough Papers, 10.

[95]   Bruce Smith to Sir J. Symon, 16 Jan. 1906 on the setting aside of 'the philosophical school of Liberalism', Symon Papers, 10/470, National Library of Australia; see, too, Glynn Papers, Diaries, e.g. 20 Oct. 1907.

Canadian General Election of 1911 of Laurier's proposed reciprocity treaty with the United States, the long-standing alternative to federation, with strong appeal to Canadian farmers and free traders.[96] The issue of preference was also sustained later with reference to India (for example, in debates over tea duties in 1911) and Bonar Law gave the issue considerable prominence in 1912 and 1913 when vainly seeking to convert Lancashire to tariffs.[97] Yet, for the most part, by 1914 even the keenest imperialists gathered in the Round Table Movement recognized that advocacy of preference could only be an obstacle to imperial consolidation.[98]

The Liberals themselves, anxious to conciliate and to reinforce imperial sentiment, displayed a growing appreciation of the economic and strategic importance of the Empire before 1914.[99] Here, Liberal policy looked both ways, for, as Offer has shown, the primary strategy evolved under the Liberals depended upon an 'Atlanticist' approach, looking to close Anglo-American co-operation in the event of war with Germany, a war that they believed tariff reform would make inevitable.[100] On the other hand, there was considerable support for non-tariff encouragement to imperial trade, and the Colonial Conference of 1911 initiated an important investigation of the economic resources of the British Empire. This resulted in the Royal Commission set up in 1912, leading to a string of reports during the First World War, endorsing non-tariff means to imperial welfare.[101] While, therefore, free trade remained unchallengeable on the surface, new considerations of defence and economic warfare increasingly encroached upon the old Liberal ideal of empire deployed and defended in 1906.

The Liberal free trade ideal of Empire was also challenged from other directions before 1914. For example, Home Rule for Ireland proceeded on the basis of the reluctant acceptance by the Irish nationalists of fiscal dependence upon England, while Liberals sometimes feared, and tariff reformers hoped, that an improbable deal might be struck, with protection held out as the bait to Irish farmers to accept the Union.[102] With Irish electors reputedly 'food taxers to a man', free trade in Ireland seemed confined to a few academic oases, as the exiled Cambridge Apostle Meredith found when he took up the Chair of Economics at Belfast in 1911. Ironically, after separation (and fiscal autonomy) in 1921, free trade was better placed to stage an intellectual and political recovery in Ireland, although

---

[96]   A. Offer, *The First World War: An Agrarian Interpretation* (Oxford, 1989), 160–3.

[97]   e.g., *Hansard*, 5th ser., 26, cc. 63–4, R. D. Holt, 22 May 1911; B. Chatterji, *Trade, Tariffs, and Empire: Lancashire and British Policy in India, 1919–1939* (Delhi, 1992), 189–94.

[98]   J. E. Kendle, *The Round Table Movement and Imperial Union* (Toronto, 1975), 166–70; G. Drage, *The Imperial Organisation of Trade* (1911).

[99]   For example, in 1911–12 Britain negotiated various relaxations in her commercial treaties to allow the Dominions more easily to withdraw from them: de Bernhardt, *Handbook of Commercial Treaties* (1912), 226 (Colombia), 280 (Denmark), 378 (France), 934 (Sweden).

[100]   Offer, *First World War*, Part Three; below, 296–7.

[101]   Startt, *Journalists for Empire*, 162–75, 190, 195–9; Offer, *First World War*, 158–63.

[102]   P. Jalland, *The Liberals and Ireland: The Ulster Question in British Politics to 1914* (Brighton, 1980), 47, 161, 202, 263; Green, *Conservatism*, 297–304.

the 1930s were to see the Anglo-Irish tariff war anticipated by free traders in the 1880s.[103]

A further impetus to economic heterodoxy continued to emanate from the West Indies, whose problems in the 1890s had most directly stimulated Chamberlain's drive towards a new imperial policy. In particular, in 1910 the Liberal government had sent the Unionist free trader Balfour of Burleigh to conduct an inquiry into trade between Canada and the West Indies. This recommended, besides improved communications, the grant of preference by the West Indies to Canada.[104] Balfour of Burleigh had strongly opposed preferential food taxes in 1907 ('the means of causing friction and difficulty and must cause the break-up of the empire more quickly than any other method which could be devised'), but believed his minor proposals in 1910 were consistent with 'broad-minded free trade'.[105] The Liberals favoured growing ties, even political federation between Canada and the West Indies in the long term, but in the interim there followed in 1912 a reciprocal extension of preference.[106]

Liberal suspicion that elasticity of mind on the issue of free trade led directly to protection was amply vindicated, for, as we have seen, under the pressures of the First World War, Balfour of Burleigh, now in charge of the Reconstruction Committee on Commercial and Industrial Policy after War, came down firmly in favour of imperial preference.[107] To many dismayed Liberals, this was a more decisive break with the past than either the McKenna Duties or the Paris Resolutions, and took imperial designs far further than the Royal Commission set up in 1912. Imperial preference was now back at the centre of British policy-making, embraced by the Imperial War Cabinet and less enthusiastically by the coalition government, and providing the lead Austen Chamberlain needed to give fiscal vent to his (and his father's) tariff reform beliefs in his budget of 1919. Preference was, of course, still very limited in its impact, and was to be checked by Tory defeat in 1923, by Labour in government, and, indirectly, by Churchill's abolition of tea duty in 1929, but the pre-war Liberal ideal and practice of empire—of free-standing nations, linked by sentiment and history—had been repudiated, stretched to breaking-point by the demands of war and the demands of the colonies.

One of the weak links in that old ideal had always been India, for while, on the

---

[103]   H. O. Meredith, 'The Irish Fiscal Inquiry', *Economic Journal*, 34 (1924), 135–7; C. O'Grada, *Ireland: A New Economic History, 1780–1939* (Oxford, 1994), 385–9; P. Canning, *British Policy Towards Ireland, 1921–41* (Oxford, 1985), 122–75.

[104]   Balfour, *Balfour*, 141; 'There is no Protection in our proposals', Balfour of Burleigh to Strachey, 28 Sept. 1910, Strachey Papers, S/2/5.

[105]   Balfour of Burleigh to Long, 18 Dec. 1907 (copy), Balfour of Burleigh Papers, TD 93/55/58; various letters, memos, etc. *re* Commission, ibid. 24, 69, 72, 80, 90; Balfour to A. Elliot, 8 Aug. 1910, EP 19497: 'I have gone pretty far but not I think further than a broad-minded Free Trader might in the interests of the Empire.'

[106]   C. P. Lucas to Hopwood, 8, 15 July 1908, Southborough Papers 7; D. R. Annett, *British Preference in Canadian Commercial Policy* (Toronto, 1948), 39.

[107]   Turner, *British Politics and the Great War*, 334–53; above, 281.

one hand, Cobden had looked forward to the end of British rule in India, a growing body of native opinion believed that free trade had acted as the ideological disguise for imperial(ist) exploitation. As we have seen, Lancashire had consistently opposed the imposition of cotton duties, whether or not designed for revenue or protection. As late as 1903 Manchester had campaigned against both import and excise duties on cotton goods.[108] But as recent studies have suggested, fiscal and monetary policy in India always owed more to the financial imperatives of the India Office and the City of London than they did to 'the interests of Manchester', although the latter often proved a useful and popular defence.[109] India also placed tariff reformers in a dilemma, for while some supporters urged the inclusion of India in any preferential scheme, others rarely looked beyond the 'White Empire' of the Dominions.[110] In Britain, therefore, while former Indian civil servants and some City men with Indian links, urged preference, this met stout resistance on the grounds of inevitable harm to Lancashire, to the Indian government, and to the Indian people, who would face higher prices (for native goods) through the artificial encouragement of Indian production.[111] In India itself, much domestic opinion, as in Australia or Canada, favoured protection rather than preference, a desire less readily dressed up in the garb of imperial sentiment than it was in the Dominions.[112] As a result, India rarely came to the forefront of the tariff reform debate. The possibility of preference in the Indian market provided no attraction to those who had waged successive campaigns for free entry into India, and whose Edwardian summer had been based on Indian demand. Nor did Liberal and progressive opinion seem any readier to endorse protection when advocated by Indian nationalist millowners rather than by English tariff reformers.[113]

After 1918, however, Indian demands for protection and autonomy proved far less easy to resist. The central issue at stake remained, as in 1865 and 1894–6, the imposition of import duties on (Lancashire) cotton goods. These had been reintroduced in 1917, as a wartime fiscal expedient. The collective protests of Lancashire had proved unavailing, and, as the cotton lobby feared, wartime precedent served

---

[108]   Above, 216; Redford, *Manchester Merchants*, vol. 2, 43.

[109]   P. J. Cain and A. G. Hopkins, *British Imperialism* (2 vols, 1993), vol. 1, ch. 10; Chatterji, *Trade, Tariffs and Empire*; for the 'Peelite' fiscal aims of Bertram Currie, see G. Peel, *Free Trader*, 251 (1951), 134–9.

[110]   Oddly, India is almost completely ignored in the two most thorough accounts of the Tariff Reform movement: Sykes, *Tariff Reform* and Green, *Conservatism*.

[111]   The Colonial Conference acted as one spur to debate, see R. Lethbridge, *India and Imperial Preference* (1907); cf. S. Mitra, *India and Imperial Preference* (1907). Lethbridge was a 'devoted follower of Hamilton and List', Mitra, a Cobden Club author. See, too, H. B. Lees-Smith, *India and the Tariff Problem* (1909).

[112]   Lethbridge made a determined effort to make the 'imperial' case, scoffing at the notion that preference would lead to tariffs against Lancashire. Lethbridge to Deakin, 11 Apr. 1907, Deakin Papers, 1540/1/1400. Lethbridge had earlier informed Deakin that 'the Cobdenite idea is not only rejected in India . . . but is actually loathed and detested by Indians', 9 Apr. 1907, ibid. 1540/1/1395.

[113]   Crewe and *Manchester Guardian*, 14 Dec. 1912, cited in Chatterji, *Trade, Tariffs and Empire*, 191–2.

merely as the prelude to the Fiscal Autonomy Act of 1919, itself engendering a series of increases in duties, as well as the abolition of the countervailing excise in 1925. As has been shown, this was no simple case of Lancashire's power being replaced by that of Indian manufacturers, for, as before 1914, the fiscal and political needs of the Indian government remained uppermost in decision-making.[114] Yet Indian millowners, having mounted the bicycle of protection, pedalled furiously, leaving the Lancashire cotton lobby bitter and disconsolate in their wake, with tariff rates rising to 25 per cent on British textiles by 1931.[115] The wider rationale of the India Office—that fiscal autonomy might slow down the demand for self-rule—provided little comfort for the employers who believed themselves swindled, and cotton operatives who found themselves unemployed.

In these circumstances, it was not perhaps surprising that it was the Labour Party, heavily dependent upon Lancashire for its seats in Parliament, that proved in the 1920s to be the ultimate upholder of the Liberal empire. For not only did Snowden in his budget of 1924 end the preference granted by Chamberlain in 1919, but Labour was strongly hostile to preference in principle, with the under-secretary for the Colonies, for example, warning against the 'slippery slope', for 'the whole policy of preference is economically unsound, and is really based upon the principle of protecting Dominion and colonial interests at the expense of the people of the Mother Country, and that means mainly the worker'.[116] By 1929 some Labour ministers, above all Thomas, were ready to take a different line (as were some Liberals) and in office even strong free traders such as Graham were obliged pragmatically to accept some degree of preference and even to extend it, especially in the face of rising Indian protectionism.[117] Nevertheless, few politicians doubted the extent of the electorate's attachment to free trade, such that the general election of 1931 neatly sidestepped the issue of free trade and tariff reform in its call for a 'doctor's mandate'. But with the National Government safely in power, Chamberlain, with due filial piety, was openly to espouse imperial preference, and J. H. Thomas, in the approach to the Ottawa Conference, was even forced to abandon unilateral preference, the figleaf by which preference-seekers had sought to avoid the charge of sordid tariff-bargaining.[118] Within the Cabinet the free trade rump was no more able to resist preference than it had protection, but Snowden, Sinclair, and 'the imperial Cobdenite' Samuel resigned from the National Government in protest against what Snowden considered the 'final and complete triumph of the Tory protectionists'.[119]

---

[114] Chatterji, *Trade, Tariffs and Empire, passim.*

[115] Drummond, *Economic Policy*, 121–31; Chatterji, *Trade, Tariffs and Empire*, chs. 4–6.

[116] Quoted in Drummond, *Economic Policy*, 177. For a valuable account, see P. S. Gupta, *Imperialism and the British Labour Movement, 1914–1964* (1975), 19–32, 60–71, 145–61, 212–19. Leonard Woolf influentially rejected preference as indistinguishable from protection in *International Economic Policy* (?1916), 5–6.

[117] Drummond, *Economic Policy*, 127–8; Chatterji, *Trade, Tariffs and Empire*, 337–8, 340–1.

[118] Drummond, *Economic Policy*, 90 ff.

[119] Snowden, *An Autobiography* (2 vols, 1934), vol. 2, ch. 85, Letter to MacDonald, 29 Aug. 1932; Wasserstein, *Herbert Samuel*, 356 ff.; Samuel, *Empire Free Trade* (1930).

Yet these Cobdenite laments were but dignified whispers amidst the Chamberlainite *feu de joie*.[120] The Ottawa Agreements, and subsequent bilateral commercial treaties, which implemented this new 'National policy', were of course susceptible to a quasi-'liberal' interpretation, in the search for intra-imperial free trade, and aggressive tariff-bargaining against foreign nations.[121] But this was a gloss convincing only to those who also believed that the Chamberlains, *père et fils* (and List before them), were more Cobdenite than Cobden.[122] A clearer guide to the policy implications of 1931–2 came in the lengthening pages of the tariff schedules, as thousands of duties were now imposed, erecting a structure of consumer prices which would last until Britain's entry to the European Common Market in 1973.[123] For the first time since the 1830s, customs revenue contributed a rising share of total government revenue, while its absolute growth in the early 1930s outstripped that of income tax by 75 per cent.[124] Here were clear signals that one hundred years of progressive fiscal policy had eventually been reversed.

'Traders and heroes':[125] *war, peace, and free trade, 1906–46*

If Cobdenite ideas retained any substantial influence after 1932, it was within the gamut of instincts and principles that informed the 'idealist' strand in British foreign policy and public opinion on issues of war and peace.[126] That free trade would lead to peace had been the Utopian expectation of the 1840s. Such simplicities had been under stern challenge, as we have seen, since the Franco-Prussian War, but had survived the weight of evidence against them. Not only had there been a significant strengthening of the European peace movement after 1889, but in the wake of the Boer War and as part of the renewal of free trade, Cobdenite notions of foreign policy had been conspicuously revived.[127] The electoral ascendancy of free trade provided a new opening for the pursuit of international peace,

---

[120] *Hansard*, 5th ser., 269, cc. 27–146, 154–264, 338–479 [18, 19, 20 Oct. 1932]; *The Economist*, 27 Aug., 3 Sept., 1 and 22 Oct. 1932.
[121] Drummond, *Economic Policy*, 114; for detailed accounts of British policy in the 1930s, see I. M. Drummond, *Imperial Economic Policy, 1917–39: Studies in Expansion and Protection* (1974) and Rooth, *British Protectionism*.
[122] Cf. [F. W. Hirst] 'Ottawa and the Cobden Treaty', *Manchester Guardian*, 24 Sept. 1932, 10.
[123] A. S. Harvey, *The General Tariff of the United Kingdom* (1933).
[124] P. Mathias, *The First Industrial Nation* (1969), Table 12, 462; in absolute numbers, customs revenue grew by 74% between 1930 and 1931, and 1936 and 1937; income tax revenue fell by less than 1%: *Statistical Abstract for the United Kingdom* (1938, Cmd. 5627), 170–1.
[125] W. Sombart's *Händler und Helden: Patriotische Besinnungen* (Munich, 1915) influentially contrasted the English traders' world-view, life as the sum of commercial transactions, with the Germanic heroic understanding of sacrifice and duty. See F. Ringer, *Decline of the German Mandarins: The German Academic Community, 1890–1933* (Camb. Mass., 1969), 183–4; F. Y. Edgeworth, *Economic Journal* (Dec. 1915), 604–10; J. H. Clapham, *An Economic History of Modern Britain, Vol. 2: Free Trade and Steel* (Cambridge, 1st edn., 1932; 1967) 238 n. 2.
[126] P. M. Kennedy, *Strategy and Diplomacy, 1870–1945* (1980), 15–39; M. Ceadel, *Pacifism in Britain, 1914–1945* (Oxford Historical Monographs: Oxford, 1980), and id., *Thinking about Peace and War*; D. Long and P. Wilson (eds.), *Thinkers of the Twenty Years' Crisis: Inter-War Idealism Reassessed* (Oxford, 1995).
[127] Above, 226–7.

while, ideologically, 'Angellism', following the publication of Norman Angell's *The Great Illusion* in 1911, powerfully reinforced Cobdenism.[128] The outbreak of world war in 1914 proved the greatest falsification of the Cobdenite belief that the greater economic interdependence of nations would result in peace. Yet, as in 1870, the very shock of war revitalized the desire to avoid war. It was in this context that the Edwardian revival of Cobdenite thinking was carried over into inter-war perceptions of foreign policy.

'Free trade, peace, and goodwill'—the simple catchwords of the 1860s—continued to express an optimistic vision which linked Campbell-Bannerman, the Cobden Club, and the bulk of Radical–Liberal opinion. Between 1903 and 1906, the Cobdenite world-view had gained a wide audience through projects such as Campbell-Bannerman's League of Peace, and through the promotion of free trade as part of the rational case for peace, the cause of 'sane internationalism' to which men such as Bertrand Russell had rallied, and which had formed an important strand in the Cobden celebrations of 1904.[129] In many respects, the very success of this Radical vision heightened the rift that historians have frequently detected between Liberal imperialist policy-makers led by Grey and Asquith and 'the trouble-makers', the anti-war Radical critics of foreign policy who proved so vocal in Edwardian Britain.[130] Yet to emphasize this undoubted tension is to ignore the substantial common ground held by both policy-makers and Radical opinion, and to ignore the success of the Radical vision, a success that vastly enhanced Radical aspirations before August 1914, and the extent of their disillusionment thereafter.

Moreover, despite the truism that Liberal foreign policy followed directly from that of the Unionists, it is usually forgotten that, had tariff reform succeeded in 1906 or 1910, Unionist policy would have been very different. For, at the very least, the Conservatives were committed to Lansdowne's 'big revolver', the threat of commercial retaliation, the view that Britain should be ready to join those other states in Europe whose engagement in tariff wars had done not a little to contribute to the growing tensions of pre-war Europe.[131] As Cromer, diplomat and Unionist free trader, urged, 'if we are to adopt a policy of Protection . . . the danger [of war with Germany] will be a good deal increased'.[132] This view itself had become a

---

[128]   See, *inter alia*, H. Weinroth, 'Norman Angell and *The Great Illusion*: An Episode in Pre-war Pacifism', *Historical Journal*, 17 (1974), 551–74; J. D. B. Miller, *Norman Angell and the Futility of War. Peace and the Public Mind* (1986), and id., 'Norman Angell and Rationality in International Relations', in Long and Wilson (eds.), *Thinkers*, 100–21; Blaazer, *Popular Front*, 89 ff.

[129]   H. Samuel, 'The Cobden Centenary and Modern Liberalism', *Nineteenth Century* (June 1904), 904; *Cobden Centenary: Programme Souvenir* (1904), 3 (G. H. Perris); Cobden Club leaflets, 167, *Cobden on International Peace* (1904).

[130]   A. J. P. Taylor, *The Trouble Makers: Dissent over Foreign Policy 1792–1939* (1957); A. J. A. Morris, *Radicalism Against War, 1906–1914*; id. (ed.), *Edwardian Radicalism, 1900–1914*, chs. 10–15.

[131]   W. B. Harvey, *Tariffs and International Relations*; *Parl. Papers*, 1904, 95 [Cd. 1938] Tariff Wars between certain European States.

[132]   To A. Elliot, 28 Nov. 1909, EP 19497.

virtual commonplace among British diplomats before 1914. Its obverse was well expressed in the famous memorandum of Eyre Crowe, the son of Joseph, Britain's first commercial attaché:

[I]n proportion as England champions the principle of the largest measure of general freedom of commerce, she undoubtedly strengthens her hold on the interested friendship of other nations, at least to the extent of making them feel less apprehensive of naval supremacy in the hands of free trade England than they would be in the face of a predominant protectionist Power. This is an aspect of the free trade question which is apt to be overlooked.[133]

Yet several shadows were cast across Crowe's reassuring linkage between free trade as a 'public good' for the world, and British power as dependent upon naval predominance. First, its value had been eroded by the threat of tariffs in Britain, for free trade, no longer a policy above party, seemed to have at best a limited lifespan, dependent upon electoral vicissitudes. Prussian ministers now encouraged free trade in Britain, just as British diplomats warned of the dangers that protectionism at home held for Anglo-German relations.[134] This argument incurred the wrath of tariff reformers, but their response reinforced the perception that free trade had become a party rather than a public good, and provided a further sign of the temptation that 'commercial war' held for the tariff reformers. Second, the colonies, with their growing tendency towards protection and preference, challenged the notion of an open door, a fear increased by the long-simmering tariff war between Germany and Canada.[135] Third, despite progress in the codification of naval laws, Britain had resolutely refused to accept the immunity of private property in time of war as part of international law. This appeared to detract from the 'disinterestedness' of British policy, and remained a vitally controversial issue, in which British strategy seemingly outweighed international morality.[136] Even so, despite this lacuna, Britain's role in the world depended upon her ability to uphold free trade; only in this way could her people be assured of food, her traders of markets, and her enemies of her good intent. These assurances might sound hollow to those German traders who had attempted to penetrate the tariff barriers of the self-governing colonies, but Britain was the world's emporium, and German

[133] 1 Jan. 1907. Quoted in K. Bourne, *The Foreign Policy of Victorian England, 1830–1902* (Oxford, 1970), 482.

[134] P. M. Kennedy, *The Rise of the Anglo-German Antagonism, 1860–1914* (1980), 264, 282; Spring-Rice to G. W. Balfour, 7 June 1909, Balfour of Whittingehame Papers, 116.

[135] e.g. *Nation*, 8 Aug. 1908; *War and Peace*, 3 (Aug. 1916), 168 (Lowes Dickinson); for Hamilton's earlier fears, see Diary, 25 May 1903, Add. MS 48680.

[136] B. Semmel, *Liberalism and Naval Strategy* (1986); J. W. Coogan, *The End of Neutrality: The United States, Britain and Maritime Rights, 1899–1915* (Ithaca, 1981); A. Offer, 'Morality and Admiralty: "Jacky" Fisher, Economic Warfare and the Laws of War', *Journal of Contemporary History*, 23 (1988); id., *The First World War*; K. Neilson, '"The British Empire Floats on the British Navy": British Naval Policy, Belligerent Rights, and Disarmament, 1902–1909', in B. J. C. McKercher (ed.), *Arms Limitation and Disarmament: Restraints on War, 1899–1939* (Westport, Conn., 1992), 21–41.

merchants remained, after those of India, her best customers.[137] Britain therefore remained charged, as Cobden had urged in the 1840s, with the mission not only of keeping the faith, but upholding the international economic order.

This goal by no means seemed an impossible one, for despite the predictions of the tariff reformers, the world had not by 1914 disintegrated into hostile trading blocs. If this was not quite the high tide of internationalization valorized by Keynes after the war, world trade had continued to grow steadily, and despite intimations of decline, Britain's share had grown between 1886 and 1913.[138] British commercial diplomacy had also proved far from impotent. For example, the Anglo-French entente cordiale had been underpinned by a series of agreements with the British colonies, culminating in the Franco-Canadian Convention of 1907. Some sources of friction remained, and attempts to secure a new Anglo-French commercial treaty in 1908–9 failed. But good commercial relations with France were valued as an important asset to the free trade case, while, among the more optimistic, even the prospect of the Channel Tunnel was revived.[139] Britain, as in the late 1870s and early 1880s, had also concluded a series of commercial treaties in Eastern Europe, in response to the German attempt at a 'commercial diplomatic revolution'. This included treaties with Bulgaria and Romania (both 1905), Serbia (1907), Montenegro (1910), even if these were mere wicket-gates compared with the growing ring-fence round the Austro-German market. Further afield, Britain also negotiated a new commercial treaty with Japan in 1911, an important rejoinder to the tariff reform case for preference and retaliation.[140]

More encouragingly still, the United States itself, the long-standing bane of the Cobdenites, showed new signs of economic liberalism before 1914. In 1910 Hirst enthused: 'What a wonderful insurrection there is against your tariff. If it succeeds we shall very soon have to take a second place in international trade. But we shall all benefit.'[141] Above all, the Underwood Act of 1913, while designed to uphold moderate protection for American industry, was hailed by *The Economist* as 'the

---

[137]   Significantly, the British tariff occupied a mere 5 pages in Kelly's *Customs Tariffs of the World* (1911 edn.); cf. Canada, 26 pages; Germany (excluding colonies), 45; France (excluding colonies), 46; the United States, 32.

[138]   Keynes, *Economic Consequences of the Peace* (1919), 10; W. A. Lewis, 'The Rate of Growth of World Trade, 1830–1973', in S. Grassman and E. Lundberg, *The World Economic Order: Past and Prospects* (1981), 62–73.

[139]   Memoranda *re* Anglo-French commercial relations, CAB 37/93/74, 78; 94/96, 98, 103; W. Behrens, *The Proposed Franco-British Treaty of Commerce* (1908); British Chamber of Commerce of Paris, *Annual Report 1906* (Paris, 1907), 169 ff.

[140]   *The Economist*, 8 and 15 Apr., 10 June 1911; interestingly, in January 1911 Japan had also floated a loan in London which some financiers had wished to link to tariff reductions (D. Kynaston, *The City of London* (vol. 2, 1995), 504); I. H. Nish, *Alliance in Decline: A Study in Anglo-Japanese Relations, 1908–23* (1972), 36–40. Other negotiations were less successful, for example those with Portugal, hampered by the perennial issue of wine duties, CAB 37/98/29, 38, 41 [12 Feb. 1909 et seq.]; 103/49 [1 Mar. 1911]; 105/29 [17 Mar. 1911]; 106/38 [27 Mar. 1911]; 107/99 [9 Aug. 1911], C. Hazlehurst and C. Woodland (eds.), *A Liberal Chronicle. Journal and Papers of J. A. Pease, 1st Lord Gainford, 1908–1910* (1994), 203, 220.

[141]   To E. A. R. Seligman, 8 Oct. 1910, Seligman Papers, Colombia University Library.

heaviest blow that has been aimed against the Protective system since the British legislation of Sir Robert Peel between 1842 and 1846'.[142] Arguably, this was not so much a victory for the free traders as for the tariff reformers, fear of whose success had prompted this change in American policy.[143] Yet here at least was some indication of the long-sought commitment of the United States to an open world system, which, despite the lengthy caesura of war and isolation, would be taken up by Cordell Hull in the 1930s.[144] It also offered some confirmation of the Atlanticist commitment that British strategists had sought under the Liberals in the pre-war period, as an alternative to the imperial perspective of the tariff reformers.[145] Britain had to that extent successfully restrained before 1914 the economic conflict that free traders believed tariffs presaged.

Liberal foreign policy after 1906 had also shown considerable zeal in the causes of both disarmament and the codification of international law, particularly maritime law. These issues have been extensively discussed by recent historians, and it remains only to underline the continuity with the Cobdenite past.[146] For example, retrenchment and disarmament were goals given their modern shape in the 1840s, although after the 1870s they had been increasingly taken over by international lawyers, concerned with creating a special body of law and machinery far beyond the vision of Cobden himself. The inspiration behind these efforts remained fundamentally aligned with that of the Cobdenites. For example, Sir Edward Fry (1827–1918), chief British commissioner at the Second Hague Conference, bridged the world of Cobden and that of the League of Nations: the son of a strong, free trade, Liberal Quaker, Fry was a schoolboy friend of Bagehot in the 1840s, and, like him, an early enthusiast for free trade, a cause he actively defended in 1903–6, and which he proclaimed in 1917 as a post-war necessity.[147]

After 1906, therefore, goals which had been primarily associated with 'troublemakers' had in fact become the goals of government policy, however remote from realization they remained in the state of international politics. Yet some advances were made. For example, Britain had agreed arbitration treaties with several foreign powers (including Italy and Spain), while pursuing seriously, if unsuccessfully, the cause of disarmament at the Second Hague Conference in 1907.[148] Second, the London Conference, 1908–9, did go some way towards codifying international maritime law, a subject strongly linked with the Cobdenites since the

---

[142]   12 Apr. 1913, quoted in D. A. Lake, *Power, Protection and Free Trade* (Cornell, 1988), 155.
[143]   Lake, *Power, Protection and Free Trade*, 153, highlights the possible heightened costs of protection for America from a tariff reform policy in Britain, although it is not clear how strongly such a fear actually influenced American policy-making.
[144]   For a pessimistic forecast of America's place 'in the family of nations', see Lord E. Percy to J. Bryce, 22 Mar. 1914, Bryce Papers, 117; cf. Bryce at Cobden Club, *Daily News*, 21 Mar. 1914.
[145]   Offer, *First World War*, part III, 'The Atlantic Orientation'.
[146]   See n. 136 above.
[147]   *DNB*; Agnes Fry, *A Memoir of the Rt. Hon. Sir Edward Fry, G.C.B.* (Oxford, 1921), 34, 237–8.
[148]   A. T. Sidorowicz, 'The British Government, the Hague Peace Conference of 1907, and the Armaments Question', in McKercher (ed.), *Arms Limitation*, 1–19.

1850s, and which had beeen revived in late 1905 by Robert Reid (Lord Loreburn), as part of a Cobden Club campaign against naval expenditure.[149] The Liberals' return to office presented him with the opportunity to press this campaign, which he did successfully, as Semmel has shown.[150] Ultimately, the complete immunity of private property at sea in time of war, seen by free traders as a necessary step to remove German (and American) fears of British naval supremacy, remained strategically anathema to the Navy, and the Declaration of London was rejected by the House of Lords in 1911. This debate neatly polarized 'the neutralist and free trade world-view and the belligerent and neo-mercantilist outlook',[151] but in doing so it brought Cobdenite goals to the centre of Liberal governance. Only in post-bellum retrospect did Loreburn's profession of faith in 'the old doctrines of Cobden' appear unduly quaint.[152]

Nevertheless, the Liberal government was never able to satisfy its abundant Radical critics, whose persistent campaigns for public economy and arrestment of arms continued to mobilize shoals of its backbench MPs. Such criticism may be written off as 'naïve Cobdenism', but this powerful polemicism was itself part of the Edwardian transformation of Liberalism, representing not merely a survival of outmoded Manchester School views, but the reaffirmation of democratic expectation in the sphere of foreign policy. This rethinking of the issues of war and peace both subsumed and transcended the Cobdenite ideas it had inherited. By its means, the echoes of the 1840s reverberated strongly, sounding through the gunfire of the war, harmonizing well with the predisposition of Woodrow Wilson, and resounding distinctly in the birth cries of the League of Nations.[153]

Foremost in this legacy was Cobden's distinctive belief in the intertwining of free trade and peace through the interdependence of nations. This was no simple market philosophy, but encouraged the form of cultural diplomacy Cobden himself had undertaken in the 1840s, and which was now replicated by countless groups of workers, ministers of religion, scholars, and businessmen, whose experience contributed to the 'art of international government'.[154] Cobdenite goals suffused a range of cultural and commercial associations, such as the Anglo-German Friendship Society, with Lubbock and Perris, old Cobdenite hands, or the Entente Cordiale Society and British Chamber of Commerce at Paris, orchestrated by self-proclaimed Cobdenites such as Sir Thomas Barclay.[155] The Manchester variant of

---

[149]   Above, 263; *The Times*, 4 Dec. 1905, Cobden Club meeting at Oxford.
[150]   Semmel, *Liberalism and Naval Strategy*, 95–6 ff.
[151]   Ibid. 98.
[152]   Cited in Bentley, *Liberal Mind*, 212.
[153]   e.g., Grey's creed, 'L. of N. plus Free Trade plus co-partnership in industry': cited in Bentley, *Liberal Mind*, 89; L. Martin, 'Woodrow Wilson's Appeal to the People of Europe: British Radical Influence on the President's Strategy', *Political Science Quarterly*, 74 (1959), 498–516. For Wilson's free trade propensities, see W. Diamond, *The Economic Thought of Woodrow Wilson* (Baltimore, 1943), 24–6.
[154]   *Nation*, 1 Aug. 1908, 629.
[155]   Hutchinson, *Lubbock*, vol. 2, 216 ff.; Perris to Bryce, 23 and 31 Oct., 10 and 21 Nov. 1905, Bryce Papers, 118; T. Barclay, *Thirty Years: Anglo-French Reminiscences (1876–1906)* (1914), 303–4, 307–8.

this form of international co-operation was that undertaken by Sir Charles Macara, epitome of the Edwardian business diplomatist, ready both to organize international federations of cotton spinners and to undertake peace missions to Germany.[156] This internationalization of economic life served to underpin the intellectual case for peace, derived from Ricardo and Cobden, but persuasively restated in Norman Angell's *The Great Illusion*.[157] For Angell adduced the economic interdependence of nations and the costs of warfare as the most powerful arguments against the (rational) waging of warfare.

Angell's ideas provided a tremendous boost to Edwardian pacifism, but really only brought up to date a long-standing strand of argument, supplementing the industrial case for peace by attention to the growing financial and commercial links between nations. This took its part alongside the pacifist and Cobdenite elements in the Liberal conscience. For the link between free trade and peace had long been a commonplace in a series of national and international institutions since the 1870s, with groups such as the International Arbitration and Peace Association and the Interparliamentary Union promoting numerous conferences, including a series of peace congresses since 1889. The journal *Concord* illustrates this strand, sharing an editor with the Cobden Club (G. H. Perris), and tracing its essential ideas back to Cobden.[158] To the insistent, if traditional, connection between retrenchment and warfare was added the new link, that savings on armaments might well finance expenditure on social reform, an essential plank in the redoubled efforts by groups such as the National Peace Council as the Edwardian arms race escalated.[159]

In other ways, Cobden's own analysis of foreign policy remained central to the Edwardian Radical movement. For example, from the 1830s he had most vigorously asserted the need for an end to aristocratic diplomacy. The arguments for democratic control of foreign policy adduced by critics such as Ponsonby derive very clearly, if not explicitly, from Cobden and the arguments upheld by the Cobden Club in the 1870s.[160] Cobden had also been the most vociferous critic of the 'balance of power'. Here, the essentials of the Edwardian Radical critique of the dangers of the search for a balance, drawing Britain into an alliance system and so into unnecessary wars, was, in its essentials, identical with the case made by Cobden against Palmerstonian diplomacy.[161] This was true both in substance and terminology, with, for example, the origins of wars in 'panics' got up by warmon-

[156] C. W. Macara, *Recollections* (1921); W. H. Mills, *Sir Charles W. Macara, Bt. A study of Modern Lancashire* (1917).
[157] For the tradition, see J. K. Whitaker, 'The Economics of Defense in British Political Economy, 1848–1914', in Goodwin (ed.), *Economics and National Security*, 37–60. For one Edwardian example, see R. Rea, *Free Trade in Being* (1908), 213–15.
[158] e.g. *Concord*, May and June 1904, esp. 78 (Hobson and S. Buxton), 81–2 (Perris), 83–4 (F. Passy), on the Cobden centenary.
[159] Minutes, 4 Nov. 1908, 16 Mar. 1910, National Peace Council Archives, 1/1, BLPES.
[160] R. Jones, *Ponsonby; The Politics of Life* (1989), *passim*.
[161] H. Weinroth, 'British Radicals and the Balance of Power, 1902–1914', *Historical Journal*, 13 (1970), 653–82; H. Brailsford, *The War of Steel and Gold* (1914); F. M. Leventhal, *The Last Dissenter: H. N. Brailsford and His World* (Oxford, 1985), 92–113.

gers deployed by critics such as Hirst and Hobson.[162] For many, the resemblance between Grey and Palmerston was irresistible, with the Radicals *en masse* forming a collective reincarnation of Cobden. This perspective perhaps varied in only one detail, for where Cobden had demonized the services and the court, his Edwardian heirs discovered the iniquities of the arms trusts and traders, groups whose antipathy both to free trade and peace could not be more clear cut.[163] To some extent, therefore, the old Radical analysis was given a modern gloss, but the continuity of argument from Cobden to the Union of Democratic Control was clear and direct.

If the Radical analysis of foreign policy owed its essential inspiration to Cobden, increasingly its vision of the future extended beyond Cobden's belief that free trade itself offered the most powerful antidote to war. Few Edwardians doubted that a free trade world would be pacific, but non-market, non-voluntary mechanisms were necessary to secure peace, which might itself be a necessary condition for trade to be free. The movement for international arbitration had already begun to put in place a legal framework for the regulation of international disputes, and it was the intertwining of this body of thought with the Cobdenite vision, as well as a new strand of socialist thinking, which encouraged a new wave of internationalist thought, centred on institutions for collective security. This direction was already signposted by some pre-war thinkers, for example Brailsford, but it was the outbreak of war that precipitated the search for new institutional mechanisms to prevent war, for which neither its economic irrationality nor the existing structure of diplomacy had been sufficient. Here, then, was the impetus for groups such as the After War League, the Bryce Group, and the League of Nations Society, which all sought to build an element of collective security into international relations. Protection had undoubtedly fostered armed conflict and international anarchy, but the goal of free trade now required such a League as a necessary part of a new international order.[164] Thus, while these thinkers shared a clear belief that in a free trade world peace would be enjoyed, free trade itself might only be realized within such a peaceful world order. Both political order and nations were preconditions for the workings of international trade. To some extent this conclusion had been implicit as far back as the 1860 Anglo-French Treaty, yet fashionably 'new internationalists' like Zimmern distanced themselves from such Cobdenite panaceas.[165]

---

[162] Hirst, *Six Panics* (1913); Hobson, *The German Panic* (Cobden Club, 1913); Cobden Club minutes, 28 Apr. 1913, CP 1190, WSRO.

[163] G. H. Perris, *The War Traders* (1913); C. Trebilcock, 'Radicalism and the Armament Trust', in Morris (ed.), *Edwardian Radicalism*, ch. 11.

[164] In addition to works cited above, see, especially, M. D. Durbin, 'Towards the Concept of Collective Security: The Bryce Group's "Proposals for the Avoidance of War", 1914–1917', *International Organisation*, 24 (1970), 288–318; also, typically, G. L. Dickinson, *The International Anarchy, 1904–14* (1926), 19.

[165] A. Zimmern, *Nationality and Government* (1918), ch. 12; id., *The Prospects of Democracy* (1925), 233–56; Trentmann, 'The Strange Death of Free Trade', in Biagini, *Citizenship and Community*, 236–41.

Others, however, more freely acknowledged the Cobdenite inspiration in the League of Nations. Above all, Hobson's *Richard Cobden: The International Man* (1918) resurrected Cobden as a forerunner of international government, consolidating the juncture between free trade and the 'League of Nations mind'.[166] However uneasy men such as Morley and Hirst felt at this transition, New Liberals such as Hobhouse welcomed the recognition of Cobden as a pioneer of internationalism and democracy.[167] The rational direction of nations towards peace was also reasserted in the social reformer Helen Bosanquet's *Free Trade and Peace in the Nineteenth Century* (1925).[168] And the free trade vision guided the direction of Conservatives such as Lord Robert Cecil towards the League of Nations Union.[169] These post-war Cobdenite echoes became an ingrained part of the inter-war thinking on foreign policy, so much so that by the mid-1920s their derivation had become of little immediate interest, as W. H. Dawson, expert on Germany and social insurance, found to his disappointment on the publication of *Richard Cobden and Foreign Policy* in 1926.[170] The Cobden Club itself remained resolute, if insignificant, promoting several efforts to reconvert Europe to universal free trade. It bravely summoned International Free Trade Conferences in 1920, 1921, and 1922, edited the *World Free Trader*, and supported Sir George Paish's quixotic attempt to evangelize Europe on the model of Cobden's journey of 1846–7.[171] At home, the Cobden family, including by marriage F. W. Hirst, did much to keep alive the memory of Cobden, with the Fisher-Unwins donating Cobden's Dunford House as the basis for the Cobden Memorial Association in 1927.[172] From 1929 a series of Cobden Memorial Lectures formed a elegiac chorus to the lost world of Richard Cobden, with tributes from the Asquithian Charles Mallet, Grey, Simon, George Peel, and Hirst. Liberal nostalgia was reinforced by the laments of continental witnesses, to the rising tide of arms, autarky, and dictatorship. Yet such European despondency was balanced by a more vital stream of Anglo-American liberal sentiment, deriving above all from the Carnegie Endowment for International Peace,

---

[166]　H. C. G. Matthew, 'Hobson, Ruskin and Cobden', in M. Freeden (ed.), *Re-appraising J. A. Hobson* (1990), 23–30; 'Cobden, the Pacifist', *New Statesman*, 8 Feb. 1919; D. Long, 'J. A. Hobson and Economic Internationalism', in Long and Wilson (eds.), *Thinkers*, 161–88.

[167]　*Manchester Guardian*, 3 Apr. 1919, 5.

[168]　Cf. review, R. Harrod, *Economic Journal*, 35 (1925), 294–6.

[169]　R. Cecil, *A Great Experiment* (1941); Cowling, *The Impact of Labour*, 62; J. C. Heim, 'Liberalism and the Establishment of Collective Security in British Foreign Policy', *TRHS*, 6th ser., 5 (1995), 91–110.

[170]　G. P. Gooch to Dawson, 6 Jan. 1926, Dawson Papers 880, University of Birmingham; more appreciatively, Victoria Webster-Wemyss (daughter of Cobden's admirer, R. B. D. Morier) to Dawson, 20 Jan. 1927, ibid. 945. For a random example, see *Southport Guardian*, 25 July 1928: 'Cobden and Bright . . . were the pioneers of international peace which now finds its expression both in the League of Nations and the Kellogg Pact' (press cutting, CP 1142, WSRO).

[171]　Above, 287; *Proceedings, International Free Trade Conferences* (London, 1920; Amsterdam, 1921; Frankfurt, 1922); *The World Free Trader*, 1926–9, for the activities of the Committee for Universal Free Trade.

[172]　*The Dunford House Association. Report and Proceedings* (1928).

whose collective efforts did so much after 1911 to promote the study of war, free trade, and peace.[173]

Indirectly, this strand of Cobdenite thought influenced diplomacy between the wars, both through the international policy of the Labour Party and through the economic aspirations of the League of Nations.[174] The economic diplomacy of the League of Nations, however remotely, still looked back to the model of the Cobden treaty system, while directing its efforts towards a more technical approach to the world economy, and to the political preconditions for free trade.[175] As the prospects for international economic agreement collapsed in 1929–31, British free traders drew some comfort from both the emerging idea of a 'United States of Europe' and from more limited regional free trade schemes, whilst keeping alive the remote prospect of universal free trade amidst the encircling tariff walls.[176]

More importantly still, in the 1930s Cobden's prediction—that the economic leadership of the world would pass to the United States—was on the verge of fulfilment. With that ascendancy, a little-heralded 'Cobdenite' strain arose in hitherto invincibly protectionist America, as Cordell Hull pushed to the centre of American commercial diplomacy the belief that free trade meant peace.[177] Freer trade thus became the goal of American diplomacy in the 1930s, as it had been of Huskisson in Britain in the 1820s, such that the Anglo-American trade agreement of 1938 appeared, like the Cobden–Chevalier Treaty of 1860, the instrument towards the opening of the world economy.[178] During the Second World War, this

[173] W. J. Barber, 'British and American Economists and Attempts to Comprehend the Nature of War, 1910–1920', in Goodwin, *Economics and National Security*, 61–86. See, too, the journal, *International Conciliation*. Hirst, Brailsford, and Paish had been early recruits to the Carnegie Endowment's work. Its head N. M. Butler initiated the Cobden Memorial Lectures in 1929.

[174] L. Woolf, *International Economic Policy* (?1916); Boyce, *British Capitalism*, esp. ch. 7 for League diplomacy.

[175] E. Grossmann, *Methods of Economic Rapprochement* (League of Nations, Economic and Financial Section, Geneva, 1926); W. E. Rappard, *Post-War Efforts for Freer Trade*, Geneva Studies, 9 (2 Mar. 1938) based on his Cobden Lectures at the LSE; de Marchi, 'League of Nations' Economists'; 'At Geneva recently the business leaders of Europe all talked Cobdenism without knowing it.' *The Nation*, 6 June 1927.

[176] '*United States of Europe*' (Dunford House (Cobden Memorial) Association, 1930); D. Abel, *A History of British Tariffs, 1923–42* (1945); 'The Restoration of World Trade', *International Conciliation* 311 (June 1935). For a French example, see C. Taquey, *Richard Cobden* (Paris, 1939), with an introduction by the leading French financial civil servant Jacques Rueff; Herriot also paid due tribute to Cobden in his *United States of Europe* (Eng. edn., 1930), 'the most complete type of the modern apostle' (37).

[177] R. L. Buell, *The Hull Trade Programme and the American System* (New York, 1939); J. Pennar, 'Richard Cobden and Cordell Hull. A Comparative study of the Commercial Policies of Nineteenth-Century England and Contemporary United States', unpublished Ph.D. thesis, Princeton University (1953), chs. 4 and 5. Hirst found Hull 'a Jeffersonian Liberal Free Trader, simple and direct' when lunching with him and Snowden in June 1933, 'all three uncompromising free traders': Hirst, *Diary*, 28. See, too, A. W. Schatz, 'The Anglo-American Trade Agreement and Cordell Hull's Search for Peace', *Journal of American History*, 57 (1970–1), 85–103.

[178] F. W. Hirst, 'Cobden and Cordell Hull', *Contemporary Review*, 155 (1939), 10–17; C. Kreider, *The Anglo-American Trade Agreement* (Princeton, 1943); I. M. Drummond and N. Hillmer, *Negotiating Freer Trade: The United Kingdom, the United States, Canada and the Trade Agreements of 1938* (Waterloo, Canada, 1989); Rooth, *British Protectionism*, 282–303.

goal became a focal point of Anglo–American co-operation, enshrined in the Atlantic Charter, Article VII of the Mutual Aid Agreement, the plans for the International Trade Organisation (ITO), and its more modest successor, the General Agreement on Tariffs and Trade (GATT).[179] Here it is possible to see the emergence of the distinctive post-war liberal international order, in which free trade was linked to peace not through a natural harmony of interests, but through a framework of rules and institutions designed, like the commercial treaties of the 1860s, to facilitate free exchange between nations.[180]

Peel's hope in 1846 that the British example of free trade would extend to the United States seemed, therefore, on the point of realization. For in the competing schemes for the post-war international economic order, the British nineteenth-century model remained central to conceptions of a multilateral free trade system held by both British and American policy-makers. For example, Meade's commercial union scheme in 1942 clearly repudiated British policy since 1930 in favour of 'large and bold ideas' of world-wide free trade.[181] Similarly, Lionel Robbins's ideas on policy consistently displayed his admiration for the ideal of the nineteenth-century world order, as the basis for peace, prosperity, and individual freedom.[182] This harmonized well with readiness of American policy-makers to seize their opportunity to free the executive from the power of vested interests in tariff-making, and, less importantly, to force the abandonment of British imperial preference.[183] Keynes, ever keen to rescue politicians from their enslavement to defunct economists, disliked those ideas in American and British policy which smacked too much of the nineteenth century, yet the post-war world order that he helped shape was in many respects a testament to the enduring legacy of the Cobdenite ideal and Keynes's own return to the free trade internationalism of his youth.[184] Above all,

[179] A. P. Dobson, *The Politics of the Anglo–American Economic Special Relationship, 1940–1987* (1988); L. S. Pressnell, *External Economic Policy since the War* (vol. 1, 1986); R. N. Gardner, *Sterling–Dollar Diplomacy: Anglo–American Collaboration in the Reconstruction of International Trade* (Oxford, 1956); W. Diebold, *The End of the I.T.O.* (Princeton, 1952); D. Irwin, *The GATT's Contribution to Economic Recovery in Post-War Western Europe* (International Finance Discussion Papers, 442, Board of Governors of the Federal Reserve System, 1993).

[180] R. O. Keohane, 'International Liberalism Reconsidered', in J. Dunn (ed.), *The Economic Limits to Modern Politics* (Cambridge, 1990); above, 103.

[181] 'Project of a Commercial Union', Board of Trade, 5 Nov. 1942, in PRO T160/1378/18003/021/1 (Committee on Post-War Commercial Policy); printed in S. Howson (ed.), *Collected Papers of James Meade* (vol. 3, 1988), 27–35.

[182] Robbins, *Economic Planning and International Order* (1937) best expresses his vision of international liberalism, while his *Economic Causes of War* (1939) perhaps most clearly approximates to a Cobdenite tract. The imprint of both remains strong in his wartime diaries, see S. Howson and D. E. Moggridge, *The Wartime Diaries of Lionel Robbins and James Meade, 1943–45* (1990); see, too, D. P. O'Brien, *Robbins* (1988).

[183] R. B. Woods, *A Changing of the Guard: Anglo–American Relations, 1941–1946* (Chapel Hill, 1990).

[184] R. F. Harrod, *The Life of John Maynard Keynes* (Harmondsworth, 1972), 734–7; D. J. Markwell, 'John Maynard Keynes, Idealism and the Economic Basis of Peace', in Long and Wilson (eds.), *Thinkers*, 189–213, esp. 207.

therefore, while the long-lived British experiment in free trade had collapsed in the crisis of 1931, American economic policy, as one British official noted, was 'away from their old heresies . . . and towards what our own economic policy had been until the 1930s'.[185] To that extent, it was only in the 1940s that the United States imbibed the ideological lessons of the repeal of the Corn Laws in 1846, above all, the desirability of the world's leading economic power fostering a multilateral trading system, 'a network of relations more international than ever'.[186] The *pax Americana* after 1945 was thus to be built upon the liberal aspiration towards a universal commercial republic, the vocation foreseen by Cobden in the 1830s, but only now belatedly enshrined in American diplomacy.[187]

This was a global ideal which British Liberals enthusiastically endorsed, acclaiming what they (too readily) saw as the abandonment of Ottawa, preference, and protection, and the rebirth of 'the conception of a new order for the civilized world based on Cobden's teachings'.[188] Labour's welcome was to be necessarily more guarded, as it attempted in its first majority government to balance the Atlanticist, European, and imperial elements in Britain's post-war and Cold War diplomacy, while open to the charge on the Left that its international economic policy represented 'a return to the 19th century . . . it is mid-Victorian'.[189] But Labour had little real choice or desire but to participate in the re-creation of a multilateral trading system, embodied in GATT, which Harold Wilson was to defend against both the party's advocates of 'socialist planning' and its early supporters of a Federal Europe.[190] The goal of Anglo-American policy commended by *The Times* on the centenary of Repeal, 26 June 1946, was thus to 'reinstate the broad principles and flexible practices of the system of world commerce ushered in by the events of 1846'. The *Manchester Guardian* on the same occasion recalled the link between Repeal and the avoidance of an Anglo-American war over the Oregon

---

[185]   Memorandum by Hall-Patch, FO 3 Aug. 1945, in R. Bullen and M. Pelly (eds.), *Documents on British Policy Overseas*, ser., 1, vol. 3 (1986), 3.

[186]   W. Röpke, 'The Centenary of British Free Trade', in *Against the Tide* (1969), 101–10; for doubts as to whether America had learnt that exports required free imports, see J. H. Clapham, 'Corn Laws Repeal, Free Trade and History', *Transactions of the Manchester Statistical Society, 1945–46*, 5.

[187]   'The latter power [Britain] now sees, in America, a competitor in every respect calculated to contend with advantage for the sceptre of naval and commercial dominion': 'England, Ireland, and America', in *Political Writings*, 45; W. R. Louis and R. Robinson, 'The Imperialism of Decolonization', *Journal of Imperial and Commonwealth History*, 22 (1995), 494–5. For incomplete realization of this aspiration, see K. W. Stiles, 'The Ambivalent Hegemon: Explaining the "Lost Decade" in Multilateral Talks', *Review of International Political Economy*, 2 (1995), 1–26.

[188]   F. W. Hirst, *Richard Cobden and John Morley* (1941), 30; Abel, *British Tariffs*, 140 ff.; R. Harrod, *Tory Menace. What is article 7?* (Feb. 1942); *Britain, the USA and Free Trade* (Liberal Publication Dept., c.1945), copies in Liberal Party Archives, BLPES; *The Free Trader* (May–June, 1946): ITO 'involves something bigger and bolder than yet conceived in world history' (158), while for Harrod, article 7 was 'the modern Free Trade Charter' (ibid. 173); Harrod, *A Page of British Folly* (1946); for a comparable American view, see O. G. Villard, *Free Trade—Free World* (New York, 1947).

[189]   *Hansard*, 5th ser., 446, c. 1272 [29 Jan. 1948].

[190]   Ibid., c. 1328 et seq.; A. Morgan, *Harold Wilson* (1992), 141–2.

Question: 'We are today faced with darker confusion than ever; yet if light is to break through it can only be by our having the same faith in the freeing of human intercourse, the same attachment to peace for its own sake which moved Britain in 1846.' Repeal's relevance to the international order seemed as fresh in 1946 as in 1846.

If the desirability of international free trade seemed agreed, how far did the repeal of the Corn Laws in 1846 still hold any domestic lessons for post-war Britain under Labour? This seemed much more doubtful to contemporaries, especially those remaining Liberals for whom free trade had increasingly connoted the world of individualism and unregulated markets, far removed from the logic of planning and the enlarged state for which Britain was now geared up. Yet in 1946 it seemed by no means impossible to urge forward the synthesis of Cobden and Keynes, in which free trade internationally was compatible with state-centred welfare and the managed economy—that is, a variety of economic controls, directed above all to the goal of full employment.[191] However distasteful to the dogmatic, this ideological prescription proved eminently attractive to Labour and to many Liberals. The wartime union of Cobden and Keynes, it seemed, would not end in precipitate divorce.

Yet for the small remnant of free traders who still looked back for inspiration to the repeal of the Corn Laws, its centenary in June 1946 was clouded by the long shadow of Chamberlain, of world war, and of Labour's new ascendancy. Among the emblems of that free trade tradition, the Hon. George Peel, grandson of Sir Robert, and a prolific publicist, regretted that the simplicity of the Peelite tariff had been lost, as over seven thousand customs duties had accumulated since the Chamberlainite reversal of fiscal policy between 1915 and 1932.[192] For F. W. Hirst, the most self-conscious bearer of the Cobdenite torch, wartime controls not only embodied all the evils of bureaucratic tyranny, but had reduced Britain to a level of privation reminiscent of the 'hungry forties'.[193] For Sir Andrew MacFadyean, former Treasury official, merchant banker, and in 1945 Liberal candidate in the City of London, planning and protection threatened freedom of enterprise and

---

[191]   Liberal Sub-Committee on International Trade, *International Trade: the Future of Britain's Trade* (1943); Harrod, *Free Trader*, 33 (May–June 1946), 173. Harrod had been a Liberal candidate at Huddersfield in 1945, but in the 1930s had been linked with the New Fabian Research Bureau. H. Phelps Brown, 'Henry Roy Forbes Harrod, 1900–78', *Proceedings of the British Academy*, 65 (1979), 653–96. One of Dalton's protégés of the 1930s Colin Clark emerged as a keen post-war free trader, e.g. *Free Trade—an Immediate Remedy for Britain's Recovery* (1954); cf. B. Pimlott, *Hugh Dalton* (1985), 202, 217, 222, 237, 251.

[192]   *Centenary of the Corn Laws, 1846–1946* (Free Trade Union, 1946), 6–7. Peel's varied career included the Treasury, the Gold Standard Defence Association, the Army, and Trade Commissioner in Egypt during the First World War, Liberal MP 1917–18, and helping set up the Save the Children Fund.

[193]   *The Repeal of the Corn Laws* (Cobden Club, 1946); ironically, two days after the centenary, bread rationing was introduced for the first time.

genuine competition: '[W]e are to-day substantially back in 1846', he averred, 'and the fight must be taken up again.'[194] One hundred years after the repeal of the Corn Laws, free traders drew solace from the rebirth of the Cobdenite world order, whilst lamenting—and elegizing—the end of Liberal England.

[194] *Centenary of Corn Law Repeal, 1846–1946*, 11–15; MacFadyean shortly after became a founder of the Liberal International, as well as chairman of the FTU and the Liberal Party; he was also a leading advocate of a Federal Europe; G. Peden, 'MacFadyean', *DNB 1971–80*, 528–9.

Select Bibliography*

A. Manuscript Sources

Ampthill Papers, Public Record Office
Anti-Corn Law League Letters, Manchester Central Library
Asquith Papers, Bodleian Library, Oxford
Avebury (Sir John Lubbock) Papers, British Library
G. W. Balfour Papers, Public Record Office
Balfour of Burleigh Papers, Scottish Record Office
Balfour of Whittingehame Papers, Scottish Record Office
Bank of England Archives
Barings' Archives, Bishopsgate, and Guildhall Library, London
Barton Papers, National Library of Australia
Board of Trade Papers, Public Record Office
E. A. Bowring Diaries, William Perkins Library, Duke University
Bright Papers, British Library and Princeton University
Bryce Papers, Bodleian Library, Oxford
Burgess Papers, New York Public Library
Cabinet Records, Public Record Office
Campbell-Bannerman Papers, British Library
Carnarvon Papers, Public Record Office
Cartwright Papers, Northamptonshire Record Office
Chamberlain Papers, Birmingham University Library
Childs Villiers Papers, National Library of Australia
Clarendon Papers, Bodleian Library, Oxford
Sir Edward Clarke Papers, private possession
Cobden Club Miscellanea, private possession
Cobden Papers, British Library, West Sussex Record Office, and
    William Perkins Library, Duke University
Cobden–Alexander Letters, Bodleian Library, Oxford
Cobden–Thomasson Letters, British Library of Political and Economic Science
Cowley Papers, Public Record Office
W. H. Dawson Papers, University of Birmingham Library
Deakin Papers, National Library of Australia
Derby Papers, Liverpool Record Office
Dilke Papers, British Library
Disraeli Papers, Hughenden Deposit, Bodleian Library, Oxford
Easthope Papers, William Perkins Library, Duke University

---

* Full references are given in footnotes.

Arthur Elliot Papers, National Library of Scotland
Farrer Papers, Surrey Record Office
Foreign Office Papers, Public Record Office
Gladstone (Herbert) Papers, British Library
Gladstone (W. E.) Papers, British Library
Glynn Papers, National Library of Australia
Glynne–Gladstone Papers, St Deniol's Library (Clwyd Record Office)
Gold Standard Defence Association Papers, Royal Bank of Scotland
F. C. Gould, Autobiography, House of Lords Record Office
Grant Duff Papers, India Office Library
Granville Papers, Public Record Office
Grenfell Papers, Buckinghamshire Record Office
Grey Papers, University of Durham
Hambledon Papers (W. H. Smith plc)
Hamilton Papers, British Library
Harcourt Papers, Bodleian Library, Oxford
Harpton Court Papers, National Library of Wales (transcripts courtesy of Peter
    Mandler)
Hickleton Papers, Borthwick Institute of Historical Research, York
Iddesleigh Papers, British Library
Imperial Federation League Papers, British Library
John Johnson Collection, Bodleian Library, Oxford
Kennedy Papers, Public Record Office
Kimberley Papers, Bodleian Library, Oxford
La Nauze Papers, Archives of Business and Labour, Australian National University
Layard Papers, British Library
Lister Papers, Bodleian Library, Oxford
Mallet Papers, British Library, and private possession
Manchester Chamber of Commerce Records, Manchester Central Library
Middleton Papers, Labour Party Archives, National Museum of Labour History,
    Manchester
Minto Papers, National Library of Scotland
Morier Papers, Balliol College, Oxford
Mottistone (J. E. Seely) Papers, Nuffield College, Oxford
G. H. Murray Papers, Blair Castle
Norman Papers, Centre for Kentish Studies, Maidstone
Overstone Papers, University of London Library
Parkes Papers, Mitchell Library, Sydney
Peel Papers, British Library
Phelps Papers, Oriel College, Oxford
T. B. Potter Letters, Manchester Central Library
J. E. Thorold Rogers Papers, Bodleian Library, Oxford
Rosebery Papers, National Library of Scotland
Russell Papers, Public Record Office and William Perkins Library, Duke University
Earl of St Aldwyn (Sir M. Hicks Beach) Papers, Gloucestershire Record Office

J. B. Smith Papers, Manchester Central Library
Sidney Smith Journal, Scottish Record Office
Southborough (F. S. Hopwood) Papers, Bodleian Library, Oxford
Spencer Papers, British Library
Strabie Papers, Somerset Record Office
Strachey Papers, House of Lords Record Office
Symon Papers, National Library of Australia
Tennyson Papers, Mitchell Library, Sydney
Thornely Letters, British Library of Political and Economic Science
Treasury Papers, Public Record Office
Trevelyan Papers, University of Newcastle
George Wilson Papers, Manchester Central Library

B. Official Publications

Hansard, 3rd, 4th, and 5th series
Parliamentary Papers
Bourne, K. and Watt, D. C. (eds.), *British Documents on Foreign Affairs* (Foreign Office Confidential Print) (1983–)

C. Newspapers, Journals, and Series

Bankers' Magazine
Chambers of Commerce Journal
Cobden Club, Annual Reports, Circular, Leaflets, Lists of Members, etc.
Contemporary Review
The Economist
L'Économiste Belge
Financial Reformer
Fortnightly Review
Free Trade Union, Handbooks, Leaflets, Pamphlets
Free Trader
Hertslet's Commercial Treaties
Independent Review
Journal des Économistes
League
Liberal Publications Department, Pamphlets and Leaflets
Manchester Guardian
Morning Star
Nation
New Liberal Review
Nineteenth Century
Pall Mall Gazette
Sentinel
Speaker
Spectator
Statist

The Times
Transactions of the National Liberal Club. Political and Economic Circle
Westminster Gazette
World Free Trader
Young Scot

D. Books and Articles (Books published in London unless otherwise stated)

Abel, D., *A History of British Tariffs, 1923–42* (1945)

Allin, C. D., *Australasian Preferential Tariffs and Imperial Free Trade* (Minneapolis, 1929)

Amery, J., *The Life of Joseph Chamberlain*, vols 4–6 (1951–69)

Apjohn, L., *Richard Cobden and the Free Traders* (1883)

Armitage-Smith, G., *The Free-Trade Movement* (1st edn. 1898)

Ashley, P., *Modern Tariff History* (1st edn. 1904)

Ashton, T. S., 'The origins of the Manchester School', *The Manchester School*, 1 (1930–1), 1–13

Ashworth, H., *Recollections of Richard Cobden and the Anti-Corn Law League* (1877)

Asquith, H. H., *Trade and the Empire* (1903)

Australia and the Fiscal Problem (1903)

Barclay, T., *Thirty Years: Anglo-French Reminiscences (1876–1906)* (1914)

Barnes, D. G., *A History of the English Corn Laws, 1660–1846* (1930)

Barrington, E. I., *The Servant of All: Pages from the Family, Social and Political Life of My Father, James Wilson*, 2 vols (1927)

Beachey, R. W., *The British West Indies Sugar Industry in the late 19th century* (Oxford, 1957)

Bentley, M., *The Liberal Mind, 1914–1929* (1977)

—— *The Climax of Liberal Politics* (1987)

Bernhardt, G. de, *Handbook of Commercial Treaties* (1912)

Bernstein, G. L., *Liberalism and Liberal Politics in Edwardian England* (1986)

Beveridge, W. H., *Tariffs: The Case Examined* (1931)

Biagini, E., *Liberty, Retrenchment and Reform: Popular Liberalism in the Age of Gladstone, 1860–1880* (Cambridge, 1992)

——(ed.), *Citizenship and Community: Liberals, Radicals and Collective Identities in the British Isles, 1865–1931* (Cambridge, 1996)

——and Reid, A. (eds.), *Currents of Radicalism* (Cambridge, 1991)

Bisset, A., *Notes on the Anti-Corn Law Struggle* (1884)

Blaazer, D., *The Popular Front and the Progressive Tradition: Socialists, Liberals, and the Quest for Unity, 1884–1939* (Cambridge, 1992)

Black, R. D. Collison, *Economic Thought and the Irish Question, 1817–1870* (Cambridge, 1960)

——(ed.), *The Papers and Correspondence of W. S. Jevons*, 7 vols (1972–81)

Bosanquet, H., *Free Trade and Peace in the Nineteenth Century* (Kristiania, 1924)

Bourne, K., *The Foreign Policy of Victorian England, 1830–1902* (Oxford, 1970)

Boyce, R. W. D., *British Capitalism at the Crossroads, 1919–1932* (Cambridge, 1987)

Brent, R., *Liberal Anglican Politics, 1830–1841* (Oxford, 1987)

—— 'God's Providence: liberal political economy as natural theology at Oxford, 1825–60', in M. Bentley (ed.), *Public and Private Doctrine* (Cambridge, 1993)

Breton, Y. and Lutfalla, M. (eds.), *L'Économie Politique en France au XIXe siècle* (Paris, 1991)

Bright, J. and Rogers, J. E. T., *Speeches on Questions of Public Policy by Richard Cobden*, 2 vols (1870); single vol. (1878)

Brock, C. J. L. and Jackson, G., *A History of the Cobden Club* (1939)

Brown, B. H., *The Tariff Reform Movement in Great Britain, 1881–1895* (New York, 1943)

Brown, L., *The Board of Trade and the Free-Trade Movement, 1830–1842* (Oxford, 1958)

——'The Chartists and the Anti-Corn Law League', in A. Briggs (ed.), *Chartist Studies* (1959), 342–71

Burn, D. L., 'Canada and the Repeal of the Corn Laws', *Cambridge Historical Journal*, 2 (1928), 252–72

Buxton, S., *Finance and Politics: An Historical Study, 1783–1885*, 2 vols (1888)

Cain, P. J., 'Capitalism, War, and Internationalism in the Thought of Richard Cobden', *British Journal of International Studies*, 5 (1979), 229–47

——'Political Economy in Edwardian England: The Tariff Reform Controversy', in A. O'Day (ed.), *Edwardian Britain: Conflict and Stability, 1900–1914* (1979), 35–59

——'Introduction', *The Political and Economic Works of Richard Cobden*, 6 vols (1995)

——and Hopkins, A. G., *British Imperialism*, 2 vols (1993)

Calkins, W. N., 'A Victorian Free Trade Lobby', *Economic History Review*, 2nd ser., 13 (1960–1), 90–104

Capie, F., *Depression and Protectionism: Britain between the Wars* (1983)

——(ed.), *Protectionism in the World Economy* (Aldershot, 1992)

Chatterji, B., *Trade, Tariffs, and Empire: Lancashire and British Policy in India, 1919–1939* (Delhi, 1992)

Chomley, C. H., *Protection in Canada and Australasia* (1904)

Clapham, J. H., 'The Last Years of the Navigation Acts', *English Historical Review*, 25 (1910), 480–501, 687–707

——'*Zollverein* Negotiations, 1828–1865', in A. W. Ward (ed.), *Cambridge History of British Foreign Policy*, vol. 2 (Cambridge, 1923)

Clarke, P. F., *Lancashire and the New Liberalism* (Cambridge, 1971)

——*Liberals and Social Democrats* (Cambridge, 1978)

——'The End of Laissez-Faire and the Politics of Cotton', *Historical Journal*, 15 (1972), 493–512

——'The Treasury's Analytical Model of the British Economy between the Wars', in M. O. Furner and B. Supple, *The State and Economic Knowledge* (Cambridge, 1990)

Cobden, R., *Political Writings of Richard Cobden*, 2 vols (1867; 1878, ed. L. Mallet)

The European Diaries of Richard Cobden, 1846–49, ed. M. Taylor (Aldershot, 1994)

Cobden Club, *Cobden Club Essays. Second Series, 1871–72* (1872)

——*Free Trade and the European Treaties of Commerce*, (1875)

——*Richard Cobden and the Jubilee of Free Trade* (1896)

Cobden-Unwin, Jane, *The Hungry Forties: Life under the Bread Tax* (1904)

Coetzee, F., *For Party or Country: Nationalism and the Dilemmas of Popular Conservatism in Edwardian England* (New York, 1990)

Dangerfield, G., *The Strange Death of Liberal England* (1935)

Dawson, W. H., *Protection in Germany* (1904)

Dawson (*cont.*), *Richard Cobden and Foreign Policy* (1926)

Disraeli, B., *Lord George Bentinck: A Political Biography* (1852; new edn. 1861)

Doughty, A. G. (ed.), *The Elgin–Grey Papers, 1846–52*, 4 vols (Ottawa, 1937)

Drummond, I. M., *British Economic Policy and the Empire, 1919–1939* (1972)

Dunham, A. L., *The Anglo-French Treaty of Commerce of 1860* (Ann Arbor, 1930)

Dutton, D. J. (ed.), *Odyssey of an Edwardian Liberal: The Political Diary of Richard Dunning Holt*, Record Society of Lancashire and Cheshire, vol. 129 (Gloucester, 1989)

Edsall, N. C., *Richard Cobden, Independent Radical* (1986)

Emy, H. V., 'The Impact of Financial Policy on English Party Politics before 1914', *Historical Journal*, 15 (1972), 103–31

——*Liberals, Radicals, and Social Politics, 1892–1914* (Cambridge, 1973)

Farrer, T. C. (ed.), *Some Farrer Memorials: being a Selection from the Papers of Thomas Henry, first Lord Farrer, 1819–1899, on Various Matters* (privately printed, 1923)

Farrer, T. H., *Free Trade versus Fair Trade* (1st edn. 1881)

——*The Sugar Convention* (1889)

Fawcett, H., *Free Trade and Protection* (1878)

Fay, C. R., *The Corn Laws and Social England* (Cambridge, 1932)

Fielden, K., 'The Rise and Fall of Free Trade', in C. J.Bartlett (ed.), *Britain Pre-eminent: Studies of Britain's World Influence in the Nineteenth Century* (1969)

Forster, B., *A Conjunction of Interests: Business, Politics and Tariffs, 1825–1879* (Toronto, 1986)

Free Trade Union, *Centenary of Corn Law Repeal, 1846–1946* (1946)

Freeden, M., *The New Liberalism: An Ideology of Social Reform* (Oxford, 1978; repr. 1986)

——*Liberalism Divided* (1986)

——(ed.), *Minutes of the Rainbow Circle, 1894–1924*, Camden Soc. 4th ser., vol. 38 (Royal Historical Society, 1989)

Friedberg, A., *The Weary Titan: Britain and the Experience of Relative Decline, 1895–1905* (Princeton, 1988)

Fuchs, C. J., *The Trade Policy of Great Britain and her Colonies since 1860* (1905)

Gash, N., *Sir Robert Peel: The Life of Sir Robert Peel after 1830* (1972)

Gaston, J. W., 'Trade and the Late Victorian Foreign Office', *International History Review*, 4 (1982), 317–38

——'The Free Trade Diplomacy Debate and the Victorian European Common Market Initiative', *Canadian Journal of History*, 22 (1987), 59–82

Ghosh, P. R., 'Disraelian Conservatism: A Financial Approach', *English Historical Review*, 99 (1984), 268–96

Goldmann, L., *The Blind Victorian. Henry Fawcett and British Liberalism* (Cambridge, 1989)

Gomes, L., *Foreign Trade and the National Economy: Mercantilist and Classical Perspectives* (1987)

Goodwin, C. D. W., *Economic Inquiry in Australia* (Durham, NC, 1966)

——(ed.), *Economics and National Security: A History of their Interaction*, Annual Supplement to vol. 23, *History of Political Economy* (Durham, NC, 1991)

Gowing, R., *Richard Cobden* (1885)

Grampp, W. D., *The Manchester School of Economics* (1960)

Grant Duff, M. E., *Miscellanies, Political and Literary* (1878)

Green, E. H. H., *The Crisis of Conservatism: The Politics, Economics, and Ideology of the British Conservative Party, 1880–1914* (1995)

Grey, H. G., *The Colonial Policy of Lord John Russell's Administration*, 2 vols (1853; repr., 1970)

—— *The Commercial Policy of the British Colonies and the McKinley Tariff* (1892)

Hancock, W. K., *Survey of British Commonwealth Affairs. Vol. II Problems of Economic Policy, 1918–1939 Part I* (Oxford, 1940)

Harling, P., *The Waning of 'Old Corruption': The Politics of Economical Reform in Britain, 1779–1846* (Oxford, 1996)

Harnetty, P., 'The Indian Cotton Duties Controversy, 1894–96', *English Historical Review*, 77 (1962), 684–702

Harvey, W. B., *Tariffs and International Relations in Europe, 1860–1914* (Chicago, 1938)

Haultain, A. (ed.), *A Selection from Goldwin Smith's Correspondence* (1913)

Helleiner, K. F., *Free Trade and Frustration: Anglo-Austrian Negotiations, 1860–70* (Toronto, 1973)

Henderson, W. O., *Britain and Industrial Europe, 1750–1870* (Leicester, 1972)

Heringa, A., *Free Trade and Protection in Holland* (1914)

Hilton, A. J. B., *Corn, Cash, and Commerce: The Economic Policies of the Tory Governments, 1815–1830* (Oxford: Oxford Historical Monographs, 1977)

—— 'Peel: A Re-appraisal', *Historical Journal*, 21 (1979), 585–614

—— *The Age of Atonement: The Influence of Evangelicalism on Social and Economic Thought, 1785–1865* (Oxford, 1988)

Hinde, W., *Richard Cobden. A Victorian Outsider* (1986)

Hirst, F. W., *From Adam Smith to Philip Snowden. A History of Free Trade in Great Britain* (1925)

—— *Gladstone as Financier and Economist* (1931)

—— *A Brief Autobiographical History of the Liberal Free Trade Committee, 1931–1946* (Heyshott, 1947)

—— *In the Golden Days* (1947)

F. W. Hirst: By his Friends (1958)

Hobart, Lady Mary (ed.), *Essays and Miscellaneous Writings of Vere Henry, Lord Hobart*, 2 vols (1885)

Hobhouse, L. T., *Democracy and Reaction* (1904)

Hobson, J. A., *Canada To-day* (1906)

—— *Richard Cobden: The International Man* (1918)

Hoffman, R. J. S., *Great Britain and the German Trade Rivalry, 1875–1914* (Philadelphia, 1933)

Howe, A. C., *The Cotton Masters, 1830–1860* (Oxford: Oxford Historical Monographs, 1984)

—— 'Free Trade and the City of London, *c.*1820–1870', *History*, 77 (1992), 391–410

—— 'Towards "The Hungry Forties": Free Trade In Britain, *c.*1880–1906', in E. Biagini (ed.), *Citizenship and Commmunity* (Cambridge, 1996)

Howson, S. and Moggridge, D. E., *The Wartime Diaries of Lionel Robbins and James Meade, 1943–45* (1990)

Hutchinson, H. G., *Life of Sir John Lubbock, Lord Avebury*, 2 vols (1914)

Iliasu, A., 'The Cobden–Chevalier Treaty of 1860', *Historical Journal*, 14 (1971), 65–98

Ingham, G., *Capitalism Divided: The City and Industry in British Social Development* (1984)

International Free Trade Conferences, Proceeedings (1908, 1920–2)

Irwin, D. A., 'The Political Economy of Free Trade: Voting in the British General Election of 1906', *Journal of Law and Economics*, 37 (1994), 75–108

——*Against the Tide: An Intellectual History of Free Trade* (Princeton, 1996)

James, S. C. and Lake, D. A., 'The Second Face of Hegemony: Britain's Repeal of the Corn Laws and the American Walker Tariff of 1846', *International Organization*, 43 (1989), 1–30

Jeremy, D. J. (ed.), *Dictionary of Business Biography*, 5 vols (1984–6)

Jones, R. A., *The Nineteenth-Century Foreign Office* (1971)

Kadish, A., *Historians, Economics, and Economic History* (1990)

——(ed.), *The Corn Laws. The Formation of Popular Economics in Britain*, 6 vols (1996)

——and Tribe, K. (eds.), *The Market for Political Economy: The Advent of Economics in British University Culture, 1850–1905* (1993)

Keohane, R. O., 'International Liberalism Reconsidered', in Dunn, J. (ed.), *The Economic Limits to Modern Politics* (Cambridge, 1990)

Klein, I., 'English Free Traders and Indian Tariffs, 1874–96', *Modern Asian Studies*, 5 (1971), 251–71

Koot, G. M., *English Historical Economics, 1870–1926: The Rise of Economic History and Neomercantilism* (Cambridge, 1987)

Kynaston, D., *The City of London. Vol. II. Golden Years, 1890–1914* (1995)

Lake, D. A., *Power, Protection and Free Trade: International Sources of U.S. Commercial Strategy, 1887–1939* (Cornell, 1988)

La Nauze, J. A., *Political Economy in Australia: Historical Studies* (Melbourne, 1949)

——*Alfred Deakin: A Biography*, 2 vols (Melbourne, 1965)

Leech, H. J. (ed.), *The Public Letters of John Bright* (1885)

Levi, L., *The History of British Commerce* (2nd edn. 1880)

Lindsay, W. S., *Our Merchant Shipping: Its Present State Considered* (1860)

——*History of Merchant Shipping and Ancient Commerce*, vol. 3 (1876)

Long, D. and Wilson, P., *Thinkers of the Twenty Years' Crisis: Inter-War Idealism Reassessed* (Oxford, 1995)

Lyons, F. S. L., *Internationalism in Europe, 1815–1914* (1963)

McCord, N., *The Anti-Corn Law League, 1838–1846* (1958)

——*Free Trade: Theory and Practice from Adam Smith to Keynes* (Newton Abbot, 1970)

Macintyre, A. D., 'Lord George Bentinck and the Protectionists: A Lost Cause?', *Transactions of the Royal Historical Society*, 5th ser., 39 (1989), 141–65

Macintyre, S., *A Colonial Liberalism* (Melbourne, 1991)

McKeown, T., 'The Politics of Corn Law Repeal and Theories of Commercial Policy', *British Journal of Political Science*, 19 (1989), 353–80

McKibbin, R. I., 'Why was there no Marxism in Britain?', *English Historical Review*, 99 (1984), 297–331

McLean, I., 'Rational Choice and the Victorian Voter', *Political Studies*, 40 (1992), 496–515

Malchow, H. L., *Agitators and Promoters in the Age of Gladstone and Disraeli* (1983)

Mallet, B., *Sir Louis Mallet: A Record of Public Service and Political Ideals* (1905)

——*British Budgets, 1887–1913* (1913)

Mallet, L., *Free Exchange* (1891)

Mandler, P., *Aristocratic Government in the Age of Reform. Whigs and Liberals, 1830–1852* (Oxford, 1990)

Marrison, A., *British Business and Protection, 1903–1932* (Oxford, 1996)

Martin, A. W., *Henry Parkes: A Biography* (Melbourne, 1980)

Massingham, H. W. (ed.), *Labour and Protection* (1903)

Masters, D. C., *The Reciprocity Treaty of 1854* (1937; new edn. 1963)

Matthew, H. C. G., *The Liberal Imperialists* (Oxford: Oxford Historical Monographs, 1973)

—— 'Disraeli, Gladstone, and the Politics of Mid-Victorian Budgets', *Historical Journal*, 22 (1979), 615–43

—— *Gladstone*, 2 vols (Oxford, 1986 and 1995)

—— and Foot, M. R. D., *The Gladstone Diaries*, 14 vols (Oxford, 1968–94)

Medley, G. W., *Pamphlets and Addresses* (1899)

Mock, W., *Imperiale Herrschaft und nationales Interesse: 'Constructive Imperialism' oder Freihandel in Gross Britannien vor dem Ersten Weltkrieg* (Stuttgart, 1982)

Mongredien, A., *Free Trade and English Commerce* (1879)

—— *History of the Free-Trade Movement in England* (1881)

[Morier, R.], *Commercial Treaties: Free Trade and Internationalism: Four Letters* (1870)

Morley, J., *The Life of Richard Cobden*, 2 vols (1881)

—— *The Life of William Ewart Gladstone*, 3 vols (1903)

Morrell, W. P., *British Colonial Policy in the Age of Peel and Russell* (Oxford, new imp. 1966)

Morris, A. J. A., *Radicalism against War, 1906–1914. The Advocacy of Peace and Retrenchment* (1972)

—— (ed.), *Edwardian Radicalism* (1974)

Murray, B. K., *The 'People's Budget', 1909–1910* (Oxford, 1980)

Newton, T. W. L., *Lord Lyons: A Record of British Diplomacy*, 2 vols (1913); single vol. edn. (n.d.)

Northcote, S., *Twenty Years' of Financial Policy* (1862)

Nye, J. V., 'The Myth of Free Trade Britain and Fortress France: Tariffs and Trade in the Nineteenth Century', *Journal of Economic History*, 51 (1991), 23–46, and debate, ibid. 53 (1993), 146–58

O'Brien, D. P., *The Correspondence of Lord Overstone*, 3 vols (Cambridge, 1971)

O'Brien, P. K. and Pigman, G. A., 'Free Trade, British Hegemony, and the International Economic Order', *Review of International Studies*, 18 (1992), 89–113

Offer, A., *Property and Politics, 1870–1914* (Cambridge, 1981)

—— *The First World War: An Agrarian Interpretation* (Oxford, 1989)

Page, W. (ed.), *Commerce and Industry: A Historical Review*, 2 vols (1919)

Palmer, S., *Politics, Shipping and the Repeal of the Navigation Laws* (Manchester, 1990)

Parker, C. S., *Sir Robert Peel from his Private Papers*, 3 vols (1891–9)

Parry, J. P., *The Rise and Fall of Liberal Government in Victorian Britain* (1993)

Platt, D. C. M., *Finance, Trade and Politics in British Foreign Policy, 1815–1914* (Oxford, 1968)

—— (with Latham, A. J. H. and Michie, R.C.), *Decline and Recovery in Britain's Overseas Trade, 1873–1914* (1993)

Political Economy Club. Minutes of Proceedings, 1899–1920, Roll of Members, and Questions Discussed, 1821–1920 (1921)

Porritt, E., *Sixty Years of Protection in Canada, 1846–1907* (1908)

——*Fiscal and Diplomatic Freedom of the British Overseas Dominions* (Oxford, 1922)

Porter, B., *Critics of Empire: British Radical Attitudes to Colonialism in Africa, 1895–1914* (1968)

Potter, J., 'The British Timber Duties, 1815–1860', *Economica*, 22 (1955), 122–36

Prentice, A., *History of the Anti-Corn Law League*, 2 vols (1853); 2nd. edn. intro. W. H. Chaloner (1968).

Prest, J., *Politics in the Age of Cobden* (1977)

——'A Large or a Small Amount? Revenue and the Nineteenth-Century Corn Laws', *Historical Journal*, 39 (1996), 467–78

Priestley, F. E. L., Robson, J. M. *et al.*, *The Collected Works of John Stuart Mill*, 33 vols (Toronto, 1963–91)

Ramm, A. (ed.), *The Political Correspondence of Mr Gladstone and Lord Granville, 1868–1876*, Camden Soc. 3rd ser., 81 and 82 (Royal Historical Society, 1952)

——(ed.), *The Political Correspondence of Mr Gladstone and Lord Granville, 1876–1886*, 2 vols (Oxford, 1962)

——*Sir Robert Morier: Envoy and Ambassador in the Age of Imperialism, 1876–1893* (Oxford, 1973)

Rea, R., *Free Trade in Being* (1908)

Read, D., *Cobden and Bright: A Victorian Political Partnership* (1967)

——*Peel and the Victorians* (1987)

Redford, A., *Manchester Merchants and Foreign Trade*, 2 vols (Manchester, 1934 and 1956)

Rempel, R. A., *Unionists Divided: Arthur Balfour, Joseph Chamberlain and the Unionist Free Traders* (Newton Abbot, 1972)

Robbins, L. G., *Economic Planning and International Order* (1937)

Robson, M. M., 'Liberals and "Vital Interests": The Debate on International Arbitration, 1815–72', *Bulletin of the Institute of Historical Research*, 32 (1959), 38–55

Rogers, J. E. T., *Speeches on Questions of Public Policy by John Bright* (1869)

——*Cobden and Modern Political Opinion* (1873)

Rooth, T., *British Protection and the International Economy: Overseas Commercial Policy in the 1930s* (Cambridge, 1994)

Roseveare, H., *The Treasury: The Evolution of a British Institution* (1969)

Russell, A. K., *Liberal Landslide: The General Election of 1906* (Newton Abbot, 1973)

Russell, John, Earl, *Recollections and Suggestions, 1813–1873* (1875)

Rylands, L. G., *Correspondence and Speeches of Mr Peter Rylands MP*, 2 vols (1890)

Saul, S. B., *Studies in British Overseas Trade, 1870–1914* (Liverpool, 1960)

Schonhardt-Bailey, C., 'Lessons in Lobbying for Free Trade in 19th-Century Britain: To Concentrate or Not', *American Political Science Review*, 85 (1991), 38–58

——'Specific Factors, Capital Markets, Portfolio Diversification, and Free Trade: Domestic Determinants of the Repeal of the Corn Laws', *World Politics*, 43 (1991), 545–69

——'Linking Constituency Interests to Legislative Behaviour: District Economic and Electoral Composition in the Repeal of the Corn Laws', *Parliamentary History*, 13 (1994), 86–118

——(ed.), *Free Trade. The Repeal of the Corn Laws* (Bristol, 1996)

Schuyler, R. L., *The Fall of the Old Colonial System: A Study in British Free Trade, 1770–1870* (New York, 1945)

Schwabe, Mrs Salis, *Richard Cobden: Notes sur ses Voyages, Correspondances et Souvenirs* (Paris, 1879)

Searle, G. R., *Entrepreneurial Politics in Mid-Victorian Britain* (Oxford, 1993)

Semmel, B., *Imperialism and Social Reform* (1960)

—— *The Rise of Free Trade Imperialism* (Cambridge, 1970)

—— *Liberalism and Naval Strategy: Ideology, Interest, and Sea Power during the Pax Britannica* (1986)

Silberner, E., *The Problem of War in Nineteenth-Century Economic Thought* (Princeton, 1946)

Smith, M. S., *Tariff Reform in France, 1860–1900* (Ithaca, 1980)

Snyder, R. K., *The Tariff Problem in Great Britain, 1918–1923* (Stanford, 1944)

Southgate, D., *The Passing of the Whigs* (1962)

Soutter, F. W., *Fights for Freedom* (1925)

Spall, R. F., 'Free Trade, Foreign Relations, and the Anti-Corn Law League', *International History Review*, 10 (1988), 405–32

Startt, J. D., *Journalists for Empire: The Imperial Debate in the Edwardian Stately Press, 1903–1913* (Westport, 1991)

Steele, E. D., *Palmerston and Liberalism, 1855–1865* (Cambridge, 1991)

Stein, A., 'The Hegemon's Dilemma: Britain, the United States, and the International Economic Order', *International Organization*, 38 (1984), 355–86

Stevas, N. St John, (ed.), *The Collected Works of Walter Bagehot*, 15 vols (1965–86)

Stewart, R., *The Politics of Protection. Lord Derby and the Protectionist Party, 1841–52* (Cambridge, 1971)

Strachey, L. and Fulford, R. (eds.), *The Greville Memoirs, 1814–1860*, 8 vols (1938)

Stuart, J. M., *Free Trade in Tuscany* (Cobden Club, 1876)

Sykes, A., *Tariff Reform and British Politics, 1903–1913* (Oxford, 1979)

Taylor, A. J. P., *The Trouble Makers: Dissent over British Foreign Policy, 1792–1939* (1957)

Tooke, T. and Newmarch, W., *A History of Prices and of the State of the Circulation from 1793 to the Present Time*, 6 vols (1838–57).

Trainor, L., 'The British Government and Imperial Economic Unity, 1890–1895', *Historical Journal*, 13 (1970), 68–84

—— *British Imperialism and Australian Nationalism* (Cambridge, 1994)

Trentmann, F., 'The Strange Death of Free Trade: The Erosion of the "Liberal Consensus" in Britain, c.1903–32', in E. Biagini (ed.), *Citizenship and Community* (Cambridge, 1996), 219–50

—— 'The Transformation of Fiscal Reform: Reciprocity, Modernization and the Fiscal Debate within the Business Community in early twentieth-century Britain', *Historical Journal*, 39 (1996), 1005–48

Turner, J., *British Politics and the Great War* (1992)

Tyler, J. E., *The Struggle for Imperial Unity, 1868–1895* (1938)

van der Linden, W. H., *The International Peace Movement, 1815–1874* (Amsterdam, 1987)

Verdier, D., *Democracy and International Trade: Britain, France, and the United States, 1860–1990* (Princeton, 1994)

Verein fur Sozialpolitik, Die Handelspolitik der wichtgeren Kulturstaaten in den letzen Jahrzehten (Leipzig, 1892–3)

Free Trade Speeches of Charles Pelham Villiers, ed. 'A Member of the Cobden Club' [Agnes Lambert], 2 vols (1883)

Vincent, J., *Disraeli, Derby, and the Conservative Party: The Political Journals of Lord Stanley, 1849–69* (Hassocks, 1978)

Walker-Smith, D., *The Protectionist Case in the 1840s* (1933)

Wallace, E., *Goldwin Smith: Victorian Liberal* (Toronto, 1957)

Waller, P. J. (ed.), *Politics and Social Change in Modern Britain* (1987)

Walling, R. A. J. (ed.), *The Diaries of John Bright* (1930)

Ward, J., *Experiences of a Diplomatist* (1872)

Wemyss, R., *Memoirs and Letters of the Rt. Hon. Sir Robert Morier*, 2 vols (1911)

Williams, J. B., *British Commercial Policy and Trade Expansion, 1750–1850* (Oxford, 1972)

Williamson, P., *National Crisis and National Government* (1992)

Wilson, T. (ed.), *The Political Diaries of C. P. Scott, 1911–1928* (1970)

Wood, J. C., *British Economists and the Empire* (Beckenham, 1983)

Zebel, S., 'Fair Trade: An English Reaction to the Breakdown of the Cobden Treaty System', *Journal of Modern History*, 12 (1940), 161–85

—— 'Joseph Chamberlain and the Genesis of Tariff Reform', *Journal of British Studies*, 7 (1967–8), 131–57

E. Unpublished Theses

Adams, P., 'Tariff Reform and the Working Classes, 1903–6', M.Litt. thesis, University of Oxford (1982)

Bolchini, P., 'Anglo-Italian Economic Relations (1861–1883)', Ph.D. thesis, University of London (1967)

Cameron, K. J., 'The Anti-Corn Law Movement in Scotland', Ph.D. thesis, University of Edinburgh (1971)

Carter, L. J., 'The Development of Cobden's Thought on International Relations, particularly with reference to his role in the mid-nineteenth-century peace movement', Ph.D. thesis, University of Cambridge (1970)

Castorina, C. P., 'Richard Cobden and the Intellectual Development and Influence of the Manchester School of Economics', Ph.D. thesis, University of Manchester (1976)

Charbit, Y., 'Ideas on Population as part of Social Thought: The French Free Traders (1848–1870)', D.Phil. thesis, University of Oxford (1973)

Clayton, K. B., 'Anglo-French Commercial Relations, 1860–1882', MA thesis, University of Manchester (1954)

Davis, J. R., 'Trade, Politics, Perspectives, and the Question of a British Commercial Policy towards the German States, 1848–1866', Ph.D. thesis, University of Glasgow (1994)

Farrar, P. N., 'Richard Cobden: Educationist, Economist and Statesman', Ph.D. thesis, University of Sheffield (1987)

Fisher, J. R., 'Public Opinion and Agriculture, 1875–1900', Ph.D. thesis, University of Hull (1972)

Gaston, J. W., 'Policy-Making and Free-Trade Diplomacy: Britain's Commercial Relations with Western Europe, 1869–1886', Ph.D. thesis, University of Saskatchewan (1975)

Gatrell, V. A. C., 'The Commercial Middle Class in Manchester, *c.*1820–1857', Ph.D. thesis, University of Cambridge (1971)

Hobson, J. M., 'The Tax-Seeking State: Protectionism, Taxation and State Structures in Germany, Russia, Britain and America, 1870–1914', Ph.D. thesis, University of London (1991)

Iliasu, A., 'The Role of Free Trade Treaties in British Foreign Policy, 1859–1871', Ph.D. thesis, University of London (1965)

Marrison, A., 'British Businessmen and the "Scientific Tariff": A Study of Joseph Chamberlain's Tariff Commission, 1903–21', Ph.D. thesis, University of Hull (1980)

Pennar, J., 'Richard Cobden and Cordell Hull. A Comparative Study of the Commercial Policies of Nineteenth-Century England and Contemporary United States', Ph.D. thesis, Princeton University (1953)

Pigman, G. A., 'Hegemony and Free Trade Policy: Britain, 1846–1914 and the USA, 1944–90', D.Phil. thesis, University of Oxford, 1992

Ryan, J., 'B. R. Wise: An Oxford Free Trade Liberal', MA thesis, University of Sydney (1966)

Smith, S. R. B., 'British Nationalism, Imperialism, and the City of London, 1880–1900', Ph.D thesis, University of London (1985)

Wandrucz, A., 'Liberal Internationalism', Ph.D. thesis, University of London (1952)

Index

OCT 1 2 2000

DATE LOANED

GAYLORD 3563